D1511267

PRINCIPLES OF PERSONNEL MANAGEMENT

McGRAW-HILL SERIES IN MANAGEMENT
Keith Davis, Consulting Editor

EDWIN B. FLIPPO

Professor of Management
University of Arizona

PRINCIPLES OF PERSONNEL MANAGEMENT

FOURTH EDITION

McGraw-Hill Book Company

New York St. Louis San Francisco Auckland Düsseldorf Johannesburg
Kuala Lumpur London Mexico Montreal New Delhi Panama
Paris São Paulo Singapore Sydney Tokyo Toronto

To my wife

**PRINCIPLES
OF PERSONNEL
MANAGEMENT**

1234567890DODO79876

This book was set in Optima by Black Dot, Inc.
The editors were William J. Kane and Michael Weber;
the designer was Anne Canevari Green;
the production supervisor was Judi Allen.
New drawings were done by J & R Services, Inc.
R. R. Donnelley & Sons Company was printer and binder.

Library of Congress Cataloging in Publication Data

Flippo, Edwin B
    Principles of personnel management.

    (McGraw-Hill series in management)
    Includes bibliographies and index.
    1. Personnel management.   I.   Title.
HF5549.F583   1976   658.3   75-20426
ISBN 0-07-021316-X

CONTENTS

Ownership   Suggestion Systems   Summary

LIST OF CASES

PREFACE

After fifteen years of use, the fundamental framework on which this text is based still proves sufficiently flexible to incorporate continuing developments in the field of personnel management. The book can be summarized in one somewhat lengthy sentence: *personnel management is the planning, organizing, directing, and controlling of the procurement, development, compensation, integration, and maintenance of human resources, to the end that organizational and societal objectives may be accomplished.*

After attention is allocated to the changing responsibilities of a personnel manager within an organization, the greater bulk of the book is concerned with the processes and philosophies of obtaining personnel (procurement), developing their abilities (development), rewarding them monetarily to effect feelings of equity and motivation (compensation), aligning group and individual interests with organizational goals (integration), and preserving the mental and physical condition of this able and willing work force (maintenance).

This revision notes major changes in the role of the personnel manager. In Chapter 1, new challenges are noted, such as the altered mix of available work forces, modifications of worker values, and steadily increasing governmental legislation in the field. The continuing responsibility to assist in overall organization design is further emphasized through discussion of job enrichment programs. A new chapter on the social role and responsibilities of the firm highlights the personnel manager's obligation to assure that society's human resources are preserved, protected, and enhanced. Specific attention is allocated to female employees, minorities, and the culturally disadvantaged.

In addition to updating regular features from previous editions, this revision includes the following additions: (1) under Procurement: legal implications of testing, role analysis to improve selection, and greater emphasis on assessment centers; (2) under Development: Management by Objectives, organization development, personnel outplacement, and redesign of the management development discussion to focus on abilities required; (3) under Compensation: equity theory, expectancy theory, and managerial programs; (4) under Integration: model of informal/formal organization, human models of ethologists and behaviorists, behavior modification, analyses of roles and primary work groups, enlarged frameworks of leadership styles, Johari's Window in communication, counseling programs, conflict resolution models, productivity bargaining, and union-management relations in public employment; and (5) under Maintenance: new legislation, including the Occupational Safety and Health Act and the Employee Retirement Income Security Act, alcoholics and drug users among the work force, and the personnel manager as a change agent.

For instructional purposes, at least a dozen new charts have been provided, seven new cases have replaced old ones, and all supplementary readings have been changed and updated. Discussion questions at the end of each chapter have been substantially altered.

As the editions roll by, I hope to avoid the mounting tendency to take greater credit for the book. I still recognize the original and continuing influence of Ralph Davis of Ohio State University, Keith Davis of Arizona State University, William Voris of the American Graduate School of International Management, and Michael Jucius of the University of Arizona. I am deeply indebted to many professors, managers, and students throughout the nation and the world who have submitted comments and suggestions, as well as having conducted valuable research that led to changes in this edition. I am particularly grateful to Professor Richard Lutz of the University of Akron for his many helpful suggestions. Credit must go to my wife, Jean Gwin Flippo, for her efforts in the original editing and to Donna Brammer for rapid and accurate manuscript typing.

It is my continued hope that the framework for understanding the personnel field presented in this book will prove to be of value to students, teachers, and practitioners.

EDWIN B. FLIPPO

PART ONE

INTRODUCTION

The history of personnel management is short in one sense, but long in another. Modern personnel management dates back only to the 1940s; personnel problems requiring managerial attention date back to the time of the Industrial Revolution. In this part of the text we shall examine the managerial and operative functions of personnel. The status of the field will be analyzed in the light of its past as well as with reference to such modern challenges as are posed by changes in human values, technical demands of large corporations, increasing governmental controls, and changes in the work force skill mix.

ONE

THE NATURE AND CHALLENGE OF PERSONNEL MANAGEMENT

Institutional spokesmen have often proclaimed that the work force of an organization constitutes one of its more important system components, e.g., "People are our most important asset." In recent decades, the magnitude of this importance has transcended organizational borders. Society at large has proclaimed its human resources to have vital needs that move beyond a "work force" status. As a consequence, the modern personnel manager is located at the nexus of at least three major forces: (1) the institution, as it calls upon one to provide an able and willing work force to accomplish organization objectives, (2) institutional employees, as they ask for reasonable fulfillment of physiological and psychological needs, and (3) general society, as it demands, often through legislation, that the institution assume a larger responsibility in developing, enhancing, and protecting its human resources, with particular reference to disadvantaged groups such as the handicapped, the aged, and minority races, religions, and nationalities.

The role of the personnel manager has thus changed through time. At first, the personnel manager was an instrument of top management in procuring and maintaining an effective work force. As knowledge expanded in executing this role, the manager began to understand the necessity for ascertaining and accommodating to the needs of the human beings who constituted that work force. He or she constantly searched for that program which would support the accomplishment of *both* organizational and individual objectives. The job was made more difficult by such factors as the rise of the modern labor union, the increasing educational level of societal members, the increasing size and complexity of the organization and its technology, and the insistent and sometimes violent demands of less privileged segments of our society. This last-named factor has led to the final major alteration of the personnel manager's role. As will be discussed at length in Chapter 3, the private organization is expected to recognize, define, and attempt to fulfill a general social responsibility in addition to its originally assigned role. Though society "permits" and encourages the use of its citizens as means to organizational ends, the fact that they constitute an instrumental work force in no way detracts from the fact that they are (1) human beings with certain inalienable rights, and (2) society's citizens with assigned rights and privileges. In this newly expanded role, the personnel manager will at worst act as the organization's social conscience, and at best will work, as an informed specialist, with all members of the organization in determining and meeting the demands of this social role.

The modern personnel manager therefore requires a broad background in such fields as psychology, sociology, philosophy, economics, and management. He or she must deal with issues and problems that often do not have "right answers" obvious to all. There will be required an ability to understand that which is not logical, a capacity to project oneself into other positions without losing perspective, and a skill in predicting human and organizational behavior. Reading or studying a text such as this will not magically change one into an effective personnel executive. Study should be of material assistance, however, in giving a perspective from which to view the field, in suggesting possible answers to current problems, and in helping to define the way toward further improvement and research. Certainly, in this text the technical content of the field will be thoroughly discussed. The personnel manager who does not meet the demands of this initially assigned role may not be around to worry about the other two. We shall also emphasize and attempt to define the nature of the forces brought to bear by individuals and society. At the minimum, the personnel manager needs to keep his or her head above water while swimming in the confluence of these three major streams of influence.

DEFINITION OF PERSONNEL MANAGEMENT

It is appropriate and helpful to offer, at the beginning of the discussion, a definition of the subject to be covered. In the following definition we are presenting an outline of this entire text. In the first place, we are dealing with two categories of functions, managerial and operative. A manager is one who exercises authority and leadership over other personnel; the president of a firm is certainly a manager, and so also is the department head or supervisor. On the other hand, an operative is one who has no authority over others but has been given a specific task or duty to perform under managerial supervision. Thus, the personnel manager is a manager and as such must perform the basic functions of management. This is true no matter what the nature of the operative function. Yet a comprehensive definition of personnel management must include also the operative functions in the field. In outline form, the definition would appear as follows:[1]

[1]The listing of major management functions varies with the experts. For example, Ernest Dale, *Management Theory and Practice*, 3d ed., McGraw-Hill Book Company, New York, 1973, pp. 4–5, lists planning, organizing, staffing, direction, control, innovation, and representation. One of the early writers, Luther Gulick, in "Notes on the Theory of Organization," in Gulick and Lyndall Urwick (eds.), *Papers on the Science of Administration*, Institute of Public Administration, New York, 1937, p. 13, coined the word POSDCORB, standing for the management functions of planning, organizing, staffing, directing, coordinating, reporting, and budgeting. There is substantial agreement upon the general content of the process; only the listing of *major* elements varies.

1 Management functions
  a Planning
  b Organizing
  c Directing
  d Controlling
2 Operative functions
  a Procurement
  b Development

It is therefore possible to summarize this entire text into the following sentence: *Personnel management is the planning, organizing, directing, and controlling of the procurement, development, compensation, integration, and maintenance of people for the purpose of contributing to organizational, individual, and societal goals.* A brief elaboration of the component parts of this definition is given below.

PLANNING Effective managers realize that a substantial portion of their time should be devoted to planning. For the personnel manager, planning means the *determination in advance of a personnel program that will contribute to goals established for the enterprise.* Presumably, the process of goal establishment will involve the active and enlightened participation of the personnel manager, with his or her expertise in the area of human resources.

ORGANIZING After a course of action has been determined, an organization must be established to carry it out. An organization is a means to an end. Once it has been determined that certain personnel functions contribute toward the firm's objectives, the personnel manager must form an organization by *designing the structure of relationships among jobs, personnel, and physical factors.* One must be aware of the complex relationships that exist between the specialized unit and the rest of the organization. Because of increasing expertise in this function, many top managements are looking to the personnel manager for advice in the general organization of the enterprise.

DIRECTING At least in theory, we now have a plan and an organization to execute that plan. It might appear that the next logical function would be that of operation, doing the job. But it has been found that a "starter" function is becoming increasingly necessary. In our above definition, this function was labeled "direction," but it may be called by other names, such as "motivation," "actuation," or "command." At any rate, a considerable number of difficulties are involved in *getting people to go to work willingly and effectively.*

CONTROLLING Now, at last, the personnel functions are being performed. But what is the management duty at this point? It is logical that its function should be that of control, that is, the observation of action and its comparison with plans and the correction of any deviations that may occur, or, at times, the realignment of plans and their adjustment to unchangeable deviations. Control is the managerial function concerned with *regulating activities in accordance with the personnel plan, which in turn was formulated on the basis of an analysis of fundamental organization goals or objectives.*

It is believed that the four above-named functions are basic and common to all managers. In Chapters 4 and 5, the personnel manager's responsibilities for planning, organizing, and controlling will be discussed. The essence of the fourth function, direction, is so closely allied with the operative function of integration that its discussion will be delayed until later in this text. Though all managers must unavoidably direct their subordinates, the personnel manager should possess exceptional expertise.

There is a skill in managing that can be transferred to various operative areas, but no one will deny that an effective manager must know what it is that he or she is managing. The greater portion of this text is devoted to these personnel operative functions.[2]

PROCUREMENT   This first operative function of personnel management is concerned with the *obtaining of the proper kind and number of personnel necessary to accomplish organization goals*. It deals specifically with such subjects as the determination of human resources requirements and their recruitment, selection, and placement. Determining such requirements refers to both number and quality of personnel. Selection and placement cover the multitude of activities designed to screen and hire personnel, such as reviewing application forms, psychological testing, conducting interviews, and inducting. These activities are presented and analyzed in Chapters 6 to 9.

DEVELOPMENT   After personnel have been obtained, they must be to some degree developed. Development has to do with the *increase of skill, through training, that is necessary for proper job performance*. This is an activity of very great importance and will continue to grow because of the changes in technology, the realignment of jobs, and the increasing complexity of the managerial task. Discussion of both management development and operative training will be presented in Chapters 10 through 13, along with such supporting activities as performance appraisal and promotion programs.

COMPENSATION   This function is defined as the *adequate and equitable remuneration of personnel for their contributions to organization objectives*. Though some recent morale surveys have tended to minimize the importance of monetary income to employees, we nevertheless contend that compensation is one of the most important functions of personnel management. Where employees do indicate a decreasing interest in the importance of wages, it may be suspected that an adequate remuneration program already exists. In dealing with this subject, we shall consider only economic compensation. Psychic income is classified elsewhere. The basic elements of a compensation program are presented in Chapters 14 to 16, with an emphasis upon such subjects as job evaluation, wage policies, wage systems, and some of the recently devised extracompensation plans.

INTEGRATION   With the employee procured, developed, and reasonably compensated, there remains one of the most difficult and frustrating challenges to management. The definition labels this problem "integration." It is concerned with the attempt *to effect a*

---

[2]Few authors attempt to designate and define basic operative functions of personnel. One exception is Michael J. Jucius, *Personnel Management*, 7th ed., Richard D. Irwin, Inc., Homewood, Ill., 1971, p. 2. Jucius indicates that these basic functions are procurement, development, maintenance, and utilization.

reasonable reconciliation of individual, societal, and organizational interests. It rests upon a foundation of belief that significant overlappings of interests do exist in our society. Consequently, we must deal with the feelings and attitudes of personnel in conjunction with the principles and policies of organizations. This broad problem, as well as the narrower related problems, such as communication, informal organization, and labor unions, will be covered at length in Chapters 17 to 23.

MAINTENANCE It is only logical that the last operative function should be that of *sustaining and improving the conditions that have been established.* This would, of course, encompass the continuance of the functions mentioned above. But at this point we should like to emphasize the specific problems of maintaining the physical condition of our employees (health and safety measures) and of maintaining favorable attitudes toward the organization (employee service programs). As in all areas of general management, research can and must continue to advance the effectiveness of the entire program. Consideration of these three subjects constitutes the final section of this text in Chapters 24 to 26.

The purpose of all the activity outlined above, both managerial and operative, is to assist in the accomplishment of basic objectives. Consequently, the starting point of personnel management, as of all management, must be a specification of those objectives and a determination of the subobjectives of the personnel function. The expenditure of all funds in the personnel area can be justified only insofar as there is a net contribution toward basic goals. For the most part these are goals of the particular organization concerned. But as suggested earlier, society is tending to impose human goals upon the private business enterprise, goals that may or may not make an immediate contribution to an organization's particular objectives.

PERVASIVE NATURE OF PERSONNEL MANAGEMENT

Within an organized society, every subsidiary unit is formed for some primary purpose or objective. The economic system is designed to allocate scarce resources among competing economic ends for the purpose of enhancing the general standard of living in material things. The objective of a manufacturing firm, an economic subunit, is to produce and sell a product or service for a return of some type. Activities directly related to the primary objective are often designated "line functions." Thus, functions commonly designated as line *within* the manufacturing firm are production, sales, and finance. Performance of these enables the firm to accomplish the primary responsibility levied upon it by society.

It has been found that the performance of certain secondary activities will enhance the effectiveness of the primary. Thus, secondary functions, often designated "staff functions," are those that do not contribute directly toward the primary objective but rather do so indirectly by facilitating and assisting in the performance of line work. In the typical manufacturing firm, the personnel manager and the specialized unit are usually denoted as "staff." They assist line managers by supplying adequate numbers of personnel, assisting in their training and development, and the like. But it should be evident that it is neither feasible nor advisable to separate completely all personnel management functions from line managers. *All the responsibility for personnel work cannot and should not be centered in a staff personnel department.* In most areas, a staff service unit can only assist operating managers rather than completely relieve them of personnel responsibilities. Thus *all* executives must unavoidably be personnel managers. This responsibility does not deny the need for staff assistance. Despite the seeming simplicity of the field, it has become increasingly complex because of such factors as the growth of unions, the extension of government into the labor management field, the creation of new techniques of personnel evaluation, and the variable quality of human nature. Specialized staff activity in the personnel field can usually be justified in the medium- and larger-sized firms.

It should also be noted that society can alter its assignment of responsibilities. It can state that the firm should enhance the material standard of living but that this must be accompanied by affirmative action to assist culturally disadvantaged groups within society. In this event, the personnel manager may become the instrument of society in the enforcement of its decrees, thereby adding an element of authority that goes beyond a secondary status. In effect, the primary mission of the firm has been changed, leading to a redefinition of primary and secondary functions. Though the personnel unit is still predominantly a secondary staff activity in most firms, the trend toward greater societal concern with the operations of private organizations may well lead to changes in status in the future.

Though emphasis in this text is given to personnel management in the large organization, obviously similar functions exist in the firm with no specialized department. The line supervisor may have to carry job specifications in his or her head, recruit and hire personnel, induct and train them, and integrate them into the existing organization with little or no assistance from others. One may not be able to afford some of the more advanced and expensive techniques of performing these functions, but certain guiding concepts common to both large and small organizations should be of value.

It should also be apparent that performing personnel functions is as necessary in the office, retail store, or governmental organization as in the more commonly cited factory organization. The first personnel departments were formed for production organizations, but obviously similar problems arise in procuring, developing, and integrating clerks, engineers, salesmen, or professional government workers. Personnel management seems to transcend all functions, regardless of the nature, size, or type of personnel involved. Common problems demand common principles to assist in their analysis and solution.

NATURE OF PERSONNEL MANAGEMENT PRINCIPLES

Numerous principles of personnel management will of course be set forth in this book, and we should at this point indicate the nature of these principles. A principle is a fundamental truth, generally stated in the form of a cause-and-effect relationship. Principles are discovered by research, investigation, and analysis. Some people tend to confuse principle with policy, the latter being a rule or predetermined course of action established to guide an organization toward its objectives. It is to be hoped that when policies are established by management they will be formed on the basis of known principles. It quite often happens, however, that we lack knowledge in an area where we still have to make policy. Though we should recognize a close correlation of the two in practice, we shall do well to keep the distinction clear. Policies should not be construed as fundamental, unchanging truths, nor should principles be considered rigid rules applicable to all situations without change.

A second significant point concerning the concept of principles is that in the social sciences they are not exact in their working. When people are part of the problem, it is naïve to expect that we can follow principles as if they were rules, with sure, predetermined results. For example, a commonly accepted principle of disciplinary action is that its administration to an individual in private will usually produce the most satisfactory results in terms of future productivity and cooperation. Most managers agree that this is a principle, a fundamental truth. Yet on a specific occasion a public reprimand may well be the technique that will accomplish most for a particular worker, at a particular time, given particular circumstances. We have in personnel management an art rather than an exact science.

Many of the principles of personnel management have been discovered through practice and general observation without controlled experimentation and research. As a result, social scientists tend to deny their validity and label them "useful generalizations" or "theoretical concepts." It is suggested, however, that many of these practices have been subjected to such repeated use with reasonable success in the realistic laboratory of practical experience that their designation as truths can be substantiated. In addition, the field of personnel rests heavily upon such supporting disciplines as psychology and sociology, in which there has been much controlled research. Such researched principles would still have to be adapted to conditions of actual practice.

CHALLENGES OF MODERN PERSONNEL MANAGEMENT

We need not look far to discover challenging problems in the field of personnel management. Managers may ignore or attempt to bury personnel problems, but these will not lie dormant because of the very nature of the problem component. Many problems are caused by constant changes that occur both within and without the firm. Among the many major changes that are occurring, the following four will illustrate the nature of the personnel challenge.

1   Changing mix of the work force
2   Changing values of the work force
3   Changing demands of employers
4   Changing demands of government

Changing mix of the work force

Though each person is unique and consequently presents a challenge to our general understanding, one can also appreciate broader problems by categorizing personnel to delineate and highlight trends. Among the major changes in the mix of personnel entering the work force are: (1) increased numbers of minority members entering occupations requiring greater skills, (2) increasing levels of formal education for the entire work force, (3) more female employees, (4) more married female employees, (5) more working mothers, and (6) a steadily increasing majority of white-collar employees in place of the blue-collar.

The fourth challenge, has had much to do with many of the above-listed changes.

Prohibition of discrimination and requirements for positive action to redress imbalances in work force mix have led to greater numbers of minority personnel being hired for
all types of jobs. The proportion of blacks, for example, has increased significantly in
professional, technical, managerial, clerical, sales, and craftsman-type jobs. However,
this group still holds a disproportionately large share of the less skilled and lower-paid
jobs, such as those of service worker and laborer. Steady increases in the level of formal
education would seem to bode well for continued change. The number of black college
graduates in the work force doubled during the 1960s and it is predicted it will double
again by 1980.[3]

Improvement in the educational level for blacks has also been accompanied by
increased levels all along the line. In 1972, approximately 15 percent of the civilian labor
force had four years or more of college. This is projected to rise to 18.5 percent in 1980,
to 21.2 in 1985, and to 23.8 in 1990.[4] In 1972, the percentage of the labor force with eight
years or less of schooling stood at 33. By 1990, this is expected to decline to about 6
percent. These projections present both a serious problem and a vast challenge for
personnel managers. In the past, employers' expectations with respect to hiring
requirements have tended to rise with increases in the qualifications of the jobseekers
themselves. If not altered, this practice could contribute to continued discrimination
against better-educated minorities. It definitely will contribute to the alienation and
frustration of all employees if they are placed on jobs for which they are overly
qualified. Increased competition for promotion among greater numbers of more highly
qualified personnel can create serious conflicts and strains within our organizations.
Rather than relaxing with the feeling that more of a good thing (education) is even
better, if we do not redesign jobs to effect a match with better-qualified personnel, we
are contributing only to frustration, absenteeism, grievances, and turnover.

Laws, as well as activist groups, have contributed to greater numbers of female
employees entering the work force.[5] In 1974, approximately 32 million of a total civilian
work force of 93 million employees were female. This number is projected to rise in
1980 to 37 million female workers.[6] This would be double the number employed in
1950, reflecting a major change in life-style in this country. Also of significance to the
manager is the fact that an increasing proportion of these employees are married with
children below the age of six years. For every two married men in the work force, there
is one married woman. Ten years ago, this ratio stood at 2.6 to 1 and twenty years earlier
it was 3.5 to 1.[7] Over 40 percent of the married women in this country are in the civilian
work force. Having children below the age of six years makes it quite difficult for the
mother to become a regular employee of an organization. Yet the percentage of
mothers with children this young who have entered the work force has risen
sharply—13 percent—in the past decade. This change in the work force mix also poses
challenges for the firm. Many have met them by providing flexible hours of work,
permitting sharing of a job by two or more women, and providing child care during

[3]U.S. Department of Labor, *U.S. Manpower in the 1970's*, Government Printing Office, Washington, 1970,
p. 5.

[4]Denis F. Johnston, "Education of Workers: Projections to 1990," *Monthly Labor Review*, vol. 96, no. 11,
November 1973, p. 22.

[5]For further discussion of discrimination in regard to special groups, see Chap. 3.

[6]U.S. Department of Labor, *U.S. Manpower in the 1970's*, op. cit., p. 6.

[7]Howard Hayghe, "Marital and Family Characteristics of the Labor Force in March 1973," *Monthly Labor
Review*, vol. 97, no. 4, April 1974, p. 21.

working hours. More serious problems lie in the areas of improved job placement, promotion, and pay. These are discussed at greater length in Chapter 3.

One of the more interesting changes in skill mix that has occurred in our society is depicted in Figure 1-1. In 1956, white-collar jobholders outnumbered blue-collar workers for the first time. By 1980, almost one-half of the total work force is expected to hold white-collar jobs. Within this general category, one of the fastest-growing segments is the professional and technical class, encompassing such specialities as scientist, engineer, mathematician, accountant, lawyer, and chemist. Management of the "knowledge worker" is one of the foremost challenges that the personnel manager must face in the modern industrial society.

In researching the utilization of highly educated and skilled professionals, considerable attention has been given to their attitudes toward both the employing organization and their particular disciplines or professions. If the dominant posture is one of dedication and service to the pursuit of professional knowledge, using the organization as a means to that end, the attitude is labeled "cosmopolitan." If, on the other hand, the organization is accorded primary loyalty, with professional skills being exclusively adapted toward its ends, the attitude is termed "local." Obviously, any professional who is employed by an organization has elements of both "localism" and "cosmopolitanism." As suggested in Figure 1-2, attitudes can be positioned in one of four quadrants: (1) relatively indifferent, (2) heavily oriented toward the profession, (3) heavily oriented toward the organization, and (4) oriented significantly toward both the profession and the organization.

In a study conducted by Miller and Wager, these four different orientations were discovered among 390 engineers and scientists in two units of a major American aerospace company.[8] The researchers utilized a questionnaire technique and labeled 31 percent "cosmopolitans," since they exhibited high professional orientation accompa-

---

[8]George A. Miller and L. Wesley Wager, "Adult Socialization, Organizational Structure, and Role Orientations," *Administrative Science Quarterly*, vol. 12, no. 2, June 1971, pp. 151–162.

Figure 1-1 Changes in work force mix

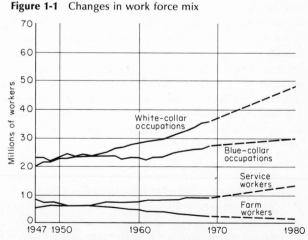

Source: U.S. Department of Labor, *U.S. Manpower in the 1970's*, p. 8.

Figure 1-2 Cosmopolitan and local
orientations

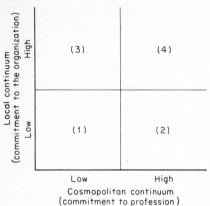

nied by a low bureaucratic attitude. Members of this group were largely physical
scientists with Ph.D. degrees working in the basic science research laboratory. They
exhibited such attitudes as "I would most like to publish a paper in the leading journal
of my profession, even though the topic might be of *minor* interest to the company,"
and "In the long run, I would rather be respected among specialists in my field outside
the company." Thus, the cosmopolitans view the universe as the field of their
profession, wherever they find themselves. They are not necessarily bound to the
current organization for which they happen to be working, and they tend to be highly
mobile. They often ask questions and make critical comments that traditional managers
feel to be bordering on disloyalty to the organization. Yet, the skills and scientific
viewpoint of the cosmopolitan are the fountainhead of the ideas that contribute to
organizational progress and growth.

Twenty-seven percent of the 390 engineers and scientists were characterized as
"locals," since they possessed a relatively low orientation to professional values with a
high concern for and loyalty to the organization. The greater bulk of these were
engineers without the Ph.D. If the professionals remain with a single organization for a
considerable time, the attitude tends to become more local in character. They tend to
agree with such statements as "Being able to pursue a career in management is very
important to me," and "Having a job which permits me to take on progressively more
administrative responsibility is important to me." Engineers, more often than scientists,
are likely to move toward this set of values. The significant reference group is
management rather than outside professionals in the field. "Locals" are usually more
cooperative and willing to take direction from management. The "cosmopolitan" often
contends that freedom and dedication to scientific values will produce greater total net
return to the enterprise, despite short-run costs caused by uncooperativeness, time
spent on projects of little value to the organization, and, at times, outright insubordination. An interesting paradox is presented by the fact that the engineer, who tends to be
more oriented to the organization than the scientist, is also more prone toward
unionization. Scientists are less likely to submit to any control, company or union. It
must be recognized that the terms "local" and "cosmopolitan" are relative in nature—

that just as engineers are more "local" than scientists, they in turn are more "cosmopolitan" than craftsmen or assembly line workers. Only a small percentage of engineers have been organized into unions, the largest of which are the American Federation of Technical Engineers and the Scientific, Professional and Engineering Association, each having approximately 13,000 members.

The remaining personnel in the Miller and Wager study were divided into the two hybrid types: 15 percent were "indifferents," with low orientation to both sets of values, and 27 percent were "local-cosmopolitans," who exhibited high orientations to both the profession and the organization. The "indifferents" were mostly engineers with long service with the organization. This suggests that an entering engineer might have begun with high orientation to either the profession or the organization or both, but was slowly transformed into an "indifferent" as he or she experienced lack of progress in both areas. The "local-cosmopolitan" was more likely to be an engineer who had worked for the company for a shorter period of time. It is apparent that the management of highly educated and skilled personnel poses a considerable challenge to personnel management.

Changing values of the work force

The changing mix of the work force inevitably leads to introduction of new values to organizations. In the past and continuing into the present, the work force of America has been heavily imbued with a set of values generally characterized by the term "work ethic." Work is regarded as having spiritual meaning, buttressed by such behavioral norms as punctuality, honesty, diligence, and frugality. One's job is a central life interest and provides the dominant clue in interpersonal assessment. A work force with this set of values is highly adapted to use by business organizations in their pursuit of the values of productivity, efficiency, and effectiveness.

There is growing evidence that the work ethic is declining in favor of a more existential view of life. Instead of organizations providing the basic guides to living, persons are responsible for exploring and determining for themselves what they want to do and become. With this philosophy, work becomes only one alternative among many as a means for becoming a whole person in order to "do one's own thing." Family activities, leisure, avocations, and assignments in government, churches, and schools are all equally viable means through which a person can find meaning and become self-actualized. The absolute worth of the individual is a value which is merged with the concept that all people are members of the great human family. Concerning specifics, full employment gives way to the full life. Climbing the organization ladder of success for its accompanying materialistic symbols becomes less important than self-expression through a creative accomplishment. Private lives outside the job and firm are relatively autonomous, accompanied by an increasing reluctance to sacrifice oneself or one's family for the good of the organization.

A vice-president of General Electric Company has predicted a number of specific changes in values for the decade of the seventies.[9] Among these are moves toward (1) quality of life over mere quantity, (2) equity and justice for the employee over economic efficiency, (3) pluralism and diversity over uniformity and centralism, (4)

[9] Virgil B. Day, "Managing Human Resources in the Seventies," *Personnel Administration*, vol. 33, no. 1, January–February 1970, p. 23.

participation over authority, (5) personal convictions over dogma, and (6) the individual over the organization. There is some evidence among a few firms that action is taking place in the proposed directions.

With respect to an increasing emphasis upon the individual as compared with the organization, a number of changes in personnel programs have been tried. Attempts have been made to *redesign jobs* to provide challenging activities that meet needs of the human ego.[10] In one company, it being well realized that some individuals prefer more repetitive, less challenging assignments, a choice was provided between the assembly line and individual assembly for the *same* product. Concerning *pay*, a few firms have moved to pay the employee for skills possessed rather than for skills demanded by the job. With respect to *fringe benefits*, a cafeteria arrangement has been proposed where the employee can periodically choose what particular benefits he or she desires while remaining within an overall cost limit. It is apparent that individuals differ over time with respect to their needs for cash, insurance, and retirement income. One writer has proposed that the *hiring* process be executed with more concern for the individual's need for information about the company.[11] Rather than the organization consuming all the hiring time in attempts to extract information about applicants, provision should be made for giving applicants data about their projected supervisors, type of personnel with whom they will be working, current statistics on absenteeism and turnover in the projected department, and recent morale survey results. Applicants make decisions about taking jobs which are as important to them as decisions made by the organization to hire them.

One of the more interesting personnel programs that reflect an increasing concern for the individual is "flexi-time." Though just now making its entry into this country from Europe, it is a program that allows flexible starting and quitting times for the employee. The schedule used by one company is as follows: (1) 7 to 9 A.M. constitutes a flexible band during which the employee may choose the time he or she begins work, (2) 9 A.M. to 11:30 is core time—all employees must be present, (3) 11:30 A.M. to 1:00 P.M. is flexible time for taking a thirty-minute lunch, (4) 1 P.M. to 4 P.M. is core time, and (5) 4 P.M. to 6 P.M. is flexi-time for quitting. All employees must still work the required hours for the week or month.

The flexi-time arrangement began in West Germany in 1967 and it is estimated that over one million of its industrial employees are under the plan. In one firm, flexi-time encompasses twenty-four hours per day, as all employees are given keys to the plant.[12] Though the plan is catering to individual needs, a number of values have accrued to the employer. Tardiness and absenteeism have been reduced, since the individual can take care of personal errands during flexi-time. Productivity has been enhanced, since individuals can arrange to work during their peak activity periods. They are also inclined to finish a job started near the end of the day, rather than postponing it with a consequent second warm-up period. Problems with the system lie in the areas of recording time, legislation governing overtime hours, supervision, and contacts with those outside the firm who are accustomed to more inflexible hours. The time clock,

---

[10]See Chap. 4.

[11]Edward E. Lawler III, "For a More Effective Organization—Match the Job to the Man," *Organizational Dynamics*, vol. 3, no. 1, Summer 1974, p. 25.

[12]Alvar O. Elbing, Herman Gadon, and John R. M. Gordon, "Flexible Working Hours: It's about Time," *Harvard Business Review*, vol. 52, no. 1, January–February 1974, p. 19.

banished as a symbol of regimentation in some firms, may have to reappear in a different role of time accumulation. Some laws require penalty payment for hours in excess of eight per day and/or forty per week. Supervisors will have to train and delegate self-supervision rights for hours when they are not present. Outsiders will have to be informed of the restricted core-time hours when they can expect to find all persons available.

Currently, it is estimated that no more than 100 firms with approximately thirty thousand employees in this country employ some type of flexi-time. Movement to a four-day week has been more popular. However, it is apparent that the four-day week does not adapt to individual differences as much as flexi-time. Of some three thousand firms that have moved to this schedule, some 15 percent have abandoned the effort as being dysfunctional. Fatigue is cited as the principal disadvantage of compressing the schedule into four days.[13]

Changing demands of employers

Changes are not all on the side of members of the work force. Organizations constantly undergo changes in their internal environments in response to competitive pressures as well as advancing technological progress. Two of the many major changes are (1) growth of the huge international organization and (2) steadily increasing attempts to automate operations. Effects of these upon personnel programs will be briefly outlined.

Of the gross world product in 1973, it was estimated that 15 percent was produced by multinational corporations. It is also predicted that by the close of this century, some three hundred giant international business firms will produce more than half of the world's goods and services.[14] Of the world's top industrial companies, over half are based in the United States.

The most important facet of the personnel process in the establishment and operation of overseas plants and facilities is that of selection and placement of key personnel. Pains should be taken to assure that selectees possess certain basic characteristics. Among these are: (1) a very real desire to work in a foreign country, (2) spouses who have actively encouraged their mates to work overseas, (3) cultural sensitivity and flexibility, (4) high degree of technical competence, and (5) a sense for politics. One survey of the opinions of 127 overseas managers revealed that they thought that the spouses's opinion and attitude should be considered the number one screening factor.[15] Cultural sensitivity is also essential if we are to avoid the image of the "ugly American." In correlating success of performance with various selection criteria, one study emphasized "the great importance of setting consistent and accurate initial expectations about the work situation" of the overseas assignment.[16] This would

[13]Janice Neipert Hedges, "New Patterns for Working Times," *Monthly Labor Review*, vol. 96, no. 2, February 1973, p. 4.

[14]Richard Eells and Clarence Walton, *Conceptual Foundations of Business*, 3d ed., Richard D. Irwin, Inc., Homewood, Ill., 1974, chap. 6.

[15]John M. Ivancevich, "Selection of American Managers for Overseas Assignments," *Personnel Journal*, vol. 48, no. 3, March 1969, p. 192.

[16]James A. F. Stoner, John D. Aram, and Irwin M. Rubin, "Factors Associated with Effective Performance in Overseas Work Assignment," *Personnel Psychology*, vol. 25, no. 2, Summer 1972, p. 317.

require considerable education of the candidate concerning the culture, country, politics, language, and business setting of the international facility.

That a challenge definitely still remains in this area is revealed by a survey of personnel activities actually undertaken for a group of overseas managers.[17] Approximately 80 percent of the firms involved used no tests in screening for these assignments; of those who did, only 20 percent attempted to validate them. Two-thirds of the firms never bothered to consult candidates' spouses concerning their attitudes and feelings about the assignment and the designated country. Two-thirds provided no pre-departure training for selectees to acquaint them with such matters as the people, their political system, and their government. Though the selectees will learn in time, this initial ignorance not only leads to many daily mistakes and gaffes, but it also contributes to disillusionment and a desire to return to home base. The personnel manager must take a more active role in this steadily increasing challenge resulting from changed employer demands.

The second illustration dealing with altered employer demands is <u>automation</u>. Though it has been given various specific meanings, in its simplest terms it is applied to machine and work processes that are mechanized to the point of automatic self-regulation. Among some of the major effects upon personnel management of automation are the following:

1 *The restructuring of production jobs.* Some of the routine, dull, monotonous jobs will be eliminated. New jobs will be created with a "systems viewpoint" rather than the "specialized task" perspective introduced by time and motion studies of the past. An increase in the number of maintenance jobs will occur as a consequence of an accelerated substitution of capital for labor.

2 *Necessity for upgrading the work force.* The restructuring of jobs will levy a considerable burden upon personnel managers to retrain and upgrade personnel to qualify for these new jobs. This will require more classroom instruction as well as on-the-job training.

3 *Structural unemployment.* A most challenging problem to all those interested in effective personnel management is the adjustment of the present work force in terms of quantity. Some jobs will be eliminated and others created that call for higher levels of skill and knowledge. Some personnel cannot be retrained because of fundamental deficiencies in education and abilities. Some personnel cannot be reabsorbed even if retrainable. The unemployment that results is a problem of such significance and complexity that it requires the efforts of not only private industry, but labor unions and all levels of government as well.

4 *Labor relations problems and adjustments.* Restructuring of jobs will also affect the organization of corresponding labor unions. Some unions will die, though unwillingly, as a specialized occupation is automated out of existence. Changes in union jurisdictions would also mean changes in seniority units. The trend may well be in the direction of larger units covering a series of jobs or occupations, or perhaps encompassing the entire plant or company.

5 *Adjustments in wage structures.* The intricate tie-in among jobs and work stations in a highly mechanized or automated plant tends to place the emphasis upon

[17]James C. Baker and John M. Ivancevich, "The Assignment of American Executives Abroad: Systematic, Haphazard or Chaotic?" *California Management Review*, vol. 13, no. 3, Spring 1971, pp. 39–44.

cooperation rather than competition. The individually oriented piece-rate wage system may have to give way to systems which reward the group. As jobs are altered to fit a system, the related pay structures will require corresponding adjustment. Basic pay plans may again be based largely on time spent at work, with extra compensation geared to improvement in *group* output.

6 *Human relations difficulties.* The restructuring and revised layout of work necessarily involves the alteration of existing patterns of interpersonal relationships. The size of any one work group could well decrease; new layouts could force people to work in comparative isolation. This may cause problems of adjustment, as evidenced by the demands of workers in one British factory for a new fringe benefit of "lonely" pay. Certainly, it is easy to predict the human problems that accompany the introduction and grudging acceptance of changes involving the loss of job or obsolescence of skills developed over the years. Automation is introduced for technical and economic reasons, but its immediate consequences and difficulties are essentially human in nature.

Changing demands of government

Throughout this text, we will deal with pertinent national legislation when undertaking the discussion of particular functions of personnel management. It is well at some point, however, to recognize and appreciate the fact that personnel management is becoming increasingly *legalized* in our society. The following incomplete listing of major items of federal regulations pertaining to each personnel function should support this contention.

Procurement

Civil Rights Act of 1964 (Prohibits discrimination in hiring on basis of race, color, religion, nationality, and sex.)

Equal Employment Opportunity Act of 1972 (Empowers federal commission to undertake direct court action.)

Executive Order 11246 (Requires contractors of federal government to establish affirmative action programs in hiring minority groups.)

Rehabilitation Act of 1973 (Requires government contractors to take affirmative action to hire handicapped personnel.)

Development

Civil Rights Act (Applies to training programs.)

Manpower Development and Training Act of 1962 (Funds special programs for the unskilled.)

Economic Opportunity Act of 1964 (Funds special programs for the hard-core unemployed.)

National Apprenticeship Program Act of 1937 (Details basic program requirements for certification.)

Compensation

Civil Rights Act (Applies to pay.)

Davis-Bacon Act of 1931 (Establishes minimum wages and overtime hours for government construction work.)

Equal Pay Act of 1963 (Requires that men and women on same job get equal pay.)

Fair Labor Standards Act of 1938 (Establishes minimum wages and overtime hours for firms engaged in interstate commerce.)

Walsh-Healey Public Contracts Act of 1936 (Sets minimum wages and overtime hours for contracts in excess of $10,000.)

Integration

Age Discrimination Act of 1967 (Prohibits discrimination against older workers.)

Labor Management Disclosure Act (Landrum-Griffin) of 1959 (Protects union members from abuse by union officials and requires numerous reports.)

Labor Management Relations Act (Taft-Hartley) of 1947 (Levies obligations for bargaining upon labor unions.)

National Labor Relations Act (Wagner) of 1935 (Protects right to form unions, levies bargaining obligations on employer.)

Norris-LaGuardia Act of 1932 (Limits use of injunctions against labor unions.)

Maintenance

Employee Retirement Income Security Act of 1974 (Protects worker rights in private pension plans.)

Occupational Safety and Health Act of 1970 (Sets standards and enforces them through inspections and fines.)

Social Security Act of 1936 (Sets up old age and survivors insurance and medicare and stimulates state unemployment compensation.)

In addition to these major pieces of federal regulation, all fifty states have legislation that impinges upon the personnel program. Prominent among these are worker's compensation laws that require employer insurance against injuries on the job, and unemployment compensation laws that require accumulation of funds for payment to workers in the event of layoff. Though one would not like to see a personnel manager design a program with a basic legalistic bent, it is undeniable that one requires the services of a lawyer to monitor compliance with the law. Our society is becoming increasingly legalistic in nature, and great emphasis has been devoted to the protection and enhancement of our human resources.

SUMMARY

A survey of the functions and challenges of personnel management supports the contention that the modern personnel manager must operate at the nexus of three major forces. First, one must plan, organize, direct, and control the procurement, development, compensation, integration, and maintenance of a work force in order that the organization may accomplish its designated objectives. In this view, the work force is an instrument of the organization, and the personnel manager provides and shapes that instrument. Organization requirements change with time, as is illustrated by the growth of large, multinational corporations and the use of more complex and automated technology.

Secondly, the instrumental work force is composed of human beings of varying types with complex and changing needs and values. The personnel manager must assist the organization in adapting to changes in mix (better educated, more working mothers, more minority employees) and values (demands for individual rights, treatment, and opportunities). The personnel manager searches for programs which have overlapping interests for both employee and organization, e.g., flexi-time, which allows individual decision concerning working hours, yet returns values in the area of tardiness, absenteeism, turnover, and productivity.

Finally, the third major force is society, represented by multiple levels of government. A brief list of the statutes and regulations of only the national level serves to illustrate the nature of this burgeoning third force. The obligations of both the organization and the personnel manager toward society will be discussed in greater detail in Chapter 3.

DISCUSSION QUESTIONS

1   Describe the position of the modern personnel manager as he or she stands at the nexus of three major forces of influence with respect to how the job is done.

2   How has the mix of the work force changed in recent years? What problems are thereby created for the personnel manager?

3   With respect to professionally trained employees, what are the nature and significance of designations such as "local" and "cosmopolitan"? What two other categories can be developed using these terms?

4   How does the employment of cosmopolitan professionals alter the task of personnel management?

5   Compare and contrast the "work ethic" with a more existential philosophy of life.

6   Assuming one wanted to alter organizational practices in the direction of catering more to individuals, what suggestions are made in the areas of hiring, pay, fringe benefits, and job design?

7   What is flexi-time? What are its values to the individual and the organization and its problems for the organization?

8   In selecting personnel for overseas assignments, what particular characteristics are desired? How well are personnel managers doing in regard to identifying and preparing these personnel?

9   For each of the personnel functions, itemize one piece of federal regulation that limits or guides the personnel manager.

10   Define and distinguish between a principle of personnel management and a policy of personnel management. Give an illustration for each.

SUPPLEMENTARY READING

ELBING, Alvar O., Herman Gadon, and John R. M. Gordon: "Flexible Working Hours: It's about Time," *Harvard Business Review*, vol. 52, no. 1, January–February 1974, pp. 18–33, 154.

HARRISON, E. Frank, and James E. Rosenzweig: "Professional Norms and Organizational Goals: An Illusory Dichotomy," *California Management Review*, vol. 14, no. 3, Spring 1972, pp. 38–48.

JOHNSTON, Denis F.: "Education of Workers: Projections to 1990," *Monthly Labor Review*, vol. 96, no. 11, November 1973, pp. 22–30.

LAWLER, Edward E., III: "For a More Effective Organization—Match the Job to the Man," *Organizational Dynamics*, vol. 3, no. 1, Summer 1974, pp. 19–29.

MYERS, M. Scott, and Susan S. Myers: "Toward Understanding the Changing Work Ethic," *California Management Review*, vol. 16, no. 3, Spring 1974, pp. 7–19.

SAXBERG, Borje O., and Robert A. Sutermeister: "Today's Imperative: Humanizing the Organization," *The Personnel Administrator*, vol. 19, no. 1, January–February 1974, pp. 53–58.

STONER, James A. F., John D. Aram, and Irwin M. Rubin: "Factors Associated with Effective Performance in Overseas Work Assignment," *Personnel Psychology*, vol. 25, no. 2, Summer 1972, pp. 303–318.

TWO
EVOLVING APPROACHES TOWARD PERSONNEL

There is usually something to be gained by taking a look at the past. We can often determine more correctly the direction in which we are headed if we view it from the perspective of past events, and we can often manage to avoid actions that have been proved, by past experience, to be mistaken. For the student of management, the past helps to give a clearer conception of the present status of the subject. For these reasons, in this chapter we shall present a brief summary of selected significant aspects of the history of personnel management.

It should be noted at this point that we shall make no attempt to cover, in detail and in chronological order, various events that have some bearing on the subject. We might debate whether to start with the Industrial Revolution, an economic and historical landmark, or to go back still further and deal with the master-slave or master-serf relationships. We shall avoid such a decision by emphasizing in this chapter the evolution of management's basic attitudes or approaches toward employed personnel. In considering these basic approaches, we note that some pressing "modern" personnel problems have been around for quite some time. Yet the fact that systematic attempts to deal constructively with them have a rather short history indicates that the basic approach has undergone considerable change in our lifetime.

MECHANICAL APPROACH TOWARD PERSONNEL

Industrial management in this country has done an excellent job in the mechanical and electronic implementation of production. For over a century managers have applied the principles of interchangeable parts, transfer of skill from human to machine, and operational specialization to machinery, equipment, layout, and the general plant. This has been accomplished with a high degree of success. It is not surprising, therefore, that the same basic mechanical approach should be applied to labor. If machines can be made more productive by extreme specialization, so can people. Jobs can be created requiring such little ability that bodies, properly numbered, can be interchanged readily. Just as we try to purchase machinery and plant with the lowest direct outlay, so we can hire labor as cheaply as possible. Just as we try to keep plant and equipment operating economically as long as possible and junk them for better when necessary, so we can use and discard human labor.

This basic approach, which we have labeled "mechanical," has also been called the "commodity approach" or the "factor-of-production concept." These titles are descriptive of the attitude which assumes that labor must be classified with capital and land as a factor of production to be procured as cheaply as possible and utilized to the fullest. The fact that a human being is involved in this factor is of little significance. In effect, we are adopting a *closed-system* stance or strategy in our approach to the management of personnel. We assume that personnel are controllable, predictable, and interchangeable. The firm is sheltered from outside forces such as government or labor unions that might attempt to "interfere" with the mechanistic approach to personnel. Related to this attitude was the "scientific management" movement, which also adopted a rationalistic, deterministic, and closed-system approach to the management of the enterprise. Its recognized founder, Frederick W. Taylor, introduced such techniques as motion study, time study, incentive wages, and specialized foremanship in the pursuit of technical efficiency. As he stated, "Each man must learn how to give up his own particular way of doing things, adjust his methods to the many new standards, and grow accustomed to receiving and obeying directions covering details, large and small, which in the past have been left to his individual judgment."[1] Man is viewed as an excessively simplistic human system who only strives to avoid pain and obtain money, the "economic-man" model.

Since labor is human, with multiple complex motives, the mechanical approach usually results in the creation of various management problems—personnel problems. Many of these problems are quite old and have their beginning with the original adoption of this approach toward labor. Though the philosophy toward personnel is changing and has changed, we are still struggling with the aftermath created by the mechanical approach, and it is evident that managers still exist whose attitudes are influenced by the old philosophy.

It is well at this point to survey briefly a few of these pressing modern personnel problems whose roots we find in the past. Without implying that these are the only such problems, we believe that this presentation should assist in providing some perspective for the personnel function as performed in the present. The selected problems are (1) technological unemployment, (2) security, (3) labor organization, and (4) pride in work. Some indication will be given of how the problems arose, what management did about them using the mechanical approach, and what the consequences were of such proposed solutions.

Technological unemployment

Loss of jobs through the development of new machines or new techniques of work is termed "technological unemployment." Labor is replaced either by machines or by management innovations that result in more work being done by fewer people. The

---

[1]Frederick W. Taylor, *Shop Management*, Harper & Brothers, New York, 1911, p. 133.

mechanical approach of management toward technical problems pays off in the immediate sense. In that same sense the losses to labor are obvious. Reactions of labor in the past were not greatly different from those of today to similar events—fear and resistance. Yesterday there were riots and attempts to sabotage the new machinery. Today there are more subtle types of resistance, such as slowdowns and union-negotiated introduction of laborsaving devices.

In dealing with this problem, we might as well admit at the outset that the introduction of technological improvements is going to create some immediate problems, particularly in the short-run displacement of personnel. The solution will then be directed toward a minimization of such unemployment and a lessening of the burden upon the personnel actually displaced.

Labor unions are not against technological progress per se. Such progress is the foundation of our high economic standard of living. Machines expend over 90 percent of the work energy demanded by production, and few would like to go back to the "good old days" of hand labor.[2] It has been demonstrated that in the economist's long run greater employment results from these technological improvements. The newer techniques result in a decrease in the price of the product; the lower price results in increased sales and production; and after the required adjustment takes place, our unemployed worker is recalled. Though the effect in the long run is beneficial, we still have the problem of the worker's need to eat and live in the short run. He or she may be recalled to another type of job. Technological improvements usually result in the modification of jobs and often in their elimination. It sometimes happens that an entire occupation, such as glass blowing, is practically wiped out by the introduction of machinery. The reabsorption of displaced personnel may require extensive retraining and often, for a time, personal adjustment to lower incomes.

What are some of the proposed solutions to the personnel problem of minimizing the adverse effects of technological changes? First, it should be pointed out that for over a century industrial managers in general did not particularly worry about the problem and that they mechanically laid off the employee. This was the free-enterprise system, in which employees looked after themselves. But growing public dissatisfaction with the manner in which this problem was being ignored stimulated the proposal of some individual solutions. A few isolated companies, such as Procter and Gamble, advanced the philosophy of sharing part of the company's profits with employees in order (1) to allow workers to benefit from the company's improved position and (2) to provide some additional funds to help tide the worker over in case of unemployment. This solution was not widely accepted, to say the least, though the Procter and Gamble plan, started in 1886, exists to this day. A few companies, such as Nunn-Bush Shoe Company, Hormel Company, and again Procter and Gamble, proposed the idea of guaranteeing an annual wage for all eligible employees. Though they might work a short week or be laid off entirely, covered employees would continue to receive pay for a limited time, a year being, in most plans, the maximum. These employer-initiated guaranteed annual wage plans did not spread.[3] In 1936 the federal government in the Social Security Act imposed a responsibility on private industry for partially financing the out-of-work employee through unemployment compensation. Funds collected

---

[2]J. Frederic Dewhurst and Associates, *America's Needs and Resources*, Twentieth Century Fund, New York, 1957, p. 787.

[3]See Chap. 16 for a more complete coverage of this type of compensation.

from taxing employers are available to eligible persons seeking work. These funds are administered by state employment agencies and provide some weekly compensation for a limited period. In the 1950s we had the union version of the guaranteed annual wage as an imposed solution to this problem. In most instances, this means an employer-financed supplementation of the unemployment compensation, which would raise the total amount paid to the employee to over 50 percent of the base wage. It should be noted that these plans cover all types of job losses other than discharge for cause and organized strikes. Perhaps the two most common reasons for job loss are technological change and layoff due to the reduction in the need for output.

All the above-cited plans—profit sharing, unemployment compensation, and guaranteed annual wages—will be discussed in this text. Our purpose at this point is to demonstrate (1) that we are dealing with a very old personnel problem, (2) that the problem was long ignored by private industry, (3) that the problem will not take care of itself through relying on the usual long-run economic adjustment, and (4) that solutions imposed from without, by government and labor unions, will fill the void left by private industry. Few thinking people oppose these technological improvements, but many are concerned with the manner and timing of their introduction in order to minimize the short-run effects on employment.

Security

It is evident that decreased economic security is also a current problem that results partially from other problems, such as technological unemployment, and in turn creates still other problems, which lead to the creation of labor organizations. The mechanization of production creates the factory system. With the forming of factories, labor must move from a predominantly agricultural environment to the locale of a city. The tool or machine assumes greater importance, and the worker is often relegated to the position of machine tender. The uncertainty of steady employment, coupled with the problem of coming old age, works to produce a greater feeling of economic insecurity.

Granting the increase in the insecurity of employees, we might ask why management should be concerned, in a free competitive society. Such unconcern was at one time the attitude of industry in general, a philosophy that was consistent with the mechanical approach. This reaction to the problem proved to be wrong, and outside forces stepped in to impose certain solutions. In the first place, the workers' insecurity led to the formation of labor unions in order that they might acquire a measure of control over some of the factors bearing on economic security. Secondly, the government again entered the picture with such requirements as the following:

1   In 1935 the government, in the National Labor Relations Act, indicated that promoting unionization and collective bargaining was to be the national policy.
2   In 1936 the Social Security Act created the Old Age and Survivors' Insurance program, which forced industry to contribute to retirement pensions.
3   In 1947 the National Labor Relations Board ordered employers to bargain with labor unions on the subject of private pension plans.
4   In 1974, the Employee Retirement Income Security Act required employers to insure their private pension plans against default, and to make provision for employee ownership of individual shares (vesting) after minimum years of service, thereby avoiding total loss of pension if separated from the firm before retirement.

This is not to say that many private employers are not today voluntarily installing various programs to promote employee security. But it is apparent that both unions and government feel that private enterprise by itself will not do enough. Increased employee security can be rationalized on the basis that it contributes to increased employee productivity. It is apparent, however, that business firms cannot "prove" this relationship to the point that it will voluntarily undertake all the programs that society feels is necessary for its human resources.

Labor organization

Management's indifference to the requirements of its personnel contributed heavily to the creation of labor unions. Immediately after the formation of factories, there were attempts to create unions in order to protect against management arbitrariness. Management often seemed unaware that it was initiating labor discontent. When unions were actually formed, various techniques were utilized to destroy them. Labor organizations grew at a very slow pace through the nineteenth century because of such factors as the following:

1   Periodic economic depressions, during which union members broke ranks to obtain any kind of employment
2   Immigration, which supplied workers willing to take less than union men
3   The frontier, which always beckoned when things got rough with an Eastern employer
4   The public attitude, which was generally opposed to labor organization, considering it antagonistic to private property rights and freedom of the individual
5   The attitude of all branches of government, which was a reflection of the public attitude cited above
6   The expenditure of union energy and funds for "uplift" unionism concerned with political reform, rather than with the "business" unionism of dealing with employers for better wages, hours, etc.
7   The aggressive efforts of most managements in actively combating the efforts toward unionization

These factors constituted a decided brake on the labor movement. As each was modified or eliminated, the membership of unions tended to grow.

The first attempt at national organization that met with any degree of success was the ill-fated Knights of Labor, a union that accumulated over 700,000 members in the 1880s. This organization had in it several defects that led to its early demise. Among them were (1) a highly centralized form of control under one man, (2) a heterogeneous membership, which included wage earners of all types and even some small employers, and (3) a great interest in "uplift" unionism. The American Federation of Labor, formed in 1886, profited by these mistakes and established a labor organization which lasts to this day. The federation based its form of unionism on the organization of homogeneous groups of employees along craft lines. The fact that it was formed as a federation is an indication of a decentralization of authority. In addition, the basic policy of the AFL was to refrain from direct participation in politics, a policy which was followed until the 1940s, when the passage of the Taft-Hartley Act jarred the organization away from this philosophy.

Almost from its inception, the American Federation of Labor dominated the labor movement. During these years, industrial management was well aware of the efforts being made along the line of employee organization. Many attempts, mostly successful, were made to halt the spread of unionism. A large number of these attempts involved force and violence. One interesting example should demonstrate the attitudes of union and management and the types of activity utilized by both sides in these contests.

The steel industry in 1892 had a union of skilled workers, the Amalgamated Association of Iron, Steel, and Tin Workers. It was a fairly strong union. The Homestead, Pennsylvania, plant of the Carnegie Steel Company had been struck by this union even though relations between company and union had been fairly friendly prior to this time. Carnegie, who had stated that he was wholly in favor of unions, was away in Europe and had left the factory in the hands of the plant manager, Henry Frick. A wage cut brought on the strike, whereupon Frick shut down the entire plant and prepared to protect it. The workers seized the mill property. Frick rose to the occasion by hiring some three hundred Pinkerton detectives, whom he armed with Winchester rifles and placed on two barges, which were towed up the Monongahela River near the plant property. For one full day a battle that would have done credit to almost any small war raged on the banks of the Monongahela. The strikers tried to sink the barges with cannons, and when this failed, they poured oil on the water and set it afire. The detectives, with three dead and several wounded, surrendered and were marched out of town. Frick then appealed to the Governor of Pennsylvania for aid, and one week later the state militia took over the town. With this protection the company reopened the plant and started to bring in outside personnel. It was estimated that only eight hundred out of nearly four thousand strikers got their jobs back. So thoroughly was the job done that it was not until the 1930s that another effective union was established in steel.

The above-cited example is not presented to secure sympathy or blame for either labor or management. Our purpose is to demonstrate the unenlightened role played by both parties. Much of the stimulus toward labor organization was provided by management activity.

By 1916 there were approximately three million members of labor unions. During the next four-year period, the number was almost doubled, because of wartime prosperity and favorable government attitudes. As usual, the movement suffered during the ensuing short depression and managed to stabilize again at about three million during the 1920s. With some further losses during the Depression of the 1930s, the membership stood at less than three million in 1933. *Twelve years later, there were approximately fifteen million union members.* The most powerful factors contributing toward this increase were the favorable public attitudes, wartime prosperity, and passage in 1935 of the Wagner Act, the Magna Charta of labor. Collective bargaining was pronounced our national policy, and the right to organize was protected. Management's authority over another function was reduced and rigorously regulated.

In 1972 union membership stood at 20.8 million, the highest numerical total in history. Most of the current membership, some 16.4 million, are in unions affiliated with the American Federation of Labor–Congress of Industrial Organizations; the rest is in nonaffiliated unions such as the Teamsters, United Auto Workers, United Mine Workers, and various local independents.[4] Approximately 21.8 percent of the total labor force is organized into unions. This represents a decline from a high of 27.1

[4]See Chaps. 22 and 23.

percent reached in 1953. It is evident, however, that despite this decline, turning back is impossible; the labor union is here to stay as a definite factor in our economy. A philosophy toward unionization different from that of pre-1935 must prevail in the future. We do not suggest that since unions have come this far, management should accept them completely. Such acceptance is neither desirable nor legal. But it should be evident that this problem of labor organization is one of the foremost of our time and requires more constructive thinking than has been evident in the past. Both labor and management would do well to disclaim pure and righteous actions in the past and to concentrate on the practical problem of mutual survival in a comparatively free economic system. Both must basically change their attitudes, and the change of management's point of view may often be a prerequisite to a change on the part of labor.

Decreased pride in work

The tightly designed organization structures and precisely planned work systems have played a role in lessening the freedom of the individual organization member. On the operative level, the increasing transfer of skills to machines has often left the worker with either a task of machine tending or no task at all. For managers, introduction of computers and data processing systems has served to regulate more closely their activities. Chris Argyris has suggested that industrial management in general has tended to underestimate the intelligence, resourcefulness, goodwill, and creativity of the American worker. He contends that jobs have been designed that call for docility, passivity, submissiveness, and short-term perspectives.[5] In his terms, the net result is psychological failure. We should, therefore, be concerned with a resulting absence of individual pride in accomplishment engendered by traditional structures of organization and operation.

As we consider this problem, we should first ask if pride in work is necessary. So long as the employee grinds the work out day after day, regulated by a system of production and managerial controls, why worry? Yet, when a problem is ignored, certain solutions are contributed by others which may not be the most desirable. This work situation, as we have briefly described it, is essentially the plight of the mass production worker, though we have the same problem in many occupations. The CIO split from the AFL in 1936 for the specific purpose of representing this group of employees. The practice of ignoring the many requirements of the mass production worker has led to more unionization. The CIO, of course, later rejoined the AFL to form the AFL–CIO in 1956.

There are no laws or union demands that require management to create employee pride in work. The management with a mechanical approach toward labor has no interest; consequently, it can see no need and therefore no possible profit in considering the employee's psychology. Further analysis of this problem has led many to change their minds and, thus, their approach to labor. If stimulated, employees can often utilize their talents to make greater contributions than the minimum required. There is a large, relatively untapped reservoir of ability, loyalty, and interest. As we shall note later, the individual human subsystem is not so simple as the economic-man

---

[5]Chris Argyris, "Personal vs. Organizational Goals," *Yale Scientific Magazine*, February 1960, pp. 40–50.

model would propose. The employee *has* options other than compliance, suggesting that a closed-system strategy is not really possible.

Of all the problems presented in this series, this is the most difficult to solve. It is even difficult to discuss, inasmuch as it cannot be seen. Many people disclaim any need or desire for pride in work. Yet the need is present, and when there is no constructive outlet, the worker's energies are diverted toward other channels which often prove to be undesirable to management. The treatment of surface symptoms by mechanical management is tantamount to inventing rubber gloves to handle leaky fountain pens. Those with less confidence in the mechanical manipulation of people have been doing some work on this problem, which will be treated in a later chapter. But it is fair to say that even now the surface has been merely scratched. To some, we are in the dilemma of choosing between high productivity through specialization and mechanization and the creation of employee satisfaction while producing. To others, there can be a considerable overlap of interests between the individual and the organization, and jobs can be redesigned that will simultaneously enhance productivity and human satisfaction.[6]

Various other problems of personnel could be classified as a part of this series. But we feel that the essential point has been made—that management has played a large part in creating many of our modern personnel problems and that these problems have been too long ignored. Much of the progress made concerning these and similar problems has taken place within the last twenty years. Personnel management is a youthful, skilled profession dealing with some old and ingrained problems.

PATERNALISM

Although not all firms and managers held with the mechanical approach toward labor, it was fairly predominant in our economy up until the 1920s. Then suddenly there was a drastic reversal of form by a substantial segment of industrial managers. Some believe that a different approach was created by a fear of labor union growth, for during World War I the union membership almost doubled in number. Employees had demonstrated that they could escape from the managerially engineered closed system. As employers observed the breakdown of total control, they attempted to reclose the system by demonstrating to employees that there was little need for an outside force, the labor union. They began to undertake "voluntarily" a number of humanistic activities that they, the "fathers," felt that the employees needed.

Paternalism is the concept that management must assume a fatherly and protective attitude toward employees. The cold, impersonal attitude of the commodity concept is now replaced by a personal, and sometimes superpersonal, attitude of paternalism. The 1920s were the period during which personnel management became known as the glamor field of management. Here is where the need arose for the "backslapper," the "personality boy," and the man whose sole qualification was "liking people." During this time very elaborate personnel programs were developed, emphasizing such activities as company stores, company homes, recreational facilities, and the like. If the objective of this approach was to contain unions, it succeeded for a time, since the

[6]See Chap. 4.

labor movement actually decreased in membership during this period. If the objective was that of buying employee loyalty and gratitude, it failed, since the employees considered themselves adults rather than children.

We do not believe that merely supplying many benefits, such as housing, recreation, and pensions, makes a management paternalistic. It is the attitude and the manner of installation that determine whether or not a management is paternal in its dealings with employees. Of firms that offer identical benefits, one might be properly labeled paternalistic and the other might not. To be paternalistic, two characteristics are necessary. First, the profit motive should not be prominent in management's decision to provide such employee services. They should be offered because the management has decided that the employee needs them, just as a parent decides what is good for the children. This is not to say that the services may not prove to be profitable, but profit is not the prime reason for their installation. Secondly, the decision concerning what services to provide and how to provide them belongs solely to management. The *father* makes the decision that he feels is best for the child. If a firm offers a program of employee services because (1) it feels that such treatment of labor is a sensible and profitable undertaking that will advance the entire organization, or (2) the employees request and participate in the establishment of such programs, or (3) the labor union *demands* such programs, then that firm cannot properly be labeled paternalistic.

It is interesting to note that the paternalistic era coincided with the initiation of a second school of management thought. Just as the first, scientific management, developed in conjunction with the mechanical approach, the second school grew out of a series of lengthy experiments at the Hawthorne plant of the Western Electric Company beginning in 1924. This school, variously titled "human relations" and "behavioral," encouraged the adoption of a new model of man as a social being. The pendulum swung from one extreme to another, from simplistic economic man to simplistic social man. Developing employee morale was viewed as a certain means to higher productivity. The interests of humans and organizations were deemed to be substantially identical. The impact of this school of thought, populated primarily by psychologists and sociologists, was felt primarily in the 1940s and 1950s. Just as the scientific management philosophy exacerbated certain human problems within the organization, the softer, human relations programs did not meet the requirements of organizational effectiveness in the experience of many managers. The problem is, instead, a highly complex one.

SOCIAL SYSTEM APPROACH

Paternalism died largely during the Depression of the 1930s, though certain managements still claim to utilize this basic approach even today. Having learned through experience of the values and dysfunctions of both prior approaches, managers and researchers began to realize that the management of personnel is no simple process. The pendulum has moved from its extreme simplistic positions to a more complex location involving analysis of multiple and often conflicting forces. We shall term this third view of personnel management a "social system" approach. In brief, the organization, or firm, is viewed as a complex central system operating within a complex environment which can be termed an "outer extended system." Managers recognize that the central system *cannot* be closed and directed in a mechanistic fashion. Options are available to central system members, both within the boundaries of the firm and on the outside with the aid of such external units as labor unions, government, and various public groups. Significant elements of the systems, depicted in Figure 2-1, will be discussed in the following sections.

System components

There are many and varied definitions of the term *system*. The definition by Beckett— "A system is a collection of interacting systems"—is perhaps most accurate, though confusing.[7] A system is a conglomerate of interrelated parts, each of which in turn can be viewed as a subsystem. Our central system, the firm, is a part of a larger system generally known as the "economic system." The economic system is a part of the political system of our nation. Our country is a part of the political system of the world. The world is a subsystem of the solar system, which in turn is a subsystem of a largely uncharted space system. Thus, when we state that a system is a collection of interacting systems, we are emphasizing the inevitable interconnectedness and relationships that management must consider if it is to develop viable programs of personnel management.

The major components of any one system, as depicted in Figure 2-1, are (1) inputs from the outer environment; (2) a processor component, consisting of people, functions, and physical factors, that transforms these inputs into another set of utilities (e.g., steel into automobiles, ill patients into healthy people, uninformed students into knowledgeable citizens); (3) a set of outputs desired by members of the outer

[7]John A. Beckett, *Management Dynamics: The New Synthesis*, McGraw-Hill Book Company, New York, 1971, p. 29.

Figure 2-1 The social system

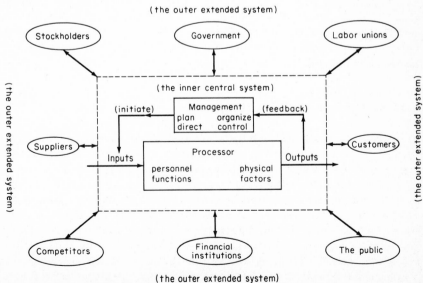

environment; and (4) a nerve system, usually designated "management," which regulates the inputs, processor, and outputs. One of the significant subsystems of the processor is termed "personnel." Though located *within* the boundaries, modern managers recognize that they do not have total control over the talents and attitudes of their employees, thereby requiring an open-systems strategy of adaptation, negotiation, persuasion, and compromise. Each individual employee is a complex human system. Employees tend to develop friendships, cliques, and associations that, in turn, become informal subsystems. We have learned that serious study of individual needs, as well as of informal group processes, can lead to personnel programs that help to align central system objectives (outputs) with the goals of the personnel component. This is a very complicated process, defying any easy assumptions growing out of the mechanistic or paternalistic approaches of the past. In some instances, alignment is not possible, and management must accept and cope with conflict in order to keep the system operating at acceptable levels. It should also be noted that the subsystem of "management" has been divided, as suggested in the preceding chapter, into the functions of planning, organizing, directing, and controlling. After plans have been developed, the processor is designed and populated through the organizing function. Direction provides the initiating impulses for the processor to begin operation, while control works from the feedback of information concerning the nature and level of ensuing operations. Thus, the management component is also a subsystem. It should be equally apparent that a personnel department, if one exists in the firm, is also a subsystem of the processor with activities and goals that can hopefully be aligned with all other subsystems.

Interfaces with outer extended system

It will be noted in Figure 2-1 that a dashed line has been drawn around the central system to indicate its boundary. Outside of this boundary line is the system's environment. It should also be noted that the line is dashed, implying openness to external forces, and is drawn through the inputs and outputs, since these inputs are drawn from the environment and outputs are returned to that environment. The inputs of this system are the outputs of other systems. General Motors requires the input of steel, a material which constitutes the output of Bethlehem Steel. General Motors produces the output of automobiles, which in turn is the input of the Avis car rental organization.

All of the eight listed members of the outer environment can bring forces to bear upon the central organization. The forces exerted by government and labor unions upon personnel programs are very apparent and will be discussed throughout this text. The public is typically less well organized, but there have been many instances where special groups have instituted boycotts or set up pickets to influence management in its treatment of selected groups of employees or potential employees.

The phrase "Everything affects everything else" is a true one, but it is of little assistance in defining and delimiting management processes. How wide and far-reaching into the outer environment should the extended-systems viewpoint take the manager? There is no arbitrary rule or guide to follow. The extended-system boundaries are likely to be vaguely defined and to undergo alteration as knowledge expands concerning the importance of various environmental groups. If the central system is significantly dependent upon other systems for its survival and success, they must be included in a concept of a more extended system. Labor unions were heavily ignored until the 1930s, when they expanded their membership fivefold. Government was either ignored or manipulated until the Depression of the 1930s, when societal demands led to a rash of social legislation which is destined to continue. In the distant past, management was inclined to look almost exclusively toward the legal owners, the stockholders. In some instances, where they have gained control over election to boards of directors, they have reduced their dependency and thus their extended-systems viewpoint. Hired managers, as contrasted with owner managers, are more inclined to expend monies in directions *other* than dividends. One study revealed that owner-manager firms returned 75 percent more income on investment than did firms managed by hired, professional managers.[8] The latter were investing funds in employee welfare, contributions to private schools, employing the hard-core unemployed, and perhaps, stockholders would contend, in a more inefficient administration of processor activities.

As any one of the members of the extended outer environment acquires power to affect the firm's processes, management must modify its decision processes. It may first attempt to contain the forces, thereby trying again to close the system. For example, public relations programs are undertaken to convince the public that the organization is "good" in its various actions. Advertising programs are developed to persuade the customer that this company's products are best. Earnings are retained to lessen dependency upon financial institutions. Multiple sources of supply are developed so that no one vendor will have too much influence. Stockpiles of finished goods are created to enable the firm to withstand strike threats from labor unions. Lobbyists are hired to contact members of government, as well as to manipulate appointment of friendly people to various regulatory commissions. Stockholder proxies are avidly pursued by managers to control board of director elections. To some, many of these actions designed to reduce central-system dependencies are antagonistic to a broader view of social utility. However, two points can be made. First, the basic requirements of all social systems involve this movement toward control and predictability. The efficiency and effectiveness of the scientific management school, which had much to do with developing the high American economic standard of living, rest on this movement toward greater rationality. The fact that certain individual managers may become "power mad" is incidental to the requirements for rationalizing organizations. Second, we must again emphasize that there is *no way* that the system can be entirely closed and made completely rational. Though they may try, managers will never be able to eliminate the contingencies (What might they do?) and constraints (They will not allow it!) imposed by members of the outer environment. The decision process is often one exemplified by, "*If* clients (customers) are willing to wait while the change-over is being made, and *if* the shareholders will accept reduced dividends this year, the production line will be automated—*if* the supplier will make certain modifications in the design of the equipment and reduce the last quotation."[9] And one might also add other *ifs*, such as "if the labor union will permit it" and "if the firm can find other jobs for all displaced personnel."

---

[8]R. Joseph Monsen, "Ownership and Management: The Effect of Separation on Performance," *Business Horizons*, vol. 14, no. 4, August 1969, p. 47.

[9]Glenn Gilman, "The Manager and the Systems Concept," *Business Horizons*, vol. 12, no. 4, August 1969, pp. 23–24.

Finally, the concept of an ever-changing extended-systems view can also be applied to personnel within the central system. As noted in Chapter 1, research has indicated that the employee's spouse can have a significant impact upon effectiveness of operation in overseas assignments. Thus, a system view would require managerial extension to include interviews with and education of the spouse as well. On the other hand, some purely domestic firms have sought to extend the view to require approval of the spouse prior to promotion. This has often been socially rejected and the boundary pushed back, on the basis that it is none of the firm's business and constitutes an invasion of privacy. Some firms have attempted to extend the system to include disciplining employees for undesirable off-the-job behavior, e.g., slugging one's supervisor in a local bar or pub. The court system helps to define the legal system limits in many such cases. In one instance, the firm was allowed to discipline the employee for hitting the supervisor—it was deemed necessary to maintain the hierarchy of authority, the backbone of the processor. When one slugs a fellow employee in an off-the-job location, however, courts have determined that it is none of the firm's business.

In sum, the social system approach to personnel is part and parcel of a larger system approach to management. Research has demonstrated that it is often possible to develop personnel programs that can simultaneously satisfy the needs of individuals, groups, managers, and the total organization. In other instances, research has also shown that total integration of these multiple interests cannot be effected. Open-system analysis and development of strategies characterized by discussion, confrontation, negotiation, and compromise will be required to manage conflicts that inevitably develop. This task is further complicated by the forces that can be brought to bear by significant others in the outer environment. These forces seem to become more numerous and powerful as time goes by. The net result is that modern management, as well as personnel management, is an exceedingly difficult and complex task. There are no easy prescriptions. We must examine each proposed and operating program on the basis of its functional and dysfunctional effects upon the central system and its component parts. Though our final decision will not ensure a home run every time we come to bat, it is highly likely to improve our batting average.

SUMMARY

In many respects one can consider personnel management to be a relatively new function in American business. Few staff personnel departments existed prior to 1920, and many that were begun during the era of paternalism were eliminated by the Depression of the thirties. The growth of unions, the greater injection of government into the field of labor-management relations, and World War II all combined to remake the face and content of the personnel function. Thus our history is short, and the development pace is rapid.

Yet, as is emphasized in this chapter, many of our modern personnel problems are in reality quite old. The mechanical approach fostered by the factory system created many of these problems. That they were so long ignored by business managements does not deny their existence. Improper handling of these problems has worked to the disadvantage of the business firms, because authority and freedom have been lost, to a considerable degree, to government and labor unions. When business did little to soften the effects of technological unemployment, to provide a greater measure of economic security, to contribute to a greater pride in the work and the firm, or to recognize the need of employees for self-expression and greater security against arbitrariness, it more or less invited the solutions of others.

Scientific management and the mechanical approach to personnel assumed that the system could be closed and buffered from all unpredictable forces. When the union movement doubled its membership during a five-year period, management attempted to reclose the system through a second approach of paternalism. Though paternalism was effective for a time, the Depression of the 1930s, quintupling of union membership, increasing governmental regulation, and on-going research into management processes led to the development of a third approach to personnel.

The social system view of personnel is largely based upon relative power analysis. The manager of the central system is dependent upon processor personnel for cooperation, ideas, and goodwill that cannot always be commanded or directed. The central system is also dependent upon multiple significant groups in the outer environment. Such multiple and complex interdependencies call for managerial strategies of an open-system type, requiring skills of analysis, adaptation, negotiation, persuasion, and compromise. Intensive study of the personnel component is necessary to develop programs that have greater chances of reconciliation with organizational goals. Recognition, acceptance, and reasonable integration of inevitable conflicts when interests do not coincide are also managerial requirements within the social system. Unusual obligations of the personnel manager with respect to assessing and coping with the government and public components of the outer system will be discussed in the following chapter.

DISCUSSION QUESTIONS

1   Define and interrelate the three approaches to personnel with the development of various schools of management thought.
2   Of the three approaches—mechanical, paternalistic, and social system—which is most likely to assume the presence of a closed system? Why?
3   Relate the growth of labor union membership to the development of the three approaches to personnel.
4   What is meant by the concept of "extended-systems" view of the outer environment? How does the manager know how far it should be extended?
5   What are the major components of a system? How can we characterize management as a nerve subsystem?
6   Concerning pride in work, what is the nature of Argyris's charge against industrial managements?
7   When private managements fail to solve such problems as technological unemployment, insecurity, and loss of pride in work, what usually happens next?
8   How can two firms have the same list of employee benefits and services and yet one be paternalistic and the other not?
9   What are the major groups making up the outer environment? Indicate how managements attempt to reduce their dependency on each group.
10   If a firm demands the right to interview a prospective employee's spouse before hiring or promoting, is it going beyond acceptable system limits? Discuss.

SUPPLEMENTARY READING

BECKETT, John A.: *Management Dynamics: The New Synthesis*, McGraw-Hill Book Company, New York, 1971, chap. 2.

COLEMAN, Charles J., and David D. Palmer: "Organizational Application of System Theory," *Business Horizons*, vol. 16, no. 6, December 1973, pp. 77–84.

MYERS, M. Scott: "The Human Factor in Management Systems," *California Management Review*, vol. 14, no. 1, Fall 1971, pp. 5–10.

PENZER, William: "Bridging the Industrial Engineering/Behavioral Science Gap," *Personnel Journal*, vol. 52, no. 8, August 1973, pp. 696–701.

SHAPIRO, H. Jack, and Mahmood A. Wahba: "Frederick W. Taylor—62 Years Later," *Personnel Journal*, vol. 53, no. 8, August 1974, pp. 574–578.

SHEPARD, Jon M.: "Specialization, Autonomy, and Job Satisfaction," *Industrial Relations*, vol. 12, no. 3, October 1973, pp. 274–281.

PART TWO

PERSONNEL MANAGEMENT FUNCTIONS

The personnel manager has both advisory and service responsibilities to fulfill for the organization. Two major areas in which specialized and expert advice is sorely needed are (1) the social obligations of the private firm (Chapter 3), and (2) the design of the total organization structure for the enterprise (Chapter 4). The major continuing service obligation is, of course, to establish and manage the operating personnel unit (Chapter 5), whose basic goal is to provide an able and willing work force for the organization (Parts Three through Seven).

THREE

TOWARD THE SOCIAL ROLE
OF THE BUSINESS FIRM

In recent decades, there has been a growing concern about a redefinition of the proper role of the business firm within our society. This concern has usually been discussed under the label "social responsibility." Obviously, every component of a society owes some obligation or responsibility in return for its rights and privileges. Traditionally, the responsibility of the business firm has been to produce and distribute economic goods and services in return for a profit. Because of the increasing size and complexity of society's needs, this narrow definition of role is no longer tenable. Decisions concerning the direction and operation of the economy and its business entities have *social consequences* that can no longer be ignored.

Successful performance of the economic role has ceased to be the *only* kind of socially responsible behavior which society requires of the business firm. Beyond this, we have become increasingly concerned with the preservation and enhancement of (1) our physical resources on this planet and (2) our human resources. Concerning the first, it has become only too apparent in recent years that our physical resources of air, land, and water are being seriously threatened by an uncontrolled pursuit of economic goals. Thus ecology and pollution abatement have come to the fore as prime additional social responsibilities of business. Secondly, with the labor union movement of the 1930s and 1940s and the civil rights movement of the 1950s and 1960s, society members have demonstrated their marked interest in the utilization and enhancement of human resources, particularly those characterized as minority groups, culturally disadvantaged, handicapped, and female.

The personnel manager of a business firm has an important and inescapable responsibility in helping the firm's management to recognize, define, and fulfill this enlarged concept of its social role. Managerial capability in terms of abilities to direct the firm toward economic goals is no longer sufficient. Today, the concept of "every man to his last" does not hold up. The modern manager in our complex society cannot enclose herself or himself in a "cultural economic cocoon" impervious to the pressing noneconomic needs of society.

Surveys of public opinion have revealed a growing antibusiness feeling among members of the general public. In one such survey conducted by the Opinion Research Corporation, the share of the public expressing low approval for business has climbed from 47 percent in 1965 to a clear-cut majority of 60 percent in 1972.[1] A part of this feeling can be attributed to not knowing the facts; e.g., the public believes that after-tax profits of corporations average 28 cents on a dollar of sales, as compared with an actual figure of about 4 cents. But more is due to the reluctance of business firms to take on added social responsibilities in the physical and human areas. A PR (public relations) job will not take care of the problem.

Inasmuch as the human resource portion of social responsibility is of direct and relevant concern to personnel managers, they will be called upon to contribute to the "social conscience" of their firms. In this chapter we shall briefly examine the background material necessary for understanding this enlarged social role, as well as devote specific attention to the societal requirements of utilizing equitably the talents of such special groups as the culturally disadvantaged, the minority groups, and the handicapped. Finally, the personnel manager's role in the execution of a periodic systematic audit of social activities undertaken by the enterprise will be discussed.

UNDERSTANDING THE SYSTEM

To understand the social role of business, the manager requires knowledge in addition to the technical and economic. He must have some acquaintance with history, politics, government, sociology, psychology, and philosophy. The requirements for a university degree in business administration have been increasingly expanded to include these elements in the potential administrator's background. The manager must come to understand that though one may operate within the economy with profit as a stimulus, one does not *own* the economy with unfettered freedom to do with it as one pleases. The United States has moved into a "postindustrial society" where business is no longer the focal point but rather takes its place as a subsystem of a complex whole. As one writer suggests, the purpose of a free economy is not production, but freedom.[2]

Though the list of significant disciplines is long, we shall concentrate here upon three major conceptual foundations underlying our social system; (1) freedom of assembly, (2) pluralism, and (3) constitutionalism. Understanding of these few concepts should assist in understanding the business subsystem role.

Freedom of assembly

Freedom to assemble and form groups and associations is a civil right that is protected by the First Amendment to the United States Constitution and made applicable to the states by the Fourteenth Amendment. Such freedom can exist only in an open society. This freedom enables us to form business organizations, labor unions, fraternities,

---

[1]"America's Growing Antibusiness Mood," *Business Week*, June 17, 1972, p. 100.

[2]Henry C. Wallich, *The Cost of Freedom*, Harper & Brothers, New York, 1960, p. x.

professional organizations, and the like. Rather than have all needs met by a monolithic government, an open society permits the invention and utilization of all types of organizations to meet the complex and changing needs of society. "The genius of America has been its capacity to sustain and foster those intermediary associations that develop the sense of participation in a meaningful community."[3] The United States has often been characterized as an "organizational society."

No freedom is absolute, and it may be modified by society for its general welfare. At one time in our history, it was illegal to form labor unions. Currently, in some states that have so-called "right-to-work" laws, it is illegal to require membership in a union. In other states, the worker cannot disassociate himself from the union if he wishes to retain his job. Men and women are relatively free to form an association called "marriage." To dissolve this association, most states have set up certain restraints. Again, if the society is truly open, citizens are relatively free to move in and out of all types of associations. The restraints placed on this freedom are deemed necessary to the long-term welfare of society.

The traditional view of the association termed a "corporation" is that it is a creature of the state. It is set up with permission to accomplish certain purposes designated in its charter, with the implication that the charter can be revoked or modified if society's welfare requires it. The increased power that has accrued to a relatively few large corporations in America and the world has led some to believe that this "concession theory" is no longer valid, that there is in these vast economic machines a power that devolves from their very great accomplishments. The multinational corporation that transcends international borders, with the assistance of budgets greater than the budgets of most countries of the world, has posed a considerable challenge in defining its social responsibility to a nation or the world.

Pluralism

The right to form associations leads to the formation of a pluralistic society. In a "free-enterprise" economic system, we have multiple competing associations producing the same good or service, with the citizen-consumer presumably benefiting by freedom of choice in the market. We utilize a pluralistic form of government when we deal with city, county, state, and national governments. Pluralism is deeply embedded in the very fabric of American society.

Americans favor pluralism in their society for at least two reasons: (1) it ensures diffusion of power among many organizations, and (2) it promotes the greatest amount of innovation and creativity. Americans are quite suspicious of any concentration of power, whether in their government or in the multiplicity of private organizations. They have taken to heart Lord Acton's famous phrase, "Power tends to corrupt and absolute power corrupts absolutely." The Sherman Anti-Trust Act is directed toward large concentrations of economic power. Despite contentions that largeness begets economies of scale and efficiency, we nevertheless do not rest easy when any one person or association possesses great power. Pluralism, issuing from rights of free association, helps to maintain freedom and liberty.

---

[3]Richard Eells and Clarence Walton, *Conceptual Foundations of Business*, 3d ed., Richard D. Irwin, Inc., Homewood, Ill., 1974, p. 104.

Pluralism also suggests that we should be suspicious of any claims of omniscience. No one person or organization is deemed to have the irrefutable truth. We feel that if many organizations and human minds are grappling with a problem, we are more likely to come up with a more innovative and effective solution. Behavioral management theorists feel that this concept, so widely utilized among our multiplicity of organizations, should also be applied *within* any one organization by encouraging widespread employee participation in solving business problems. Pluralism also connotes competition among multiple associations, which may have some favorable effect in enhancing productivity.

Again, total pluralism would be chaotic in effect. Some concentrations of power are conducive to maximum societal welfare. Like most social concepts, the extremes are objectionable and often dysfunctional. Citizens and associations continue to grapple with the problem of the appropriate mix between the values issuing from largeness and those obtained from many small, locally controlled units.

Constitutionalism

Constitutionalism also issues from the fear of excessive concentrations of power and its possible misuse or abuse. It is characterized by specific restraints imposed upon the holders and users of power. With respect to government, a constitution establishes both a grant of power and a limitation upon the use of that power. Specific constitutional devices in use in this country are those of judicial review to make the constitutional limits effective and "due process of law" to ensure that the human rights of life, liberty, and property will not be transgressed unduly.

In our national government, we have purposely divided the powers among the executive, legislative, and judicial branches. As indicated by various events involving President Nixon, we are still in the process of ascertaining the specific limitations of the powers of each branch. Thus, we have a combination of pluralism and constitutionalism to ensure that human liberties are protected and enhanced. We have even imposed territorial (state, city, and county) and chronological limitations (election for limited periods) upon the wielders of power.

Of what interest is this to a personnel manager? There are strong indications that the concept of constitutionalism may enter the *internal* operations of the firm, particularly the large corporation. When a management has the power to affect a great many lives to a high degree, concern grows for limiting the power, or at least the manner in which such power will be exercised. With respect to the decision to hire, transfer, promote, discipline, or discharge an employee, the unfettered use of decision-making power is steadily being challenged. "Due process of law" or procedure for the business employee is a form of corporate constitutionalism. The employee does not give up his societal citizenship when he enters the corporation. Perhaps the foremost branch of corporate government is the executive, but legislative functions are being undertaken to some extent by labor unions and judicial functions by government arbitrators. Rather than attack these growing restraints on the power of the executive as totally objectionable on the grounds of efficiency, the modern manager will understand the much broader and basic concept upon which this attack is based—the constitutional protection of human rights within the firm.

THE SOCIAL RESPONSIBILITY OF THE BUSINESS FIRM

If one grants that the business firm is a subsystem of the economy, which in turn is a subsystem of the total society, it still remains to determine the nature and extent of that firm's societal obligation. Normative statements of what business *ought* to do with regard to social responsibility will not ensure that action will be undertaken. There are a number of rationales or theories upon which social action can be based. Among these are:

1 Long-run profit maximization and social responsibility are substantially similar concepts.
2 The changing ethics of business managers are in concordance with the changing norms of society.
3 Firms should strive to maximize social utility rather than profits.
4 Firms will prepare a list of goals in order of priority with noneconomic social values being included.
5 Firms will be socially responsible to the degree they perceive power threats in the environment.

With respect to the coincidence of a long-term view of profit and social responsibility, it has been stated, "The longer the range a realistic business projection is, the more likely it is to find a sound ethical footing."[4] When Henry Ford II explained Ford's extensive hard-core unemployed hiring and training program to stockholders, it was justified on the basis of preventing future riots in Detroit. When insurance companies undertook extensive investments in slum reconstruction, they explained to their stockholders that they were opening up future markets for life insurance. When money is contributed to private educational institutions, stockholders are told that the firm's management is helping to develop professional employees for the future. All of these implications are logical, but exclusive benefit to the spending firm is difficult to prove. In addition, the actions of the money and stock markets are often typically based on short-run rather than long-run implications of management decisions. In many instances, this rationale for social spending is often just that—a rationale for a decision made on other grounds.

The sociological view of a movement toward greater business social responsibility rests upon the impact of changing cultural values upon the firm's managers. It is contended that as concern for physical and human resources spreads throughout society, individual managers' consciences and codes of ethics will lead them to make more socially responsible decisions. One negative note is sounded by a survey and comparison of codes of ethics of practicing marketing managers and young college students in both business and liberal arts fields.[5] In asking over 1,500 students and businessmen their views on questionable actions in twenty hypothetical situations, there were *no* significant differences in the answers from the three groups: businessmen averaged 34 percent approval, business students 36 percent, and liberal arts

---

[4]Albert Z. Carr, "Can an Executive Afford a Conscience?" *Harvard Business Review*, vol. 12, no. 4, July–August 1970, p. 64.
[5]Charles S. Goodman and C. Merle Crawford, "Young Executives: A Source of New Ethics?" *Personnel Journal*, vol. 53, no. 3, March 1974, pp. 180–187.

students 33 percent. Lowest average approval was for an action involving hiding your wife's expenses on a report of a recent business trip (4 to 8 percent), while highest approval was given to using "long-distance" telephone calls from nearby cities to reach busy executives (81 to 88 percent). Using hidden tape recorders in conducting personal interviews received approval by approximately a third of all respondents. It has also been observed that business managers will undertake decisions when thinking organizationally (for the benefit of the firm) that they would reject as personally unethical when thinking individually (for the benefit of themselves). Thus, a profit-motivated system may perpetuate some antisocial actions despite changes in personal codes of ethics.

A more optimistic note is provided by a study of 72 corporations from *Fortune's* list of the 500 largest industrial firms arranged by sales in this country.[6] It was found that the net-income-to-net-worth ratio was 75 percent higher for owner-controlled corporations than it was for those managed by hired, professional managers. It is suggested that the owner-manager tries to maximize profits, while the hired manager is either less capable or less motivated toward profit maximization. If hired managers are reducing profit in order to expend monies in the environmental or human resources areas, then their codes of ethics are leading to more socially responsible decision making. One can still worry about the areas in which they are electing to invest this "surplus." Some shudder at the thought of a few appointed business leaders determining what is good for society as a whole.

The third basis for socially responsible action requires determination of the social utilities of managerial decisions. Decisions concerning whether to build or close a plant, promote or fire an employee, or raise or lower a product price have social implications. In deciding whether to shut down a copper smelter that is polluting the surrounding air to some measurable degree, one must balance the societal gains from cleaner air against the societal losses of a reduced number of jobs in the area. Such precision of measurement, ignoring the real problem of determining lesser and more important values, makes such an approach to social responsibility extremely difficult to apply. The closest activity to this process is the systematic social audit, a subject that will be discussed at the end of this chapter. Of course, moving from a profit-maximization philosophical stance to a social utility-maximization view of decision making will require changes in either codes of ethics or total-system pressures upon the executive.

A more usable basis for injecting a greater measure of social responsibility into business decision making is the lexicographic approach.[7] The manager is induced to accept the fact that the firm has, not one goal, but *many* objectives to achieve. These are then placed in an order of priority. Once the first priority has received a *reasonable*, rather than maximum, amount of achievement, efforts are directed toward goals of lower priority. Thus, even though a manager contends that profit is the major goal of the firm, he or she strives to obtain a satisfactory level of profits rather than tries to exact the last possible dollar out of each decision. One places on the list such values as hiring and training the physically handicapped, or locating new plants in underdevel-

[6]R. Joseph Monsen, "Ownership and Management: The Effect of Separation on Performance," *Business Horizons*, vol. 12, no. 4, August 1969, p. 47.

[7]Harold L. Johnson, *Business in Contemporary Society: Framework and Issues*, Wadsworth Publishing Company, Inc., Belmont, Calif., 1971, p. 71.

oped ghetto areas. The new plant may not make a profit for the first few years, but this is not as important if sufficient profits are being generated by other activities of the firm. In the meantime, there is a social contribution in the form of providing jobs in a depressed area.

The final basis is considered by many, particularly the more cynical, to be the only viable, approach to social responsibility. It is based upon a combination of intelligent selfishness and relative power analysis. There are significant and powerful groups operating in the environment of the business firm. Labor unions and governmental units are perhaps the most powerful. Consumer groups, led by such men as Ralph Nader, are working to increase their power. Special-purpose groups, such as the Urban League and the National Organization of Women, try to bring pressure upon the managements of private business firms. Managers will assess the power of each group and its potential threat to organization activities. They will pursue what they deem to be the primary goals of the enterprise, but always with a weather eye out for constraints imposed by others. When managers go too long without responding, or when they fundamentally disagree with actions demanded, they risk the possibility of new legislation. At the minimum, socially responsible action is that of conforming to the laws of society. As will be demonstrated in a later section, the number of laws governing the utilization of society's human resources is steadily increasing. This is evidence that business management either did not read the cues thrown out by society or waited too long to voluntarily comply, thereby ensuring the creation of governmental agencies to monitor business behavior.

OBLIGATIONS OF THE PERSONNEL MANAGER

Thus far we have been speaking generally of the social obligations of the firm. We turn now to the specific responsibilities of a personnel manager in regard to this subject. These can be classified as internal and external.

Many would propose that just as survival and profit are goals of first priority for the firm, the personnel manager's first concern is to assist general management achieve its goals through procuring, developing, compensating, motivating, and maintaining a competent labor force. Certainly, if these are not accomplished to some reasonable degree, perhaps neither the personnel manager nor the firm will be around for long. With regard to added social responsibilities, the personnel manager occupies a unique position. He or she is primarily responsible for seeing that the human resources of society utilized in this firm are protected, preserved, and enhanced. We would also suggest that the personnel manager will be increasingly concerned with human rights as the movement toward corporate constitutionalism continues. In this regard, there is much to be accomplished. Surveys indicate that managements too often make decisions of supreme importance to employees with little or no consultation with them.[8] The "quality of life" within the firm can stand improvement in many areas. Beyond adequate compensation and a safe and healthy work environment, there will be growing demands in the areas of providing challenging and interesting jobs, develop-

---

[8]Rama Krishnan, "Business Philosophy and Executive Responsibility," *Academy of Management Journal*, vol. 16, no. 4, December 1973, pp. 658–668.

ing human capacities, according respect for personal privacy, tolerating dissent, and permitting greater degrees of individualism in such matters as dress and life-style.

Though varying styles and degrees of dedication will result in a diversity of internal corporate governance forms, on the external side government will introduce a measure of uniformity. Each year, a greater obligation is placed upon the personnel manager to ensure compliance with a host of laws and government rules concerning the hiring, training, compensating, and utilization of various special groups in our society. As suggested in Chapter 1, personnel management is increasingly becoming a legalistic process as society has become impatient with voluntary social action by private firms. Brief coverage of these external pressures will be presented in the following section, followed by discussion of special groups selected for protection. As one personnel manager stated, "We do our best and pray a lot."

DISCRIMINATION AND THE LAW

Though approximately forty states of the United States have passed laws related to the prohibition of discrimination in employment, discussion here will be confined to significant pieces of federal legislation and executive orders. Perhaps the most pervasive controls affecting the personnel manager and the firm are: (1) the Civil Rights Act of 1964 as amended by the Equal Employment Opportunity Act of 1972, and (2) Executive Order 11246, covering actions of government contractors. In addition, there is the Equal Pay Act of 1963, the Age Discrimination Act of 1967, and the Rehabilitation Act of 1973.

The Civil Rights Act of 1964, as amended, applies to state and local governments, employers and labor unions with fifteen or more employees, and private and public employment agencies. In brief, it prohibits discrimination in hiring, firing, pay, or other conditions of employment because of race, color, religion, sex, or national origin. The Equal Employment Opportunity Commission, the administering agency, is empowered to undertake direct court action against alleged offenders, after failing at attempts of education, persuasion, and conciliation. The Civil Service Commission is charged with the responsibility in this area for all federal employees. In administering the act, such prohibitions as the following have been forthcoming: no preference for sex can be placed in advertisements; there may be no segregation or classification of employees in any way that deprives them of opportunities or status; there may be no white and black union locals; there may be no separate seniority rosters by type; and there may be no use of selection devices without proper validation. The law does not require an affirmative action program to redress imbalances in the work force, but various courts have required preferential treatment to overcome a perpetuation of discrimination, e.g., one company was required to base promotion on company-wide seniority to overcome the continued discrimination which would have followed using job seniority. In another instance, the EEOC prevailed upon the Federal Communications Commission to refuse a rate increase for the American Telephone and Telegraph Corporation until it effected improvement in employment percentages for females and selected races. As a result, AT&T increased its number of black employees by 44 percent and its Spanish-surnamed employees by 93 percent while increasing its total work force only 14 percent. The company also agreed to place 7,000 women in jobs traditionally held by men, and 4,000 men in positions usually held by women. On occasions, companies have agreed to pay compensation for past discrimination practices, e.g., nine steel firms agreed to over $30 million back pay for 45,000 workers to reflect differences in earnings of minorities for a two-and-one-half-year period.

Contractors of the federal government are covered by Executive Order 11246, which is administered by the Office of Federal Contract Compliance. This control goes further than the Civil Rights Act in that the government can require affirmative action programs to redress work force imbalances. An example of one such plan is shown in Figure 3-1. One specific order of the government has been widely publicized as the "Philadelphia Plan." Contractors in the construction industry with minimum-size contracts are required to work toward specific percentage goals of blacks in employment. For example, the range of acceptable employment for ironworkers in 1970 was 5 to 9 percent; this increased to 11 to 15 percent in 1971, to 16 to 20 percent in 1972, and to 22 to 26 percent in 1973. Some fifty-five cities have variations of the Philadelphia Plan for the construction industry at the present time. Affirmative action programs are also required by the Federal Civil Service Commission. Under such programs the percentage of blacks employed by the federal government moved from 4.2 percent in 1940 to 15 percent in 1970.[9] In 1970, blacks constituted 11.2 percent of the total population.

[9]Larry E. Short, "Nondiscrimination Policies: Are They Effective?" *Personnel Journal*, vol. 52, no. 9, September 1973, p. 790.

Figure 3-1   Affirmative action plan

Purpose:
It is the continuing policy of the Company and its subsidiaries to ensure equal employment opportunity for and utilization of all individuals without regard to race, color, religion, sex, age, or national origin. The following Affirmative Action Plan is being adopted to further this policy and to comply with the requirements of the Office of Federal Contract Compliance under Executive Order 11246.

Responsibility:
The Personnel Manager is charged with the responsibility for carrying out the Company's Affirmative Action Plan, and will modify this plan as needed to maintain its timeliness. All individuals with supervisory authority are responsible for carrying out this policy in their respective areas.

Dissemination:
All recruiting sources will be informed of the Plan. They will be instructed to actively recruit and refer minority applications. Minority organizations, agencies, schools, and community leaders will be notified of the Plan. A civil rights clause will be continued in the labor agreement.

Recruiting:
The Company will actively seek out qualified minority applicants. Advertisements will be placed on a regular basis in newspapers known to have high readership among minority groups. The phrase "An Equal Opportunity Employer" will be used in all advertisements.

Placement:
Affirmative efforts will be made to place minority individuals on all levels in all departments. Hiring goals will be established to maintain a correct balance in the work force.
  1   By January 1, 1977, the number of minority individuals will increase by at least 48 or 50 percent of the number necessary to achieve full utilization.
  2   By January 1, 1979, the remaining 50 percent, or 48 individuals, will be employed.

Training:
Employees will be given equal opportunity for participation in all Company-sponsored and outside training without regard to race, religion, sex, color, age, or national origin.

Figure 3-1—continued.

Promotion:

All qualified employees will be given equal consideration. No job categories are closed. The Company will periodically review the qualifications and progress of its minority employees to ensure that the Plan is fully implemented.

General:

All employees are encouraged to participate in all Company-sponsored activities. All work areas, cafeterias, restrooms, lounges, and recreational areas will continue to be maintained on nonsegregated basis.

Compliance:

The Personnel Manager is responsible for ensuring that this policy is complied with and for informing management as to the degree of compliance. A report of the results of the Plan will be compiled annually in March, and the program updated as necessary.

The Equal Pay Act is an amendment to the Fair Labor Standard Act, which is administered by the Wage and Hour Division of the Department of Labor. It requires equal pay for equal work without regard to sex. The Age Discrimination Act, also administered by the Department of Labor, protects workers between the ages of forty to sixty-five from arbitrary age discrimination in hiring, firing, job referral, and the granting of fringe benefits. The Rehabilitation Act requires affirmative action programs for the handicapped by federal contractors. Finally, a summary of pertinent legislation under this subject could include the National Labor Relations Act, under which a board certifies particular labor unions as exclusive bargaining agents for employees. Unions have been decertified when discriminatory acts have been proved. Certification and protection of union organizing rights provide another possible governmental avenue to enforce prohibition of discriminatory practices.

SPECIAL CULTURAL GROUPS

As the laws and orders discussed above indicate, there are certain selected special groups which society feels should be specifically protected from continued discrimination. The groups that will be briefly discussed are (1) female employees, (2) racial groups, (3) religious and nationality groups, (4) the aged, (5) the handicapped, and (6) the culturally disadvantaged.

Female employees

In the past few years, the activism displayed by various groups of women in bringing pressure to bear upon employers has increased significantly. Approximately 40 percent of the work force is composed of female employees.

The fact that substantial discrimination against the female employee does exist in our society is undeniable. On the average, they receive slightly over 60 percent of the compensation accorded males. For females employed year round in full-time jobs, median earnings in 1972 were $8,925 for those with a college degree, $5,770 for high school graduates, and $4,305 for those who did not complete elementary school.[10] Comparable earnings for the men were $14,660, $10,075, and $7,575, respectively. These lower compensations are caused not only by a general allocation of women to lower-paying jobs and industries, but also by receipt of significantly less pay in the same job. Because of early role differentiation in our society, females constitute the majority in such industries as medical-health (nurse the sick), personal services (cook and serve food), and education (teach children). Female-intensive industries have significantly lower pay levels than those with a heavy preponderance of males.

With the assistance of the Civil Rights Act, Equal Pay Act, and group pressures, there are indications that changes are being slowly effected. The ratio of earnings of women to earnings of men has risen from 61 percent in 1959 to 64 percent in 1969.[11] The percentage of women enrolled in professional training has significantly increased during the period 1960 to 1972: from 6 percent to 13 percent in medicine, from 4 percent to 14 percent in veterinary medicine, from 4 percent to 12 percent in law, and from less than 1 percent to 3 percent in engineering.[12] Needless to say, there still remains much to be done. In a survey of 150 companies by the American Society of Personnel Administrators, it was found that though females constituted in excess of 10 percent of the total employment in most firms, they held significantly less than 10 percent of the professional, technical, and managerial positions.[13] And though 20 percent of the AFL-CIO membership is female, only a very few women hold top-level jobs in American labor unions.

The fundamental causes of discrimination on the basis of sex lie deep within our culture. From early childhood, codes of behavior and interests are taught by parents concerning what is "right" for "little girls" and "little boys." The impact is so pervasive that it has entered our language. Militant members of women's rights groups contend that "Ms" should replace "Miss" or "Mrs.," that perhaps "chairman" and "spokesman" should give way to "chairperson" and "spokesperson," and that personnel managers should substitute "human resources management" for "manpower planning programs." Fixed attitudes have developed among managers concerning the expected behavior of the female, e.g., women employees will get married and quit, mothers with small children will have high absenteeism rates, female employees will not accept transfers to other cities because of the husband's job, and women in general are more undependable emotionally. Concerning these attitudes, some are based on inadequate statistical information, while others display cultural lag in being unaware of significant changes in our society.

With respect to studies of turnover and absenteeism, it has been concluded that sex cannot be isolated as the single major contributor to these problems.[14] When

[10]Elizabeth Waldman and Beverly J. McEaddy, "Where Women Work: An Analysis by Industry and Occupation," *Monthly Labor Review*, vol. 97, no. 5, May 1974, p. 12.

[11]Victor R. Fuchs, "Women's Earnings: Recent Trends and Long-Run Prospects," *Monthly Labor Review*, vol. 97, no. 5, May 1974, p. 23.

[12]John B. Parrish, "Women in Professional Training," *Monthly Labor Review*, vol. 97, no. 5, May 1974, p. 42.

[13]Charles D. Orth and Frederic Jacobs, "Women in Management: Pattern for Change," *Harvard Business Review*, vol. 49, no. 4, July–August 1971, p. 140.

[14]Gary G. Petersen and Linda Bryant, "Eliminating Sex Discrimination—Who Must Act?" *Personnel Journal*, vol. 51, no. 8, August 1972, p. 590.

corrected for type of job, age of person, and education and background, the sounder managerial approach is to avoid general stereotyping on the basis of sex. Concerning absenteeism caused by illness, the Department of Health, Education, and Welfare reported that females lost an average of 5.9 days in 1968 compared with 5.2 for males.[15] However, workers of both sexes over age 45 lost more days, those with less than 9 years' schooling had twice the rate of those with 16 years, whites had 5.1 days while nonwhites had 8.1, workers from families earning less than $3,000 had 7 days lost as compared with 4.4 for those earning above $15,000, and employees of the federal government lost 6.8 days, those from private employment 5.4 days, and the self-employed 5.0 days.

Turnover studies of such specific occupations as chemist and lawyer show no differences in the rates for males and females. A survey of 664,321 employees in California revealed that females, constituting 36.68 percent of the labor force, accounted for 34.4 percent of the quits and discharges.[16] The conclusion again was that separation rates for men and women of similar *age* and *skills* in similar *jobs* are about the *same*.

With respect to possible cultural lag in beliefs about the female role, there are indications of changes in life-styles among the younger segments of the population. Forty percent of the female work force are mothers, one-third of whom have children under the age of six. Household responsibilities are increasingly shared, with less division on the basis of "woman's work" and the "man's job."

Some employers are beginning to move in the direction of decreased discrimination on the basis of sex. Elimination of traditional job allocations on the basis of sex as well as race must be effected. The one significant item of difference, that of child-bearing, can be adapted to through pregnancy leaves, day child-care centers, and flexible working hours. Court decisions are increasingly striking down arbitrary practices with respect to leaves and benefits for maternity. The Supreme Court has upheld a lower-court ruling that a pregnant schoolteacher could continue to work as long as physically able. A district court has found General Electric Company guilty of sex discrimination in denying disability benefits to pregnant workers. There is no portion of the personnel program that will remain unaffected by societal pressures to reduce discrimination.

Racial groups

Because of the energy with which their leaders have attacked the problem of employment discrimination, blacks would constitute a good single illustration of a special racial group. The success that has met their efforts has encouraged more activity on the part of such groups as the American Indians and Mexican- or Spanish-Americans.

A review of various economic data will reveal reasons for the high degree of activity by black leaders in regard to employment discrimination. Blacks' rate of unemployment is ordinarily about double that whites'. Approximately 60 percent of the white labor force have high school diplomas, as compared with 40 percent of the black. In

---

[15]"Days Lost from Work because of Illness or Injury," *Monthly Labor Review*, vol. 95, no. 8, August 1972, p. 48.

[16]Myra H. Strober, "Comment on Lower Pay for Women: A Case of Economic Discrimination?" *Industrial Relations*, vol. 11, no. 2, May 1972, p. 280.

reviewing the changes of the past decade, some improvement in conditions has been noted. The median family income of blacks has increased from 51 percent to 61 percent of that of whites in the period 1960 to 1970.[17] During the 1960s, black employment rose 22 percent as compared with 19 percent for whites. Black employment in white-collar jobs, crafts, and machine operation jumped 72 percent while that in professional and technical areas actually doubled. Despite these gains, blacks still hold most of the lower-paying jobs—37 percent of all black men work in service and labor occupations, as compared with 17 percent of all white men. In 1960, 38 percent of young blacks had completed high school, while in 1970 this had risen to 56 percent.

When a management wishes to introduce a special racial group into the enterprise, it is wise to be aware of possible human relations difficulties. However, studies have indicated that most managements are overly fearful of the reactions of the white majority, and that careful advance planning and preparation can do much to smooth the transition.

The first essential of such an introductory program is the adoption of a definite policy by top management. This serves the same purpose for the firm as law does for the community. If trouble does arise, supervisors are given more confidence by the existence of an explicit directive from top management. If persuasion fails, they can use the policy to force at least a minimum degree of acceptance.

The communication of the policy is of central importance. All managers must *understand* that the policy exists. As has been suggested previously, attitude changes are effected more readily through processes of discussion and conference than through orders and commands. The philosophy and techniques of group dynamics can serve to develop supervisory understanding and acceptance of minority-group members. Willing acceptance is always preferable to forced obedience. However, subordinate managers must be assured that top management mean what they have said and promulgated. Employment agencies and the union must also be informed and convinced. As usual, actions in hiring and upgrading will mean far more than a planned publicity campaign alone.

A key issue is the pace with which members of the special group are introduced into the firm in terms of number, time, and degree of concentration. Many enterprises prefer the "Jackie Robinson model" of selecting a single outstanding employee and allowing him or her to pave the way for others to follow. Black leaders contend that this leads to "tokenism" and long-delaying tactics that perpetuate economic and social discrimination. Though quotas are resisted by employers, various black groups view them as the fastest way to correct past discriminatory practices.

If the firm is serious about improving significantly the percentages of blacks employed, special efforts such as the following will have to be forthcoming in the area of recruitment: (1) Pacific Telephone and Telegraph Company uses walking employment offices—Spanish and black recruiters go to people's homes, barbershops, poolrooms, and bars; (2) Michigan Bell sends recruiting trailers to the ghetto areas; (3) Westinghouse Electric provides one-day plant orientation sessions for students from predominantly black high schools; and (4) General Electric took legal steps to open up housing for a newly hired black engineer.[18]

[17]"The Black Message: Business Must Do More," *Business Week*, Jan. 22, 1972, p. 80.
[18]Theodore V. Purcell, "Break Down Your Employment Barriers," *Harvard Business Review*, vol. 46, no. 4, July–August 1968, pp. 71–72.

In the placement process, application blanks will have to be altered to eliminate questions bearing upon race, religion, and nationality, and interviewers will have to be retrained to assure equal treatment of all applicants. If the black applicant must be rejected on the basis of inadequate qualifications, frankness is important. Acceptance of such rejections is facilitated if it is realized that other blacks have already been hired successfully by the firm. The black is sensitive because of past discrimination, and any rejection must be handled skillfully. At the least, careful rejection records must be kept.

Concerning introduction and orientation of the new black employee, the supervisor is of utmost importance. Certainly, the new employees must be carefully oriented. Though technically qualified, the new black employees may need help in adjusting not only to the industrial environment, but also to the probable "cold" initial acceptance by the majority. They should be placed in departments where supervisors are both sympathetic to the company policy and respected by present subordinates. Supervisors should speak frankly of possible prejudice and the necessity for patience and good performance. They should indicate that they and the company will not tolerate fellow employee actions when they definitely interfere with work processes or when they make it too uncomfortable for the new employees to carry on. If overt resistance is encountered, firm action in consonance with the policy is an absolute necessity. In regard to the employee himself or herself, the manager should expect acceptable levels of job performance, criticize constructively when necessary, and handle disciplinary problems in the same manner that would be employed for those of majority members.

Religions and nationality groups

During the fiscal year ending in June 1972, 47,331 complaints were filed with the Equal Employment Opportunity Commission of the federal government.[19] Only 2.5 percent of these involved religion and 11.2 percent national origin. The more common complaints lay in the areas of race (58 percent) and sex (22 percent).

One of our long-standing national norms is to permit and encourage freedom of religious belief. Our version of constitutionalism requires separation of church and state. Though courts have held that firms do not have to adapt to a limitless number of religious beliefs in the conduct of their business, selection and advancement on the basis of religious convictions are prohibited by law. Though there is less discrimination in initial hiring, there is more in upgrading to higher jobs, particularly those in the management ranks. There are relatively few complaints in the areas of nationality and religion, probably because these characteristics are less observable than those of sex and race.

The aged

There has been relatively little activity undertaken by the government under the Age Discrimination Act. One of the largest suits ever filed by the Department of Labor charged Standard Oil Company of California with using age as a basis for selecting

---

[19]"Job Rights for Women: The Drive Speeds Up," U.S. News and World Report, Dec. 11, 1972, p. 90.

employees to be terminated during a cutback in employment in 1971. Though the company did not admit to violation, it did agree to rehire 120 of its previously terminated employees, and to accompany its action with $2 million back pay for lost wages and benefits.

On a continuing basis, the Department of Labor reports that illegal advertising with respect to age requirements is the most common violation of the law. Almost 2,000 such instances were discovered during 1973. Discrimination on any basis other than qualifications to perform the job is costly to society. Research concerning older workers usually indicates that they are the equal of the younger in terms of quantity and quality of output. Older employees also offer maturity derived from experience. Older workers are less prone to accidents than the younger; caution and experience may compensate for loss in agility and dexterity. They are also usually superior in terms of turnover, inasmuch as they are, ironically, fully aware of the discrimination that exists and thus more appreciative of the job they now hold. Perhaps the greatest bar to the hiring of this class of employee is fear of excessive fringe benefit costs in the areas of retirement pensions, insurance, etc.

The handicapped

The employment of the physically handicapped rests upon economic as well as humanitarian grounds. Research has demonstrated that when properly placed, these employees are equal to or better than unimpaired employees in terms of productivity. They demonstrate even better records in terms of absenteeism, turnover, and accidents. Some additional company effort must often be undertaken with regard to analysis of jobs, re-engineering of jobs to fit selected disabilities, and modifications of entrance and service facilities. These investments will usually return good dividends in the form of dedicated workers.

In 1973, the Rehabilitation Act required government contractors and subcontractors to take affirmative action in the employment of qualified handicapped individuals. Contractors are required to make reasonable accommodation to the limitations of the handicapped, unless they can demonstrate that such accommodations would impose an undue hardship. To be covered by this law, individuals must have their handicaps certified by an agency of the Department of Labor. Written complaints will first be directed to the contractor, and then to the Department of Labor, with final decision by the Secretary of Labor. Sanctions available are the usual ones that can be applied to contractors, e.g., withholding payments, termination of contracts, judicial review for relief from breach of contract, and blacklisting.

The culturally disadvantaged

Though no national laws require that currently unqualified personnel be hired and utilized by private business firms, the federal government has attempted to encourage help for the culturally disadvantaged through various forms of subsidies. There are in our society a number of persons whose consideration for employment on the basis of current qualifications would lead to their exclusion with little hope for change in the future. Perhaps the more commonly used label for this group would be the "hard-core unemployed." In one group of ninety-eight so identified by the Lockheed Aircraft

Corporation, all were male, most were single, three-fourths were black, two-thirds were twenty years old or younger, and two-thirds were school dropouts.[20] For these persons to enter the typical business firm, regular hiring standards must be relaxed. Unless full subsidies are received from the government, such a program would certainly constitute fulfillment of a social responsibility beyond the requirements of law.

The Civil Rights Act of 1964 would not prohibit the exclusion of a hard-core unemployed applicant on the basis of lack of job skills. In many instances, the formal education level possessed is no higher than fourth or fifth grade. Consequently, the federal government has become involved on a promotional basis and has appropriated money to subsidize unusual costs of training, personal counseling, and transportation to and from work. This program is labeled "Job Opportunities in Business Sector" (JOBS) and is administered through a voluntary organization of business executives, the National Alliance of Businessmen.

The NAB encourages employer participation in assisting the culturally disadvantaged through either contracts that compensate for unusual expenses or a signed pledge in voluntary recognition of a social responsibility. Examples of such expenses sometimes include serving breakfast to create regular eating habits, education in personal hygiene, transportation door-to-door for the first week, provision of specialized counselors, and even purchasing alarm clocks to re-regulate sleeping and working hours. In a survey of 350 corporations, it was discovered that the retention rate (a crucial success factor) of firms collaborating with JOBS programs averaged 57 percent.[21] This compared with an average of 39 percent for those without formal affiliation with the program. The retention rate is of great importance because of the necessity to convert the culture of the hard-core unemployed to that deemed necessary by the hiring organization in regard to dress, work habits, punctuality, attendance, and so on.

In a study of practices of five large organizations (Boeing, Eastman Kodak, Westinghouse, UAL, Inc., and Bankers Trust Company), it was concluded that an extensive and special effort is necessary to implement a successful hard-core unemployed program. Key elements of the program include top management commitment which gets through to "majority" members, pretraining preparation of the trainee, considerable support while in training, clear linkages of training with the future job, and follow-up activities after the employee assumes the regular job. This and other studies emphasize the very crucial nature of the support activities. The assignment of a specialized counselor is one of the most effective means of increasing successful trainee adaptation. However, there should be scheduled a definite time at which this specialized support will cease, so that the regular supervisor can take over usual responsibilities for all subordinates. Successful programs require committed and understanding supervisors who are willing to work in an empathic and counseling manner.

In a study of 839 hard-core unemployed, measures of attitudes and success in adaptation to the organization's work ethic were made before and after training and six

---

[20]James D. Hodgson and Marshall H. Brenner, "Successful Experience: Training Hard-core Unemployed," *Harvard Business Review*, vol. 46, no. 5, September–October 1968, p. 150.

[21]Robert C. Sedwick and Donald J. Bodwell, "The Hard-Core Employee: Key to High Retention," *Personnel Journal*, vol. 50, no. 12, December 1971, p. 951.

months after being placed upon a job.[22] Of the multitude of variables correlated, only the degree of organizational supportiveness perceived by the trainee distinguished between success and failure on the job as measured by supervisory ratings. Measures of motivation, vigor, past experience, and education did not identify the successful trainee. It was also concluded that the major difficulty with trainees lay in their higher rates of tardiness, absenteeism, and turnover. When they were present on the job, their work was comparable to that of other regular employees. This also suggests that when trainees find the work climate nonsupportive, they cope with this frustration through avoidance activities such as absenteeism and turnover. In a study of varying organizational levels and their attitudes toward such support, it was discovered that pre- and postprogram measures for top management moved from neutrality to positive, while those of foremen and rank and file moved from positive to neutral.[23] This highlights again the considerable challenge and difficulty of preparing the regular organization members to accept the culturally disadvantaged. The supervisor who obtained her or his promotion as a result of long and arduous effort will require a new social perspective to accept and cooperate with more externally oriented top managers who have agreed to a JOBS effort for the enterprise.

SOCIAL AUDIT

Even if the personnel manager is not given the central responsibility for preparing the social audit, he or she will have a significant role to play because of concern for the firm's human resources. One should first note that social auditing is only in its infancy, with very few firms undertaking this systematic appraisal process. A *social audit* is defined as "a commitment to systematic assessment of and reporting on some meaningful, definable domain of a company's activities that have social impact."[24] Its uses are to provide internal information to management which aids in decision making and to provide external information to the public in response to pressures upon the enterprise to be socially responsible.

Four possible types of audits are currently envisaged: (1) a simple inventory of activities, (2) compilation of socially relevant expenditures, (3) specific program management, and (4) determination of social impact. The inventory is generally the place where one would start. It would consist of a simple listing of activities undertaken by a firm over and above what is required for ordinary operation. For example, one firm itemized the following social activities: (1) minority employment and training, (2) support of minority enterprises, (3) pollution control, (4) corporate giving, (5) involvement in selected community projects by firm executives, and (6) a hard-core unemployed program.

A step forward in sophistication would be an attempt to itemize the costs incurred in these socially oriented activities. Such expenditures would be more

[22]Frank Friedlander and Stuart Greenberg, "Effect of Job Attitudes, Training, and Organization Climate on Performance of the Hard-Core Unemployed," *Journal of Applied Psychology*, vol. 55, no. 4, August 1971, pp. 287–295.

[23]Brian S. Morgan, Melvin R. Blonsky, and Hjalmar Rosen, "Employee Attitudes toward a Hard-Core Hiring Program," *Journal of Applied Psychology*, vol. 54, no. 6, December 1970, pp. 473–478.

[24]Raymond A. Bauer and Dan H. Fenn, Jr., "What *Is* a Corporate Social Audit?" *Harvard Business Review*, vol. 51, no. 1, January–February 1973, p. 38.

impressive to external publics but more depressive to internal managers without some indications of offsetting benefits. One utility company determined that it had spent $30,000 in one year in the human resources area, with an additional $90,000 being allocated to pollution control. Further documentation was provided in such areas as: (1) emission levels of particulate matter, sulfur oxides, and nitrogen oxides for coal, oil, and gas used, (2) temperatures of water received and discharged from the plant, (3) workdays lost due to employee injuries and illnesses, (4) number of minority and female employees hired and trained, and (5) charitable contributions.[25]

In the program management approach, each separate project is researched to ascertain not only its expenditures but also its outputs, in terms of specific management objectives. In the Bank of America, for example, the Small Business Administration–Minority Enterprise Program is evaluated in terms of additional costs incurred for this type of loan, compared with a projected goal of new successful minority enterprises established.[26] The Student Loan Program would involve a comparison of the costs of the lower rate of interest received with a goal concerning numbers of young people financed in college. This "Management by Objectives" approach permits managerial determination of the degree of success without invading the issue of the impact of goal accomplishment upon the welfare of society.

The ideal social audit would involve determination of the true benefits to society of any socially oriented business activity. Obtaining data for this ultimate impact not only is extremely difficult but involves decisions requiring value judgments. What is the value of a hard-core unemployed program to the community? Is it greater or less than the value of a program to promote minority business enterprises? Program management evades this issue by accepting a program as generally good on the basis of logic or pressure, and then evaluating it against specific program objectives. This does not deal, however, with the development of an overall, balanced, and integrated program that could issue from an analysis of social impact. Given the embryonic stage of development in which we find the social audit, management should be willing to settle for less than this ultimate form. In searching for outside help, the company will be hard pressed to find very many consultants with experience in the area. In any event, the personnel manager will have an important part to play in the accomplishment of any type of social audit conceived by top management.

SUMMARY

Every business decision has an impact upon society. Successful performance of the economic role is no longer sufficient in and of itself. The modern business manager must understand the nature of the total societal system and the social role accorded the economic enterprise. Freedom of association, pluralism, and constitutionalism are concepts that help shape a viable philosophy of management.

Society expects socially responsible behavior in the two basic areas of human resources and the physical environment. The personnel manager possesses an unusual

[25]Steven C. Dilley and Jerry J. Weygandt, "Measuring Social Responsibility: An Empirical Test," *The Journal of Accountancy*, September 1973, pp. 62–70.

[26]Bernard L. Butcher, "The Program Management Approach to the Corporate Social Audit," *California Management Review*, vol. 16, no. 1, Fall 1973, p. 14.

responsibility with respect to the former. Unavoidable in this regard are the numerous laws and orders that seek to force the firm to behave in an acceptable manner—the Civil Rights Act, Executive Order 11246, the Equal Pay Act, the Rehabilitation Act, and the Age Discrimination Act. These regulations have great impact upon the total personnel program, especially with respect to such special groups as female employees, older employees, the physically handicapped, and minority races and to religions and nationalities. Research in regard to all of these groups indicates that, aside from the law, discrimination is economically detrimental as well as socially objectionable.

The personnel manager has an obligation to do more than ensure that the company is in compliance with the law. Concern grows regarding improving the quality of life within the firm for all employees, special group or not. Corporate constitutionalism may soon require tolerance for dissent, participation in decision making, judicial review for complaints, and freedom to pursue individual life-styles. The personnel manager should also emphasize the firm's responsibility to culturally deprived segments of our society, even though there are no laws that require hiring of personnel not currently qualified. These additional obligations in no way decrease responsibility for providing the enterprise with a competent and capable work force making possible the effective accomplishment of traditional economic goals.

DISCUSSION QUESTIONS

1 Define and interrelate the concepts of freedom of assembly, pluralism, and constitutionalism. Of what interest are these concepts to a personnel manager?
2 Discuss the five rationales for a private business firm's assuming a social responsibility beyond that of producing a product or service for profit.
3 Itemize and indicate the basic purposes of major national legislation and orders in the field of discrimination in employment.
4 What is an affirmative action program? Under what regulation can it be required?
5 A commonly asserted justification for discrimination against female employees is their higher absenteeism and turnover rates. Discuss the validity of this contention.
6 How does the average compensation of the female employee compare with that of the male? What is the explanation for the difference?
7 What is the nature of the task with respect to hiring and retaining the hard-core unemployed? What key element tends to increase the percentage of retention?
8 Discuss the four types of social audit and the role of the personnel manager in their preparation.
9 What responsibilities with respect to discrimination in employment and conditions of work are assigned to (a) the Equal Employment Opportunity Commission, (b) the Department of Labor, (c) the Office of Federal Contracts Compliance, and (d) the Civil Service Commission?
10 Discuss the specific obligations of the personnel manager with respect to the social responsibility of the firm.

SUPPLEMENTARY READING

BAUER, Raymond A., and Dan H. Fenn, Jr.: "What *Is* a Corporate Social Audit?" *Harvard Business Review*, vol. 51, no. 1, January–February 1973, pp. 37–48.
CHAYES, Antonia Handler: "Make Your Equal Opportunity Program Court-Proof," *Harvard Business Review*, vol. 52, no. 5, September–October 1974, pp. 81–89.

DAVIS, Keith: "The Case for and against Business Assumption of Social Responsibilities," *Academy of Management Journal*, vol. 16, no. 2, June 1973, pp. 312–322.

DOMM, Donald R., and James E. Stafford: "Assimilating Blacks into the Organization," *California Management Review*, vol. 15, no. 1, Fall 1972, pp. 46–51.

EILBIRT, Henry, and I. Robert Parket: "The Current Status of Corporate Social Responsibility," *Business Horizons*, vol. 16, no. 4, August 1973, pp. 5–14.

GROSSMAN, Harry: "The Equal Employment Opportunity Act of 1972: Its Implications for the State and Local Government Manager," *Public Personnel Management*, vol. 2, no. 5, October 1973, pp. 370–379.

MILTON, Charles R., and James M. Black: "The Disadvantaged: Changing Definitions and Personnel Practices," *Personnel*, vol. 51, no. 2, March–April 1974, pp. 57–65.

ROSEN, Benson, and Thomas H. Jerdee: "Sex Stereotyping in the Executive Suite," *Harvard Business Review*, vol. 52, no. 2, March–April 1974, pp. 45–58.

FOUR
ORGANIZATIONAL DESIGN

Organizations are systems of relating resources that will make possible the accomplishment of specified ends or goals. They are social and technological devices made up of people and physical factors. With the aid of technological implementation, these people execute functions, or tasks, that lead to the accomplishment of rationally determined objectives. Organizations are processing units which transform certain inputs from the environment into specified outputs desired by society; e.g., a hospital transforms ill patients into healthy people, and a manufacturing firm transforms raw material into usable products.

Every manager has the responsibility of organizaing subordinates into patterns of interactions that will facilitate accomplishment of unit goals. However, the basic, overall design of the total organization has always been the responsibility of the chief executive. As the organization grows in size, its complexity increases at an even more rapid rate. Consequently, in the larger organizations, there have been evolved specialized people and units to advise and assist the chief executive in this organizing function. One survey indicated that 100 of the nation's top 500 companies had established specialized staff units for the purpose of assisting in organizational design and development.[1]

There is growing evidence that the personnel department is the one that will be responsible for the organizational design unit, at least until the unit merits separate status under the chief executive. The study cited above revealed that *most* of the 100 existing departments were subdivisions of personnel departments. In another study of 244 personnel departments in large companies, 82 percent had been given general responsibility for organization planning.[2] In those companies placing the unit outside

[1]William F. Glueck, "Where Organization Planning Stands Today," *Personnel*, vol. 44, no. 4, July–August 1968, pp. 19–26.

[2]Allen R. Janger, *Personnel Administration: Changing Scope and Organization*, National Industrial Conference Board, Studies in Personnel Policy, no. 203, New York, 1966, p. 23.

of that department, it was usually grouped with such personnel activities as management development and human resource planning. A third survey of 245 companies indicated that organization planning and design was the fifth-ranked major concern of personnel executives, being listed behind labor relations, departmental administration, personnel techniques, and personnel policies.[3]

The above studies strongly suggest that the personnel manager should develop a special interest and expertise in organization planning and design in order to provide the service desired by the chief executive. This view also makes sense, considering the nature of the operative functions of personnel. If the three key components of any organization are people, jobs, and physical factors, the personnel manager has special knowledge of the first two. Organizations are dependent upon the caliber of personnel available, and it is no accident that organizational design is frequently grouped with personnel activities like executive training and development and the forecasting of human resource needs. The personnel unit also collects information about job content which can be of material assistance in organizational design.

The function of organizing is basically a process of tying these key components together and harnessing them so that they may be directed toward enterprise objectives. Thus, a technical definition of the formal process of organizing would be as follows: it is the process of establishing *relationships* (responsibility, authority, and accountability) among key *components* (personnel, functions, and physical factors) for the purpose of *harnessing* (line, line/staff, functionalized, and project structures) and directing toward organizational *objectives*. Thus, experts in organizational design require knowledge of such subjects as objectives, components, relationships, and structures. If the personnel manager is to provide sound and effective advice in this area, this executive must study the theory and practice of organizing as avidly as the more traditional content of the personnel functions. Brief coverage of the major elements of this definition will be presented in the following sections.

ORGANIZATIONAL OBJECTIVES

Inasmuch as organizations are intendedly rational devices established to achieve objectives, it is logical to begin a consideration of organization design with a consideration of those objectives. One of the first things recognized by most managers is that any organization has *multiple* objectives. One classification of goals of business organizations has been established as follows:[4]

I Primary objectives
   A Create and distribute a product or service
   B Satisfy personal objectives of the members of the organization, such as:
      1 Profits for owners
      2 Salaries and other compensation for executives

[3]Dalton E. McFarland, *Company Officers Assess the Personnel Function*, American Management Association Research Study 79, New York, 1967, p. 35.

[4]Adapted from Ralph C. Davis, *Industrial Organization and Management*, 3d ed., Harper & Row, Publishers, Incorporated, New York, 1957, p. 26.

      3 Wages and other compensation for employees
      4 Psychic income for all, including:
         a Pride in work
         b Security
         c Recognition
         d Acceptance
  C Meet community and social obligations, such as:
      1 Protection and enhancement of the human resources of society
      2 Protection and enhancement of the physical resources of society
II Secondary objectives
  A Economy of operation in meeting the primary objectives
  B Effectiveness of operation in meeting the primary objectives

A careful study of the above outline should reveal much concerning the nature of organizational objectives. Reasonable accomplishment of all is prerequisite to managerial success, a fact that should create some appreciation of the difficulty of the managerial task.

PRODUCT OR SERVICE OBJECTIVES Every business organization must have as one of its basic purposes the creation and distribution of some good or service. The tangible representation of this objective is the automobile, refrigerator, can of beans, or haircut. The personnel engaged in the actual creation, distribution, or financing of this product are performing the basic work of the organization. They are carrying the ball. A personnel department is *not* so engaged. It is charged with the responsibility of *assisting* those in production, who are creating the product, those in sales, who are distributing it, and those in finance, who provide the funds for its creation and distribution. Thus, the goals of a personnel department must be derived from the objectives of the entire organization.

PERSONAL OBJECTIVES An organization is composed of two or more people. These people have various and often conflicting personal objectives, which must be reasonably satisfied or individuals will withdraw from the organization. Such withdrawal can lead to collapse of the enterprise and failure to accomplish the product or service objective.

These personal objectives are of two general types, monetary and nonmonetary. In recent years, management has become increasingly aware of the nonmonetary goals of people. When the wage or salary is somewhat reasonable, other desires come to the fore, and they form the basis of today's human relations program. A particular individual has been known to change organizations and accept a lower-paying position in order to gain more prestige, recognition, security, or some similar psychic income.

On personnel management rests a large measure of the responsibility for ensuring satisfactory accomplishment of the personal objectives of employees. If the personal objectives of all groups are not reasonably achieved, the basic objectives of the entire organization will suffer. Consideration of the nature and techniques of fulfilling many of these objectives constitutes a major portion of this text.

COMMUNITY AND SOCIAL OBLIGATIONS   Society has imposed upon business a number of broad social obligations, which thereby become business objectives. It is apparent that appreciation of superordinate societal goals, discussed in the preceding chapter, will have considerable impact upon the design of complex organizations in the future.

SECONDARY OBJECTIVES   In labeling economy and effectiveness of operation as secondary objectives, one should not imply that they are unimportant. If these goals also are not satisfactorily achieved, all other goals will suffer. But again, we are not in the business of providing more economy and effectiveness in a vacuum. Some other objective must be the basic goal, which we hope to accomplish with a reasonable expenditure of money and effort.

PRIMACY OF PRODUCT OR SERVICE OBJECTIVE   Aside from their multiplicity, one aspect of the outline of business objectives that seems unusual is the emphasis on the product or service objective. The thesis of the primacy of the service objective can be defended in three areas. The first might be labeled the political area. Society, through the Constitution, has granted us the right to own property and establish a business. The right was not granted solely to enable an owner to make a profit; rather, *the right to make a profit was granted in order to provide an incentive to produce the goods and services that society needs.* Profit is the personal motivation; the good or service is the end or objective. Ours is known as the profit system, a system which is a means to the end of creating the necessary and desirable goods. The service objective exists in other types of economic systems where the profit objective does not. It is rather sobering for business managers to realize that there is no unalterable guarantee of the continuation of the right to make profits. Belief in the primacy of the service objective is essentially a *defense* of the profit system, inasmuch as providing good products at a reasonable cost is the best way to convince society that its grant of authority has been well handled.

The second defense lies in the area of organization. It is a principle of organization that all members must have one *common* goal in order to secure cooperation and coordination of action. As we have said above, the organization is composed of various people with differing personal objectives. The product or service objective is the only one in which all are immediately interested. Thus, while the objective of the business manager or owner is profit, the objective of the business organization is the product or service. Profit is an objective of *one part* of the organization, though that part is admittedly very important. The principle of a common goal designates the product or service objective as primary.

The last defense of this thesis is economic in nature. Under our competitive system, there is substantial freedom of choice in the markets for goods and services. The theory of the system is that resources will flow to the organizations that produce the best product at the lowest price. In the political area, a business may be voted out of existence or hampered by means of legislation. In the marketplace, it may be voted out or restricted by the customer's dollar. Thus, the rationale of our system is that resources, income for profits and wages, will flow to the organization that creates the best goods and services.

In the final analysis, the manager who is aware of the tremendous importance of the product or service objective, already being aware of the profit objective, will have a philosophy of management that will not be too far wrong. An *intelligent* pursuit of profits, with equitable consideration for labor and the customer, will usually lead to the same position as the principle of the primacy of the service objective.

FUNCTIONS

Objectives do not accomplish themselves. Work must be executed by people or machines in order that objectives may be achieved. The word "function" can be defined simply as *work that can be distinguished from other work*. The function of production, for instance, can be defined and distinguished from sales, just as planning can be separated from control. In manufacturing concerns, three functions are considered to be primary or organic: they are sales, production, and finance. These functions contribute directly toward the accomplishment of the basic objective of the firm, that is, the product or service objective. Since these are primary, they are generally referred to as "line" functions.

In the one-person firm, all functions are bound up in one person. This person produces, sells, and finances the product. As the volume of business increases, a process of functional differentiation occurs. This is essentially a separation of certain functions from the original performer and an assignment of them to other people who are added to the enterprise. Functional differentiation takes place in two directions— downward and outward.[5] The results of both directions of growth are the same, i.e., more functional specialization.

Functional differentiation downward

Staying with the one-person firm for the moment, we see that as the business grows, a helper will be hired. Thus, a function has been differentiated, possibly in the area of production, and assigned to the second person, as shown in Figure 4-1. The process of downward differentiation is under way, and we now have two levels of organization. As volume continues to grow, additional personnel are added to the organization, as depicted in Figure 4-2. Perhaps one or two of the subordinates are engaged in the function of selling. At some point in this process of functional splitting, the owner will

---

[5]Ralph C. Davis, *The Fundamentals of Top Management*, Harper & Row, Publishers, Incorporated, New York, 1951, pp. 216–220.

Figure 4-1 FUNCTIONAL DIFFERENTIATION DOWNWARD

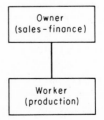

Figure 4-2

FURTHER DOWNWARD DIFFERENTIATION

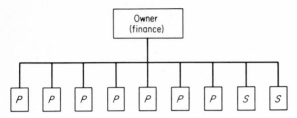

P, production employee; S, salesman

encounter a basic principle of organization known as the *span of control.*[6] This principle is basically a statement of human limitations; that is, there is a limit to the number of people and functions that one person can supervise effectively. Assuming that our owner-manager has reached that limit, we must push down to another level of organization. One of our present employees is perhaps appointed a supervisor, and now this span of control can be utilized when we add other personnel to the company. With further growth, three full levels will come into existence, as shown in Figure 4-3.

As the limits of anyone's span of control are reached, we are forced to push down and create another level of organization. In organizations of several thousand members, there may be as many as fourteen different levels. Were there no such principle as the span of control, there would be one manager, to whom all others would report. This concentration is obviously inconceivable in any except the smallest of organizations.

Let us examine this span-of-control principle more closely. What are the limits? The number of functions and personnel that one person can supervise effectively will depend upon such factors as that *person's ability*, one's *subordinates' abilities*, the *complexity* of the functions performed, the *similarity* of the functions to one another, the degree of *situational stability*, and the degree to which separate work assignments *interlock*. A series of subprinciples can thus be devised as follows: (1) the greater the degree of functional complexity, the fewer the functions that can be supervised effectively, and (2) the greater the degree of dissimilarity of functions, the fewer the functions that can be controlled effectively. Research by Joan Woodward indicates that the type of technology has impact upon spans of controls actually used in business organizations.[7] Classifying technology on the basis of unit or small-batch processing, mass production, and process production with continuous flow, she discovered that the spans were largest in mass production enterprises and relatively smaller in the other two. Jobs of those being controlled were more routine and similar in mass production, thereby lengthening the effective span.

Traditional managers tend to prefer smaller spans, which permit a higher degree of

[6]As in the case of the exception principle, the span-of-control concept is quite old. Exodus 18:25 states, "And Moses chose able men out of all Israel, and made them heads over the people, rulers of thousands, rulers of hundreds, and rulers of fifties, and rulers of tens."

[7]Joan Woodward, *Management and Technology*, Her Majesty's Stationery Office, London, England, 1958, pp. 8–30.

Figure 4-3

THREE FULL LEVELS OF ORGANIZATION

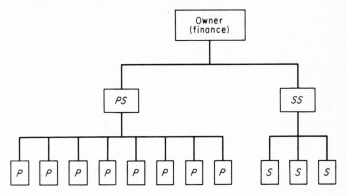

PS, production supervisor; SS, sales supervisor; P, production employee; S, salesman

control of communication and operations. Psychologists and sociologists, on the other hand, advocate broader spans, which necessitate a greater degree of freedom for the subordinate. It is apparent that there are no valid formulas that will indicate the theoretically perfect span for any situation. The particular philosophy of management, analysis of the limiting factors cited above, and a reasonable amount of trial and error will all doubtlessly be involved in answering this question for each manager.

Functional differentiation outward

The lack of managerial specialization becomes increasingly serious with increased growth in size of organization. This situation results from the effect of another principle known sometimes as *the law of functional growth.* This law states that as the volume of business grows, the complexity of the functions necessary for performance increases at an even more rapid pace. For example, the establishment of a wage and salary structure for a shop of four or five people is considerably less difficult than the performance of the same function for a concern of several hundred or thousand employees. The effect of this principle is to emphasize the need for managerial assistance through specialization. Certain activities are differentiated outward from the chain of command previously established by means of downward differentiation. Secondary or staff functions are established in areas *other* than production, sales, or finance. The objective of these secondary functions is the assistance and facilitation of the performance of line functions. Thus a staff function is *one that has been separated from the line for purposes of specialization.* Its separation is justified only so long as it is believed that the function can be performed more effectively and economically by a specialist than by the line from which it was evolved. All staff functions come from the line and are returned to the line in the event that economy and effectiveness are not produced.

The above description can be clarified by an example. Functional differentiation downward of the three primary functions creates a pure line organization. All members are producing, selling, or financing, or are in the direct chain of command above these three functions. The production supervisor in Figure 4-4 has been having trouble training new personnel because of the rapid growth of the firm. He or she has asked that a line machine operator be assigned as a training assistant to assume much of the responsibility in that area. Training done by the training assistant is a staff function. As the business continues to grow, there may be more work than the training assistant can handle alone. He or she is provided with a subordinate, which means, of course, that functional differentiation is pushing downward within the staff function of training. This movement results in the formation of a staff section, the training section. The process illustrates the formation of a secondary chain of command within a staff function.

While the above functional differentiation outward and downward is going on, the law of functional growth has forced other functions out of the line into staff assignments. The production supervisor may have the usual subordinate line personnel but will also have a multitude of staff engaged in such activities as training, production control, inspection, hiring, safety, and the like. To reduce the span of control, one may prefer to regroup some of the staff sections to form a staff department. Thus the personnel department may consist of the sections of hiring, training, safety, and other functions deserving of specialization at this stage of growth. It should be noted in passing that it is impossible to separate *completely* any staff function from the line. Some residual responsibility has to remain for coordination purposes at the very least. In the personnel area, it will be found that a very large proportion of the responsibility, because of its very nature, *simply cannot be removed from the line*.

Functional differentiation outward can take place at *any* level in the primary chain command. It may take place gradually and go through the above-described steps: (1)

Figure 4-4

ADDITION OF STAFF TO A LINE ORGANIZATION

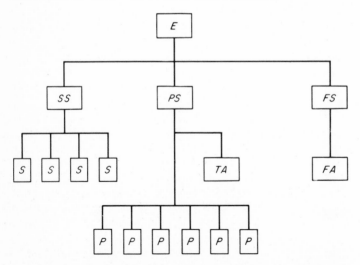

E, executive; PS, production supervisor; SS, sales supervisor; FS, financial supervisor; TA, training assistant (staff); S, salesman; P, production worker; FA, financial assistant

assignment of the function to one person, a staff assistant; (2) creation of a staff unit by adding personnel; and (3) creation of a larger staff unit by grouping with related specialized units. In addition, with further growth the staff unit may develop an internal support structure. For example, if the training effort becomes sufficiently large, the organization may be able to afford a training *research* subunit. Thus, if production is primary to the goal, and training secondary in that production is facilitated, then training research is tertiary in that it facilitates the secondary function of training. In effect, we have experienced functional differentiation downward in training to create a secondary chain of command, followed by functional differentation outward to create a "staff-to-staff."

The pattern of functional growth is universal—first *down* in the primary or line functions and secondly *out* into staff functions. This can be summarized as follows:

Principle	Process	Result
Span of control	Functional differentiation downward	Operative specialization and added organizational levels
Law of functional growth	Functional differentiation outward	Managerial specialization and creation of staff

Finally, if the firm grows quite large, the staff function can be separated on multiple levels from top to bottom in the organization. As shown in Figure 4-5, there can be a personnel director for the entire organization, as well as personnel units for each of the product managers. The top central unit serves as a clearinghouse for personnel information and activities throughout the enterprise. It may also provide certain central services, such as negotiating the master contract with the labor union. This parallel functional development also acts as a specialized channel of communication and constitutes a career promotion ladder. It should be noted that even though the staff director is reporting directly to the president, and may even be accorded vice-presidential standing, this in no way transforms the unit into line status. The incidence of service toward primary organizational goals is still controlling.

Figure 4-5

PARALLEL PERSONNEL STAFF

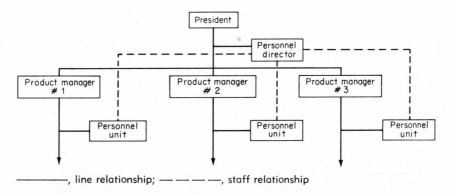

————, line relationship; — — — —, staff relationship

RELATIONSHIPS

The process of organizing is one of *relating* the component parts of the organization to one another and to the organization objective. Knowledge of these parts—functions, personnel, and physical factors—is prerequisite to understanding the relationships that should exist among them. Characteristics of personnel and physical factors assigned to differentiated functions will also, of course, have impact upon the design. Though treatment of these two components will not be undertaken at this point, various illustrations will appear in this and later chapters. Organizing is the process of binding the parts together into a unified whole that can operate effectively. The immediate result of this process is the establishment of organization structure, a subject that will be discussed later in this chapter.

The relationships that will be established among the components of organization are of two general types, formal and informal. Formal relationships are those which are *officially* established and prescribed in the organization manual, charts, and job descriptions. The three basic relationships of this category are *responsibility*, *authority*, and *accountability*. Informal relationships are those created by the particular people in the organization; these are not officially recognized, defined, or regulated. These relationships are most closely identified with the general field of human relations and will be discussed under the function of integration.

Responsibility

Responsibility is *one's obligation to perform the functions assigned to the best of one's ability in accordance with directions received.* It is logically the first relationship that should be established and is based on an analysis of *functions* required to accomplish the organization *objective.*

There are many principles governing the formal assignment of responsibility. Perhaps the foremost one is the *principle of functional similarity*. This principle states that *the functions assigned to an individual should be grouped on the basis of similarity to one another in order to facilitate specialization.* Insofar as possible, the functions to be assigned to make up a job, section, department, or division should be sufficiently related one to another to take advantage of specialized backgrounds.

The greater the volume of work, the greater is the opportunity to apply the principle of functional similarity. In small organizations one person's job frequently consists of many different and varied tasks. In the large enterprise a full-time job may comprise only one function or two closely related functions. As has been pointed out previously in this text, there are dangers involved in carrying this principle too far. Problems of boredom and monotony, reduced interest in work, lack of the broad background necessary for top management, and narrow and restricted viewpoints are often characteristic of excessive application of the principle of functional similarity.

Other principles applicable to responsibility are: (1) there should be no overlapping responsibilities—the same function should not be assigned to two or more persons; (2) responsibility limits should be clearly defined; (3) there should be no gaps in responsibility assignments—work that should be done must be assigned to some person; and (4) responsibility should not be assigned for work that is unnecessary and does not contribute toward organization objectives. It should be noted that responsibility is assigned through delegation from superiors. The significance of the word "delegation" is that the process in no way reduces the superior's original amount of responsibility. This concept is what puts the risk in a manager's job. Responsibility is still full and complete although execution of the task has been largely relegated to others.

Authority

Authority is the *right to decide what should be done and the right to do it or to require someone else to do it.* The basic principle governing this relationship is the principle of coequal authority and responsibility. This principle states that a commensurate amount of authority should accompany a delegation of responsibility. Just as responsibility is derived from functional analysis, authority is derived from responsibility. A person should have no authority without having a prior responsibility.

Industrial managers do a fairly good job of informing an individual of responsibilities; these are often written down. The job of informing a person of organizational rights is done less well. A few companies, however, specify the limits of authority for each unit of responsibility. For example, one responsibility of a department head may be to procure competent personnel for the department. Opposite this requirement is a specification of authority which could be at any one of several levels, such as the full right to recruit and hire, the right to reject recommendations of the personnel department but no rights of recruitment, or no rights of rejection of the people sent by the staff personnel department. There is some feeling that a too rigid specification of authority and responsibility is undesirable because it may frustrate the influence of the individual over the job and its makeup. The manager may want the person to grow and assume greater responsibility and authority as time goes by. In low-level jobs, the specification is often rather exact and highly controlled.

The source of authority is from above through delegation. It should always be viewed as an official or formal concept, thereby precluding the use of the term "informal authority." The latter should be subsumed in analyses of power, a concept that will be discussed under the function of integration.

Accountability

Accountability is the *requirement of answerability for one's performance.* It is the opposite phase of responsibility, in that responsibility is delegated downward while one is accountable upward to some superior for proper performance. If one has been delegated an amount of authority commensurate with responsibility, one can, logically, be held accountable for results. Just as responsibility is a derivative of functions and authority is a derivative of responsibility, accountability is a derivative of authority. If insufficient authority has been delegated, it is not logical to hold a person fully answerable.

Perhaps the foremost principle governing the formal relationship of accountability is that of single accountability. This principle states that *the most desirable relationship is that each person be accountable to only one superior.* Divided accountability to multiple superiors imposes considerable difficulties upon the subordinate. It often means that one must perform a managerial function of coordinating superiors, particularly when receiving conflicting orders, or when finding that the total demands made are in excess of personal capacity. As the size of the organization increases with concurrent expansion in the number of staff specialists, this principle of single accountability is placed in considerable jeopardy. Specialists seem to have a built-in tendency to give orders rather than advice. In addition, at the upper levels of organization, it is extremely difficult for one person to review closely all recommendations and specifically approve them in order to convert them to personal orders and thereby preserve the desired unity of command.

It has been suggested that a related concept, the principle of unity of command, is more important than single accountability. Though a person has two bosses, *if* those bosses are coordinated, unity of command can be preserved despite the loss of single accountability. It may well be that future large-size organizations will see the increased introduction of "plural executive," that is, a number of executives operating as one office. Single accountability should be preserved as long as possible to reduce the danger of possible disunity. The more bosses, the greater the opportunity for conflict, poor coordination, and misplaced emphases. But single accountability can be sacrificed when complexity demands multiple experts, *provided* that unity of action is preserved. This requires stability of membership within the "plural executive group," as well as reasonable specification of the various jurisdictions.

To summarize the organizing process to this point, we started with a determination of organizational objectives. From this, a specification of necessary functions to accomplish these objectives was developed. When personnel are introduced to execute functions, responsibility is established. On the basis of this responsibility, authority is allocated to make accomplishment possible. Assuming sufficient authority, then accountability can be imposed. Thus, the logical derivation is in the sequence of (1) objectives, (2) functions, (3) responsibility, (4) authority, and (5) accountability.

ORGANIZATION STRUCTURE

The immediate result of the organizing process is the creation of organization structure. This structure is a framework of the formal relationships that have been established. Some compare it to a harness that defines the position of the team members in relation to one another and to the common objective. The purpose of the structure is to assist in regulating and directing the efforts put forth in an organization so that they are coordinated and consistent with organization objectives.

There are several basic types of organization structure, any one of which may be adopted. If responsibility, authority, and accountability are established in one way, the result is *line structure*. If these relationships are set up in another way, the *line and staff structure* is created. The third arrangement of relationships is known as the *functional type of structure*. Each of these structures will be briefly described and the location of the personnel functions noted. In addition, the project structure will be briefly discussed to indicate how activities can be fitted into this most recent structural adaptation.

Line organization structure

The nature of line organization structure has been largely described in the earlier discussion of functional differentiation. Line structure is created by the functional differentiation downward of primary or basic functions. In manufacturing, these basic functions are production, sales, and finance. Thus in the line organization, all personnel are either producing, selling, or financing, or are in the direct chain of command above these three functions. There is no functional differentiation outward.

In the line organization, the personnel functions exist but are performed by line personnel. A supervisor is responsible for procurement of personnel and their development and integration in the workplace. He or she has no assistance in these matters beyond what superiors can supply.

The advantages of this type of structure are (1) simplicity, (2) ease of comprehension by all members, (3) rapidity of decision making and action, inasmuch as there are few people to consult, (4) clear and inescapable accountability, and (5) the possibility of developing general backgrounds for most personnel. The most outstanding disadvantage is the increasing loss of effectiveness with growth, due to the lack of managerial specialization. The law of functional growth will sooner or later force an evolvement of certain functions from the line in order that they may remain competitive.

One of the decisions common to all types of structure is the selection of bases for grouping divided activities. What has been divided must be combined, if possible, to effect coordinated and unified progress toward organization goals. Perhaps the two most significant bases of grouping are (1) functions and (2) product or service. Line organizations typically group on the basis of the first—that is, all activities related to production, for example, are placed in one unit, while all those related to the selling function are placed in another. This ensures specialization and requires the top manager of the enterprise to coordinate the total task.

With increasing size, firms typically move to the product or service base. Each unit has its own production and sales subgroupings, thus leading to a seeming duplication of activities throughout the firm. Each may be established as a separate profit center designed to produce such values as a "whole" approach to each product, more rapid decision making, and greater development and motivation of personnel responsible. Rarely, though, are all functions given to a product manager. The General Motors Corporation, for example, is basically a product grouping, but the finance function and significant portions of labor relations are retained near the top level.

In addition to these two bases of grouping, other choices available are (1) geography, (2) customers, (3) time, and (4) numbers. Recognition of the first will result in territory managers. The second reflects recognition of peculiar customer requirements, e.g., teenage shops and budget basements in department stores. Time and numbers may call for multiple supervisors on different work shifts. Specific applications of these possible bases will be discussed with reference to the personnel unit in the following chapter.

Line and staff organization structure

Functional differentiation downward *and* outward produces a line and staff organization. Most business organizations, except the very small, have this type of structure. The problems of management have become sufficiently complex so that presumably expert attention will produce more effective results in selected areas. This expertise is introduced into the organization in an advisory or facilitative manner. In theory, line managers are free to reject the specialized advice or service on the basis of overriding general objectives. Examples of specific guides for combining line and staff activities will be discussed in the following chapter with specific reference to the staff personnel unit.

Functional organization structure

The adoption of the functional form of organization structure involves the violation of some principles of organization previously cited. A functional relationship is established when *a staff function is brought directly to bear on line functions with authority to command rather than to advise*. Thus, the integrity of the line is broken and some personnel are accountable to multiple superiors. If the personnel unit, for example, is set up on a functionalized basis, it does not recommend that a supervisor accept an applicant; it *orders* that it be done. The unit can overrule lower line managers on matters of wages, grievances, training, and the like. Thus in matters pertaining to personnel, the supervisor must look to the personnel unit; in other areas, the supervisor looks to the appropriate line superior.

No firms today are completely functionalized in all specialized functions. The significance lies in the provision of a third alternative. Organizers can choose among the following: (1) a function such as hiring can be allocated to the supervisor (line organization); (2) it can be given to a specialized personnel unit with rights of advice only (line and staff); or (3) it can be assigned to the personnel unit with rights of command (functionalized). The third alternative should be used sparingly to prevent distortion of basic general objectives.

Project structure

A variation of the functionalized form now coming into wider use, particularly in the aerospace industry, is the project structure. If a management desires to emphasize strongly a specific undertaking or project, a special structure can be created. Such projects are usually unique and unfamiliar to the existing organization and complex in nature. They require interaction among specialists and have limited time objectives. A project manager is given authority to assemble temporarily the necessary talents and facilities to accomplish an undertaking. In some instances, the usual line and staff departments do the work, but the project manager specifies what effort is needed and when it will be performed. The operating unit manager may decide who in his or her unit is to help and how the work is to be accomplished. It is apparent that, though the unit manager has line or command authority over personnel, the project manager has functionalized authority in connection with the work on the particular project. ("The Case of Two Masters" at the end of this part provides an example of a personnel specialist who was caught between the conflicting demands of his unit supervisor and his project manager.)

Business managers have found the project structure supplement to be highly effective in assuring the accomplishment of important goals. The project cannot get lost between departments. It has been found that one person can work for two or more "masters," and that a "master" can effectively influence those over whom he or she has no clear authority. The possibility of conflict and frustration is great, but the opportunity for prompt, expeditious, and effective accomplishment is even greater. The coordinative power of the knowledge and expertise of the participating specialists makes up in part for the vagueness and complexity of formal organizational relationships. Both project managers and supporting unit managers must maintain an open mind and be willing to negotiate. The typical role of personnel managers in project structures is to provide supporting personnel specialists and be willing to share in their supervision.

JOB DESIGN

Moving from general groupings to the specific, the personnel manager should have an even greater interest in the design and specification of individual jobs within the organization. Excessive specialization and concentration upon technical efficiency have had an adverse impact upon the motivation of personnel responsible for executing these narrow jobs.

The design of an effective work unit for an individual employee is a highly complex task. It should not be left solely to the line supervisor, the union business agent, or the industrial engineer. The personnel manager has a responsibility to represent the interests of the individual, which hopefully will be reflected to some degree in the interests of the total organization. Among the many factors that will affect job design are (1) the proven values of specialization and repetitive operations, (2) changing technology, (3) labor union policies, (4) abilities of present personnel, (5) available supply of potential employees, (6) the interaction requirements among jobs within the system, and (7) psychological and social needs of human beings that can be met by the job.

Specialization tends to lead to greater productivity as well as ease of manning the work unit. The resulting unit of work undergoes constant modification because of the impact of mechanization and automation. Some jobs are eliminated, others created, and still others altered in content, resulting in different specifications of education, experience, personality, and breadth of viewpoint. Labor unions are necessarily involved and seek to retain both present employee security and union control of these units of work. Thus, the firm may be required to respect jurisdictional lines of traditional crafts or to delay alteration of job content despite advances in technology. Economic and organizational values lost in job design may be recouped in part through enhanced union cooperation.

Management must also be concerned with the practical considerations of quantity and quality of personnel presently available, both within the firm and in the labor market generally. It does little good to design a job in terms of the ideal if the resulting unit cannot be supplied with workers. Consequently, changes in job content may be made to reflect particular characteristics of specific people available for transfer or hire.

It is apparent that the interrelationships among various jobs will levy an interaction requirement upon job incumbents. Work systems should be designed to minimize points of friction. For example, Whyte's restaurant study found that when lower-status personnel, such as runners, initiated action for higher-status personnel, such as chefs, the potential for explosions and dish breakage was increased.[8] He hypothesized that work will flow more smoothly when those of higher status are in a position to originate work for those of lower status. What appear to be personality conflicts between two

---

[8]William Foote Whyte, *Organizational Behavior*, The Dorsey Press and Richard D. Irwin, Inc., Homewood, Ill., 1969, chap. 4.

individuals may actually be defects in job design which tend to go counter to the needs and cultures of personnel handling the jobs.

Behavioral scientists have continually stressed the importance of designing jobs and systems of work in a manner that will satisfy psychological and sociological needs of people. One of the most commonly cited human relations problems in this area of job design is employee dissatisfaction with jobs that are repetitive, narrow, meaningless, and routine. Engineering efficiency has led to the creation of the production and assembly lines. Such lines have proved themselves on the basis of the quantity and quality of production that can be exacted from such a productive arrangement. The major deficiency, however, lies in the human relations area, with such specific problems resulting as the boredom of the worker, loss of pride in work, insecurity, and obsessive thinking. These problems are compounded when a moving conveyor links all positions together. The conveyor is a "monster" whose pressure never ceases.

Traditionally, the solution to excessive specialization of job assignments has involved some means of periodic rotation to provide variety, e.g., change tasks every few hours, or work up the moving assembly line. In recent years, considerable research has been undertaken with respect to more unusual and seemingly risky changes in job content. Among these are job enlargement, job enrichment, and sociotechnical groups.

Job enlargement

In response to criticisms concerning the dehumanization of work through excessive specialization, an obvious suggestion would be to enlarge job content to utilize more of the abilities of employees. If the additional responsibilities are of a horizontal nature, variety has been introduced and the process is termed "job enlargement." If the additional responsibilities are of a vertical nature encompassing self-control, the process is termed "job enrichment." Job enrichment is the approach to job design most recommended by behaviorists and will be discussed in the following section.

Variety can be produced by adding functions, thus possibly reducing monotony. An added psychological value can be derived if the added functions make possible the completion of an identifiable unit, thereby producing a sense of closure. As a case in point, research reported by Louis Davis demonstrated that the breaking up of a conveyorized assembly line is not necessarily disastrous in terms of output.[9] The product studied was a hospital appliance that was to be assembled by nine operators spaced along a moving conveyor. Figure 4-6, part a, shows the daily productivity index of this old method at 100. Part b shows the results of the mere removal of the conveyor, with the work stations remaining as before. Production dropped to an index of 90, thus demonstrating the power of the moving conveyor. Part c shows the record of a new system of production, in which one worker performed all nine operations, thereby applying the concept of job enlarement. Part d refers to the same system of work, one worker for all operations, but with the work taking place in the main production area rather than in a room adjacent to the production floor as in the case of c. Parts c and d refer to the same system of production, and the increase of d over c reflects both an increase in experience with the new system and a change in work location. It should be noted that the production rate of the original conveyor was never reached through the

[9]Louis E. Davis, "Job Design and Productivity: A New Approach," *Personnel*, March 1957, pp. 418–430.

job enlargement methods. However, the experiment covering parts c and d lasted for only forty-three days. Production with the moving assembly line method of operation had been going on for years.

Though quantity was slow in returning under job enlargement, quality was immediately and significantly improved. The percentage of rejects dropped to one-fourth of the original total. When the accountability for proper performance can be effectively determined for each employee, rather than divided up among the group, quality usually improves.

In a study of various assembly line jobs in a home laundry manufacturing firm, attempts were made over a five-year period to increase the number and variety of tasks in single jobs.[10] For example, a pump assembly line of six operators required an average of 1.77 minutes per unit. In moving to single-operator work stations where the operator would perform the full assembly, the time was reduced to 1.49 minutes. In thirteen other similar job changes, there was an average decrease in quality rejects from 2.9 to 1.4 percent. However, there was an average decrease in output efficiency from 138 percent to 126 percent.

Regardless of the contentions of some business researchers, it should not always be concluded that all employees prefer an enlarged job assignment. In a study of 202 television set assemblers, 104 indicated a preference for smaller task assignments, 24 preferred job enlargement, and the remaining had no preference.[11] When General Motors attempted to increase the number of tasks assigned to personnel on the Vega

[10]E. H. Conant and M. D. Kilbridge, "An Interdisciplinary Analysis of Job Enlargement: Technology, Costs, and Behavioral Implications," *Industrial and Labor Relations Review*, vol. 18, no. 3, April 1965, p. 377.

[11]M. D. Kilbridge, "Do Workers Prefer Larger Jobs?" *Personnel*, September–October 1960, p. 47.

Figure 4-6

AVERAGE DAILY PRODUCTIVITY INDEXES

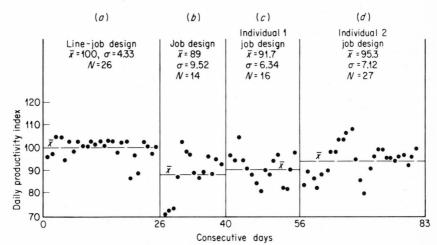

N, number of days in each job-design period

Source: Louis E. Davis, "Job Design and Productivity: A New Approach," *Personnel*, March 1957, p. 425.

assembly line, the immediate reaction was a wildcat strike protesting the "speed-up" of work. Though variety and a sense of closure are desirable elements of a mature job assignment, they are often insufficient if not accompanied by elements introduced by job enrichment.

Job enrichment

Enrichment of jobs would include not only horizontal enlargement, but also vertical enlargement to permit subordinate participation in managerial decisions concerning tasks assigned. Total freedom for the employee is not envisaged. However, if one is delegated the right to determine the method to be used (entailing elimination or transformation of the motion study engineer into a resource consultant), the speed or rate of output (suggesting elimination of the staff time study engineer), and the degree of acceptable quality produced (eliminating need for the quality control inspector), then a high degree of job enrichment has been introduced. Perhaps the foremost theorist advancing the concept of job enrichment is Frederick Herzberg. He strongly believes that self-management of job performance is the key to tapping tremendous motivational potentials in human beings.

Concerning the practicality of such enrichment programs, various organizations have undertaken experiments to determine possible effects upon performance. In the Imperial Chemical Industries Limited of Great Britain, the content of the laboratory technician job was changed for members of an experimental group.[12] The newly enriched job provided for technician writing and signing of final research projects without checking by supervision prior to issue, participating with superiors in work planning and target setting for the job, requisitioning materials and equipment needed on one's own signature, and conducting training programs for junior staff normally assigned.

On evaluation of the quality of research reports written, the fifteen members of the experimental group received ratings of 5, $8^{1}/_{2}$, and $7^{2}/_{3}$ at the end of the first, eighth, and fifteenth months. The control group of 29 laboratory technicians received corresponding ratings of $4^{1}/_{2}$, $6^{1}/_{3}$, and $4^{3}/_{4}$. It should be noted that the groups did not begin to diverge until about the eighth month. When eleven members of the control group were reassigned to the new experimental approach, their ratings rose from 6 to $8^{1}/_{2}$ in a five-month period.

In another reported experiment involving outside sales personnel, the newly enriched jobs entailed self-determination of customer calling frequency, self-determination of what customer information was to be passed on, authority to make immediate settlement of claims up to $250, authority to vary prices up to 10 percent, and the right to buy back unwanted stock without prior approval. All of the above rights were withheld from a control group of twenty-three salesmen. After the nine-month study, the experimental group of fifteen salesmen had increased their sales 19 percent over the level of the preceding year. The control group's average performance had decreased 5 percent over their previous year. The managerial implications of such job enrichment programs can be summarized in the form of the ideal job. Such a job would have (1) variety to allow use of multiple skills, (2) identity of task, thus permitting

[12]William J. Paul, Jr., Keith B. Robertson, and Frederick Herzberg, "Job Enrichment Pays Off," *Harvard Business Review*, vol. 47, no. 2, March–April 1969, p. 63.

psychological closure, (3) task significance in the eyes of the incumbent and others, (4) feedback of task performance results, and (5) autonomy in selecting methods of work, pace of work, and determination of acceptable quality.[13]

There is evidence that the theory of job enrichment is far in advance of its actual acceptance and practice on the part of management. In a survey of 125 of our largest industrial firms, only 5 reported having formal job enrichment programs.[14] However, almost 30 indicated having plans for possible use in the future. It should be apparent that job enrichment is no panacea, but that specific analysis of each work situation will be required to determine its practicality. Assuming that the firm's managerial philosophy is favorable to the sharing of management with subordinates, one still must consider such factors as qualifications and desires of available personnel, degree of interaction currently required with other jobholders, whether the job can be restructured to permit identity and feedback of performance levels, and degree to which the work process is dominated by inflexible and expensive technology. Job enrichment strikes at the technological "guts" of the organization, requiring considerable investment in both time and money. Finally, when job enrichment has been tried, the economic results have not always been uniformly favorable. A systematic review of ten studies of situations in which jobs had been enriched revealed an increase in work quality in all ten but increases in work quantity in only four instances. Thus, the decision-making situation involves the possibility but not the certainty of improvements in employee morale, a high degree of certainty with respect to improved product quality, and a substantial probability of a decrease in quantity, at least in the short run.

Sociotechnical groups

The interaction requirements of many jobs would call for "work group enrichment" rather than job enrichment. Research in the British coal industry indicated that work divided by the mining cycle rather than the shift made possible the formation of self-sufficient, largely self-managed work groups that were able to effect considerable gains in productivity.[15] Davis suggests that the sociotechnical approach would entail (1) identifying a group task that can logically be self-regulated, (2) providing for the full range of necessary skills, (3) delegating authority for group self-assignment of tasks and roles, (4) developing internal communication opportunities within the group, and (5) providing for a group monetary reward system.[16]

With the stimulus of research, a few firms in the United States have experimented with the sociotechnical approach to team development. In one pet-food manufacturing plant, all tasks were assigned to teams of seven to seventeen members.[17] Each worker learns every job performed by the team, and the pay rate rises as teammates decide that skills have been acquired. There are no conventional departments or appointed

---

[13]Robert Janson, "Job Design for Quality," *The Personnel Administrator*, vol. 19, no. 7, October 1974, p. 15.

[14]William E. Reif, David N. Ferrazzi, and Robert J. Evans, Jr., "Job Enrichment: Who Uses It and Why," *Business Horizons*, vol. 17, no. 1, February 1974, p. 74.

[15]E. L. Trist, G. W. Higgin, H. Murray, and A. B. Pollack, *Organizational Choice*, Oxford University Press, London, 1965.

[16]Louis E. Davis, "The Design of Jobs," *Industrial Relations*, vol. 6, no. 1, October 1966, p. 44.

[17]Richard E. Walton, "How to Counter Alienation in the Plant," *Harvard Business Review*, vol. 50, no. 6, November–December 1972, pp. 74–78.

supervisors. Rather, there are team leaders who work as equals with other members. New employees are jointly hired by team members. Work teams have authority to solve manufacturing problems, to deal with task redistribution caused by absenteeism, and to perform equipment maintenance, housekeeping, and quality control. After eighteen months of operation, the results were favorable in economic terms: overhead costs were 33 percent lower than in comparable plants, absenteeism 9 percent lower, and quality rejects 92 percent lower, and superior records were effected in the areas of turnover and safety. Problems arising included some intra-team disputes over certifying members as qualified, refusal of some members to take on greater responsibilities, inability of some team leaders to stop acting like bosses, and the confusion of some outside vendors who found themselves negotiating with operatives when they were accustomed to managers. It should also be noted that certain elements made this approach possible—the technology could be redesigned for team application, it was a new plant isolated from other parts of the corporation, the size of the work force was small, and there was no labor union.

In the automobile industry, perhaps the most publicized attempt to incorporate sociotechnically designed work groups is that of Volvo in Sweden.[18] The long final assembly line has been broken up into multiple shorter lines, interspersed with storage areas. Each line is under the control of a properly designed group with authority to alter production speeds and assignments within imposed limits. The owners estimate an increase in original costs of 15 percent over more typical plants but hope to derive values in the areas of product quality and human relations.

SUMMARY

This chapter has ranged from the general to the specific, from the basic overall objectives of an organization to the specific job content of an individual task. On the thesis that the personnel manager will be increasingly called upon for advice and expertise in the field of organizational design, knowledge must be obtained on such diverse subjects as objectives, functions, relationships, structure, job enlargement and enrichment, and sociotechnical teams.

Organizing is the process of establishing formal relationships (responsibility, authority, and accountability) among key components (functions, personnel, and physical factors) for the purpose of harnessing (line, line/staff, functionalized, or project structure) and directing toward common enterprise objectives (service, member, and social). Objectives govern the specification of functions, which tend to be differentiated, both downward and outward, with increasing size of organization. Primary, secondary, and tertiary contributions to the primary objective can be identified. If a production manager does training research, the function has been allocated to the line. If a personnel unit performs that research, it has removed to a secondary status of staff service. If a specialized subunit within the personnel department performs that research, its relationship to the basic general objective is tertiary. These analyses of objectives and functions are necessary for the understanding and design of basic instrumental structures.

[18]"Job Redesign on the Assembly Line: Farewell to Blue-Collar Blues?" *Organizational Dynamics*, vol. 2, no. 2, Autumn 1973, pp. 61–63.

Whether an organizational expert or not, the personnel manager must study the design of specific job and group assignments. Psychological and sociological research suggests that redesign of work content to provide variety, permit closure, and meet needs for mature self-regulation can often provide considerable returns to the organization. Returns in the areas of product quality and such human values as morale, absenteeism, and turnover are highly probable. The major worries usually encountered revolve around the considerable investment in time and talent required for such redesign, accompanied by serious doubts about the net impact upon work output.

DISCUSSION QUESTIONS

1   Give the complete definition of the formal process of organizing.
2   Cite the major arguments in favor of looking toward the personnel manager as the prime expert adviser on the function of organizing.
3   Beginning with training being performed by immediate line supervisors, trace the process of functional differentiation outward to its organizational allocation in a large, multiplant firm.
4   What are the derivative relationships among the concepts of function, authority, responsibility, accountability, and objectives? What, therefore, is the justification for authority?
5   For each of the three basic types of organization structure—line, line/staff, and functionalized—indicate the nature and location of the personnel functions.
6   Define and distinguish between job enlargement and job enrichment.
7   How do the set of recommendations issuing from sociotechnical system studies compare with those issuing from job enrichment?
8   Describe the relationship of a personnel department manager to a project officer under the project form of structure.
9   Defend the thesis of the primacy of the service or product objective.
10   Is a manager's effective span of control likely to be longer or shorter when supervising other managers as compared with nonmanagers? Why?

SUPPLEMENTARY READING

CHILD, John: "Predicting and Understanding Organization Structure," *Administrative Science Quarterly*, vol. 18, no. 2, June 1973, pp. 168–185.
LUTHANS, Fred, and William E. Reif: "Job Enrichment: Long on Theory, Short on Practice," *Organizational Dynamics*, vol. 2, no. 3, Winter 1974, pp. 30–38.
MORSE, John J.: "A Contingency Look at Job Design," *California Management Review*, vol. 16, no. 1, Fall 1973, pp. 67–75.
THAMHAIN, Hans J., and Gary R. Gemmill: "Influence Styles of Project Managers: Some Project Performance Correlates," *Academy of Management Journal*, vol. 17, no. 2, June 1974, pp. 216–225.
WALTON, Richard E.: "How to Counter Alienation in the Plant," *Harvard Business Review*, vol. 50, no. 6, November–December 1972, pp. 70–81.
ZENGER, John H., and Dale E. Miller: "Building Effective Teams," *Personnel*, vol. 51, no. 2, March–April 1974, pp. 20–29.

FIVE

MANAGING THE PERSONNEL UNIT

It was stated previously that the basic functions common to all managers are planning, organizing, directing, and controlling. In this chapter we are assuming that a specialized personnel unit exists within a complex organization, and we shall examine the managing task of its leader. Attention will be given to only three of the functions—planning, organizing, and controlling—with discussion of the fourth, directing, delayed until coverage of the operative function of integration. The directing function is heavily concerned with motivation of others to contribute to organizational objectives, a task that is essential to integration. If the personnel manager is obligated to assist other managers in this area, it would seem logical that this same expertise could be brought to bear upon the immediate organizational unit.

That more attention should be devoted to management of personnel activities is substantiated by frequent and persistent criticism of personnel units as uneconomical and useless appendages to vital living structures of productive organizations. A former chairman of the Avis Rent-A-Car Corporation recommended "firing the whole personnel department."[1] Herzberg complains that the unit's major goal is too often that of "peace," thereby calling for numerous hygienic programs to "clean up" the workplace and prevent dissatisfaction.[2] Though criticism of specific company programs is often justified, it is undeniable that a considerable potential for value creation exists in specialized units whose primary concern is the organization's human resources. With increasing pressures brought to bear by both government and labor unions, there is little danger that the unit will be "fired." However, a professional personnel manager will not settle for this protective, maintenance, and peacekeeping role and will search

[1]Robert Townsend, *Up the Organization*, Alfred A. Knofp, Inc., New York, 1970, p. 144.
[2]Frederick Herzberg, *Work and the Nature of Man*, The World Publishing Company, Cleveland, 1966, chap. 9.

for approaches that will simultaneously enhance values derived by people, organizations, and society. That this is one of the most difficult tasks imaginable perhaps provides us with an excuse, but it does not serve to justify excessive absorption in relatively unimportant activities. Top management can lead the way by insisting that personnel managers establish definite goals for the personnel system, that continuous planning be practiced because of the dynamic nature of the subject, that more human resource information be made available in a form that facilitates sound decision making, and that the multiple, splintered, and technique-oriented operative activities be integrated into a coordinated system.

Opportunities do exist for personnel managers to act decisively and professionally. In a survey of large enterprises, 126 of the 249 top personnel executives carried the title "vice-president."[3] In a second study of 132 personnel managers in business organizations, 71 percent had earned a bachelor's degree, 21 percent a master's degree, and 8 percent a law degree.[4] Almost all had taken college courses in industrial psychology, principles of personnel management, labor problems, and human relations. Approximately 35 percent had been in personnel work for their entire career, the average tenure being fifteen years. Both the opportunity and the skills are available in many organizations to make personnel a vital and value-adding function.

ORGANIZING THE PERSONNEL UNIT

Inasmuch as we have just completed discussion of the personnel manager's responsibility to advise in the area of organizational design, we shall discuss first the same task with respect to the specialized personnel unit.

Bases of departmentation

As indicated in the preceding chapter, a manager can organize the department area on a number of different bases. Perhaps the functional base is most common within personnel departments. In the example shown in Figure 5-1, the basic grouping revolves around procurement (employment), development (training), compensation

[3]Allen R. Janger, *Personnel Administration: Changing Scope and Organization*, National Industrial Conference Board, Studies in Personnel Policy, no. 203, New York, 1966, p. 14.

[4]O. Jeff Harris, "Personnel Administrators: The Truth about Their Backgrounds," *Business Topics*, vol. 17, no. 3, Summer 1969, pp. 22–29.

Figure 5-1

PERSONNEL DEPARTMENT–FUNCTIONAL BASE

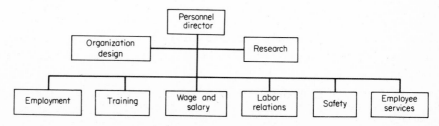

(wage and salary administration), integration (labor relations), and maintenance (safety and employee services). The exact breakdown would obviously vary with the enterprise, inasmuch as it is affected by such variables as size, abilities of personnel, and top management philosophy regarding the role of personnel.

One behavioral critic has suggested that most personnel time and budget have been improperly spent upon hygienic activities designed to prevent employee dissatisfaction. Though the importance and extent of such activities will not decline, Herzberg contends that an even more significant activity should be undertaken, that of promoting employee satisfaction.[5] As indicated in Figure 5-2, the first functional grouping should be on the basis of purpose or service: (1) prevent dissatisfaction through hygienic maintenance and (2) promote satisfaction through motivators. The functional breakdown of the hygiene division would be similar to that in Figure 5-1. The suggested breakdown of the new motivator division would be as follows: (1) an educational function to convince all managers that satisfaction comes basically from the job content and not the surrounding environment, (2) a job design function to enhance interest and pride in work (see preceding chapter), and (3) a remedial function involving training and education to overcome technological obsolescence, poor performance of specific individuals and groups, and administrative mistakes in policy, practices, and assumptions regarding the sources of motivation. Though a few enterprises are undertaking programs of this type, they are not usually allocated the status suggested by Herzberg.

Sokolik suggests a third basis on which modern departments might be organized: clientele.[6] He feels that modern crises as well as the varying requirements of different types of employees might dictate specialization on this particular base. As indicated in Figure 5-3, he recommends that subunits be developed to concentrate separately upon scientific and technical personnel, workers new to industry (hard-core unemployed), managers, women, and labor organized into unions. Instead of a "total market" approach to all personnel, market or personnel segmentation would be more likely to lead to differentiation of programming and treatment. In most instances, the particular personnel department organization that is adopted is a combination of bases, rather than any single one.

With respect to the size of the personnel department, various studies have

[5]Frederick Herzberg, op. cit., pp. 171–181.

[6]Stanley L. Sokolik, "Reorganize the Personnel Department?" *California Management Review*, vol. 11, no. 3, Spring 1969, p. 48.

Figure 5-2

PERSONNEL DEPARTMENT–SERVICE BASE

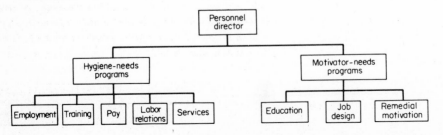

Figure 5-3

PERSONNEL DEPARTMENT–CLIENTELE BASE

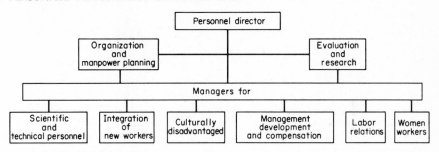

Source: Stanley L. Sokolik, "Reorganize the Personnel Department?" *California Management Review*, vol. 11, no. 3, Spring 1969, p. 48; © 1969 by The Regents of the University of California, reprinted by permission of The Regents of the University of California.

reported the ratio of personnel employees to total employees. A survey of 107 member firms of the American Society of Personnel Administrators revealed that the number of persons on the staff of the personnel department per 100 employees ranged from 0.15 to 4.76, with a median of 0.89.[7] Approximately 60 percent of the firms had more than 1,000 employees. That this is reasonably representative of average size is supported by a second survey of sixty-three manufacturing firms in the state of Arizona, the average ratio being 0.78.[8] Because of organizational difficulties of dividing job assignments, the ratios tend to be larger in the smaller-size firm. Ratios also tend to vary by industry, with comparatively greater investments in specialized personnel units in finance, manufacturing, and government.

Line and personnel staff relationships

When a specialized staff unit is introduced into an organization, formerly clear interunit relationships often become highly complex. In organizing, what has been divided to secure specialized expertise must ultimately be combined to secure unity of organized action. Various guides or principles of line/staff relationships have been proposed as means of effecting greater coordination and cooperation. Four examples will be given, the first two of which emphasize the primary status of line; the latter two defend the necessary contribution of the personnel staff unit.

PRINCIPLE OF STAFF ADVICE This is the most frequently cited principle in this area and states that staff can only *advise* line what to do, never command or order. The wholeness or integrity of the line should not be broken. But what if the personnel manager has recommended that a superintendent follow a proposal and the latter refuses? According to the principle, personnel cannot force compliance. But the personnel manager is convinced that the proposal is sound. The formal organization

[7]"Planning and Budgeting the Personnel Program," *ASPA-BNA Survey No. 23*, The Bureau of National Affairs, Inc., Washington, D.C., June 6, 1974, p. 1.

[8]Edwin B. Flippo, Patricia Bauman, Jose G. Gutierrez, and Michael L. Bettega, "The Personnel Manager in Arizona Manufacturing Companies," *Arizona Review*, vol. 22, no. 1, January 1973, p. 9.

allows appeal to a common superior, in this case the vice-president of production. If this official agrees, the staff recommendation becomes a line order, which the superintendent must follow. The integrity of the line has been preserved, but the personnel manager may have difficulty in working with the superintendent in the future. Many staff specialists feel that they can be more effective in their work by avoiding such actions as this except in extremely important situations. They prefer to rely upon persuasion and sometimes upon "politicking" to achieve their aims.

In terms of specific grants of decision-making authority, research has discovered a high degree of variability, not only among different firms but also among different personnel operative functions within the single enterprise. In interviews with seventy-five executives in twenty-five firms varying in size from 100 to 15,000 employees, French and Henning discovered that the authority varied from little or none to unilateral rights of decision making in some personnel functions.[9] Over half reported that personnel directors are particularly strong in terms of unilateral action in decisions concerning the use of psychological tests, reference checks, and determination of bargaining strategy. They play a weaker role in decisions concerning the creation of new positions, maximum bargaining concessions, and granting of unusual and new fringe benefits. They are most authoritative in the procurement function and least authoritative in determining wage-level policies.

PRINCIPLE OF LIMITATION OF STAFF ECONOMY   This principle emphasizes the *service* relationship of staff. It states that in order for the line to operate at maximum economy and effectiveness, it is sometimes necessary for the serving staff to operate with reduced economy. The line is to be served by staff, not vice versa. Sometimes the staff official may have to run his or her department in a manner that is considered undesirable in order properly to serve the line. For example, a company may be desperately short of machinists. There is some chance that if the personnel department stays open at night some machinists may be encouraged to look around for another job after working hours. Also, these long hours may be extremely unpopular with personnel employees, and the budget may take a beating, but the hardship is necessary for the welfare of the line organization. Too often staff tends to prescribe what line must do to adjust to its requirements. The tail attempts to wag the dog.

PRINCIPLE OF COMPULSORY STAFF ADVICE   The first two principles stated above emphasize the importance of the line. If staff is necessary in an organization, its contribution must be defended. Staff functions are separated from the line and sometimes line resents this loss. There may be a tendency in the line to ignore or refuse to utilize staff, in the hope that they will go away and leave the line alone. If such is the case, a considerable investment has been made in staff personnel with little or no return. The line official is making all decisions with no assistance.

The principle of compulsory staff advice does not compel a line official to accept and follow the advice; it compels the line person only to listen. For example, the personnel unit should be consulted when jobs are being redesigned by line managers. Too often, only engineers and line managers are involved, thereby leading to job contents that may be technically feasible but humanly objectionable.

---

[9]Wendell French and Dale Henning, "The Authority-Influence Role of the Functional Specialist in Management," *Journal of the Academy of Management*, vol. 9, no. 3, September 1966, pp. 187–203.

PRINCIPLE OF STAFF INDEPENDENCE   Staff may not only be ignored by some line officials, but it may sometimes be dominated by others. The principle of staff independence indicates that staff personnel should have sufficient security to be able to give truthful advice to their superiors without fear of losing their jobs. This is the opposite of the "yes man" atmosphere. If we are to profit by the presence of expertness, then that expertness requires a certain amount of freedom within which to operate. If the staff specialist is merely to echo line ideas, the investment is wasted and the function should be returned to the line, formally as well as informally.

An example of this concept has sometimes been observed with respect to pending unionization of a firm. Research and study may lead the personnel manager to conclude that cooperation with the unionizing attempt, within the confines of the law, may be to the long-run best interest of the organization. Recommendation of such a policy to an owner-manager in some instances has been tantamount to immediate discharge. Again, line officials are not compelled to accept or follow the advice of expert specialists; but they are exceedingly shortsighted if they refuse to listen at all, or if they punish and reward in a manner leading to suppression of rational thought.

PLANNING THE PERSONNEL PROGRAM

Defined in its simplest terms, *planning is the determination of anything in advance of action.* It is essentially a decision-making process which provides a basis for economical and effective action in the future. Effective planning sets the stage for integrated action to take place, reduces the number of unforeseeable crises, promotes the use of more efficient methods, and provides the basis for the managerial function of control, thereby assuring focus on organization objectives.

Decision making

The personnel manager, despite the nebulous and complex nature of the field, can increase program effectiveness through a more judicious decision-making process. The suggested sequence of steps in more scientific decision making would encompass the following: (1) recognize and define a problem that calls for action, (2) determine possible alternative solutions, (3) collect and analyze facts bearing upon the problem, and (4) decide on a solution. Recognition of personnel problems calls for experience and background that make it possible for cues and clues to be observed and synthesized into patterns of probable cause and effect. In the personnel field, one must be always alert to possible dysfunctional human effects issuing from many technical programs promulgated in the name of rationality and profit; e.g., controls such as budgets often stimulate internal warfare. In generating solutions, creative imagination as well as interpersonal contacts will lead to generation of multiple possible answers. "Brainstorming" and other artificial creative stimulants have been applied to personnel problems on occasions.[10] After imagination abates temporarily, judgment takes over in the collection and analysis of facts. Operations research and quantitative methods show

---

[10]"Brainstorming" is a group ideation process where judgment is prohibited, "wild" ideas are encouraged, quantity rather than quality is the immediate goal, and chain reactions from idea to idea often develop. It has most often been used in the field of advertising.

some promise of being able to assist the personnel manager in collating and understanding gathered data. Ultimately, the essence of the manager's position is *choice*.
One must extend one's neck and commit time and talent to a program that one figures
will work. The manager must never forget, however, that acceptance of the program by
those concerned is often as important as its technical quality; an 80 percent "perfect"
solution with 100 percent employee acceptance may be worth more than the reverse.

Programs and policies

Policies and programs are human-made guides to action. In theory, they are based on
an analysis of enterprise objectives as well as on the available knowledge in the subject
area concerned. Personnel managers are often called upon to establish guides in areas
where the state of the art is incomplete, and able persons can differ concerning best
approaches. For example, is it a true principle that the higher the employees' morale,
the higher their productivity? If this were a universal fact, the development of various
programs would be a simpler task. The available research indicates, however, that the
relationship is not a simple one. A review of a number of studies by Vroom, for
example, shows a median correlation of plus .14 between employee satisfaction and
output (1.00 would indicate a perfect relationship, while 0 would suggest that they are
unrelated).[11] All is not lost, however, for certain of the studies in particular companies
revealed a very high correlation (in the .60s and .70s), suggesting that personnel
managers *here* would do well to develop morale-building activities. In a few firms, the
correlation was inverse, placing the personnel manager in a considerable quandary,
torn between moral and economic values.

The subject matter of personnel requires that the manager become somewhat
familiar with decision-making techniques involving the use of probability estimates.
Illustrative of this concept, the Xerox Corporation has developed an approach to permit
more objective assessment of proposed programs. As Figure 5-4 indicates, a proposed
personnel program in job enrichment can be assessed by the manager in four major
areas: (1) the state of the art with respect to designing enriched jobs, (2) the ease with
which it can be implemented in the organization, (3) the projected economic benefits
to the firm, and (4) possible economic risks associated with the program. Under the
category of economic benefits, it should be noted that the manager must estimate the
probability of obtaining each specific benefit. There are no certain probabilities (1.0),
but it is calculated that it is almost certain (.8) that job enrichment would reduce
absenteeism because of greater interest in the job. With the assistance of accountants,
estimates can be made concerning dollar savings. When these are multiplied by
probability estimates, the *expected* values can be ascertained ($2,132,500 \times .8 =$
$1,706,000 for absenteeism).

Despite the high marks given the job enrichment program in areas of state of art,
economic benefits, and economic risks, the very low score allocated to "ease of
implementation" led the management to rate the proposal as "moderately desirable."
As suggested above, technical quality is not enough. One must also consider line
manager attitudes, organization structure, technology, the outer environment, and
preferred leadership styles. A difficult implementation process is envisaged. Perhaps
another program, an educational one, could be devised to reduce predicted managerial

[11]Victor H. Vroom, *Work and Motivation*, John Wiley & Sons, Inc., New York, 1964, p. 183.

Figure 5-4 Personnel program evaluation form

1. Define and describe the program.	**PROGRAM NAME**: Service Force Job Enrichment Program Program No. 16
	DESCRIPTION (objectives, target population, implementation schedule):
2. Identify and segregate legally required efforts.	To extend the job enrichment program for the service force — as piloted in Spring Falls, Avon Hills, and Maplewood branches — to all branches between 1972 and 1976.
	Is program legally required? ☐ Yes ☒ No
3. Evaluate feasibility: (a) State-of-the-art implications.	**STATE OF THE ART** ☒ High ☐ Medium ☐ Low
(b) Ease of implementation.	**EASE OF IMPLEMENTATION** ☐ High ☐ Medium ☒ Low
(c) Net economic benefits...	**ECONOMIC BENEFITS** ☒ High ☐ Medium ☐ Low

	Potential revenue impact	Probability of occurrence	Probable gross benefit (cost)
Identifiable benefits: Reduction in service force turnover of 1 point.	$ 450,000	.2	$ 90,000
Extension of 1.2 point reduction in absenteeism, as demonstrated in pilot project.	$ 2,132,500	.8	$ 1,706,000
Extension of 5% increase in service force productivity, as demonstrated in initial efforts.	$85,500,000	.1	$ 8,550,000
Total benefits	$88,082,500	.12	$10,346,000
Tangible costs to Xerox of acting: Group personnel staff time to develop program, and line management time to implement program in all branches.	($ 472,950)	9	$ 425,655
Total costs	($ 472,950)	.9	$ 425,655
Probable net benefits (cost)			$ 9,920,345

... and intangibles.

Intangible benefits

Increased morale in service force, with improved customer service and satisfaction.

"Contagious effect" of job enrichment to other groups, e.g., sales and clericals.

Improved service manager development with concurrent sharpening of their motivational skills. As an extreme example, one manager at Avon Hills increased his team's productivity 70%.

(d) Economic risks.

ECONOMIC RISKS ☒ High ☐ Medium ☐ Low

Possible consequences of not acting:
Continued escalation of service costs as a percent of revenue.

ASSUMPTIONS AND OTHER CONSIDERATIONS:

Cost estimates assume 4.4 man years of group staff time, .26 man years of branch manager time, and 15.8 man years of service manager time to implement program in a population of 1,053 service managers.

Benefit estimates assume elimination of 3 days absenteeism per month for each of 1,053 service teams, favorable productivity, and that turnover experience in pilot branches can be cascaded to all branches.

Source: Logan M. Cheek, "Cost Effectiveness Comes to the Personnel Function," *Harvard Business Review*, vol. 51, no. 3, May–June 1973, p. 99. Used with permission.

resistance, thereby upgrading the "ease of implementation" assessment to at least the "medium" level.

The "seat-of-the-pants" approach to decision making in the field of personnel is increasingly jeopardized by the size of the stakes involved. Systematic study and assessment of possibilities in all the functions of personnel will have to be undertaken to design value-producing programs as well as to reduce potential conflict with government agencies and labor unions. In *procurement*, better answers are necessary in determining minimum hiring qualifications, use of psychological tests, and employment of the culturally disadvantaged. Improved *development* requires comprehensive, balanced, and assessable training programs for managers and operatives, as well as sound policies of promotion and performance appraisal. *Compensation* policies are particularly difficult to devise in times of extreme inflation, for the state of the art in this area is not well developed. The difficulty of choosing appropriate *integration* programs was demonstrated above in discussing the relationship between morale and productivity. Collective bargaining with organized labor has been, and will continue to be, equally demanding. Programs and policies in the *maintenance* function would seem to be a little easier inasmuch as we have so many fringe benefits to emulate, as well as those programs absolutely required by law. But even here, the challenge remains in the possible transformation of routine, peace-keeping programs into programs providing positive value to the organization.

The computer and personnel

It would appear that one hope for more scientific decision making in the personnel field issues from the steady invasion of computer processing. In many firms, the answers to personnel questions are highly dependent upon the memories of existing personnel specialists. Pertinent information exists within the file drawers, but the search process is of necessity highly limited. For example, who in the company is qualified for a new job opening in electrical engineering for a new plant to be opened overseas? A search of the files is a partial search. If a skills inventory were available in a computer memory bank, *all* qualified personnel would at least be brought to the attention of the personnel manager. And if this split-second, comprehensive survey of all internal personnel reveals that none are qualified, an external city, state, or national skills data bank would undoubtedly provide a list of qualified alternatives. Naturally, the computer does not make the hiring decisions. It merely provides the available alternatives.

If a management wishes to develop an automatic data-processing system for personnel data, certain minimum essentials must be met. In the first place, there must be established a personnel data base that includes each piece of personnel information necessary for making decisions. In the study of one organization, it was found that over 2,100 items of data were used, but further analysis reduced this to only 160 items or elements that proved to be distinctly different.[12] One of the significant by-products of the creation of this data base was a reduction in the costs of maintaining and transacting personnel information; in this instance, the reduction was in excess of $6 per employee per year. Another study of twenty-five companies showed that the average firm uses 340

[12]Philip L. Morgan, "Automatic Data Processing of Personnel Data," *Personnel Journal*, vol. 45, no. 9, October 1966, p. 554.

separate and distinct personnel documents involving an average of 197 separate and distinct items of information.[13] Each item of information was repeated an average of 9.7 times within the array of 340 documents. It is apparent that a single data bank would reduce both repetition and the opportunity for error.

Within this single personnel data bank, many items of information must be available and current. With respect to skills, each person's record should show past jobs held, preference for job type, geographic preferences, foreign languages known, level of formal education, and special courses completed both within and without the firm. Many companies lose blue-collar workers who have just completed requirements for a college degree because somehow the word got to the personnel department only through the exit interview. Specific and systematic collection of skills information on a continuing basis will emphasize to all employees that none will be overlooked or forgotten when personnel decisions are made. In addition, a comprehensive and current record must be maintained concerning each employee's in-company history with respect to such items as changes in job, department changes, salary increases, updated insurance, seniority levels, leaves of absence, and benefits received. With respect to the last item, a yearly accumulation report mailed to the employee's home should do much to convince him or her that 25 percent of the income does not appear in the periodic paycheck. As suggested in Figure 5-5, a more complete personnel management information system would include this personnel data base in conjunction with the payroll file and the benefits records. Each of these bases is often maintained and updated separately; e.g., the personnel data might be updated once a month or once every six months, while the payroll file is updated daily or weekly.

[13]John V. MacGuffie, "Computer Programs for People," *Personnel Journal*, vol. 48, no. 4, April 1969, p. 255.

Figure 5-5 Personnel management information system

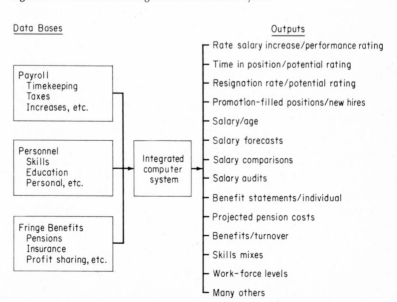

The use of information from all three data bases can be integrated through proper computer programming. As suggested, the personnel manager can call upon the total system for answers to questions that will permit more effective utilization of human resources. For example, a report of the rate with which salary increases are meted out to individuals in comparison with their performance ratings will doubtlessly prevent able, but unrewarded, personnel from quitting. The amount of time spent in each position in comparison with assessed potential will indicate the degree to which the firm is utilizing its prized human assets. Comparing the number of positions filled from within by promotion with those where the firm was forced to go outside gives some measurement of the effectiveness of personnel development programs.

The integrated personnel data-processing system also facilitates the control function. Identification of significant exceptions to standards can be programmed for such on-going problems as determining those employees for whom salary increases are overdue, determining which specific recommended pay changes are in excess of or below authorized limits, flagging personnel or organizational units that have excessive lost time, and specifying employee requisitions that have remained unfilled for excessive periods of time.

Planning for the future is facilitated through projected simulations. Negotiators with labor unions might want to know the specific costs if vacation allowances were extended one additional week for employees with ten years of service instead of the present fifteen years. What specific jobs will become open throughout the total organization by reason of retirement within the next five years? What has been the experience of this company with respect to the relationship between age and salary when educational level is held constant? There are many things that a manager would like to know in order to determine the direction and speed with which the organization is moving or drifting. An automatic personnel data-processing system should make many of these answers available. Surveys of practice generally indicate increasing utilization of the computer in the personnel functions by the larger-size firms; e.g., of 210 firms with 500 to over 25,000 employees, 74 percent reported use of electronic data processing in personnel, particularly with respect to records, wages and salaries, and service benefits.[14]

Standards

A very important part of the personnel manager's responsibility for general administration of the personnel program is the establishment and maintenance of many standards by which performance can be judged. A *standard* can be defined as an *established criterion or model against which actual results can be compared.*

Many different types of standards can be used in controlling business activities. The foremost type would be standards governing the nature of the operating *results*, commonly called "performance standards." Operating results generally concern such variables as quantity, quality, time, and costs. Personnel control must also be concerned with these same standards of quantity, quality, time, and costs. At the present stage of development, the latter two variables, time and cost, are more adaptable to the

[14]Frederick H. Black, Jr., "The Computer in the Personnel Department," *Personnel*, vol. 46, no. 5, September–October 1969, pp. 67–68.

personnel field than are quantity and quality. It is quite common to work against personnel budgets that specify cost standards. Similarly, work schedules which give time objectives are usually established for particular personnel functions. The more important standards of quantity and quality are much less adaptable to exact quantification and control. In the following section, we shall itemize and briefly discuss certain specific standards that are concerned with quantity and quality in the personnel field.

Sometimes it is difficult if not impossible to specify exactly the performance standards desired. In such cases, standards governing the process may be established and used as a basis for control in an attempt to promote the maximum in results. These other types of standards cover (1) *method or function*, (2) *personnel*, and (3) *physical factors*. The reader will recall that these three factors are the basic ingredients of all organizations, and they effect the accomplishment of work. Consequently, if lack of knowledge prevents the establishment of exact and accurate standards of operating results, control over the *manner* of operative execution will contribute to a better result than could otherwise be obtained. Thus, if the best-known methods of performance are utilized by high-quality personnel, who have available the latest in equipment, we can logically expect a high order of results in terms of quantity and quality.

With reference to standards of function, a basic method, often termed a standard operating procedure, can be devised and enforced. Presumably, if this procedure is followed, the desired result will be obtained. If it proves difficult to establish either or *both* a performance standard and a standard of function, selection of a high-quality person to do the job may effect the desired result. This approach would be favored by behaviorists even in cases where accurate performance standards were feasible. A specification of human characteristics required to execute a task thus constitutes a standard of personnel. Standards of physical conditions are also important since they can drastically affect the work of people. If the machinery, equipment, and general working conditions leave much to be desired, the best person using the best method may yield inadequate results in terms of quantity, quality, time, and costs. Examples of each of these seven types of standards are given in Figure 5-6 with reference to the hiring or procurement function.

Figure 5-6   Examples of standards applicable to procurement function

Type of standard	Example
Performance results	
1 Quantity	20 Assembly Technicians to be obtained for new project
2 Quality	Turnover rate for technicians to be less than 1 percent per month
3 Time	20 Technicians to be obtained and placed by June 15
4 Cost	Budget for hiring not to exceed $4,000
Process	
1 Function	Hiring procedure to encompass reference checks, dexterity tests, and interviews
2 Personnel	Interviewers to possess college degrees and undergo retraining every two years
3 Physical factors	Testing and interviewing to be conducted in locations where total privacy is assured

CONTROLLING THE PERSONNEL UNIT

The personnel manager must oversee and collect information concerning the performance of personnel functions and compare these results with predetermined standards. Continuous comparison is expensive. The period of time over which results should be accumulated before making a comparison is a matter of judgment. The period tends to be shorter under conditions of highly centralized control and repetitive operations. In the personnel field the periods are relatively *long*. For example, it may take years to determine the true effectiveness of a new psychological testing program to be used in selection. This is not to say that some comparisons will not be made within a year, but the situation is certainly not like that which exists in production, where comparisons may be made hourly. *Monthly* reports on such factors as absenteeism, turnover, and accidents are quite typical of business operations; comparisons can be made with both past performance and the published data in the industry. *Yearly* comparisons are usually made on wage and fringe benefits. Training results as revealed through productivity rates can be made *daily* or even *hourly*.

When the comparison of performance with standards is made, there must be a decision as to the significance of the deviation discovered. If it is deemed a significant exception to planned behavior, corrective action will follow. There are two general types of corrective action—immediate and basic. Those actions directed toward solution of the discovered exception are considered to be immediate, e.g., issue new instructions, work overtime, appeal for unusual cooperation, and revise the plan. Those actions directed toward correcting the underlying conditions that led to this and other similar emergencies are deemed to be basic, e.g., replace personnel, discipline personnel, revise the operating procedure, and change the organizational relationships. In general, immediate corrective action should be taken first in order to provide the time necessary for the analysis of underlying causes.

Strategic control points

In this text we are primarily concerned with the management of personnel. How does one ensure that the personnel program is returning value for the investment that was made in it? To understand the presentation that follows, the reader needs familiarity with the nature of personnel operations. Since operative performance precedes or is concurrent with control, the proper reading sequence might well demand that this be placed at the end of the text. But in the interest of demonstrating the interrelationships within the management cycle, we have included the discussion of control in this section.

Although we cannot separate precisely the operative functions of personnel one from another, we find it desirable to organize the presentation of control points by the operative functions. For example, if procurement is a basic operative function of personnel, how can one check to ensure that it is being done effectively? The specific measures that are applied to procurement may also shed light on integration or development, but we believe that some type of classification will help the reader to understand and remember.

PROCUREMENT The objective of the procurement process is to secure the proper number and kind of personnel for the organization. Successful procurement will result not only in the organization's acceptance of the person, but also in the person's acceptance of and satisfaction with the job and the company. The following various points can be utilized to check upon the effectiveness with which the procurement process is administered:

1 *Formal placement follow-up* to determine (1) the supervisor's satisfaction with the employee, and (2) the employee's satisfaction with the job, department, supervisor, and company.

2 *Requests for transfer.* Such requests should be analyzed to determine whether they are caused by poor procurement activities or are created by causes outside the control of the organization.

3 *Voluntary quits.* The greatest number of voluntary quits ordinarily occur during the first few months on the job. This suggests poor selection and induction. Either the new employee has been oversold by recruiters or has been treated in a manner considered undesirable after being placed on the job. In addition, the employer has possibly been guilty of the technical error of failing to match properly the person's qualifications with specified job requirements.

4 *Involuntary layoffs.* In these days of unemployment compensation and guaranteed annual wages, involuntary layoffs caused by poor planning of human resources requirements are to be avoided. Consequently involuntary layoffs can be taken as an index of the effectiveness of personnel planning, with, of course, proper consideration for the exigencies of particular situations, stage of the business cycle, etc.

We do not imply that the above-listed points constitute a complete coverage of the methods of controlling a procurement program. But the list does suggest that control is necessary and can be effected without watching every step that the line manager, recruiter, or employment interviewer may take. Among other points sometimes used to judge the quality of the personnel obtained are sales in dollars per employee, output in units per person-hour, and the level of aging of the work force because of its effect upon long-range manpower planning.

DEVELOPMENT Measuring the effectiveness of training and development is one of the manager's more difficult tasks. In many instances, an evaluation of the program by the trainee is the prime source of information. This point is not to be ignored, but it is clear that a wide discrepancy often exists between trainee acceptance and trainee performance on the job. Better techniques of measuring training effectiveness will have to be developed in the future, particularly as closer scrutiny is being given to training expenditures by top management. Some suggested control points are listed below.

1 *Productivity.* Where it is adaptable to the problem, specific information concerning productivity after training is the best control point for a training program. Often, however, the objectives of training are more intangible. For example, how does one measure the effectiveness of a human relations training program for first-line supervision? This is a highly subjective area, but even here managers should attempt to deal with concrete results by either observing the trainee in action or receiving reports from others with whom he or she comes in contact.

2 *Quality losses.* This index is closely related to the productivity record, emphasizing quality in addition to quantity. As we have indicated above, trouble with quality control can issue from other sources besides training, and it is generally impossible to state that a particular observed result issues from a single stimulus. Nevertheless, quality losses can provide a clue to the adequacy of training.

3 *Adequacy of talent reservoir.* How many incumbents of key jobs are backed up by trained replacements with the potential for promotion? What is the status of the available talent for new jobs to be created with the expansion of the firm? Investigation of these two questions often provides information that is shocking to the top management of a firm. An index that may also be helpful in judging the adequacy of the talent reservoir is the number of higher-level positions that were filled from within the organization. Within particular development programs, points to watch would include the percentage of participants completing the course, costs per person-hour, and percentage of key personnel who are currently involved in organized development. Certainly, the developmental history of each key individual should also be reviewed from time to time.

COMPENSATION The function of compensation, as defined in this text, is concerned solely with monetary remuneration. It would therefore seem that control points in this area should be more objective, since we are dealing with concrete figures. The determination of a correct wage, however, is not a completely objective process since "correctness" also denotes fairness and equitableness. Whether a wage is fair and equitable involves subjective decision on the part of labor, management, and often the labor union. The following measures of a compensation program are suggested for control purposes:

1 *Community wage rates.* The going wage in the community can be used as a basis for comparison with the company's wage structure. Though ordinarily some argument is raised concerning the selection of firms to be surveyed and the geographic area to be covered, the community wage rate is a fairly objective measure of the entire compensation system.

2 *Wage and salary budgets.* In addition to ensuring that the firm is generally competitive in terms of salary, the manager must also make sure that expenditures are within allocated budgets. The average pay of employees in particular jobs can be compared with the midpoint in the salary range. Salary distribution by decile throughout each range will provide a more complete picture. Salary range limits for each job classification are monitored by the personnel specialist, and specific line approval must be sought when limits are to be exceeded.

3 *Grievances concerning compensation.* One of the objectives of any systematic wage and salary program is to reduce employee discontent with wages. The number of formal and informal complaints submitted by individuals is an indication of discontent. This measure should not be applied immediately after the introduction of any new compensation program, for the difficulties and publicity that go with the introduction often serve to increase the number of grievances filed.

4 *Incentive earnings: number of employees.* The number of employees earning bonus in excess of the standard rate of pay constitutes an index of the effectiveness of the incentive compensation program. If only a very small percentage of the employees on incentive jobs actually earn extra income, obviously very little incentive exists and some part of the incentive program is not working.

5   *Incentive earnings: amount.* Analysis of the amount of incentive earnings per employee will provide valuable data for appraising the effectiveness of an incentive program. If we find that most or all employees are earning *uniform* bonus amounts, possibly the group has agreed concerning the amount that should be produced.

INTEGRATION   The function of integration is one of the most intangible and difficult parts of a personnel program to evaluate. In this area we are dealing with feelings and attitudes. Several measures have been developed which give clues to the effectiveness of an integration program:

1   *Morale surveys.* Surveys of opinions and attitudes on various and sundry subjects of interest to the organization can be made and will give an index of morale. Comparisons of results can be made in various ways—department by department, this company with other companies, or by comparing a present survey with one taken in the past. The direction of progress within the firm can thereby be determined, as well as progress in relation to other firms in the industry.

2   *Absenteeism, tardiness, and turnover.* The reasons for absenteeism, tardiness, and turnover are many. It is the belief of many in personnel management that these factors often reflect a basic attitude—a feeling of irresponsibility and indifference. Though this may not be true in any one particular instance, a record accumulated over a period of time can give a good measure of interest in and acceptance of the job and the company.

3   *Number of grievances.* The number of grievances submitted by employees is a frequently used index of morale in industry. It should be pointed out that a simple statistical count can be misleading. Other important variables to be considered along with the number are the types of grievances submitted, the organization source, and the timing of other related actions such as the introduction of a new program. In many instances the number of grievances filed is compared with the number settled as well as the number entering arbitration proceedings. This comparison can give some indication of the degree of successful grievance processing within the company.

MAINTENANCE   The maintenance of personnel is concerned primarily with preserving the physical, mental, and emotional condition of employees. Measures of the effectiveness of programs designed to achieve this are as follows:

1   *Accident rates.* Using the accepted measures of accidents and comparing company rates with those of one's competitors provide a basis for considering the desirability of corrective action. The most commonly used measures of accidents are frequency rates and severity rates.

2   *Insurance premiums.* One of the most telling measures of a safety program is the out-of-pocket costs in the form of insurance premiums. When we realize that other indirect costs of an accident amount to four times the out-of-pocket insurance premium costs, we appreciate more the material importance of this particular measure.

3   *Employee participation in service programs.* When participation is absolutely required in a particular program, such as a retirement system, the extent of such participation is obviously no measure of its effectiveness. But for the various systems that are optional, such as recreational programs and some forms of economic assistance, a count of voluntary participants is a measure of the effectiveness of the plan, at least in the eyes of the employees. Proving that an employee service program is of benefit to the company is considerably more difficult.

The personnel audit

Few top managements fail to see the necessity for periodic internal and/or external audits of the financial resources of the enterprise. The obtainment, preservation, and expenditure of the human resources would appear to be an equally important responsibility of a management interested in long-term viability of the enterprise. The personnel audit is a systematic survey and analysis of all operative functions of personnel, with a summarized statement of findings and recommendations for correction of deficiencies. In many cases, the auditing tool is a simple worksheet of basic questions to be answered during interviews with personnel specialists and, at times, selected personnel throughout the enterprise. This systematic interviewing process should be preceded by collection and comparison of pertinent statistical data available in the control points previously discussed.

The orientation of the auditing process is toward the ways and means of program execution. A series of questions, which can be answered either "yes" or "no," is prepared, covering the five operative functions. Many of the questions deal with the myriad of details pertaining to the establishment of systematic procedures in any field. For example:

1   Are the required federal and state labor bulletins properly posted?
2   Is the firm in compliance with labor laws concerning overtime hours and rates, female employees, rest periods, and employment of minors?
3   Is the firm in compliance with state and federal minimum wage laws?
4   Are multiple sources for personnel utilized in recruitment?
5   Have employee handbooks on rules, policies, and benefits been prepared and distributed?
6   Are enrollment cards for available life insurance programs on file for each insured employee?
7   Does each job have a written description that has been approved by the personnel manager during the past twelve months?
8   Has each specified key employee had a formal appraisal during the past twelve months?
9   Has each employment interviewer undergone retraining during the past two years?
10   Do new employees receive an orientation tour?
11   Have all first-level supervisors received specific training prior to assumption of the position?

The above list of questions by no means covers the entire personnel program, but it does indicate the basic nature and approach of an audit. The fact that a personnel manager knows that he or she is subject to periodic systematic inspections by outside consultants, or representatives of top management, tends to stimulate a serious concern for internal planning and control.

Human resources accounting

Though extremely difficult to implement, interest is growing in the possibility of establishing a system of accounting for human resources. The significance of this is highlighted by the following question: Supposing that tomorrow a major catastrophe wiped out all of the human resources in your organization, how long would it take and how much would it cost to replace them with equivalent talent and interpersonal competence? Typical estimates of costs range from three to five times present payroll.[15] Typically, the first set of costs for human resources are those associated with their obtainment. Firms can determine with some accuracy costs of (1) recruiting, (2) hiring and placing, (3) initial orientation, and (4) continued training programs. Mere collection of such costs serves to impress upon all managers the seriousness of economic loss when personnel leave the organization.

Likert contends that even more important significant aspects of human resources lie in the area of general employee satisfaction and motivation. Consequently, he suggests periodic measures of attitudes toward the job, company, supervision, security, and opportunity. Though these can be obtained and evaluated on a comparative basis, conversion into dollar costs is quite difficult. Conceivably one could establish individual asset accounts, thus highlighting the more valuable humans to be retained at all costs. It is recommended, however, that human resource accounting be directed only toward aggregates. The state of the art, as well as dysfunctional side effects upon individual morale and motivation, would suggest that these measures be used for the overall control of the organization or major subdivisions thereof. Preservation and enhancement of our human assets should lead to savings in costs (turnover and absenteeism) and, desirably, improvements in values (productivity and quality).

SUMMARY

The management of a specialized unit charged with accomplishment of nebulous but important goals is no easy task. The personnel manager should not rely on the "softness" of the field to provide exemption from improving managerial practices. In organizing the unit, choice lies among multiple bases of departmentation—functions, clientele, and service. A considerable obligation must be assumed in tying the unit into the entire organization, following such guides as compulsory staff advice, limitation of staff economy, and staff independence.

In planning the personnel program, the manager should approach the decision-making process in a systematic and objective manner, calculating and comparing probabilities, costs, risks, and benefits. Specific policies, procedures, and standards will have to be established, even in subject areas where the state of the art is not well developed. The introduction of the computer and electronic data processing present new opportunities to manipulate data and obtain answers to questions of considerable significance to managing human resources more effectively.

In controlling the personnel unit, the manager must identify selected strategic control points that can be monitored on an exception basis. Periodically, a systematic

[15]Rensis Likert and David G. Bowers, "Organizational Theory and Human Resource Accounting," *American Psychologist*, vol. 24, no. 6, June 1969, p. 588.

and comprehensive audit of personnel activities and practices can be undertaken to assure that the program is being accomplished as planned. If in the future a reasonably accurate and acceptable system of accounting for human resources is developed, personnel management will improve in practice, visibility, and status.

DISCUSSION QUESTIONS

1 Compare and contrast the various bases of departmentation on which a personnel unit can be organized.
2 Suppose that you have been appointed the new personnel manager of a new department in a manufacturing firm with 800 employees. What size personnel department would you recommend be established? How would you organize it? How would you establish the department's relationship with the production division?
3 If you, the personnel manager, established the line supervisory training class as meeting at 8 A.M. daily because that is your free period, what principle of line/staff relationship are you likely to be violating? How?
4 For each of the seven types of standards, cite one example that a personnel manager might use in controlling his hiring section.
5 What approach to decision making is recommended in selecting specific personnel programs to install in the firm?
6 If an electronic personnel management information-processing system is available, what types of questions would a modern personnel manager ask of it?
7 What is human resources accounting? Of what possible value is it to the organization?
8 What is the nature of a personnel audit?
9 For each of the operative functions of personnel, cite two strategic control points to monitor.
10 What problems are posed to a personnel manager by the research finding that the median correlation coefficient between morale and productivity, in a number of different companies, is plus .14?

SUPPLEMENTARY READING

BAKER, Geoffrey M.: "The Feasibility and Utility of Human Resource Accounting," *California Management Review*, vol. 16, no. 4, Summer 1974, pp. 17–23.
CHEEK, Logan M.: "Cost Effectiveness Comes to the Personnel Function," *Harvard Business Review*, vol. 51, no. 3, May–June 1973, pp. 96–105.
FRANTZREB, Richard B., Linda L. T. Landau, and Donald P. Lundberg: "The Valuation of Human Resources," *Business Horizons*, vol. 17, no. 3, June 1974, pp. 73–80.
POWELL, Reed M., and Paul L. Wilkens: "Design and Implementation of a Human Resource Information System," *MSU Business Topics*, Winter 1973, pp. 21–27.
SHEIBAR, Paul: "Personnel Practices Review: A Personnel Audit Activity," *Personnel Journal*, vol. 53, no. 3, March 1974, pp. 211–215.
TOMESKI, Edward A., and Harold Lazarus: "The Computer and the Personnel Department," *Business Horizons*, vol. 16, no. 3, June 1973, pp. 61–66.

CASES FOR PART TWO

THE CASE OF THE REDESIGNED JOBS: THE DEKKER COMPANY*

The Dekker Company was a large manufacturer of electrical equipment for control devices and for the radio and television industry. In its Louisville, Kentucky, branch plant the company manufactured a complicated switching mechanism used in specialized electrical apparatus. The switching mechanism was produced in Department C, one of the three major operating departments shown in Figure 1.

The works manager was responsible to the company-wide vice-president of production for plant operations. Reporting to the works manager were six division managers. Each division was separated into departments, such as the switch department (Department C). Each department was further divided into sections and groups.

The production employees of the company, including those in Switch Department C, were represented by a local of an international labor union. The labor contract specified a typical grievance procedure of five steps beginning with "informal, oral discussion between the Section Chief and the Authorized Representative," except that grievances regarding a job wage rate could not be initiated until "60 days subsequent to the setting of such rate," in order to give the new rate a fair trial.

About 75 piece parts were required for each switch made in the switch department. The switches were assembled on an "assembly conveyor" by about 15 girls. They were then placed on an overhead conveyor which carried the assembled switches to an "adjusting conveyor" in an adjoining area. Here, 13 men performed about 50 electrical and mechanical adjustments on each switch. The adjusted switches were sample-

*Keith Davis, *Human Relations in Business*, McGraw-Hill Book Company, New York, 1957, pp. 581–585. Used with permission.

Figure 1 The Dekker Company (Louisville branch). Partial organization chart.

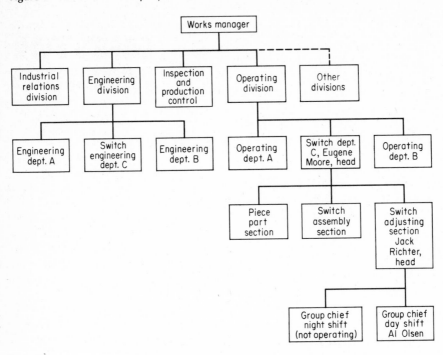

inspected by members of the inspection division, and then loaded on a transport rack for delivery to another building. The standard output from this adjusting conveyor was 60 switches per hour. The adjusting line was set up on this basis.

The 50 switch adjustments were broken down by the engineering department so that each of the 13 men performed only a few adjustments on *each* switch as it went past on the conveyor belt. Through the use of time-study data, the engineer on the job balanced the line so that each position required an equal amount of time.

Certain adjustments were more difficult to make than others. In recognition of this, the men who made the difficult adjustments were assigned a higher labor grade. The four labor grades on the adjusting line ranged from Grade 10 (the second lowest grade in the factory) to Grade 14. The rate difference between each grade was 5 cents, and each grade had a within-grade range of 8 cents. All adjusters were paid a day rate.

Engineering Department C serviced the switch shop. The engineers determined the method of manufacture, established time standards for each job, and authorized the purchase of all new machines and equipment. They prepared manufacturing layouts which the operating department was responsible for following. For example, a written layout by the engineering department covered the switch-adjusting operations for the 13-man assembly line. The sequence of adjustments and the duties of each position on the conveyor were described in this layout.

The department head in the switch shop, Eugene Moore, had been with the company for twenty-four years. He had been a department head for twelve years. His subordinates considered him to be a "company man," that is, he had a firm management viewpoint and lacked close touch with employees in his department.

The section head in the switch-adjusting section, Jack Richter, was a young man about thirty years of age. He had been recently transferred to his present line supervision job, after working several years at a desk job in the production-control department. He was energetic and aggressive. He wanted to "get ahead." The adjusters did not like him, although he got along well with most other persons in the switch department.

The group chief on the adjusting conveyor, Al Olsen, had been with the company less than two years. He was young, had a pleasant personality, and was well liked by the adjusters. He was conscientious but not aggressive. He found it difficult to discipline his men, many of whom were young men in their first job.

Ten weeks ago the daily production schedule was increased from 480 switches to 720 switches by management in the company home office. Thus the standard hourly production, or "SHP" as the men called it, had to be increased from 60 to 90 switches, if the plant was to remain on a one-shift basis. It was not feasible to install another conveyor, and it was company policy to manufacture on a one-shift basis insofar as possible. The existing conveyor, with minor modification, was capable of taking care of as many as 24 men.

Upon notification of the new schedule, the engineer revised the adjusting operations, adding some preliminary operations and changing the sequence of others, in such a manner that 18 men could adjust 90 switches per hour. Time standards, previously established for each element of work, were used as the basis for rebalancing the "line" to turn out the increased schedule. Because each adjuster had less time to spend on each switch, it was necessary in some cases to divide a complicated or lengthy adjustment into two parts, a preliminary adjustment and a final adjustment. One man would make the preliminary adjustment, and a second man on the line would make the final adjustment. The new method used the same number of higher labor grades that the old one used.

From the engineering standpoint, the new method of adjusting switches was just as good as the old method. The new method was covered by an engineering layout and given to switch-shop supervision through regular channels (i.e., lines of authority). The project engineer realized that some "bugs" might develop in a change of this magnitude, so he notified Al Olsen informally that when the new method was introduced on the conveyor, the engineers would watch operations carefully for possible trouble.

When Richter and Olsen received the new engineering layout and instructions, they protested that they did not want to use the new method because:

1   They believed they could not meet the higher SHP, even though the time standards indicated that they could.
2   They did not have the five additional trained switch adjusters required by the new layout.

They wanted to continue adjusting according to the old method on the day shift, but to hire 5 new men to work on this day shift, thus relieving 5 experienced men to work on a second shift. The second-shift line would run on a kind of partial conveyor basis. Operating in this manner, and by working an overtime day on Saturdays, they believed that the increased schedule could be met.

At Moore's insistence, backed by the project engineer, the 18-man line was placed in operation without giving much consideration to the alternate proposal. Some minor "bugs" in the adjusting procedure were discovered but readily eliminated, and it was proved to the satisfaction of the engineering department that the new method would work. The SHP of 90 was not met at first, but this was expected by the engineers, since the men needed time to gain experience.

From the very first day, however, the adjusters did not like the new arrangement. They felt that the new sequence of operations would not work. They did not like the idea of subdividing some of the lengthy adjustments into two parts. They thought that the new SHP was too high. In general, they griped to Olsen, to the engineer, and to anybody who would listen. One habit which they developed at this time was to place metal tote boxes on the floor under the adjusting table and drum and pound on them with their feet while they worked. Often they did this in unison several times a day, making a terrific noise which disturbed nearby departments. The men were not disciplined because Richter felt he needed their goodwill and cooperation in order to meet the increased schedule. The schedule had to be met within a few weeks; otherwise the backlog of adjusted switches would be exhausted, which would idle several hundred employees in later production stages.

This unsettled situation continued for four weeks. Output gradually increased, but it leveled at 5 to 10 switches above the old SHP of 60 switches. In addition, the quality declined precipitously. The inspector rejected many of the completed lots. The stock of adjusted switches became so short that Richter took the following emergency actions:

1   He established a partial second shift using 4 new men and 5 regular adjusters. The regular adjusters were replaced on the first shift by 5 new men.

2   He placed both shifts on a ten-hour day. This required that the two shifts overlap from 1:30 to 5:30 P.M. Since there was adequate space, the second shift during this overlap sat at side benches and reworked switches that had been rejected by the inspectors.

3   He scheduled one Saturday shift using as many persons from both shifts as wished to work.

While checking the night shift, about six weeks after the change, Richter privately approached one of the adjusters who was quite friendly with him, and asked him to "check up" on the activities of the other adjusters. Richter wanted him to report any adjuster who was not working diligently. This adjuster told several of the other adjusters, and the men began to "simmer." At about 10 P.M. the adjusters refused to work any longer. One of the men called Al Olsen, who was at home, and told him about the trouble. Olsen called Moore and they both came to the plant. The adjusters were told by Moore to go back to work, and they did. So much hard feeling developed from this incident that management decided to transfer Richter to another plant in another city during the following week to give him a fresh start. An experienced supervisor named Gene Smith was brought from another department to fill Richter's job.

Aside from this incident, whenever the supervisors did advise and lecture the men about maintaining high quality, the men answered by pointing a finger of blame at defective switch parts. They claimed that adjustments were too difficult to make because of poor piece parts which made up the switch.

Some adjustments concerned a clearance between moving parts. For example, one part had to clear another part by at least 0.005 and not more than 0.01 inch. The first part also had to be parallel to the second part. Therefore, if during piece-part manufacture the parts were not deburred properly, were not milled properly, or were not polished smoothly, the adjustments were very difficult to make.

Another adjusting trouble resulted because one adjustment might affect adversely a prior adjustment. For example, the thirteenth man might make an adjustment which would "throw out" the adjustment which the ninth man made. In a case of this kind, the thirteenth man was supposed to recheck the adjustment made by the ninth man to make sure that it was not disturbed. All of the adjustments were involved to this extent. It was, therefore, difficult for inspectors to pinpoint causes of poor quality without a special investigation. There was a special investigating staff for that purpose.

Ten weeks after the changeover, production was still below 90 switches hourly, quality was bad, and the stock of finished switches was almost exhausted. The operating division manager called a conference to try to determine a solution to the adjustment problem. He invited the project engineer and his manager, the project inspector and his manager, the switch-department head (Moore), the three switch-section heads, and Olsen.

THE CASE OF TWO MASTERS

The Adamson Aircraft Company has in the last decade expanded its product line to include the design, development, and production of missiles for the United States government. For this purpose a missile division was established, and over 5,000 personnel were gathered to man this portion of the firm.

The traditional type of organization in aircraft manufacturing calls for functional specialization like that found in the automobile industry. Aircraft are made up of such items as engines, radios, wheels, and armament. The manufacture of component parts was standardized and the aircraft put together on an assembly line. It was quickly recognized that such a simplified approach would not meet future requirements, as the demand for greater capability and effectiveness increased and forced the designers to insist upon optimum performance in every part or component. Several components, each with an operational reliability of 99 percent, may have a combined reliability of only 51 percent. Even with the most judicious selection and usage of standard parts, a system could end up with a reliability approaching zero. To overcome this reliability drop, it became necessary to design the entire system as a *single* entity. Many of the parts that were formerly available off the shelf must now be tailored to meet the exacting demands of the total system. Thus, the "weapons system" concept was developed, which necessitated a change in organization and management.

For each weapons system project, a chief project engineer is appointed. He assembles the necessary design personnel for every phase of the project. In effect, he organizes and creates a small, temporary company for the purpose of executing a single weapons system. On his staff are representatives of such functional areas as propulsion, secondary power, structures, flight test, and "human factors." The human factors specialist, for example, normally reports to a human factors supervisor. In the human factors department are men with training in psychology, anthropology, physiology, and the like. They do research on human behavior and hope to provide the design engineers with the basic human parameters applicable to a specific problem.

James Johnson, an industrial psychologist, has been working with the missile division of Adamson for six months as a human factors specialist. His supervisor, George Slauson, also has a Ph.D. in psychology and has been with the firm for two years. Johnson is in a line relationship with Slauson, who conducts his annual review for pay purposes, and prepares an efficiency report on his work. Slauson is responsible for assembling and supervising a group of human factors experts to provide Adamson with the latest and most advanced information in the field of human behavior and its effect on product design.

Johnson has been assigned to a weapons system project, which is under the direction of Bernard Coolsen, a chief project engineer. In a committee meeting of project members, Coolsen stated, "I am thinking about a space vehicle of minimum weight capable of fourteen days' sustained activity, maneuverability, and rendezvous with other vehicles for maintenance and external exploration. How many men, how big a vehicle, and what instruments, supplies, and equipment will we need?" Johnson immediately set to work on his phase of the project. The data for the answer to this request were compiled and organized, and a rough draft of the human factors design criteria was prepared in triplicate. Johnson took the original to his supervisor, Slauson, for review, retaining the other two copies. Using one of the copies, he began to reedit and rewrite, working toward a smooth copy for presentation to Coolsen. A week later Johnson was called in by Slauson who said, "We can't put out stuff like this. First, it's too specific, and secondly, it's poorly organized." Slauson had rewritten the material extensively and had submitted a draft of it to *his* immediate superior, the design evaluation chief. In the meantime Coolsen had been calling Johnson for the material, insisting that he was holding up the entire project. Finally, taking a chance, Johnson took his original copy to Coolsen, and they sat down together and discussed the whole problem. An illustrator was called in, and in two days the whole vehicle was sketched up ready for design and specification write-up. The illustrator went to his board and began converting the sketches to drawings. Coolsen started to arrange for the writing of component and structural specifications, and Johnson went back to his desk to revise his human engineering specifications in the light of points brought out during the two-day team conference.

Three days later the design evaluation chief called Johnson into his office and said, "Has your supervisor seen this specification of yours?" Johnson replied that he had and that this was Slauson's revision of the original. The chief then asked for the original, and Johnson brought in the third original copy. Two days later the chief's secretary delivered to Johnson's desk a draft of his original specification as modified by Slauson as modified by the design evaluation chief. Johnson edited this for technical accuracy and prepared a ditto master. Slauson and the design evaluation chief read the master, initialed it, and asked for thirty copies to be run off. One copy was kept by Johnson, one by Slauson, one by the chief, five put into company routing, and the balance placed in file. Those in company routing went to the head of technical staff, head of advanced systems, and finally to the project engineer, Coolsen. Coolsen filed one copy in the project file and gave the other to Johnson. The latter dropped it in the nearest waste basket, inasmuch as several days previously, Coolsen had combined his, the illustrator's, and Johnson's material and submitted it to publications. Publications had run off six copies, one each for Coolsen, the illustrator, Johnson, the head of advanced systems, the U.S. Patent Office, and one for file. Also, by this time, the vehicle had been accepted by the company management as a disclosure for patent purposes. Johnson breathed a sign of relief, since he thought that he had gotten away with serving two masters.

THE CASE OF THE DISGRUNTLED RESEARCHER

The Hartley Manufacturing Company is a nationwide concern engaged in producing and distributing electrical products of various types. There are several factories scattered throughout the United States. Recently the personnel division of the home office has undertaken the task of analyzing and describing middle-management jobs throughout the company. The information gathered is to be used primarily in selecting and training persons for these crucial positions. It is part of a broader executive inventory and development program designed to provide a continuing and adequate supply of middle-management talent.

George Hoskins, the head of the personnel research section, was given the responsibility of assembling a team of job and organization analysts to undertake this research project. He got together a team of five persons, all possessing master's degrees and showing indications of high general ability. These five persons were given an intensive training program in job analysis, management principles and policies, and the organization structure of Hartley Company. The immediate objective for the team was to prepare job descriptions of managerial jobs. There seemed to be little knowledge available about managerial job analysis, and the group, under the guidance of Hoskins, worked to develop a standard approach and, insofar as possible, a list of standard attributes of middle-management jobs. Each analyst would then utilize this approach and outline as he interviewed job incumbents and prepared written job descriptions. The difficulty of the analysis involved was highly variable, depending upon the nature and complexity of the job being analyzed. It was difficult for Hoskins to control closely the work of these analysts because of the variable, subjective, and inexact nature of the process. This difficulty was compounded because of the necessity for frequent trips to the field by the analysts, separately at times, often as a group under Hoskins' direct supervision. In view of these situations, Hoskins had purposely hired top-notch personnel, who would require little supervision.

The five analysts on the team were Wilma Hansen, Joe Gordon, Howard Finley, Ronald Peters, and George Halton. They all seemed to get along very well, and Hoskins was proud of his work team and its efforts. There seemed to be few human relations problems.

The remainder of this report is in the words of George Halton.

"In general, we seem to have a pretty good group of guys on this job. The work is very interesting and you have a lot of freedom. But there is one thing about it that bothers me—Howard Finley. Howard is a very nice fellow. I like him personally. He has a good sense of humor, but he is—well—he's a 'goof-off.' While the rest of us are slaving away on job descriptions, he is striding up and down the aisle of the office, reading Shakespeare in loud, resonant tones. At times, he even attempts to improve upon portions of the Bard's works in a humorous way, and we all greatly enjoy his antics. Yet I think all of us—Ron, Joe, and myself for sure—are irritated with the small amount of work he turns out. He always has a good story for Hoskins, and I know that the work is hard to evaluate. The thing that gripes us most is that he gets the same pay as all the rest of us. I really don't think Hoskins knows what is going on. None of us feel like laying it on the line. We are all just generally disgruntled. Ron and I have deliberately cut down a third or so on the amount of work we are turning out. Even at that we're doing more than Howard is. Yet, I don't want to do anything to jeopardize my future in Hartley. I guess I need some advice."

THE CASE OF EVERYBODY'S BUSINESS

James Ryan, a young lieutenant in the military, had been placed in charge of a section of a military personnel division of a large headquarters establishment. The section was divided into five units, each with a supervisor reporting directly to Ryan. The section was authorized fifty-five people and had forty-one assigned: seven military and thirty-four civilians. There were thirty-one female civilians and two WACs; the rest were men, five of whom were military personnel. The average age of the female civilians was about fifty. A difficult and touchy personnel problem arose and is related as follows by Ryan.

"One of the WACs became pregnant without benefit of wedlock and by her own admission was unable to identify the prospective father closer than four or five possibilities. She held no hope for a timely marriage. This girl had been a good worker on the job and her work continued to be good after her condition became generally known. Soon thereafter, however, word reached me that this girl was receiving the 'silent treatment' from nearly all of the civilian women. One exception was a supervi or and the other was a worker who was usually at odds with the other women.

"I called the supervisors together and discussed the matter with them. Three of the supervisors were men and two were women. The man with the largest unit had a female assistant, but she was not present at the meeting. They all agreed that this was unjust treatment and said that they would do their best to have it discontinued. The male supervisor who had the largest number of women in his unit was very pessimistic about his chances of success. Three days later he came to me with the information that the women in his unit did not feel that they should be 'compelled' to work in the same building with a person of such low morals and threatened to put in for transfers or report sick if she was not removed. It was ten o'clock in the morning when I learned of this.

"I immediately called a meeting of all the supervisors and sought their advice. They all agreed that they felt the women would do as they threatened, although perhaps not the very next day. One of the women said she felt this trouble was being caused by only one or two women, whom she declined to mention by name. One man felt I should turn the problem over to my boss, while the majority felt that the solution to the problem was to have the girl transferred. It would not have been difficult for me to arrange a transfer for her. I thanked them for their advice and the meeting ended.

"The comment about only one or two women possibly causing this situation interested me. I thought about the problem and then came up with this plan. At two o'clock that same afternoon I arranged to see each one of the female civilian employees privately in my office. I scheduled them in alphabetical order, and each came to my office from her work when called and returned to her work immediately after leaving my office.

"When each woman entered my office I told her that I would appreciate it if she would voluntarily answer some questions to help me make this section a better place in which to work. Then I asked each woman about five questions. The first was how much contact she had with the girl in question in doing her normal duties. For those who had much contact, I asked them how effective they felt this girl was in doing her work. I asked them if this girl had done or said anything to them which they considered offensive. I asked each one if she had seen this girl do anything or had heard her say anything which she had found offensive. Then I asked each if there was anything she had come in contact with which she felt made this section an unpleasant place in which to work. Although I knew the answer beforehand, I asked each married woman if she had any children of her own. Finally, I asked each if she would come in and see me before she put in for a transfer. Then I thanked each, asked her not to talk to any of the women that I had not yet seen, assured her that anything she had said to me would not be repeated elsewhere, and called for the next woman.

"The women's responses and reactions were interesting. All said they would help me or try to help me by answering the questions if they could. A few first asked if they were suspected of any wrong-doing, and some asked if their replies would be confidential. They all said that the girl did satisfactory work, and many said good. None had any experience with her which she considered offensive. Most of those who had children of their own simply told me yes, or perhaps the number, but some quickly assured me that their children arrived long after marriage. In those cases I remarked that if they could remember the problems involved with an expected arrival, could they imagine facing them without a spouse? There was a little response to that, but many lowered eyes. All promised to come in to see me before considering a transfer, and most of them acted completely surprised at the mention of the word.

"There were no affirmative answers to the question about an unpleasant place in which to work, which was really amazing for two reasons, neither of which I had thought of when I framed the question. One, there were several changes in procedure at that time, which caused our section, already shorthanded, a great deal of extra work. Secondly, it was exceptionally cold during this time and the temperature in our old building did not get above 60 degrees much before noon each day. I knew that working in those cold rooms was very difficult for the older women, who were in the majority. However, as I mentioned above, I hadn't thought of that, and not one of the women mentioned it.

"I said nothing else to anyone and spent a great deal of time pacing the floor that night. The next day everyone was at work, in spite of a snowstorm, and no transfers were ever forthcoming. By the time the girl was ready to stop working—some four months later—the women working near her were doing practically all of her work, although she was more than able to do it herself. I never heard any more about the matter.

"I must admit I'm afraid I'm bragging a little, but for twenty-four years old and just a year out of college, I thought I had done pretty well. There's safety in numbers, but nobody wants to 'bell the cat.'

"The sequel to the story is that the girl, who was discharged from the WAC, later returned to exactly the same section as a civilian employee and worked there at least three more years. Another fact that really didn't have any bearing on the case but I think is interesting is that my boss and boss's boss were both women!'"

PART THREE

PROCUREMENT

The management functions are to plan, organize, direct, and control. The operative functions of personnel are procurement (Chapters 6 to 9), development (Chapters 10 to 13), compensation (Chapters 14 to 16), integration (Chapters 17 to 23), and maintenance (Chapters 24 to 26).

In this part, we will discuss the procurement process. The first step in a personnel program is to obtain personnel to execute the work of the organization. This involves two basic subprocesses: (1) the determination of the number and type of personnel required (Chapter 6), and (2) the recruitment and screening of applicants for job openings (Chapters 7 and 8). Special attention is given to managerial talent (Chapter 9). Procurement ends with the induction or orientation of the newly hired employee to the job, other employees, and the organization.

SIX
JOB ANALYSIS AND HUMAN RESOURCES REQUIREMENTS

The first operative function of personnel management is the procurement of personnel for the organization. In a large concern, much of the procurement function is delegated to specialists, e.g., an employment section of a personnel department. In the smaller organization, each manager may well do the recruitment, interviewing, and placement without specialized assistance. In either case, there is a necessary first step that must precede recruitment. There must be some determination of the *kind* of personnel desired for each job as well as a specification of the *number* to be hired.

Decisions concerning human resources requirements are not confined to a personnel department. It will be found that the line supervisor has much to contribute, as well as certain other staff elements such as time study and production control. This chapter is devoted to the general question of human resources requirements and is divided into two parts. The first part deals with the process of determining the kind or quality of personnel needed. This is followed by a presentation and analysis of the problem of determining the quantity of personnel required to operate the organization properly. The immediate tangible result of these two analyses is the creation of an *employee requisition* authorizing the hiring of a certain number of people of a specified type.

QUALITY OF PERSONNEL

In order to hire personnel on a scientific basis, one should establish in advance a standard of personnel with which applicants can be compared. This standard should establish the minimum acceptable qualities necessary for adequate performance of the job duties. Establishing such qualities entails (1) the design of the job and (2) a study of the job duties and responsibilities to determine human abilities required for execution. The establishment of the job is a part of the organizing process, and was discussed in Chapter 4. The study of job content to determine human requirements is termed "job analysis." Personnel specialists in large organizations should be intimately involved in both activities. In the small firm, these two tasks must also be performed and, of necessity, will be executed by line managers.

Job terminology

In most areas of study, a certain amount of technical terminology is necessary in order to facilitate communication. It is therefore desirable to list and define terms in the job analysis field, as well as some terms that are related to and often confused with job analysis. An understanding of these terms should contribute to an appreciation of the nature and significance of the job analysis process.

POSITION[1] A position is a *group of tasks assigned to one individual*. There are as many positions in a firm as there are personnel. The term is used in this narrow technical sense to facilitate more precise analysis of the job analysis technique.

JOB A job can now be defined as a *group of positions that are similar as to kind and level of work*. In some instances only one position may be involved, simply because no other similar position exists. For example, in the typical firm the position of personnel manager also constitutes a job since there is only one personnel manager in the organization.

OCCUPATION An occupation is a *group of jobs that are similar as to kind of work and are found throughout an industry or the entire country*. An occupation is a category of work found in many firms. The United States Employment Service has attempted to survey and define the occupations of the United States in the *Dictionary of Occupational Titles*.[2] It has also prepared occupational descriptions for various industries. These descriptions are necessarily general in nature and can be used only for background purposes for a particular firm's job analysis program. To show the relationship among these first three definitions, we can say that one person can hold a position, a job, and an occupation simultaneously. One must always have a position and a job, but may not be in a type of work that is found generally throughout an industry and thus may have no occupation.

JOB ANALYSIS Job analysis is the *process of studying and collecting information relating to the operations and responsibilities of a specific job*. The immediate products of this analysis are job descriptions and job specifications, which are defined below.

MOTION STUDY Job analysis is often confused with motion study, which also involves study of the job. There are two different ways of studying the same job. Motion study is

---

[1]This definition is not widely used in business. It does, however, have certain values in problem analysis. Examples of authors who utilize this definition are Carroll L. Shartle, *Occupational Information*, 2d ed., Prentice-Hall, Inc., Englewood Cliffs, N.J., 1952, p. 25; and Jay L. Otis and Richard H. Leukart, *Job Evaluation*, 2d ed., Prentice-Hall, Inc., Englewood Cliffs, 1954, p. 12.

[2]*Dictionary of Occupational Titles*, 3d ed., U.S. Employment Service, 1965.

a *process of analyzing a job to find the easiest, most effective, and most economical method of doing it or portions thereof.* The significant differences between job analysis and motion study are outlined in Figure 6-1 by various factor headings. If the job is to be subjected to both processes of study, motion study should preferably *precede* job analysis.

JOB DESCRIPTION   A job description is an *organized, factual statement of the duties and responsibilities of a specific job.* In brief, it should tell *what* is to be done, *how* it is done, and *why.* It is a standard of function, in that it defines the appropriate and authorized content of a job. A more complete explanation of this document follows in a later section.

JOB SPECIFICATION   A job specification is a *statement of the minimum acceptable human qualities necessary to perform a job properly.* In contrast to the job description, it is a standard of personnel and designates the qualities required for acceptable performance. This product of job analysis is also covered at greater length in a later section.

Figure 6-1   Major differences between job analysis and motion study

Factors	Job analysis	Motion study
Purpose	Descriptive	Change and improve job
Scope	Broad, covering duties, responsibilities, supervision, etc.	Change and improve job
Degree of detail	Less detailed	Very detailed
Organization	Executed by personnel departments	Executed by industrial engineers
Techniques used	Observation, interview, questionnaire, log	Observation, photography, stopwatch, etc.
Uses of results	Procurement, training, wages, etc.	Methods improvement and standardization

JOB CLASSIFICATION   A job classification is a *grouping of jobs on some specified basis such as kind of work or pay.* The term is placed in this series because it is often confused with job analysis and job evaluation. It can refer to a grouping by any selected characteristic but probably is used most often in connection with pay and job evaluation. The *Dictionary of Occupational Titles* utilizes a number of different classification bases as indicated by the following codes: "0" and "1" cover professional, technical, and managerial occupations; "2" refers to clerical and sales; "3" is for service occupations; "4" is used for farming, fishery, and forestry work; "5" is for processing work; "6" for machine trades; "7" for bench work; "8" is reserved for structural work; and "9" is for miscellaneous occupations. The second and third digits of a code number provide a finer breakdown with respect to function or industry. For example, "50" is for metal processing, "52" for food processing, and "56" for wood processing. The last three digits show the relation of the occupation to data, people, and things. The occupational code for a chief housekeeper is 187.168: "1" indicates that it is a managerial occupation, the "87" identifies the service industry, the "1" after the decimal point indicates a coordinating function with respect to data, the "6" shows a speaking-signaling relationship with people, and the "8" reveals no significant relationship with things. It is apparent that this classification system rests on a number of different bases and is usable by the personnel manager of a private firm for background information only.

JOB EVALUATION Job evaluation is a *systematic and orderly process of determining the worth of a job in relation to other jobs*. The objective of this process is to determine the correct rate of pay. It is therefore *not* the same as job analysis. Rather it should *follow* the job analysis process, which provides the basic data to be evaluated. Job evaluation is discussed at length in a later chapter and is included at this point in order to reduce confusion with the term "job analysis."

Job analysis process

The process of analyzing a job after its design is essentially one of data collection. Various approaches can be utilized in studying a job, and the four currently most popular are (1) questionnaires, (2) written narratives, (3) observation, (4) interviews. A survey of 899 firms ranging in size from under 500 employees to over 100,000 revealed that the most widely used method was the interview; 85 percent reported using this research method for both salaried and hourly workers.[3] The second most popular was observation, which was used more widely for hourly employees. Questionnaires and written narratives were about equally divided in popularity, ranking behind the other two. In addition, there were many miscellaneous sources of information such as old job descriptions, time and motion studies, and daily diaries or logs.

The questionnaire technique places great faith in the jobholder's ability to organize the reporting of the job. It has not been found that this ability is very widespread, even among holders of managerial jobs. We believe, therefore, that the questionnaire technique is a highly inadequate job analysis method. The information received is often found to be incomplete, unorganized, and sometimes incoherent. Such a questionnaire can be used, however, in providing background information for the interview, which must necessarily follow, in order to analyze the job properly. It can also be helpful in focusing the job incumbent's attention, so that more intelligent cooperation can be effected during the interview.

Narrative descriptions can be requested of both the job incumbent and the supervisor. This approach is used more often on salaried jobs. A more detailed reporting of this type would be the daily diary or log. Under this system, the employee keeps a daily record of major duties performed, marking the time when each task is started and finished. Narratives, logs, and questionnaires can be of material assistance to the job analyst, but as single techniques unsupported by follow-up interviewing and observation, they leave much to be desired.

The third and fourth methods of collecting job information hold the greatest promise of completeness, accuracy, and better utilization of time. If a particular job is simple and repetitive, observation may be the only technique required. In most cases, however, interviews coupled with observation constitute the preferred approach. The interview will provide information not readily observable plus the verification of information obtained by means of other techniques.

Since the job analyst will use the interview as a prime method of data collection,

[3]*Summary of National Job Analysis Methods Survey*, California State College, Bureau of Business Research, Long Beach, 1968, p. 9.

there are several basic attitudes and techniques that will serve to elicit the maximum of accurate and complete information. These attitudes and techniques will also help to reduce the natural suspicion of both employee and supervisor toward a staff specialist operating out of the personnel unit. Among these are the following:

1 *Introduce yourself so that the worker knows who you are and why you are there.* The supervisor can be of material assistance in helping to explain in advance what the job analysis program is and how it affects various personnel activities such as procurement and compensation. A job analyst's superior or condescending attitude, generated either through ego or through newness and insecurity, will provoke a negative response. The employee should be assured that the objectives of the process are not detrimental to his or her well-being. On the contrary, the program may easily result in more realistic training, better organization, and more equitable compensation for the job.

2 *Show a sincere interest in the worker and the job being analyzed.* It is difficult to fake sincerity, and a periodic, mechanical "uh-huh" in response to worker contributions is insufficient and often irritating. The job constitutes a large proportion of this employee's life. If the analyst can demonstrate a sincere interest in both the job and the employee, increased receptivity and openness generally follow.

3 *Do not try to tell the employee how to do the job.* In this process, the incumbent is the job expert and the analyst's task is to extract the information and organize it in a significant manner. The job analysis process is basically descriptive in nature. Correction of mistakes and possible changes in job content should be initiated by those with authority in the area concerned. The job analyst should view herself or himself as an expert in studying and reporting jobs, not as an expert in the job itself.

An interesting question might be raised at this point. What type of background should a job analyst possess? To ask intelligent questions about a job, one must know something about it. Yet, if a large number of different types of jobs are covered, how can one be expert in all? The preceding paragraph gives the correct answer. The job analyst's skills are in extracting correct information, organizing that material in logical order, and presenting it in understandable and usable form. One need not be expert in the job, though preliminary familiarization with certain aspects is necessary in order not to appear too ignorant during the interview. At times it is actually very difficult to ask an intelligent question. This is where the other techniques, such as questionnaires and logs, prove very useful in providing background information.

4 *Try to talk to the employees and supervisors in their own language.* This will involve some preparation, particularly when the analyst covers many different fields; but the establishment of rapport is facilitated if the worker feels that the analyst is not a complete novice. This process can, however, be overdone. It is wise to confine oneself to the jargon that a member of the firm would reasonably be expected to acquire; an attempt to use all the shop terminology smacks of "getting down to their level" and thereby incurs resentment. The analyst will have to learn to read the perceptible reactions of the interviewee as he or she uses certain words, makes various statements, and asks specific questions.

5 *Do not confuse the work with the worker.* The particular worker being interviewed is the medium through which information is derived about the job. The objective is not to describe this particular employee but rather the job that the incumbent performs and, later, the abilities necessary for proper execution of job duties. The fact that this particular jobholder has a college degree does not necessarily mean that such a degree is a minimum requirement. This could be caused by either a personnel mismatch or temporary assignment from other regular duties. In this process of data collection, the basic approach should be scientific insofar as it attempts to distinguish between fact and inference and between fact and opinion. This is a type of applied research, and the analyst requires considerable judgment in order to filter the answers to his or her questions.

6   *Do a complete job study within the objectives of the program.* The information desired in job analysis is of the type that will assist in various personnel activities. Job analysis is not motion study, and we do not need a "blow-by-blow" physical description of what the worker does. Suppose that the worker tells the analyst that a production part is placed in a solution to be electroplated and is taken out when done. A motion study analyst may be interested in how the item is dipped and how it can be removed most efficiently. The job analyst must have information that will reveal the *skill* and *knowledge* required. One may ask the worker, "*How* do you know when the item should be removed from the solution?" The usual response is, "I just know by experience." This is not sufficient to show skill level, and the job analyst must get *behind* the "just know how." Knowing *what* information one wants and knowing *how* to question an employee to get that information are different things. There is very definitely a need for knowing how to ask intelligent and discerning questions.

7   *Verify the job information obtained.* Data collected from one employee should be checked by consultation with others holding the same job. The analyst may thus obtain additional information and may find some contradictions and inconsistencies. Resolution of such discrepancies, if they are factual, is the responsibility of supervision. The analysis should *not* be confined to work done by the best worker on the job; a reasonable sample is necessary when the job is composed of a considerable number of positions.

In the previously cited survey, most large organizations assigned the responsibility for job analysis to the wage and salary section of the personnel department. The average time for completing the analysis of one job was less than four hours for hourly jobs, and four to eight hours for the salaried. Automatic data-processing systems for storage of job information were reported by only 10 percent of the surveyed companies.[4]

The job description

The first and immediate product of the job analysis process is the job description. As its title indicates, this document is basically descriptive in nature and constitutes a record of existing and pertinent job facts. These facts must be organized in some fashion in order to be usable. A suggested order is as follows:

1   Job identification
2   Job summary
3   Duties performed
4   Supervision given and received
5   Relation to other jobs

[4]Ibid., pp. 5, 8, and 9.

6   Machines, tools, and materials
7   Working conditions
8   Definitions of unusual terms
9   Comments which add to and clarify the above

The identification section includes such information as job title, alternate titles, department, division, plant, and code number for the job. The job summary has two purposes: (1) to provide a short definition that will be useful as additional identification information when the job title is not sufficient, and (2) to serve as a summary to orient the reader toward an understanding of the detailed information that follows. In practice, it is easier to write this section *after* writing section 3.

The duties-performed section is the heart of the job description and is the most difficult to write properly. It is supposed to tell what is being done, how it is done (without involving the detail of a motion study), and the purpose behind each duty. It is often found advisable to list major duties with a statement of "what" and "why," followed by subduties detailing the "how." These should, if possible, be arranged in chronological order. In addition, an estimate concerning the approximate percentage of time devoted to each major duty is helpful. Research has indicated that employees are reasonably accurate in estimating these time percentages. When checking the actual times against the estimates, Hinrichs discovered that 232 technical employees were within 5 percent of the time proportions obtained through work sampling.[5] A study of sixteen clerical workers, done in the same manner, revealed that differences were no larger than 6 percent, one of the larger errors being in an excessively small estimate of idle time.[6] Despite these differences, the estimates are sufficiently accurate to be used as a general guide in recruitment, training, compensation, and reorganizing.

It should be noted that there is a definite writing style for the duties-performed section. It is terse and direct, giving the impression of action. There are many detailed rules, such as: (1) start each sentence with an action verb; (2) use present tense; and (3) use the word "may" when only some workers perform the duty and the word "occasionally" when all workers perform at irregular intervals. The purpose of this style is to facilitate communication through completeness, conciseness, and clarity. It should be noted, however, that a job analyst with a facility with words can make a job appear much more impressive than it actually is. This can best be illustrated by an example. What is the worth of the job whose duties are described in Figure 6-2? A somewhat more terse description is found at the end of this chapter.

Figure 6-2   An example of how job descriptions can mislead

Proposed Job Description
1   Job identification
   a   Title: Director of Industrial and Agrarian Priorities
   b   Dept.: Maintenance
2   Job duties
   a   Directs, controls, and regulates the movement of interstate commerce, representing a cross

---

[5]J. R. Hinrichs, "Communications Activity of Industrial Research Personnel," *Personnel Psychology*, vol. 17, no. 2, 1964, pp. 193–204.
[6]Stephen J. Carroll, Jr., and William H. Taylor, Jr., "Validity of Estimates by Clerical Personnel of Job Time Proportions," *Journal of Applied Psychology*, vol. 53, no. 2, 1969, pp. 164–166.

Figure 6-2—continued

section of the wealth of the American economy. Exercises a broad latitude for independent judgment and discretion without direct or intermediate supervision.

b   Integrates the variable factors in an evolving situation utilizing personal judgment, founded on past experience, conditioned by erudition, and disciplined by mental intransigence. Formulates a binding decision relative to the priority of flow of interstate and intrastate commerce, both animate and inanimate, such decisions being irreversible and not subject to appellate review by higher authority or being reversed by the legal determination of any echelon of our judicial complex. Influences the movement, with great finality, of agricultural products, forest products, minerals, manufactured goods, machine tools, construction equipment, military personnel, defense materials, raw materials, end products, finished goods, semifinished products, small business, large business, public utilities, and government agencies.

c   Deals with all types of personalities and all levels of education, from college president and industrial tycoon to truckdriver, requiring the exercise of initiative, ingenuity, imagination, intelligence, industry, and discerning versatility. Implements coordinated motivation on the part of the public, which is consistent with the decision of the incumbent, failure of which could create a complex objurgation of personnel and equipment generating a catastrophic loss of mental equilibrium by innumerable personnel of American industry, who are responsible for the formulation of day-to-day policy, and guidance implementation of the conveyances of transportation, both interstate and intrastate.

d   Appraises the nuances of an unfolding situational development and directs correction thereof commensurate with its seriousness and momentousness.

The remaining sections of the job description are based on the duties-performed section. The section on supervision tells (1) the titles of jobs that are immediately over and under this job and (2) the degree of supervision involved, such as general direction, intermediate, or close supervision. The section on relation to other jobs identifies vertical relationships of promotion and the horizontal relationships of work flow and procedures. The machines, tools, and materials portion lists and defines each major type, giving trade names when necessary. This information is helpful in devising training programs. Checklists are often used to indicate working conditions, using such alternatives as hot, cold, dry, dusty, oily, noisy, etc. Hazardous conditions should be particularly noted. Any technical or unusual words used in the duties-performed section should be listed separately and defined; they thus become a kind of job glossary. Because the requirements of the job-description style are somewhat confining, it seems wise to permit the analyst to add any extra comments that he or she feels are appropriate and helpful in understanding the job. The comments section provides for this freedom of expression.

The job descriptions of managers tend to be more concerned with goals and situational factors. As shown in Figure 6-3, situational information is provided that indicates size of work group, type of employees, and degree of delegation. This particular illustration suggests that goals should be subdivided according to physical resources, sequences of functions, other persons, achievement, and groups. Opposite each set of goals are the prescribed activities that will lead to their accomplishment.

Role analysis

Dissatisfied with the somewhat simple and sterile nature of existing job descriptions that highlight formal duties, various critics have suggested that job analysis should be

Figure 6-3 Job description which identifies situational factors, goals, and activities

Name: John Doe   Title: General Plant Manager
Supervisor: President   Company: General Paper Company
Number of employees in the plant: 40 exempt, 36 nonexempt salaried, and 150 hourly paid. Reporting directly to him are 7 department heads. General manager has full authority to take action necessary to meet the goals for which he is responsible. He is supported fully in this by the company president.

Objects (physical resources)

Goals	Performance activities
1 To assure acquisition, operation, and maintenance of physical facilities.	1 Plans for authorized expenditures for plant physical resources.
2 To improve and develop products and equipment.	2 Plans for and coordinates product and equipment development and improvement.

Sequences and events (process, schedules, and accounting systems)

Goals	Performance activities
1 To assure the development and use of systematic and effective work flow, operation processes, and accounting systems.	1 Coordinates the processes, schedules, and accounting controls between departments.
2 To schedule work operation and transportation.	

Other persons (human relations)

Goals	Performance activities
1 To maintain a favorable organization climate.	1 Maintains an atmosphere of acceptance and support.
2 To maintain a warm and friendly relationship with employees and associates.	2 Communicates well the expectations and results of subordinates.
	3 Reduces threat to security.
	4 Recognizes the needs of others in working with them.
	5 Cooperates with others in work.

Achievement (profitability, productivity, marketing, etc.)

Goals	Performance activities
1 To establish policies, objectives, and plans for overall plant profitability, productivity, marketing, physical and financial resources, and personnel.	1 Prepares written policies, broad objectives, and plans for the plant.
2 To assure efficient operation and coordination of department functions for maximum profitability, productivity, and sales.	2 Participates in group meetings with department heads for the establishment of objectives.
	3 Stimulates accomplishment of objectives and conduct of plans. Discusses results of performance with subordinates.
	4 Approves product grade change and allocates new grades to machines.
	5 Maintains cost control and proper balance of financial expenditures.

Purposeful groups (organization and leadership)

Figure 6-3—Continued

Goals	Performance activities
1 To provide the overall leadership functions for the plant.	1 Performs leadership functions for the plant.
2 To assure the effective design, development, and staffing of the organization.	2 Works with subordinates to provide organization structure, proper delegation, and coordination.
3 To motivate and develop subordinates.	3 Establishes effective managerial control through delegation and coordination.
4 To assure participation of all subordinates in group management.	4 Establishes policies and procedures for personnel programs to maintain group satisfaction, stimulate their achievement, and evaluate performance.
5 To initiate and assure completion of actions.	5 Works effectively with superiors, peers, and subordinates.
	6 Conducts regular participative meetings.
	7 Initiates the actions toward meeting broad goals.

Source: J. C. Wofford, "Behavior Styles and Performance Effectiveness," *Personnel Psychology,* vol. 20, no. 4, Winter 1967, pp. 470–471.

extended to include *role analysis.* The concept of role is broader than that of job. A role would consist of the total pattern of expected behavior, interactions, and sentiments for an individual holding an assigned job. As such, the job incumbent is exposed to a number of personnel who often expect different attitudes and behavioral patterns, thus establishing the potential for substantial role conflict. For example, the supervisor is expected by assigned subordinates to protect and promote their interests in the organization. Simultaneously, superiors levy expectations of operating the unit at its most productive and efficient level, which often entails actions deemed detrimental by subordinates. The ability to cope with such built-in job conflicts is a definite and important job requirement. Mere listing of official duties will not necessarily reveal the behavioral expectations of multiple and various groups that impinge upon the job incumbent.

Role analysis of personnel holding boundary-spanning jobs provides a good example of its potential value in the making of personnel decisions.[7] A boundary-spanning job is one whose incumbent is commissioned to deal with some significant element of the *outer* environment, e.g., credit officer, purchasing agent, finance officer, sales personnel, and personnel manager. The credit officer, for example, is expected by the finance department to minimize losses due to bad debts, thereby lessening organizational dependency upon outside banks. Simultaneously, the sales department views the task as one of facilitating growth of sales and creation of new customers. Thus, the credit officer, finance officer, and sales manager are all boundary-spanners, providing the basis for conflict spillover into the organization itself. The personnel manager is also a spanning agent as new employees are obtained from the outside. When strong labor unions are present in the environment, particularly stressful conflicts are generally encountered. Coping with these inevitable internal and external conflicts is a role requirement.

---

[7]Dennis W. Organ, "Linking Pins between Organizations and Environment," *Business Horizons,* vol. 14, no. 6, December 1971, pp. 73–80.

With reference to contacts with significant external personnel, the boundary-spanning agent must deal with persons and organizations over whom absolute control is denied. Thus, flexible personalities and pragmatic personal value systems are often requisites. If the organization is particularly dependent upon the external unit, preference is for solutions that work even though they are not beautiful and elegant in their configurations. Such roles often require superior verbal skills, sensitivity to the values of external personnel, and an aptitude for remembering details. Thus, when the personnel manager is required to deal with a powerful labor union, effective role behavior requires the selective use of words that do not incite emotional resistance, an understanding of union leadership values and motives, and the ability to remember names, dates, places, and events of significance to union negotiators.

Organizations, viewed as entities, also establish different climates based on different philosophies, thereby leading to different behavioral expectations. The job descriptions for two supervisors in two different companies may look the same, but the role requirements could be substantially different. If one company's philosophy regarding leadership is basically democratic, role requirements would necessitate behavior characterized by helping, supporting, persuading, talking freely and cheerfully, and empathic understanding. If the second company's philosophy is more authoritarian, the expected behavioral pattern is likely to include aggressiveness in relation to others, insistence upon adherence to prescribed patterns, impatience with faulty performance, and supportive relationships with superiors rather than with subordinates. As noted in Chapter 1, role analysis of behavioral requirements is of considerable importance in the selection of personnel for overseas assignments.

Though the importance of the expected behavioral style cannot be denied, it is seldom diagnosed, recorded, and used systematically in the hiring process. For this reason, the face-to-face interview will doubtlessly remain an important part of the hiring process despite its frequently reported low validity as a predictor of job success. The accuracy of the job analysis process would be improved considerably if attention were given to role expectations surrounding each prescribed activity or duty.

Job specification

Preparing a complete and correct job description is relatively simple as compared with preparing a complete and correct job specification. After reading a job description, we may find ourselves in considerable disagreement concerning the human requirements for the work. Does this job properly call for a high school diploma or is some college education necessary? What is the minimum degree of intelligence required? What experience level and how much? Because of the admitted impossibility of presenting a completely objective and accurate standard of personnel, some firms have discarded the idea of preparing job specifications. Instead, they prefer to deliver the description to the employment interviewer, for they are sure of the accuracy of *that* information. But it should be pointed out that the job specification has *not* been thereby eliminated. It now exists in the minds of the interviewer or interviewers. Instead of having one standard of personnel for this job, we have as many as there are readers of the job description.

The establishment of basic minimum human requirements for work is a decision of concern to our entire society. It has been commented by some observers that organizations in general establish excessively high requirements for formal education and training backgrounds, a process that results in overly qualified personnel being placed on routine jobs, e.g., requiring a college engineering degree for a routine draftsman's job. Not only do such practices lead to frustrated and discontented personnel, the Supreme Court decision in the Duke Power case indicates that it may be illegal if such requirements work to the proven disadvantage of certain classes of citizens.[8] Section 703 of Title VII of the Civil Rights Act of 1964 specifies that "it shall be an unlawful employment practice for an employer—to limit, segregate, or classify his employees in any way which would deprive or tend to deprive any individual of employment opportunities or otherwise adversely affect his status as an employee, because of such individual's race, color, religion, sex, or national origin." In the Duke Power Company, a minimum hiring requirement of a high school diploma had been established for initial assignment to any department except labor. Such a requirement worked to prevent the employment of larger numbers of blacks than whites. This does not mean, however, that the high school requirements is illegal per se. As Chief Justice Burger's opinion stated, "Congress has placed on the employer the burden of showing that any given requirement must have a manifest relationship to the employment in question." In other words, the employer can stipulate possession of a high school diploma if it can be proven that such possession results in better job performance than by those without the degree. This would, of course, be merely sound personnel practice. Hiring requirements should not be established in a vacuum by fiat with little regard for their appropriateness to job success. Nevertheless, the court decision requiring such research has led many firms to abandon stipulations of human minimums, particularly in the area of formal education.

Systematic personnel research can provide information that can lead to realistic and legal hiring requirements. For example, one research study revealed that employees with highly anxious personalities are more susceptible to fatigue on extremely repetitive jobs than are those who can be classified as low in anxiety.[9] Perhaps the job should be redesigned; but if it does exist in this particular form, study of successful and unsuccessful job incumbents can lead to research-based minimum hiring requirements. Performance requirements in the more subjective areas of personality and attitudes either may not result in discriminatory classifications deemed illegal, or may not tend to attract the attention of militant groups. Nevertheless, sound personnel practice requires that *all* stipulated minimum hiring requirements have a foundation of fact rather than intuition.

Uses of job analysis information

Job analysis is one of the most pervasive tasks of personnel management. Its products, descriptions and specifications, have many and varied uses beyond those mentioned previously. A brief listing of these uses is as follows:

1   *Procurement.* A job specification is the standard of personnel against which a job

---

[8]Floyd L. Ruch, "The Impact on Employment Procedures of the Supreme Court Decision in the Duke Power Case," *Personnel Journal*, vol. 50, no. 10, October 1971, pp. 777–783.
[9]Bernard Hanes and Edwin B. Flippo, "Anxiety and Work Output," *Journal of Industrial Engineering*, vol. 14, no. 5, September–October 1963, pp. 244–248.

applicant can be measured. The content of the specification provides the basis for the construction of a selection procedure.

2   *Training.* Description of duties and equipment used is of material assistance in developing the content of training programs.

3   *Job evaluation.* Job descriptions and specifications of human requirements are evaluated in terms of worth, with the ultimate objective of determining dollar value.

4   *Performance appraisal.* Instead of rating an employee on characteristics such as dependability and initiative, there is now a tendency toward establishing job goals and appraising the work done toward those goals. In this type of appraisal, a job description is useful in defining the areas in which job goals should be established.

5   *Promotion and transfer.* Job information helps in charting the channels of promotion and in showing lateral lines of transfer.

6   *Organization.* Job information obtained by job analysis often reveals instances of poor organization in terms of the factors affecting job design. The analysis process, therefore, constitutes a kind of organization audit.

7   *Induction.* For the new trainee, a job description is most helpful for orientation purposes. It may not be as meaningful as for veteran employees, but it erects some signposts that aid understanding of the job and of the organization.

8   *Counseling.* Job information is, of course, very valuable in occupational counseling. More of such counseling is advisable at the high school level, since many graduates are unaware of the types of jobs that exist. It is not unknown for a firm to do some occupational counseling also when an employee does not seem suited to the present position.

9   *Labor relations.* A job description is a standard of function. If an employee attempts to add to or subtract from the duties listed therein, the standard has been violated. The labor union as well as the management is interested in this matter. Controversies often result, and a written record of the standard job jurisdiction is valuable in resolving such disputes.

10   *Job reengineering.* If employers wish to adapt to any special group, such as female employees or the physically handicapped, they must usually alter the content of certain jobs. Job analysis provides information that will facilitate the changing of jobs in order to permit their being filled by personnel with special characteristics.

The survey of 899 firms showed that 75 percent used the results of the job analysis process in making job specifications, approximately 60 percent for training, over 90 percent in setting wage and salary levels, approximately 60 percent in appraising personnel on salaried jobs as compared with 44 percent on hourly jobs, 70 percent in transfers and promotion, 50 percent in organizing, 36 percent in orienting new employees, 25 percent in counseling, 25 percent in restructuring hourly jobs for the handicapped, and 33 percent and 43 percent respectively for conducting labor negotiations and handling grievances in hourly jobs.[10] It is apparent that most firms find many uses for job analysis information in their personnel programs. The job is one of the major "stocks in trade" of a personnel manager. Whether job knowledge is gained formally or informally, it is necessary for scientific management of personnel. Only in

[10]*Summary of National Job Analysis Methods Survey,* pp. 4–5.

this way can we adequately determine the type of personnel we need in the organization.

HUMAN RESOURCES REQUIREMENTS

The second decision concerning the organization's need for human resources is a determination of the *number* of personnel of each type that should be provided. This problem can logically be divided into two parts: (1) projection of the firm's needs for some finite period of time, and (2) analysis of present work force capability to meet those needs. Discrepancies between (1) and (2) would call for contraction through layoff, adjustment through internal transfers, or expansion through the hiring process.

Forecasting of needs

In undertaking the extremely difficult task of forecasting human resource needs, significant inputs would come from economic forecasts, more specific sales forecasts, and top management decisions concerning investment plans for new plant and equipment. Obviously, the information necessary for a reasonably sound forecast comes from areas in the firm other than the personnel unit. The personnel manager must make sure that she or he is privy to these significant items of information so that the unit will not be caught short and surprised by events that drastically affect the level of personnel required. In addition, if obligations are met in the area of social responsibility, the personnel manager will assist in top management planning for resources required to meet these added social goals. This text is not the place to discuss the techniques of time series analyses, trend extrapolation, economic analyses, or criteria for investment decisions. It is sufficient to state here that efficient personnel procurement will be seriously affected by the accuracy of major plans affecting the future of the enterprise. Poor performance can easily lead to major layoffs of personnel as well as insufficient lead times to procure special and unusual human talents.

Specific sales forecasts for the coming year can be translated into a work program for the various parts of the enterprise. For production, this is variously titled "production program," "master schedule," and "department schedule." In the sales portion of the organization, the problem revolves around sales quotas and sales territories. Some plans must be made concerning the amount of work that *each* segment of the firm is expected to accomplish during some coming period. If possible, this plan should be expressed in the form of a work unit, such as parts produced, products assembled, tons produced, boxes packed, customer calls, vouchers processed, and pounds received and issued. In many cases, particularly in staff activities, the work unit has to be the person-hour. But it is more desirable to determine the work load in some tangible unit and then, by proper study of that unit, translate it into person-hours required per unit.

There are various ways of translating work loads into person-hour requirements. Past experience can, of course, be utilized for this purpose. If the work unit is the voucher or statement processed, the number of such units completed can be ascertained for a selected period in the past. This figure can be divided into the number of person-hours *actually* expended to determine the person-hours required per work unit. The planned work load for a coming period can then be multiplied by the person-hours per unit to obtain the number required. For example, suppose that each voucher requires an average of 0.09 person-hour to process. This time automatically includes all delays and interruptions, since it was determined by dividing total hours expended into the work load actually undertaken. Many would say that the figure may also include a substantial amount of loafing and general inefficiency. The manager concerned is the best judge of the quality of the effort that is being obtained.

Let us assume that 22,000 vouchers are to be processed in the coming month. This figure multiplied by 0.09 gives a total of 1,980 person-hours of work. Theoretically, one person can contribute approximately 180 hours of work next month, working $4^{1}/_{2}$ weeks. Dividing 1,980 by 180 gives an answer of 11 persons needed to undertake the predicted work load.

The above analysis may appear to be highly theoretical in nature, but the basic approach is sound. How much work is scheduled to be done? How much work can one person do? Division of the former by the latter gives the number of personnel needed. What if the number does not come out even? Can we hire half a person, for example? There are many possible answers. Overtime can extend one individual's capacity beyond 180 hours, though it should be recognized that the 0.09 standard will probably increase to 0.10 or 0.12 during the overtime hours. If similar skills exist, perhaps an employee can be transferred in and used part time. In some situations part-time help can be leased. It must also be remembered that neither of the figures, the 0.09 person-hour standard per work unit or the 22,000 predicted volume of vouchers, is highly exact and accurate. Such realization may well preclude any great degree of concern over carrying the analysis out to a fine point.

Past experience is often codified into a number of rules-of-thumb; e.g., one new sales person will be added for each $100,000 increase in sales, or one new production employee will be added when overtime exceeds $1,000 per week for four continuous weeks. Such shortcuts are heavily based on experience and are most useful for short-run applications. For more accurate answers, attention is usually turned to more systematic study. Among these are computer simulations, the Delphi technique, linear programming, and systematic time study of jobs. Computer simulations have been utilized to determine the number of personnel and servicing stations required to process a work load that varies in amount during the day. Within the personnel unit, for example, applicants arrive at random hours during the day, and we must determine how many personnel interviewers are required to meet the anticipated work load. In one computer modeling for an office handling 150 applicants per day on the average, it was determined that waiting time and transit time are least when there are four interviewers processing seventy-five applicants.[11] Thus, eight interviewers was stipulated to be the number required to minimize applicant waiting without excessive ineconomy on the part of the firm.

The Delphi technique of decision making has been used in determining the number of highly professional personnel of varied types that firms will require in the future. Essentially, it is an iterative questionnaire technique where recognized experts are asked to make specific estimates of needs, followed by feedback of summarized

[11]Robert H. Flast, "A Computer Simulation of a Corporate Employment Office," *Personnel Journal*, vol. 53, no. 1, January 1974, pp. 52–58.

results, followed by new estimates, etc. It is a "judgment refining" process that is quite lengthy and should be confined to estimates that have considerable cost impact on the firm, where the state of the art is not well developed.

Linear programming is a mathematical technique of limited general applicability. It is confined to resource allocation problems where constraints impose a degree of certainty in which the most efficient allocation of personnel, and other resources, can be determined mathematically. Use of this operations research technique is predicated on the availability of reasonably accurate information, some of which is often provided by systematic time study of work operations.

Time study of repetitive operations should provide more accurate figures on the amount of work that can be accomplished by the average employee, exerting average effort, working under average conditions. Returning to the voucher example, time study may convert the 0.09 figure into 0.08 or 0.07, particularly if attention is also devoted to devising better methods of operation. In addition, if the standard selected is coupled with incentive wages of some type, the output per person-hour may increase even more. This will result in a reduction of the minimum number of personnel required to do the job.

The immediate result of the work load analysis is a determination of the number of personnel necessary to execute that amount of work during some specified period. Such a figure is not usually highly exact, for obviously the output per person is influenced by many factors. Yet it has been proved that detailed and systematic study of outputs and work loads produces economies in staffing beyond those that prevail in a department or section that "just grows."

The above-described approach is an excessively simplified analysis adaptable to short-range projections. However, it is becoming increasingly apparent that the need for human resources should be anticipated sooner than one year in advance of requirement. Though aerospace firms have attempted to translate new long-term government contracts into specific needs, surveys show that most firms are not preparing full-scale projections covering long periods. They tend to stick to short periods for rank and file employees, and concentrate upon the problem of replacing key professional and managerial personnel. Inasmuch as most large firms do prepare long-range forecasts in marketing, research, and capital investment, it is surprising that more attention is not given to human resources projections. Wikstrom suggests that if estimates are only within 15 to 20 percent of actual requirements, they would be of considerable value.[12]

Determining and planning for long-range human resources needs are affected by such complex factors as (1) the population age distribution, (2) technological developments in both products and processes, (3) competition, (4) levels of economic activity, and (5) specific enterprise plans for growth. The varying birth rate from time to time provides differing amounts of population in each age group. Rapid advances in technology lead to increased demand for new technical and professional personnel. Social and legal changes exert a considerable impact on the constitution and nature of the work force. Though all of these are nebulous and difficult to pin down with exactitude, the professional personnel manager will constantly be alert to cues that will indicate the nature of the personnel procurement task that lies ahead.

[12]W. S. Wikstrom, "Planning for Manpower Planning," *Business Management Record*, National Industrial Conference Board, New York, August 1963, p. 33.

Work force analysis

Returning to the specific short-range projection problem of the voucher clerks, let us assume that work load analysis demonstrates that eleven voucher clerks are required as an absolute minimum for the coming month. The section supervisor consults the records and discovers that eleven such clerks have been assigned. There would seem to be no problem since the eleven required equals the eleven available. Such a conclusion is risky if there has been no work force analysis. Is there any assurance that these eleven will be available for work every day of the coming month? In general, the answer is no. There are at least two major problems that must now be considered—absenteeism and turnover. Both work to reduce the number of personnel available to a figure *less* than the eleven names showing on the payroll.

ABSENTEEISM   "Absenteeism" is the title given to a condition that exists when a person fails to come to work when properly scheduled to work. The absenteeism rate is the ratio of days lost to the total number of days for which employment was available. The rate is expressed in the following formula:

$$\text{Absenteeism} = \frac{\text{worker-days lost}}{\text{worker-days worked} + \text{worker-days lost}}$$

There is probably some irreducible minimum of absenteeism in most organizations, and 3 percent is projected by some as this figure. A survey of 931 firms revealed an average absenteeism rate of 3.73 percent, with the highest average reported by firms in manufacturing, 4.41 percent, and the lowest by those in the banking industry, 2.79 percent.[13]

Excessive absenteeism constitutes a considerable cost to the firm even when the absent employee receives no pay. Work schedules are upset and delayed, quality of product tends to deteriorate, overtime may be required to make up work, and many fringe benefits are still paid regardless of attendance. When sick pay is authorized, the costs mount up even more rapidly. It was estimated in one instance that for a plant of 1,000 employees, an increase in the absentee rate of 1 percent costs approximately $150,000 per year.[14] It is therefore desirable that management should attempt to reduce the rate, and, in any event, include the known rate in their decision concerning human resources requirements.

Since the subject of absenteeism is covered only in this one place in this text, it is advisable to turn briefly to a discussion of ways and means to reduce the number of absentees. Reducing absenteeism is achieved through an analysis of its causes. Each absence can be classified according to characteristics, and patterns may emerge which will aid in analysis and reduction. Basic characteristics and some patterns are given as follows:

1   *Name of the employee.* It is often found that there are absence-prone persons in

[13]Prentice-Hall Editorial Staff and American Society for Personnel Administration, *Absenteeism and Lateness: How Much Is Too Much?* Prentice-Hall, Inc., Englewood Cliffs, N.J., 1974, p. 12.

[14]John C. Kearns, "Controlling Absenteeism for Profit," *Personnel Journal*, vol. 50, no. 1, January 1970, p. 50.

an organization. One survey discovered that about 10 percent of the employees usually accounted for 45 percent of all absences.[15] After appropriate counseling and help, dismissal is sometimes the only solution. In the overwhelming majority of reported surveys, poor attendance can be a sole basis for dismissal.

2 *Reasons given.* Illness is doubtlessly the number one reason given for an absence, accounting for well over half of the cases. Correction of this involves a combination of private and organizational health programs. Other reasons given are frequent transportation difficulties, personal requirements, and care of children. One of the foremost values of the flexi-time schedule, discussed in Chapter 1, is the reduction of official time lost for these personal requirements. Problems related to care of children could also be alleviated by employer-sponsored child-care centers.

3 *Projected reasons.* Many employers contend that the real reason for high absenteeism is a lack of an employee sense of responsibility. Though some will blame the gradual switch from a work ethic to one of a more existentialistic character, we would do well to also look at the environment in which we expect employees to live daily. Monotonous and demeaning jobs, relatively poor pay, oppressive and pressureful supervision, and poor working conditions do not inspire daily loyalty. Correlations of absenteeism rates by general desirability of the job serve to support this contention.

4 *Age.* In 1972, the part-week unscheduled absence rate for teenage employees was the highest of all age groups.[16] The rate for the fifty-five-to-sixty-four-year category was lowest. However, the full-week absence rate was just the reverse. The young employee tends to be absent for short periods more frequently, suggesting placement in low entry jobs or personally compensating for the business practice of according longer vacations to senior employees. Older employees tend to be out for longer periods, suggesting problems related to health.

5 *Sex.* Many studies show a higher rate of absenteeism for females as compared with males. Such statistics are very misleading inasmuch as they are often not analyzed for the factors of job and pay. Females as a group tend to have higher absence rates because they have been improperly allocated to lower-paid, less desirable jobs. When corrected for job type, compensation levels, and formal education, the difference between the sexes tends to disappear.

6 *Date.* Tabulating absences by date often shows such interesting patterns as high rates on Mondays and Fridays, after paydays, before and after holidays, and on opening days for various seasons such as hunting and baseball. A top manager in one automobile firm stated that the rate sometimes amounted to 13 to 15 percent on Monday and Friday. The four-day, forty-hour week has been proposed to provide an officially approved three-day time-off period. Others suggest that the real problem lies within the structure of the job and work situation.

To go back to our illustration cited above concerning the voucher clerks, let us assume that the absence rate in the past has been about 9 percent. This excessive rate demands investigation, for it means that on the average one clerk has failed to show up for work each day. If the situation shows no immediate improvement, work force

[15]Lawrence L. Steinmetz and Peter P. Schoderbek, "What You Can Do about Absenteeism," *Supervisory Management,* vol. 12, no. 4, April 1967, p. 14.

[16]Janice Neipert Hedges, "Absence from Work: A Look at Some National Data," *Monthly Labor Review,* vol. 96, no. 7, July 1973, p. 28.

analysis would indicate that we need twelve clerks, not eleven, to fulfill the work load requirements.

TURNOVER Further analysis may lead to a modification of the answer of twelve clerks. We have not investigated the possibility of loss of personnel through retirement, death, quits, or any of a number of factors forcing separation from the firm. Consequently some analysis of labor turnover is required.

In the broad sense, "turnover" refers to the movement into and out of an organization by the work force. This movement is an index of the stability of that force. An excessive movement is undesirable and expensive. When an employee leaves the firm, such costs as the following are usually involved:

1   Hiring costs, involving time and facilities for recruitment, interviewing, and examining a replacement.
2   Training costs, involving the time of the supervisor, personnel department, and trainee.
3   The pay of a learner is in excess of what is produced.
4   Accident rates of new employees are often higher.
5   Loss of production in the interval between separation of the old employee and the replacement by the new.
6   Production equipment is not being fully utilized during the hiring interval and the training period.
7   Scrap and waste rates climb when new employees are involved.
8   Overtime pay may result from an excessive number of separations, causing trouble in meeting contract delivery dates.

An estimate of $500 turnover cost per rank and file employee is considered to be conservative by the American Management Association.[17] Greater appreciation of the significance of these costs has stimulated considerable managerial interest in the problem of labor turnover. In a survey of twenty-four California firms, the greatest turnover costs issued from lost production while the position was vacant and the substandard production of the replacement while learning.[18] These were estimated to be 70 percent of the total. Next in order of significance were costs of supervision, employment, formal training, taxes, and exit procedure.

The turnover rate can be expressed by a number of different formulas. We should always make sure that the same method is being utilized by two firms before trying to make a comparison. These various formulas involve such terms as *accessions*, additions to the payroll; *separations*, quits, discharges, retirements, deaths; *replacements*, one accession plus one separation; and *average work force*, number at the beginning of the period (usually a month) plus number at the end, divided by 2.

Suppose that our work force averages 800 employees this month, during which time there were 16 accessions and 24 separations. The accession rate is $^{16}/_{800} \times 100 = 2$ percent; the separation rate is $^{24}/_{800} \times 100 = 3$ percent; and the replacement rate is

[17]F. J. Gaudet, *Labor Turnover: Calculation and Costs*, American Management Association, Research Study 139, 1960.
[18]Joseph C. Ullman, "Using Turnover Data to Improve Wage Surveys," *Personnel Journal*, vol. 45, no. 9, October 1966, p. 529.

$^{16}/_{800} \times 100 = 2$ percent. The replacement rate is always the smaller of the two figures, accessions and separations, since we must have one entry and one exit to equal a replacement. The replacement rate, entitled "net labor turnover" by the Bureau of Labor Statistics, emphasizes the costs of turnover entailed by hiring and training a replacement. In 1973, the annual accession rate in manufacturing was 4.8 percent while the separation rate was 4.6 percent.[19]

Each separation can be analyzed much as we analyzed the problem of absenteeism. Separations can be classified by department, reasons for leaving, length of service, and personal characteristics, such as age, sex, marital status, home ownership, and amount of insurance. High turnover from certain departments suggests a need for improvements in working conditions and/or supervision. When the Connecticut General Insurance Company moved from Hartford to a new and luxurious building in a country club setting in Wethersfield, the quit rate for women dropped from 9 percent to 5.1 percent in one year.[20] Reasons given for leaving must be analyzed carefully to ascertain their truth. Because of the difficulty of getting real answers in exit interviews, a few firms try to elicit them by questionnaire after the exiting employee has had time to procure another position. In a comparison of reasons given at the exit interview with those obtained through follow-up questionnaires, one firm discovered agreement between the two sources in only 11 out of 116 cases.[21]

Analysis of length of service often indicates that a large percentage of voluntary quits occur in the first six months of employment, a fact that suggests errors in placement and orientation. In a statistical study of quits and stays in a relatively routine clothing manufacturing job, one firm discovered that stable employees (in relation to turnover) were over the age of twenty-nine at hiring, owned their own homes, had prior work experience, and had no more than nine years of formal schooling.[22] Each of these characteristics could be credited with point values on the application blank. Other things being equal, the stable employee is favored during the hiring process. It would not appear that any of the stipulated characteristics would significantly discriminate against any group protected by the Civil Rights Act. However, statistical proof of effective prediction of job success, in terms of tenure, would tend to follow the guidelines established by the agencies and courts.

Returning to our original problem, we may discover, in an analysis of the work by individuals, that a retirement is imminent or that an application for transfer has been submitted. Retirements, in particular, are subject to advance analysis, and preparations should be started well enough ahead to allow effective handling of the problem of replacement. Thus, our work load analysis may indicate a need for eleven clerks. Absenteeism rates require the addition of one more, and an analysis of turnover factors and rates may add another. Though we now have eleven voucher clerks on the payroll, a requisition is necessary for *two* additional voucher clerks. An employee requisition can now be prepared specifying both quantity and quality of personnel required.

[19]"Current Labor Statistics," *Monthly Labor Review*, vol. 97, no. 7, July 1974, p. 96.

[20]Raymond F. Pelissier, "Successful Experience with Job Design," *Personnel Administration*, March–April 1965, p. 12.

[21]Jerry Levine, "Labor Turnover," *Personnel Administration*, vol. 33, no. 6, November–December 1970, p. 35.

[22]Gordon C. Inskeep, "Statistically Guided Employee Selection: An Approach to the Labor Turnover Problem," *Personnel Journal*, vol. 49, no. 1, January 1970, p. 21.

SUMMARY

Before recruitment and selection of personnel can be undertaken, one must know the nature of the problem to be solved. The requirements for human resources must be analyzed in terms of quality of personnel needed as well as the number of each type. Job design and analysis are the basic processes that provide information leading to the establishment of personnel standards regarding quality. The immediate result of the processes is the creation of a job description (standard of function) and a job specification (standard of personnel). These two documents have multiple uses in a well-planned personnel program, but their immediate use at this stage of the text is as a standard by which we can measure applicants for jobs. A somewhat more terse statement of the duties described in Figure 6-2 is: "At highway construction projects where only one-way traffic is possible, this person waves a red flag and tells which car to go first." Job analysis jargon can be misleading. It can also be misleading in that it leaves out the many values provided by proper role analysis. Common job descriptions in two different organizations often have different behavioral expectations.

The second major question concerning human resources requirements is that of specifying the number of each type of personnel needed. This involves a prediction of the volume of work for the coming period and a translation of this into the number of people necessary to undertake that volume. Long-term predictions of requirements require consideration of such major variables as population distribution, technology, and company plans for growth. Short-term projections can be based on immediate past experience or on data derived from detailed and systematic time studies of standard operations. The total work to be done divided by the work one person can do equals the number of people required. Work force analysis must follow work load analysis in order to determine exactly how many personnel can reasonably be expected to report to work daily. Analysis of absenteeism and labor turnover rates may reveal that though eleven names are on the payroll we cannot reasonably expect eleven people to be available each day. The first approach should be that of analyzing causes of such absences and turnover in order to develop a program for their reduction. At the very least, these rates must be incorporated into an estimate of personnel requirements so that the preparations for the procurement of additional personnel can be completed if such addition is found to be necessary. Intelligent and effective recruitment and hiring require an adequate amount of lead time as well as accurate information concerning the number and quality of human resources desired.

DISCUSSION QUESTIONS

1 In what way is private-firm establishment of job specifications subject to review and approval by society?
2 Define and distinguish between job analysis and role analysis.
3 What peculiar human requirements are often characteristic of boundary-spanning jobs?
4 Define and distinguish between job analysis and job design. What roles should the personnel manager play in both processes?
5 Explain how the role requirements of two supervisors could differ even though their job descriptions are substantially identical.

6 Define and distinguish among the terms "job," "position," and "occupation." Why is the job description most useful? Of what value is an occupational description?

7 In translating sales and growth projections into specific human resources plans, of what assistance are computer modeling simulations? The Delphi technique? Time study?

8 When correlating absence rates with individual employees, reason given, age, calendar dates, and sex, cite one specific finding likely for each.

9 If you were given the assignment to submit a proposal to reduce the separation rate, how would you proceed to analyze the problem?

10 If the work schedule requires processing of 44,000 vouchers during the next month ($22\frac{1}{2}$ working days of 8 hours each), and time study has set 0.09 person-hour as the voucher-processing standard time, how many persons will be required to meet the schedule? If the average absenteeism rate is 5 percent, how would this change your answer?

SUPPLEMENTARY READING

BRYANT, Don R., Michael J. Maggard, Robert P. Taylor: "Manpower Planning Models and Techniques: A Descriptive Survey," *Business Horizons*, vol. 16, no. 2, April 1973, pp. 69–78.

CASSELL, Frank H.: "Manpower Administration: A New Role in Corporate Management," *Personnel Administration*, vol. 34, no. 6, November–December 1971, pp. 33–43.

FLAST, Robert H.: "A Corporate Simulation of a Corporate Employment Office," *Personnel Journal*, vol. 53, no. 1, January 1974, pp. 52–58.

HEDGES, Janice Neipert: "Absence From Work: A Look at Some National Data," *Monthly Labor Review*, vol. 96, no. 7, July 1973, pp. 24–30.

PRENTICE-HALL EDITORIAL STAFF AND THE AMERICAN SOCIETY FOR PERSONNEL ADMINISTRATION: *Absenteeism and Lateness: How Much Is Too Much?* Prentice-Hall, Inc., Englewood Cliffs, N.J., 1974, pp. 1–30.

PRIEN, Erich P., and William W. Ronan: "Job Analysis: A Review of Research Findings," *Personnel Psychology*, vol. 24, no. 3, Autumn 1971, pp. 371–396.

TELLY, Charles S., Wendell L. French, and William G. Scott: "The Relationship of Inequity to Turnover among Hourly Workers," *Administrative Science Quarterly*, vol. 16, no. 2, June 1971, pp. 164–172.

SEVEN

RECRUITMENT AND HIRING

Once a determination of human resources requirements has been made, the recruitment and hiring processes can begin. *Recruitment* is the process of searching for prospective employees and stimulating them to apply for jobs in the organization. It is often termed "positive" in that its objective is to increase the selection ratio, that is, the number of applicants per job opening. Hiring through selection is negative in that it attempts to eliminate applicants, leaving only the best to be placed in the firm. In this chapter, we shall be concerned with both these processes; in the following chapter more attention will be devoted to interviewing and testing aspects.

RECRUITMENT

In general, the sources of employees can be classified into two types, internal and external. Filling a job opening from within the firm has the advantages of stimulating preparation for possible transfer or promotion, increasing the general level of morale, and providing more information about job candidates through analysis of work histories within the organization. In addition, it avoids the problem of people coming in one door of the firm while highly similar talent leaves by another. An internal search of the computer personnel data bank can flag personnel with minimum qualifications for the job opening. Dissatisfaction with such skills inventories have led some to a more personalized job posting and bidding system. Such a system is more compatible with adapting the organization to the needs of individuals.

Internal job posting should take place at least one to two weeks prior to external recruiting. Policies vary as to whether an interested present employee must inform the supervisor of the bid for a new job. Usually, this is required only when the person is tentatively accepted and scheduled for the screening interview. If accepted for the posted job, the former supervisor is allotted approximately a month to provide for a successor. The personnel unit often acts as a clearinghouse in screening bids that are unrealistic, preventing an excessive number of bids by a single employee, and counseling employees who are constantly unsuccessful in their attempts to change jobs. If an even more open climate exists, employees may be allowed to place a "position wanted" ad in publications used in the job posting system. A well-designed and administered job posting and bidding system should effect better utilization of the firm's human resources, despite some reluctance of supervisors to let go of personnel with the qualifications to move on.

Inevitably, the firm must go to external sources for lower-entry jobs, for expansion, and for positions whose specifications cannot be met by present personnel. Among the more commonly used outside sources are the following:

1 *Advertising.* There is a trend toward more selective recruitment in advertising. This can be effected in at least two ways. First, advertisements can be placed in media read only by particular groups; e.g., *The Tool Engineer* is ordinarily read by production engineers. Secondly, more information about the company, the job, and the job specification can be included in the ad to permit some self-screening. Trade publications usually stay in circulation for a longer period of time, thereby increasing the number of potential applicants. They can also contribute to image- and prestige-building for the organization. A prime disadvantage is the longer lead time required for their publication. When time is limited, the daily newspaper, particularly the Sunday edition, will reach the maximum number in the shortest period.

2 *Employment agencies.* Additional screening can be effected through the utilization of employment agencies, both public and private. Today, in contrast to their former unsavory reputation, the public employment agencies in the several states are well-regarded, particularly in the fields of unskilled, semiskilled, and skilled operative jobs. In the technical and professional areas, however, the private agencies appear to be doing most of the work. The public agency and selected private agencies provide a nationwide service in attempting to match personnel demand and supply. Many private agencies tend to specialize in a particular type of worker and job, e.g., sales, office, executive, or engineer. A recent innovation, the videotaped interview, promotes more effective decision making with easier scheduling and more time saving for the hiring organization. When job specifications are somewhat nebulous, as they generally are in the higher types of jobs, the addition of a thirty-minute videotaped interview to the usual, more sterile résumé enables representatives of the hiring organization to quickly narrow the pool of candidates to a few finalists. Often, the representative will stop the tape after a few minutes, concluding at this point that the candidate is not suitable. This would be far more difficult to accomplish in a tactful fashion in a regularly scheduled interview. Videotaped interviews can be collected over a period of weeks and then shown to the employer during a single day.

3 *Recommendations of present employees.* When present employees are asked to recommend new hires, a type of preliminary screening takes place. The present employee knows both the company and the acquaintance and presumably would attempt to please both. In one company employing 1,600 clerical workers, it was found that long tenure was related to obtaining employees from this source.[1] The separation

---

[1]Joseph C. Ullman, "Employee Referrals: Prime Tool for Recruiting Workers," *Personnel,* vol. 43, no. 3, May–June 1966, p. 33.

rate of referred employees was lower than that of those obtained through either want ads or employment agencies. A second study of clerical employees in three insurance firms tended to confirm this finding with the additional modifying elements of (1) degree of friendship, (2) accuracy of company information conveyed, and (3) subsequent employee performance rating.[2] In two of the firms logic prevailed, with closeness of friendship and more accurate information contributing to hiring of superior employees. In the third firm, however, the close-friend recruit with accurate information received significantly lower subsequent ratings. The failure was attributed to the low level of morale in the third organization; generally negative but accurate information was being passed, with the result that only lower-quality recruits would act upon it. Thus, one must assess the morale of present employees before according their recommendations heavier weight.

4 *Schools and colleges.* Jobs in business have become increasingly technical and complex to the point where high school and college degrees are widely demanded. Consequently, many firms make special efforts to establish and maintain constructive relationships with school faculties and administrations. In recruiting at the college level, inquiries from 255 new technical college graduates, both before and one year after hiring, revealed that the most important influences affecting choice of firm and job were work-related factors, such as the nature of the assignment, degree of responsibility, and possibilities for advancement.[3] Bachelor's-degree candidates were more interested in training opportunities and precise definition of the initial assignment in order to reduce first-job anxiety. Master's candidates were also interested in the nature of the work but, in addition, exhibited considerable concern about the human organization and the personalities with whom they would be working. Doctoral-degree candidates indicated a significantly greater interest in the first job assignment than in future allocations. They were also interested in the human organization as well as the status of the industry in which the employing organization was located. It is apparent that successful attraction of college graduates will necessitate some study of their needs, as well as some attempt to transmit information concerning the degree to which these needs can be met.

5 *Labor unions.* Firms with closed or union shops must look to the union in their recruitment efforts. Disadvantages of a monopolistically controlled labor source are offset, at least partially, by savings in recruitment costs. With one-fifth of the labor force organized into unions, organized labor constitutes an important source of personnel.

6 *Casual applicants.* Unsolicited applications, both at the gate and through the mail, constitute a much-used source of personnel. These can be developed through provision of attractive employment office facilities and prompt and courteous replies to unsolicited letters.

7 *Nepotism.* The hiring of relatives will be an inevitable component of recruitment programs in family-owned firms. Such a policy does not necessarily coincide with hiring on the basis of merit, but interest and loyalty to the enterprise are offsetting advantages.

8 *Leasing.* To adjust to short-term fluctuations in personnel needs, the possibility of leasing personnel by the hour or day should be considered. This practice has been particularly well developed in the office administration field. The firm not only obtains

[2]Raymond E. Hill, "New Look at Employee Referrals as a Recruitment Channel," *Personnel Journal*, vol. 49, no. 2, February 1970, p. 147.

[3]J. R. Beak, "Where College Recruiting Goes Wrong," *Personnel*, vol. 43, no. 5, September–October 1966, pp. 22–28.

well-trained and selected personnel but avoids any obligation in pensions, insurance, and other fringe benefits.

RECRUITMENT EVALUATION

Not every firm can afford to develop every source of labor to the fullest extent. Sources utilized should be evaluated and judged in terms of the degree of success in obtaining competent personnel. For each major category of jobs, present personnel can be evaluated in terms of job success. If a correlation is discovered between successful personnel and particular labor sources, those sources should be further developed with money and effort. Within certain general sources, such as schools and colleges, the firm may find that particular schools provide better personnel for its purposes than other schools. A continuing study by the Division of Research, Harvard Business School, suggests that a firm's image or style has something to do with the type of student talent it can attract.[4] Firms are characterized by such variables as size, discouragement of risk taking, stability, emphasis upon profits, plainly stated policies, and well-structured chain of command. In correlating student preferences concerning these variables and student preferences regarding religion, the study suggested that Jewish students may wish to work for a smaller and less well-structured company. Catholics tend to prefer the well-structured company with clear policies, while Protestants and agnostics tend to fall in between Catholics and Jews. Thus, if firms wish to attract personnel from diverse ethnic backgrounds, certain alterations in practices and image may facilitate this process.

If the most successful sources of employees can be ascertained, the recruitment program can be more carefully aimed. A large insurance company has discovered that three sources of personnel provide them with most of their better employees. These are (1) high schools, (2) present-employee recommendations, and (3) newspaper advertising. Michigan Bell discovered that present employee recommendations constituted the best single source. A New York bank, regularly utilizing seven sources, discovered that quit rates varied from a 21 percent low for one source to a 40 percent high for another, a pattern that was sustained over a four-year period.[5] If the bank had confined its recruiting to the best four sources (reemployment of former workers, referees from high school, present-employee recommendations, and walk-ins), it would have reduced its quit rate by 9 percent, resulting in estimated savings of $180,000 over the four years. Of course, one would have to make sure that sufficient personnel are actually available from the more restricted set of sources.

The computer is readily adaptable to recruitment problems where job requirements must be matched with human characteristics and capabilities. One private employment agency for middle executives requires a six-page questionnaire to be completed by all job applicants. Information extracted from this is placed into a computer. When a client company sends in a job specification to be filled, the agency can obtain from the computer a list of candidates who most nearly match the position. A similar approach has been used in some universities for graduating seniors, thus

---

[4]"How Does Religion Influence Job Choice?" *Business Week*, Apr. 17, 1965, p. 178.

[5]Martin J. Gannon, "Sources of Referral and Employee Turnover," *Journal of Applied Psychology*, vol. 55, no. 3, June 1971, pp. 226–228.

providing company recruiters with the names and addresses of students who appear to qualify for their job specifications. This same process has been used in the past on a manual filing basis, but its application to the computer with its large memory-storage capability makes the process far more complete and current.

Recruitment is not an inexpensive process, particularly for professional personnel. Though forty companies were surveyed in the Washington, D.C., area, only eleven were able to provide concrete data concerning costs of recruitment.[6] In hiring 841 professional personnel, the average cost reported was $1,467; this compares with an average of $175 when hiring 1,879 nonprofessional personnel. The major costs in the professional personnel category were relocation costs (22 percent), private agency fees (18 percent), newspaper advertising (15 percent), and efforts of the employment staff (16 percent).

To reduce the costs of recruiting, a few of the larger organizations attempt to utilize such techniques as linear programming and Performance Evaluation and Review Technique (PERT). International Business Machines Corporation has centralized the control of college recruiting and divided the task into four geographic areas. Desired personnel are classified as engineering, other technical, and nontechnical. With a goal of filling specified quotas in each of the three types of personnel at the least cost in terms of recruiter travel and time, applicant visiting costs to company, and moving costs of new hires, a series of linear equations was developed to aid in allocating assignments to the four geographic areas.[7] It was concluded that the order and logic that linear programming brought to an increasingly large and complex task made possible a more effective distribution of recruitment assignments.

In undertaking an organized college recruitment program in a single company, Schoderbek has demonstrated how all the components can be programmed using the PERT approach.[8] In brief, PERT forces attention upon the interrelationships of multiple components of complex projects, with the goal of determining the shortest time needed to complete the overall project, as well as ascertaining possible slack times within particular portions. A PERT network is a flow diagram showing activities and events that must be executed to reach the program objectives. In preparing for a large college recruitment program, various activities are necessary, such as the following:

1 Determination of college graduate requirements
2 Determination of the college budget
3 Obtainment of authority to hire
4 Development of job specifications
5 Survey and selection of colleges and universities to be visited
6 Determination of number and type of recruiters needed
7 Determination of this year's starting salary
8 Development of recruitment pamphlets
9 Assembly of recruitment packages of literature

[6]Anthony B. DePasquale, "Personnel Digests," *Personnel Administration*, vol. 32, no. 1, January–February 1969, p. 56.

[7]Leon Teach and John D. Thompson, "Simulation in Recruitment Planning," *Personnel Journal*, vol. 48, no. 4, April 1969, pp. 286–292.

[8]Peter P. Schoderbek, "PERT in College Recruiting," *Management of Personnel Quarterly*, vol. 3, no. 4, Winter 1965, pp. 40–43. See this article for a comprehensive PERT network for college recruitment.

10 Sending of advance materials to selected colleges
11 Establishment of interviewing dates at colleges
12 Obtainment of reservations for lodging for recruiters

It is apparent that some of the above activities must be carried out in a specific sequence, and others may take place at any time. To the appropriate sequencing must be added estimates of the time necessary for execution of each activity. The final network would consist of a series of time lines (representing activities) and circles (representing milestones or completed events). The critical path would be the series of activities and events that requires the greatest amount of time from the beginning to the end of the project. Such a systematic and planned approach to recruitment would prevent embarrassing episodes, such as the case where representatives of three divisions of the same company showed up on one campus, telling different stories about jobs and salaries while professing no knowledge of the presence of the other representatives.[9]

Success in the function of recruitment can be judged by utilizing a number of criteria, among which are, in order of increasing importance: (1) the number of applicants, (2) the number of offers made, (3) the number of hirings, and (4) the number of successful placements. The number of job applicants would appear to have least value in determining the effectiveness of the program, for applicants can be attracted by methods that do not result in successful hirings. The number of offers made is a better indication of the quality of the recruits. The number of acceptances of hirings is getting closer to the real objective of securing an adequate number of qualified personnel. But the true test of a recruitment program can be determined only by means of a hiring follow-up. Was the placement successful? Did the employee quit because of misunderstanding the nature of the job and company? Is the person a good employee in terms of productivity and attitude? Admittedly, such an evaluation will include an appraisal of the selection procedure as well, but we believe that one cannot properly evaluate recruitment without considering the end result, a successful placement. Placing the control point earlier in the cycle could well lead to an overemphasis on the wrong types of recruitment. It could result in a glowing picture of recruitment activity in terms of numbers of applicants, offers, and hirings, and a dismal result in terms of the recruits' performance on the job. Too few firms attempt to evaluate their recruitment programs by considering the successful placement.

NATURE OF THE HIRING PROCESS

In order to initiate the procedure for hiring, we must satisfy the three preliminary requirements depicted in Figure 7-1. First, there must be the authority to hire, which comes from the employment requisition, as developed through analysis of the work load and work force. Secondly, we must have a standard of personnel with which we can compare prospective employees. This is represented by the job specification, as developed through job analysis. And finally, we must have job applicants from whom we can select the persons to be hired. A planned recruitment program provides us with these applicants.

[9]George S. Odiorne, "How to Get Men You Want," *Nation's Business*, vol. 52, no. 1, January 1964, p. 30.

The hiring procedure is essentially a series of methods of securing pertinent information about the applicant. At each step we learn more about the prospect. The information obtained can then be compared with the job specification, the standard of personnel. If the applicant qualifies, he or she advances to the next step. Thus, the job specification and the job applicant are present at each step in the hiring procedure. The step constitutes the means by which the applicant's qualifications can be compared with the minimum requirements established in the job specification.

Evaluating the abilities of a human being is an extremely difficult task. There are no easy shortcuts, and the hiring procedures used by the more advanced firms are long and complicated. This fact has not entirely prevented the use of various techniques of quick appraisal, some of which are well organized and can be called "pseudosciences." Among such practices are the following examples.

PHRENOLOGY   This is a system which proposes to evaluate the qualities of a person by an analysis of the skull, its shape and protrusions. Like many pseudosciences, phrenology has a semblance of a scientific basis, inasmuch as it has been discovered that certain parts of the brain are concerned with specific sensory or motor functions of the body. From this concept an entire system has been conceived, which proposes to evaluate quickly the qualities of any person.

PHYSIOGNOMY   Few people practice phrenology in evaluating personnel. Perhaps more fall into the trap of using physiognomy, that is, of evaluating a person on the basis of facial features. This approach attributes meaning to such features as the heavy jaw, receding chin, shifty eye, and high forehead. Appearance is important in many jobs and should be appraised in the light of job requirements. The use of physiognomy, however, is the practice of judging psychological qualities on the basis of certain physical features.

ASTROLOGY   This is one of the oldest pseudosciences. It should be evident that there is

Figure 7-1

FRAMEWORK FOR PROCUREMENT

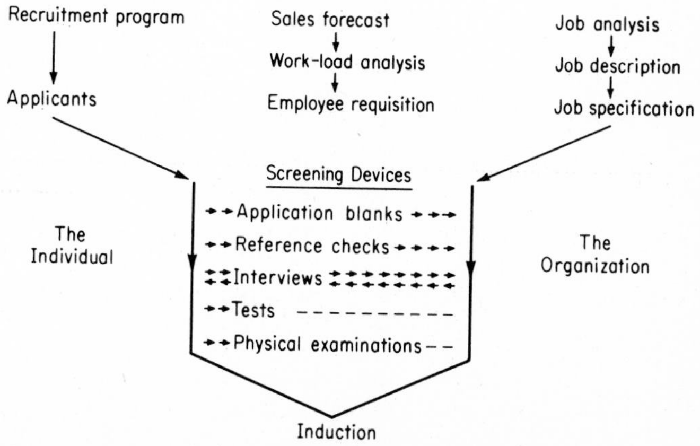

little relationship between date of birth and vocational aptitude. Nevertheless, some otherwise intelligent people have been attracted to astrology and attempt thereby to obtain aid in making various decisions.

PIGMENTATION   One widely known system of analyzing character is the blonde-brunette theory. According to this system, blondes are positive, dynamic, aggressive, and domineering, whereas brunettes are negative, serious, patient, and conscientious. Of course, one serious defect of this system has arisen in our modern society. How does one tell the true color of a person's hair?

GRAPHOLOGY   Graphology is a technique of analyzing a person's character by means of his or her handwriting. For example, heavy writing shows strength of will, and large lettering indicates a person with ambition. To the graphologist the way in which letters are formed is significant. In one unnamed company, supposedly among the nation's 500 largest corporations, an experiment in graphology and selection was tried.[10] Seventeen employees who were rated very superior by the graphologist were rated again fifteen years later; fourteen were rated very superior by the company, one adequate, and two inferior. Nevertheless, it is still significant that the company did not permit its name to be used in the article.

Most people do not consciously practice any of the above-listed pseudosciences, but many have favorite techniques of their own, judging by such things as how a person shakes hands, whether one looks you in the eye, and how one holds a cigarette. Again we must emphasize that there is no easy shortcut to the accurate evaluation of a human being under any circumstances. The length and complexity of the modern selection procedure are tangible evidence of this fact. Obviously, the attractiveness of all the above-mentioned shortcuts lies in the ease with which the desired information can be obtained. The graphologist needs a sample of handwriting; the astrologist requires only the birth date; and the physiognomist's only requirement is a photograph or two. Often it is not even necessary to see or talk with the applicant. Such a prospect may be quite appealing if one is thinking of the economy and effectiveness of hiring. It is quite impossible if one recognizes the nature and complexity of the human mind and personality.

THE HIRING PROCEDURE

As we have learned more about studying and measuring the individual, we have seen a continuous development of hiring procedures over the years. There are, of course, numerous aspects of a person that can be accurately measured, such as the attributes of height, weight, age, and eyesight. Other qualities, such as hearing and hand dexterity, are subject to less accurate evaluation. Psychological capabilities are even more difficult to measure, but even here there is a hierarchy of accuracy ranging from the testing of abstract intelligence, which can be done quite well, to the judging of that most nebulous of all qualities, personality. Though personality is probably the most difficult

[10]Ulrich Sonnemann and John R. Kernan, "Handwriting Analysis: A Valid Selection Tool?" *Personnel*, November–December 1962, p. 12.

characteristic of all to measure, it is one of the most important determinants of job success.

In the hiring procedure varying methods are used to discover significant information about an applicant, which can then be compared with the job specification. Though there is no standard procedure adopted by all firms, the following is an example of a popular method:

1 Initial or preliminary interview
2 Application blank or blanks
3 Check of references
4 Psychological tests
5 Employment interview
6 Approval by the supervisor
7 Physical examination
8 Induction or orientation

It is not suggested that these specific steps or this particular sequence constitutes a model to be followed. The procedure will vary with the size of the company, the type of job to be filled, and the philosophy of the personnel management. In a survey of 202 Canadian manufacturing firms, 40 percent of those with over $50 million in sales utilized four or more selection instruments, as compared with only 7 percent of those with sales under $500,000.[11] It will be noted in Figure 7-2 that the procedure followed by the Champion Paper and Fibre Company very nearly approaches the one outlined above.

In the sections that follow, a brief explanation of the nature and objectives of each step will be presented. Two of the steps, testing and interviewing, require considerably more space and will be discussed in the next chapter.

Preliminary interview

The more nonselective the recruitment program, the more likely it is that a preliminary interview will be required. This initial interview is usually quite short and has as its

[11]Harish C. Jain, "Managerial Recruitment and Selection in the Canadian Manufacturing Industry," *Public Personnel Management*, vol. 3, no. 3, May–June 1974, p. 212.

Figure 7-2 Example of hiring procedure

Champion Paper and Fibre Company Employment Procedure
1 The first step in hiring an applicant into the Champion organization is the initial interview, during which time an attempt is made to screen out undesirable candidates.
2 If the results of the initial interview are favorable, the applicant is given an application blank to fill out. This can be filled out while in the employment office or at his home and mailed back to the employment office.
3 After reviewing the application, the applicant may be called to the employment office to take a battery of screening tests such as: Wonderlic A (general intelligence), PTI Numerical (arithmetic achievement), Bennett Mechanical AA (mechanical comprehension), Brainard Occupational Interest (occupational interest), and Thurstone Temperament (personality).
4 A check of references is next made and a phone call made to the present employer, if any.

Figure 7-2—continued

---

5 The next step in the procedure is a call to the Hamilton Credit Bureau for credit references on the applicant. The credit report is a written report and includes the credit ratings and a check for police record, if any.

6 A final interview is arranged, at which time all facts at hand are considered and a decision is made as to whether or not the applicant will be hired. During this interview the employment-section representative discusses with the applicant conditions of work, type of job, rate of pay, bonuses, etc.

7 The final step in the employment procedure is to arrange for a physical examination in the medical department. Employment, of course, is based on any applicant's passing a physical examination.

8 After the examination, the applicant is returned to the employment office for a brief discussion concerning rules and regulations, payday, and hours of work. He is then taken to the clock house and shown how to ring his timecard. After this he is introduced to his supervisor.

Source: Champion Paper and Fibre Company, Hamilton, Ohio. By permission.

object the elimination of the obviously unqualified. In many instances it is a stand-up interview conducted at a desk or railing.

The more obvious facts and impressions are of the type generally obtained in an initial interview. Appearance and facility in speech are quickly evaluated. Applicants are often asked *why* they are applying for a job with this particular organization. Salary requirements are ascertained. An idea of education and experience can be obtained by asking for the last grade finished in school and the names of jobs previously held. Many firms do not bother to initiate any paper work at this early stage. If the applicant appears to have some chance of qualifying for existing job openings, he or she is given the application blank to complete.

Application blank

After reviewing several application blanks used by various organizations, the impression received is that "when you have seen one, you have seen them all." There is a remarkably high degree of similarity among the blanks of various companies. Perhaps this uniformity is caused by the fact that these blanks deal with basic information that all firms consider important; or companies may be following each other like sheep and including questions for which they have little use. With the passage of the Civil Rights Act of 1964, discrimination in employment on the basis of race, creed, nationality, and color is prohibited. This requires eliminating from the application blank questions that would reveal such information. It is not clear, as yet, how far regulations will proceed in this regard. A review of federal legislation and the rights laws of most states indicated that the following are illegal questions: (1) asking applicants if they have ever worked under another name, or for the birthplaces of their parents, spouse, or other close relatives; (2) asking how abilities to read, write, or speak a foreign language were acquired; (3) asking for a list of names of all clubs, societies, and lodges in which membership is held; (4) asking for religious affiliation, name of church, or religious holidays observed; and (5) asking whether and when the applicant was ever arrested.[12] In general, these questions can be interpreted as seeking information which would reveal national origin, race, creed, or color of the applicant. Firms can ask what foreign

---

[12]Robert L. Minter, "Human Rights Laws and Pre-Employment Inquiries," *Personnel Journal*, vol. 51, no. 6, June 1972, pp. 431–433.

languages are spoken as potentially usable for job assignment. They can also ask for prior convictions of crimes, but not for arrests, inasmuch as one does not always lead to the other.

Figure 7-3 is an example of the first page of the usual type of application blank found in many companies. Three additional pages are also included in this particular blank, asking for detailed information on prior military service, all jobs held since leaving school, and a series of personal references. Some companies use a second preliminary short form which is inspected to determine whether an applicant can proceed to the longer form; it is apparently a substitute for a preliminary interview.

One of the general principles of hiring procedures is to assign to each step

Figure 7-3

THE EMPLOYMENT APPLICATION BLANK

EMPLOYMENT APPLICATION
KSC 806 R-3

Kaiser Steel
BOX 217 FONTANA, CALIFORNIA

ANY INFORMATION GIVEN ON THIS BLANK WILL BE REGARDED AS STRICTLY CONFIDENTIAL. IT WILL BE TO THE APPLICANT'S ADVANTAGE TO ANSWER EACH QUESTION FULLY AND ACCURATELY. THE USE OF THIS BLANK DOES NOT INDICATE THERE ARE ANY POSITIONS OPEN AND DOES NOT IN ANY WAY OBLIGATE THIS COMPANY.

PLEASE PRINT ALL INFORMATION

SOCIAL SECURITY NO. | DATE

FULL NAME: LAST | FIRST | MIDDLE | PHONE NO. | CHECK ✓: Own Phone ☐ Neighbor's ☐

PRESENT ADDRESS: NO. AND STREET | CITY | STATE | LENGTH OF RESIDENCE

IF YOU NOW LIVE ON A RURAL ROUTE, COMPLETE THE NEXT LINE

NAME OF NEAREST CROSS STREET | HOW FAR AWAY | WHICH DIRECTION

FORMER ADDRESS: NO. AND STREET | CITY | STATE | LENGTH OF RESIDENCE

POSITION DESIRED | MINIMUM WAGE YOU WILL ACCEPT | HAVE YOU APPLIED TO US BEFORE ☐ YES ☐ NO WHEN | WHEN CAN YOU REPORT FOR WORK

MALE ☐ FEMALE ☐ | HEIGHT FT. IN. | WEIGHT | PHYSICAL DEFECTS | SINGLE ☐ MARRIED ☐ WIDOW ☐ WIDOWER ☐ DIVORCED ☐ SEPARATED ☐ | HOW MANY DEPENDENT CHILDREN HAVE YOU

DATE OF BIRTH: MONTH | DAY | YEAR | AGE | TOWN, STATE AND COUNTRY OF BIRTH | ARE YOU A UNITED STATES CITIZEN YES NO | DATE NATURALIZED

NAME OF NEAREST RELATIVE (HUSBAND OR WIFE, IF MARRIED) | RELATIONSHIP | SERIAL NUMBER | PLACE

EDUCATION

TYPE OF SCHOOL	NAME OF SCHOOL	LOCATION	CIRCLE NUMBER OF YEARS COMPLETED	DATE OF COMPLETION	MAJOR AND MINOR COURSES TAKEN	DIPLOMA, DEGREE, OR CERTIFICATE
Last Elementary			3 4 5 6 7 8		X X X X X X X X X X X X X X X X X	
High Schools			1 2 3 4			
College or University			1 2 3 4 5 6			
College or University			1 2 3 4 5 6			
College or University			1 2 3 4 5 6			
Business College			1 2 3 4			
Trade School			1 2 3 4			
Other			1 2 3 4			

OTHER TRAINING NOT SHOWN

WHAT WAS YOUR AVERAGE GRADE IN HIGH SCHOOL? | BASED UPON WHAT SYSTEM

WHAT WAS YOUR GRADE POINT AVERAGE IN COLLEGE? | BASED UPON WHAT SYSTEM

SCHOLASTIC HONORS AND AWARDS

EXTRA-CURRICULAR ACTIVITIES, ORGANIZATIONS, SPORTS, OFFICES, ETC.

WHAT PART (%) OF YOUR COLLEGE EXPENSE DID YOU EARN | HOW

information objectives that can best be obtained by the methods of that particular step. Factual information should be obtained by means of an application blank. We should not ask embarrassing questions or questions that can be easily misinterpreted. We should not automatically assume, however, that all information written on the blank by the applicant is accurate. In a study of 111 blanks completed by applicants for the job of nurse's aide, systematic checking with previous employers produced some marked discrepancies: one-fourth disagreed on "reasons for leaving prior position," while over half of the applicants overstated both salaries received and duration of previous employment.[13] It was also discovered that 15 percent had never worked for employers they had indicated on the blank. On hopefully rare occasions, newspapers carry stories of the highly successful medical doctor who has never graduated from medical school, the reasonably effective professional who does not have the degrees claimed, and the properly credentialed and classroom-effective professor who held three *full-time* college jobs simultaneously within a hundred-mile radius.

Some firms are now attempting to increase the value of the application blank by studying the relationship between certain biographical data ordinarily requested on the form and success on the job. If the specific value of any of the factual items can be determined, these items can then be weighted. In general, the approach is that of studying carefully the qualities of both your present successful employees and the unsuccessful ones. If one group possesses certain qualities and the other does not, these may well be distinguishing characteristics. For example, it may be discovered that successful employees are married and have families and that unmarried ones have poorer records. If so, a scale of points can be established for such variables as single, married, and married with children. There are several factors that have been discovered to be of value in specific business situations. Weights have been determined for such items as educational level, amount of life insurance, experience, age, and number of jobs held in the last five years. In a study of 1,525 life insurance salesmen in Metropolitan Life Insurance Company, a combination of high prior income and more than two dependents at the time of application was found to be descriptive of subsequent high producers.[14] Low producers could be identified by low earnings prior to their employment by this company. The factors of age, education, marital status, and sales experience were of little importance in this study. When one company was pressured by a union into granting a new fringe benefit of company-paid automobile insurance, analysis of driver risk designations revealed that the "low-risk" employee-driver averaged 7 days' absence per year, the "average risk" driver had 11 days per year, while the "high-risk" driver averaged 13 days per year.[15] Good drivers also were less likely to receive reprimands, have their wages garnisheed, be late to work, or receive injuries on the job. A review of twenty-one studies of biographical blanks by Schuh revealed one or more items with a predictive relationship with turnover in almost every case.[16] Contrast of the predictive accuracies of biographical data versus psychological

[13]Irwin L. Goldstein, "The Application Blank: How Honest Are the Responses?" *Journal of Applied Psychology*, vol. 55, no. 5, October 1971, p. 492.

[14]Robert Ranofsky, R. Ronald Shepps, and Paul J. O'Neill, "Pattern Analysis of Biographical Predictors of Success as an Insurance Salesman," *Journal of Applied Psychology*, vol. 53, no. 2, pp. 136–139.

[15]Dale Zechar, "Auto Insurance Rating: Measure of the Man?" *Personnel Journal*, vol. 49, no. 4, April 1970, p. 315.

[16]A. J. Schuh, "The Predictability of Employee Tenure: A Review of the Literature," *Personnel Psychology*, vol. 20, no. 2, Summer 1967, pp. 133–152.

Figure 7-4 Weighted application blank for secretary

Item	Percentage		Weight
	Short-term	Long-term	
Age:			
20 or under	10	0	0
21–25	50	12	−4
26–30	20	12	0
31–35	10	23	0
Over 35	10	53	+5
Marital status:			
Married	20	47	+2
Single	63	41	−1
Widowed	0	0	0
Divorced	10	6	0
Separated	7	6	0
Education:			
Attended grade school	0	0	0
Grade school graduate	0	0	0
Attended high school	0	12	0
High school graduate	33	41	0
Attended college	40	41	0
College graduate	27	6	−1
Business school	10	29	0
Years on last job:			
Less than 1	50	0	−5
1 to 1½	7	35	+2
1½ to 2½	37	12	−1
2½ to 3	0	6	0
More than 3	10	35	+2
Years of experience:			
0	3	18	0
Less than 1	20	0	−1
1 to 2	20	0	−1
2½ to 3	30	0	−3
More than 3	27	71	+5

Use of the cutting score of +2 would have eliminated 83 percent of the short-term employees and 13 percent of the long-term employees.

Source: Stanley R. Novack, "Developing an Effective Application Blank," *Personnel Journal,* vol. 49, no. 5, May 1970, pp. 421–422. Used with permission.

tests (intelligence, aptitude, interest, personality) with regard to job proficiency showed substantially higher validities for the former.[17] Such results would suggest that serious attention be devoted to the "hard" data on biographical inventories in order to improve selection effectiveness.

The weighted application form must be established and used with caution. First, objectives must be determined. Many firms have established as the prime objective the

[17]James J. Asher, "The Biographical Item: Can It Be Improved?" *Personnel Psychology,* vol. 25, no. 2, Summer 1972, p. 255.

selection of more stable employees to decrease labor turnover. They have discovered and utilized the particular data that denote stability—facts relating to home ownership, marital status, age, and sex. An example of the weighting process is shown in Figure 7-4 on page 143 with respect to one company's experience in retaining secretaries. Classification into categories of "short-term" and "long-term" employment was correlated with factual items on the blank. The pattern of findings was then translated into points, as indicated in the illustration. Other firms have established job proficiency as the major objective and have correlated biographical items with production records, merit-rating scores, or sales volume. The criterion of success must be selected before significant factors can be determined.

A second problem is concerned with the breadth of coverage of any particular factor in success. It may be found that age, for example, is a distinguishing factor in one company or one department but not so in another. Job conditions differ substantially, and the differences alter the relationship between any one factor and job success. Consequently, each firm must develop its own weighted form, taking cognizance of the varying conditions within the organization. In addition, the blank must be continuously updated. A survey previously cited demonstrates consistent decreases in predictive accuracy of the blank with the passage of time.[18] It is recommended that the entire blank be restudied and reweighted every three years at the minimum. It is also suggested that separate scoring studies be established for different ethnic groups.[19]

Finally, we must emphasize that no firm should try to select an employee solely on the basis of one or two important facts. The application form constitutes only one step of a long and complicated procedure. Information discovered elsewhere may weigh more heavily than any that is discovered here. Besides, no one factor on a blank is weighted sufficiently to have great bearing on the final decision. In effect, we are saying that if other things are equal, we shall prefer the applicant who fulfills the conditions that have proved to be significant in the past. The weighting is just one more attempt to improve the accuracy and the selectivity of the various steps in the hiring procedure.

References

There is a considerable amount of controversy concerning the value of checking applicant references. Some managers feel that little usable information is obtained, owing to the reluctance or inability of the reference giver to cite factual information. Others believe that if references are checked in the correct manner, a great deal can be learned about a person that an interview or psychological test cannot elicit. In a survey of 473 manufacturing firms of 250 employees or more, it was discovered that approximately 90 percent check work references in some manner or other, 66 percent check school and personal references, and 35 percent ask for a credit check.[20]

In general, three types of references are of value in hiring procedures: (1)

---

[18]A. J. Schuh, op. cit., p. 146.

[19]David L. Toole, James F. Gavin, Lee B. Murdy, and Saul B. Sells, "The Differential Validity of Personality, Personal History, and Aptitude Data for Minority and Nonminority Employees," *Personnel Psychology*, vol. 25, no. 3, Winter 1972, pp. 661–672.

[20]National Industrial Conference Board, *Personnel Practices in Factory and Office*: *Manufacturing*, Studies in Personnel Policy, no. 194, New York, 1964, p. 12. This study worked from replies from 1,834 firms, but the segmenting of the sample into four groups resulted in any one question being answered by only 400 to 500 respondents.

character, (2) work, and (3) school. Today, character references are of very little value in applying for jobs. Since a character reference is selected by the applicant, one can usually predict the nature of the information that will be obtained—expression of high praise of the individual's ability and integrity. It is generally agreed that a check on work experience constitutes the most important type of reference. Many desired items of information about an employee only experience will divulge. For example, the many attempts to test for accident proneness have met with little success. Consequently, if we can obtain a check on the safety record of a job applicant, this information will be of considerable value.

School references are of value in hiring students directly out of high school or college. The items that a teacher is in a position to evaluate, however, are often not those that are significant in hiring. At the very least, a check can be made on the honesty of the applicant in giving accurate information on the application form as to his level of schooling.

There are various ways of obtaining the required information on a reference check. Among them are:

1   Letter of reference sent to the hiring company at the request of the applicant
2   Letter of reference sent to the hiring company at the request of the hiring company
3   Telephone call to the reference giver
4   Personal visit or contact with the reference giver

In general, the principle holds that the closer one can get to the reference giver, the more accurate and valuable will be the information obtained. Thus, if the last technique, a personal visit, is utilized, the information obtained will probably prove to be of material value in the hiring process. Some companies, such as Nationwide Insurance Company, follow the practice of checking all work references by telephone. It is hoped that references can be completely checked while the applicant is completing the remaining steps of the hiring procedure.

The values of checking by direct conversation, face to face or by telephone, lie in the greater amount of information that is obtainable. Not only is the reference giver usually willing to speak more freely, but one also has the advantage of hearing the voice and its inflections. When information is to be written and signed, there is a natural tendency to modify it to the point of becoming primarily laudatory or meaningless. People generally speak more freely than they write. If the two parties know each other personally, the value of the information received can be extremely high.

The most widely used method of checking references is that of a letter of reference sent to the hiring company at its request. Within this technique there can be varying approaches. The most unsatisfactory is an inquiry which forces the reference giver to compose a general letter concerning the applicant's qualifications. Such a letter is likely to be quite general and meaningless. Most firms use some type of checklist letter of inquiry. This may take the form of a type of rating scale similar to that shown in Figure 13-1. Another approach consists of asking specific questions which can be answered in brief form, questions such as (1) What is the attendance record? (2) Why did she or he leave your employ? (3) Would you reemploy? (4) Was the person cooperative? (5) What is the accident record? and (6) Did the employee gamble or drink to excess? These same questions can also be used as a basis for a telephone check.

Because of the considerable pressures leading toward excessively laudatory responses by reference givers, a forced-choice format has been recommended by some researchers. This approach has been used more frequently in performance appraisal and will be explained in more detail in Chapter 13. In general, the reference-giver is asked to check which of two items is most descriptive of the applicant, e.g., "(1) has many worthwhile ideas or (2) requires little supervision." Since both items are laudatory, the reference-giver is forced to choose the single one most descriptive. Cross-validation research with actual job performance at a later date may well reveal that one laudatory phrase is more predictive of success than the other. One such study dealing with selection of clerical employees obtained a correlation coefficient of .56 between the forced-choice scoring key and a composite measure of employee effectiveness and low turnover.[21] Such accuracy was only possible when previous jobs were similar to the present one, when references were obtained from former immediate supervisors with more than two months' contact with the applicant, and when similarities existed between applicant and reference-giver in terms of race, sex, and national origin. It is obviously quite difficult to transform the reference into an accurate selection device.

Psychological tests

The next step in the procedure outlined above is that of testing. If all organizations, large and small, are considered, it is apparent that most are *not* using psychological tests. However, there is a direct relationship between the size of firm and the use of tests in hiring. In the above-cited survey, 81 percent of 473 firms, each with over 250 employees, used one or more psychological tests in selection.[22] Most of the larger companies that can afford to have a more detailed and accurate selection procedure do utilize some form of employment testing. It is the smaller company that frequently does not bother with tests, but places greater reliance upon the interview. Since psychological testing is a complex subject, it will be discussed at greater length in the next chapter.

Employment interviewing

Probably few companies would consider hiring anybody without benefit of an interview. The interview is a much-maligned method of human evaluation, and it is also probably the oldest. It is quite probable that if companies were restricted to the use of a single method of evaluation in a hiring procedure, they would choose interviewing most frequently. Although highly subjective and frequently inexact, the interview is essential.

Because of the importance of the interviewing step, we shall cover the subject at greater length in the next chapter. The basic purpose of the employment interview is to obtain significant information about the applicant. It often turns out to be the "catchall"; that is, if no other step can adequately extract the desired information, the task is automatically assigned to the interview, and consequently it gathers much highly subjective (and highly important) information. In a sense, progress in selection can be measured by the degree of success we have in narrowing the scope of the interview.

[21]Stephen J. Carroll, Jr., and Allan N. Nash, "Effectiveness of a Forced-Choice Reference Check," *Personnel Administration*, vol. 35, no. 2, March–April 1972, p. 45.

[22]NICB, *Personnel Practices*, p. 14.

For example, one purpose of the interview used to be to arrive at an estimate of intelligence. However, with the widespread availability of good intelligence tests, there is little necessity for such an estimate now.

In an attempt to improve the selection procedure, a few firms are now experimenting with a device called "leaderless group discussion."[23] At present, most appraisals of an applicant's leadership potential are made by means of the interview plus an analysis of his past. Leaderless group discussion is an attempt to improve the measurement of this quality. This method usually operates as follows: A number of job applicants are convened around a conference table. A brief, written résumé of some general problem is given to each of them. It could be some problem such as, "Should a firm like ours undertake a program of hiring the hard-core unemployed in final assembly jobs although our present policy is against such hiring?" Additional facts are supplied. The group is told that they have a definite length of time to discuss this problem and arrive at some specific decision. At this point, the group is left alone. They have a problem and no leader.

The measurement process in leaderless group discussion is accomplished by a series of observers. The applicants obviously know it is some type of test but do not know exactly what qualities are being measured. Observers are watching for such participant activities as (1) taking the lead in the discussion, (2) influencing others in the discussion, (3) summarizing and clarifying issues, (4) mediating arguments between two other participants, (5) speaking effectively. It has been found in various experiments that different observers can agree with one another on the score to be given to members of the group for each form of participation. The reliability of this measurement process is quite good. The problem, however, lies in attempting to relate these measures of performance to later success on the job.

The leaderless group discussion is cited primarily to emphasize that continued attempts are being made to improve the accuracy and predictability of the selection process through a reduction in the scope of the interview. Despite present and potential progress, it is believed that the subjective employment interview will remain a basic part of the procedure. The human being is far too complicated to be subjected to a comprehensive, objective measurement process.

Approval by the supervisor

Following the outlined procedure, we should now be of the opinion that a candidate who has successfully completed all steps thus far should be hired. This is often the opinion of a staff personnel department that is administering certain phases of the hiring procedure. Though many staff departments have the authority to hire, the principles of line and staff relationships require that the candidate be submitted to the supervisor of the job opening for acceptance or rejection.

At this point in the process, a third interview is conducted. The information objectives of this interview may well overlap those of the preceding one. This overlap is not undesirable for at least two reasons. First, the organizational relationships often require that the supervisor be given the right to pass upon personnel; otherwise he or she cannot be held accountable for their performance. Thus we preserve the equality of

[23]See Jules Z. Willing, "The Round-table Interview: A Method of Selecting Trainees," *Personnel*, vol. 39, no. 2, March–April 1962, pp. 26–32.

authority and responsibility. Secondly, the qualities that are generally appraised in an interview are highly intangible, such as personality, ability to get along with others, and leadership potential. In such matters it is helpful to have an appraisal by both the staff employment interviewer and the supervisor, who is better acquainted with the actual job conditions and the type of personnel at present in the department.

In executing the personnel unit screening functions, the emphasis tends to be more on formal qualifications and general suitability. When the supervisor takes over, the emphasis tends to switch toward more specifically job-oriented worker characteristics such as training and relevant past experience. For this reason, some firms reduce the role of the supervisor in a socially oriented program of hiring the culturally disadvantaged. If such is the case, the personnel unit may also have to supplement its increased authority in hiring with more personal-support counseling services for the disadvantaged person when transferred to the regular supervisor.

Physical examination

The physical examination is an employment step found in most businesses. It can vary from a very comprehensive examination and matching of an applicant's physical capabilities to job requirements, to a simple check of general physical appearance and well-being. In the hiring procedure the physical examination has at least three basic objectives. First, it serves to ascertain the applicant's physical capabilities. Can the applicant work standing up? Can a 10-pound weight be lifted? Is his or her eyesight sufficiently keen to meet the job requirements? This is a particularly important step when hiring the physically handicapped. Proper study of job requirements and of a person's physical assets often results in a far greater utilization of physically handicapped personnel than many in industry deem possible. A currently difficult problem facing many personnel units is that of screening to detect the addicted drug user.[24] Such detection is quite difficult and adds to the expense of the physical examination, involving such techniques as thin-layer chromatography or ultraviolet spectro-photofluorometry. In pre-employment screening in areas like New York City, it is reported that as many as 10 percent of job applicants have morphine in the urine.

The second objective of the examination is to protect the company against unwarranted claims under workers' compensation laws, or against lawsuits for damages.[25] As lawsuits are won, physical examinations change. In recent years, employees have won settlements for loss of hearing even though no lost time occurred on the job. If a record of a new employee's physical condition at the time of entry does not exist, a claim could possibly be filed for injuries greater than were incurred after starting to work. It is important to have an adequate record of the physical condition of the employee at the time of entry for legal as well as selection purposes.

A final objective of the physical examination is to prevent communicable diseases from entering the organization. It is obvious that this is a continuing objective and will constitute part of the regular work load of a medical department after personnel are hired and placed.

In the suggested procedure, the physical examination is located near the end. We do not suggest that this sequence should be rigid; some firms place the examination

[24]David Sohn, "Screening for Drug Addition," *Personnel*, vol. 47, no. 4, July–August 1970, pp. 22–30.
[25]See Chap. 24.

relatively early in the process. There are some good reasons for locating it last. One is that this step is rather time-consuming and expensive, and that the number of applicants who reach it will be considerably less than the number who fill out application blanks. And then again, there is sometimes an interval of time elapsing between initial screening by a personnel department and actual entry into the firm. Giving the physical examination near the end ensures that we are informed of the employee's physical condition at the time of actual entry.

Induction

If the physical examination has been passed successfully, the employee is hired. The examination is the last step at which a rejection can be made, and thus it is the actual end of the selection process. The induction function, however, immediately follows and is generally considered to be a part of the hiring procedure.

Induction is concerned with the problem of introducing or orienting a new employee to the organization. In the past, this was a step of little consequence. The applicant was hired and told to report to work at a specified time. Little or no help was provided in finding the way to the assigned department, where relatively brief instructions were received from the supervisor. Gradually, over a period of time, the new employee got to know some of the other members of the unit, found out where the cafeteria was, discovered the approved mode of dress, learned how to punch a time clock, etc. Too often during this period, the employee quit. Various firms have reported that over half of the voluntary quits occur within the first six months on the job. It is believed that a large portion of these may well be due to poor introduction and orientation.

Induction constitutes a significant part of what Bakke calls the "fusion process," which is a "simultaneous operation of the socializing process by which the organization seeks to make an agent of the individual for the achievement of organizational objectives and of the personalizing process by which the individual seeks to make an agency of the organization for the achievement of his personal objectives."[26] A degree of integration and agreement between organization goals and personal goals must be effected. The organization begins by attempting to select compatible personnel and then communicating to them its philosophies, policies, and customs of doing business.

The first phase of the program is ordinarily conducted by a personnel department. It is generally concerned with some explanation of the nature of the company and its products. Sometimes a motion picture is shown concerning the history and operations of the firm, the purpose of which is to begin the building up of some pride and interest in the organization. In addition to this, information is usually given concerning specific employee services, such as pensions, health and welfare plans, and safety programs. This general orientation consumes considerable time, during which the new employee usually accumulates a substantial amount of literature and, not infrequently, confusion. Research has shown that providing a realistic preview of the job, as compared with a sales indoctrinational pitch, will lead to more rapid fusion as well as reduce the potential for voluntary resignation. In a controlled experiment with eighty newly hired telephone operators, half were shown a fifteen-minute film of the traditional type—

[26]E. W. Bakke, *The Fusion Process.* New Haven, Conn.: Yale University Labor and Management Center, 1955, p. 5.

mostly good information about the company.[27] The other half were given a fifteen-minute film containing both good and bad information about the job; only four minutes of film were identical. Though the realistic job preview had no effect on the decision to take the job, those given the realistic information had lower initial expectations, fewer subsequent thoughts of quitting, and ultimately a slightly higher survival rate in the job.

After the general introduction, the induction is continued by the job supervisor. Proper induction takes time, and if the supervisor is too busy, some older employee should be designated to undertake this task. Here begins the merger of the employee not only with the company but with the specific personalities of fellow workers. The new hire may or may not be accepted by the work group. Not only must the new employee accept the organization, the supervisor, and the work group, but they must accept her or him if successful fusion is to occur. Induction at this point is quite specific and requires skill on the part of the supervisor. The employee is shown the department and its workplaces, introduced to several of the present employees, and informed of the locations of the cafeteria, locker rooms, and time clock. Information is provided concerning specific practices and customs, such as whether the personnel bring or buy their lunch, timing and length of rest periods, and manner of dress. In other words, the basic problem that is being attacked here is one of adjustment. The new employee will have to adjust to a new work environment that makes specific demands. The company can make this adjustment process considerably easier by undertaking many of the activities cited above. If, on the other hand, the new person is allowed to sink or swim, the adjustment period either is considerably lengthened with consequent losses in productivity, or it is eliminated altogether by a resignation, with consequent losses in turnover costs. In a study of 405 operators conducted at Texas Instruments, it was discovered that the first days on the job were anxious and disturbing ones, and that informal initiation procedures by peers intensified this anxiety.[28] The new employees indicated reluctance to discuss these feelings with supervisors. As a consequence, a special experimental induction program was devised with the specific goals of assuring new hires that their chances of success were very good, asking them to disregard the hazing games of older employees, and encouraging them to get to know their supervisors and take the initiative in communication. They were told that most supervisors preferred to answer questions and that they would not be considered dumb for asking. In the subsequent comparison of this experimental group with a control group at the end of the first month of employment, the former was producing 93 units per hour with an absentee rate of 0.5 percent and training hours required of 225. The control group inducted in the usual manner was producing 27 units per hour with an absentee rate of 2.5 percent and training hours required of 381. This study would suggest that initial difficulties are largely caused by anxiety and fear of the unknown. Good induction is good business for the firm and a basic desire of most, if not all, new employees.

The complete induction program will provide for a follow-up some weeks after the initial hiring and orientation. This interview, conducted by either the supervisor or a

---

[27]John P. Wanous, "Effects of a Realistic Job Preview on Job Acceptance, Job Attitudes, and Job Survival," *Journal of Applied Psychology*, vol. 58, no. 3, December 1973, pp. 327–332.

[28]Earl R. Gomersall and M. Scott Myers, "Breakthrough in On-the-Job Training," *Harvard Business Review*, vol. 44, no. 4, July–August 1966, pp. 62–72.

specialist from personnel, is concerned first with whether the employee is reasonably well satisfied with the job. How successful was the placement? Such a follow-up should also include the supervisor, to determine how well satisfied she or he is with the new employee after some work experience. If the employee has not been oversold or misled during the recruiting and hiring process, and if a good job of matching employee capabilities with job requirements has been done, the follow-up will probably indicate a successful placement. At times, dissatisfactions are cleared up by explanations and more information concerning particular points. In any event, the interest in the employee that is evidenced by the mere act of having a follow-up interview will actually help to raise the level of employee satisfaction.

SUMMARY

A hiring procedure works best on a foundation provided by job analysis, labor budgeting, and recruitment. Job analysis, through a job specification, tells us the kind of person that is necessary to fulfill properly the responsibilities of the job. An analysis of work load and of the characteristics of the present work force enables us to budget or plan our work force requirements from the standpoint of number. Skillful recruitment provides a number of reasonably satisfactory job applicants. Thus, knowing what kind of people we want and how many are to be hired, we can choose from the available job applicants.

The selection or hiring procedure is basically a series of personnel studies. We are attempting to discover the qualifications and characteristics of the job applicant. Each step in the sequence should contribute new information. Information objectives should be assigned to the step that can best extract that type of data. A preliminary interview can do little but effect a "meat-ax" type of selection—elimination of the obviously unfit. The application blank can elicit more factual information. A reference check can provide the experience of others, often information about certain qualities which defy accurate measurement by other means. Psychological tests can measure such qualities as intelligence and aptitude. To the interview is assigned a number of difficult objectives. If we can obtain information in no other way, we will usually attempt to obtain it through an interview.

The supervisory interview can also make a contribution toward successful selection and placement by adding the specialized, on-the-job knowledge of the department head. The physical examination enables us to match the applicant's physical capabilities with the job requirements. Though induction is not actually a step in selection, it is *always* the final step in the hiring process. Proper orientation and introduction, both in general for the company and specifically for the workplace, can be justified on a dollars-and-cents basis.

DISCUSSION QUESTIONS

1   Outline the total framework of the procurement function, denoting the major components.
2   Discuss "present-employee recommendations" as a prime source of new employees.
3   Indicate ways in which the entire recruiting program can be evaluated with respect to effectiveness.

4 What is a weighted application blank? How does one go about the process of setting one up?

5 In what ways can the traditional reference be improved to derive more accurate information about job applicants?

6 What impact does the induction program have upon voluntary resignations? What suggestions have been made to improve this type of program?

7 What is the relation between recruitment and such analytical, quantitative decision-making techniques as linear programming and PERT?

8 How can progress in improving selection procedures be measured by the assigned goals of the interviewing step?

9 How many interviews were specified in the procedure presented in this chapter? Indicate the goals of each.

10 Why is the hiring procedure so long and complicated? What are some of the questionable shortcuts that have been used?

SUPPLEMENTARY READING

BASSETT, Glenn A.: "The Psyche of Selection," *The Personnel Administrator*, vol. 18, no. 3, May–June 1973, pp. 19–23.

DIAMOND, Daniel E., and Hrach Bedrosian: "Job Performance and the New Credentialism," *California Management Review*, vol. 14, no. 4, Summer 1972, pp. 21–28.

HUGHES, Charles L.: "Help Wanted. Present Employees Please Apply," *Personnel*, vol. 54, no. 4, July–August 1974, pp. 36–45.

JAIN, Harish C.: "Managerial Recruitment and Selection in the Canadian Manufacturing Industry," *Public Personnel Management*, vol. 3, no. 3, May–June 1974, pp. 207–215.

SCHWAB, Donald P., and Richard L. Oliver: "Predicting Tenure with Biographical Data: Exhuming Buried Evidence," *Personnel Psychology*, vol. 27, no. 1, Spring 1974, pp. 125–128.

WANOUS, John P.: "Effects of a Realistic Job Preview on Job Acceptance, Job Attitudes, and Job Survival," *Journal of Applied Psychology*, vol. 58, no. 3, December 1973, pp. 327–332.

EIGHT

TESTS AND INTERVIEWS

Two of the more important screening devices used in hiring procedures are psychological tests and employment interviews. Both of these are quite complex in substance and difficult to utilize properly. In this text, we can only survey rather quickly each of these two selection methods in order to indicate their place in a personnel program, with particular emphasis upon the function of procurement. Both methods are adaptable to specialization and constitute occupational areas in themselves. To devise, administer, and evaluate psychological tests properly, a considerable background in industrial psychology is required. Similar training is necessary to become skilled in employment interviewing. For more detailed coverage of these two subjects, the student is referred to numberous texts and treatises on industrial psychology, group and individual testing, counseling, and interviewing.[1] Our purpose at this point is to present a brief picture of these devices, to indicate their place and importance in the personnel program, and to suggest some principles and approaches to be utilized in their administration.

PSYCHOLOGICAL TESTS

An employment test is an instrument designed to measure selected psychological factors. The purpose of this measurement process, at least in business, is to enable one to predict what a person will do in the future. Actually we are measuring what we feel to be a representative sample of human behavior and utilizing that measurement to predict future behavior. As indicated above, the factors measured are usually of the

[1]For selected sources, see Supplementary Reading at the end of this chapter.

psychological type, such as ability to reason, capacity for learning, temperament, and specific aptitudes. Usually the term also includes those tests designed to measure certain physical or motor abilities, such as manual dexterity or hand-eye coordination.

The use of tests in industry today is not so widespread as the volume of literature on the subject would lead one to believe. Their use has steadily expanded, however, and testing has definitely earned a place in a scientific selection procedure. One survey of personnel practices in business has revealed that 81 percent of 473 firms having 250 employees or more indicated that they were using one or more tests in hiring.[2] Most smaller firms do not make use of standardized tests, but rely more heavily upon interviews and background checks. Many have tended to abandon testing in the light of validation requirements made evident by the Supreme Court decision in the *Griggs v. Duke Power Company* case, a subject that will be discussed later in this chapter.

In the discussion that follows, emphasis will be given to two aspects of a testing program. First, we shall present certain basic testing principles to which a program must adhere in order to become and remain successful. Secondly, we shall survey briefly the various types of tests given in industry. The purpose of this survey is to give some conception of the nature of tests and the factors that are being measured. Obviously, no comprehensive listing of the literally thousands of tests being published and sold today could be attempted in a book of this type.[3]

Basic principles of testing

One of the first principles of testing is that tests must be selected or designed on the basis of a sound job analysis program. Since the purpose in testing is to predict future success in a job situation, the beginning point of analysis is obviously the job. What are the basic human qualifications that are required for successful job performance? We must return to the job specification. At this point a decision must be made concerning which of the required characteristics are adaptable to measurement by tests. If we have specified a requirement for a certain level of ability to reason, we can select some type of intelligence test that will measure this characteristic satisfactorily. If we have specified a requirement for some type of capacity for leadership and motivation of others, we must find out whether or not a relevant test is available or can be designed. If an important selection factor cannot be measured by a test, we shall have to measure it by means of some other technique, such as interviewing. In sum, the development of a testing program must rest on a foundation of job analysis that reveals the types and degrees of specific qualifications required for job performance. As government challenges of testing programs are increasing, it is extremely important that such programs rest on a solid foundation of job descriptions and job specifications.

A second principle of testing is to ensure that the test selected or designed for use is a reliable instrument. "Reliability" refers to the degree of *consistency* of results obtained. If a test possesses high reliability, a person who is tested a second or third time with the same test under the same conditions will obtain approximately the same score. If the results obtained vary drastically, it is doubtful if we are testing anything.

---

[2]National Industrial Conference Board, *Personnel Practices in Factory and Office: Manufacturing*, Studies in Personnel Policy, no. 194, New York, 1964, p. 14.

[3]For a comprehensive listing of tests, see O. K. Buros, *The Seventh Mental Measurements Yearbook*, The Gryphon Press, Highland Park, N.J., 1972.

Certainly, no decisions can be based on any one of these highly variable scores. If consistent scores are obtained, we are assured that we are measuring something. Whether that measurement is of value in predicting job success is another subject, that of validity.

Tests selected for use in employment must possess the characteristic of validity. Does the test do what we want it to do? Validity is highly specific in nature. A particular test may be valid for one objective and invalid for another. Thus, by means of job analysis we may have determined that a certain level of intelligence is required for adequate job performance. We select a well-known and valid intelligence test. It has been determined, through previous research, that the selected test is valid for the objective of measuring intelligence. However, we have now *altered* the objective to that of predicting success on a particular job. For this specific purpose, the test's degree of validity is generally much lower, for many other variables influence job success besides intelligence. This concept also helps to explain why no tests or group of tests can be used in hiring except in conjunction with application blanks, interviews, references, and the like. The validity of the entire selection process can be higher than the validity of the testing phase alone.

Not only is validity specific with respect to objective, but it is also specific with respect to the particular business situation. It has happened that one firm has achieved a measure of validity in using a particular test for predicting future job performance. You have determined that your company has a similar problem, that is, the selection of satisfactory personnel for the same type of job. It is dangerous to assume that the same test will be of equal validity in both situations. The factors which influence job success under certain conditions may not have equal influence under other conditions. It may happen that the same test is of no value whatsoever for prediction about the same type of job in your particular situation. It is almost certain that you will derive a different level of validity.

The specific nature of validity leads to an obvious conclusion: one must determine degree of validity for oneself. An employer can generally accept with some assurance the research of others concerning reliability, for this is a determination of the degree of precision that a particular instrument possesses; but with validity, each employer has a somewhat differing set of objectives and situations. Though too many firms do not do so, each should attempt to determine the degree of effectiveness of each testing instrument. Relying upon the claims of other companies or pointing to the reputation of the test designer does not constitute a defense when the testing program is challenged.

The degrees of validity and reliability are often presented in the form of a coefficient of correlation. These coefficients range from 0, indicating a complete absence of a relationship between two variables, to 1, which indicates a perfect relationship. With respect to reliability, if the test gives completely consistent results, it is said to have a reliability coefficient of 1. If the scores vary slightly each time given, the coefficient may drop to the .90s. When one considers the nature of reliability, it is obvious that reliability coefficients must be quite high to make the test usable for anything. If there is little reliability, there can obviously be no validity. Coefficients in the .90s are quite common for psychological tests and are acceptable. Those that drop into the .80s should be regarded with suspicion. Some place the cutoff point, below which the test will not be accepted, at .85.

The validity coefficient of correlation indicates the relationship between the test score and job performance. The test score is obtained during the hiring procedure. We must now find some means of obtaining a measure of job performance, the *criterion* by which we judge the validity of the tests. There are various indexes of job performance that can be used, such as production quantity, quality, merit ratings, salary increases received, and number of promotions received.

Perhaps the most commonly used criterion is supervisory ratings. As will be discussed in a later chapter, these ratings often suffer from low reliabilities and can vary in accuracy from supervisor to supervisor because of difference in skills, prejudices, leniency, and severity. More concrete and quantifiable criteria are preferred, such as output, turnover, absenteeism, lateness, and accidents. However, these are sometimes not available and may be incomplete or even irrelevant to job success. It is obvious that the specific criterion selected can influence greatly the degree of validity determined. When we select a specific criterion, such as production quantity, what we are saying is that our test can predict success with respect to production. A person selected on the basis of one test for this job may still be a failure because of not measuring up to other requirements. Thus, many firms, in considering the multiplicity of criteria, have turned to the use of test batteries to measure the multiple facets of job success. Multiple correlations are required between many tests and many criteria.

In validating our tests we must also decide upon the group of personnel that should be studied, present employees or new employees. If present employees are used, the result is termed "concurrent validity"; if new applicants constitute the data source, we are developing "predictive validity." The latter is considered to be the more accurate. Using present employees means that we can obtain the correlations quickly by administering the selected tests to them. We already have the criteria of job success, such as production records and ratings. The problem here, however, is that of the desire to do well on the test. Present employees *already* have a job and may regard such testing procedures with either indifference or great suspicion. A considerable amount of orientation will be required. In addition, present employees are usually older and more experienced—which sometimes leads to more generous supervisory ratings than their ability would justify. They also have been previously selected by some type of screening process, and thus the range in abilities is more restricted than it would be for new applicants. We lack information on how effectively people making lower test scores would have fared on the job. In many instances, we would have few if any representatives of minority groups on the work force, thus precluding subgroup validations, as suggested by guidelines published by the Equal Employment Opportunity Commission. Using new applicants would solve the problem of incentive, as well as provide a wider range of predictor scores. However, the problem of obtaining the criterion has been created. We shall have to hire various types of people and wait to observe their job performance in order to correlate it with the test scores. This will involve a considerable length of time.

If a test predicts future job success perfectly, it has a validity coefficient of 1. The persons who score highest on the tests turn out to be the most competent on the job, or at least in the phase of the job represented by the selected criterion. If, by using the test, we are still operating at no higher level than sheer chance, the correlation is 0.

The sample used in the validation process must be sufficiently large to reduce the standard error. "The most efficient of our correlation coefficients, the Pearsonian, has a standard error which is equal to .10 when the 'true' coefficient is zero and the group from which it is obtained numbers 100."[4] This means that a correlation of plus .10 would arise by chance once in every six times, and one of plus .196 would occur by chance once in every twenty times. With smaller groups, this error will be larger, and Bennett feels that studies of fewer than fifty employees do not deserve publication in the literature. If, however, the "true" correlation is greater than 0, the standard error decreases slightly.

Many years of experience have shown that validity coefficients seldom exceed .50, and are higher in predicting training success than job success. "Taking all jobs as a whole . . . it can be said that by and large the maximal power of tests to predict success in training is of the order of .50, and to predict success on the job itself is of the order of .35."[5] The range of validity coefficients discovered by Ghiselli in a survey of published research was from .27 to .59 for training criteria and from .16 to .46 for job success criteria. Over the years, there has been little movement toward greater validities.

The reasons for this prediction ceiling lie on both sides; the human being is an open system and works within a larger, varied system. "The same digit span score can be obtained by a strategy of grouping or by a wax-like memory . . . the same score on a verbal analogy test by a good vocabulary or by superior ability to see the relationships. . . ."[6] Thus the same score on a particular test may come from two people using very different basic processes. These processes, rather than the test score, are the basic determinants of training or job success.

On the other side, job success means different things in different environments. In a firm with an authoritarian climate, the "good" employee will be different from the "good" employee in a democratically administered organization. In addition, various research studies have *not* shown specific types of behavior to be always successful. In the same organization, it is entirely possible that both autocratic supervisors and permissive superiors will achieve the same results as measured by quantity and quality of output. Thus, the other half of the equation, the criterion of job success, also contributes to the creation of a prediction ceiling.

The relationship between test scores and criteria of job success can be presented in other ways than coefficients. Figure 8-1 portrays this information by means of a scatter diagram. Such a diagram is of assistance in determining the critical score required to pass the test. In Figure 8-1, if the minimum acceptable score is placed at 30, we should have eliminated nineteen employees, sixteen of whom were rated 4 and below by their supervisors. This score would have prevented the hiring of three employees who were rated 5 and above and none who were rated 6 through 9. Thus, there is a usable relationship between test scores and the ratings of supervisors. A critical score of 30 will permit most of the better employees to be retained and most of the poorer ones to be rejected.

There are numerous other principles underlying personnel testing programs, such as the following: (1) tests should be regarded as additional selection instruments and are not to be used as the sole basis for hiring decisions; (2) the administration of tests must be controlled and standardized in order to make test results comparable; and (3)

[4]George K. Bennett, "Factors Affecting the Value of Validation Studies," *Personnel Psychology*, vol. 22, no. 3, Autumn 1969, p. 267.

[5]E. E. Ghiselli, *The Validity of Occupational Aptitude Tests*, John Wiley and Sons, Inc., New York, 1966, p. 125.

[6]Edward A. Rundquist, "The Prediction Ceiling," *Personnel Psychology*, vol. 22, no. 2, Summer 1969, p. 11.

Figure 8-1

SCATTER DIAGRAM OF TEST SCORES AND SUPERVISORY RATINGS

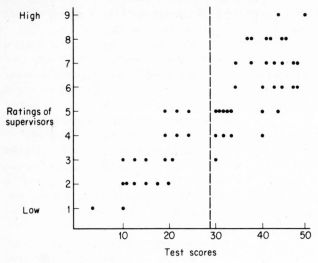

— — — — —, possible critical score

insofar as possible, tests should possess face validity in addition to statistical validity; that is, the appropriateness of the test questions to the task at hand should be apparent to the candidate.

Types of tests

Various ways of classifying psychological tests bring out and emphasize certain characteristics. Tests may be taken by pen or pencil or by trying out through performance, e.g., a typing test. Most tests have time limits and are designated "speed" tests; while others, classified as "power" tests, have no time limit but questions asked become progressively more difficult. Tests may also be classified by the type of questions, e.g., objective, descriptive, or projective. For the present purpose of briefly sketching the nature of psychological testing in business, we may classify the various methods as (1) intelligence tests, (2) aptitude tests, (3) achievement tests, (4) interest tests, and (5) personality tests. We shall discuss each type. In the previously cited survey, of the 384 firms having a testing program, 74 percent used intelligence tests; 30 percent, interest tests; 38 percent, personality tests; 76 percent, mechanical aptitude tests; and 92 percent, clerical tests.[7]

INTELLIGENCE TESTS The intelligence test is probably the most widely administered standardized test in industry. It is also one of the first types developed by the psychologists. Intelligence has been given various definitions. One of the first intelli-

[7]NICB, op. cit., p. 14.

gence tests, the Binet-Simon, assumed that intelligence was a general trait, a capacity for comprehension and reasoning. Thurstone later differentiated primarily mental abilities from the general trait of intelligence and created more specialized types of intelligence tests; they were reasoning, word fluency, verbal comprehension, numbers, memory, and space.[8] The Wechsler-Bellevue Intelligence Scale utilizes a multiple measurement of such factors as digit spans both forward and backward, information known, comprehension, vocabulary, picture arrangement, and object assembly. This test can be used to score general intelligence quantitatively and underlying character structure in a qualitative fashion. As such, it has been used in the assessment of both intelligence and personality.

In a survey conducted by Ghiselli and Brown of several studies of the use of intelligence tests in business, it was discovered that the importance of intelligence to job success varies with the type of job.[9] Median validity coefficients tended to be higher when selecting skilled workers (.55), supervisors (.40), and clerical workers (.35). They were substantially lower in predicting job success for unskilled workers (.08) and sales clerks (.09).

Intelligence tests, though among the more widely used, have come under serious attack as discriminating against minority-group members with little or no validation being effected. The general measure, in particular, suffers from imprecision. For example, occupants of both drafting and secretarial types of jobs tend to have about equal scores on general intelligence tests. However, those in drafting tend to have higher component scores in spatial relations and numbers, while those holding secretarial positions have higher component scores in perceptual speed and verbal fluency. Thus, the general intelligence test may prove to be too dull a tool to utilize for procurement in a society that proposes to eliminate inadvertent and unintended discrimination.

APTITUDE TESTS   Whereas intelligence is frequently defined as a general trait, an aptitude is a more specific capacity. "Aptitude tests measure whether an individual has the capacity or latent ability to learn a given job if he is given adequate training."[10] As suggested, the use of aptitude tests is advisable when an applicant has had little or no experience along the lines of the job opening. We are interested in selecting persons who will show a higher degree of success after the training period.

Examples of specific capacities or aptitudes are as follows: mechanical, clerical, linguistic, musical, and academic. In addition to these examples, some psychologists include in this category certain motor capacities such as finger dexterity, hand dexterity, and hand-eye coordination.

Two of the more widely known mechanical-aptitude tests are the Bennett Test of Mechanical Comprehension and the Stenquist Mechanical Aptitude Test. Questions are asked which fall into the general area of understanding mechanical relationships. Some questions relate to knowledge of actual shop machines, tools, and similar

[8]L. L. Thurstone and T. G. Thurstone, "Factorial Studies of Intelligence," *Psychometric Monograph*, no. 2, University of Chicago Press, 1941, p. 37.

[9]Edwin E. Ghiselli and Clarence W. Brown, "The Effectiveness of Intelligence Tests in the Selection of Workers," *Journal of Applied Psychology*, vol. 32, no. 6, December 1948, pp. 575–580.

[10]Joseph Tiffin and Ernest J. McCormick, *Industrial Psychology*, 6th ed., Prentice-Hall, Inc., Englewood Cliffs, N.J., 1974, p. 137.

equipment. Others deal with certain practices such as the type of fastener to be used to fasten a board to a box or a hinge on a door. In one study conducted by Tiffin, a correlation of .36 was found between the Bennett Test and a supervisor's ratings of job performance of forty-seven paper-machine operators.[11] Such a correlation was usable in differentiating the better employees by means of the test.

Tests of clerical aptitude deal with questions concerning office vocabulary, arithmetic, spelling, and detail checking. There are many tests in the manipulative and dexterity field. The O'Connor Finger Dexterity Test requires the applicant to place three pins, 1 inch in length and 0.072 inch in diameter, into a hole 0.196 inch in diameter. The holes are spaced $1/2$ inch apart, ten in each row. The reliability of this test has been found to be .98. A correlation obtained with the Otis Test of Mental Ability was .07, thus indicating that these two tests are measuring widely different characteristics.

Business managers are much concerned with the task of identifying potential leaders from among rank and file employees. While interviews and intelligence tests are widely used in this regard, the heart of some programs, such as that of American Telephone and Telegraph, is a series of test situations that *simulate* actual managerial problems.[12] Procter and Gamble has designed "MATRIX," standing for Management Trial Exercise, to provide a realistic simulated exercise in plant management.[13] Decisions are required in employee relations, community relations, and human resources planning, and they are administered in an "in-basket" fashion. The test has been established not only as a means of identifying management potential, but also of orienting potential managers (college graduates) to the pressures and problems of a plant manager.

There are, of course, many other examples of tests of aptitude. The examples cited illustrate the nature of these tests. The correlation coefficients given emphasize the necessity for validating tests of this type in the situations in which they are to be used. An aptitude is a capacity to learn in one specific direction; thus an aptitude test will not ordinarily show an unusually high correlation with future success.

ACHIEVEMENT TESTS Whereas aptitude is a capacity to learn in the future, achievement is concerned with what one has accomplished. When applicants claim to know something, an achievement test is given to measure how well they know it. Trade tests are the most common type of achievement test given. Questions have been prepared and tested for such trades as asbestos workers, punch-press operators, electricians, and machinists. There are, of course, many unstandardized achievement tests given in industry, such as a typing or dictation test for an applicant for a stenographic position. Obviously all tests, aptitude and intelligence included, reflect some degree of achievement on the part of the applicant. If the test—achievement, intelligence, or aptitude— will enable us to predict job success, its specific classification as to type is of secondary importance. With the courts demanding a more demonstrable relationship between test content and job performance, it is predicted that the usage of achievement tests will grow at the expense of the more intangible general intelligence, aptitude, and personality tests.

[11]Ibid., p. 119.

[12]"Sharper Tools for the Talent Hunt," *Business Week*, Mar. 27, 1965, p. 70.

[13]John W. Plattner and Lowell W. Herron, *Simulation: Its Use in Employee Selection and Training*, American Management Association, Management Bulletin 20, 1962.

INTEREST TESTS   Most people realize that a person who is interested in a job or task will do much better than one who is uninterested. At times superior interest offsets lack of basic ability. Interest is a factor that should contribute to success on the job.

Two of the more widely used tests of interest are the Strong Vocational Interests Blank and the Kuder Preference Record. These tests utilize two basically different approaches. The Strong has been validated in specific occupations; that is, it determines the degree of agreement between the applicant's interests and the interests of successful personnel in specific professions and occupations. The applicant is asked whether he likes, dislikes, or is indifferent to many examples of school subjects, occupations, amusements, peculiarities of people, and particular activities. Patterns of interests have been developed for some sixty occupations, among which are accountant, architect, dentist, engineer, personnel manager, production manager, and teacher. When instructed to fake specific interests, individuals can increase their scores by one to five standard deviations, suggesting extreme caution in the use of the Strong in a selection situation. However, research with respect to the degree of faking that does occur under actual selection conditions indicates that "there is neither a significant nor consistent tendency for applicants to increase their selection scores."[14] Thus, test-taking behavior under artificial faking instructions may not parallel that usually practiced under actual conditions.

The Kuder Preference Record is scored in terms of more basic interest groupings. These areas are mechanical, computation, scientific, persuasive, artistic, literary, musical, social service, and clerical.[15] Techniques of scoring the Preference Record have been developed to differentiate between the honestly answered blanks and those designed to make a good impression. Methods also exist for identifying the carelessly or randomly completed test. Both interests and personality measures are of considerably greater value in counseling situations where the subject is sincerely interested in finding out more about herself or himself in an attempt to solve pressing personal problems.

PERSONALITY TESTS   The importance of personality to job success is undeniable. Often an individual who possesses the intelligence, aptitude, and experience for a certain job has failed because of inability to get along with and motivate other people. As a result, there has been a considerable amount of interest in the possibility of developing some measurement of personality traits in order to aid in selection and placement.

Personality tests are similar to interest tests in that they, also, involve a serious problem of obtaining honest answers. Such tests have been of great use in counseling situations. In the employment situation, however, the applicant is highly motivated to make a good impression. Consequently an applicant is often led to alter answers when that is possible. In one study of the Humm-Wadsworth Temperament Scale, sixty-five college students were asked to answer the 318 questions on the test as frankly and honestly as possible. After this they were asked to answer as if they were applying for a job. The desirable personality traits showed a marked increase and the undesirable a substantial decrease.[16]

---

[14]N. M. Abrahams, Idell Neumann, and W. H. Githens, "Faking Vocational Interests: Simulated versus Real Life Motivation," *Personnel Psychology*, vol. 24, no. 1, Spring 1971, pp. 5–12.

[15]*Kuder Preference Record: Vocational*, Science Research Associates, Inc., Chicago, Ill.

[16]Tiffin and McCormick, op. cit., p. 175.

In an attempt to obtain a more realistic assessment of personality, projective tests have been designed. "The essential feature of a projective technique is that it evokes from the subject what is, in various ways, expressive of his private world and personality process."[17] One of the more popular projective tests is the Thematic Apperception Test. The subject is shown a series of pictures, one at a time, and is asked to make up as dramatic a story as he can for each. Examples of such scenes are (1) a short, elderly woman stands with her back turned to a tall young man, and (2) a boy lies on the floor next to a couch with a revolver by his side. The subject is asked to tell what led up to the event, what is happening at the moment, what the characters are feeling and thinking, and what the outcome of the situation will be. The psychologist analyzes the story in terms of such factors as length, vocabulary, cohesiveness, bizarre ideas, plot, mood, and symbols used. It has been charged that the resulting description is as similar to the personality of the psychologist as it is to the subject. The well-known Rorschach test is also projective in technique; the subject is asked to organize unstructured inkblots into meaningful concepts. The resulting projections are analyzed in terms of such factors as use of color and shadings, use of part or the whole of a blot, seeing of movement, and definiteness and appropriateness of forms seen. An integrated picture of the subject's personality is then formulated. The use of all personality tests, whether of the projective or questionnaire types, requires the services of a trained psychologist.

Ghiselli and Barthol conducted a survey of the testing literature for research studies on personality tests in business situations. They found that the average of the coefficients in relating personality test scores to job success was not high, ranging from .36 for sales clerks to .14 for general superintendent.[18] Many feel more confident with projections based on biographical data obtained through more sophisticated application blanks. In assessing personality characteristics of potential managers, greater efforts are being directed toward the use of multiple simulations in a specially designed assessment center.[19]

To test or not to test

Because an overwhelming preponderance of the larger organizations utilize some type of testing program, it would appear that testing will always make a positive contribution to hiring effectiveness. Previous discussion would suggest that applied research must be undertaken in each case to prove worth, that face validity should not be used to the exclusion of statistical validity.

The worth of a testing program will depend not only upon validity coofficients, but upon the selection ratio as well. If there is but one applicant to one opening, testing will not be necessary. A third important factor is the range of performance existing in the presently untested group of employees. If the best performer is ten times as good as the worst, testing can make a material contribution in screening future applicants. If the work environment is closely structured, as in the case of an assembly line operation, the performance range may well be one of 10 to 9. Testing in this situation is

[17]L. K. Frank, *Projective Methods*, Charles C Thomas, Publisher, Springfield, Ill., 1948, p. 47.
[18]Edwin E. Ghiselli and Richard P. Barthol, "The Validity of Personality Inventories in the Selection of Employees," *Journal of Applied Psychology*, vol. 37, no. 1, 1953, p. 18.
[19]See Chap. 9.

not likely to improve hiring effectiveness. Haire points out that if the selection ratio is 10 to 4 (ten applicants for four openings), if the test's validity coefficient is .45, and if the range of performance among present personnel is a not unusual 3 to 2, the improvement in hiring effectiveness will be about 4 percent.[20] He suggests that performance improvements through good training and supervision of unscreened personnel could easily be 30 to 40 percent, thus downgrading the role of selecting in comparison with subsequent training and supervision. Where the range of possible performance qualities is great, such as in executive and management positions, screening through testing can easily improve placement effectiveness as much as 10 to 15 percent.

William H. Whyte, Jr., suggests that testing, particularly personality testing, constitutes an invasion of privacy. In his popular book, *The Organization Man*, he provides a psychological set to enable the applicant to pass any personality questionnaire, thereby evading the firm's invasion of his privacy.[21]

Research concerning the seriousness of the invasion of privacy contention does not indicate that it is a widespread, general phenomenon. It is more a matter of significant subgroupings. In one study, younger females expressed annoyance at 35 out of a total of 361 questions; older males found all but 4 questions to be acceptable.[22] In a second study of approximately 1,400 subjects, more precise patterns were encountered: (1) older employees were less concerned about questions concerning values and interests than were younger, (2) the more educated were less concerned about personal history items but more concerned with questions about personal finances, and (3) female employees were less concerned with personal financial inquiries but more concerned with topics involving personal history data.[23] Greatest general sensitivity was experienced with questions concerning religious beliefs, racial or ethnic background, description of brothers and sisters, loans being paid, savings, other sources of income, and how income is budgeted. It should be recalled that inquiries about the first two items are prohibited by law.

Others are concerned about the use of polygraphs or lie detectors in attempts to verify information provided on the application blank without the necessity of undertaking a background check. Sometimes the applicant, faced with a week's delay before beginning work, and the organization, faced with an expensive background check, will both agree to quicker and cheaper polygraph checks on the accuracy of the information given. Such tests are also used for making periodic security spot checks in organizations where theft is likely, as well as in situations where a specific investigation of a theft is being undertaken. The Zale Corporation, a retail jewelry chain, reports that 10 to 15 percent of applicants for positions in that organization fail to pass the polygraph test.[24] Another company reported that 7 percent of all applicants for plant-protection jobs were discovered to be unfit on the basis of the test.[25]

---

[20]Mason Haire, *Psychology in Management*, 2d ed., McGraw-Hill Book Company, New York, 1964, p. 135.

[21]William H. Whyte, Jr., *The Organization Man*, Doubleday & Company, Inc., Garden City, N.Y., 1957, pp. 449–456.

[22]Ronald C. Winkler and Theodore W. Mathews, "How Employees Feel about Personality Tests," *Personnel Journal*, vol. 46, no. 8, September 1967, pp. 490–492.

[23]Bernard L. Rosenbaum, "Attitude toward Invasion of Privacy in the Personnel Selection Process and Job Applicant Demographic and Personality Correlates," *Journal of Applied Psychology*, vol. 58, no. 3, December 1973, pp. 333–338.

[24]"Corporate Lie Detectors Come under Fire," *Business Week*, Jan. 13, 1973, p. 88.

[25]"Lie Detector Seeks Out Misfits," *Factory*, vol. 119, no. 1, January 1961, p.240.

The use of polygraphs in employment have been objected to on the basis of invasion of privacy, self-incrimination, violation of human dignity, and questionable accuracy of measurement in the hands of unskilled practitioners. Twelve states have laws prohibiting the use of polygraphs as a condition of employment. Only 16 states have polygraph licensing laws stipulating minimum educational and training backgrounds as necessary for operating the device. Though the justification of any test must first rest on proved contributions to hiring effectiveness, any business practice is subject to veto by society. That polygraphs are not fully in good standing is indicated by the fact that their results cannot as yet be entered as evidence in civil procedures. Labor arbitrators of grievance disputes generally show a considerable distaste for the use of lie detectors in disciplinary and discharge cases. Employees who are discharged for refusal to take the test are often given their jobs back by the arbitrators. Those finally discharged for this reason are seldom disqualified from receiving unemployment compensation by state agencies. Though the employer justifiably is concerned about more effective hiring and the prevention of theft and embezzlement, it would appear that the trend in social values may well restrict the choice of screening instruments.

Finally, there is a growing concern about inadvertent discrimination against various "culturally deprived" groups when using standardized psychological tests. It is contended that the makeup and validation of most such tests have been geared to the majority, white, middle-class segment of our population. This problem first came to general public attention in the famed Motorola, Inc., case in 1963 when that company had rejected a black applicant who had failed a pre-employment ability test. Research has suggested that different predictive validities exist for different subgroups of job applicants.

In a study by Ruda and Albright of 1,034 applicants screened for office jobs, it was found that (1) high scores on a weighted application blank were predictive of low turnover for both blacks and whites, (2) high scores on the Wonderlic Personnel Test were associated with high turnover for whites but not for blacks, and (3) there was no predictive validity for either group on the job performance criterion.[26] This company had been giving preference to high Wonderlic scorers, and research indicated that the test was being used incorrectly for whites and was irrelevant for blacks.

In a second study, reported by Lopez, three selection instruments were used to screen applicants for the job of toll collector; these were a clerical speed and accuracy test, a mental ability test, and a standardized ten-minute biographical data interview.[27] Criteria of job success used in the validation process were absence rates, toll-accuracy rate, continued employment, and supervisor's ratings. In the study of 182 toll collectors, it was found that black applicants achieved significantly lower scores on the mental ability test and the interviewer's rating sheet. However, there was *no* significant difference in job performance between white and black employees. On other criteria, high scores on the predictors meant poor attendance, high toll accuracy, and high turnover for blacks, and only poor toll accuracy and high turnover for the white group. If the supervisory rating is used as a single criterion, the two tests were predictive of job success for the whites but showed no significant relationship, pro or con, for the black

---

[26]Edward Ruda and Lewis E. Albright, "Racial Differences on Selection Instruments Related to Subsequent Job Performance," *Personnel Psychology*, vol. 21, no. 1, Spring 1968, p. 31.

[27]Felix M. Lopez, Jr., "Current Problems in Test Performance of Job Applicants," *Personnel Psychology*, vol. 19, no. 1, Spring 1966, pp. 10–18.

group. The interview was predictive for black job success but showed no relationship for the white group. It is apparent that different hiring practices could be justified depending upon the groupings utilized. As indicated in the following section, current guidelines issued by the Equal Employment Opportunity Commission require the compilation of validity statistics for significant minority groups within the enterprise.

Despite the frequently encountered finding of different validity coefficients for various subgroups, some researchers have indicated that the jury is still out on the issue because of the widespread lack of proper test validation in most organizations. A nonvalidated test frequently excludes a disproportionate number of blacks for reasons unrelated to job performance. Analysis of 160 validity coefficients in thirteen research studies dealing with black-white validities in employment revealed that 100 were not significant for either group.[28] In thirty-three cases where there was a difference, the criterion utilized tended to be supervisory ratings rather than more objective measures such as output, quality, attendance, and turnover. The criterion is as vulnerable to possibilities of bias as predictor. "What results is that nonvalidity (or unknown validity) masquerades as differential validity."[29] Nevertheless, even if true differential validities are not as widespread as reported, even the occasional instance can have undesirable social repercussions. Probably few personnel programs have ever been harmed from over research.

Testing and the law

As indicated in preceding chapters, Title VII of the Civil Rights Act of 1964 prohibits discrimination in employment because of race, color, religion, sex, or national origin. Psychological testing, perhaps because of its presumed objectivity, has received a substantial amount of challenge and criticism by aggrieved applicants and the EEOC (Equal Employment Opportunity Commission). In one year, 20 percent of the complaints filed under Title VII concerned the use of tests, two-thirds of which were decided in favor of the aggrieved. The Commission has received substantial backing from various federal courts, e.g., *Griggs v. Duke Power Company*, wherein the Supreme Court not only declared a high school diploma stipulation illegal because of unproved relationship to job performance, but also directed its verdict toward similar use of the Wonderlic Personnel Test and the Bennett Test of Mechanical Comprehension. In 1973, a federal district court ordered Detroit Edison to pay $4 million and Local 223, Utility Workers of America, to pay $250,000 in punitive damages to blacks victimized by union-supported company practices in hiring. In addition, the company was ordered to increase the number of black employees from 8 percent to 30 percent, and to halt the use of intelligence and aptitude tests which worked to exclude blacks with no substantiating validation data.

The thrust of both the Commission and the courts is to require personnel managers to provide validating proof of the effectiveness of procurement practices. Among various guidelines established by the Commission, perhaps the foremost one concerns the manner of establishing validity. *Empirical statistical validity*, showing a significant relationship between the predictor and specific measures of job performance, is the

[28]Virginia R. Boehm, "Negro-White Differences in Validity of Employment and Training Selection Procedures: Summary of Research Evidence," *Journal of Applied Psychology*, vol. 56, no. 1, February 1972, pp. 33–39.

[29]Ibid., p. 37.

preferred approach. Within this category, "predictive validity" studies on incoming applicants are deemed to be better evidence. If "concurrent validity" based on present employees is utilized, there may be no representative groups of minorities among the work force; in this event, only "provisional" acceptance is granted. In the event that empirical studies are impracticable, the Commission has established the use of *content* and *construct* validities. In content validity, the test itself must be a representative sample of job duties, e.g., a typing test for a clerk, a welding test for a welder. In using this approach, the firm must provide evidence in the form of job descriptions that supports the use of selected content testing. In construct validity, a test is developed to measure an ability or trait less directly observable than in content validity, e.g., a test of spatial relations ability is potentially usable for jobs requiring blueprint reading. Validation of such a test requires that the test actually measure the trait in question. Evidence must also be provided that the trait is in fact required for job performance. In all statistical studies, the Commission expects the obtained correlation coefficients to be significant at the .05 level, that is, where there is only one chance in twenty that the correlation was obtained by chance.

With respect to minority employees, the Commission requires generation of separate validation studies for each minority group. Where a test is valid for two groups but one group tends to obtain higher test scores without a corresponding difference in job performance, multiple cutoff scores in hiring must be set to predict the same probability of job success. The Supreme Court, in the *Griggs v. Duke Power Company* case, frequently referred to Aesop's fable of the fox, stork, and shallow dish of milk. Though a firm may protest that the same test and cutoff score are fair for all, the Court decreed that the vessel in which the milk is proffered be one *all* seekers can use. The Commission requires graphical presentation of cutoff scores in order to ascertain their impact upon separate groups of employees.

In general, the federal courts have established the premise that "good intentions" constitutes no defense against an accusation of discrimination. If a practice which operates to exclude a minority group cannot be shown to be significantly related to job performance, the practice is prohibited. "Built-in headwinds" must be removed. The law does not guarantee a job to every person regardless of qualifications. Qualifications, in fact, now stand out as the *single* major legal basis for making hiring decisions. But selection devices must be "useful servants" in this regard, and not "masters of reality."

A study of private organization practices in the aftermath of the *Griggs v. Duke Power Company* case shows some changes in company personnel programs.[30] Prior to the case, 53 of 60 companies were using testing; after the case, the number had decreased to 45, many of the smaller companies abandoning such programs. Prior to the case, 14 of the 53 testing companies were not properly validating their tests; afterward, this number had decreased to only 2. Concerning predictions for the future, some personnel managers foresaw a similar EEOC crackdown on all selection devices (weighted application blanks, references, interviews, etc.), with ultimate abandonment of selection programs in favor of random hiring, subject to a probationary period. If this should occur, those firms that do continue to utilize properly validated selection

---

[30]Donald J. Petersen, "The Impact of Duke Power on Testing," *Personnel*, vol. 51, no. 2, March–April 1974, pp. 30–37.

devices will be able to skim the cream off the available labor force. The wiser course is to practice the *profession* of personnel management.

INTERVIEWING

Interviewing is probably the most widely used single method of selection. This preference exists despite the subjectivity of the interviewing process. Many studies have indicated that two or more interviewers often disagree concerning the evaluation of a candidate. As an example, a study of the practices of 100 managers in the life insurance industry showed a great deal of disagreement as to favorability of items of information and, consequently, disagreement concerning the evaluation of applicants.[31] On two applicant items, "being active in eight outside groups" and "feeling that he's gotten nowhere for the last five years," the distribution was bimodal; that is, almost as many managers considered these items highly favorable as would no longer consider the man for a job. In rating seven hypothetical "applicants" the average correlation between pairs of raters was .16, and each of the applicants was ranked best by some raters and worst by others. The overall conclusion was that interviewers do not hold an identical picture of the ideal applicant for the job of insurance agent.

A substantial amount of subjectivity, and therefore unreliability, is to be expected from interviewing when it is used as a tool of evaluation; one human being is evaluating another under somewhat strained circumstances. The more objective factors have been removed from the interviewer's province and allocated to such steps as application blanks, tests, and physical examinations. Things which cannot be measured otherwise must be measured in the interview. There is nothing wrong with this; it is a sound principle of personnel selection. But the fact that some disagreement results among various interviewers is no sound basis upon which to indict the interview as a basic selection technique. For example, in a study of the ability of interviewers to distinguish between honest and dishonest interviewees, it was concluded that their accuracy was better than chance in spite of the fact that the same cues frequently led to opposite conclusions.[32] Intuitive judgments were made with a degree of accuracy; however, they were far more accurate in identifying the dishonest interviewee. Later research showed that the accuracy could be further *improved* by *reading* a recording of the interview.[33] Evidently, the presence of the interviewee serves to lessen the concentration of the interviewer on what is actually being said.

The concentration of the interviewer is also affected by the larger control system of which he or she is a part. As suggested by one comprehensive review of decision making through interviewing, the process is often a search for *negative* information.[34] Various studies show a greater impact upon the final decision by information that is

[31]Eugene C. Mayfield and Robert E. Carlson, "Selection Interview Decision: First Results from a Long-term Research Project," *Personnel Psychology*, vol. 19, no. 1, Spring 1966, pp. 41–53.

[32] Norman R. F. Maier, "Sensitivity to Attempts at Deception in an Interview Situation," *Personnel Psychology*, vol. 19, no. 1, Spring 1966, pp. 55–56.

[33]Norman R. F. Maier and James A. Thurber, "Accuracy of Judgments of Deception When an Interview Is Watched, Heard, and Read," *Personnel Psychology*, vol. 21, no. 1, Spring 1968, pp. 23–30.

[34]Edward B. Webster, *Decision-making in Employment Interview*, McGill University, Industrial Relations Centre, Montreal, 1964.

unfavorable to the hire. This could well issue from an organizational reward system that criticizes the interviewer for recommending misfits while failing to praise the interviewer when the decision is correct. Consequently, interviewers acquire a sensitivity to negative information that leads to a general attitude of caution.

In the American Telephone and Telegraph management assessment center, the reliability of the interview was vastly improved by separating the information-gathering function from its later assessment.[35] Each two-hour assessment interview was recorded on tape and later evaluated by multiple raters. The median reliability coefficient for college-educated interviewees was .82; for the noncollege group, it was .72. Ratings were made on eighteen different variables with the higher reliabilities being attained for forcefulness, oral communication skills, need for security, need for advancement, and social objectivity. The lower reliabilities were obtained from assessments of behavioral flexibility, ability to delay gratification, range of interests, and Bell System value orientation. This separation of collection and evaluation may have contributed to the improvements in reliability. The intangible objectives that are assigned to the interview are important to job success, and some evaluation by a trained person is preferable to no evaluation at all.

It has been found in many employment situations that proper training of the interviewer and better construction of the interview will contribute substantially to improved reliability and validity. Seventeen years of experience in interviewing applicants for the job of stock broker, or customers' man, were summarized by Ghiselli. Using the criterion of survival with the company for a three-year period, his interview ratings correlated with the criterion at the level of .35, a figure that compares quite well with validity coefficients often reported from psychological testing. When corrected for restriction of range, since Ghiselli interviewed only those already screened by the personnel officer and other managers, the correlation rose to .51. His conclusion is that "The ordinary personnel interview is not necessarily and invariably invalid, but rather that its validity may be at least equal to, if not greater than, the validity of tests."[36] After examining over three hundred articles in the psychological literature, Mayfield is still quite critical of the validity of interviews.[37] He did find, however, that those studies reporting the greater degrees of reliability were characterized by the use of structured formats. Interviewing is largely an art, and considerable improvements in reliability and validity can be effected through proper training of the interviewer and proper ordering of the interviewing process.

Types of interviews

In general, there are two types of interviews, guided and unguided. Alternate titles sometimes used are "directed and nondirected" and "patterned and unpatterned." In the guided interview, a list of questions is prepared based on an analysis of the job

---

[35]Donald L. Grant and Douglas W. Bray, "Contributions of the Interview to Assessment of Management Potential," *Journal of Applied Psychology*, vol. 55, no. 1, 1969, p. 28.

[36]Edwin E. Ghiselli, "The Validity of a Personnel Interview," *Personnel Psychology*, vol. 19, no. 4, Winter 1966, p. 394.

[37]E. C. Mayfield, "The Selection Interview: A Revaluation of Published Research," *Personnel Psychology*, vol. 17, no. 3, Autumn 1964, pp. 239–260.

specification. Such a list is quite helpful to the untrained interviewer, but with the passage of time and development of skill, one tends to depart from this detailed pattern. A survey of 273 firms revealed that only 26 percent used a patterned interview form.[38] The typical employment interview is guided, nonetheless, as its average length is 30 minutes for plant employees and 45 minutes for office employees.

The unguided interview is more often used in situations other than hiring, such as counseling, processing of grievances, and exit interviews. This type of interview is largely unplanned, and the interviewee does most of the talking. On the surface, this would seem to be an easier job for the interviewer, but actually it involves a considerably higher degree of skill if the objectives of the interview are to be accomplished. The theory of the unguided interview is that the interviewee will reveal more of her or his desires and problems. The greater use of this type is by skilled counselors in seeking to help disturbed people. Advice and reassurance are avoided, and listening is emphasized. It is often found that release of emotional tension through talking to someone is the major value of such interviews. A permissive atmosphere is most important, and such an atmosphere is difficult to create in the normal business situations by any except staff counselors. Although the typical employment interview is guided, the use of the unguided approach for higher types of job openings is not unknown. More time is devoted to interviewing the candidate, frequently by many different interviewers. In the study cited above, the average length of the unguided employment interview was 90 minutes for college graduates, 2 hours for engineers, and 3 hours for supervisors and executives.

Another basis for classifying interviews is the situation in which the interview is conducted. We are discussing here primarily the employment interview. In addition to this type, there is the counseling interview, the merit-rating or appraisal interview, the grievance interview, and the exit interview. A list of this kind emphasizes the fact that the interview is a basic management tool that is used in various situations. Thus, even though the staff-specialist interviewer is expected to be most expert, each manager must interview another person from time to time. The following principles of interviewing should therefore be of interest and concern to all managers.

Principles of interviewing

There are many principles of good interviewing, and it is helpful to classify them in some manner to facilitate their retention. Perhaps the most useful means of classification is by the typical sequence of functions that occur within the interview: (1) preparation, (2) setting, (3) conduct of the interview, (4) close, and (5) evaluation.[39] The following is a discussion of the principles of interviewing for each of the steps.

PREPARATION   There should be preparation of some type for all interviews, scheduled or unscheduled. Obviously, a considerable amount of planning is needed for interviews that are scheduled in advance, such as employment and appraisal interviews. However,

[38]Milton M. Mandell, *The Employment Interview*, American Management Association Research Study 47, New York, 1961, p. 23.

[39]After that found in Paul Pigors and C. A. Myers, *Personnel Administration*, 6th ed., McGraw-Hill Book Company, New York, 1969, pp. 272–282.

many interviews conducted on the spot, such as the initial processing of a grievance, allow for no preparation. In spite of the fact that the degree of preparation may be less than when one has advance notice, the following principles are still applicable:

1 *Determine the specific objectives of the interview.* In employment interviews, some decision must be made as to which information objectives are to be accomplished in the interview. There should be little overlap with other employment steps; the interviewer should not, for example, repeat all of the basic information questions given on the application blank. In general, the employment-interviewing objectives are largely intangible, dealing with such traits as character, social adjustment, attitude, oral expression, and capacity for growth and advancement. As we have noted earlier, the intangibility of the objectives contributes to the unreliability of interviewing ratings.

The objectives of other types of interviews should be similarly spelled out. The general purpose of a grievance interview is resolution of the controversy to the satisfaction of both the employee and the company. The purpose of an exit interview is to obtain the real reason for quitting the employ of the company, and, at times, it is an attempt to persuade an employee to remain. The purpose of an appraisal interview is to inform the employee of his or her standing concerning performance and to motivate the individual toward improvement. Thus, in a sense, every interview is capable of being preplanned with respect to objectives.

2 *Determine the method of accomplishing the interviewing objective.* In general, this principle involves a decision to utilize either the guided or the unguided approach. It involves such questions as whether to use a standard rating form or a less systematic evaluation; whether to take notes or to rely upon the memory. Systematic notetaking definitely increases the amount of information that can be recalled from the interview. In a study of forty managers viewing a twenty-minute videotaped interview, those managers who took notes were able to answer almost all of twenty straightforward, factual questions about the interview (the average number correct was ten).[40] Managers who retained less information tended to systematically rate the interviewee higher and with less variability on component traits and abilities, a type of halo effect. Those with more information allocated lower ratings and recognized intra-individual differences. Thus, less qualified applicants have reason to become concerned when the interviewer begins to write things down!

Finally, one must decide whether the interview should be recorded. Multiple ratings can be conducted of taped and videotaped interviews, often with an increase in accuracy. A decision must also be made concerning the number of interviews—this involves organizational problems regarding interviewers with the authority to hire.

3 *Inform yourself as much as possible concerning the known information about the interviewee.* For the employment interviewer, this means a study of the application blank. For the supervisor handling an unexpected grievance, this emphasizes the traditional need of "knowing your people."

SETTING Establishment of the setting is not exactly a separate step in the interviewing process, but it deserves special emphasis. The setting for an interview is of two types, physical and mental.

---

[40]Robert E. Carlson, Paul W. Thayer, Eugene C. Mayfield, and Donald A. Peterson, "Improvements in the Selection Interview," *Personnel Journal,* vol. 50, no. 4, April 1971, p. 271.

1 *The physical setting for the interview should be both private and comfortable.* The value in the use of this principle lies in the encouragement of talk on the part of the interviewee. Readers can probably recall occasions when they were interviewed standing up at an office rail or at a desk in a room full of people. Numerous interruptions by telephone or by a secretary not only reduce the privacy but dramatically indicate the lower status of the interviewee. Such conditions are not conducive to frank conversation. A few firms are taking advantage of the principle of comfort. An individual who is sitting in a comfortable padded chair has a tendency to relax and talk more freely, thus providing more and truer information for the interviewer to evaluate.

2 *The mental setting should be one of rapport.* An initial effort should be made by the interviewer to establish an atmosphere of ease. Instead of plunging directly into the business at hand, some seemingly idle conversation should take place first. Some interviewers still use the weather as the favorite ice breaker; others utilize more specialized subjects gained from a reading of the interviewee's application blank. The interviewer must be aware of nonverbal behavior. Impatience, irritation, hostility, and resentment can be conveyed by body language. If one seldom smiles and always keeps a physical barrier between oneself and the interviewee, very little rapport will be established.

CONDUCT OF THE INTERVIEW   This is the step in the process where most of the action takes place. It is here that we obtain the information desired and supply the facts that the interviewee wants to know. Several sound principles could be cited here, but the following few examples should be sufficient to indicate the nature of the problem:

1 *The interviewer should possess and demonstrate a basic liking and respect for people.* This principle is considered by some to be the most fundamental in interviewing. It is not a specific rule to follow but, rather, a fundamental philosophy. It has been pointed out previously that liking people does not automatically qualify one for the job of personnel management. That fact, however, does not deny the importance of liking people in certain specific areas of personnel management, and interviewing is one of these areas.

The interviewer who likes to talk with people and is truly interested in them will find out the most about them. He or she creates a general atmosphere which leads the interviewee to open up. Above all, such an interviewer is not condescending in approach and avoids provoking needless feelings of inferiority on the part of the applicant.

2 *Questions should be asked in a manner that encourages the interviewee to talk.* Instead of asking if the person being interviewed has trouble getting along with supervisors, the interviewer should ask what type of supervisor the interviewee would like to work for and why. Questions that can be answered by "yes" or "no" are not the type that will reveal the true nature of the applicant. Leading questions should be avoided, as well as questions that reveal the interviewer's biases and prejudices. Even in guided interviews the interviewee should do the greater amount of the talking. The interviewer should not feel it necessary to speak if the interviewee pauses. Silence almost always implies a request for more information, and the interviewee usually continues to supply it.

In unguided interviews questioning is almost nonexistent. To make it truly unguided, the interviewer must be careful to give no clues to his or her own thinking and biases. In fact, restatement of thoughts presented by the interviewee is the basic technique of keeping the conversation going. Such a statement is made to indicate interest and encourage further talk, but one must be careful to restate, and not reinterpret, in order to avoid guidance.

In all good interviewing, the interviewer is successful in getting the interviewee to talk freely and reveal the true self. This is the reason behind the principles of privacy and comfort. It is the reason for the establishment of rapport. It is the reason for the importance of an atmosphere of mutual respect. This same desired result must be reflected in the type of questioning that is utilized.

3 *Listen attentively and, if possible, projectively.* At the very least the interviewee must have the full attention of the interviewer. Marginal listening not only prevents the obtaining of full information but is insulting to the interviewee. One cannot successfully fake attentive listening.

To understand fully the meaning of what is being said by the interviewee, projective listening is required. The interviewer who can listen much faster than the interviewee can talk must utilize that time by attempting to project into the position of the interviewee. One must possess the characteristic of empathy, the ability to project one's consciousness into that of another person. This will require an imaginative study of the personal background of the individual as revealed by his application blank. It will require an understanding of the manner in which the interviewee uses particular words. Projection does not necessarily mean that the interviewer must agree with everything that is said. One still must retain a measure of objectivity by means of which the applicant and her or his capabilities can be assessed.

CLOSE Some have compared the interview to a situation of controlled polite conversation. Civility makes certain requirements—for instance, that the interview should open and run smoothly, without awkwardness and embarrassment. There is a similar requirement for its close.

1 *The interviewer should make some overt sign to indicate the end of the interview.* One of the problems often mentioned by applicants is that they are never sure when the interview is ended. They do not wish to be embarrassed by assuming that the interview is over when it is not, or by overstaying their time and being asked by the interviewer to leave. In employment situations, the interviewer has a definite responsibility for bringing the conversation smoothly to a close and so indicating in some obvious manner, thus enabling the interviewee to make a reasonably poised exit. The interviewer may lay a pencil down, push back a chair, stand up, or do any of a number of things to indicate that the conversation is coming to a close. The interviewee is often highly appreciative of such signs, particularly after having been caught in embarrassing situations in the past.

With reference to the requirements for civility, the above principles are applicable to most employment-interviewing situations. Some firms, however, employ the "stress" interview and purposefully place the interviewee in demanding and embarrassing situations in order to observe the person's resulting behavior. In this type of interview, many of the above-cited principles are not applicable. The stress interview should be used, however, only where the job specification justifies its use as a technique of selection.

2 *The interviewee should be given some type of answer or indication of future action.* One should not be left hanging in the air, wondering what, if anything, happens next. This is true even for the processing of gripes and grievances, when the supervisor is not in a position to give a definite answer. In such a case the complainants should be told of the steps that will be undertaken to provide an answer, and, if possible, another interview should be scheduled to communicate the results.

In employment interviewing, any one of several things can happen. The applicant can be accepted, in which case she or he is informed of further employment processing. Or the applicant can be rejected for not measuring up to the job specification. There is much discussion concerning the best method of rejection. The old bromide, "Don't call us. We'll call you," is still used occasionally. Many prefer to avoid a face-to-face rejection and rely upon more impersonal means, such as a letter. Others prefer to speak frankly to interviewees and inform them of the rejection and of the reasons for it. When the reasons concern objective facts, such as age, schooling, and experience, the explanation is not difficult. When it is based on an evaluation of personality, the communication requires a higher degree of skill. There are a few interviewers who will, after the rejection, assume a counseling role in trying to aid the person through advice or referral to other employers.

EVALUATION When the door closes, the interviewer must immediately undertake the task of evaluating the candidate while the details are fresh in mind. If notes have not been previously taken, details should be recorded now. If a rating sheet has been provided for the structured interview, entries and supporting information should be entered. Some decision must be reached concerning the applicant.

In addition to evaluating the candidate, the interviewer should always evaluate herself or himself at this point. Interviewing is largely an art, the application of which can be improved through practice. One should be constantly aware of the dangers and pitfalls of face-to-face contact. Among these are assuming that habits are general rather than specific, permitting one outstanding trait to overshadow all others for better or worse, being unduly influenced by the nervousness of the applicant, and having a bias toward the applicant with no outstanding faults. The person with no significant faults may also be the one with no significant assets, thus constituting a "faultless mediocrity." The interviewer should possess a level of ability at least equal to the ability of those being interviewed. One should not be a power seeker who glories in the role of judging other human beings and making decisions that affect their very lives. Such maturity, perspective, and stability should be evident in the manner in which the interview is conducted as well as in the deliberation processes surrounding the decision.

SUMMARY

In this chapter, we have attempted to summarize the salient points of two large fields of personnel management. Each of these fields constitutes the basis for an occupation to which many people devote their entire lives. Our purpose in a text of this type is to (1) familiarize the student of personnel management with the general outline of the content of each field and (2) attempt to integrate these areas into a broader program of personnel management.

Brief familiarization with the types of psychological tests used in industry can best be obtained by following the classification of (1) intelligence, (2) aptitude, (3) achievement, (4) interest, and (5) personality. The intelligence test is the oldest and best developed. At the other extreme, the personality test is largely in a developmental stage as far as its uses in selection are concerned. The cardinal principle in the use of a test of any type is that such a test must be validated under the actual conditions of use. Validity is highly specific in nature and must be proved to exist for each proposed use in each company. That this is no longer just a requirement of the profession is made evident by the Civil Rights Act of 1964, guidelines established by the Equal Employment Opportunity Commission, and the Supreme Court decision in the case of *Griggs v. Duke Power Company*. Empirical statistical validity utilizing new applicants is the preferred method; concurrent statistical validity and content and construct validities are required in its absence. Special attention will have to be devoted to the problem of testing minority groups using instruments generally validated on characteristics of a white majority class.

The most widely used, and some would say misused, selection method is that of interviewing. Familiarity with the nature and importance of this device can best be obtained by following a series of interviewing steps: (1) preparation, (2) setting, (3) conduct, (4) close, and (5) evaluation. Citing specific principles under each of the steps indicate both the nature and the difficulty of the interviewing process.

It will be recalled from Chapter 7 that in a good hiring procedure several steps generally follow the employment interview. Approval by the line supervisor is often required, which will result in another interview. The supervisor would do well to undertake a continual self-review of interviewing processes, since the interview is a basic managerial tool of use in all phases of the job. After a physical examination, the new employee is inducted into the company, the department, and the job. The next logical step is that of developing skill in doing this job. Such development is presented as the second operative function of personnel. Before turning to this, special attention will be devoted to the planning and provision of an important type of talent for the organization. The problems and approaches to assuring an adequate supply of managers or executives are considered in the following chapter.

DISCUSSION QUESTIONS

1 Define and differentiate among the following types of validities: empirical statistical predictive validity, concurrent validity, content validity, and construct validity.

2 Discuss the impact of the *Griggs v. Duke Power Company* decision upon the profession and practice of personnel management.

3 What is meant by the statement, "validity is specific as to objective and situation"? Cite examples of varying validities with changes in objectives.

4 Discuss the use of polygraphs and personality tests with respect to their social implications versus their contribution to improving hiring procedures.

5 In dealing with testing of minority groups, what is the nature of the problem and the position taken by the Equal Employment Opportunity Commission?

6 What is the "prediction ceiling" with respect to the validation of tests? Why does it exist?

7 Discuss the role and accuracy of the employment interview as a part of the selection procedure.

8 Itemize the basic steps of the interviewing process, citing at least one guiding principle for each step.

9 What is the nature of the task of criteria selection in validating selection instruments? If supervisory ratings are chosen as the main criterion, what implications are probable?

10 In what ways can the reliability of the interview be improved?

SUPPLEMENTARY READING

AUSTIN, David L.: "Transactional Interviewing: or, Who Does What to Whom?" *Personnel Journal*, vol. 53, no. 6, June 1974, pp. 450–453.

CARLSON, Robert E., Paul W. Thayer, Eugene C. Mayfield, and Donald A. Peterson: "Improvements in the Selection Interview," *Personnel Journal*, vol. 50, no. 4, April 1974, pp. 268–275.

FOX, Harvey, and Joel Lefkowitz: "Differential Validity: Ethnic Group as a Moderator in Predicting Job Performance," *Personnel Psychology*, vol. 27, no. 2, Summer 1974, pp. 209–223.

MINER, John B.: "Psychological Testing and Fair Employment Practices: A Testing Program That Does Not Discriminate," *Personnel Psychology*, vol. 27, no. 1, Spring 1974, pp. 49–62.

PETERSEN, Donald J.: "The Impact of Duke Power on Testing," *Personnel*, vol. 51, no. 2, March–April 1974, pp. 30–37.

SAFREN, Miriam A.: "Title VII and Employee Selection Techniques," *Personnel*, vol. 50, no. 1, January–February 1973, pp. 26–35.

TAYLOR, Duane F.: "Test Validation: A Look at the Basics," *The Personnel Administrator*, vol. 18, no. 6, November–December 1973, 66–69.

NINE

EXECUTIVE TALENT PROCUREMENT

In Chapter 6 we examined the general problem of determining human resources requirements. In this chapter, we shall give attention to one specific type of resource that is becoming increasingly scarce, executive or managerial talent. To some degree, the content of the preceding three chapters can be applied equally well to executives, but we believe that the nature of the problem is sufficiently different and significant to merit separate treatment. For the purposes of this chapter, such terms as "manager," "executive," and "administrator" are interchangeable. The problem is one of ensuring an adequate supply of the abilities to plan, organize, direct, and control the work of others on all levels of organization.

Managerial or executive talent is quite limited in quantity, and business must look for it diligently and husband and develop the talent that it discovers. There are several reasons for the scarcity of such talent. The period since World War II has seen a tremendous expansion in the size of the national economy. This growth alone would result in the creation of numerous new positions of management. Along with growth in the private sector, the number of managerial positions in governmental organizations has burgeoned. Concomitant with the sheer growth in numbers has been the increasing complexity of the management task in large, complex organizations, as one is forced to deal with advanced technology internally and with multiple powerful groups externally. The time required for employees to qualify for managerial positions has been extended because of the more technical requirements entailed. The problem of procuring executive talent is further compounded by analysis of population statistics. Because of the lower birth rate during the depression of the 1930s, the percentage of people in the thirty- to forty-five-year category is significantly lower during the 1970s. It is from this category that the bulk of tomorrow's top executives will be derived. One researcher is even alarmed about the growing scarcity of managerial inclinations among young college graduates.[1] Marking the beginning of student activism during mid-1960s,

---

[1] John B. Miner, "The Real Crunch in Managerial Manpower," *Harvard Business Review*, vol. 51, no. 6, November–December 1973, pp. 146–158.

he notes a steadily decreasing tendency in young college graduates to aspire to managerial positions in business enterprises. In any event, the forward-looking management will be greatly concerned *now* with the problem of an adequate talent supply for executive positions in the future.

The increasingly widespread appreciation of the value of properly qualified and well-trained executives has underlined the slowness and uncertainty of conventional channels of promotion. Because of the importance of this type of talent, hit-or-miss planning of needs can no longer be tolerated. Needs must be anticipated far enough in advance to make possible the discovery, recruitment, and development of talent to meet planned requirements. In more and more firms, systematic attention is being devoted to executive resource planning, inventory, and analysis. This chapter will deal with the basic components of a program of this type.

ELEMENTS OF EXECUTIVE TALENT PROCUREMENT

An executive talent planning program can be defined as an *appraisal* of an organization's ability to perpetuate itself with respect to its management and a *determination* of the measures necessary to provide the essential executive resource. It includes, first, the determination of needs, in both number and kind. Owing to the length of the executive development cycle, determination of needs must be made years in advance to permit adequate time for education, training, and development. Secondly, executive resource planning must include an inventory of present talent in order to (1) determine the status of the present supply of available management personnel and (2) discover undeveloped talent presently within the organization. The final stage of planning would be concerned with decisions with respect to the *difference* between demand and supply; that is, if future needs exceed available talent, this imbalance becomes the basis for a program of executive recruitment and development. Thus, "executive talent planning" is a broad term that includes the forecasting of needs, executive inventory and analysis, and recruitment and development of management talent to fill the gap.

The executive talent planning program has four basic elements, two of which will be covered in this chapter. These elements are (1) organization planning of executive needs, (2) executive inventory and analysis, (3) executive recruitment, and (4) executive development. The first two elements actually establish the nature of the resource problem. Recruitment and development must naturally follow and are discussed in other chapters.

The element of organization planning is primarily concerned with a prediction of the growth and replacement needs of the business. A combination of the abilities to forecast and to organize is the essential requirement for this phase. Growth of the enterprise must be anticipated, and the effect of this growth on the internal organization structure must be determined. Since executives are not all alike and jobs have varying requirements, some attention must also be paid to the question of the kind of executive talent required. These subjects are discussed more fully in the following section.

Executive inventory and analysis is, as the term suggests, a counting of heads. More accurately, it is a counting of specific talents available. It appraises the depth of replacements for each management position, searches out personnel who have qualifications for advancement, and decides what additional education, training, and experience would be valuable. It encompasses a systematic study of the present and potential management talent of an organization, with a view toward the future problem of quickly and effectively filling positions that become vacant or are newly created by growth and reorganization.

Most of the firms that have developed systematic executive talent programs are large in size. Most have followed the four-element program listed above. Typical of these are the plans of Chrysler Corporation, Westinghouse Electric Corporation, General Motors Corporation, and Trans World Airlines. The computer has greatly facilitated the process of storing the talent inventory in the large organization so that it can be quickly checked against immediate and future needs. Smaller firms, however, can similarly profit from a systematic approach to planning. In Edgerton, Germeshausen, and Grier, Inc., a set of manually prepared cards has been established—one card for each skill or talent deemed significant to the organization.[2] Each card has 480 numbers, sufficient to provide for all key personnel in this firm. On the basis of questionnaires and interviews, each person's set of talents is uncovered, and her or his code number is punched in the appropriate skill cards. All personnel possessing a single talent are readily identifiable on a single skill card. However, a combination of several talents is frequently demanded by the organization. A set of such skill cards can be assembled, and any personnel possessing *all* the selected talents will be immediately identified.

The need for revised policies to accompany a central talent bank is made evident by observed practices in many business organizations. Too often, conventional practice makes it possible for managers to hoard talent to the detriment of the total organization. In addition, when filling departmental openings, it is usual to restrict the selection to other members of the department, or to outsiders whom the manager knows simply by chance. From the career viewpoint of the employee, his or her future depends excessively upon the present supervisor's abilities and attitudes. Alfred makes a powerful argument in favor of a more open, centrally administered internal job market.[3] Such an approach could include (1) widespread advertising of all key openings throughout the firm, (2) requiring any hiring manager to consider at least five people for each opening, including three located outside the immediate department, (3) strongly discouraging or prohibiting any manager from preventing a subordinate from applying for an opening outside the immediate department, and (4) requiring that each applicant refused for an advertised opening be granted an interview to discuss both reasons for rejection and recommendations for personal development. Such an approach would open up the entire organization in staffing key jobs. It would also open up the entire organization for career planning by individual employees, which could well lead to reduced resignations of able personnel because of limited opportunities. In one company that pursued such policies, approximately one out of every five management openings was filled by someone who would have been overlooked under the more typical closed system.

Whether a firm is large or small, the four fundamental elements of a talent planning program are present. Organizational needs must be compared with an accurate

[2]Richard J. Bronstein, "Setting Up a Skills Inventory," *Personnel*, March–April 1965, pp. 66–73.

[3]Theodore M. Alfred, "Checkers or Choice in Manpower Management," *Harvard Business Review*, vol. 45, no. 1, January–February 1967, pp. 163–165.

inventory of present talent, and differences must be provided for through either new hires or training and development, or both. Large size merely requires that this process be handled systematically with the aid of such instruments as records, computers, and sorting devices. The manager of a very small firm may be able to do the same thing in her or his head; the fundamental process is the same.

ORGANIZATIONAL PLANNING OF EXECUTIVE NEEDS

The planning of executive talent needs necessarily involves dealing in the future and to some extent "gazing into the crystal ball." Some firms claim that executive needs are too intangible to forecast, that management cannot be defined or planned for in any constructive manner. One by one, the major elements of business activity have been isolated and studied. We are not surprised when a particular firm predicts its sales for the coming year with a high degree of accuracy. Companies analyze and control their inventories of raw materials. Requirements for cash are accurately predicted. With a factor as important to an organization as management, with something as difficult to obtain and develop as management, how long can a firm ignore planning for it? More and more firms are recognizing that management resource planning is a problem that can be analyzed and systematically attacked. Many parts of the problem are subjective and inexact, but the somewhat primitive nature of this area of personnel management should not deter us from trying to develop it.

Under the heading of organizational planning of executive needs, four subsidiary problems can be identified. First, can we determine a rate of loss of present executive personnel and, thus, predict the needs for their replacement? A substantial portion of this decision can be quantified. Secondly, can we predict the supply of talent available at various stages of development? If we require a certain number of top-level executives seven years hence, the pipeline feeding into this level must be properly filled. Thirdly, can we predict the need for new executive personnel required as a result of growth and expansion? And finally, can we determine the abilities specifically necessary to meet job requirements, so that hiring, promotion, and training processes can be facilitated? A brief examination of each of these problems follows below.

Rate of loss

Forecasts are based, at least in part, on an analysis of historical data. Indications are that the factors causing past occurrences will also play a similar role in the future. This projection of historical data into the future must be adjusted in the light of other known information. Certain losses of key personnel can be predicted with a substantial degree of exactitude. These include losses from retirement, physical disabilities, and cases of substandard work performance.

Retirement is the most common type of anticipated separation. One method of visually portraying the effect of future retirements of management personnel is to prepare a retirement profile. An example of one type of profile is shown in Figure 9-1 for one section of a large company. This profile includes key operative as well as managerial personnel. Though firms are generally aware of the problem of retirement, since a fixed retirement age is frequently set, too often it is ignored or forgotten until

Figure 9-1 Retirement profile: development engineering

	Chief engineer	Assistant chief engineers	Staff engineers	Section engineers	Senior project engineers	Project engineers
1976						
1977						
1978		J. Worley				
1979						
1980				D. Green		J. Roth
1981						
1982					A. Crow	
1983					P. Stimson	
1984	B. Simpson					
1985		M. Whiting				
1986						
1987						
1988		C. Cox				

too late. Insufficient lead time is provided to select and properly prepare a replacement. Systematizing the presentation of retirement times serves to highlight the scope and significance of the problem, thus stimulating some preparatory activity.

In like manner, losses for known physical disabilities and for substandard work performance can be predicted. We realize that difficult human relations problems are involved here; but the significant thing at this point in the analysis is that some losses of key personnel can be anticipated with some degree of exactness. The management that does not recognize and prepare for these losses is shortsighted indeed.

There will, of course, be other losses of management personnel. Some will quit and take other jobs; some will transfer to other departments in the company. Since all management personnel are not completely interchangeable, variations in growth rates of various portions of one organization will cause problems. One department may be expanding while another is contracting, though the overall size of the organization may well remain constant. Coping with these unknown losses is of course much more difficult. One possible approach is to try to establish an annual average rate of loss by department or division. Personnel records can be examined over a considerable period of time to uncover data on losses, including quits, discharges, mutually satisfactory releases, leaves, deaths, retirements, and transfers. From these, all predictable losses can be subtracted as known. The remaining separations can be used in determining an annual rate of loss, by dividing the number of executive separations each year by the total number of executive personnel. For example, in one particular year there was a total of forty managerial personnel in a developmental engineering area. Out of a total of five persons who left the organization, there were two retirements, one physical-disability separation, and two resignations. Retirements and disability separations should be known and predictable. Only two separations, then, were unanticipated. The rate of loss of this type for this year was 5 percent. If the experiences of five to ten years are figured, one can derive an average annual rate of loss due to unpredictable causes. Projection of this rate into the future should provide some basis for anticipating the need for replacements from this source.

Maintaining the talent pipeline

If, for example, five new branch managers must be available seven years from now, *more* than five should have entered the firm *this* year, assuming that seven years is the average developmental time. Obviously, some will quit before the seven years is up, and others may not qualify for promotion. Most firms do not do any systematic analysis of the pipeline behind higher positions, preferring to just hire and keep hiring so that a constant stream is maintained. Should there be a mismatch of supply and demand in any one year, correction is in the form of either layoff or searching externally for a branch manager type.

It has been suggested that this type of planning problem can be approached as a Markov chain. Let us assume that the pipeline behind the branch manager consists of three definite stages: (1) trainee status, (2) specialist assignment, and (3) section manager. In order to approach this problem systematically, we need to know the number of personnel present in all four positions (trainee, specialist, section manager, and branch manager), the normal rate of personnel loss in each category (see preceding section), and the normal percentage of promotions from one stage to another. Without getting into the mathematics, it should be apparent that we can determine the changing states in each category with the passage of time.[4] We can also manipulate the model to ascertain the effects of speeding up or slowing down the promotion rate, of increasing or decreasing the number of new trainees hired, and of changing the turnover rates to reflect conditions in the economy. Management does have some control over these factors and thus can influence the varying levels of personnel at each stage of the pipeline. Periodic and systematic looks at the situation by the personnel manager should ensure that the firm is not caught short in time of need, or at least that its managers are forewarned.

Predicted expansion or contraction

Thus far, we have dealt with forecasting talent needs as a result of losses of present personnel. We should not need to consider any other data if the national economy, the industry, and the company were stable and would remain so. But this is not the case. Even when the economy is expanding generally, many firms contract in size and some will fail. Predicting growth or contraction of a particular firm is a problem which has broader ramifications than those that concern us in personnel planning. Such prediction must affect *all* portions of the business. The thesis here is that such predictions should be as effectively utilized in planning executive requirements as they are in planning the expansion of capital facilities.

If executive resource planning is to be undertaken by the personnel manager, he or she must of necessity be privileged to sit on the management committees that plan the future of the enterprise. Just as financial planning must take place before a new plant is built, a personnel department should be allotted at least an equal amount of lead time to make necessary personnel plans. Such planning will be affected by anticipated

[4]See Gordon L. Nielsen and Allan R. Young, "Manpower Planning: A Markov Chain Application," *Public Personnel Management*, vol. 2, no. 2, March–April 1973, pp. 133–144, for an exceedingly simple illustration of the application of Markov chains to this type of problem.

growth of the firm, major organizational changes in objectives and policies, and changes in such environmental influences as new legislation and major social changes. The personnel manager cannot simply be a reactor who responds only when someone calls for a service. If deserving of the title "executive," the manager must be an active participant in the very vital planning process for the total enterprise.

Again, we can obtain assistance in predicting the future by examining the past. The past record of growth provides a basis for forecasting. It is important to study the major segments of the firm, for one area may be growing faster than another. With the trend toward automation, for example, the number of supervisory personnel in engineering areas may be growing while the number in production may be declining. Capital expenditures forecasts make an excellent source of information for the resources planner. These forecasts generally encompass a longer period, and investment in a new plant and equipment provides good, solid ground for predicting personnel needs. If the number of operative personnel is known, application of the usual span-of-control ratios in each area can give some help in predicting the need for supervisory personnel. If sufficient attention is devoted to the problem, a reasonably good estimate of future needs for executive personnel can be made.

Executive job analysis

As was indicated in Chapter 6, few firms attempt to analyze and describe the content of an executive job. A growing number, however, believe that a more realistic accomplishment of executive selection and training could be effected if more were known about the particular characteristics of the executive job. Consequently, some of the larger firms are undertaking the task of executive job analysis in order to assist in planning the needs for executives in terms of particular skills or talents required.

One of the first problems in this area is that an executive job is nonrepetitive in nature. Besides, all such jobs seem to be quite different in content. How can one obtain a complete picture of the job? Various research projects have been undertaken to develop a basic pattern for analyzing and describing executive jobs.[5] In most such studies, it has been found that all executive jobs have certain functions and elements in common; thus, each analysis can be directed along the following lines:

1 *Job objectives.* What is the scope and nature of this job? What is the purpose of the segment of the firm over which this job is placed?
2 *Organizing.* What is the authority to select? How many subordinates are there? What are the responsibilities for personnel development? Can the job incumbent alter the organization structure?
3 *Planning.* What types of projects are undertaken in this job? An executive job description cannot cover every plan developed by the job incumbent, but sufficient examples should be shown to indicate the range in scope and complexity.
4 *Policy making.* On what committees does the job incumbent sit? What problems

[5]See Jack Mendleson, "Improving Executive Job Descriptions," *Management of Personnel Quarterly*, vol. 8, no. 1, Spring 1969, pp. 27–35; and Edward N. Hay and Dale Purvis, "The Analysis and Description of High-Level Jobs," *Personnel*, January 1953, pp. 344–351. In addition, the author participated in a job and organizational analysis of a segment of the United States Air Force. Though no publications issued from this study of command and staff managerial jobs, the approach taken was similar to the above-cited studies.

are discussed? What part is played in decision making within and without this particular segment of the firm?

5   *Direction.* How are subordinates stimulated and motivated? With what type of personnel does this job incumbent come into contact?

6   *Control.* What is the nature of the control problem—timing, type of data, pressure, and authority to make corrections?

7   *Operation.* In most managerial jobs, there is at least one operative function directly executed by the manager. For example, the personnel manager may help to write the labor contract, or a sales manager may actually sell to a few of the more important accounts.

In addition to specifying job duties, it is very important in executive jobs to undertake some type of role analysis. As was suggested in Chapter 6, a manager occupies a central position subject to multiple and often conflicting role demands. One researcher has suggested a role typology of behavioral demands based on work patterns (other- or self-generating, fragmented or steady), types of uncertainty encountered (number of crises, degree of inexact information in decision making, and extent of future that must be foreseen), responsibility for resources (degree to which shared, consultative opportunities, and degree to which mistakes can be traced), demands on personal private life (relocation, trips, and overtime), and extent and nature of contacts (who, length of relationship, internal or external, and time spent in talking). As indicated in Figure 9-2, seven basic job types have been identified, along with typical business examples for each category. It is apparent that though certain managerial functions may be held in common, executive jobs do vary in degree of risk entailed, social skills in interacting with others, degree of dependence, and amount of role conflict. These findings have important implications for executive selection and development.

Some people, practitioners as well as theorists, object to the entire process of preparing executive job and role descriptions. They feel that such specifications confine the manager and inhibit exercise of much-needed initiative. Though that danger is ever present in formalizing organizations with growth, values received may offset such costs. Structuring provides the basis for establishing reasonable goals to be accomplished and, thus, the foundation for a "Management-by-Objectives" program.[6] Identifying certain regular portions of the assignment assists in developing an equitable salary structure that reflects varying levels of responsibility, skill, and risk. Certainly, if we are to plan for future executive talent requirements, we must have some idea of the nature of the job responsibilities envisaged. Without setting up such job and role descriptions as fences constructed in stone, they are of considerable use in a planned and systematic personnel program.

EXECUTIVE INVENTORY

As a result of organization planning of executive talent needs, we should have a good idea of the number and kind of management personnel we shall require in the future.

---

[6]See Chap. 13.

Figure 9-2 Job typology of behavioral demands of managerial jobs or equivalent status in industry and commerce. (Excludes top management jobs where the occupant can largely adapt the role as he wishes.)

Job Types	Relationship, Direction of*	Main Characteristics	Subdivisions	Main Characteristic(s) of Subdivisions	Examples of Jobs
I	*Responsibility for separate unit* [Downwards] (Outwards) (Up)	Few or no peer relations. Little or no role conflict. Evaluation possible.	1. Primarily internal contacts.	People management high. Hard information. Responding known contacts.	Retail store manager. Some works managers
			2. Entrepreneurial.	External contacts, particularly customers. Can choose balance self-starting/responding.	Branch bank managers. Some general managers.
II	*Field supervision* (area responsibility for separate units) [Downwards & Up]	No interlocking subs. Few or no peer relations. People management high. Known contacts. Demands on private life.	1. Structured.	Responding. Similar tasks. Hard information.	Superintendent, retail chain stores. Various area management jobs
			2. Relatively unstructured	High uncertainty. Self-generating.	Regional director of overseas operations
III	*People management* (relatively self-contained dept. or section) [Down] (Up)	People management key relationship. High contact time. Fragmented. Responding.	(Could be subdivided by leadership situation.)		Some administrative jobs. Some production management.
IV	*Work-flow jobs* [Down and sideways] (Up)	Peer dependence. Obtaining co-operation without authority. Role conflict. Meetings. Known contacts.	1. Line management	People management high.	Chief engineer, chief accountant, production manager
			2. SERVICE VARIANTS a. nonselling – customers come to you.	Time deadlines. Responding.	Some computer management. Transport manager
			b. selling.	Self-generating. Role conflict very high.	Training manager. Some personnel. Some computer mgt.
			c. ext.	External contacts, time deadline.	Service manager
			3. Co-ordinator (non-subs)	Peer dependence very high.	Product manager
			4. Control (over non-subs)	Risk unpopularity. Role conflict very high.	Quality control manager. Some accounting
V	*Solo jobs* [Alone]	Sustained attention. High alone time. Plan work.			Some planning jobs. Various specialist jobs
VI	*Consulting and advisory* [Upwards] (Sideways & down)	Sustained attention. Time with senior mgt. Wide contacts.	1. Structured. Continuing.	Known contacts, hard information. Low uncertainty.	Some accounting jobs
			2. Unstructured, often one-shot jobs.	Risk incurring unpopularity. No, or low, people management. Self-generating.	Internal consultancy and special assignments
VII	*External Jobs* [Outwards]	Conflict objectives. External contacts high. Uncertainty high.	1. People management important.	People management high. Demands on private life.	Some sales management
			2. Dealing with specialist contacts.	Conflict job objectives very high. Known contacts.	Purchasing manager. Advertising manager
			3. P.R., varied contacts.	Short-term relations. Demands on private life.	Public relations. Some general managers

* *Main direction in [ ] other in ( )*

Source: Rosemary Stewart, "The Manager's Job: Discretion vs. Demand." *Organizational Dynamics*, vol. 2, no. 3, Winter 1974, p. 70. Used with permission.

To establish the nature of the recruitment and development problems, we now need to determine the number and kind of management personnel at present available within the organization. "Inventory" is a term often used in relation to the counting of tangible objects such as raw materials, goods in process, and finished products. In executive inventory, however, the items inventoried are generally intangible. The inventory is not simply a counting of heads; it includes a cataloging of present and potential abilities and aptitudes. We must count not only the abilities that are evident and being used, but also those which thus far have remained undiscovered. The count of abilities must be modified by a count of motivation; that is, it sometimes happens that a person who appears to be properly prepared for an advancement to a designated position indicates a desire to transfer, to change occupational area, or to remain on the present job. In executive inventory, the things to be counted are considerably more intangible than physical property.

The first step in the procedure is a determination of *who* is to be included in the inventory. Certainly, present lower- and middle-management personnel will be listed. Higher-management personnel should also be covered, since grooming a successor to the president is one of the most important talent planning tasks. In some companies all salaried personnel compensated on a monthly or semimonthly basis are included. To be more sure that all available talent has been canvassed, certain operative employees must be added. Each first-level supervisor may be asked to submit recommendations of personnel who seem to have the potential to advance within the organization.

After the above decision has been made, detailed information about each individual must be gathered. This information will first consist of existing information brought up to date. Items of particular importance are education, experience, retirement date, merit-rating history, health status, and psychological-test results. If some of the included personnel, such as selected hourly paid employees, have not been given the necessary psychological tests, they will have to take them at this time. In addition, some of the categories of information, education in particular, could easily have become obsolete and must be brought up to date.

To ensure that the factual record is currently correct, an interview is ordinarily conducted with each person. This is an interview that not only serves to check the accuracy of the above-listed data but also attempts to uncover unknown abilities and motives. Questions are asked about subjects which are often not found in personnel records, such as recreational interests, hobbies, civic groups in which the person is active, and various offices held in organizations outside the business enterprise.

Canadian National Railways in its inventory of 7,500 middle managers has found it important to include the attitudes of the employee concerning training and development needs.[7] Certainly, the employee's particular career preference as well as willingness to relocate are important variables in determining talent availability. Any information that will assist in determining whether the person concerned has advancement potential is a proper objective of this interview. In addition, it might be noted that this particular interview is often the first tangible evidence the employee has had of the existence of an executive talent planning program. It is therefore quite important to explain thoroughly the nature and objectives of the program, of the inventory, and of this particular interview. Knowledge of this type of program is a very real morale

---

[7]A. T. Mathews, "Keeping Tabs on 7500 Middle Managers," *Personnel*, vol. 43, no. 3, May–June 1966, p. 27.

stimulant to many people. On the other hand, some who lack the motivation or desire for advancement will make known their feelings at this time and may well be removed from the inventory schedule.

At this point it is advisable to establish a catalog of talent. For each of the individuals, a summary record containing all of the above-cited information should be made. An example of such a record is found in Figure 9-3. Filing these records on the basis of element of organization has the advantage of grouping together the records as they would most probably be used in talent planning. These records provide a solid factual foundation for the executive talent planning program. As indicated earlier, these skills can be transferred to storage on cards or computer memory drums, thereby making possible rapid searches for unusual combinations of talents needed.

EXECUTIVE ASSESSMENT

The third step in making the inventory must involve an appraisal of the personnel included in the talent catalog. Predicting managerial success for specific people and groups is increasingly becoming an important research area. In general, the research has taken two directions: (1) a determination of significant personal characteristics or behaviors that seem to presage future success, and (2) the establishment of clinically oriented assessment centers modeled somewhat after the Office of Strategic Services Assessment Program of World War II.

Early identification through characteristics

Since the managerial development process consumes extended periods of time, it would be helpful to identify particular human talents that give rise to potential managerial success. One early measure that can be assessed is performance in college as measured by grades. Two research programs of the American Telephone and Telegraph Company found a definite relationship between grades in college and salary level achieved.[8] In the 1960 study of 10,000 managers, 51 percent of those in the top tenth of their college class were located in the top third of the salary levels in the company. The correlation between grades and salaried level was .33; in the earlier study of 1,300 managers, it was .37. In a study of top managers at General Electric, it was found that individuals who received salary increases of 30 percent or more at least once in a single year had a much higher probability of reaching the top within this company.[9] Such increases reflected one or more rewards for outstanding behavior.

One of the earliest research programs, undertaken by Sears, Roebuck in 1942, resulted in the development of a number of significant characteristics and attitudes that were associated with successful managerial performance.[10] Among these were a

---

[8]F. R. Kappel, "From the World of College to the World of Work," *Bell Telephone Magazine*, Spring 1962, pp. 3–21.

[9]Lawrence L. Ferguson, "Better Management of Managers' Careers," *Harvard Business Review*, vol. 44, no. 2, March–April 1966, p. 146.

[10]*Research toward the Development of a Multiple Assessment Program for Executive Personnel*, Sears, Roebuck and Co., Psychological Research and Services Section, June 1965.

Figure 9-3 Sample inventory record

(Front)

| Photograph | Birth date: 3/1/25   Service date: 5/22/63   Retirement: 3/1/90
Family status: Married, 3 children
Outside activities: Member of Big Brothers and Boy Scouts; interested in boating and hobby-shop work connected with boating; has been member of city council and chief of volunteer fire department
Education: 2 years high school; quartermaster service school, auto mechanic and body-work course, 2 weeks, 1961; State College, basic management course, 2 weeks, 1968
Military history: U.S. Army 1964–1966, S./Sgt. in charge of basic training platoon; not in reserves
Previous employment: 1945–1963, auto mechanic (self-employed)
In-plant experience: 1963, patrolman (85); 1967, sergeant (85) |

JOHN DOE

(Reverse)

JOHN DOE

Appraisals

Date	By	Reviewer	Result
6/15/70	A. K. Allison	H. J. Bright	Potential for future promotion
8/20/72	''	H. J. Bright	''
5/25/74	''	D. G. Doll	Immediately qualified for promotion

Interests: Strong in mechanical, computation, persuasive, musical, social service, and clerical

Personality: Normally stable, extroverted, dominant, and confident

Mental alertness: 40th percentile

Mechanical comprehension: 85th percentile

Remarks

Centerville credit bureau: Credit rating satisfactory, no record of convictions

Management screening investigation: Reported to be industrious, civic-minded, quiet, and a good neighbor

Health: Has recurring bronchitis and acute asthma

marked preference for orderly thought, overt and even aggressive self-confidence, a leaning toward "number-related tasks," personal values of a practical and economic nature, and high general activity. The Sears researchers used a battery of standard tests, and it has been discovered that though the test scores of the same person can differ significantly until the age of thirty is reached, thereafter personality tends to stabilize and test results show little change. A study of 443 managers of Standard Oil of New Jersey attempted to relate job success to measurements produced by such devices as a general intelligence test, a nonverbal reasoning test, personality tests, an individual background survey, a management judgment test, a self-performance report, and an attitude inventory.[11] The most significant relationships were found between the background survey (.64) and the management judgment test (.51). The latter test described managerial problems and presented several choices for action or decision. The least valuable predictive device was the personality test. The criteria for job success included the organization level of job held, salary, and general ratings. An appraisal

---

[11]*A Summary of the Early Identification of Management Potential Research Project*, Standard Oil Co. of New Jersey, Social Science Research Division, Employee Relations Department, August 1961.

approach using such statistical analyses would provide guiding information to the supervisors responsible for making selection and development decisions for each employee included in the talent inventory.

Moving from abilities that could possibly signal success in management, Miner proposes that motivation is equally important. Ability is impotent if not accompanied by desire. As suggested earlier, his research has discovered a steadily decreasing trend in college student motivation to aspire to managerial positions. The measurement scale consists of ascertaining degree of possession of the following attitudes: (1) favorable attitude toward authority, (2) desire to compete, (3) assertive motivation to take charge and make decisions, (4) desire to exercise power, (5) desire for attention of others, and (6) a sense of responsiblity.[12] Research has indicated that high scores on these six measures correlate with managerial success. In a study of sixty-one managers in one oil company, those whom the company "would rehire" had average scores of 8.9, while those whom they would "not rehire" averaged 3.3, a significant difference. In another study, executives who had not been promoted scored 3.7, those promoted one or two levels had 6.2, and those promoted three or more organizational levels scored 8.6. Business managers in general have an average score of 6 points, nonbusiness managers (largely school administrators) score 1 point, while the average scores of 1,400 students in five universities have declined from approximately 4 points to minus 2 points over the period of 1960 to 1972. The last result has been attributed to changing social values and increased emphasis upon democratic and participative leadership styles in collegiate teaching. Though the behavioral participative model is ethically appealing, Miner contends that it is currently not a viable strategy for most business organizations. In any event, the motivational measure can be employed to identify personnel who desire to utilize their abilities in managerial positions in organizations that are led in a basically autocratic manner.

One final, highly interesting human ability that may make possible identification of effective managerial performance in entrepreneurial positions is precognition or extrasensory perception (ESP). In guessing which of ten numbers (0 through 9) has been generated by a computer, the probability of being right, and thus the average score, is 10 percent. Some people can achieve scores as high as 24 percent, while others score as low as 2 percent. In a study of twenty-five executives heading up small manufacturing companies, twelve had doubled their companies' profits in five years.[13] Of these, eleven had above-average precognition scores (12.8 percent). One who had increased profits fifteenfold had a score of 16 percent. Of the thirteen who had not doubled profits, seven scored below chance, one at chance, and five above. The five above chance had increased profits from 50 to 100 percent. The implication is that intuition plays a significant role in decision making, and one more measure has been added to the process of identifying talents that bode well for success.

Assessment centers

The assessment center concept for examining and identifying personnel with potential for managerial success began with the German military in World War II. It spread to

---

[12]John B. Miner, op. cit., p. 148.

[13]"Do Successful Executives Have ESP?" *Business Week*, Jan. 26, 1974, p. 77.

Great Britain in the form of a War Office Selection Board, moved to the United States in selecting agents for the Office of Strategic Services, and was finally introduced to American business by the American Telephone and Telegraph Corporation in the mid-fifties. It was estimated that in 1972 there were approximately a dozen large business firms operating executive assessment centers.[14] The following year saw a jump to over 150 such companies.

The hallmark of the assessment center is the utilization of performance simulations as a primary means of obtaining valid information about executive candidates. Figure 9-4 presents a skeleton outline of a typical 2½-day assessment center schedule. A survey of thirty-three companies reveals that the three most widely used simulations are in-basket exercises (thirty-one firms), business games (thirty firms), and leaderless group discussion (thirty-one firms).[15] An in-basket is a set of notes, messages, telephone calls, letters, and reports that the candidate is expected to handle within a period of one or two hours. The candidate's decisions can be rated by assessors with respect to such abilities as willingness to take action and organizing of interrelated events. A business game is a competitive simulation where teams are required to make decisions concerning production, marketing, purchasing, and finance in competition with each other. The leaderless-group-discussion simulation was briefly described in an

[14]Allen I. Kraut, "Management Assessment in International Organizations," *Industrial Relations*, vol. 12, no. 2, May 1973, p. 175.

[15]Joseph M. Bender, "What Is 'Typical' of Assessment Centers?" *Personnel*, vol. 50, no. 4, July–August 1973, p. 51.

Figure 9-4 Typical assessment center schedule

Day 1:
Orientation of dozen candidates
Break-up into groups of four to play a *management game* (Observe and assess organizing ability, financial acumen, quickness of thinking, efficiency under stress, adaptability, leadership.)
Psychological testing (Measure and assess verbal and numerical abilities, reasoning, interests, and attitudes) and/or *depth interviews* (Assess motivation.)
Leaderless group discussion (Observe and assess aggressiveness, persuasiveness, expository skill, energy, flexibility, self-confidence.)
Day 2:
In-basket exercise (Observe and assess decision making under stress, organizing ability, memory and ability to interrelate events, preparation for decision making, ability to delegate, concern for others.)
Role-playing of employment or performance appraisal interview (Observe and assess sensitivity to others, ability to probe for information, insight, empathy.)
Group roles in preparation of a budget (Observe and assess collaboration abilities, financial acumen, expository skill, leadership, drive.)
Day 3:
Individual case analyses (Observe expository skill, awareness of problems, background information possessed for problems, typically involving marketing, personnel, accounting, operations, and financial elements.)
Obtain *peer ratings* from all candidates.
Staff assessors meet to discuss and rate all candidates.
Weeks later:
Manager, with assessor experience, meets with each candidate to discuss assessment with counseling concerning career guides and areas to develop.

earlier chapter. In addition, various other exercises are often designed to fit the firm's particular situation, e.g., J. C. Penney utilizes the Irate Customer Phone Call, made by an assessor, in order to rate the candidate's ability to control emotions, demonstrate tact, and satisfy the complaint.[16] Psychological tests and depth interviewing are frequently used techniques but generally show lower levels of accuracy in predicting future success. Personality tests, in particular, appear to be the weakest predictor.

In determining the predictive accuracy of the assessment center approach, the initial study of AT&T was most impressive. Assessor ratings were not communicated to company management for a period of eight years in order not to contaminate the results. In a sample of fifty-five candidates who achieved the middle-management ranks during that period, the center correctly predicted 78 percent of them.[17] Of seventy-three persons who did *not* progress beyond the first level of management, 95 percent were correctly predicted by the assessment staff. As a result, this company has maintained its centers, processing an average of 10,000 candidates a year. Reviewing ratings and actual progress of 5,943 personnel over a ten-year period demonstrated a validity coefficient of .44 for assessment center predictions.[18]

Other firms have had similar success in the use of the assessment center technique. A study of ninety-four men from two divisions of a large electronics firm revealed that a combination of assessments produced higher correlations with the criterion of increased managerial responsibility three years after assessment.[19] When an overall subjective rating was utilized, the correlation was .37. Multiple correlations of paper-and-pencil tests with the criterion produced a .45 level. When tests, ratings of characteristics, and assessment center simulations and exercises were utilized, the correlation rose to .62. It was concluded that the assessment center procedure made a substantial and unique contribution to the prediction of management success.

In a survey by Korman of over thirty such studies, he concludes that "judgmental" prediction methods as exemplified particularly by assessment procedures are better predictors than psychometric procedures alone.[20] Intelligence tests are ruled out since the restriction of the range of applicants does not allow significant differentiation between the successful and unsuccessful. Personal history data as predictors are usable primarily for first-level managerial jobs but tend to be less valuable for higher positions. Personality inventories tend to have the least predictive value in assessing executive potential on all levels.

Assessment centers are not without their disadvantages. Obviously, there are considerable costs involved, particularly when the ratio of assessors to candidates averages three to one. Most assessors are higher line managers, who are thus provided a valuable by-product in their training to evaluate personnel more effectively. Psycholo-

[16]William C. Byham, "Assessment Centers for Spotting Future Managers," *Harvard Business Review*, vol. 48, no. 4, July–August 1970, p. 158.

[17]Douglas W. Bray and Donald L. Grant, "The Assessment Center in the Measurement of Potential for Business Management," *Psychological Monographs*, whole no. 625, vol. 80, no. 17, 1966, p. 24.

[18]James R. Huck, "Assessment Centers: A Review of the External and Internal Validities," *Personnel Psychology*, vol. 26, no. 2, Summer 1973, p. 198.

[19]Herbert B. Wollowick and W. J. McNamara, "Relationship of the Components of an Assessment Center to Management Success," *Journal of Applied Psychology*, vol. 53, no. 5, October 1969, p. 352.

[20]Abraham K. Korman, "The Prediction of Managerial Performance: A Review," *Personnel Psychology*, vol. 21, no. 3, Autumn 1968, p. 319.

gists are also used, particularly when the techniques of psychological tests and depth interviews are being utilized. Possible dysfunctional consequences of the use of the center include the "crown prince or princess effect," the "kiss of death effect," and possible demotivation of low-rated personnel who are competent in present positions. Studies of the operations of the International Business Machines center over a five-year period indicate that fears concerning these adverse by-products are not well founded.[21] High ratings received in the center were not sufficient in and of themselves to secure a promotion for a particular individual. High ratings increased the likelihood of advancement but did not assure it. Low ratings were not necessarily the "kiss of death," but they did slow a candidate down. Concerning possible disillusionment leading to resignation, this study showed that the proportion of low-rated candidates who quit was not significantly different from the proportion of the high-rated group. Touchy human relations problems do exist with respect to those not receiving invitations to attend a center, as well as in the stress situations created by the obvious competitive elements of assessments through simulation. However, most organizations evidently conclude that the values far outweigh the costs and problems. Selection in this manner should help meet governmental requirements with respect to nondiscrimination on the basis of race, color, creed, nationality, or sex. In a Labor Department study, 250 black and Indian trainees were assessed through conventional written tests, and only 15 percent were deemed to have potential for promotion.[22] When this same group was measured through the simulation approach of an assessment center, approximately 50 percent were found to have advancement potential. Thus, the center which utilizes performance exercises provides a vessel from which all can drink.[23]

Supervisory assessment

It is the belief of most managers that responsibility for appraisal of potential for promotion *must rest with line superiors.* A personnel specialist can do the spadework in assembling the background information discussed above, but the decision concerning promotability must be made by supervisors. All employees included in the inventory should be rated in some fashion. In addition to this rating, added written comments are helpful, such as listing of examples of commendable work, specific limitations, positions for which the employee is presently or potentially qualified, additional training or experience recommended, and a judgment as to whether the employee is properly placed at present. Since this is a group of key employees, it is advisable to obtain and record their reactions to these appraisals, and employee reactions should be reviewed by the supervisor of the appraiser or appraisers and moved up through the chain of command to the heads of the major organization elements.

On the basis of this formal evaluation, managers can determine which employees have some potential for advancement. These individuals can then be separated for detailed study. We can now become concerned with the problems of *timing* and the

[21]Allen I. Kraut and Grant J. Scott, "Validity of an Operational Management Assessment Program," *Journal of Applied Psychology*, vol. 56, no. 2, April 1972, pp. 124–129.

[22]"Where They Make Believe They're the Boss," *Business Week*, Aug. 28, 1971, pp. 34–35.

[23]In reference to the *Griggs v. Duke Power Company* case when the Supreme Court utilized Aesop's fable of the fox and stork attempting to drink milk from a shallow dish.

type of promotion that should be made. Among these persons, which are immediately qualified for advancement to what positions? Who has the potential for promotion to what job within a year or two years? We must return to the appraisers for the answers to these questions. Because of the subjective nature of this appraisal, it is important to obtain *multiple* ratings. If possible, at least three evaluations should be made of each employee who has advancement potential. Executive appraisal is a difficult task, and, when possible, multiple opinions are preferred. Figure 9-5 shows a tabulation of appraisals of the type discussed here. The promotion status for the individuals listed on the chart is arrived at by averaging the results of two or more raters. In this instance, only a general rating of promotability was made with no detailed evaluation of individual traits.

For each individual who is deemed to have some potential for advancement, we now have a factual inventory record covering background and some subjective but systematic appraisals made by the superiors. This record provides the foundation for a program of individual development. It tells management what it needs to know concerning the adequacy of the supply of available executive talent now and in the future. It deals specifically with particular individuals and gives a detailed picture of the inventory of present talent. Thus, we have created a catalog or schedule of present and future executive talent within the company. It cannot be completely accurate, but the

Figure 9-5

ANALYSIS OF MANAGERIAL PROMOTABILITY OF SALARIED EMPLOYEES

Employees graded on salaried-personnel appraisal as having some degree of promotability	*Question*: Is employee now qualified for promotion into or within management, or will he, within eighteen months, become qualified for promotion into or within management							Resultant promotable status
	Interviewers:							
	P. Calhoun	A. Brown	C. Alton	R. Smart	D. Hardy	W. Mathy	H. Hill	
R. W. Alton					Q	Q		Q
U. P. Baker			Q			P		P
J. J. Brown								
A. E. Bruner			P			P		P
D. E. Hardy						Q	Q	Q
R. C. Klipstein					Q	Q		Q
R. G. Morris		P			Q	Q		Q
L. L. Poly				Q	Q	Q		Q
H. N. Reammer					Q	Q		Q
C. R. Saltz						P		
W. O. Sloneker	Q				Q	Q		Q
R. D. Smart					P	P		P
L. O. Tully					Q	P		

Q, qualified; P, potential (will become qualified within eighteen months).

probability is that it is more complete and accurate than an unsystematic impression of the general status of the organization.

EXECUTIVE TALENT PLANNING IN ACTION

During the course of executive inventory and forecasting, much information will be obtained. It is of little value unless it can be organized and communicated to the points in the organization where it can be used. Though a central computerized talent bank would seem to be most conducive to total organization effectivenes, one of the more popular ways of recording the current status of executive talent Is the modified organization chart as shown in Figure 9-6.

In Figure 9-6, the basic form is the current organization structure of the unit. Only key positions are covered. Additional information depicted on the chart includes the age of each job incumbent, number of years of management experience, and promotion status of three types: persons who are qualified immediately for promotion, those who have potential for promotion within a reasonable period of time, and persons who do not have the qualifications or potential for advancement. If the chart is coded in various colors, one can see at a glance those jobs that contain either an abundance or a definite lack of reserve potential. Ages are important, for they point out future losses to retirement. Some organizations color-code this factor to highlight the replacement problem. When a near-retirement is indicated, and the name of no qualified or potentially qualified subordinate appears on the chart, it is evident that a problem exists *now* and not just on the day of retirement. In some organizations, years of management experience are considered important. If an individual coded as "not qualified" is at the lowest level of management and has been there for a long period of time, it is fairly safe to conclude that he or she has "leveled off." If, however, a person coded as "not qualified" has been in the lowest level of management for only a short period of time, this subordinate position could well be an indication that she or he is still inexperienced but has potential for advancement at a time later than that shown on the chart.

One particular firm shows on its promotability organization chart each person's desires and special capabilities for promotion. Sometimes a particular person has the potential for promotion within his or her part of the organization but desires promotion in another area. This desire for transfer serves to reduce the talent reservoir of one department and augment the other. This situation can also be portrayed in the form of a list, as shown in Figure 9-7. C. E. Brubaker, for example, is not promotable to a higher position in the inspection department (see Figure 9-6) where presently employed. Because of either personal desires or specific capabilities, she is promotable to a higher position in direct manufacturing. This represents no problem because, as shown in Figure 9-6, we have both Ulter and Root to back up Armes. To be more specific, there is no problem here of finding adequate replacements, but a difficult managerial problem still exists. Who shall be promoted, Ulter or Root? And how can we obtain the cooperation of Ray in accepting the promotion of either Ulter or Root?

Analyses of this type can also lead to a discovery of an excess of talent in one area, which can lead to other human relations difficulties that should be recognized. Referring again to Figure 9-6, we find that group supervisor Kirby has no subordinate to replace him. Perhaps either Ulter or Root can be transferred. We still may have trouble,

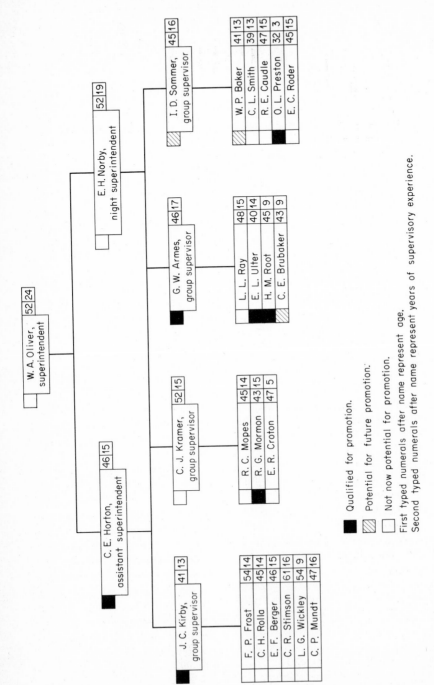

Figure 9-6 Promotability chart

Figure 9-7 Promotion direction chart: Inspection Department

Name	Promotability is for positions in the following areas:		
	Inspection	Direct manufacturing	Other areas
G. W. Ames	X		
W. P. Baker	X	X	
C. E. Brubaker		X	
C. E. Horton	X	X	
J. C. Kirby	X		X
R. G. Mormon	X		
O. L. Preston			X
H. M. Root	X		
I. D. Sommer	X		
E. L. Ulter	X	X	X

since Frost, Rolla, Berger, Stimson, Wickley, and Mundt may well resent such a transfer as infringing upon their rights of succession. Management's evaluation of capabilities and potentialities of subordinates often does not consider the subordinate's degree of self-education. This is compounded by the worship of seniority that exists in many firms, an attitude which does not permit recognition of the superiority of greater ability. Though the six supervisors previously named may recognize and admit the superior ability of Ulter or Root, there is nevertheless a strong feeling that the senior person deserves the promotion. Executive talent planning in action can be tremendously complicated by the feelings, emotions, and expectations of the persons around whom we are planning. But it is still advisable to lay out the problem and possible solutions as objectively as possible before tackling the human relations difficulties. If the law of the situation is discovered and applied, the selling job will become that much easier, particularly when working with higher-caliber personnel. One last interesting difficulty might be pointed out in the charts given. What happens to R. G. Mormon? She is qualified to replace Kramer, but Kramer is not qualified to move up. Neither is Kramer near retirement. Perhaps steps can be taken to provide some assistance for Mormon through transfer. Proper analysis can spot problems like these. It is generally true in business that the demand for properly qualified persons in management is greater than the available supply of such talent.

It has been appropriately pointed out that correctly determined transfers and promotions are not without their costs, particularly in large companies.[24] In moves involving relocation to a different plant and community, there are social losses for the family in the disruption of selling a home, leaving friends, purchasing a new house, and reestablishing the family unit in a new community. The latter involves the myriad of problems in locating doctors, dentists, appliance repairmen, and the like. The disruption of schooling of children was so severe in one case that tutors were provided at the expense of the company. These worries undoubtedly have some effect upon the short-term performance of the new appointee. In addition, there are societal costs resulting from development of a transient group that is tempted to take little interest in community social and political problems. This is particularly true if the usual practice

[24]Peter L. Mullins, "The Price Tag on Employee Transfers," *Personnel*, vol. 46, no. 2, March–April 1969, pp. 34–39.

involves moving key personnel every two or three years. This contributes to development of a narrow company-business-oriented society of friends and acquaintances which may lead to loss of contact with more general social values. Just as there is often an "American colony" in foreign cities having overseas branches, a transient executive society may lead to a "business only" parochialism that reacts with astonishment when the business system is criticized and regulated by general society. As in most decisions in business management, multiple values conflict to some degree in the formulation of a career program. At least, the manager responsible should be aware of the disvalues, as well as values, of a career program geared primarily to the needs of the company, secondarily to the needs of the employee, thirdly to the needs of family, and lastly to the noneconomic interests of society.

SUMMARY

The increasing shortage of competent executives in this country has given rise to special efforts to discover and develop executive talents. The development cycle for executives is not short and requires a considerable amount of planning and anticipation of problems that are distant in terms of years as well as months. A systematic program of executive talent planning should include certain basic elements: (1) organization planning of executive needs, (2) executive inventory and analysis, (3) executive recruitment, and (4) executive development. The first element, organization planning of executive needs, can in turn be broken down to include: (1) a determination of the rate of loss of present executives, thus establishing the replacement problem; (2) maintaining the talent pipeline; (3) a prediction of expansion of the firm, thus establishing the requirements of new positions; and (4) a determination of the qualities necessary properly to fill these positions.

Executive inventory and analysis should follow in order to ascertain the present status of available talent within the organization. This inventory is comprised of four steps: (1) a determination of the personnel to be inventoried, (2) a cataloging of factual background information on each individual, (3) systematic and detailed appraisal of those individuals included in the inventory, and (4) detailed study of those individuals deemed to possess potential for development as viewed by ratings of multiple line superiors.

It has been found that clinically oriented assessment centers are fairly effective in the appraisal of individual potential for executive positions. Various statistical studies on selected characteristics have shown some relationships with performance, as measured by jobs, salary, and ratings.

The results of executive talent planning can be portrayed in various ways, the most common method being a modified organization chart depicting, for each position, the age of the incumbent, qualifications for advancement, desires for advancement, and years of service in management positions. This information is of value in appraising the reserve potential for each position. It provides the basis for initiating transfers to supplement the personnel in critical areas and is of particular value in directing the recruitment, hiring, and development programs for executives within the organization. The executive inventory is individually oriented, thus providing an excellent foundation for the establishment of individual development programs. The amount of talent presently available in most organizations is much larger than is commonly suspected. A systematic approach toward its discovery and cataloging will do much to solve the talent shortage.

DISCUSSION QUESTIONS

1 What reasons give rise to a possible "crunch" in the procurement of executive talent in the future?

2 What is the nature of and approach to the task of maintaining the "pipeline" of talent leading to the filling of higher positions?

3 What specific statistical indexes have been utilized to identify potential executive talent early in a person's career?

4 Describe the operation of a typical assessment center.

5 In assessing the effectiveness of an assessment center, what are some of the reported findings?

6 Discuss the pros and cons of preparing job descriptions for executive positions. How can role descriptions add to their value?

7 Identify the four basic elements of an executive talent planning program, and indicate what techniques can be utilized to improve their effectiveness.

8 Of what value is a color-coded organization chart in executive talent management? What values could be added by a central talent data bank in a computer?

9 In what ways do assessment centers more fully meet governmental requirements with respect to discrimination in hiring?

10 Of what importance is personal motivation in identifying potential for managerial success? What are some of Miner's findings with respect to motivation of business managers, nonbusiness managers, and students?

SUPPLEMENTARY READING

GRIMSLEY, Glen, and Hilton F. Jarrett: "The Relation of Past Managerial Achievement to Test Measures Obtained in the Employment Situation: Methodology and Results," *Personnel Psychology*, vol. 26, no. 1, Spring 1973, pp. 31–48.

HOWARD, Ann: "An Assessment of Assessment Centers," *Academy of Management Journal*, vol. 17, no. 1, March 1974, pp. 115–134.

HUCK, James R.: "Assessment Centers: A Review of the External and Internal Validities," *Personnel Psychology*, vol. 26, no. 2, Summer 1973, pp. 191–212.

MINER, John B.: "The Real Crunch in Managerial Manpower," *Harvard Business Review*, vol. 51, no. 6, November–December 1973, pp. 146–158.

NIELSEN, Gordon L., and Allan R. Young: "Manpower Planning: A Markov Chain Application," *Public Personnel Management*, vol. 2, no. 2, March–April 1973, pp. 133–144.

STEWART, Rosemary: "The Manager's Job: Discretion vs. Demand," *Organizational Dynamics*, vol. 2, no. 3, Winter 1973, pp. 67–80.

CASES FOR PART THREE

THE CASE OF THE WORRIED ATTORNEY

George Helms paced the floor of his den. It was 2 A.M., and his wife had urged him to stop worrying and go to bed. George felt, however, that he had to make a decision before he could sleep. Which of the two young law graduates should their law firm of Harrison, Holmes, and Helms hire? Since the one chosen would presumably be a partner some day, the decision was doubly important.

As he worried about the choice, his thoughts returned to his own graduation day fifteen years ago. While growing up near San Francisco, he had always felt that his family, especially his father, had kept him on a particularly tight leash. Sometimes Helms resented the fact that his father was such a prominent judge in the Bay area. Despite doing well in school and sports, he was never sure he had done as well as his father had expected. Upon graduation from law school he had been accepted by the State Department for a foreign assignment in France. Instead of his father's being pleased, he had strongly advised him to turn down the appointment and come back to San Francisco to enter the firm of Harrison and Holmes. The discussion concerning this had been long and sometimes bitter. In the end, George had returned to San Francisco, and as he reflected now, it had been for the best. He had been quite happy with this old San Francisco law firm.

Helms's mind next moved to the first of the two applicants who were being considered. Eleven in total had applied or been asked to apply for the opening in the firm. All were recent law school graduates. The field had been narrowed to two, Bruce

Hargraves, who had received his law degree from Michigan four years ago, and Roger Parnes, who was graduating from Stanford this year. As George pondered his decision, he asked himself why Harrison and Holmes had left so much of this decision on his shoulders. Bruce Hargraves . . . surely a top-flight student . . . second in his class . . . had been one of the editors of the school's law review . . . had also done some teaching . . . was active in local Democratic politics . . . wonder where he got the time for all of this? Helms recalled that Hargraves had taken a job with an oil company in Iran after graduation. He recalled in the interview that he had asked why, and that Hargraves had snapped back that it was for the money. Hargraves then had told him about his childhood and teen-age years in Columbus—how he had always had some kind of job since he was twelve, and how he had been arrested for street fighting when he was fifteen. Helms recalled that Hargraves had won an engineering scholarship at MIT but had turned it down. He had gone to Michigan instead. Hargraves told how he had it figured out that he had enough money to get through the football season without taking a job. In the winter, he got a six-hour-a-day factory job in Willow Run and also received a small athletic scholarship. Helms recalled asking if he had ever played varsity ball at Michigan. Hargraves had replied that he and the coach had had an argument, and that he quit the squad as a result. Hargraves added that he was able to make more money playing semipro industrial football on Saturdays and Sundays. George recollected that Hargrave's grades in college were surely outstanding; in fact, he had graduated a member of Phi Beta Kappa. Other data concerning Hargraves came to mind. He had turned down a bid from a fraternity because he could not afford it. He had been quite active in campus political clubs. That, he said, had helped him get a summer job in the Governor's office one year. When Hargraves graduated from college, he was almost immediately drafted. He had told Helms that he had become a sergeant and had seen quite a bit of action. When asked about his marital status, Hargraves had artfully dodged the question. He said he had no plans to settle down until he was a tired old man of forty. Helms remembered smiling at the remark but thought it a little brash. George decided that there was something in Hargraves's manner that disturbed him. He remembered the day the two of them had driven to Oakland in Hargraves's Austin-Healey. He had felt the same way that day. He just could not put his finger on what it was, though.

Helms's attention now shifted to Roger Parnes. He could not quite get used to the idea of young Roger Parnes becoming a member of his or any other law firm. Though he had not really known Roger before he had made application to the firm, he had seen him around the San Francisco area for years. Roger's father had been a friend of the family, though he could not remember his ever coming to the house. He and Roger had played golf in the same foursome a time or two. George laughed to himself as he recalled that until recently he had thought that golf was Parnes's greatest accomplishment in life. Reading Roger's transcripts had shown George that Roger's brain was more agile than he had realized. Though not brilliant, he had been in the top third of the Stanford Law School class during his first two years. This did not stack up to Hargraves's record, but it was certainly acceptable. Actually, Roger had a bit more legal experience than the other man. He had spent the past six summers working as a law clerk. Hargraves's job with the oil company had not been in the legal field, though he was hired for his law training. Thinking back to Hargraves, George reflected he had sort of a take-charge quality that many people probably admired. He was unable to find such a quality in Roger, though he knew that Roger got along well with people. He reasoned, therefore, that people must certainly have looked to Roger for leadership. When Roger was very young, he had considered him to be a "mamma's boy," with his carefully combed hair and almost too well-groomed clothes. Later recollections included him on the golf course, racing his sailboat, and at a dance or two with Charlotte Gilmour. Charlotte's family had been very close friends of George's, so he had gotten to know Roger a little in this way. Roger's only years away from California were two spent in the service. George did not recall where.

George lighted another cigarette and paced some more. Why had Fletcher Harrison and Charles Holmes left the decision up to him when they were the senior partners? He very well knew how each stood. Fletcher had said that George should make the decision, and then added that, from the interviews, young Parnes appeared to be very capable. George then thought back to his own father's comments that when Helms, Sr., and Harrison were in law partnership, Fletcher sometimes took days to express an opinion or make a decision. Charles Holmes had made his feelings more obvious. Charles had been given his first job by George's father. He said he thought Hargraves was the sharpest young fellow he had seen in a long time.

Helms smoked and paced some more. He sat down and decided that Roger Parnes would make a fine member of the firm. Feeling relieved, he went to bed. On getting up the following morning, he thought a bit more about his decision. Although not completely satisfied, he decided that all had worked out for the best.

THE CASE OF THE FULL WORK ASSIGNMENT

Brooks Valu Center was a large discount grocery-department store located in the Midwest. It was the only store of its kind in the city and was the main shopping outlet for many people in the town. Due to the inventory and profit policies, the grocery and department areas were each autonomous, separated by a wide aisle. Each had its own manager, staff positions, and check-out counters. The only person having authority over both grocery and department operations was Mr. Brooks himself.

The department store had a staff of cashiers which included four full-time cashiers, working during the days, and five part-time cashiers who usually worked evenings, Saturdays, and Sundays. All of the cashiers were under the authority of Mrs. Foster, head cashier. She, in turn, reported directly to Mr. Een, department store manager.

One evening an incident arose which greatly disrupted the unity of the department store cashiering staff and alienated the department store manager from the cashiers.

As reported by one of the cashiers:

"Mr. Brooks always placed great emphasis on speed of check-out. He would just see red if he came in and saw long lines at the check-out counters. On the other hand, he hated to see a cashier with nothing to do. These attitudes created a problem. If we had enough cashiers to immediately take care of the customers, we would invariably be idle part of the evening.

"Mr. Brooks, Mr. Een, and Mrs. Foster discussed this problem and decided that the cashiers could be responsible for marking prices on items during the slower parts of the evening. They would do this at the check-out counters, marking only items which were small and would not require much room. In this way, they would be available in case a line of customers formed. This was all right with us, as we didn't like to just stand with nothing to do.

"One evening business was unusually slow. There were three cashiers, but very few customers. Mr. Een had looked for some small merchandise for us to mark but had found none. Finally he brought us a dust cloth and said one of us would have to dust the racks in the men's and women's clothing departments. We were angry at this, as we felt this was not part of our job. The janitors came every evening, and we thought they should be doing the cleaning. Evidently they never touched those racks as, we found out later, they were positively filthy.

"We decided among us that Sue should go and dust while Barb and I stayed at the registers. We knew Mrs. Foster wouldn't be happy at her cashiers being demoted to janitors, as she thought a cashier's job was a very important one and took great pride in it. We were also angry at taking orders from Mr. Een, as none of us particularly cared for him anyway.

"Around eight o'clock business picked up and both Barb and I had short lines at our registers. Rather than call Sue on the intercom to come and help, we decided that if Mr. Een wanted us to be janitors, we would comply with his wishes. Our lines grew longer and we were very surprised to see Mr. Brooks come through the door. He took one look at the situation and without a word to Barb or me, strode over to the third register and began to check customers through that lane.

"Barb picked up the intercom and called Sue to the register but, as we found out later, she had just finished dusting and had gone to the restroom to wash her hands. I guess she also took a short rest and smoked a cigarette too, figuring she deserved a break after completing her extra job. The intercom wasn't hooked up to the restroom, so she didn't know about our dilemma until it was over.

"As the lines diminished, Mr. Brooks closed the register and, still without a word, went immediately to Mr. Een's office. I guess he demanded to know how many cashiers had been scheduled to work and where they all were. Later, both of them came down and ushered Sue back to Mr. Een's office. They were really angry and both of them were very harsh with Sue—said she had to be accessible at all times in case she was needed. I don't know whether she would have been fired or not. As it was, she was so upset she quit her job on the spot.

"Barb and I also got a talking to after the store closed. Brooks was angry that we hadn't called Sue when the lines began to form. Mr. Een, however, was trying to smooth over the situation, and he emphasized how all the groups had to work together for a good store, how important morale was, and all that. We were both upset about Sue, so didn't listen to either one.

"Mrs. Foster heard all about the situation the next morning from Mr. Een. As we thought, she was upset about the cashiers having to dust the fixtures, but she couldn't do much about it. She was also disgusted with Mr. Brooks and Mr. Een for being so condemning with Sue—forcing her to quit. She had been a good cashier and now Mrs. Foster would have to take additional time to train someone else for the job.

"Things finally cooled down. As long as I worked there Mr. Een never again asked us to dust. I guess Mrs. Foster made it clear that cleaning wasn't a cashier's job and that we didn't have to do it. However, the morale of the cashiering staff was much lower than it had been before, and many of the other store employees blamed Mr. Een for what had happened, thereby choosing sides."

THE CASE OF THE FIRM IN SEARCH OF LEADERSHIP:
ARCHER COMPANY*

Upon the death of their father, the two sons of Frederick Archer each took part of their father's original business and set up separate establishments. James Archer set up the Archer Company, an advertising specialty manufacturing firm, making metal, wood, and paper advertising items.

The Archer Company organization was set up by James Archer when he was 40 years old. He operated the business as its sole owner and principal executive for 15 years. The company employed about 150 people in the plant, on the average, and had a staff of nine salesmen. Most of the business of the firm was special order work. The Archer Company was highly regarded for the quality of its work.

James Archer, at the age of 55, began formulating plans for the future of his organization in the light of his planned retirement from active management a few years hence. His primary objective was to leave a strong, going concern. The plan, as matured by Archer, provided for the establishment of three key positions in the organization. These three positions were general manager, sales manager, and factory manager. It was Archer's purpose to have the men holding these three positions act as the executive committee of the company in determining policy and making important decisions. Initially, Archer would maintain active connection with the company, but he would gradually give over operating authority to the general manager, who would make use of the executive committee in formulating policy.

Up to the time this plan was developed, the Archer Company was a one-man organization operated by Archer himself. After a careful survey of his existing staff, Archer felt it necessary to go outside the firm to fill the newly created positions.

As general manager of the concern, Archer selected his son-in-law, Samuel Barton. At the time of his employment, Barton was not well acquainted with the business. He was rated by associates as a man of superior mental ability. He demonstrated an excellent capacity at long-range planning and organizing and was considered an average administrator. Some of his associates said he was moody at times and attributed what was called "personality difficulties" to the fact that he was hard of hearing and used a hearing aid. Barton had an obvious personal interest in the position by virtue of family connections and undertook his new job with enthusiasm.

For the position of sales manager, Archer selected James McCarthy. McCarthy was an outstanding salesman with a record of great success in this industry. He had a tremendous amount of drive and had achieved his reputation through his personal sales efforts. He had limited experience as a sales executive. At the time he was hired, his administrative skill in directing a sales force was an unknown quality. Archer was motivated in selecting McCarthy by the belief that his knowledge of salesmanship in this industry and his obvious success would serve as an example and inspiration to the sales force.

William Stevens was hired by Archer for the position of factory manager. Stevens had no direct production experience in this industry. However, for some years he had sold equipment throughout this industry and had a thorough knowledge of the machinery, its use, and its capabilities.

---

*Robert Dubin, *Human Relations in Administration*, 2d ed., Prentice-Hall, Inc., Englewood Cliffs, N.J., 1961, pp. 485–490. Used with permission.

Shortly after these three principal executives were installed in office, they made plans for achieving an annual volume of business of one million dollars. The business was to be expanded over a five-year period to reach this goal. This represented a substantial increase from the present volume of about $600,000 a year. Archer participated in this planning as the source of final authority in approving the work of the new executive committee.

Anticipating the expanding business, a decision was made to hire two additional specialists. Will Harrison was selected to fill the job of plant superintendent under Mr. Stevens. Harrison had worked in the industry for many years and had a fine reputation for his technical knowledge. Arnold Jefferson was hired as chief designer. He came to the Archer Company with an excellent background in product design, having done such work with several companies and with a design consulting firm in New York.

Also in line with the expansion program, an order was placed for a considerable amount of new production equipment. At this time a major contract was secured covering a 10-year period and calling for an estimated annual sales of $250,000 to this single account, the largest in the company's history.

In the face of sales expansion and plant modernization, Archer personally hired Sidney Fremont, an industrial engineer, to work on plant layout and production processes. Fremont was hired only on a project basis, but did such a creditable job that he was retained permanently to work out industrial engineering problems.

The final stage of staff expansion was reached when a decision was made to secure a new man to take over the job of Jefferson, the chief designer. Jefferson was considered a competent designer capable of developing other people's ideas. He was considered weak, however, on originality in design. The decision was made to move him into the sales department, where his talents would be particularly useful in servicing established accounts. To replace him, Wayne Klinger was employed as chief designer. In previous positions, Klinger had demonstrated exceptional promotional talents; he gave every promise of being the idea man desired for the position.

About a year after the organization began to expand, its structure was as shown in the chart (Phase I) on page 204.

In the course of the development of Phase I in the growth of the Archer Company, a number of problems arose. First of all, it became reasonably clear that the executive committee idea was not serving in the manner intended by Archer. He had retained very direct participation in the organization and his staff continued to look to him as the active chief executive. This was particularly true of McCarthy, the sales manager. Although nominally reporting to Barton, McCarthy often bypassed Barton and took problems directly to Archer. Archer's reaction to this was to continue to permit Barton to be bypassed. Archer viewed such action by McCarthy as a natural continuation of the sort of consultation he was used to as active head of the business.

At the same time that McCarthy seemed to be making an effort to work around Barton, he was frequently a minority of one in the executive committee in opposing the creation of new jobs and persons hired to fill them. This was particularly true of Klinger, to whom McCarthy took an instant dislike. Part of McCarthy's dislike for Klinger may have been related to the fact that Klinger soon developed direct contacts with customers and was responsible for securing some important accounts on his own. In the nature of his work as new-idea man in the organization, Klinger had a lot of opportunity to contact customers and, if possible, secure their accounts through such contacts.

Archer Company organization: Phase I

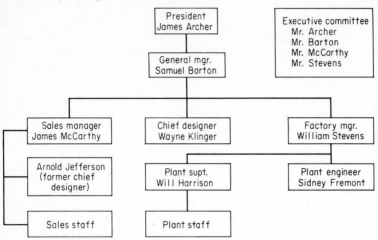

McCarthy was the object of considerable discontent among the salesmen. They felt that he was seldom at the office to help them, and in fact, was never really available for consultation or help with sales problems. McCarthy was on the road a great deal. Some of his sales staff undoubtedly viewed him as a potential threat in their own territories, since, by virtue of being sales manager, he could work in any territory he chose.

Barton soon found himself on the most friendly and cordial terms with Klinger. This friendship extended even to after-hours recreation, in which the two men spent considerable time together. This friendship was ultimately viewed by many of their associates as the cause of Barton's wife divorcing him. These observers said that Barton and Klinger had developed quite a reputation for "painting the town red" to the point where Mrs. Barton could no longer ignore her husband's activities.

McCarthy had by this time become so enraged with Klinger that he successfully delved into Klinger's past and sent a report to Archer outlining some of the more undesirable features of Klinger's career. Archer was not disposed to fire Klinger, since, on business grounds, his work was entirely satisfactory. However, the report from McCarthy, together with Klinger's connection with the events leading to the Barton divorce, put him in a frame of mind to accept Klinger's resignation when it was offered at the time of the divorce. (Klinger also had gained knowledge of the fact that Archer had the McCarthy report on Klinger's unsavory past. The combination of Klinger's close connection with Barton's divorce and Archer's knowledge of his past probably led him to submit his resignation.) The removal of Klinger from the organization tended to relieve McCarthy's feelings only temporarily.

Barton also offered his resignation to Archer at the time of the divorce. In spite of Archer's obvious hurt at seeing his daughter seek a divorce, he told Barton that he was doing a good job and did not have to resign. Archer pointed out that "A man's personal life has nothing to do with his business life. He would be judged on the job only as he was successful in the latter."

At about this juncture in the affairs of the company, Archer became increasingly

Archer Company organization: Phase II

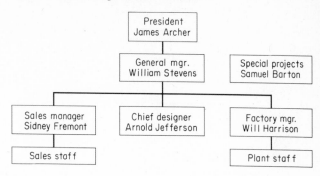

aware that the strong organization he had envisioned had not yet materialized. He had this view confirmed when a personnel consultant hired by Barton discussed the organization with him. Archer came to the conclusion that he would have to shake up the organization drastically.

McCarthy was let go. In his place, Sideny Fremont, the industrial engineer, was appointed. Arnold Jefferson, the former chief designer, was given his old position back to take the job left vacant by Klinger's resignation. William Stevens was moved up from factory manager to general manager in place of Barton, who was retained in the company but given no specific assignment other than to be available for work on special projects. Finally, Will Harrison, plant superintendent, was moved up to factory manager and his old position was abolished. The executive committee was discontinued.

In the second phase of the growth of the Archer Company, the organization was as shown in Phase II.

The replacement of McCarthy by Fremont has been viewed by the sales staff as a distinct improvement. Fremont spends considerable time working individually with the salesmen and confines most of his work to the office, leaving direct sales to the salesmen. Jefferson is said to have improved and seems to display more creative ability than he first showed upon joining the organization. Stevens occasionally encounters difficulties in making decisions, according to some of his associates, but he has easy access to Archer's advice and counsel on such occasions. Harrison is doing a capable job of running the factory. Barton is called in on special projects to lend his assistance whenever and wherever needed.

PART FOUR

DEVELOPMENT

The final phase of the procurement function is induction. Immediately after induction, and usually combined with it, is the function of developing the employee's ability to do the job on which he or she has been placed. In this section we shall examine the training of operative employees (Chapter 10) and the development of managerial personnel (Chapter 11). Since the opportunity to advance is essential to an effective development climate, we shall next present discussions of the means and avenues of advancement (Chapter 12), as well as of the function of appraising employee performance (Chapter 13) so that the nature and direction of employee development can be determined.

TEN

TRAINING OPERATIVE PERSONNEL

After the employee has been selected, placed, and inducted, she or he must next be trained. Training is the act of increasing the knowledge and skill of an employee for doing a particular job. No firm has a choice of whether to train or not; the only choice is that of method. If no planned program of training is established, training costs have not thereby been eliminated. The employee must engage in self-training by trial and error or by observing others. It has been proved that the absence of a systematic training program generally results in higher training costs, not only because of the considerably lengthened learning period but also because of the likelihood that the employee will not learn the best operating methods.

In the establishment of a sound training program, the interests of labor and management should be close if not identical. The values to a firm of skilled and knowledgeable employees are many, and they will be discussed in the following section. Adequate training is equally desirable for the employee. A learned skill is an asset that can be taken away only by the complete elimination of the need for that skill. It is valuable to the employee in terms of better security and greater opportunity for advancement within or without the present organization. The untrained job applicant should be as much interested in a firm's training program as in the starting salary, for it often happens that the lower-paying job offers a greater training opportunity and may well prove to be the sounder choice in the long run. Training is one of the areas of management in which employer and employee have a mutual interest.

Because of the breadth of the subject and the multiplicity of approaches, we shall split the discussion of training into two parts, the training of operative personnel and the development of managers. Although basic principles of teaching should be applicable to both types of personnel, the widely different nature of their duties and responsibilities requires different approaches. We shall cover training of operative personnel in this chapter and shall discuss managerial development in the next.

IMPORTANCE OF TRAINING

The importance of training to a business firm or any other type of organization should be readily apparent. The major values are:

1 *Increased productivity.* An increase in skill usually results in an increment in both quantity and quality of output. The increasingly technical nature of modern jobs demands systematic training to make possible even minimum levels of accomplishment.

2 *Heightened morale.* Possession of needed skills helps to meet such basic human needs as security and ego satisfaction. Elaborate personnel and human relations programs can make a contribution toward morale, but they are hollow shells if there is no solid core of meaningful work done with knowledge, skill, and pride.

3 *Reduced supervision.* The trained employee is one who can perform with limited supervision. Both employee and supervisor want less supervision, but greater independence is not possible unless the employee is adequately trained.

4 *Reduced accidents.* More accidents are caused by deficiencies in people than by deficiencies in equipment and working conditions. Proper training, in both job skills and safety attitudes, should contribute toward a reduction in the accident rate.

5 *Increased organizational stability and flexibility.* Stability, the ability of an organization to sustain its effectiveness despite the loss of key personnel, can be developed only through creation of a reservoir of trained replacements. Flexibility, the ability to adjust to short-run variations in the volume of work, requires personnel with multiple skills to permit their transfer to jobs where the demand is highest. There is no greater organizational asset than that of trained and motivated personnel.

The above-listed values demonstrate the importance of training to the organization. In the past three decades, automation and technology have intensified the importance of training in assuring the survival of both employees and organizations. The task of converting the skills of huge segments of our labor force is one that demands the best efforts and thinking of management, labor unions, and government.

The development of human resources through training and education is a subject of considerable importance to society in general. Unemployment rates of 5 to 6 percent of the work force usually generate a number of governmentally sponsored programs to develop initial hiring skills for the young and to retrain personnel who have been displaced by mechanization or automation of work processes. It is estimated that enrollment in federally funded work-training programs had grown from 50,000 in the early 1960s to approximately 1 million persons in any given month in 1971.[1] One of the earlier legislative attempts in this regard was the Manpower Development and Retraining Act of 1962, which was designed to assist in the conversion to new skills of those persons thrown out of work by changing job requirements. Eligible persons received training in skills needed in the local labor market at special skill centers or training schools outside the regular school system. Subsistence and transportation allowances were also provided. In 1964, the Economic Opportunity Act was directed toward providing training help for young entrants in the job market: there were established

---

[1] Sylvia S. Small, "Statistical Effect of Work-Training Programs on the Unemployment Rate," *Monthly Labor Review*, vol. 95, no. 9, September 1972, p. 7.

Neighborhood Youth Corps to help school dropouts acquire usable skills in the local area, Job Corps that provided training away from home for those needing a change in environment, and a College Work Study program for full-time undergraduate students whose resources were inadequate to enable them to stay in college. In all these, immediate training objectives were emphasized to the possible detriment of job placement; there were high graduation rates, followed by low placement. Some poor Americans were being trained three and four times; training, in effect, became the occupation.

Later programs attempted to relate more effectively the training given to an actual job placement. The Work Incentive Program (WIN), replacing a prior program, was designed to move people from welfare rolls into meaningful permanent employment. State employment service personnel provided on-the-job training, counseling, and job referral. Employers are allowed a 20 percent tax credit for wages paid WIN recipients for the first twelve months of employment. In this program, females constituted 60 percent of the total participants. The Public Service Careers program, specifically oriented toward placing the disadvantaged in government work, usually involved hiring first and training later. The Job Opportunities in the Business Sector (JOBS), previously discussed in Chapter 3, was oriented toward initial placement of the hard-core unemployed, followed by supportive counseling and training to effect permanent employment.

It has been estimated that the overall effect of these many federally sponsored programs has been to reduce the unemployment rate approximately 0.3 percent.[2] The principle has been established that training is no longer the exclusive concern of the hiring organization, that society has established as a primary goal the more effective development and utilization of its human resources. The modern personnel manager, with an enhanced sense of social responsibility, will find that this societal goal will cross the borders of the organization, resulting in hiring, counseling, and coaching programs that may or may not be underwritten by governmental funds. Training cannot occur in a vacuum; the cooperative efforts of multiple private organizations are absolutely essential.

TRAINING AND EDUCATION

At this point in the discussion we must distinguish between training and education. As defined earlier, training is concerned with increasing knowledge and skill in doing a particular job, and the major burden for training falls upon the business organization in which the job is located. On the other hand, education is concerned with increasing general knowledge and understanding of our total environment. Business firms are also involved in the educational process, since they want their employees to have knowledge and understanding of the economic environment. But the major burden for educating falls upon our formal school system.

The difference between training and education is not precise. It resembles a continuum ranging from general to specific, i.e., from general background for proper understanding to specific skill for proper execution. Thus, when we teach a person how to assemble two objects and tighten a nut, we are without doubt training to do a

[2]Ibid., p. 12.

specific job. At the other extreme, a course in the appreciation of art or music can be certainly labeled education. In between there can be many gradations. A course in motion and time study is found in many colleges. Is it training or education? It is education in the sense that no one specific technique or procedure can be taught, and the certain fundamentals common to all business situations are emphasized. The student will have to be trained by the business firm in its particular motion and time study philosophy and technique.

A course in human relations is also offered by many colleges and universities. In contrast to the motion and time study course, it is considerably less specific and lays more emphasis upon building background and attitudes. Thus, one might observe the human relations class and label it education, and study the motion and time study class and call it training. Properly speaking, we should state that the motion and time study class approaches a training situation more closely than the human relations class. This illustration should serve to demonstrate the nature and relationship of training and education, and an attempt has been made in Figure 10-1 to portray this concept. Both training and education are involved in the development of personnel to the desired level of skill, knowledge, and attitude. In general, the higher the job in the organization, the more important education becomes as a job requirement. This principle may explain the increasing emphasis upon the recruitment of college graduates for

Figure 10-1

THE TRAINING-
EDUCATION CONTINUUM

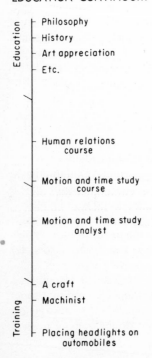

Education
- Philosophy
- History
- Art appreciation
- Etc.

- Human relations
  course
- Motion and time study
  course
- Motion and time study
  analyst

- A craft
- Machinist
- Placing headlights on
  automobiles

Training

positions from which one can advance in the organization. We shall give more attention to education in the following chapter on management development.

PRINCIPLES OF TRAINING

As one observes a new, unskilled employee during the time when she or he is acquiring a skill, it is very evident that a complex process is under way. On the basis of extensive research, a number of principles have been evolved which serve as guides toward imparting skills, knowledges, and attitudes. Among these guides are the following:

1 *Motivation.* The more highly motivated the trainee, the more quickly and thoroughly a new skill or knowledge is learned. The means (training) must be related to an end which the trainee desires (more money, a job, recognition, promotion, etc.). Motivating a new employee is usually much easier than motivating an older person who is undergoing a process of upgrading or retraining. It must also be recognized that the motivation within the classroom, as provided by the trainer, is not always consistent with motivation back on the job as provided by the supervisor. When undergoing retraining in particular, the trainee's prestige is at stake, and he or she must usually have a means of rationalizing failure, if it should occur. The typical trainee approaches the training sessions motivated by many needs, and the trainer would be wise to assume neither their apparentness nor their simplicity.

2 *Progress reports.* Various research studies have demonstrated a relation between the specificity and amount of progress information and the rapidity and effectiveness of learning. Care must be taken, however, to assure that neither excessive information nor information that can be misinterpreted is given. The trainee is having a sufficiently difficult time absorbing a new skill without also having to learn to handle too much or the wrong type of progress information.

3 *Reinforcement.* When skills are learned, the effect should be reinforced by means of rewards and punishments. Promotions, pay increases, and praise are typical positive reinforcements. Management should be careful to ensure that rewards are properly forthcoming to successful trainees and that the operational parts of the organization are consistent with the training segment. When behavior is not the type desired by the organization, experts in operant conditioning suggest that it should be ignored or met with a neutral response.[3] Though punishment is the most typical response to undesirable behavior, it is contended that penalties work to the long-term detriment of the trainer through incurring resentment and ill will. It is also contended that positive reinforcement dispensed on a variable ratio schedule (after a varying number of responses unknown to the trainee) will be more effective in sustaining desired behavior over a longer period. Again, the more widespread practice in the beginning is to reward the trainee after *each* time success is attained, thus following a fixed and continuous reinforcement schedule. In time, the reward schedule will become more variable as the trainee is given less and less attention by the trainer.

4 *Practice.* To effectively acquire a skill, knowledge, or attitude, active participation

---

[3]Fred Luthans and David Lyman, "Training Supervisors to Use Organizational Behavior Modification," *Personnel*, vol. 50, no. 5, September–October 1973, pp. 38–44.

by the trainee is essential. Carefully spaced practice periods are essential to effective learning. Learning plateaus are often encountered in various types of operative jobs, and trainees must be informed of their significance. Otherwise, they will become discouraged and feel that they will never successfully meet the norm. In the elemental method of training, it is claimed that these plateaus can be avoided by teaching basic skills.[4] Jobs are broken down into elements from which are extracted the fundamental physical, sensory, and mental skills. Training exercises are provided for each skill, incorporating the rhythm, motions, and tempo of the expert from the outset. Using this particular approach, a group of dry-cleaning trainees achieved average incentive rate in eight weeks as compared with the usual twenty weeks.

5 *Whole versus part.* The research is not clear concerning whether it is best to teach the whole job at once or to establish a series of subgoals for various parts. The longer and more complex the job, the more likely that subportions will be taught. The trainee then has the task of putting the parts together into an effective whole. When parts are taught, training usually proceeds from the known to the unknown, from the easy to the difficult. Providing for the motivation of the trainee is always an important task of the trainer.

6 *Individual differences.* Though group training is often an economic necessity, it is apparent that individuals vary in intelligence and aptitude. Consequently, the most effective training would adjust pace and complexity to individual abilities. With the introduction of individual teaching machines, adjustment to these differences will become more practicable.

SYSTEMS OF OPERATIVE TRAINING

Though the basic principles of teaching are applicable to both training and education and to one system of training as contrasted with another, still it is important to be aware of the training systems that are available and used in business. In the operative area, there are four: (1) on-the-job training, (2) vestibule school, (3) apprenticeship, and (4) special courses. The most commonly used system is that of on-the-job training. This system places the primary burden upon the immediate supervisor or a selected representative. The reasons for the widespread use of this system are many. In the first place, most of the jobs in industry are of the type that can be learned in a relatively short period of time—a week or two at most—and no elaborate program is necessary as far as subject content is concerned. Automation will gradually change this situation. On-the-job training also has the advantage of simplicity, because there is no division of responsibility between a training department and line supervision. It may be pointed out that this method of training is highly economical since no additional personnel or facilities are required. This economy is sometimes false, however, particularly if the line supervisor (1) does not know how to train subordinates, (2) does not have time to train properly, or (3) does not appreciate the importance of adequate training.

ON-THE-JOB TRAINING   This is a basic system which must be utilized to some degree by all organizations. It has the advantage of strongly motivating the trainee to learn. It is

---

[4]Charles P. Horgan, "A New Approach to Training: The Elemental Method," *Personnel,* July–August 1963, pp. 39–44.

not located in an artificial situation, either physically or psychologically. The fact that the success of the system depends almost entirely upon the immediate supervisor, the trainer, means that even in on-the-job training systems the personnel department has a great responsibility for making a good, effective teacher out of every supervisor. Because of the pervasive nature of on-the-job training and the present fundamental importance of the approach, we shall give more attention later to the process of teaching that the teacher-supervisor should follow.

VESTIBULE SCHOOLS   These are adapted to the same general type of training problem that is faced by on-the-job training. A vestibule school is operated as a specialized endeavor by the personnel department. It usually trains for the same type of job as on-the-job training, i.e., work of the semiskilled machine operator or tender. Why, then, have a vestibule school? The reason lies in the law of functional growth, as described in Chapter 4. When the amount of training that has to be done exceeds the capacity of the line supervisor, a portion of this training is evolved from the line and assigned to staff through a vestibule school. When the volume of training becomes too great, the supervisor can no longer cope with the on-the-job technique and still fulfill other responsibilities of production, quality, housekeeping, and so on.

It should be noted also that this situation sometimes creates typical line-staff difficulties of the kind that were discussed in Chapter 5. The staff school trains the employee and turns him or her over to the supervisor. If the employee is deficient in performance, who is to blame? The supervisor may "pass the buck" to the school and attribute the poor performance to improper training. The school may return the ball to the supervisor and attribute it to poor induction that led to the confusion of the employee. Any time a staff function is evolved from line, myriad opportunities for conflicts arise. In fact, a function in its entirety cannot be removed from the line; some vestige must remain for control purposes. This calls for careful definition of line and staff responsibilities plus continuing indoctrination concerning the values of line and staff cooperation toward the common objective.

The advantages of using the vestibule-school system are the advantages of specialization. The instructor, a specialist, should be more skilled at teaching. The student avoids the confusion and pressure of the work situation and thus is able to concentrate on learning. One can also often attain a given level of skill more quickly in the specialized learning situation. We have more assurance that adequate time and attention will be given to training and that it will not be slighted in favor of other problems. More individualized instruction can be given, and training activities do not interfere with the regular processes of production.

Just as specialization has advantages, so it also creates difficulties. As noted above, the splitting of responsibility leads to organizational problems. This type of schooling is limited to jobs that utilize equipment which can be duplicated without excessive investment. A final disadvantage is that the training situation is somewhat artificial, a fact which, though it may facilitate learning, may also inhibit adjustment when the employee is placed on the job. The immediate supervisor must still assume the burden of orientation so that learned skills can be put to productive use.

APPRENTICESHIP PROGRAMS   The third system of training, apprenticeship programs, is designed for a higher level of skill. Apprenticeship programs tend toward more education than on-the-job training or vestibule schools, in that knowledge and skill in doing a craft or a series of related jobs are involved. The usual apprenticeship program combines on-the-job training and experience with classroom instruction in particular subjects.

The basic federal law establishing apprenticeship policy is the National Apprenticeship Act of 1937, which is administered by the Bureau of Apprenticeship and Training of the Department of Labor. In addition, some thirty states have their own apprenticeship laws.

Specific apprenticeship programs are administered by joint labor and management committees for each craft. These committees, called JACs, establish the selection qualifications for entry into a program. Though they vary from craft to craft, general requirements include a high school education, letters of recommendation, specified intelligence and aptitude scores on standard tests, and willingness of a particular employer to hire the applicant for the apprenticeship period, usually three to five years. Because of the length and expense of these programs, the last qualification is perhaps the most confining.

The values of registering a program with the government agencies are several: (1) the certificate of completion awarded to journeymen is widely recognized and accepted, (2) public school facilities can be used for classroom instruction, and (3) though little used, the employer is legally empowered to pay an apprentice less than the minimum wage. Smaller employers tend to support programs in order to increase the number of journeymen available for operative jobs. Larger employers often look upon apprenticeship programs as a major source for first-level supervisors.

The JACs are responsible for the content of apprenticeship training programs under the general guidelines established by the government. This includes decisions concerning course content, means of instruction and examination, and allocation of time between organized group instruction and work on the job. Federal guidelines call for a minimum of 144 hours of classroom time each year. In the building trades, the administration of these programs is largely left in the hands of the labor union members of the committee.

Any program approved or financed in part by the federal government must be free of discrimination on the basis of race, creed, color, sex, or nationality. It is contended that various labor unions and firms utilize apprenticeship programs not only as a means of controlling the supply of labor but also as a means of preventing entry of certain minority groups into higher-skilled occupations.[5]

Programs registered with the government are required to use "objective standards" and to provide "full and fair opportunity for application." The Civil Rights Act of 1964 specifically prohibits discrimination in all phases of employment, including training. Because of the previously discussed problem of culturally biased psychological tests, discrimination can continue on a legal basis; e.g., in one major Southern city, every JAC was in compliance with the law, yet there were no black apprentices in any major program.[6] In one celebrated case, a black in Houston, Texas, when denied entrance to a program at the Hughes Tool Company, appealed to the National Labor Relations Board, declaring that the union committed an unfair practice in refusing to press his case. The NLRB agreed and decertified the union as bargaining representative.

[5]Irving Kovarsky, "Management, Racial Discrimination and Apprentice Training Programs," *Journal of the Academy of Management*, vol. 7, no. 3, September 1964, pp. 196–203.

[6]Ray Marshall and Vernon M. Briggs, Jr., "Remedies for Discrimination in Apprenticeship Programs," *Industrial Relations*, vol. 6, no. 3, May 1967, p. 305.

It was subsequently replaced by a local of the United Steel Workers, and the applicant successfully passed the examinations and was admitted to the program. Thus, it is possible to use both the National Labor Relations Act and the Civil Rights Act in attempting to reduce discrimination in admission to apprenticeship programs.

Apprenticeship programs are available in a number of crafts such as machinists, electricians, pipefitters, welders, tinners, carpenters, and millwrights. The mechanical apprenticeship program in Champion Paper and Fibre Company, for example, encompasses a period of four years. Four hours per week must be spent in classroom training for which instructors are provided by the company. Progress reports are given every three months for the first year and every six months thereafter. The apprentice has the same status as other employees with respect to insurance, vacations, and bonuses. In a survey of 193 manufacturing firms, approximately 14 percent reported having formal apprenticeship programs.[7]

SPECIAL COURSES The last system of operative training may be classified by some as education rather than training. Yet special courses, such as shop math or blueprint reading, cannot be labeled as general education and can be directly related to a person's particular job.

A particularly difficult problem in this regard is the maintenance of professional skills when technological knowledge grows at a rapid pace. Analysis of the experiences of 2,500 engineers in technology-based industries indicated that the performance ratings of engineers tend to peak during the age period 31 to 35.[8] The more challenging assignments involving new technology tend to be given to younger personnel. Performance appraisal systems that pit employee against employee tend to discourage personnel occupying the lower half of the curve. Realizing the greater mobility of the younger engineers, management may allocate a disproportionate share of salary increases to this sector to discourage movement. Though having been out of college for only about fifteen years, the older engineer begins to lose heart and to view the future with pessimism.

That technical skills rapidly become obsolete is a fact that both the operative engineer and the employing organization will have to face. Rather than solving the problem by constantly bringing in new engineers, and thereby wasting the talents of large numbers of middle-aged personnel, the more appropriate course of action would seem to be the constant reeducation of existing technical talent. The burdensome requirement of taking night courses without end could be solved for the older engineer by bringing such activities into the plant during the working day; e.g., some firms in the Dallas area have TV classrooms in the plant that are connected to engineering courses given at Southern Methodist University.[9] A case can also be made for periodical sabbatical leaves that provide the employee sufficient time to acquire new technologies. Certainly, training on the job can be enhanced by a more equal sharing of challenging assignments among older and younger engineers. And, finally, appraisal programs could be redesigned to reduce the demotivating effects of pitting person against person. In any event, the continuous offering of specialized technical course

---

[7]National Industrial Conference Board, *Personnel Practices in Factory and Office: Manufacturing*, Studies in Personnel Policy, no. 194, New York, 1964, p. 56.

[8]Gene W. Dalton and Paul H. Thompson, "Accelerating Obsolescence of Older Engineers," *Harvard Business Review*, vol. 49, no. 5, September–October 1971, p. 59.

[9]*Ibid.*, p. 64.

work appears to be an essential element of a training program geared to preventing technological obsolescence among professional personnel.

The teaching machine, a device originated by Sidney L. Pressey of Ohio State University in 1924, has become a popular technique in the past two decades. Programmed learning has been used in a number of ways, as in a textbook, for example, but its adaptation to a machine has stimulated more widespread use. Advantages to the trainee are that one can select a personal pace of learning, go back over material when desired, and use the machine when it is convenient. A slow learner will be forced to go through every portion in the program, while correct responses by fast learners will permit more rapid completion. The material is very carefully divided and programmed in the form of "frames," each of which requires a response of the trainee. After material has been presented, the trainee is asked a question. In one system, if a correct response is chosen, the student is praised and given new information followed by another question. If an incorrect response is chosen, one is directed to a frame giving the reason why the choice is incorrect and additional clarifying information, and then directed back to the original question. If the initial response is so completely wrong that it shows total lack of understanding, the trainee may be directed to a subprogram for intensive training in that aspect before returning to the main program. It is apparent that this method of instruction is utilizing the basic learning concepts of (1) establishing explicit goals, (2) breaking the subject into bits of logically sequenced knowledge, (3) requiring an active role on the part of the learner, (4) making learner self-pacing possible, and (5) providing immediate reinforcement of learning through feedback of results.[10]

Programmed learning through teaching machines has been best adapted to the transmission of facts rather than attitudes. Programs have been developed to instruct in grammar, mathematics, languages, and electronic troubleshooting. The approach has been used by such companies as Eastman Kodak in teaching statistics, International Business Machines in teaching maintenance of data-processing systems, and New Jersey Bell in teaching basic electronics.[11] An opinion survey of 117 directors of firms on *Fortune's* list of the top 500 corporations indicated that they rated programmed instruction as the most effective method for the acquisition of knowledge (case studies and conferences ranked second and third, while the lecture method was rated last).[12]

Concerning the relative effectiveness of programmed learning as compared with other more conventional methods, attention can be allocated to three factors: savings in learning time, amount of immediate learning, and long-term retention. A survey of over 150 studies reveals that programmed instruction is clearly superior in only the first factor, learning time.[13] On the average, the time saved was approximately one-third of that normally taken by competitive methods. Time saved issues largely from individual flexibility in establishing one's own pace. It has been suggested that studies should be made concerning actual learning time on the program as compared with actual learning time in a conventional classroom situation. Perhaps if the conventional method were

---

[10]John W. Buckley, "Programmed Instruction in Industrial Training," *California Management Review*, vol. 10, no. 2, Winter 1967, p. 73.

[11]Anthony C. Nicoletti, "The Use of Small Teaching Machines in Industry," *Advanced Management Journal*, vol. 29, no. 1, January 1964, pp. 61–64.

[12]Stephen J. Carroll, Jr., Frank T. Paine, and John J. Ivancevich, "The Relative Effectiveness of Training Methods: Expert Opinion and Research," *Personnel Psychology*, vol. 25, no. 3, Autumn 1972, p. 497.

[13]Allan N. Nash, Jan P. Muczyk, and Frank L. Vettori, "The Relative Practical Effectiveness of Programmed Instruction," *Personnel Psychology*, vol. 24, no. 3, Autumn 1971, pp. 410–411.

pruned of all its unessential and superfluous material, it might well be possible for it to compete more effectively with programmed instruction. The findings concerning degree of immediate learning as well as degree of retention over time did not reveal significant differences between programmed learning and more conventional approaches; there were an approximately equal number of studies with favorable results for each side.

One can still conclude that programmed learning is of considerable value in cutting the training time by a third with no loss in either immediate learning or long-term retention. In a previously cited study of 193 firms, 20 percent used some form of programmed instruction.[14]

There is no one best system of operative training. In any one firm, it would not be unusual to find all four systems in use simultaneously. As stated earlier, the on-the-job system is by far the most commonly used. With the advent of automation and the consequent upgrading of skill level, it may be that special courses and classroom instruction will receive a much greater degree of emphasis in the future.

THE TRAINING PROCEDURE

One of the better personnel programs to come out of World War II was the Training within Industry Program of the War Manpower Commission. This was basically a supervisory training program to make up for the shortage of civilian supervisory skills during the war. One of the parts of this program was the job instruction training course, which was concerned with *how* to teach. If on-the-job training is to be the basic approach used in industry, it is essential that each training supervisor possess teaching skills. The training procedure discussed below is essentially an adaptation of the job instruction training course, which has been proved to be of great value.

PREPARATION OF THE INSTRUCTOR The instructor must know both the job to be taught and how to teach it. The job must be divided into logical parts so that each can be taught at a proper time without the trainee losing perspective of the whole. This becomes a lesson plan. For each part one should have in mind the desired technique of instruction, that is, whether a particular point is best taught by illustration, demonstration, or explanation. The physical workplace should be made ready for the instruction process, along with the equipment, tools, and teaching aids, if any.

PREPARATION OF THE TRAINEE As in interviewing, the first step in training is to attempt to place the trainee at ease. Most people are somewhat nervous when approaching an unfamiliar task. Though the instructor may have executed this training procedure many times, he or she should never forget its newness for the trainee. The quality of empathy is a mark of the good instructor. In addition to minimizing any possible apprehension, the instructor should emphasize the importance of the job, its relationship to the work flow, and the importance of rapid and effective learning. One of the most common errors committed by an industrial instructor is neglecting to prepare properly the mind of the trainee to receive the instruction and being prone to plunge headlong into the step that follows.

[14]NICB, op. cit., p. 56.

A study cited earlier with reference to induction demonstrates the considerable importance of this preparation function. At Texas Instruments Incorporated, experiments were conducted to determine the effect of trainee preparation upon the length of time required to reach satisfactory production on jobs involving the assembly and welding of microminiature circuitry units.[15] With an experimental group, special attempts were made to reduce the anxiety that usually accompanies any new training experience. One full day was devoted to relaxed interchanges between managers and employees. Time was taken to get acquainted with specific supervisors, and trainees were repeatedly assured that records showed that "your opportunity to master the job is very good." They were encouraged to seek out the supervisor for help at any time, and were cautioned against the hazing games that old employees often play to frighten newcomers. A control group was prepared in the conventional manner which included very brief introductions to busy supervisors, warnings of the consequences of failure, and little or no attention to possible trainee fears. As Figure 10-2 indicates, the experimental group achieved a competence level during the second month of training, as compared with the fourth month for the control group. The experimental group achieved the mastery level within the third month as compared with the fifth month for the control group. It was concluded that the reduction in anxiety accounted for the entire gap between the two curves.

PRESENT THE OPERATION   There are various alternative ways of presenting the operation. An instructor almost always uses the method of explanation. In addition one may illustrate various points through the use of pictures and other training aids. When the job is essentially physical in nature, demonstration is an excellent device. The following sequence is a favorite with some instructors:

1   Explain the sequence of the entire job.
2   Go through the procedure slowly and explain each step.

[15]Earl R. Gomersall and M. Scott Myers, "Breakthrough in On-the-job Training," *Harvard Business Review*, vol. 44, no. 4, July–August 1966, pp. 62–72.

Figure 10-2

MASTERY ATTAINMENT BY EXPERIMENTAL AND CONTROL GROUPS

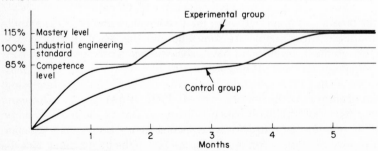

Source: Earl R. Gomersall and M. Scott Myers, "Breakthrough in On-the-job Training," *Harvard Business Review*, vol. 44, no. 4, July–August 1966, p. 69.

3 Go through procedure slowly and have the trainee explain each step that the instructor is performing.

4 Have the trainee explain the entire job.

Key points in each step should be emphasized. When demonstrating the operation, the instructor should stand beside the trainee rather than in front, so that the latter may better adapt his or her movements to those of the instructor. Questions should be encouraged in order to be sure that the learner really understands.

TRY OUT THE TRAINEE'S PERFORMANCE As a continuation of the presentation sequence given above, the trainee should be asked to start upon the machine or operative procedure. Some instructors prefer that the trainee explain each step before doing it, particularly if the operation involves any danger. It has been discovered by many teachers that one of the better ways of learning something thoroughly is by trying to teach another.

In the initial phases of the tryout period, the supervisor must be very close and must see that help is constantly available. It may be that in the beginning the supervisor will continue to do the more difficult steps while the trainee concentrates upon the easier ones. As the latter becomes more proficient, he or she will gradually assume execution of all steps. An attitude of patience and goodwill on the part of the instructor is prerequisite to a proper trainee attitude.

Gradually the supervision will be lessened. The trainee, through repetitive practice, will acquire more skill. It has been found in many types of operations that a learning plateau will occur; that is, a time will come when the trainee seems to make no further progress, though being still below the desired skill level. The problem, during this difficult period, is largely one of motivation. The presentation of learning curves of other trainees, which locate and identify such plateaus, is quite helpful in convincing the present trainee that the trainee's progress is normal.

FOLLOW-UP The final step in most management procedures is that of follow-up. When people are involved in any problem or procedure, it is unwise to assume that things are always constant. Such follow-ups can be adapted to a variable reinforcement schedule as suggested in the discussion of learning principles. It is doubtful, however, if undesirable behavior will be totally ignored by the practical supervisor. But, instead of pouncing upon the employee with a punitive attitude, the approach should be a supportive one of providing help in doing the job correctly. Of course, if the reward most desired by the trainee is supervisor attention, rather than correct job performance, a continuation of undesirable behavior will be effected. *Such* are the hazards involved in behavior modification through operant conditioning processes.

EVALUATING THE WORTH OF THE TRAINING PROGRAM

Though training is desirable in theory, in business organizations the worth of the training program must be proved by evidence. The position of the training program will be greatly bolstered if it rests on quantitative proofs of its value to the organization. Personnel management must move from arguments based on faith and logic to those based on factual evidence. Therefore it would be well to have a picture of the situation *before* training and *after*.

The specification of values given at the beginning of this chapter forms a basis of evaluation. In operative training, the prime measure of worth is that of productivity. Production rates, covering both quantity and quality, are good indicators of the values of training. In most business situations, these rates will have to be obtained on a before-and-after-training basis. In an experimental situation, a control group that does not receive training could be compared with one that does in order to ascertain the effect of training. Industrial managements will generally look first at production and scrap rates to determine the worth of operative training.

As we have pointed out previously, proper operative training has other values which can be determined quantitatively. Before-and-after figures on accident rates may show an improvement as a result of training, but it will take a longer period of time to produce sufficient evidence in this area. Analysis of absenteeism and labor turnover rates may demonstrate morale values. These, along with accidents, can be translated into dollars-and-cents costs for the benefit of management. Effects on morale in general are the most difficult to determine. Except in experimental situations, when all other factors are held constant except training, conclusions concerning the specific effects of training on a particular group are based on somewhat inaccurate information. In the ordinary business situation, analyses of the type indicated above must form the basis for practical training evaluation.

General observation should not be overlooked as a means of training evaluation. The immediate supervisor is often a good judge of the skill level of subordinates. For on-the-job training programs, the supervisor is in effect the judge of his or her own efforts. If the supervisor is treated as a part of the professional management of the organization and has been properly selected and trained, this self-analysis and appraisal can be quite accurate and objective.

In the immediate sense, the specific course of training can be evaluated in terms of written and performance tests. The test is supposedly a sample of what the trainee knows or can do. Successful accomplishment of the tests would indicate successful training. But the true test is whether that which was learned in training is successfully transferred and applied to the job. It is dangerous to rely upon tests alone to demonstrate the true value of training.

SUMMARY

Training is any process by means of which skill and knowledge are increased to do a particular job. The term "training" contrasts with the term "education," which is concerned with increasing our general knowledge, understanding, and background. Both are desirable for any employee. In this chapter our concern has been primarily with training.

There are two broad groups of personnel to be trained, operatives and managers. The four basic systems of operative training are (1) on-the-job training, (2) vestibule schools, (3) apprenticeship programs, and (4) special courses. This list in itself demonstrates the continuum of specific to general types of training. On-the-job training is highly specific; vestibule schools are specific but somewhat more general; apprenticeship programs deal with a series of jobs or a craft; and special courses in the classroom demonstrate a tendency toward education. On-the-job training is by far the most common system of operative training because of the semiskilled nature of most jobs in industry. Automation may effect a change in the direction of special classroom courses. The objective of all training is to effect a change in organizational behavior; and the adherence to basic principles of learning—motivation, progress reporting, reinforcement, practice, and adjustment to individual differences—will facilitate the process.

Effective operative training will usually produce such values as (1) increased production in terms of quantity and quality, (2) reduced accidents, (3) lessened burden on supervision, (4) increased organizational flexibility and stability, and (5) heightened morale. The person responsible for training would do well to collect all possible evidence in these areas to determine whether the training program is producing desired results.

DISCUSSION QUESTIONS

1   Defend the thesis that training programs contribute to broad social objectives.

2   In federally funded training programs, indicate specifically how the emphasis has shifted in the past decade.

3   Discuss the programmed learning method of training in terms of specific learning principles and concepts.

4   How does programmed learning compare with more conventional methods of training in terms of effectiveness?

5   When a firm's work force is heavily populated by professional and technical personnel, what impact does this have upon the objectives and design of a training program?

6   Of what significance is trainee preparation to training effectiveness? What are the Texas Instruments findings in this regard?

7   Contrast the four systems of operative training from the viewpoints of purpose, organization, costs, and educational characteristics.

8   Distinguish between training and education. Are you trained or educated by a university? By a business firm? By a business college within a university?

9   What indexes can be used to judge the effectiveness of training efforts? How would you design a training evaluation effort to obtain a measure of effectiveness?

10   If you wish to train a fellow student to underline key elements of this chapter, what would be the content of each of the major steps in the training procedure?

SUPPLEMENTARY READING

CARROLL, Stephen J., Jr., Frank T. Paine, and John J. Ivancevich: "The Relative Effectiveness of Training Methods: Expert Opinion and Research," *Personnel Psychology*, vol. 25, no. 3, Autumn 1972, pp. 495–509.

HIRSBRUNNER, Jack E.: "Manpower Training and Development in Multinational Companies," *Public Personnel Management*, vol. 3, no. 5, September–October 1974, pp. 378–384.

LUTHANS, Fred, and David Lyman: "Training Supervisors to Use Organizational Behavior Modification," *Personnel*, vol. 50, no. 5, September–October 1973, pp. 38–44.

NASH, Allan N., Jan P. Muczyk, and Frank L. Vettori: "The Relative Practical Effectiveness of Programmed Instruction," *Personnel Psychology*, vol. 24, no. 3, Autumn 1971, pp. 397–418.

PARKER, Treadway C.: "Evaluation: The Forgotten Finale of Training," *Personnel*, vol. 50, no. 6, November–December 1973, pp. 59–63.

SCHNEIER, Craig Eric: "Training and Development Programs: What Learning Theory and Research Have to Offer," *Personnel Journal*, vol. 53, no. 4, April 1974, pp. 288–293.

ELEVEN
EXECUTIVE AND ORGANIZATION DEVELOPMENT

One of the most prominent areas of personnel management is that of executive development. The activity in this field since World War II has been of such a quantity and type that it is often labeled a "management revolution." The tremendous volume of burgeoning development programs is properly deserving of this label, particularly when contrasted with the small amount of such activity prior to 1940. In fact, the management development movement has often taken on the aspects of a fad. So many firms have adopted such programs, and so much publicity has issued therefrom, that it is believed that many have undertaken these activities in order to appear up to date. Under the circumstances, some organizations do a considerable amount of copying of particular techniques of training and development without examining the fundamental philosophy on which these specific approaches rest.

Perhaps the foremost justification for a planned and systematic executive development program is the very complex nature of the job itself. The executive job is typically open-ended, fragmented, interpersonal, verbal, and active. Job descriptions, if they should exist, cannot possibly capture the nature of the job in its entirety. Though we may theoretically specify that the executive plans, organizes, directs, and controls, the typical day is not that neat. A few minutes might be devoted to checking up on a project (control), followed by a few seconds to issue an order on another project (direct); then follows a meeting to coordinate with a fellow manager on a continuing conflictful situation (organizing), interrupted by an emergency telephone call from the assistant manager (control), etc. An immediate supervisor may have over 500 separate incidents during the day, many of which are of limited importance. In many instances, the manager may devote no more than one-half of her or his time to contacts with subordinates, the remainder being allocated to persons outside of the chain of command, so that skills of persuading, negotiating, coordinating, and facilitating are called for. In the active climate in which the manager operates, it is often quite difficult to find the time, as well as the inclination, to devote to the planning function. "The manager is not a planner in a reflective sense, and no amount of admonition in the literature will make him so. His milieu is one of stimulus-response."[1] Nevertheless, the organization does require purposeful direction, and some time must be spent by some group within the firm on the problems of the future.

Managerial talent is essential to organizational success. At the minimum, managers provide the communication linkups among separate organizational components to make it possible for coordinated action to take place. Managers are usually allocated the primary responsibility for ensuring the attainment of organizational goals. This requires design of a sociotechnical system that facilitates work accomplishment internally, as well as adjusting to external changes in the outer environment. Though nonmanagers or operatives who accomplish the operative tasks pertinent to objectives are obviously essential, their efforts could well be duplicative, at cross purposes, directionless, or even absent were it not for the hierarchical glue provided by occupants of managerial positions.

Though arguments abound as to whether or not management constitutes a profession, the complex and essential nature of the task requires that conscious and systematic attention be allocated to development of managerial skills. There is no specified formal educational requirements, as in the cases of law and medicine. There is, however, a strong tendency on the part of the larger firms to require possession of a college degree for admission to executive development programs. Some have suggested that the Master of Business Administration (MBA) will become for the manager what the M.D. is to the physician and the LL.D is to the lawyer. Given the open-ended, complex, and variable nature of the task, this situation is less likely to come about on the basis of proven need. Executive development typically calls for a combination of experience, training, and education, thus requiring collaboration among employing organizations and a variety of private and public educational enterprises.

Experiences in executive development programs have demonstrated that isolated changes in executive skills and attitudes can often add up to nought if the culture of the rest of the organization remains unaltered. With particular reference to promoting utilization of improved interpersonal skills, some firms have moved to attempt "organization development." Thus one can attempt to train a whole organization, or some component portion, as well as develop particular individuals within that enterprise. As a concluding section of this chapter, brief attention will be given to the task of organization development.

PRINCIPLES OF EXECUTIVE DEVELOPMENT

After two decades of experience, business firms have evolved a number of basic guides in creating and maintaining an effective executive development program. In the beginning, the philosophy seemed to be one of creating a "development factory"

---

[1] Henry Mintzberg, *The Nature of Managerial Work*, Harper and Row, Publishers, Incorporated, New York, 1973, p. 182.

through which executive material was to be processed. Management, presumably, controlled the entire process of development. When, upon graduation day, many of the products of this "factory" did not live up to expectations, a reexamination of the fundamental philosophies underlying the approach was undertaken. Many managements realized that people are developed not so much by others as by themselves. This does not mean a return to the philosophy of learning solely by experience, but it does emphasize the importance of the individual candidate's inner motivation and basic abilities. He or she must be helped, and a well-planned program can create an environment in which self-development is stimulated and facilitated.

Thus, the first cardinal principle upon which a management development program should be based is that *all development is self-development*. A corollary of this is that developmental efforts on the part of the firm should be geared to individual differences. There is even less justification for uniformity of developmental efforts for managers than for operative employees. A third concept that must be recognized is that executive development is a long-range process with individual programs running into years, if not decades. A manager is not usually developed by taking a course, reading a book, holding one job, or attending a university-sponsored conference. Development is more closely akin to education than it is to specific training in skills.

If self-development is the main guiding concept, the establishment of an effective organizational climate is the second most important factor. Developmental facilities must be available, and their use must be associated with importance and prestige. Rewards granted candidates who exhibit interest and activity in development should be appropriate when compared with benefits granted those candidates who do not exhibit these qualities. The candidate's immediate supervisor is important as a key influence in the environment. Insistence upon high-quality performance, and supportive coaching and counseling, are supervisory activities conducive to effective learning. In a study of over one thousand college graduates experiencing development in fourteen companies, the two most valued experiences reported were (1) help and guidance from one specific supervisor and (2) being tossed into a job and held accountable for results.[2] The two values are not incompatible.

The key position of the immediate supervisor makes the main *organizational* responsibility one of line rather than staff. This does not, however, preclude the existence of management development activities on the part of a personnel department. The key decisions and environment must be provided by line, but much of the facilitative work, as well as off-the-job developmental opportunities, can be provided by a staff element. Though the primary responsibility must rest upon the person to be developed, the organization, through efforts of both line and staff, can make this development possible.

EXECUTIVE NEEDS AND DEVELOPMENTAL PROGRAMS

Among firms which profess to believe in some type of planned systematic executive development, a great variety of developmental techniques are used. The selection of techniques must rest on one's philosophy of development. In Figure 11-1 is a por-

[2]National Industrial Conference Board, *College Graduates Assess Their Company Training*, Studies in Personnel Policy, no. 188, New York, 1963, p. 13.

Figure 11-1 Executive development needs

The Job

Decision-making skills	Job knowledge	General knowledge
	Other Needs ?	
Interpersonal skills	Organization knowledge	Specific individual needs

trayal of the various types of development needs typically required by an executive position. In each of the categories, a number of alternative methods are available to achieve the designated goal. *Decision-making skills* can be enhanced through use of such techniques as the in-basket, business games, and case analysis. Much-needed *interpersonal skills* can be promoted through a variety of means, including role playing, sensitivity training, and structured insight. Obviously, the executive requires *job knowledge* in the assigned position, and thus the methods of on-the-job experience, coaching, and understudies are available. The job is performed within an organizational environment, and such required *organizational knowledge* can be obtained through position rotation and multiple management.

In the interest of long-run general development of executive talent, efforts are often allocated to the acquisition of *general knowledge*. It is here that a variety of educational organizations are usually involved in offering special courses, meetings, and selective reading lists. In adapting to the principle of individual differences, analysis of managerial candidates may reveal *specific individual needs* unique to them. Special projects and selected committee assignments are often utilized to attack these developmental problems. Again, demonstrating the open-ended nature of the managerial task, Figure 11-1 portrays a category of "Other Needs." Though the above itemization covers most of the standard developmental methods utilized in business organizations, one cannot contend that they cover all the foreseeable developmental needs on all types of management jobs.

There is no ideal best combination of executive development methods. Each organization must design its own particular program to suit the climate of the firm, the organizational level for which training is required, the particular characteristics of the personnel to be developed, the recognized specific developmental needs, and the availability of economic resources that can be allocated to training and education. There is no one best program of management development. Without itemizing the listed methods used by any one firm, a survey of 225 personnel directors in firms having at least 1,000 employees reported the following rank order of importance for development methods: (1) on-the-job experiences and transfers, (2) seminars, (3) conferences, (4) role playing, (5) in-basket technique, (6) quantitative techniques, and (7) sensitivity training.[3] Over two-thirds designated on-the-job methods as most effective. In general, the closer the development to the job, the greater the motivation of the candidate.

[3] William J. Kearney and Desmond D. Martin, "Quantitative Methods in Management Development," *Business Horizons*, vol. 17, no. 4, August 1974, p. 55.

When training and education occur away from the job, one has problems of relating theoretical concepts to the actual work situation, besides encountering problems of philosophical disagreements between trainer and supervisor.

Both on-the-job and off-the-job developmental approaches have a place in a well-rounded executive development program. In the sections that follow, we shall briefly outline the content of the various training and educational methods, classified by the developmental needs to which they are directed.

DECISION-MAKING SKILLS

To many, the essence of the executive job is making decisions, the great majority of which are correct. Though this skill can be approached in a variety of ways, including special courses in decision making, there has been a marked tendency to utilize methods entailing simulation of the executive environment. Among these methods are the in-basket, business games, and case studies.

In-basket

As indicated in an earlier chapter, the in-basket is a popularly used device in identifying executive potential in executive assessment centers. It can also be utilized in teaching decision-making skills. After trainees are given background information on a simulated company and its products, organization, and key personnel, they are provided with an in-basket of assorted memoranda, requests, and data pertaining to the firm. The trainee must make sense out of this mass of paper work and prepare memos, make notes, and delegate tasks within a limited time period. Not all the items are of equal importance, and one must often relate one item to another. Abilities that can be developed encompass (1) situational judgment in being able to recall details, establish priorities, interrelate items, and determine need for more information, (2) social sensitivity in exhibiting courtesy in written notes, scheduling meetings with involved personnel, and explaining reasons for actions taken, and (3) willingness to make a decision and take action. In one variation, the trainee is allowed to place simulated phone calls for more information. If he or she calls the correct person in the organization, more written data on the issue will be provided. Group conference discussions on separate individual handlings of the in-basket can elicit further developmental values.

Business games

Over the years, a variety of simulations have been developed to portray the operations of a firm, or some component part. These exercises introduce some uncertainty inasmuch as they are often played on a competitive basis. Teams of trainees are formed to meet, discuss, and arrive at decisions concerning such subjects as production amounts, research and development, inventories, sales, and a myriad of other activities for a simulated firm. Games can be relatively simple, permitting rapid decision making to be effected, or extremely complicated, entailing long and detailed analysis of trends in costs, inventories, and sales. Obviously, the requirement that decisions be made as a team provides trainee experience in cooperative group processes. The multiple facets

230

of a realistic simulation lead to appreciation of the complex and interlocking nature of business systems, necessitating decisions that require breadth of viewpoint as well as attention to detail.

One general business firm simulation requires seventeen decisions from each team for each round (usually covering a quarter of a year). There are three products, differentiated only by price level. For each product, decisions must be made concerning price to be charged in the next quarter, amount to be produced, costs to be placed in product as a measure of quality, advertising expenditures, and research and development investment. Teams must also determine if the physical plant should be expanded in view of anticipated production and decreasing size caused by depreciation. Conversion of cash into interest-earning securities can also be done if desired. General industrial information is provided that is accurate within 10 percent, e.g., other competitors' prices, sales, share of market, etc. Special versions of games are often designed for a particular portion of the enterprise, e.g., the marketing analysis training exercise is a refinement of the Carnegie Tech Management Game and concentrates on pricing, advertising expenditures, sales force size, call-time allocation to brands, and retail allowance.[4]

As in the case of the in-basket, playing a business game provides practice in sticking one's neck out and making a decision. Immediate feedback of results demonstrates the relative accuracy of the decision, taking into account the uncertain nature of competitors' decisions. Interjection of major changes in the environment can give practice in achieving flexibility. Organizational ability, financial acumen, quickness of thinking, and the ability to adapt under stress can also be developed through the use of game simulations.

Case studies

The case method of development utilizes actual case examples collected from various organizations for diagnostic purposes. The trainee must (1) identify the major and minor problems in the case; (2) filter out the significant facts from the insignificant; (3) analyze the issues and use logic to fill in the gaps in the facts; and (4) arrive at some means for solving the identifiable problem. Cases in personnel management are presented after each major section in this text.

In ensuing group discussions concerning the case, the trainee will usually see that other candidates differ from himself or herself about what is important and what action should be undertaken. One is thus taught tolerance of others' viewpoints as well as the difficulty of arriving at absolutely correct answers in complex problems. It has been found that some candidates are excellent in analysis and can pursue ramifications endlessly, sometimes to the point of self-immobilization. They clearly see that any decision chosen will have some undesirable dysfunctional consequences. Nevertheless, the instructor must press for some stand to be taken. Decision choice is an inescapable responsibility of a manager.

[4]Kalman J. Cohen et al., *The Carnegie Tech Management Game*, Richard D. Irwin, Inc., Homewood, Ill., 1964.

INTERPERSONAL SKILLS

Traditional managers are likely to emphasize the rational portion of a manager's task, thereby emphasizing its decision-making elements. Behaviorally oriented managers contend that acceptance of the decision is just as important as its quality, thereby emphasizing the necessity for developing interpersonal competence. Management is "getting things done through others." "Things" to do result from decision processes, but getting the "others" to do them willingly and effectively calls for unusual skills in interpersonal or human relations.

Role playing

Role playing is a simulation in which the trainee is asked to play a part in a problem situation requiring interaction with others. Basic mental sets are stated for all participants, but no dialogue is provided. For example, a supervisor, on the advice of a motion and time study engineer, has decided to change the work methods of subordinates. The supervisor's role may contain, among other items, such statements as, "You get along well with your people; this idea of the methods man makes pretty good sense for both the employees and the company; the data provided by the expert are fairly clear." Roles are also provided for each of the subordinates. One may exhibit great suspicion against the motion and time study expert. Another may be structured as a potential ally of the supervisor in the projected change. Still another may show a fear of working himself or herself out of a job if methods are improved. All will probably reflect the usual human resistance to any change, good or bad. No dialogue is provided, and the trainees attempt to play themselves in the roles as structured. They are not actors. Each will have to respond to the impromptu statements and questions of the other role players.

Role playing is close to a laboratory situation in dealing with people in job situations. Playback of the tape, if recorded, provides opportunities for the trainee to examine his or her performance with the additional insight of participants and experienced observers. Videotapes can be utilized to provide models of behavior for the trainee. Ensuing role-playing sessions can be directed toward influencing behavior toward this model. Sorcher and Goldstein report effective use of behavior models for such interpersonal problem areas as giving recognition to an employee, stimulating acceptance of proposed changes, conducting a subordinate performance appraisal, persuading an employee to improve performance levels, and inducting a newly hired employee into the organization.[5] Trainees were rewarded for successful role emulation with praise by peers and trainers. It was found that attitude changes on the part of the trainee tended to occur *after* the modeled behavior was successfully duplicated. In order to reduce dissonance created by differences between the modeled behavior and previously held managerial beliefs, the trainees moved toward beliefs that were supportive of their newly learned behavior, e.g., importance of maintaining the

---

[5]Melvin Sorcher and Arnold P. Goldstein, "A Behavior Modeling Approach in Training," *Personnel Administration*, vol. 35, no. 2, March–April 1972, pp. 35–40.

subordinates' esteem by not backing them into a corner and the essentiality of making it clear that you are interested in the employee's personal success and of not demanding immediate solutions to employee adjustment problems but allowing the employees to assist in working out an accommodation.

Sensitivity training

As the title indicates, the general goal of sensitivity training is the development of awareness and sensitivity to behavioral patterns of oneself and others. More specifically, goals frequently announced include (1) increased openness with others, (2) greater concern for others, (3) increased tolerance for individual differences, (4) less ethnic prejudice, (5) understanding of group processes, (6) enhanced listening skills, and (7) increased trust and support. Unlike content-oriented methods, sensitivity training swings to the other extreme in establishing a laboratory situation in which one learns about oneself. It involves face-to-face learning about ongoing behavior within a small group that meets continually for periods as long as one or two weeks. It is less artificial than role playing inasmuch as the trainee plays *himself* or *herself* rather than a structured role.

A critical factor in this approach to learning is the absence of structure. The trainer is a moderator who is there to facilitate the feedback process so that each trainee can learn how she or he is perceived by others. The moderator is also there to prevent serious psychological damage to persons who cannot bear up under the stresses of openness, honesty, and truth. Frustration and conflict are deemed necessary to promote "gut-level" interchanges on such subjects as one's need for intimacy and support, reactions to authority figures, and one's need to control and dominate. Learning takes place on a feeling level rather than on an intellectual plane, as is the case in most of the other methods.

The general goal of this type of training is to open up the organization through increasing managerial sensitivity and trust, as well as increasing respect for the contributions of others, whether peers, subordinates, or superiors. The technique has not received majority approval by business managers. Among the reasons for this resistance is limited acceptance of the open, supportive, and trusting organizational model that various behavioral theorists have visualized. It is contended that most managers must make unpleasant decisions that work to the short-term detriment of particular people. Excessive empathy and sympathy will not necessarily lead to a reversal of the decision, and may exact an excessively high emotional cost from the manager. As one critic stated, "The normative prescriptions implied in laboratory training may be totally inappropriate for the business environment."[6] Many business organizations have environments characterized by competition and autocracy. The power inequality that goes with hierarchical structures is not entirely compatible with openness, trust, and equalitarian ideology. The single executive who undergoes effective sensitivity training and returns to the company may well be a "sitting duck" if others have not altered their behavior. The managements of some companies, such as

---

[6]John Drotning, "Sensitivity Training Doesn't Work Magic," *Management of Personnel Quarterly*, vol. 7, no. 2, Summer 1968, p. 19.

TRW Systems, have emphasized the necessity of training all managers, or at least a substantial proportion, if there is to be a significant change in total organizational behavior.

Structured insight

Traditional methods of courses, lectures, discussions, conferences, and cases have been found lacking in effecting significant behavioral changes in trainees. Their knowledge is increased, but much is lost in the transition to operational applications. On the other hand, the laboratory approach of sensitivity training usually causes behavioral changes but is quite costly in terms of time, money, and psychological inputs. A third approach has been developed in recent years that strives to attain the personal insight of sensitivity training without many of its costs. Emphasis is placed upon systematic collection of the trainee's attitudes and assumptions concerning the motives, abilities, and attitudes of others, particularly subordinates. This is followed by a similar questionnaire assessment of preferences in leadership style, e.g., close authoritative supervision, establishment of good human relations, or a continually expanding degree of subordinate participation and self-direction. In one particular scheme, these assessments are located upon a 9 by 9 "managerial grid," with concern for people shown on the vertical scale and concern for production on the horizontal.[7] A score of 1 indicates trainee low concern and a score of 9 indicates high concern. Such assessments are then followed by thorough group discussion of the meaning of the measured location of each trainee, usually with the admonition that the group should move to a more balanced position of equal concern for both people and productivity.

Chris Argyris suggests the use of another method that will provide self-insight into leadership practices of top-level executives.[8] Executives are first asked to write out descriptions of their espoused theories of leadership, particularly in reference to how they deal with people. Secondly, a tape recording is made of an actual meeting conducted by the executive. In a later gathering of all executives involved in the development program, each is asked to diagnose and describe the actual theory in use revealed by his or her own tape. In addition, they must do the same for the tape of one other executive in the group. The ensuing discussion involves a comparison of the espoused theory with the theory actually in use as revealed by the two separate tape diagnoses. The goal of this process is to reveal the inevitable difference between stated beliefs and actual behavior; to reduce dissonance, one must change either the espoused theory or the theory in use. Assuming a desire to change behavior, a specific program of action is then prepared by each executive. Rather than presenting general resolutions such as "I'll be less autocratic," the executive is asked to specifically indicate what will be said and done in probable situations. Three months later, another tape is made of an actual meeting conducted by the subject executive, and this is analyzed in a fashion similar to that described above. Any systematic device that furthers understanding of one's actual behavior in comparison with preferred behavior can be labeled "structured insight."

[7]Robert R. Blake and Jane S. Mouton; Louis B. Barnes and Larry Greener, "Breakthrough in Organization Development," *Harvard Business Review*, vol. 42, no. 6, November–December 1964, p. 133.

[8]"Conversation with Chris Argyris," *Organizational Dynamics*, vol. 3, no. 1, Summer 1974, pp. 51–55.

JOB KNOWLEDGE

Regardless of the degree of prior possession of decision-making and interpersonal skills, the executive must acquire knowledge concerning the actual job to which he or she is assigned. As shown in the survey of personnel directors previously cited, on-the-job approaches are simultaneously most widely used and most highly valued.

On-the-job experience

Learning by experience cannot and should not be eliminated as a method of development, though as a sole approach it is wasteful, time-consuming, and inefficient. On-the-job learning is not confined to personnel assigned to relatively simple tasks. In a survey of 290 scientists and engineers engaged in research and development activities, it was found that they keep up to date through a variety of activities which are largely unrelated to formal continuing-education courses.[9] On-the-job problem solving and colleague interaction were reported as being most important for professional growth by 62 percent of the respondents. Interactions with fellow professionals on the job were seen as a major source of both motivation and information. Publishing, independent reading, formal courses, and outside professional meetings were deemed important, but not as important as on-the-job activities.

That experience alone is insufficient is suggested by studies conducted and reviewed by Fiedler. In correlating length of managerial experience with measures of effectiveness for 385 leaders in five different organizations, the median correlation was minus .12.[10] Rather than suggesting that experience is actually harmful, the intent was to demonstrate that other characteristics besides sheer seniority are essential to managerial success.

Coaching

On-the-job experience in conjunction with a skilled coach with authority, one's boss, is deemed by many to be the single most effective training technique. Teaching is individualized and one learns by doing. There is increased motivation for the trainee, with minimization of the problem of learning transfer from theory to practice. The foremost disadvantages lie in frequent neglect by the superior, both in time and quality of teaching efforts, and the tendency to perpetuate customary practices and solutions.

Effective coaching is a difficult skill to master. It requires a delicate balance of direction and freedom. The coach should help by explaining the relevance of information and through helping to generate alternatives for problems. Trainees must also be given the "right to fail" on occasions, if they are ever to stand on their own. Coaching also involves teaching by example. If an open problem-solving organization is deemed desirable, the superior must demonstrate this in her or his own style by asking for suggestions, encouraging subordinate participation in the superior's own decisions, and generally encouraging a free flow of information.

[9]Newton Margulies and Anthomy P. Raia, "Scientists, Engineers, and Technological Obsolescence," *California Management Review*, vol. 10, no. 2, Winter 1967, p. 44.

[10]Fred E. Fiedler, "Leadership Experience and Leader Performance: Another Hypothesis Shot to Hell," *Organizational Behavior and Human Performance*, vol. 5, no. 1, January 1970, p. 10.

Understudy

The understudy system can be considered a somewhat different approach from those described above, in that a certain person is specifically designated as the heir apparent. The understudy's future depends upon what happens to his or her superior. The advantages of this technique pertain to the practical and realistic situation in which the training is conducted. In addition, on-the-job learning is acquired in a situation where the trainee is not responsible for operating results. Serious mistakes are thus reduced, and the strain on the trainee is relieved. The disadvantages are numerous. Since the understudy has been specifically designated, there is often the feeling that the competition for promotion is over, with a consequent reduction in motivation for both the one designated and the other personnel as well. Besides, progress is uncertain, since the position must be vacated before the understudy can move up. Full-time understudies are somewhat expensive to maintain over a long period. And finally, this approach to training suffers the same disadvantages as all on-the-job training. The trainee learns the ways of the superior, who in turn learned them from *his* or *her* superior. Outside contacts through other development techniques constitute a desirable supplement.

ORGANIZATIONAL KNOWLEDGE

Programs designed to increase the trainee's knowledge of the total organization necessarily involve exposure to information and events outside the confines of the immediate job. Perhaps the most popular of these methods is that of position rotation. If a firm espouses the participative philosophy as a way of managing, the multiple management method can also be utilized.

Position rotation

The major objective of position-rotation development is that of broadening the background of the trainee in the business. On-the-job experience, coaching, and understudying are narrow, in the sense that the trainee acquires skill and knowledge in the one job. If the trainee is rotated periodically from one job to another, he or she acquires a general background. In a planned rotation program, the job switches are made in periods of from six months to a year. Obviously, almost everyone changes from one job to another during a lifetime, thereby gaining broader experience. In the Procter and Gamble Company, for example, a trainee may enter a department as an assistant supervisor. Gradually, the assistant learns the supervisor's job, function by function. Over a period of time, the supervisor is trained *out* of a job by transferring the duties, one by one, to the assistant supervisor. The original supervisor is then rotated to another department as an assistant and will there undergo a similar process.

The advantages of planned position rotation are: (1) it provides a general background and thus an organizational point of view; (2) it encourages interdepartmental cooperation, since managers have seen multiple sides of issues; (3) fresh viewpoints are periodically introduced to the various units; (4) it promotes organizational flexibility through generating flexible human resources; (5) comparative performance appraisal can be accomplished more objectively; and (6) it acquires all the advantages of on-the-job coaching in each situation. Position rotation can also be used as a "new experience" reward for competent managers without the qualities to move higher. The primary disadvantages of this method are that productive work may suffer because of the obvious periodic disruption caused by such changes, and the limitation on the amount of job skill that can be developed during these shorter periods of time. Managers on planned rotation programs may be discouraged in developing and pursuing long-term projects. They may also be tempted to "liquidate the human assets" in the interest of enhancing personal records for maximum output and minimum cost. These drawbacks can be ameliorated somewhat by lengthening the interval of rotation, limiting the rotation to positions of assistants, and measuring the "human assets" through morale surveys.

Multiple management

It is not possible to classify multiple management as exclusively a development method or a philosophy of management. Certainly both elements are involved. As a method of executive development, it is a special, off-the-job device, inasmuch as it utilizes specially constituted committees.

In 1932, Charles P. McCormick, president of McCormick and Company of Baltimore, introduced the idea of establishing a junior board of directors. The greatest value of this additional board was the training of junior executives.[11] The board was given the authority to discuss any problem that the senior board could discuss, and its members were encouraged to put their minds to work on the business *as a whole*, rather than to concentrate on their specialized areas. From such a method, a value may be derived similar to that achieved by rotation—the encouragement of a general viewpoint.

The junior board at McCormick consists of sixteen department managers of their assistants. At the end of each six-month period, on a ballot taken among themselves, six of these members are dropped from the committee. Nominations are then made, and an election by the remaining ten is conducted to fill the six vacancies. Membership on this board is considered to be a high honor as well as an excellent training experience. In addition, membership on the junior board has become a prerequisite to membership on the senior board of directors.

The junior board of directors discusses a wide variety of subjects. All recommendations that are forwarded to the senior board must be unanimous, and they remain as recommendations until the senior board approves them. In practice, the senior board turns down a negligible number of these submitted recommendations. Thus, though the major objective is training, the firm is also being benefited by productive ideas.

GENERAL KNOWLEDGE

It has been suggested that executive development, as compared with operative training, tends to move toward the education end of the training-education continuum. Thus, it is not surprising to find a considerable role for formal educational institutions of various types. In these developmental attempts, there are unusual problems of learning transfer from class or conference room to the job situation.

[11]Charles P. McCormick, *Multiple Management*, Harper & Row, Publishers, Incorporated, New York, 1938.

Special courses

The method of special courses requires the trainee to leave the workplace and devote her or his entire time to development objectives. Development is primary, and any usable work produced while training is secondary. Special training and/or educational courses can be established in numerous ways by a business organization as a part of its executive development program. First, there are the courses which the firm itself establishes, to be taught by members of the firm. Some companies have regular instructors assigned to their training departments. In the case of General Motors, this approach grew into the General Motors Institute of Technology, which is actually an industrial university.

A second approach to the special-course technique is for the business organization to work with a school or college in establishing a course or a series of courses to be taught by school instructors. In the training-education continuum, these courses usually tend toward the education end. There is an increasing amount of cooperation between schools and business organizations in the area of business and management education.

A third approach is for the firm to send personnel to programs established by the school or college. These programs vary quite widely in length, content, and methods of administration. The first such program was the Sloan Fellowship Program, established in 1931 at the Massachusetts Institute of Technology.[12] Most have been established since 1950. Among them are the programs at Michigan State University, Harvard University, Indiana University, Marquette University, University of Arizona, and a host of others. The American Management Association should also be mentioned at this point. It is a private organization engaged in the business of management education and has been in operation for approximately sixty years. Among its many activities, it offers seminars in the various specialized fields of finance, management, insurance, international management, manufacturing, marketing, office management, packaging, personnel, and research development. It also operates an academy at Saranac Lake, N.Y., where a basic four-week course in management principles is offered.

Special meetings

In the category of special meetings are placed such activities as the one- or two-day meetings on special subjects held by various organizations. For example, one of the activities of the American Management Association is the holding of periodic two- to three-day conferences in various fields, such as personnel or production management. Attendance varies from a few hundred to, in some instances, over two thousand participants. The meeting consists of a series of speeches with subsequent question periods. The practice of the Society for the Advancement of Management is to hold local chapter meetings once a month. At each of these meetings a talk or demonstration is presented on some management subject.

Schools and colleges are also engaged in the business of holding one- or two-day conferences. Many of these are annual conferences, such as the Personnel Institute of Ohio State University. Various associations, such as the American Institute of Industrial

---

[12]Reed M. Powell, *The Role and Impact of the Part-time University Program in Executive Education*, University of California, Graduate School of Business, Division of Research, 1962.

Engineers, the Industrial Relations Research Association, and the American Society for Personnel Administration, also conduct a series of meetings in their respective fields. Many firms are interested in sending selected personnel to special meetings held in their geographic area. The values are largely educational in nature, adding to the general knowledge of these personnel. An additional value is the interchange of information among personnel of various companies in informal sessions outside of the formal presentations.

Selective reading

Many executives claim that it is very difficult to find time to do much reading other than that absolutely required in the performance of their jobs. In most instances proper organization of the daily routine will provide some time for reading which will advance the general knowledge and background of the individual.

Business magazines, such as the *California Management Review* and *Harvard Business Review*, are purchased by some firms for management personnel. The management of the Johnson and Johnson Corporation feels that higher-level executives, who have progressed well beyond the stage where their needs can be met by organized classes, can be stimulated by an attractive book-reading program. Their "Ideas and Authors" program involves face-to-face small-group discussions with authors of stimulating books.[13] Executives are given four to six weeks to read assigned books, after which a dinner meeting is arranged with the author to discuss his major ideas. These meetings take place about six evenings a year and are designed to develop greater conceptual ability, to stimulate new ways of looking at issues that are both internal and external to the business firm, and, in general, to broaden the executives' thinking. Among the authors who have appeared are Peter F. Drucker, Leonard R. Sayles, and Whitney M. Young, Jr.

SPECIFIC INDIVIDUAL NEEDS

Most of the previously described programs require placement of the executive trainee into a group situation of a somewhat uniform character. If we are to tailor the development program to individual differences, each candidate will have to be studied to determine which of these programs will meet an observed need. In addition, this study is likely to reveal specific needs peculiar to the individual for which no standard developmental program is available. The two most popular methods of attacking this problem are special project assignments and judiciously chosen committee memberships.

Special projects

A special assignment is a highly useful and flexible training device. Such assignments ordinarily grow out of an individual analysis of weaknesses and, thus, are likely to be highly valuable training. An example of this would be to ask a trainee to develop a

---

[13]Robert V. Moore, "Meet the Author," *Personnel*, vol. 43, no. 2, March–April 1966, pp. 46–50.

system of cost collection in the production of an order. This project not only would provide valuable experience in systems analysis, but would also have the other values of indoctrinating the trainee with the importance of costs and increasing the trainee's knowledge of organizational relationships with the accounting department. At times, a task force is created consisting of a number of candidates representing different functions in the organization. Trainees not only acquire knowledge of the assigned subject but also learn how to work with and relate to others possessing different viewpoints. Other examples of this type of training are given in Figure 11-2.

Many able young college graduates have been "turned off" by routine, extended, and unexciting developmental programs to the point where a substantial majority change jobs within three years of graduation. In response, a few firms have begun special projects programs of a fast-track, "high risk/high reward" type. In one instance a recently graduated trainee was given a list of canceled accounts adding up to a half-million dollars in sales.[14] His project was to design a strategy for recouping these

[14]Lawrence Stessin, "Developing Young Managers: 'Immediacy' Sets the Tone," *Personnel*, vol. 48, no. 6, November–December 1971, p. 34.

Figure 11-2 Individual development program

Name: Oak, T.   Position: Shift foreman, rolling

Department: Continuous-weld pipe

Description of development need	Recommended method of development	Proposed dates From	To	Date completed	Comments
Planning and organizing	Increased attendance at departmental planning meetings.	As scheduled			
	More guidance in formulating plans in own group.	As need for planning occurs			
Development of subordinates	Discuss importance of systematic methods of training subordinates, delegating authority and responsibility, and reviewing their performance.	At once		3/20/75	Realizes problem, but requires more help.
	Coach him in development of subordinates and delegation of authority. Review his performance and offer help.	Monthly			
Working with and utilizing staff departments	Have him assist in budget preparation and review performance figures.	Regularly			
	Have him work with engineers and maintenance department on relocation of equipment.	Now	3/31/75	3/31/75	Excellent response. Repeat whenever possible, including other departments.

accounts; he was then shoved out the door to carry out the plan. Other unusual challenging assignments included developing a plan to recruit minority employees, preparing material for proxy battles in attempted organization take-overs, composing position papers for executive testimony in court, and designing and introducing a personnel program into a small branch plant. Such projects have usually been assigned in the past to more experienced and higher-ranking personnel. Because of the high risk, there is usually little stigma attached to any failures that may occur. Of course, someday the trainee is going to have to occupy a regular job, which, though challenging, will probably not approach the excitement of the special project.

Committee assignments

This method of training and/or education is very closely related to the one immediately preceding, but committee assignments differ from special projects in that they are regularly constituted or ad hoc committees. They are not training committees per se. Each has assigned objectives and responsibilities related to the work of the organization, and as such they must be peopled by competent personnel. This does not prevent them from being used as training devices under special conditions. If a certain executive seems to be unappreciative of the contributions of another department, appointment to a committee involving members of that department may lead to a change in attitude; or another executive may require a broader knowledge of a problem which involves diverse elements of the firm. Committee assignments could very well provide the necessary general background.

EVALUATION OF EXECUTIVE DEVELOPMENT PROGRAMS

The evaluation of executive development is considerably more difficult than measuring the worth of operative training. The executive job is more intangible, and data concerning changes in job performance are difficult to obtain.

In examining the results of over four hundred experimental studies in the evaluation of management development programs, House indicates that the general reaction is one of disappointment and disillusionment.[15] There are various methods of evaluation. The one most frequently found and least effective is measurement of the group *after* the training has been completed. In most programs, the opinions obtained from trainees about the worth of the experience are almost always favorable. Ninety-four percent of business participants in one university program rated the experience as valuable; over fifty percent indicated it had "high value."[16]

A sounder approach is that of measuring the group both before and after the training. Comparisons can then be made to determine if organizational behavior has improved within the group. A still better method is measuring the group both before and after training and applying an identical measurement process to a *control* group

[15]Robert J. House, "A Commitment Approach to Management Development," *California Management Review*, Spring 1965, p. 15.
[16]Reed M. Powell, "Two Approaches to University Management Education," *California Management Review*, Spring 1963, p. 102.

that has been carefully selected as equivalent to the trained group in all things except the training experience. Finally, an even more effective method is to use a "post-post" research design by adding an additional measure some time after training, e.g., six months or a year. In one study of the effects of training sessions on leadership styles, the immediate post-measure after completion of training showed no significant difference between the experimental and control groups.[17] Another measure eighteen months later showed that the experimental group had significantly higher scores on self- and other sensitivity measures and in showing consideration for others, both of which were goals of the training course. With reinforcement by organizational superiors, the values taught by the training program began to take form in the work situation.

In a survey of research examining the effectiveness of sensitivity training, Dunnette and Campbell conclude that, except in the case of ethnic prejudice, this type of training has not effected significant and lasting changes in attitude, outlook, and orientation.[18] In the Rubin study concerning prejudice, self-acceptance and ethnic prejudice were measured before and after training, and the scores compared with similar measures for a control group.[19] No changes were discovered in the control group, but there were substantial and significant changes toward increased self-acceptance and decreased ethnic prejudice after two weeks of sensitivity training. With respect to job behavior changes, one study has shown that those undergoing sensitivity training exhibited a greater quantity of changes than those in two other groups, one which had no training and another which was subjected to a standard lecture-discussion human relations training program.[20] Most of the changes were in the areas of greater openness and more consideration, the typical announced goals of sensitivity training. There were no reported changes in analytical skills, ability to resolve conflict, or increasing overall effectiveness in the job.

A final example illustrates the interesting, but often frustrating, nature of training evaluation. In a course specifically designed to improve problem-solving and decision-making abilities, a measurement of group opinion at the end of the course revealed that 87 percent thought the course was worthwhile.[21] The Watson-Glaser Critical Thinking Appraisal was administered to the group both before and after the training. A control group of managers on the same organizational levels in another plant of the firm was also administered this test both before and after the training of the first group. The results showed a *decline* in post-training scores for the trained group and an *increase* for the untrained control group. The differences were not statistically significant, but they still serve to illustrate the often discouraging nature of management development.

[17]Herbert H. Hand and John W. Slocum, Jr., "A Longitudinal Study of the Effects of a Human Relations Training Program on Managerial Effectiveness," *Journal of Applied Psychology*, vol. 56, no. 5, October 1972, pp. 412–417.

[18]Marvin D. Dunnette and John P. Campbell, "Laboratory Education: Impact on People and Organizations," *Industrial Relations*, vol. 8, no. 1, October 1968, p. 12.

[19]Irwin Rubin, "Increased Self-Acceptance: A Means of Reducing Prejudice," *Journal of Personality and Social Psychology*, vol. 5, 1967, pp. 233–239.

[20]J. B. Boyd and J. D. Elliss, *Findings of Research into Senior Management Seminars*, Hydro-Electric Power Commission of Ontario, Toronto, 1962.

[21]Dannie J. Moffie, Richard Calhoon, and James K. O'Brien, "Evaluation of a Management Development Program," *Personnel Psychology*, Winter 1964, pp. 431–440.

ORGANIZATION DEVELOPMENT

When personnel are subjected to individually oriented training and development programs, the application of accepted evaluation research designs often "proves" that learning was accomplished. Despite such proof, in all too many instances the impact upon organizational functioning was nil. The trainee must reenter the culture of the on-going organization, and if it has been unchanged during training, it, rather than the training, is more likely to ultimately control actual behavior. As a consequence, beginning in the 1960s, there sprang up a considerable interest in altering the organization's culture through an *organization development* program.

Bennis defines organization development (OD) as "*a complex educational strategy* intended to *change* the beliefs, attitudes, values, and structure of organizations so that they can better adapt to new technologies, markets, and challenges, and the dizzying rate of change itself."[22] It is a planned and calculated attempt to move the organization as a unit to the climate of the behavioral, open, organic model. More specific goals are (1) decision making on the basis of competence rather than authority, (2) creatively resolving conflict through confrontation designed to replace win-lose situations with win-win types, (3) reducing dysfunctional competition and maximizing collaboration, (4) increasing commitment and a sense of "ownership" of organization objectives throughout the work force, (5) increasing the degree of interpersonal trust and support, (6) creating a climate in which human growth, development, and renewal are a natural part of the enterprise's daily operation, and (7) developing a communication system characterized by mutual openness and candor in solving organizational problems. Bennis has forecasted the eventual demise of the more mechanistic type of organization as having outlived its usefulness.

Team development

One of the major techniques in the arsenal of the OD consultant is team development. Instead of sending isolated individuals off to a sensitivity training session attended by strangers, a type of sensitivity session is conducted for the members of an operating unit, off site away from the job. To overcome the natural reluctance for subordinates to exhibit candor with colleagues and superiors, the services of an outside third-party consultant are deemed essential. In effect, the outsider serves three functions: (1) contacting all members separately to determine what they feel are the major obstructions to effective functioning of the unit, (2) feeding this gathered information to the convened group in a manner that preserves the confidence of information contributors, and (3) serving as a catalyst in the ensuing discussion, which is designed to encourage honest feedback, leveling, and candor. Obviously, the entire process is ego-threatening to the superior, and he or she must first be willing to engage in such an examining process.

With the support of the consultant, the supervisor may be expected to demonstrate openness to constructive comment and suggestions concerning how the unit's collaborative processes are functioning. When one group generated the courage to tell the boss that he was a cold, unfeeling, and impersonal supervisor, he admitted it but

---

[22]Warren G. Bennis, *Organization Development: Its Nature, Origins, and Prospects*, Addison-Wesley, Reading, Mass., 1969, p. 2. Emphasis added.

simultaneously reported his intention *not* to change. He did provide the reason for his style, issuing from unhappy wartime experiences when many close friends were lost in combat; he had resolved never to become close to anyone again. Though there was no desired behavior change, the climate was significantly improved because of general understanding of the supervisor's behavior. Also, members of the group discovered that he was equally unfriendly to all—he did not discriminate! In another instance, the superior was disturbed with failures of subordinates to follow instructions communicated by memo, feeling that there might be instances of outright insubordination. At the suggestion of the consultant, several of his memos were gathered, with instructions to all who had received any to write out their interpretations. The net conclusion was that there was no insubordination—just confusion! The executive resolved to rely less on memos and more on face-to-face oral instructions.

Survey feedback

Perhaps the second major method in the OD repertoire is the systematic collection and measurement of subordinate attitudes through anonymous questionnaires. Likert-type scales ranging from disagreement to agreement are formulated on such subjects as communication, the reward system, collaboration, manager style, and decision making. The role of the consultant is again crucial, as he or she provides the anonymity necessary to truthful collection of information. Ordinarily, the results are shown first to the superior in order to avoid surprise and embarrassment during the group meeting that will follow.

When the group is convened, the specific distributions of ratings on each item are presented. Members are questioned concerning whether they feel that the rating is truly reflective of the thinking of the group. Ordinarily, the response is noncommittal for the first several items, but the superficiality of the process usually irritates one of the more secure, risk-taking members, and more discussion of one of the earlier items is requested. Ordinarily, an item is selected which everyone knows is a real "thorn in the side" of the group's processes. When the superior demonstrates a nonpunitive openness to the initial tactfully stated criticisms, other members of the group tend to own up to their own responses on the questionnaire. For example, in one group the manager was rated rather low on communicative ability. After the unfreezing process had taken place with the catalytic help of the consultant, one member revealed why he had rated the leader so low. He stated that every time that he came in with a problem, inside of two minutes the manager would switch the subject to something that was bothering *him*, with the effect that the subordinate's problem was never discussed. When a few others chimed in with agreement, the manager indicated that he had not been aware of this particular behavioral pattern. He said that he would attempt to correct it, and on the spot authorized each person to stop him and point it out should it happen again. This, again, is an example of the daily interpersonal processes that can have significant impact upon both the work and member feelings about their job and their superior.

In addition to the two basic methods of team development and survey feedback, many specially designed methods are created at once to attack particular processes that seem counterproductive. Intergroup sessions can be developed to calm the warlike gestures between production and engineering, engineering and sales, or line supervisors and the personnel department. The subject under discussion is "What Interferes with the Effective Processing of Work in This Organization." The dysfunctional consequences of specialization of functions, compounded by reward systems that encourage intraorganizational competition, can be alleviated somewhat by therapeutic efforts of OD consultants. One should also note, however, that redesign and restructuring of the organization and its reward systems can often lead to reduction in interpersonal conflicts without the necessity for such therapy.

SUMMARY

The development of executive talent is one of the most important and complex tasks of personnel management. As a consequence, a myriad of developmental techniques have been invented and utilized in attempting to meet executive needs in decision making, interpersonal skills, job knowledge, organizational knowledge, and general knowledge, and to plug specific weaknesses discovered in individual candidates.

The major conclusions to be derived from an analysis of executive and organization development programs are the following:

1   The primary emphasis in executive development should be on self-development. There is no substitute for personal drive, initiative, and ability.
2   There is no one best method of executive development. Each has its specific objectives. The better programs consist of a variety of methods.
3   Development which occurs on or near the job has the advantages of providing motivation and being practicable.
4   The higher the position in the organization, the more important become off-the-job methods. They are more closely identified with education than with training.
5   Much of the present evaluation of executive development programs has been disappointing. The fundamental test is whether or not a favorable change has occurred in job behavior.
6   Much of the developmental effort is wasted if skills and attitudes taught are not reinforced on the job. As a consequence, organization development may be necessary to alter the culture and environment in which the trainee is to work.

DISCUSSION QUESTIONS

1   Contrast and compare sensitivity training for executive development with team development.
2   Contrast and compare sensitivity training with that of structured insight.
3   Assuming that a course in leadership attitudes is to be given in your firm, design an evaluation scheme to determine its effectiveness.
4   Classify the executive development techniques into on-the-job versus off-the-job methods.
5   What is organization development? What type of organization is envisaged?
6   Describe the role of the OD consultant.
7   What executive skills are emphasized in the in-basket method? How does the method contribute to their development?
8   Briefly describe the major executive development methods designed to increase general organizational knowledge.
9   In what ways can role playing be utilized in increasing interpersonal skills?
10 Describe the desired behavior of an effective coach of executive talent.

SUPPLEMENTARY READING

ALPIN, John C., and Duane E. Thompson: "Successful Organizational Change," *Business Horizons*, vol. 17, no. 4, August 1974, pp. 61–66.

ARGYRIS, Chris: "The CEO's Behavior: Key to Organizational Development," *Harvard Business Review*, vol. 51, no. 2, March–April 1973, pp. 55–64.

IVANCEVICH, John M.: "A Study of a Cognitive Training Program: Trainer Styles and Group Development," *Academy of Management Journal*, vol. 17, no. 3, September 1974, pp. 428–439.

SMITH, H. R.: "Executive Development Programs," *Business Horizons*, vol. 17, no. 2, April 1974, pp. 39–46.

STRAUSS, George: "Organizational Development: Credits and Debits," *Organizational Dynamics*, vol. 1, no. 3, Winter 1973, pp. 2–19.

ZEIRA, Yoram: "Job Rotation for Management Development," *Personnel*, vol. 51, no. 4, January–February 1974, pp. 25–34.

TWELVE
ADVANCEMENT

One the oldest and most publicized features of the free-enterprise system is the opportunity to advance. The general thesis is that this system is sufficiently free and competitive to stimulate firms and individuals of greater abilities to move ahead. The opportunity for advancement is considered to be fundamental to the progressive organization and also to the function of personnel development. A person has little incentive toward self-development if she or he has no opportunity to advance.

Advancement within an organization is ordinarily labeled a "promotion." A promotion involves a change from one job to another that is better in terms of status and responsibility. Ordinarily the change to the higher job is accompanied by increased pay and privileges, but not always. In fact, the term "dry" promotion refers to an increase in responsibility and status without an increase in pay. Promotion is distinguishable from transfer in that the latter term refers to changes in jobs that involve little or no change in status, responsibility, and pay.

It must be noted at the beginning of this discussion that not all people within an organization want to advance. The widespread publicizing of the desire to get ahead has led many to believe that all people want to be promoted. It comes as a shock when an employee turns down a promotion to supervisor, for example. There are many reasons behind this refusal of advancement. For one, the difference in pay is often not sufficient to provide the incentive to advance. Occasionally a highly skilled operative receives more pay than the boss. Secondly, many operatives do not wish to forgo the association and acceptance of other workers. There is a universal need to conform and a wish to be socially accepted. Promotion ordinarily separates a person from the group to a degree and makes more difficult personal acceptance by the great majority of former associates. A third possible reason for refusing advancement lies in the individual's desire for security. A new job involves change and risk. The present job has been mastered and the achievement has brought great personal, social, and economic security. Failure in the higher job may result in loss of work, loss of self-confidence, and loss of "face." Not all people desire advancement, and the manager should not be surprised when certain offers of promotion are turned down by her or his subordinates.

Even if a number of employees do not want to be promoted, it is nevertheless important to make provision for their advancement. Many like to know that the opportunity is there even though they do not choose to take advantage of it, and, of course, those who do desire promotion must be given the incentive to develop. Consequently, every organization should have some type of formal and systematic promotion program. There are two basic essentials to such a program. First, clear paths of advancement must be charted through the organization. Dead-end jobs should be labeled, and the path upward well marked. The second essential is that a definite system should be established for the identification and selection of the particular people who are to be advanced. This involves not only the establishment of the means for obtaining and recording data about individuals, but also a policy decision concerning the bases of selection for promotion. The latter question must certainly involve consideration of the old controversy of merit or performance versus seniority. We shall discuss these two essentials of a promotion program—lines of promotion and bases of selection—in the following sections of this chapter.

LINES OF PROMOTION

As pointed out in Chapter 6, job analysis provides the fundamental information required to chart the lines of promotion within an organization. The questions are generally asked of a job incumbent, "To what jobs does this job lead?" and "From what job were you promoted to this job?" In addition to this information, a careful analysis of the duties of the lower job must be made to determine the adequacy of preparation for higher jobs. Too often lines of advancement are restricted to a single department and are more or less obvious to anyone who studies an organization chart. Analysis of job duties generally leads to the discovery of multiple lines of advancement to several jobs in different areas.

Figure 12-1 is a chart depicting two avenues of advancement to the top personnel job in a large manufacturing firm. With a common entry point of Personnel assistant, one avenue emphasizes advancement through a series of management positions in various-sized plants, while the other route is through multiple specialized functions within the personnel area. Some jobs may well be dead ends, and a person hired for this type of job should be informed of its nature.

If the proper atmosphere for personnel development is to be established, employees must know that opportunities for promotion exist. Promotion charts are useful devices to demonstrate that careful planning has been done in this area. Obviously, the existence of a line or channel between jobs A and B does not promise or guarantee the promotion of the incumbent of job A. It merely points out that the avenue for advancement has been surveyed and recorded. Whether or not the employee moves along this line is dependent, first, upon personal abilities, and second, upon the organization and the opening up of possible jobs. It has been indicated previously that labor turnover is not completely undesirable in an organization, and that it does have one advantage in that it frees jobs to which subordinate personnel can be advanced.

Figure 12-1 Line of promotion in personnel management—large manufacturing firm

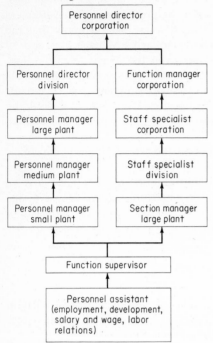

It should also be noted that a particular person is not confined to the line of advancement denoted on the chart. These are the lines of logical progression based on an analysis of job duties. Each person has qualities, desires, and experiences peculiar to him or to her. It may be that some qualities and experience qualify one for promotion outside normal channels. Often certain persons want to change their type of work. It is necessary to recall again the type of analysis and charting depicted in Chapter 9, in which the reservoir of available talent is inventoried for each key position. The preparation of such charts is based in part on the lines of logical relationships, as shown in Figure 12-1, and also on an analysis of the qualities, desires, and experiences of the particular personnel currently employed in the organization, as they have been determined by interviews and a study of personnel records.

One of the more interesting questions concerning lines of promotion is the identification of the route to the top job, the presidency of an organization. In a survey of the presidents of 239 of the 500 largest industrial firms during the period from 1945 to 1964, it was found that the main routes lay in general management, production, marketing, and finance.[1] The proportion of presidencies contributed by these fields remained fairly stable over the twenty-year period, the average being 21.6 percent for general management, 21.5 percent for production, 17.6 percent for marketing, and 15.9 percent for finance.

[1]William P. Dommermuth, "On the Odds of Becoming Company President," *Harvard Business Review*, vol. 44, no. 3, May–June 1966, p. 66.

Recent findings from a longitudinal study of presidencies of 100 large corporations reveal a dramatic increase in the number of marketing personnel occupying the top position. During the 1970 to 1972 period, marketing personnel accounted for 29 percent of the chief executive spots, followed by 22 percent for production personnel, and only 18 percent for those with financial backgrounds.[2] In the post-World War II period, financial specialists were in great demand as firms grew through mergers and acquisitions. In recent years, the rising tide of consumerism and the rapid rate of new-product introductions dictate an organizational need for skills in marketing. It is apparent that the environmental situation facing the firm will exert a considerable influence upon the choice of chief executive officer.

FORMAL BASES FOR PROMOTION

The two formal bases on which a decision can be made concerning promotion are (1) merit and (2) seniority. Management personnel generally prefer merit as determined by job performance and by analysis of employee potential for development. In this way they ensure that competence shall be the fundamental determinant of progression. The argument for merit has little foundation unless conscientious and systematic attempts are undertaken to measure merit. Measuring the worth of individual performance is sufficiently complex to deserve a full chapter. Chapter 13 is devoted in its entirety to this difficult but important subject.

Distinguishing among persons on the basis of seniority is as old as civilization itself. *Seniority* is defined here as the length of recognized service in an organization. In family organization, the eldest son has traditionally been the successor to the head of the family. Seniority is widely recognized in all types of organizations; it is highly regarded in military and governmental institutions; it is becoming increasingly important in business and economic organizations. Unless one believes that seniority and merit are always present in equal degree in the same person, there is likely to be a conflict between these factors, particularly when we attempt to establish the basis for promotion to a higher-level job.

The fact that the percentage of white-collar employees is steadily increasing in our society is no basis for ignoring the importance of seniority in decision making. In order to survive and grow, organized labor must increase its membership levels among white-collar employees. These employees are generally known for their greater identification with the organization and its management. There is, however, increasing evidence that many are beginning to seek power restraints upon unilateral decision making by management. Schoolteachers, nurses, and government employees are demonstrating a growing interest in the protection of an organized union. Unions have traditionally sought to impose decision-making systems on management which would reduce the latter's power and discretion. Seniority is an objective system with a reliability coefficient of 1 if carefully constructed. When used as the sole decision-making base, it effectively removes the personnel decision-making function from the manager. Managers are naturally disturbed inasmuch as they feel that, though seniority is a reliable measure, its validity in making many decisions is highly questionable.

---

[2]"More Room at the Top for Marketing Men," *Business Week*, Aug. 12, 1972, p. 27.

Before considering the bases of decision making that are more acceptable to management, we must first understand the mechanics of seniority which give it the reliability that the union seeks.

MECHANICS OF SENIORITY

There are at least four major tasks in the design and establishment of a seniority system. The first is specifying *when* seniority is to begin, how it may be affected by a number of different types of service interruptions, and under what conditions it terminates. In effect, this is the problem of establishing the ground rules which govern the accumulation of seniority. The second duty is determining what groups are to be given special treatment in the seniority system. Often both labor union and company want to favor their respective key personnel in the union and the firm. The third task is determining the range or area over which seniority can be accumulated, that is, whether over the entire plant or over some organizational element thereof. The final problem is determining what aspects of the employment situation will be affected by seniority. Should it be applied to promotion, layoff, and other related problems? In all such tasks, it is important that rules be carefully and specifically spelled out. If they are not, seniority can generate more personnel problems than it eliminates.

Accumulation of seniority

In many companies, seniority does not begin immediately upon hiring. There is usually a probationary period of one to six months. After this period it is usual for the recognized service to start as of the time of original employment. Even here, problems arise. Frequently, when several people are hired on the same day, it becomes important to keep exact times of hiring during the day. When there are several hires at the same time, some predetermined rule for distinguishing among personnel must be established, e.g., alphabetical by last name, lowest employee identification number, etc. Seniority's greatest asset is its ability to distinguish among all personnel on an objective basis. Details, therefore, are highly important in defining the exact length of service.

One of the more difficult problems in the accumulation of seniority is that of specifying the effect of interruptions in service. If, for example, the employee leaves a job to enter military service, many firms will allow the continued accumulation of seniority and will thus create a type of "synthetic seniority." Another, more serious type of interruption is that of leaving the collective bargaining unit through promotion to a supervisory job. It is important that the company protect the seniority of persons so promoted, for otherwise there is a great loss of incentive to accept the higher job. When such protection is provided, the newly appointed supervisor usually continues to accumulate seniority. A smaller number of companies provide that when one reenters the bargaining unit after serving as supervisor, one's seniority stands where one left it at the time of promotion. As we have indicated earlier in this chapter, there are many difficulties in stimulating qualified personnel to accept promotion to supervisory ranks. It is therefore quite important that the valuable asset of seniority should be fully protected for such personnel.

There are a number of conditions under which seniority is usually terminated.

Among them are:

1 Being discharged for proper cause
2 Voluntary resignation
3 Overstaying leave of absence
4 Absences in excess of a stipulated period, such as three working days, without notifying the company
5 Failure to report to work after layoff when properly notified
6 A layoff in excess of a stipulated period, such as a year or eighteen months

The last two reasons are the source of much controversy. To reduce the controversy surrounding reason 5, the manner of notification of the recalled employee should be spelled out in the policy or in the labor contract.

The controversy concerning the sixth reason is that many people feel that no employee should lose seniority for reasons beyond his or her control. Seniority is a highly valuable commodity, and the trend is in the direction of an increase in its value. Involuntary layoffs are outside the employee's control. From the company's viewpoint, there must be a time limitation, in order that they may maintain some control over the situation. In two-thirds of 1,845 union-management contracts covering almost 8 million employees, a stipulated period of layoff is designated for loss of seniority; one-half specify periods of less than two years, while the rest stipulate periods ranging from two to five years.[3]

Special groups

The second task in establishing a seniority system is that of deciding what groups are to be given special treatment in the form of exemptions from the rules. The labor union generally requires that its officials and shop stewards be awarded a superseniority over all others. The reason for this stipulation is to keep the representative personnel intact, particularly in times of layoff and cutbacks when they are most needed. Unless accompanied by requirement of ability to do assigned work, this superseniority can result in the layoff of highly qualified employees and the retention of stewards and union officials who may not be qualified. The essential question is whether or not the superseniority is paramount or whether it is operative only when the union official can actually perform the job in question. These exceptions must be carefully written or disputes can easily arise.

If the union requires that its organization be protected through the granting of superseniority, it is not unreasonable that the company should be able to trade those exceptions for some special treatment for certain key employees. For example, such special groups as the following may be exempted from the seniority provisions: (1) tool and die makers, (2) graduates of technical and professional schools, (3) personnel classified by management as indispensable for maintaining the flow of production, and (4) apprentices or those receiving special training and schooling. Sometimes it is specified that the number of management-protected personnel cannot exceed the number of union personnel who are granted superseniority.

[3]Winston L. Tillery, "Layoff and Recall Provisions in Major Agreements," *Monthly Labor Review*, vol. 94, no. 7, July 1971, p. 44.

Seniority unit

Our third problem in setting up a seniority system is that of specifying the area or unit over which it operates. Seniority can be computed on the basis of company, plant division, department, or occupation. Any one or all of these areas can be used for different objectives. For example, the influence of seniority in promotion may be confined to occupational seniority, whereas in the matter of vacation choice it may be company-wide. When decisions have to do with matters involving employee competence to do work, management generally prefers the narrower area.

When the seniority unit is restricted, the problem of "bumping" during layoff is reduced. A longer-service worker can displace personnel of shorter service in only a restricted unit. When the area is company-wide, the layoff of one person might well generate a dozen or more "bumps." The disruptive effects of "bumping" can be reduced by stipulating that the displaced employee can "bump" only the least senior employee in a unit, or that the number of "bumps" per displacement cannot exceed a certain number. The narrower unit coverage, however, does cause problems for management. If seniority is accumulated only by occupation or department, personnel are naturally reluctant to accept transfers from one department or occupation to another. This is a problem similar to that of promoting an operative to supervisor. Here again, it may be necessary to protect such seniority when the transfers are made at the request of the management. When such transfers are initiated by the employee, the seniority is lost.

It is important specifically to indicate the particular units in which seniority can be accumulated. It is also important for the company to maintain exact and accurate seniority lists of all personnel. To management, company-wide seniority for most objectives seems rather ludicrous. However, though occupational seniority does ensure a certain minimum of job competence, such units may be too narrow. When a job is eliminated by changes in work processes, the seniority of all assigned personnel is wiped out. If occupational seniority is utilized, it is quite important to utilize also other seniority units, such as the department or division. Departmental seniority provides some flexibility, because it is unlikely that an entire department will be eliminated. It also ensures that the employee will have some general knowledge of the jobs to which he or she might fall heir in case of layoff.

In a recent U.S. district court decision, the Crown Zellerbach Corporation and the United Paperworkers and Papermakers Union were ordered to replace a job seniority system with a plant-wide system for making promotion decisions.[4] The employer and the union were charged with violating Title VII of the Civil Rights Act of 1964 since the job seniority system was effectively utilized as an instrument in maintaining a pervasive pattern of discrimination against blacks with respect to promotion and training opportunities. Though there is nothing in the job seniority system that is inherently prejudicial to blacks, its continued use in conjunction with past discriminatory practices in hiring led to the order to abolish the system. Its replacement by a plant-wide unit effectively opened up promotion possibilities for blacks which offset any economic disadvantages that the organization might experience. The court did not hold that the plant-wide unit was the only way to correct discrimination, but any management- or

[4]*United States v. Local 189, United Paperworkers and Papermakers* (D.C.—E.D. Louisiana, Mar. 26, 1968).

union-proposed substitute would have to receive judicial approval. Thus, to the factors considered in selecting an appropriate seniority unit must be added the power of federal courts under the Civil Rights Act.

Employment decisions affected by seniority

The last and perhaps most important problem in designing a seniority system is to specify the employment privileges which seniority can affect and the weight of that effect. Certain employment factors are often affected by seniority. Among them are (1) promotion, (2) layoff, (3) transfer, (4) choice of shifts, (5) choice of vacation periods, (6) separation or severance pay, and (7) choice of machine, jobs, runs, etc. For some factors, management is often entirely willing that seniority shall be *completely* controlling. The choice of vacation periods, machinery, and shift assignments is an example of this type. Decisions concerning demotion, transfer, layoff, and promotion are more complex, and management often wishes to use the merit base in place of or in addition to seniority.

Demotion is the opposite of promotion. The employee is changed to a job which has lower pay, status, or responsibilities. The use of demotion as a tool of disciplinary action is highly questionable. Demotion may also be caused by a contraction of the work force in whole or in part. As noted earlier, if seniority governs layoff, employees with longer service can "bump" personnel in lower jobs with shorter service. This type of demotion is more acceptable to management than demotion for disciplinary reasons, but it has the disadvantages noted earlier; that is, a series of "bumps" can disrupt the entire organization. In addition, the demoted employee may be either overqualified for the present job if it is within the occupational area or underqualified if "bumping" cuts across occupational lines.

As defined earlier, a transfer is a change in job where the new job is substantially equal to the old in terms of pay, status, and responsibilities. There are various types of transfers such as (1) those designed to enhance training and development, (2) those making possible adjustment to varying volumes of work within the firm, and (3) those designed to remedy a problem of poor placement.

It is important that company policy be formulated to govern the administration of all types of employee transfers. Rather than decide each case solely on the characteristics of that case, effective management needs to establish some uniformity of treatment. The policy should cover such subjects as (1) the acceptable reasons for a transfer, (2) the organization area over which a transfer can be made, (3) the effect of seniority on such changes as shift transfers, (4) the posting of available job openings, (5) the classification of transfers as permanent or temporary, and (6) the effect, if any, of the transfer upon the pay of the employee. In general, the policy governing transfers should consider first the interests of the organization as a whole. This policy does not, however, prevent the granting of requests for remedial personnel transfers. Ordinarily company policies are flexible enough to permit some individual treatment of particular employee problems.

Layoff is a very difficult problem not only for the employee but for the company and the labor union as well. Since layoff involves the loss of income, the employee and the union are prone to restrict the company's freedom of decision. The company, again, is desirous of emphasizing the factor of ability and merit in layoff. It wishes to be sure that employees who "bump" other employees can adequately fulfill the job requirements. On the other hand, because of the seriousness of the event to the employee, the employee tries to regulate layoff decisions through seniority systems. It is generally found that seniority is a *stronger* factor in layoff than it is in promotion. In a previously cited analysis of union-management contracts, seniority was the sole factor controlling layoff decisions in 25 percent of the contracts, a primary factor in one-half (seniority controlled if employee could meet minimum performance requirements), and a secondary factor in the remainder (seniority controlled only if the displaced employee was relatively equal to the person to be "bumped").[5]

With respect to promotion, management feels that it has the strongest case in advocating merit as the sole or most important basis for the decision. Unions and employees still contend that seniority should be given significant influence. This brings us to the complex and significant problem of merit versus seniority in making various employment decisions. It will be found that compromise is not out of the question.

MERIT VERSUS SENIORITY

The utilization of seniority in making various employment decisions has a number of advantages, the most outstanding being that it is an objective means of distinguishing among personnel. There is no doubt that the person who has ten years and two months of continuous recognized service is superior in service to the one with nine years of such service. The measurement is exact. It is also contended that the measurement is simple; and it does have the advantage of simplicity, provided that the seniority system is explicitly set up and defined. A reading of the preceding section would suggest that the measurement of seniority is not so simple as many people believe.

In the realm of human relations, seniority has the value of being accepted by employees. As we stated earlier, the use of length of service in awarding rights and privileges is very old and widespread. Thus, when employment decisions are made strictly on the basis of an objective measurement of length of service, it is probable that the majority in a group will accept the decisions. Thus, the use of seniority promotes more peace than does the use of merit, the latter being more easily affected by bias and favoritism. Another value in the use of seniority is security; an employee is able to predict when and how certain changes will be made. The use of this objective measure protects one from the whims and biases of management by removing the decision-making power from management and giving it to a system.

A final value of the use of seniority, which is more acceptable to members of management, is that it effects a reduction in labor turnover. An asset as valuable as seniority is not easily given up. Employees will remain with an organization even when they are aware of better opportunities elsewhere, one reason being the loss of seniority that will result from quitting.

There are several reasons against the use of seniority, particularly when it becomes the sole base for decision making. In the first place, seniority often ignores merit or ability. The job must be done if the organization is to accomplish its objective. Length of service will not do it, and there is no guarantee that the experience indicated by

[5]Winston L. Tillery, op. cit., p. 42.

seniority will produce ability. In one study in a steel firm, it was discovered that there was little relation between ability to do the job and length of service for journeyman machinists.[6] Ten tests of ability were correlated with length of service, and only four tests showed a positive relationship, the highest correlation being a plus .30. Thus, though experience is a great teacher, there is no guarantee that a person will consent to be taught or that one will be able to learn. In addition, if the seniority system is rigidly followed, where is the incentive to learn and improve? The only incentive one has is to "stick around" and accumulate service. The use of length of service, therefore, places a considerable burden on the hiring process. In theory, if you hire effectively at the bottom, the use of seniority will not prevent good employment decisions from there on. This may be good logic, but it is practically impossible to demonstrate in practice; as indicated earlier, our selection techniques are not that good.

The use of seniority overvalues experience. It does not guarantee the selection of competent personnel. It provides no incentive toward preparation for advancement. It drives the ambitious and able person, with little service, out of the firm. A rigid seniority system makes it extremely difficult to attract and recruit capable new personnel unless they are placed in the exempt category.

This is not to say that seniority is valueless to the organization. Possession of organizational experience is an asset to any employee, but it is *only one* desirable characteristic and not necessarily the most important. If the oldest were always the ablest, our problem of measuring the performance of both people and firms would be greatly simplified.

From the viewpoint of productivity, the stronger argument is on the side of merit and performance. However, if the organization makes little or no attempt to measure merit or performance systematically, it has a very poor case to put against the more objective values of seniority. It should be recognized that much of the clamor for recognition of seniority is founded on a fundamental distrust of management.

In the event that a promotion decision made on the basis of merit is challenged, management should have evidence of the factual basis of the decision. Such data as the following can be used: scores on both written and performance tests, production records, merit ratings, absences, tardiness, education and training accomplishments, physical qualifications, age, experience, commendations, and warnings. Many arbitrators of disputes concerning promotion decisions will accept the results of tests as a measure of differences in ability. Well-designed merit-rating programs also lead to acceptance of merit scores as a legitimate basis for decision making. The management that does not attempt to improve its evaluation of individual performances and keep its employees informed of their standing should not be surprised at the force with which the employees demand recognition of seniority.

We do not advocate that seniority be completely ignored. It does have value. Many compromises have been worked out in practice between the extremes of pure seniority and pure merit, one of which can be phrased, "When ability is substantially equal, seniority will govern." This compromise is weighted in favor of ability, inasmuch as ability is rarely ever equal between two or more individuals. Obviously there will be many disputes over the word "substantially." A similar compromise has been placed into many contracts in the steel industry. Here is an example.

---

[6]George Hill, "Seniority in Industry," Address before the Cincinnati chapter of the Society for the Advancement of Management, May 3, 1956.

It is understood and agreed that except as hereafter provided, seniority is defined as the length of an employee's continuous service in a particular department of the Company, as set forth in paragraph B of this section, and shall be applied on a *departmental basis* in all cases of *upgrading* or *downgrading*, and of increase and decrease of forces. The following factors shall be considered, and *when factors 2 and 3 are relatively equal, length of continuous service* will govern.

1   Length of continuous service
2   Productivity and ability to perform the work required by the company
3   Physical fitness

A second type of compromise is written more in favor of seniority. This would be an agreement that the senior person able to do the job should be assigned to it. Suppose, for example, persons A, B, and C were being considered for a job opening. A has ten years of service, B has five, and C, three. If A can meet the *minimum* requirements for the job, it is assigned to him or her even though B and C may be of substantially higher ability. Our problem here is how to tell whether A can do the job. The labor union generally insists that A be given a trial on the job. If after a few weeks she or he proves inadequate, the company may then turn to B. It is evident that the administration of this compromise agreement can consume a substantial amount of time. In a few instances, the union has accepted the results of various written and performance tests as a shortcut in a procedure of this type. Minimum scores are established, and the person with the greatest seniority among those who have passing scores is the one who gets the job.

Many firms establish, for a class of jobs, a rate range which permits varying rates of pay for different personnel on the same job. The purpose of the rate range is to recognize and compensate individual differences. This again becomes the scene of a merit and seniority controversy. Organized labor generally prefers either a single rate for all personnel or a rate range operated on a seniority basis. Many managements prefer a rate range operated on a merit or performance basis. Various compromises in the area have also been worked out. For example, as shown in Figure 12-2a, seniority may govern in the lower half of the range and merit in the upper half. In this manner, each employee is assured of receiving the middle rate, which is often assumed to be the going rate, by merely serving the required amount of time on the job. However, if one

Figure 12-2   Merit and seniority compromises in the wage structure

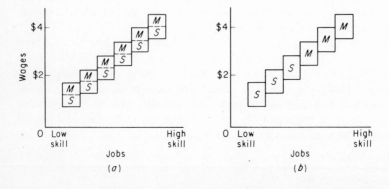

expects to receive higher than the going rate, he or she must be a better-than-average employee. Many feel that this type of compromise provides the greatest hope for a solution of the problem.

A second type of compromise is depicted in Figure 12-2b. Seniority governs completely the progression through the rate range in the lower job classes, and merit governs completely the progression through the rate range in the higher job classes. The primary reason behind this arrangement is the amount of influence an employee can rightly be expected to exert in the two types of jobs. In the lower job, the employee is more restricted and controlled; in the higher job, the individual employee can exert a stronger influence on the manner in which the job is performed. Thus, one can obtain rate increases through length of service in the lower jobs but only through good performance in the higher jobs. The height of the rate range for lower-skilled jobs is usually much smaller than for the higher-skilled type. This finding is also consistent with the distinction based on the employee's ability to exert influence and affect the content of the job.

PROMOTION OF MANAGERS

It would be naïve to insist that all promotions are made on the basis of either precisely measured seniority or objectively assessed ability. The intangible and complex nature of assessing both people and vacant positions leads to the entry of subjective and informal bases for promotion decision making. When the open positions are in the management ranks, the increased importance of the decision to the long-range interests of both person and organization practically guarantees the creation of arenas of political maneuvering.

In a study of the promotion of managers at Milo, Dalton found much disagreement concerning the importance of ability in a consideration of advancement to managerial positions.[7] Age and seniority were definitely not important factors in this firm. In analyzing the characteristics of 226 managers, he discovered that educational level was an important differentiating factor: first-level supervisors possessed 10.5 years of formal schooling, general supervisors averaged 11.2 years, departmental superintendents had 12.5 years, division chiefs averaged 13.7 years, and the plant head and his assistants had 15.3 years. Perhaps of greater importance for the higher management positions were (1) having membership in the Masonic fraternity, since 69 percent of all managers were Masons as compared with 78 percent for the top three levels, and (2) having Anglo-Saxon ancestry. Over 70 percent of the top three levels of management were Anglo-Saxon as compared with 50 percent for first-level supervisors. "Thus, ethnics composing probably less than 38 percent of the community filled 85 percent of Milo's advisory and directive forces."[8] All the higher-level managers were either overt and practicing Republicans or pretended to be. Membership in the yacht club held some relationship to position level, but was not nearly so important as Masonic membership or Anglo-Saxon ancestry.

A later study of 240 managers in forty firms by Powell tended to confirm this pattern

---

[7]Melville Dalton, *Men Who Manage*, John Wiley & Sons, Inc., New York, 1959, chap. 6.
[8]Ibid., p. 184.

of informal bases for promotion.[9] As developed from carefully introduced question-naires, it was concluded that there were many factors leading to an advancement in rank. Managerial capability was first to be stipulated but lost its importance as a screening device for higher positions as it was deemed to be a common denominator held by the entire pool of candidates. Beyond this, such factors as the following were reported: spouse and family, religion, ethnic group, educational level, seniority, luck, influence of important customers, informal relations in the firm, and refusal of a prior promotion offer. On the basis of the 240 case studies of actual promotions, Powell characterized the successful promotee as being a capable leader, white, Anglo-Saxon, healthy and energetic, Protestant or Catholic, an effective decision maker, a college graduate, ambitious, loyal, a member of a reputable social club, aided socially by his wife, a Republican, member of the chamber of commerce, tall, clean-cut, conservative-ly dressed, a social drinker, participant in charitable and professional community organizations, and lucky.[10]

In making the complex and important decisions concerning managerial promo-tions, there is considerable evidence that one tends to prefer people with qualities and interests similar to the appointing authority. Consciously or not, the manager looks for backgrounds and attitudes that will provide a basis for common understanding and cooperation. Homogeneity in terms of values will improve communication, decrease dissent, and enhance morale.[11] The primary risks lie in the areas of creativity and risk taking, inasmuch as heterogeneity tends to enhance ideation processes. In addition, the Civil Rights Act of 1964 will tend to reduce homogeneity of values by requiring advancement of members of minority groups. When AT&T says that it will increase females in second-level management jobs by 33 percent and in upper-level jobs by 50 percent in 1975, and General Motors indicates promotion of one woman for every three men on most levels, the traditional pool of white male candidates is destined for some emotional shocks. The decision-making process with respect to promotion will be increasingly governed by the same socially decreed criteria as for initial selection. Union suspicion and distrust of managers has led to seniority programs, and society's distrust has led to governmental review and threatened punitive action. The only justifiable and defensible basis for promotion decisions is that of ability to do the job. Neither unions nor government are content to accept simple management assertions that A is better than B. There must be a return to sound professional personnel practices of job analysis, publicized and equal opportunities to apply through internal job postings, systematic analysis of candidates without regard to race, religion, nationality, or sex, and willingness to explain the rationale on which a promotion decision has been based. Where such programs are not sufficient to redress imbalances in personnel assignments caused by past practices, accelerated hiring and advancement have been decreed or negotiated by the Equal Employment Opportunity Commission and the Office of Federal Contracts Compliance. In these instances, the personnel manager must be prepared to deal with dissatisfactions and complaints of "reverse discrimination" from qualified candidates from the majority group.[12]

[9]Reed M. Powell, "Elements of Executive Promotion," *California Management Review*, Winter 1963, pp. 83–90.

[10]Ibid., p. 86.

[11]John Senger, "Managers' Perceptions of Subordinates' Competence as a Function of Personal Value Orientations," *Academy of Management Journal*, vol. 14, no. 4, December 1971, pp. 415–423.

[12]"Up-the-Ladder Blues," *Wall Street Journal*, Feb. 28, 1974, p. 1.

PERSONNEL OUT-PLACEMENT

Though the typical rank and file employee is governed by the layoff provisions of the contract as discussed earlier, there is growing evidence of organizational concern for personnel displacements not covered by such contracts. In particular, the personnel units in more than 200 large corporations have developed an out-placement function to assist in large-scale dismissals of professional, technical, and managerial employees. When firms are required to make substantial cutbacks in personnel, there are very difficult decisions to make concerning which activities should be retained and which personnel within the firm should be let go. In general, most firms utilize a cutback situation to remove poorer-performing personnel, those whose salaries have grown to exceed their foreseeable value, and those who, though not incompetent, have no identifiable real strengths on which to build in the future. A personnel out-placement activity is based on the ideas that these personnel have salable skills usable to other firms, and that the extent of the market for these types of skills is largely hidden.

When the firm has identified the particular people to be dismissed, after presumably conducting an internal search for possible transfers, the next and most difficult steps are to prepare the termination letter and conduct the termination interview. Though general knowledge of a cutback has helped to prepare the way to some degree, the individual is never fully prepared for the shock of the axe on his or her employment neck. Thus, it is strongly recommended that termination notice should be given early in the workweek, and never on Friday. Immediate activity, rather than solitary brooding, is the avenue to positive action to overcome the current difficulty.

In one organization, a special out-placement unit was developed to handle the dismissal of 200 professionals and managers. Displaced persons were referred to this unit, which included consultants, psychologists, and a line manager, immediately upon the ending of the termination interview by the supervisor. The immediate major problem is to rebuild the confidence and self-esteem of the rejected employee. Assessment of his or her potential through depth interviews and psychological testing will provide the data necessary for an effective new job search program. Consultants helped personnel to prepare resumes and develop contacts through letters and telephone calls as well as in sustaining their morale during the inevitable lag period before offers began to be received. This firm was also generous in providing severance pay to finance the job search and in allowing dismissed employees to retain an office base from which the job search could be conducted. It is important, however, to quickly remove the employee from his or her regular work environment to reduce loss of "face" and to permit full-time efforts to be devoted to working with out-placement specialists and the job market. Daily conversations and exchange of job tips among the group of displaced personnel also help considerably. This firm reported that 90 to 95 percent of all displaced personnel who used the service had been placed on a new job with equivalent salaries within a four-month period.[13] When this task is contracted to an outside firm of consultants, the usual fee per displaced employee is 10 to 15 percent of annual salary.

[13]Basil Robert Cuddihy, "How to Give Phased-out Managers a New Start," *Harvard Business Review*, vol. 52, no. 4, July–August 1974, pp. 61–69.

SUMMARY

In this chapter, factors and conditions surrounding the question of advancement within the organization have been examined. We have shown that a promotion program must rest in part upon a job analysis program. Lines of logical advancement can be determined only by an analysis of job responsibilities. The more important question, at least to the employee, is that of the basis for selecting candidates for promotion. In general there are two bases, seniority and merit.

The advantages of utilizing seniority as the determining factor in promotion and layoff are its (1) objectivity, (2) simplicity, (3) wide acceptance, (4) promotion of a greater feeling of security, and (5) reduction of labor turnover. Its disadvantages are that (1) seniority and competence do not necessarily coincide; (2) it provides little incentive to improve skill and knowledge; (3) it does not serve to attract capable personnel to the organization; (4) it tends to drive out the younger capable employees; and (5) it places too great a burden upon hiring practices. In decisions concerning promotion and layoff of rank and file, the pressure of management for competence and of the worker for seniority often results in various types of compromises, such as: (1) when ability is substantially equal, seniority will govern; (2) the senior person able to meet the minimum requirements is selected; and (3) seniority is used as a sole requirement in some areas, with ability as a sole requirement for other decisions.

The selection of personnel for advancement into managerial positions is not usually afflicted with the seniority issue. The resulting freedom of management choice, presumably based on ability, is threatened by informal practices that unduly emphasize preservation of existing homogeneous values, as well as by the Civil Rights Act, Equal Employment Opportunity Commission, and the Office of Federal Contracts Compliance. Firms that have not developed systematic and professional personnel practices are in a weak position in arguing against injunctions and quotas from various governmental agencies. They have been equally vulnerable in the past when arguing with the labor union on the seniority issue. One of the keystones of a program to defend against both the union and the government, as well as positively promote the welfare of the enterprise, is a properly designed performance appraisal program, a subject covered in the following chapter.

DISCUSSION QUESTIONS

1 On what basis can the federal government force selection of a plant-wide seniority system for promotion and layoff?

2 Contrast the reliability and validity of seniority systems with the reliability and validity of assessment centers for the purpose of making promotion decisions.

3 What impact will the Civil Rights Act have upon promotion programs of private business firms?

4 What are the various types of compromises that can be effected between merit and seniority in making employment decisions?

5 In what ways can the reliability of seniority systems be reduced?

6 If the union-management contract should stipulate promotion *solely* on the basis of seniority, what impact would this have on the hiring process? Would your recommendations be consistent with the Civil Rights Act?

7 What are the usual routes to the presidency in industrial firms? Why does the pattern vary from time to time?

8 If a firm's management should feel a responsibility for out-placement of professionals and managers, what would be the nature of such a program?

9 Why do unions promote the use of seniority in employment decision making?

10 In effecting merit-seniority compromises in pay increases, (1) what is the rationale for dividing each pay range into two parts? and (2) what is the rationale for dividing the total job structure into two parts?

SUPPLEMENTARY READING

CUDDIHY, Basil Robert: "How to Give Phased-out Managers a New Start," *Harvard Business Review*, vol. 52, no. 4, July–August 1974, pp. 61–69.

FULMER, Robert M., and William E. Fulmer: "Providing Equal Opportunities for Promotion," *Personnel Journal*, vol. 53, no. 7, July 1974, pp. 491–497.

HERSHEY, Robert: "Effects of Anticipated Job Loss on Employee Behavior," *Journal of Applied Psychology*, vol. 56, no. 3, June 1972, pp. 273–276.

KING, Geoffrey R.: "Seniority, Technological Change, and Arbitration," *The Personnel Administrator*, vol. 19, no. 6, September 1974, pp. 23–27.

MORRISON, Robert F., and Maria-Luise Sebald: "Personal Characteristics Differentiating Female Executive from Female Nonexecutive Personnel," *Journal of Applied Psychology*, vol. 59, no. 5, October 1974, pp. 656–659.

TILLERY, Winston L.: "Seniority Administration in Major Agreements," *Monthly Labor Review*, vol. 95, no. 12, December 1972, pp. 36–39.

THIRTEEN

PERFORMANCE APPRAISAL AND MANAGEMENT BY OBJECTIVES

No firm has a choice as to whether or not it should appraise its personnel and their performance. Just as training must and does take place after hiring, it is inevitable that the performance of the hired personnel will be evaluated by someone at some time. The choice is one of method.

In general, it can be said that the choice lies among three possible approaches:

1 A *casual*, unsystematic, and often haphazard appraisal
2 The *traditional* and highly *systematic* measurement of (a) employee characteristics, (b) employee contributions, or (c) both
3 Mutual goal setting through a Management by Objectives program (MBO)

Though the casual approach is perhaps the most commonly used, various studies have revealed an increase in the number of firms choosing some formal type of appraisal. A survey of 426 firms resulted in 67 percent reporting a formal rather than casual attempt to evaluate employees.[1] There was a direct relationship between size of firm and incidence of formal plans, with 87 percent of those having more than 5,000 employees using a systematic approach. A more recent survey of approximately one thousand firms indicated that 80 percent have some type of formal appraisal system, the greater bulk of which were begun within the past decade.[2] One-third of the firms having

---

[1] National Industrial Conference Board, *Personnel Practices in Factory and Office: Manufacturing*, Studies in Personnel Policy, no. 194, New York, 1964, p. 17.
[2] Glenn H. Varney, "Performance Appraisal: Inside and Out," *The Personnel Administrator*, vol. 17, no. 6, November–December 1972, p. 16.

programs reported utilization of the most recent innovation, Management by Objectives. Most of the growth in usage is in relation to administrative and professional employees. The tendency is to rely upon seniority or quantitative measures of quantity and quality of output for rank and file personnel. With the previously mentioned expansion of the white-collar segment of our economy, it is logical that performance appraisal should continue to grow in importance.

When formal programs of appraisals are utilized, most organizations use one of the many variations of traditional and systematic measurement by superiors. This type of appraisal is systematic in that it evaluates all performances in the same manner, utilizing the same approach, so that the ratings obtained of separate personnel are comparable. Such systematic appraisals are undertaken periodically according to plan; they are not casual or left to chance. The essential purpose in this systematic and periodic appraisal is the accurate measurement of human performance. It attempts to reduce, if not to eliminate, human bias and prejudice by means of a system, particularly a system that is subject to impartial review and check.

In both the traditional and Management by Objectives (MBO) approaches, the trend is in the direction of attempting to evaluate *what the person does*, rather than *what he or she is*. In the past emphasis has been on the evaluation of the employee's worth as a person. This approach resulted in an appraisal of initiative, dependability, personality, etc. More recently emphasis has been given to measuring the results of the employee's performance. Thus both elements, the qualities of the person and the facts of job performance, may enter into any rating process. But considering the recent emphasis upon performance and deemphasis of the more indirect appraisal of the person, the term "performance appraisal" is more appropriate than the older ones of "merit rating," "employee rating," and "service rating."

The third approach to appraising the performance of others has issued largely from the criticism of traditional management practices in general. In the famous phrase of McGregor, traditional measurement asks that the supervisor "play God" and sit in judgment upon his fellowman.[3] As a result, much space has been devoted to the promotion of an appraisal approach involving a much higher degree of subordinate participation. A key element of this type of evaluation is provision for mutual goal setting and appraisal of progress by both the appraiser and the appraisee. This philosophy issues from the behavioral value of fundamental trust in the goodness, capability, and responsibility of human beings.

SYSTEMATIC APPRAISAL BY SUPERIORS

Appraisals of subordinates by superiors is deemed by many to be an essential part of the executive job. A systematic and periodic appraisal process is deemed superior to a casual, intuitive, and, at times, haphazard evaluation which will always take place in the absence of such preplanning. In the sections that follow, we shall examine the particular values issuing from systematic appraisal, survey several alternative measurement systems, and indicate the prominent features of a program of installation.

---

[3]Douglas McGregor, "An Uneasy Look at Performance Appraisal," *Harvard Business Review*, May–June 1957, pp. 89–94.

Values of the systematic approach

Perhaps the first and basic value of systematic performance appraisal is that it provides information of great assistance in making and enforcing decisions about such subjects as promotions, pay increases, layoffs, and transfers. It provides this information *in advance* of the time when it may be needed, thereby avoiding spot judgments when a decision must be made. The reported uses of formal appraisals in the National Industrial Conference Board study was 73 percent for promotion decisions, 69 percent for salary adjustments, 61 percent for stimulating employee improvement, 46 percent in deciding upon discharges, and 27 percent in determining layoffs.[4] The decision is not colored unduly by the events which have happened most recently or by those which the appraiser can remember. In addition, the systematic approach provides the information in *a form that permits the making of comparisons.* All persons have been appraised in the same manner. It has been found that the records established by the systematic rating of personnel are of great value in *backing up decisions* which have been challenged. Employees have more respect for a record that is religiously and accurately maintained. Arbitrators of labor-management disputes in grievance procedures will accept management records of performance appraisals as legitimate evidence in the hearing, whereas they will accept with much less credence the testimony from memory of the supervisor.

With respect to the appraisal of administrative personnel, the current trend seems to be in the direction of less prescribed format. One automotive firm asks the rater to appraise overall performance as "marginal," "competent," or "excellent," and to compose a narrative under "evaluation of performance" and "plans for future action."[5] The emphasis of this less structured, and consequently less comparable, approach is upon individual growth and development, rather than upon making justifiable decisions about pay, transfers, and promotions. Thus, the typical organization is likely to use a number of approaches and formats as it appraises the performance of multiple types of personnel.

A second value of systematic appraisal of employee performance is that it serves to *stimulate and guide employee development.* Most people like to know how they are doing. A good appraisal program provides this information in a form that can usually be communicated to the employee. The factors utilized in the rating process form a pattern of desired behavior, and a comparison of the individual's performance with the approved pattern will indicate areas of weakness. These weaknesses provide the basis for an individual development program.

The requirement for periodic and accurate appraisal levies a burden upon supervision that tends to produce *better and more competent supervisors.* An immediate superior should be well acquainted with employees and their performance. The existence of a formal requirement tends to condition and train her or him in the essential functions of judging and helping personnel. Additional values of systematic appraisal would include provision of one criterion for validation of selection and training devices, and attraction of higher-caliber personnel to an organization that recognizes and rewards better-than-average performance.

[4]NICB, op. cit., p. 17.

[5]Stanley L. Sokolik, "Guidelines in the Search of Effective Appraisal," *Personnel Journal*, vol. 46, no. 10, November 1967, p. 663.

TRADITIONAL PERFORMANCE APPRAISAL SYSTEMS

There are a number of different types of systems for measuring the excellence of employee performance. It will be found that many of the same systems that are utilized in measuring the worth of jobs (job evaluation) are also used in measuring the worth of a person on the job. These two techniques, job evaluation and performance appraisal, often provide the rational foundation for a wage and salary system.

In the discussion that follows, several performance appraisal systems will be described briefly. Among them are:

1   Ranking
2   Person-to-person comparison
3   Grading
4   Graphic scales
5   Checklists
6   Forced-choice description
7   Selection of critical incidents

We shall present briefly the rationale of each system and make some comparison of its merits with those of other approaches.

Ranking

The oldest and simplest system of formal systematic rating is to compare one person with all others for the purpose of placing them in a simple rank order of worth. In doing this, the appraiser considers person and performance as an entity; no attempt is made to systematically fractionize what is being appraised into component elements.

One of the objections to the ranking process is that we are asking the rater to perform an impossible feat. The analysis of one person's performance is not simple. Yet we are asking the rater to compare several people simultaneously and turn out an accurate rank order. Can the human mind handle all these variables at one time? To simplify this problem, the paired-comparison technique of ranking can be used. Each person can be compared with every other person, one at a time. For example, suppose there are five employees. Employee A's performance is compared with B's, and a decision is made concerning whose is the better performance. Then A is compared with C, D, and E in order. Next, B must be compared with all others individually. The same approach is used for the other personnel. Thus, the use of the paired-comparison technique with these five employees would mean a total of ten decisions, only two people being involved in each decision. The number of decisions can be determined by the following formula:

$$\text{Number of comparisions} = \frac{N(N-1)}{2}$$

In this formula, N equals the number of personnel to be compared. The results of these comparisons can be tabulated, and a rank created from the number of times each person is considered to be superior.

Person-to-person comparison

One of the first attempts to break the person's performance apart and analyze its components was the person-to-person rating system, used by the Army during World War I. Certain factors, such as leadership, initiative, and dependability, were selected for purposes of analysis. A scale was designed for each carefully defined factor. Instead of defining varying degrees of leadership, *particular people* were used to represent these degrees. The rater had to develop his or her own scale by evaluating the leadership qualities of persons known in the past. The person who demonstrated the highest degree of leadership was placed at the upper end of the scale, and particular other key people were assigned to the lowest and intervening degrees. Thus a scale of persons was created for each selected factor.

It is apparent how the title "person-to-person" was derived. Instead of comparing whole people to whole people, personnel are compared to *key persons*, one factor at a time. This system of measurement is utilized today in job evaluation, being known as the "factor-comparison" system.[6] Though it is highly useful in measuring jobs, it is of very limited use in measuring people. The devising of scales would evidently be extremely complicated. Besides, if each rater must use, for different degree definitions, particular people one has known, the ratings would not be comparable from one department to another.[7]

Grading

In the grading system, certain categories of worth are established in advance and carefully defined. In the federal civil service, for example, there are three categories of personnel: outstanding, satisfactory, and unsatisfactory. Employee performance is then compared with these grade definitions, and the person is allocated to the grade which best describes his or her performance. The employee can receive only an O, S, or U. There can, of course, be more than three grades. This is the same basic system of measurement that is used in the job evaluation system, called "grade description." The federal civil service is consistent in that it uses the grading approach for both people and jobs. As indicated earlier, the automotive firm used the three grades of marginal, competent, and excellent, which were to be supported by narrative descriptions.

The grading system is sometimes modified into a forced-distribution system, in which certain percentages are established for each grade. For example, 10 percent of the total personnel *must* go into the top grade, 20 percent *must* be assigned to the second grade, 40 percent to the middle, 20 percent to the fourth, and 10 percent to the bottom grade. It has the advantage of forcing a separation of the personnel in the group, so that the rater cannot relax and judge them all as average, superior, or below average. As in all systems that force the rater to do something, there is considerable resistance on the part of the evaluator. This system also introduces a zero-sum game for all ratees. Even though a person rated in the bottom 10 percent should significantly improve performance, he or she would not rise in ratings if all others had improved similarly. Imagine the frustration of such an employee, as well as the dismay of the

---

[6]See Chap. 14.

[7]A recent attempt to devise a person-to-person rating system based on a combination of an out-of-department reference group and an anchored rating scale can be found in Paul F. Ross, "Reference Groups in Man-to-Man Job Performance Rating," *Personnel Psychology*, vol. 19, no. 2. Summer 1966, pp. 115–142.

superior while communicating recognition of the improved performance with the same low rating.

Graphic scales

Perhaps the most commonly used traditional, systematic method of performance appraisal is that of establishing scales for a number of fairly specific factors. It is an approach similar to that of the person-to-person system except that the degrees on the factor scales are represented by *definitions* rather than by key people. Figure 13-1 is a

Figure 13-1 Graphic rating scale for hourly personnel

CPF-8472

APPRENTICE PERFORMANCE RATING - TRAINING SECTION, INDUSTRIAL RELATIONS DEPARTMENT

NAME	CLOCK NUMBER	DEPARTMENT	JOB CLASSIFICATION
DATE STARTED ON JOB	DATE OF LAST RATING		DATE OF THIS RATING

TO THE RATER: This rating will represent your appraisal of the trainee's actual performance on his present job or in related classroom work. The value of it depends upon the impartiality and sound judgment you use. You should keep in mind both the interest of the company and the personal interests of the individual, when making the rating.

TO HELP YOU MAKE A CAREFUL ANALYSIS, THE FOLLOWING SUGGESTIONS ARE OFFERED:

1. CONSIDER ONLY ONE FACTOR AT A TIME. DO NOT LET YOUR RATING IN ONE TRAIT INFLUENCE YOUR RATING OF ANOTHER.
2. BASE YOUR JUDGMENT ON THE REQUIREMENTS OF THE JOB AND HIS PERFORMANCE IN IT AS COMPARED TO OTHERS DOING SIMILAR WORK.
3. CAREFULLY READ THE DESCRIPTION OF EACH TRAIT AND SPECIFICATIONS FOR EACH GRADE BEFORE MAKING YOUR ENTRY, THEN CHECK THE SPACE WHICH MOST NEARLY DESCRIBES YOUR OPINION.
4. UPON COMPLETION, REVIEW AND CHECK YOUR RATING.
5. MAKE ANY COMMENTS IN PROVIDED SPACE WHICH YOU BELIEVE WILL FURNISH ADDITIONAL INFORMATION CONCERNING TRAINEE.

PERFORMANCE FACTORS	PERFORMANCE RATING				
	DOES NOT MEET JOB REQUIREMENTS	PARTIALLY MEETS JOB REQUIREMENTS	MEETS JOB REQUIREMENTS	EXCEEDS JOB REQUIREMENTS	FAR EXCEEDS JOB REQUIREMENTS
QUALITY OF WORK: ACCURACY, SKILL, THOROUGHNESS, NEATNESS	CONSISTENTLY UNSATISFACTORY ☐	OCCASIONALLY UNSATISFACTORY ☐	CONSISTENTLY SATISFACTORY ☐	SOMETIMES SUPERIOR ☐	CONSISTENTLY SUPERIOR ☐
QUANTITY OF WORK: OUTPUT; CONSIDER NOT ONLY REGULAR DUTIES, BUT ALSO HOW PROMPTLY HE COMPLETES "EXTRA" OR RUSH ASSIGNMENTS.	CONSISTENTLY BELOW REQUIREMENTS ☐	FREQUENTLY BELOW REQUIREMENTS ☐	USUALLY MEETS REQUIREMENTS ☐	FREQUENTLY EXCEEDS REQUIREMENTS ☐	CONSISTENTLY EXCEEDS REQUIREMENTS ☐
DEPENDABILITY: FOLLOWS INSTRUCTIONS, GOOD SAFETY HABITS, INITIATIVE, PUNCTUALITY AND ATTENDANCE	REQUIRES CONSTANT SUPERVISION ☐	NEEDS OCCASIONAL FOLLOW-UP ☐	ORDINARILY CAN BE COUNTED ON ☐	NEEDS VERY LITTLE SUPERVISION ☐	COMPLETELY TRUSTWORTHY IN JOB REQUIREMENTS ☐
ATTITUDES: TOWARD COMPANY, JOB AND FELLOW WORKERS; COOPERATION.	SELDOM WORKS WITH OR ASSISTS OTHERS. INDIFFERENT ☐	FREQUENTLY UNCOOPERATIVE. TOO CRITICAL OF OTHERS ☐	GENERALLY WORKS WELL WITH OTHERS. NORMAL INTEREST ☐	EAGERNESS OFTEN DISPLAYED. A GOOD TEAM-WORKER ☐	EXTRAORDINARY INTEREST. INSPIRES OTHERS TO WORK ☐

COMMENTS:

DEPARTMENT SUPERVISOR	CLASSROOM SUPERVISOR

Source: Champion Paper and Fibre Company, Hamilton, Ohio. By permission.

rating form for operative personnel which utilizes four factors. Five degrees are possible for each factor. General definitions appear at points along the scales. It is interesting to note that this same basic approach is the most commonly used system for measuring the worth of jobs—the "point system" of job evaluation. Perhaps one of its outstanding advantages is its face validity, which engenders acceptance on the part of the supervisor. The listing of personnel factors appears to many to be a logical, and therefore acceptable, approach.

The selection of factors to be measured is a crucial part of the graphic scales system. As indicated previously, they are of two types: (1) characteristics, such as initiative and dependability, and (2) contributions, such as quantity and quality of work. Since certain areas of job performance cannot be objectively measured, it is likely that graphic scales will continue to use a mixture of characteristics and contributions, with the emphasis upon the latter.[8]

The number of factors ordinarily used varies from nine to twelve and is adjusted to the particular occupational category being considered, e.g., hourly personnel, sales and financial, etc. Commonly used factors are quantity and quality of work, cooperation, personality, versatility, leadership, safety, job knowledge, attendance, loyalty, dependability, and initiative. Research shows that it makes no appreciable difference in rating results ". . . whether (a) the 'good' end of a graphic scale is located at the left, right, top, or bottom, (b) graphic scales or numerical ratings are used, or (c) the order of presentation is one name at a time, one trait at a time, or a matrix with free choice or order. . . ."[9] Such research usually demonstrates that there should be less concern with form and technique and more emphasis placed upon rater selection and training.

Though popular in use, graphic scales impose a heavy burden upon the rater. One must report and evaluate the performance of subordinates on scales involving as many as five degrees on twelve different factors for perhaps twenty to thirty people. The use of a continuous-line scale would seemingly provide for an infinite number of decision gradations on a single factor, as compared with the five per factor in Figure 13-1. The fact that the manager actually reports a decision for each factor in all cases does not necessarily mean that an accurate decision can be made. For such reasons as this, other systems of appraisal have been developed.

Checklists

To reduce the burden upon the appraiser, a checklist system can be utilized. The rater does not evaluate employee performance; it is merely reported. The evaluation of the worth of *reported* behavior is accomplished by the staff personnel department.

An example of the checklist system is shown in Figure 13-2. In this form a series of questions is presented concerning the subject employee and his or her behavior. The rater checks to indicate if the answer to a question about the employee is yes or no. The value of each question may be weighted. The rater is not aware of the specific values, but can distinguish the positive questions from the negative and thus introduce bias if desired. It will be noted that an attempt is made to determine the degree of consistency

---

[8]See Chester R. Harris and Reinald C. Heise, "Tasks, Not Traits: The Key to Better Performance Review," *Personnel*, May–June 1964, pp. 60–64.

[9]Herbert H. Blumberg, Clinton B. DeSoto, and James L. Kuethe, "Evaluation of Rating Scale Formats," *Personnel Psychology*, vol. 19, no. 3, Autumn 1966, p. 253.

Figure 13-2 Checklist for appraising supervisors

		Yes	No
31	Does he or she usually volunteer good ideas?	___	___
32	Is a marked interest shown in the job?	___	___
33	Is consistent treatment meted out to all subordinates?	___	___
34	Does he or she usually back up subordinates?	___	___
35	Is equipment maintained in good condition?	___	___
36	Does the supervisor display a good working knowledge of the job?	___	___
37	Does he or she know and try to follow the provisions of the labor contract?	___	___
38	Do subordinates show respect?	___	___
39	Is the departmental area usually maintained in a neat and clean condition?	___	___
40	Does the supervisor show favoritism to particular subordinates?	___	___
41	Does he or she usually find time to listen to employee troubles?	___	___
42	Has he or she ever reprimanded an employee in public?	___	___
43	Does he or she complain about treatment accorded by superiors?	___	___
44	Does the supervisor maintain control over emotions?	___	___
45	Is the buck usually passed to higher management?	___	___
46	Are orders usually followed?	___	___
47	Are the supervisor's orders usually followed?	___	___
48	Is recognition and praise accorded a well-done job?	___	___
49	Are schedules usually met?	___	___
50	Does he or she ever make mistakes?	___	___

of the rater by asking the same question twice, but in a different manner (numbers 33 and 40).

One of the disadvantages of the checklist system is that it is difficult to assemble, analyze, and weigh a number of statements about employee characteristics and contributions. The scoring key is often derived in a manner like that described in the following section covering the forced-choice system. In addition, a separate listing of questions must be prepared for different types of jobs, since those used for clerical positions cannot be used for management. The checklist approach does have the advantage of requiring only a reporting of facts from the rater. One does not have to distinguish among various degrees for each of nine to twelve factors for each of twenty to thirty employees.

Forced-choice description

None of the above-described systems can eliminate one of the major criticisms of performance appraisal, the charge that the rater may be biased or prejudiced. One of the fundamental objectives of the forced-choice approach is to reduce or eliminate the possibility of rater bias by *forcing* a choice between descriptive statements of seemingly equal worth. For example, a pair such as the following will be presented to the rater.

1 Gives good, clear instructions to subordinates.
2 Can be depended upon to complete any job assigned.

The rater is asked to select the one statement most characteristic of the ratee. Even though one may claim that both are equally applicable or inapplicable, he or she is *forced* to select the one that is closer to describing the person in question.

The rater is also forced to choose between statements that are seemingly equally unfavorable, such as the following pair.

1   Makes promises that he or she knows cannot be kept.
2   Shows favoritism toward some employees.

Again, though feeling that neither or both are applicable, one must select the statement that is more descriptive. Only one of the statements in each pair is correct in identifying the better performance, and this scoring key must be kept secret from the raters. In this manner, bias is removed from the appraisal process. For example, in one research project involving the rating of fourteen instructors by 1,046 students, the use of a forced-choice scale effectively eliminated the leniency error, while the use of a graphic scale format allowed bias to be introduced.[10]

The manner in which the secret scoring key is devised is substantially as follows: The correct answers are determined on the basis of a *study of present personnel.* By some other method of rating, present employees are placed into two or more categories. A committee can often pretty well agree upon which employees are the best and which are the poorest. The paired-comparison technique is sometimes used to make these choices. A great deal of time, discussion, and effort are put into the process of dividing up present employees as to overall worth, for the committee must be assured that these resulting divisions are as accurate as they can be made. Though rarely done, the approach could be similar to the two- to three-day assessment of potential executives in the American Telephone and Telegraph assessment center discussed in a previous chapter. For accurate assessment of human performance and potential, there is no substitute for group evaluation utilizing a number of measuring devices. The forced-choice technique represents a "shortcut" approach designed to produce the answers that the longer, more valid process would obtain.

The next step in the process is to devise a series of paired statements similar to the examples given above. At first there may be as many as 100 such pairs. Present employees are then rated in a forced-choice manner. A pair of statements must definitely distinguish between the better and the poorer employees to be accepted and incorporated into the system. If, for example, the statement, "Can be depended upon to complete any job assigned," is checked as being most descriptive for most of the good personnel and the other statement is checked for the poor employees, this pair is discriminating and can be used in the system, with the second statement indicated as the correct answer. It is often found that many paired statements do not distinguish among the categories of personnel; such pairs must be eliminated.

In effect, the forced-choice system represents an attempt to devise an objective method of arriving at the *same answers* that the committee reached after their long discussions and hard work. At the same time, it is an attempt to eliminate rater bias, since the correct answers are not apparent. Reports of reliability coefficients as high as

[10]Amiel T. Sharon and C. J. Bartlett, "Effect of Instructional Conditions in Producing Leniency on Two Types of Rating Scales," *Personnel Psychology*, vol. 22, no. 3, Autumn 1969, pp. 251–263.

.70 to .90 have been indicated in various studies.[11] This compares with the usual reliability of from .60 to .80 for most merit ratings.

There are certain primary disadvantages of the forced-choice system. First, it is difficult, if not impossible, to keep the key secret. Secondly, the system is a very poor one to use if employee development is to be emphasized. Neither the rater nor the ratee can figure out from the form the desired mode of behavior, and in fact, if the form is shown to the ratee, he or she is usually unable to accept it or the philosophy behind it. In addition, raters often object to being *forced* to make decisions which they feel cannot or should not be made. Because of these disadvantages, the use of forced-choice systems is not widespread.

Selection of critical incidents

In searching for a simpler yet more accurate system of appraising performance, the critical-incidents method was developed out of the research conducted by the Armed Forces in World War II. The theory on which this approach rests is that there are certain key acts of behavior that make the difference between success and failure on a job. Supervisor-raters must record or check certain kinds of events that occur in the performance of the ratee's job. These events are the critical incidents. For example, the materials manager may be trained to look for and recognize such critical incidents in a purchasing agent's performance as: (1) treated a salesman in a markedly discourteous fashion, (2) helped a buyer to prepare an unusually difficult purchase order, (3) persuaded a local vendor to stock a particularly important material needed by the firm, (4) rejected a bid that was excessively overpriced, (5) failed to return an important phone call, and (6) improved the design of the internal materials requisition form.[12]

The manner in which particular critical incidents are discovered is through a study of present personnel while on the job. Observers of performance must agree that certain types of behavior are critical. Then the collected incidents may be ranked in order of frequency and importance. In this manner numerical weights can be obtained, thereby providing the basis for a rating score. Several scales have been developed in industry based upon this approach. However, Flanagan feels that the greatest use of the approach lies in development rather than appraisal.[13] Specific acts of behavior can be discussed with the subordinate and their critical and significant nature emphasized. Improved performance, changed attitudes toward duties, and increased interest in making suggestions are among the anticipated values.

As an example of how critical incidents can be converted into scales, a group of store managers and researchers developed separate scales for major portions of the store manager's job. Among the major activities were supervising sales personnel, handling customer complaints, meeting deadlines, ordering merchandise, running

[11]See Ludwig Huttner and Raymond Katzell, "Developing a Yardstick of Supervisory Performance," *Personnel*, January 1957, pp. 371–379; and Lee W. Cozan, "Forced Choice: Better than Other Rating Methods?" *Personnel*, July–August 1959, pp. 80–83.

[12]Richard D. Scott, "Taking Subjectivity Out of Performance Appraisal," *Personnel*, vol. 50, no. 4, July–August 1973, pp. 45–49.

[13]John C. Flanagan and Robert K. Burns, "The Employee Performance Record: A New Appraisal and Development Tool," *Harvard Business Review*, September–October 1957, pp. 95–102.

promotions, assessing sales trends, using company systems, communicating information, and diagnosing special problems. Taking the first duty of supervising sales
personnel as an example, a scale of nine intervals was developed in the form of nine
critical incidents. One of the lower-rated critical incidents was, "Could be expected to
go back on a promise to an individual whom he had told could transfer back into
previous department if she/he didn't like the new one."[14] A medium-level incident was,
"Could be expected to remind sales personnel to wait on customers instead of
conversing with each other," while a higher-valued one was, "Could be expected to
give his sales personnel confidence and a strong sense of responsibility by delegating
many important jobs to them." Research indicated that this approach was not subject to
many of the typical rating errors, such as excessive leniency or harshness on the part of
the rater.

THE APPRAISAL PROGRAM

More important than the rating form or method is the quality of the rater. Certainly
adequate time and attention must be given to the selection and design of a rating
system, but even more time and effort must be expended in deciding such questions as
who is to rate, how he or she should be trained, and how the accuracy of the ratings can
be maintained. In the following sections, certain fundamental aspects of a formal
appraisal program are considered.

Who is to rate

In most situations, the rater is the immediate superior of the person to be rated.
Because of frequent contact, he or she is most familiar with the employee's work. In
addition, many organizations deem it essential to support the leadership and authority
position of the supervisor by considering employee appraisal as an integral part of the
supervisory task. Supervisor ratings are often reviewed and approved by higher
management, thereby maintaining hierarchical control over the appraisal process.

    If more involvement is deemed desirable, the appraisal process can be undertaken
by a group of raters. Various surveys show that 15 to 18 percent of business firms utilize
group ratings of administrative and professional personnel.[15] Members of the group
can be superiors, peers, and subordinates. If they are all superiors, group appraisal
ventures only a small distance from classical management theories. If they are all
subordinates, it involves a considerable move toward behavioral theories. A few firms
have given serious consideration to evaluation by peers. For example, over 3,000 agents
in three life insurance companies have been asked to nominate three other agents with
whom they work in connection with such questions as, "Who would you prefer to have
accompany you on a tough case?"[16] Such "buddy nominations" were not turned over

[14]John P. Campbell, Marvin D. Dunnette, Richard D. Arvey, and Lowell V. Hellervik, "The Development
and Evaluation of Behaviorally Based Rating Scales," *Journal of Applied Psychology*, vol. 57, no. 1, January 1973,
p. 17.

[15]Mitchell Novit, "Performance Appraisal and Dual Authority: A Look at Group Appraisal," *Management of
Personnel Quarterly*, vol. 8, no. 1, Spring 1969, p. 3.

[16]Eugene C. Mayfield, "Peer Nominations: A Neglected Selection Tool," *Personnel*, vol. 48, no. 4,
July–August 1971, p. 40.

to the firms, but were kept to assess their effectiveness in identifying future successful assistant managers. In general, the higher the "buddy score," the higher the success rate as managers. Of those promoted, 65 percent of those accorded high peer approval were deemed successful, as compared with only 36 percent of those receiving low peer nomination. A similar study of middle managers at International Business Machines Corporation revealed that those receiving the higher peer ratings were definitely more likely to be promoted.[17] Superiors, nevertheless, tend to show suspicion of peer ratings, as suggested by a study at North American Aviation.[18] Peer ratings were significantly higher on the system scales than manager ratings of particular subordinates. Superiors tended to emphasize initiative and work knowledge, while peers deemed getting along with others to be more important in the overall rating. This does not negate the previously cited findings that peers can accurately predict actual success of promoted managers.

The final possibility, which is most behavioral in orientation, is to allow subordinates to rate themselves. The major values lie in the development and motivation areas, it being claimed that this approach (1) results in a superior upward flow of information, (2) forces the subordinate to become more personally involved and to do some systematic thinking about self and work, (3) improves communication between superior and subordinate, in that each is given more information by the other when disagreements are discovered, and (4) improves motivation as a result of greater participation.

The usual fear of this approach is that of excessively high ratings. This fear has some basis in research. In a study of ninety-two technical employees, subordinates rated themselves more favorably than did their supervisors.[19] There was good agreement on ratings concerning creative ability and human relations skills, but little concerning technical competence. Believing that higher-level employees would show more restraint, Thornton analyzed the self-ratings of sixty-four high-level managers in one large corporation.[20] He discovered that the mean self-rating was higher than the mean superior rating, and that the self-ratings correlated negatively with the promotion chart, which showed personnel immediately promotable, those promotable at a later date, and those not promotable. Those not promotable tended to show the greatest differences with evaluations by superiors.

On the other hand, a study of eighty-one subordinates in the General Electric Company resulted in multiple values to the organization when self-ratings were requested.[21] Forty subordinates were asked for self-ratings, while forty-one were rated in the usual manner by their managers. More defensiveness was noted among those rated by superiors, eight of the forty-one feeling that criticisms brought up in the interview were unwarranted. Only two of the forty who were interviewed after

[17]H. E. Roadman, "An Industrial Use of Peer Ratings," *Journal of Applied Psychology*, vol. 48, no. 4, August 1964, pp. 211–214.

[18]D. Springer, "Ratings of Candidates for Promotion by Co-Workers and Supervisors," *Journal of Applied Psychology*, vol. 37, no. 5, October 1953, pp. 347–351.

[19]W. K. Kirchner, "Relationship between Supervisory and Subordinate Ratings for Technical Personnel," *Journal of Industrial Psychology*, vol. 3, 1965, pp. 57–60.

[20]George C. Thornton, "The Relationship between Supervisory and Self-Appraisals of Executive Performance," *Personnel Psychology*, vol. 21, no. 4, Winter 1968, pp. 441–455.

[21]Glenn A. Bassett and Herbert H. Meyer, "Performance Appraisal Based on Self-Review," *Personnel Psychology*, vol. 21, no. 4, Winter 1968, pp. 421–430.

self-ratings felt that ensuing criticism was unwarranted. In a three-month follow-up after the appraisal interviews, superiors reported that sixteen of the forty-one manager-appraised subordinates were not measuring up to the job, as compared with only eight of the forty self-rated subordinates. Twenty-three of the thirty-five managers involved believed that the self-rating approach was clearly superior.

If the basic participatory management approach continues to grow, it is certain that the self-rating aspect of the process will also become more widespread. It is completely consistent with McGregor's recommendations concerning how performance appraisal can be improved. In most instances where its use is noted, the ratees are managerial and professional personnel. It is also suggested that if the subordinate knows that the superior is also preparing ratings, the former is more likely to do a realistic job. The use of self-ratings as an additional input of information to provide the basis for a mutually beneficial interview has considerable merit. There is no suggestion that the rating must stand as the officially accepted decision. Miner suggests that multiple ratings of managerial and professional personnel by superiors, peers, and subordinates will be *the* approach in the future.[22]

When to rate

The usual schedule in the timing of ratings is twice yearly. New employees are rated more frequently than older ones. The Kaiser Steel Corporation, for example, requires two ratings of probationary employees within the first six weeks of employment. A practice recommended by a consulting organization is that each employee be rated three months after being assigned a job, after the sixth month on the job, and every six months thereafter. In this way, ratings of all employees will not fall due on the same day. When the supervisor must rate twenty to thirty employees at the same time, the pressure of other duties will probably prevent him or her from giving adequate time and attention to this task.

Training of the rater

The initial training of raters must, of course, incorporate complete explanations of the philosophy and nature of the rating system. Factors and factor scales, if any, must be thoroughly defined, analyzed, and discussed in conference sessions. Though training should be positive in nature, it has been found advisable to stress certain negative aspects of the rating process and to warn the raters about the more common errors of traditional rating in order that they may be on guard against them. Among these errors are:

1 The halo error
2 The central tendency
3 Constant errors
  a Too harsh
  b Too easy
4 Miscellaneous biases
  a Length of service

[22]John B. Miner, "Management Appraisal: A Capsule Review and Current References," *Business Horizons*, vol. 11, no. 5, October 1968, p. 86.

b   Race, religion, and nationality
c   Sex
d   Position

The halo error can be recognized quite easily on factor scales. It takes place when the rater allows one aspect of a person's character or performance to influence the entire evaluation. No person is likely to be either perfectly good or perfectly bad; one is generally better in some areas than in others. The halo error sometimes becomes a "pitchfork" error when the rater allows one adverse instance of behavior to color for the worse an entire appraisal of an individual. The best correction for the halo error is education. Often a rater is not aware of this tendency and needs only to have it pointed out to correct it.

The central tendency is perhaps the most commonly found error in performance rating. This error is evidenced when the rater marks all or almost all personnel as average. In this manner the rater avoids "sticking one's neck out" when in doubt, or possessing inadequate information, or giving the rating process little time, attention, and effort. It is possible, of course, for this type of rating, all average, to be a true rating, but its probability is less than its frequency.

There are "easy" raters and "tough" raters in all phases of life. There are teachers who rarely award A's and those who give them to most of the class. These errors are known as constant or systematic errors. Figure 13-3a illustrates the situation created by a lenient rater. Ratings are distributed in a normal curve, but the supervisor is utilizing only the upper half of the scale; the average rating is 7. The harsh rater utilizes the lower half of the scale, as shown in Figure 13-3b. He or she also has a normal distribution, with an average rating of 3. If these ratings are valid for these two groups, we have no rating problem. If they are constant errors, the rating of 7 by the first rater is equal to the rating of 3 by the second. Education, again, is the basic solution. Harsh and lenient raters should be informed of the distribution of ratings by other supervisors, just as the harsh or lenient teacher should be apprised of the grade distributions of other teachers. Should this educational process fail, there is a system, used by some organizations, that translates the raw rating score into percentiles. The rating of 7 becomes a rating of the 50th percentile, as does the rating of 3. In general, the better solution is to reeducate the rater rather than manipulate the ratings. As indicated earlier, the use of the forced-choice system will effectively reduce the leniency bias. It was also found that if ratings have to be justified to the ratee, the ratings on graphic

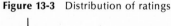

Figure 13-3   Distribution of ratings

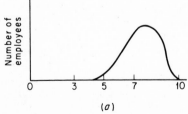 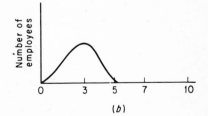

(a)   By the lenient rater
(b)   By the harsh rater

scales will be significantly higher in anticipation of the justification interview session.[23] Ratings obtained for use in administrative decision making will be significantly higher than those obtained for research purposes only.

There are a number of miscellaneous biases which the rater must guard against. Some supervisors show bias against members of the opposite sex or of another race, religion, or nationality. Often a supervisor will give higher ratings to senior employees. Either one gets used to their deficiencies or does not wish to admit that they have not improved under one's leadership. Often the rater is influenced by organizational position and gives the higher ratings to those holding the higher positions.

Finally, the supervisor must be trained to conduct the periodic appraisal interview. This, to many, is the most painful part of the process. Supervisors do not mind "playing God" if they can be a benevolent god. But when criticism is deemed necessary, they resort to the widely used "human relations sandwich"—criticism sandwiched between initial statements concerning one's good points and ending exhortations that improvement must be forthcoming in the future. In the traditional interview, the appraiser is clearly superior and acts in judgmental fashion. The distaste for this process, as well as research findings indicating its negative effects, have led a great many organizations to consider Management by Objectives programs.

Monitoring the effectiveness of the appraisal program

Maintaining surveillance over the systematic appraisal program is usually a job for a staff personnel department. The department is in a position to obtain the ratings of the various raters and to make basic analyses to determine the reliability and validity of such ratings. Systematic performance appraisal is a measurement process and as such must be reliable, which means that it must be accurate and consistent. The reliability of a rating system can be obtained by comparing the ratings of two individuals for the same person. It can also be obtained by comparing the supervisor's rating given now with another rating in the future. There should be a reasonable degree of agreement between the two for the system to be described as reliable. Whereas the reliability coefficients for psychological tests are generally in the .90s, and .85 is often taken as a minimum, the coefficients for merit-rating systems are generally lower. In fact, an .85 would be considered quite good for merit rating. Ordinarily, the performance appraisal reliabilities, when determined, range from .60 to .80. We are dealing with a measurement system which is not as accurate as a psychological test; it is essentially an attempt to objectify an estimate and it deals with more intangible subjects.

Validity is concerned with the truthfulness of the measurement results. How can we be sure that the ratings obtained are true and representative of the ratee? Sometimes the same process of checking with other informed raters is utilized to determine validity. Ratings can also be checked against certain objective evidence, such as production quantities, quality, and absenteeism. Other comparisons can be made with a curve of normal distributions, if the number of ratees is sufficiently large. As we indicated earlier, there are some systems that attempt to incorporate checks for bias or inconsistencies by comparing the answers with several related questions about the ratee. Sometimes validity is determined by comparing the results of one system with

[23]Sharon and Bartlett, op. cit., p. 262.

those of another. For example, the ratings of the forced-choice system are compared with the prior categorization of selected personnel by means of committee discussions, hard work, and serious individual study. This criterion of validity, however, is rarely available.

The ratings must be made by the immediate superiors of the ratees, but a staff department can assume the responsibility of monitoring the system. The personnel department should not change any ratings. They do have the obligation to point out certain inconsistencies to the rater, such as harshness, leniency, central tendency, inconsistencies, and high correlations between ratings given and the position or seniority of the ratee.

MANAGEMENT BY OBJECTIVES

In all of the methods of traditional and systematic appraisal, the manager is sitting in judgment on the performance of subordinates, hoping to obtain an impartial, objective, factual, and acceptable measurement score. In recent years, the critics of this philosophy of rating have increased in number and loudness. Though an attack has been mounted upon the low reliabilities and validities of traditional systems, the fundamental criticism has been based on the judgmental role of the manager and the antagonistic response of the subordinate. The initial leading critic was Douglas McGregor, who seized upon an approach previously suggested by Peter Drucker in 1954.[24] Instead of sitting in judgment, the superior should devote attention to establishment of goals, so that subordinates can exercise self-control in pursuit of those goals—Management by Objectives. Though early efforts inspired by McGregor led to subordinate self-determination of goals followed by self-appraisal of subsequent accomplishment, such programs have evolved into ones where management takes a more prominent role. Early efforts tended to enter the firm through the personnel department as a program for motivating subordinates. Admitting the increment in motivation, management was nevertheless concerned that a multitude of individuals "doing their own things" might not add up to the common good of the organization. Consequently, modern Management by Objectives (MBO) approaches tend to emphasize a participative but *joint* determination of objectives, followed by a participative but *joint* evaluation of success in periodic appraisal interviews. Each of these major program elements will be discussed in the following sections.

Establishment of objectives

Management by Objectives is far more than just an appraisal process. To many, it is a fundamental way of managing, in which periodic appraisal is but a part. Organizations are composed of a multitude of people, performing various and specialized activities, supposedly thereby contributing to basic organizational objectives. Merton and Selznick pointed out long ago the dysfunctional consequences of activity specialization and rules: that such organized segmentation and directives often lead to human behavior characterized by rigidity, impersonality, and inward orientation; to wit, a

---

[24]Peter F. Drucker, *The Practice of Management*, Harper & Row, Publishers, Incorporated, New York, 1954, p. 121.

pathological bureaucrat.[25] Odiorne, in his development of an MBO philosophy, has characterized this phenomenon as an "activity trap"; the individual becomes so enmeshed in performing assigned functions that he or she loses sight of the goal, the reason for performance.[26] Even greater dysfunctions occur when the goals change but the individual activities do not. Thus, an MBO program asks that specific objectives or end results be established for each key position. A modern MBO program stipulates that this process of establishment be a joint effort shared between superior and subordinate.

The statement that objectives should be established for key positions is a simple one that belies its complexity. It often requires days, rather than hours, to compose a set of meaningful and measurable goals that will objectify the everyday fuzzy world of work. The first step usually entails a conference between superior and subordinate with the purpose of securing agreement upon the *key tasks* included in the job description. More accomplishment will be achieved if one focuses on a limited number of goals. It is here that the superior ensures that the objectives developed are actually related to the needs of the enterprise.

Various classifications of objectives have been suggested, but most could be designated as routine, nonroutine, or personal development. Referring to the examples in Figure 13-4, the objective of the production manager to improve the percentage of due dates met could be classified as covering a routine phase of the job. Nonroutine goals would encompass both the solution of major problems encountered and the meeting of perceived innovative needs. In Figure 13-4, the personnel manager's objectives of installing a new supervisory program would be a nonroutine objective that is designed to cope with the problem of inadequate grievance processing. Adding a "return on assets employed" section to reports for cost centers on the part of the director of management information systems could well be a nonroutine objective of the innovative type. A personal development objective would specify planned accomplishment in training, education, or experience, e.g., to attain reading competence in a foreign language within one year.

In preparing objectives, research indicates that goals expressed in quantitative terms tend to result in more effective accomplishment. In a study of appraisal systems in General Electric, it was found that when specific, quantitative goals were mutually established, the average accomplishment noted later was 65 percent. In cases where such specific goals were not set, the average accomplishment was estimated to be 27 percent.[27] Thus, in writing goals, special attempts should be made to phrase them in such terms as volume, costs, frequency, ratios, percentages, degrees, phases, and calendar dates.

For each objective suggested by the subordinate and accepted by the superior, a basic strategy for assessment should be planned. The superior should do what he or she can to help in providing information that will enable the subordinate to evaluate and measure on-going accomplishment. For example, in proposing an objective within

[25]R. K. Merton, "Bureaucratic Structure and Personality," *Social Forces*, vol. 18, 1940, pp. 560–568; and P. Selznick, *T.V.A. and the Grass Roots*, University of California Press, Berkeley, 1953.

[26]George S. Odiorne, "Management by Objectives: Antidote to Future Shock," *Personnel Journal*, vol. 53, no. 4, April 1974, p. 263.

[27]Herbert H. Meyer, Emanuel Kay, and John R. P. French, Jr., "Split Roles in Performance Appraisal," *Harvard Business Review*, vol. 43, no. 1, January–February 1965, pp. 123–129.

Figure 13-4 Examples of objectives for MBO program

Position	Objectives
Director of finance	Reduce bad debt losses from 5 percent to 3 percent of sales by January 1. Reduce number of accounting employees 10 percent, through transfer of operations to computer, by June 1.
Director of management information systems	Add "return on assets employed" to reports for each cost center by January 1. Reduce by 20 percent the number of copies of EDP reports prepared by June 1.
Marketing manager	Complete field testing of Product X by June 1, and add to regular line by January 1. Increase share of market of Product J from 15 percent to 20 percent in Northeast territory by January 1.
Personnel manager	Decrease turnover of clerical employees from 20 percent to 10 percent by January 1. Complete planning and installation of supervisory training program on grievance processing by June 1.
Production manager	Reduce welding rejects from 6 percent to 3 percent by January 1. Improve percentage of due dates met on production schedule from 90 to 95 percent by June 1.
Research and development manager	Complete design and development of Product X by June 1, within a cost budget of $150,000. Provide two new products for marketing field testing within the next 12 months.

the Department of Health, Education, and Welfare, an agency head specified that 10,000 additional alcoholics would be treated during the coming year.[28] Feeling that the real goal was actual *rehabilitation*, information had to be developed as a basis for assessment of this more advanced and intangible objective. "Rehabilitation" was then defined as being gainfully employed one year after treatment. In such an instance, the previously suggested numerical objective of 10,000 may have to be scaled downward if applied to the more fundamental end result. The superior should make sure that established objectives are neither too easy nor too difficult, and that they are reasonably controllable by the subordinate concerned. The ideal immediate result of the goal-establishment process is the subordinate departing from the meeting with (1) knowledge of significant goals that are clear, concise, realistic, challenging, and assessable, and (2) a strong feeling of commitment to their accomplishment. A probability of accomplishment of .5 is deemed by many theorists as best to elicit effective motivation.

[28]Rodney H. Brady, "MBO Goes to Work in the Public Sector," *Harvard Business Review*, vol. 51, no. 2, March–April 1973, p. 73.

Appraisal interview

Though abhorred and often feared in the traditional approach to appraisal, the interview is one of the more fruitful elements of an MBO program. In the previously cited General Electric study, it was found that the traditional approach resulted in such responses as the following: (1) criticism issues from the very nature of the system, (2) criticism within the appraisal interview had a negative effect upon improvement and tended to increase antagonism and defensiveness, and (3) praise during the interview has *little* effect, either good or bad.[29] The very nature of the traditional interview where the superior acts as judge tends to stimulate one to adopt a role stereotype of supervisor—critical, evaluative, and often defensive.[30] One tends to display superiority, lack of concern, an inclination toward control or manipulation, and an attitude of certainty and finality at the end of the interview.[31]

In the MBO appraisal interviews, the atmosphere for discussion tends to be characterized by empathy, mutual respect, equality, supportive informational contributions, shared definitions, and provisional, rather than definitive, conclusions on the part of the superior at the end. The sequence of interview phases followed in one large corporation is as follows.[32] First, the subordinate usually takes the lead in a discussion of accomplishment and failures since the last meeting. The superior participates through asking questions and interjecting comments. Reasons for nonaccomplishment are examined and suggestions for changes in objectives or strategies are discussed. The atmosphere is that of two persons working on common problems with common goals, rather than of one sitting in judgment upon the other. In the second stage, the manager takes the lead in establishing goals for the next period that will fit into organizational purposes. The subordinate will submit proposals for the new set of goals. During the third stage, both manager and subordinate are equally involved in establishing criteria for assessing progress toward goals arrived at in stage two. The fourth and final stage is devoted to discussions about the subordinate's future and a determination of personal development goals. In this stage, the superior acts in the capacity of counselor.

When interviews are conducted in this performance-goal–oriented fashion, the level of satisfaction on the part of both parties tends to be high. Burke and Wilcox correlated the interview characteristics of (1) high level of subordinate participation in appraisal, (2) helpful and constructive (not critical) attitude by superior, (3) solution of job problems hampering performance, and (4) mutual setting of specific goals, with ensuing attitudes and behavior of the subordinate.[33] In a study of 323 employees in six offices of a large public utility, a composite of the above four variables correlated .75 with subordinate satisfaction with the interview, .56 with subordinate's stated motivation to improve performance, and .44 with actually improved performance. Solem discovered that when the superior talked for less than 40 percent of the interview, there

[29]Meyer, Kay, and French, op. cit., pp. 123–129.

[30]Philip G. Hanson, Robert B. Morton, and Paul Rothaus, "The Fate of Role Stereotypes in Two Performance Appraisal Situations," *Personnel Psychology*, vol. 16, no. 3, Autumn 1963, pp. 269–280.

[31]William N. Butler, "Supportive Communication and Performance Appraisal," *Personnel Administration*, vol. 32, no. 1, January–February 1969, p. 50.

[32]Edgar F. Huse, "Putting in a Management Development Program That Works," *California Management Review*, vol. 9, no. 2, Winter 1966, p. 78.

[33]Ronald J. Burke and Douglas S. Wilcox, "Characteristics of Effective Employee Performance Review and Development Interviews," *Personnel Psychology*, vol. 22, no. 3, Autumn 1969, pp. 290–305.

were significantly fewer arguments, greater mutual understanding, higher felt motivation, more positive feelings toward each other, fewer cases where subordinates failed to recognize any problems, and more cases where the superior's impression of the subordinate was materially improved.[34]

Limitations of MBO

Like all basically good and simple ideas, widespread overly enthusiastic exhortations and poorly prepared installations can move them to the status of "fads." MBO is no cure-all, no panacea for all managerial ills. It, too, has its dysfunctional consequences. Just as the original Taylor approach to measuring, separating, and motivating rank and file operatives had undesirable, as well as desirable, consequences, so also highly individualistic approaches to establishing position objectives can lead to breakdowns in interpersonal and intergroup cooperation. Meeting the 95 percent goal in due dates on the part of the production manager may lead him or her to interfere with the objectives of the quality control manager; production tries to slip marginal products by the inspectors. When multiple activities are closely interrelated, one will have to move to establishment of *group objectives* prior to identifying individual responsibilities. "A medium-size service company experimented with this approach (teams) and finally decided to ignore individual objectives altogether, reasoning that too much interlinking, support, and cooperation are required to blame or reward any individual for the production of any single end result."[35]

A second limitation of the approach is the difficulty of applying it to many nonmanagerial positions. Certainly, such an approach to blue-collar employees on the assembly line would be impracticable, though Herzberg would suggest that such jobs be redesigned so that meaningful goals and feedback of information could be developed. One could establish the goal for a receptionist, for example, of "producing" satisfied and informed visitors to the organization. Means of assessing accomplishment would be quite difficult to devise and implement, e.g., no more than 1 percent complain about the receptionist during a given period, visitors are not left waiting for more than five minutes, etc. Considering the time and effort that must be allocated to a well-designed MBO plan, most firms restrict its application to managerial, technical, and professional personnel.

A final limitation is that MBO makes *comparative* assessment of multiple personnel rather difficult. In traditional assessment methods, all personnel are rated on common factors. In MBO, each person will have different sets of goals of noncomparable complexity and difficulty of accomplishment. Management must still make various decisions on a comparative basis—who gets the pay increase or who is to be promoted. Superiors will, however, develop a strong impression of a subordinate's effectiveness in a MBO program, not only in performances related to goal accomplishment, but also in his or her conception of the job and its major goals. Certainly, the joys of intrinsic satisfaction from goal accomplishment will wear thin if not accompanied by a fair share of extrinsic rewards available in the system, e.g., money, promotion, status symbols, etc.

[34]A. R. Solem, "Some Supervisory Problems in Appraisal Interviewing," *Personnel Administration*, vol. 23, no. 3, May–June 1960, pp. 27–35.

[35]Richard E. Byrd and John Cowan, "MBO: A Behavioral Science Approach," *Personnel*, vol. 51, no. 2, March–April 1974, p. 48.

SUMMARY

One of the best bulwarks against the increasing utilization of seniority in business is the development and administration of a sound philosophy and program of performance appraisal. A philosophy and system that recognize and compensate performance not only provide the stimulus to improve and develop, but also result in superior performance in the long run.

All supervisors appraise the performance of their subordinates. It is suggested that a better job of appraisal will be effected if some conscious and planned approach is adopted. In general, planned approaches can be divided into systems through which superiors can appraise on a comparative basis (ranking, person-to-person comparison, grading, graphic scales, checklists, forced-choice description, and critical incidents), and those in which there is joint superior-subordinate establishment and appraisal of position goals accomplishment. The former approach relies on sound training of supervisors to rate objectively through avoiding errors such as leniency, harshness, halo effect, bias, and central tendency.

Management by objectives is a philosophy of management which incorporates a differently oriented appraisal process. Central to MBO is joint and mutual establishment of end results for individual key personnel. Equally essential is periodic joint appraisal when assessments are made concerning degrees of accomplishment. When organizational activities are closely interlocking, it is recommended that team or group goal establishment precede the identification of individual responsibilities and goals.

DISCUSSION QUESTIONS

1   What specific values are derived from a traditional and systematic assessment of personnel and their performance?
2   Compare and contrast the following pairs: (a) graphic scales—checklists, (b) person-to-person comparison—graphic scales, (c) forced choice—forced distribution, (d) grading—graphic scales.
3   Describe the process of designing a forced-choice system of rating.
4   What is Management by Objectives?
5   Compare and contrast the interviews conducted in a traditional performance appraisal program with those held in a MBO program.
6   Describe the characteristics of an effective "objective" in a MBO program.
7   Identify common errors of rating in traditional programs of performance appraisal. Cite possible solutions and adjustments.
8   Contrast the approaches of superior rating, peer rating, and self-rating in systematic appraisal.
9   How can critical incidents be utilized to improve the objectivity of graphic scales?
10   In what ways can the personnel department monitor the effectiveness of traditional appraisal programs?

SUPPLEMENTARY READING

BRADY, Rodney H.: "MBO Goes to Work in the Public Sector," *Harvard Business Review*, vol. 51, no. 2, March–April 1973, pp. 65–74.

BURKE, Ronald J.: "Why Performance Appraisal Systems Fail," *Personnel Administration*, vol. 35, no. 3, May–June 1972, pp. 32–40.

"Conversation with Peter F. Drucker," *Organizational Dynamics*, vol. 2, no. 4, Spring 1974, pp. 34–52.

ODIORNE, George S.: "The Politics of Implementing MBO," *Business Horizons*, vol. 17, no. 3, June 1974, pp. 13–21.

PATTON, Arch: "Does Performance Appraisal Work?" *Business Horizons*, vol. 16, no. 1, February 1973, pp. 83–91.

SCOTT, Richard D.: "Taking Subjectivity Out of Performance Appraisal," *Personnel*, vol. 50, no. 4, July–August 1973.

STONE, Thomas H.: "An Examination of Six Prevalent Assumptions concerning Performance Appraisal," *Public Personnel Management*, vol. 2, no. 6, November–December 1973, pp. 408–414.

CASES FOR PART FOUR

THE CASE OF THE TRAINING STAFF MEETING*

The Central Corporation had four plants, each employing at least 1,000 people, and a central office with a staff of approximately 250. At the central office James R. Simpson headed the training division with general staff responsibility in the area of company-wide training, and specific responsibility for running the training programs of the central office. Each of the four plants had a plant training staff operating under a director of training responsible for carrying out the plant training programs. The plant training directors reported directly to their respective plant managers. Mr. Simpson had no direct line authority over the plant training directors. His position, however, in the central office, and particularly his direct contact with the principal officers of the corporation permitted him to exercise a great deal of influence over the plant training directors.

The board of directors had determined to undertake an executive training program and gave a general directive to Mr. Simpson to develop such a program to be worked out in detail with the plant training directors. The four plant managers were informed of the directors' decision to carry on the executive training program, and were urged to get their plant training staffs working on the program in the near future. As a result, Mr. Simpson had called a conference of the plant training directors and they were meeting with him at the central office. The discussions at the meeting were recorded as the simplest means for providing each participant with a record of discussions and decisions. Following is a segment of the recorded staff meeting on the first day. As Mr.

*Robert Dubin, *Human Relations in Administration*, 2d ed., Prentice-Hall, Inc., Englewood Cliffs, N.J., 1961, pp. 575–578. Used with permission.

Simpson indicates in his opening comment, the group has been talking about the program prior to the incident recorded here.

Mr. Simpson. We seem to be in general agreement as to what the executive training program ought to accomplish—what we're shooting at. Perhaps it would be a good idea to take a look at methods—how are we going to do it. There are lots of different methods—conferences, group discussions, lectures, work shops, and the like—and we ought to have some agreement among us on which we propose to use at our plants. I, of course, can't tell any of you what methods should be used here, but I do want to throw out the idea that we consider using role-playing in our training. I have had . . . .

Carl Halvorsen (Plant I training director). I've read a little bit about that role-playing stuff, Jim, but I can't say it has impressed me particularly.

Mr. Simpson. I've used it some here and I think I can say without any qualification that it is successful. We have had amazing results with it after we once broke the ice. I know it is kind of a new thing and some of you may hesitate to undertake it because you are not familiar with it. If we decide to go ahead with it we could very easily run some practice sessions here before we break up and that would give us all a chance to see it in operation.

Harold Hicks (Eastern plant training director). Jim, before we talk about this role-playing maybe we ought to find out what plans the fellows already have, if any. Some of us have been thinking about this program ever since we knew it was coming and I'll bet some of us have even been doing some executive training already. What I mean is, let's not decide on a method until we find out what some of the ideas on that are.

Mr. Simpson. That's a good point, Hal. I guess I just assumed that would come out in the discussion, but let's do it that way to start. What are some of the plans you fellows have? How about your plant, Randy?

F. R. Randall (Plant 2 training director). Well, as you know, our plant manager hires personally all the executives at our plant and he is pretty proud of his executive staff. I think I will be able to sell him on this training program. I frankly haven't given much thought to methods—of course, we all know the usual methods—but I'll go along with anything we decide here.

Charles Pinkerton (Western plant training director). I know this role-playing business is supposed to be hot stuff; but we have used it for some time. I think all of us used it some way during the war with JMT and JRT.* I've found it works all right with workers and supervisors. But executives are likely to think it is kid stuff and just laugh it off. I have some reservations about using it in this executive training program.

Mr. Simpson. I'm glad you brought that point up, Charley. We were kind of worried about the same thing. Once we tried it here, however, we found that the executives ate it up. I know it takes some real technique in introducing it but if you do a careful job it will work. I remember one of our top executives here who just acted bored when the others were role-playing. I could see he didn't like it. Then he played the role of a department head catching hell from his division chief. He really did a superb job and had the boys in the aisles with his acting. After that he was really enthusiastic about the method. After all, executives are human, too, and they get a kick out of really participating in the training. That's what role-playing does—it gives everyone a chance to participate without having to make speeches and shoot the bull.

Mr. Pinkerton. Well, maybe the executives here at the home office have time to play games like that. But seriously, Jim, I wonder if we are going to have the time at our plants to make use of this role-playing. If we are going to do a well-rounded training program we'll have to cover an awful lot of ground. I think you'll admit that role-playing is slow going, particularly, as you say, when you have to spend so much time to put it over in the first place.

Mr. Simpson. You are right, Charley, and I wouldn't argue with you for a minute about the time it

---

*Job Management Training and Job Relations Training, standardized training programs used during the war.

takes to do role-playing. My own feeling about the matter—and this is, of course, just my personal opinion—is that the lessons learned in role-playing are really learned and stick with people. Sure, you can cover more ground quicker by the conference method or by lectures, but how much of that stuff sticks with a fellow?

Mr. Halvorsen. That's just one of the things I've worried about in role-playing. Now, I'm not an expert on it like you, Jim—I can only speak about what I've read about it—but I wonder how you evaluate its effectiveness. That's one of our biggest headaches in training—evaluation—and I don't think we know enough about evaluating role-playing to be sure we have a good thing in it.

Mr. Simpson. Carl, we all know that evaluation is a headache, and I'd be the first to admit that we are a long way from having that one licked. My own observations are that role-playing sticks with the participants and does a teaching job. What do you think, Charley?

Mr. Pinkerton. Oh, sure, I go along with you in saying it sticks with the participants, but so does at least some of most training. I still feel that we would have a real problem of getting executives to take it in the first place, and I don't think we will have the time back home at the plant to use it anyway.

Mr. Simpson. You haven't said much, Randy. What's your reaction to this?

Mr. Randall. As I said, I'll go along with anything you decide here. If you want us to try role-playing, I'll try it. It doesn't make much difference to me because training is training, after all.

Mr. Simpson. I'm sorry you put it that way, Randy. I'm not trying to force anything on you. You all know you are perfectly free to run your training programs as you please. I don't want any of you to have the impression that we at the home office are trying to insist on anything. Our purpose in getting together is to exchange ideas and develop a unified program so we will all be accomplishing the same things when we get our executive training under way. I just threw out this suggestion on role-playing because I thought it was valuable, but of course that is just one of many things out on the table. We have a lot to get over in the next couple of days so maybe we ought to move on to something else and come back to methods later.

THE CASE OF THE AMBITIOUS, UNHAPPY ENGINEER

In 1962, the Newman Test Laboratories was started with a complement of three employees and very little equipment. At present, the company has over 300 employees and assets in excess of $10 million. The rapid growth has been largely due to the introduction of missiles and complex aircraft, which require a considerable amount of environmental testing, this being Newman's primary business.

Environmental testing attempts to simulate the actual conditions under which a part will operate. For example, a valve might be subjected to extremes of heat, cold, vibration, moisture, and countless other conditions to see if it will operate properly when in actual use. The testing division of Newman is broken down into the following seven branches: mechanical, hydraulic, pneumatic, fuel, electronic, dynamic, and cryogenic. When any part is to be examined, it will be tested in any one or a combination of the seven branches. There is a head of each branch who reports directly to the vice-president in charge of the testing division. At present, the personnel department occupies a relatively low position in the structure of the Newman Laboratories. It is small in size and is largely manned by former technical personnel. Its activities are confined primarily to screening applicants (with no authority to hire), administering the employee benefits, directing company security, and maintaining personnel records. All personnel who hold supervisory or executive positions at Newman have strong technical backgrounds.

Joe Shaner, who is twenty-nine years of age and has been with the company four years, is a *lead technician*. The lead technician is in charge during the actual performance of any one test. Joe's job goes a little further, since he has a better-than-average technical and educational background. He is capable of writing formal test reports, and because of this he feels that he is entitled to the position of *junior engineer*. A junior engineer is in charge of a particular test or project. A *test engineer* designs a test and turns it over for execution to the junior engineer. The latter is then responsible for scheduling the test, issuing work assignments to lead technicians, and completing the final test report. He supervises not only technical people but some clerical personnel as well.

In the opinion of his supervisor, Joe would be qualified for advancement to junior engineer except that he has not demonstrated good ability in supervising the work of others. To some he gives too much and too detailed instruction, and they soon feel that their intelligence is being insulted. Others feel that they are not getting enough information, that they are lost and do not know what to do. Joe is neither particularly liked nor disliked by the people with whom he comes in contact. His shortcomings have been brought to his attention. He says that he realizes that he has a problem, but, as yet, has given little evidence of improvement. He is unhappy in his position as lead technician and has appealed to his supervisor for support in being promoted to junior engineer. Joe's supervisor is also an engineer in his early thirties, and this is his first management position. He points out to Joe his shortcomings and makes it clear that they will have to be remedied before he can be considered for promotion. Joe has said that if promotion is not forthcoming soon, he will have to look for another position. Neither Joe's supervisor nor the personnel department wants to see the company lose a man who, they feel, has a tremendous technical potential.

THE CASE OF THE AMBITIOUS INADEQUATE

In 1951, George Folts was hired by the Show Case Corporation as a bookkeeper trainee. Prior to this job he had worked for a short time on a weekly newspaper, but had been replaced by a man who could sell as well as write. He had also had a brief job as an apprentice sign painter. From 1946 to 1957, he had shown little promise of success in his job, advancing only one step from bookkeeper to teller.

In 1962, a public relations department was organized in the company. A woman was brought in from the outside to initiate and develop this activity. She had had a considerable amount of experience in the public relations field. After the war, she had worked for a large newspaper, had been a business writer for the *Wall Street Journal*, and had headed her own advertising agency.

George Folts asked for a transfer to this new department because of his earlier experience in writing for the weekly newspaper. He was assigned to writing publicity for the new department. During the period from 1962 to 1972, he handled his task reasonably well. He was also sent to a special workshop school during two summers to study public relations. After his completion of this workshop program, he was given his second promotion in the organization to a junior-executive level. He never interested himself in any outside activities with any organization or group. He did not wish to appear before any group to give speeches or to attend any other functions that were required in the public relations program.

In the past few years, the public relations department has grown and expanded.

Several young people have been added to the department. A couple of these have already passed the level of executive authority that is still held by George Folts. George performs the duties assigned to him quite adequately. He has developed into a capable writer. In general, management is convinced that he performs his assigned tasks well enough, but that he does not have an outgoing personality. He is considered to be too introvertive ever really to succeed or to attain a position of higher authority. He also has a tendency to receive rather than to initiate.

One day last week, George approached the head of the public relations department and said that he wanted to be given more important tasks to handle. He believes that as a long-time employee of the company, next to the department head in terms of time, he should be given more responsibility. In short, he feels that he should be at least an assistant to the department head. He thinks that it is quite unfair and ungrateful of the company to promote younger and less experienced persons to positions higher than his.

The public relations head does not feel that George is qualified to handle problems any more complex than those he deals with at present. Yet George is a steady, dependable worker. She does not want to hurt his feelings or discourage him in his present job. She is convinced that George cannot now or in the future be promoted to a position involving more responsible work. And if George should quit, his departure would constitute a serious loss to the department. She has asked George for some time to think over the request.

THE CASE OF THE PART-TIME ASSISTANT

While attending college, Jerry Watt felt a need for both money and business experience. Knowing that George Weatherby, an old high school friend, was a buyer for the men's furnishings department of a local department store, he successfully applied for a part-time job. George Weatherby was a young man in his middle twenties. He had worked his way from stock boy to buyer in about five years and was one of the coming stars of the store.

Previous to Mr. Weatherby, the men's furnishings department had seen four buyers come and go, most of them pressured into resigning because of the department's failure to meet its quotas. Consequently, the present buyer was also on the spot, and felt the pressure to succeed.

After agreeing to hire Jerry, Mr. Weatherby took him up to the personnel office and personally introduced him to Mrs. Smith. In the words of Jerry, "She was a large-framed woman, and at first appearance, she seemed to tower over you, and I was, to say the least, impressed by the size of this woman. It wasn't necessary to stand too close to her while conversing. Her voice was so loud that sometimes one would have felt more comfortable if he were standing in the next room. I found out later that she was an ex-sergeant of the Women's Marine Corps. My interview with her lasted about fifteen minutes, and when I left, I felt that I had impressed her favorably.

"About a week later, the store called part-time personnel in for a special inventory, and I, along with another college man, was placed in the basement counting china and housewares. This was a long way from the position that the buyer, George Weatherby, had promised me. But, periodically, George would come down and tell me that my current position was only temporary.

"It wasn't too long until Mrs. Smith again called and asked me to come to work the next Monday. I was instructed to wear a suit because I would be working on the main floor. My faith in Mr. Weatherby was confirmed, and the next Monday, all dressed up, I showed up ready to work. Work I did! My job was to haul all of the sale merchandise up from the basement and lay it out on the counters and tables where the customers could handle the goods.

"This was the first time that I came into contact with Elenor and Tammy. They were arch-rivals and throughout the years had reached an agreement suitable to both—they didn't speak to one another. The competition to see which one could outdo the other was fierce, and each of them would do anything to outsell the other. They both worked on commission and their compensation was dependent upon their sales for the day.

"The first day of the big sale was absolutely hectic. People would buy shirts, ties, socks, and other men's clothing by the arm-loads. People began coming to me to ask if I could help them. So after receiving permission from Mr. Weatherby, I proceeded to help customers select their goods. The problem of my not knowing how to write up a sales ticket then arose. So when I had finished helping a customer, I would ask one of the sales clerks to write up the sale. Elenor was always right there, willing and ready to do so. Because I was working in her general area, the natural thing to do was to pass the sales on to her. To say the least, this infuriated Tammy because Elenor was getting most of the business from me. And, as it turned out, Elenor, because of my assistance, outsold everyone on that particular day.

"Soon afterwards, I went through what was known as a 'sales check,' wherein the Personnel Director instructed all sales clerks about company policy, writing up sales tickets, lay-away, credits, and the store's history. Unfortunately, the major portion of the time was spent on the latter subject.

"During this 'training session,' I was told that one of the store's policies was that everyone should write his own sales tickets and must not pass on merchandise to other sales people. Another store policy was that a sales clerk was only supposed to wait on one customer at a time. This was contrary to what I had seen during the sale.

"Each day thereafter brought new problems to the employees working in the men's furnishings department. It was difficult to make friends with Elenor and Tammy, but after an effort on my part, a small friendship began. But, between Elenor and Tammy, the silence persisted. Several times Mr. Weatherby called them into his office and tried to talk them into cooperating a little more. It even reached the point where they were told by Mrs. Smith, the personnel director, to try to act more pleasantly while working together. Even the customers were able to notice the bickering that went on between the two saleswomen. Yet, when the top ten sales clerks were listed at the end of the year, both Elenor and Tammy were found near the top.

"Six months from the time I started working on the selling floor as a clerk, my fellow workers accepted me as assistant buyer even though I had not formally been placed in that position. My nature was such that I volunteered for additional responsibilities, and when the buyer was out of town or not in the store, he, along with the personnel director, made it understood that I should deal with any problems encountered on the floor. Soon I was cleared to okay checks, which elevated me in the eyes of the other workers. All ran rather smoothly until it came time for the next sale.

"On the first day, several new part-time people came to me complaining about the fact that Elenor was writing up sales in her book for customers with whom they had been working. The new clerks would wait on a customer and help him select merchandise; then when they would reach for their sales books, Elenor would step in and quickly write up the sale.

"Since I was the one who had helped them with other problems, they brought this one to me. Trying to be understanding, while at the same time a little aggravated, I approached Elenor and asked her to be more patient and help the new clerks, instead of using them to do her work. She became angry, accused me of calling her a thief, and threatened to go upstairs and tell Mrs. Smith of my accusation. She said, 'No young punk is going to call me a thief.' Instead of going upstairs, she went back to work until her next coffee break arrived. Then she went storming into Mrs. Smith's office with a story that I had insulted her. By this time, I had gone to school for afternoon classes.

"When I got back to work that evening, I was immediately summoned to the personnel office and asked to relate my side of the story. I told what had happened, explaining how the part-time clerks had told me how Elenor would take advantage of their sales. To this statement, Mrs. Smith replied that it wasn't the first time that such a problem had arisen and that it was high time something was done about both Elenor and Tammy."

PART FIVE

COMPENSATION

If the abilities of employees have been developed to the point where they meet or exceed job requirements, it is now appropriate that they be equitably *compensated* for their contributions. The factors affecting the determination of equitable compensation are many, varied, and complex, and management must come to some decision concerning the basic wage or salary (Chapter 14). To reward and motivate improved performance on the job, various systems of incentives have been developed (Chapter 15). And finally, organizations have devised numerous ways of providing supplementary compensation over and above base and incentive pay (Chapter 16).

FOURTEEN

BASE
COMPENSATION – JOB

One of the most difficult functions of personnel management is that of determining rates of monetary compensation. Not only is it one of the most complex duties, but it is also one of the most significant to both the organization and the employee. It is important to the organization, because wages and salaries often constitute the greatest single cost of doing business; in 1929 employee compensation amounted to 58 percent of the nation's income, as compared with 70 percent in recent years. It is important to the employee because the paycheck often is the sole means of economic survival; it is also one of the most influential factors determining status in society.

There have been many attempts to develop an adequate and practical theory of wages that would help in determining how much pay a person should receive. When a company determines that a particular individual should receive $3.13 an hour for performing the duties of a particular job, how do we know that $3.13 is the correct amount and not $4, $3.15, or $2.50?

The answer is that one does *not* know exactly how much pay is the scientifically correct amount that *any* person should receive. There is *no definite, exact, and completely accurate means* of determining the correct wage. Some practical and systematic approaches have been developed and applied, such as job evaluation, but there remains much research and fact-finding to be done to prove the validity of such systems. Yet, despite the lack of objective and accurate means of wage determination, every employer *must* establish a wage or salary for each employee.

The compensation of organization members will be discussed in this and the following two chapters. Total compensation has been divided into three parts: (1) base compensation for the job, (2) variable or incentive compensation for separate people on that job, and (3) supplementary compensation provided by the organization for *all* or large groups of employees. In this chapter, the complex and multiform nature of monetary compensation will be discussed, followed by an analysis of the single most-used system of wage and salary determination—job evaluation.

SIGNIFICANT FACTORS AFFECTING COMPENSATION

Though a considerable amount of guesswork and negotiation are involved in salary determination, certain factors have been extracted as having an important bearing upon the final dollar decision. Among these factors are the following: (1) supply and demand for employee skills, (2) labor organizations, (3) the firm's ability to pay, (4) productivity of the firm and the economy, (5) cost of living, and (6) government. Each of these will be discussed briefly in order to demonstrate the exceedingly complex nature of compensation. Perhaps a realization of these complexities will lead to a greater appreciation and acceptance of job evaluation despite its arbitrariness and scientific failings.

SUPPLY AND DEMAND   Though the commodity approach to labor, as discussed in Chapter 2, is not completely correct, it is nevertheless true that a wage is a price for the services of a human being. The firm desires these services, and it must pay a price that will bring forth the supply, which is controlled by the individual worker or by a group of workers acting in concert. The primary practical result of the operation of this law of supply and demand is the creation of the "going-wage rate." It will be demonstrated later how the wage and salary survey of this going rate is incorporated into a job evaluation approach to wage determination.

This simple statement of the effect that the demand and supply of labor have on wages belies its complexity. It is not practicable to draw demand-and-supply curves for each job in an organization, even though, theoretically, a separate curve exists for *each* job. But in general, if anything works to decrease the supply of labor, such as restriction by a particular labor union, there will be a tendency to increase the compensation. If anything works to increase the employer's demand for labor, such as wartime prosperity, there will be a tendency to increase the compensation. The reverse of each situation is likely to result in a decrease in employee compensation, provided other factors, such as those discussed below, do not intervene.

LABOR UNIONS   In the structure of economic relationships, the labor union attempts to work primarily on the supply side. In a strike for higher wages, the employer's demand for labor to meet a market need is pitted against a supply withheld by the union. Union leaders are often very adroit in selecting the appropriate time to strike as judged by the markets for the employer's products.

To strengthen their control over the supply of labor, unions seek such goals as union or closed shops, regulated or restricted substitution of capital for labor through technology, and controlled entry into apprenticeship programs. All of these activities serve to restrict the number of alternatives open to the employer, who must see that other groups besides labor are properly compensated. Bondholders must have their interest and stockholders their dividends, or else equally needed support will be withdrawn from the enterprise. All compensation must come from products sold in a market which is usually competitive in nature. Inequitable compensation to any or all will create trouble in maintaining the health of the organization. The increase in the strength of labor unions is due, in part, to the fact that employees' interests had not been receiving attention equal to that given to other components of the enterprise.

ABILITY TO PAY Labor unions have often demanded an increase in compensation on the basis that the firm is prosperous and able to pay. However, the fundamental determinants of the wage rate for the individual firm issue from supply and demand. If the firm is marginal and cannot afford to pay competitive rates, its employees will generally leave it for better-paying jobs. Admittedly, this adjustment is neither immediate nor perfect because of problems of labor immobility and lack of perfect knowledge of alternatives. If the firm is highly successful, there is little need to pay far more than the competitive rate to obtain personnel. Ability to pay is an important factor affecting compensation, not for the individual firm but for the entire economy or industry. If *most* firms are generally successful and require more labor, this success affects the compensation level through a general increase in the demand for labor. Or, if most organizations are having difficulty, their ability to pay is lessened and this may be reflected in a lesser demand and a lesser compensation.

PRODUCTIVITY Beginning with the famed General Motors contract with the United Automobile Workers (UAW) in 1948, much attention has been paid to the effect of general productivity increases in the economy upon the specific compensation of huge aggregations of employees. In the battle against inflation, representatives of the federal government have attempted to use computed productivity gains as guidelines in the settlement of wage disputes between managements and unions. Between 1947 and 1966, the computed average annual productivity increase in manufacturing was set at 2.9 percent, leading to the establishment of a "noninflationary" guideline for wage increases of 3.2 percent.[1] With growing inflation, resulting briefly in short-term wage and price controls, the validity of this guideline suddenly vanished. The Cost of Living Council moved its acceptable guideline up to 5.5 percent, but actual increases of 5.8 percent in 1971, 8.5 percent in 1972, and 7.6 percent in 1973 indicated the limited effect of the proposed norm upon actual behavior.[2] With inflation levels reaching double-digit figures, the governmental approach of "jawboning" to influence negotiated settlements has been placed under serious handicaps. Nevertheless, the contract negotiated by the UAW still has within it the 3 percent annual improvement factor *plus* an unlimited periodic adjustment for increasing cost of living.

Though some have hailed the widespread use of a productivity index as a major breakthrough in compensation, there are several serious drawbacks to its use. Among these are the following: (1) there is no precise and accurate measure of productivity acceptable to all; (2) the reported percent increases are generally a long-term average and are not achieved each year; (3) not all industries participate equally in productivity gains; and (4) use of any index does not materially reduce controversy in bargaining, since the index is used as the base from which to bargain.

---

[1] Martin Ziegler, "Productivity in Manufacturing," *Monthly Labor Review*, vol. 90, no. 10, October 1967, p. 3.

[2] "Wages Leave 5.5% Far Behind," *Business Week*, Feb. 2, 1974, p. 16.

COST OF LIVING   Another formula hailed by many as the answer is the cost-of-living adjustment of wages. Among the problems engendered by this approach are the following: (1) no cost-of-living formula will indicate what the base compensation should be—it merely indicates how that rate should vary; (2) this approach tends to vary monetary income but freeze real income, a result with which labor is not content; and (3) as in the case of productivity indexes, there are certain measurement problems in ascertaining cost-of-living increases. The Consumer Price Index of the Bureau of Labor Statistics, however, is widely accepted and followed by many employers and labor organizations.

Cost-of-living adjustment of compensation constitutes no fundamental solution to equitable compensation of employees. It is useful as a stopgap device in times of inflation when labor is pressed to keep up with the rise in prices. It is an essential ingredient of long-term labor contracts unless provision is made to reopen the wage clause periodically. In 1974, approximately one-fourth of major union agreements (covering at least 1,000 workers) had cost-of-living escalator provisions.[3] The UAW agreement provides for a 1-cent increase for every 0.3 percent advance in the Consumer Price Index. In contrast to past years, when an overall ceiling, such as 12 cents, was placed on the amount of such increases, the most recent contract provides for no such limit. Revisions of wage levels are usually made on a quarterly basis.

GOVERNMENT   Our varying levels of government often have very specific things to say about wages and salaries despite the theoretical and nebulous nature of equitable compensation. There are at least three major federal laws which deal directly with the subject of compensation. The Fair Labor Standards Act, often called the Wage and Hour Law, specifies *a minimum hourly wage and a standard workweek* for all firms engaged in interstate commerce. Since the law's inception in 1938, the minimum wage has moved from 25 cents to $2.30 per hour in 1976, but the standard workweek has remained at forty hours. This minimum applies to the originally specified group, which now numbers approximately 37 million persons. Two additional groups have been added: (1) 18 million employees of hotels, restaurants, hospitals, schools, and all levels of government, who will reach the $2.30 mark in 1977, and (2) 2 million farmworkers, who will reach the $2.30 minimum in 1978. Full-time students may be paid 85 percent of the specified minimum.

The Equal Pay Act of 1963 is an amendment to the Fair Labor Standards Act and specifies that equal work requiring equal skill, effort, and responsibility under equal working conditions shall be accorded equal pay, regardless of sex of employee. Any differences must be rationally justified through systematic study, usually in the form of a job evaluation plan. Adjustment of differences cannot take the form of reducing pay of the higher-paid person.[4] One airline has been ordered to pay about $25 million in back wages to stewardesses who since 1968 were paid less than male employees doing the same work.

Hours worked in excess of forty per week must be compensated at the regular rate *plus a penalty* of half time. Thus, if an employee's rate is $3 an hour, a 50-hour

[3]Jerome M. Staller and Loren M. Solnick, "Effect of Escalators on Wages in Major Contracts Expiring in 1974," *Monthly Labor Review*, vol. 97, no. 7, July 1974, p. 27.

[4]Robert D. Moran, "Reducing Discrimination: Role of the Equal Pay Act," *Monthly Labor Review*, vol. 93, no. 6, June 1970, pp. 30–34.

workweek would result in a straight-time pay of $150 (50 × $3) and overtime pay of $15 (10 × $1.50) for a total of $165. Employees assigned to executive, administrative, or professional positions are usually excluded from coverage by the act. Labor organizations constantly press for increases in the minimum wage, decreases in the standard workweek, and increases in the penalty for overtime hours, all in the interest of increasing total compensation for labor.

The Walsh-Healey and Bacon-Davis Acts apply to employers dealing with the federal government as contractors, the former applying to those with contracts whose value is in excess of $10,000 and the latter to those having public works contracts with values in excess of $2,000. Under these two acts, the minimum wage is the *prevailing rate* as established by the Department of Labor; it is usually higher than that of the Fair Labor Standards Act. The standard straight-time period is the eight-hour workday rather than the week. Hours worked in excess of this standard must be compensated with the half-time penalty.

In addition to these three acts, there are numerous state laws specifying minimum wages. Usually these rates are lower than those placed in federal legislation. It can also be contended that the federal government is instrumental in salary determination through its insistence upon collective bargaining with organized labor as required by the Wagner and Taft-Hartley Acts.

EQUITY AND COMPENSATION

Compensation will affect the behavior of people, and the employing organization desires that it do at least two things: (1) attract and keep personnel in the organization, and (2) motivate them to higher levels of performance. The first goal involves problems of employee perceptions of equity, while the second entails analysis of employee expectations of future reward for desired higher performance. We shall deal briefly with the problem of perceived equity as establishing a need for systematic job evaluation processes which desirably lead to greater equity. Discussion of employee expectancies of reward is more appropriately allocated to the following chapter dealing with incentive compensation.

Equity is concerned with felt justice according to natural law or right. Homan's exchange theory predicts greater feelings of equity between people whose exchanges are in equilibrium.[5] When an employee receives compensation from the employer, perceptions of equity are affected by two factors: (1) the ratio of compensation to one's inputs of effort, education, training, endurance of adverse working conditions, etc., and (2) the comparison of this ratio with the perceived ratios of significant other people with whom direct contact is made. Equity usually exists when a person perceives that the ratio of outcomes to inputs is in equilibrium, both internally with respect to self and in relation to others.

In Figure 14-1, nine different situations are proposed. Equity theory would hypothesize that the correlation of pay and contribution that exists in cells 3, 5, and 7 would result in feelings of equity. In all other cells, feelings of dissonance are likely to exist. Research conducted with respect to under-reward situations (6, 8, and 9) clearly

[5]George C. Homans, *Social Behavior: Its Elementary Forms*, Harcourt Brace Jovanovich, Inc., New York, 1961.

Figure 14-1 Equity in compensation

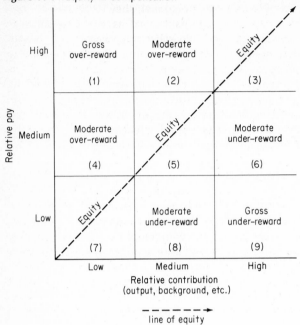

line of equity

indicates that employee satisfaction is lower than in either the equity or over-reward situations.[6] Employee contributions exceed their outcomes of money. Resulting dissatisfaction often leads to efforts to reestablish equilibrium, e.g., "borrowing" from the supply room to increase rewards, trying to adversely affect the efforts and pay of others, convincing self that pay is not out of line, quitting or frequently absenting oneself from the organization, promoting labor organization, etc.

Concerning the over-reward situations (cells 1, 2, and 4), original research conducted by Adams suggested that feelings of discomfort and guilt resulting from inequitably higher pay would lead to actions to reduce dissonance. He led an experimental group of employees to believe that the pay allocated was significantly in excess of their qualifications.[7] In one experiment, the overpaid group, compensated on an hourly basis, produced a quantity significantly *in excess* of an appropriately paid control group. In a second experiment under a system of incentive piecework, the overpaid group tended to reduce dissonance by *restricting output* so that total pay was more in line with equity expectations. And in a final experiment, the overpaid group restricted its quantity but increased its quality in order that total pay received might be in line with contributions. Other research has not demonstrated the same strength of

[6]David J. Cherrington, H. Joseph Reitz, and William E. Scott, Jr., "Effects of Contingent and Noncontingent Reward on the Relationship between Satisfaction and Task Performance," *Journal of Applied Psychology*, vol. 55, no. 6, December 1971, pp. 531–536.

[7]J. Stacy Adams, "Wage Inequities, Productivity, and Work Quality," *Industrial Relations*, vol. 2, no. 4, October 1963, pp. 9–16.

impact upon an overpaid group as for an underpaid one. For example, a second study supported hypotheses with respect to underpaid personnel; they tended to *decrease* inputs over time in comparison with those equitably paid as well as with those overpaid.[8] The overpaid group, however, tended to parallel the equity group in output. Concerning satisfaction, however, overpaids did express more *overall* dissatisfaction than did those from equitably paid groups. Thus, there is some indication of guilt from receiving more compensation than deserved, but such feelings were not translated into action. In many instances, overpaid employees convinced themselves that the high rewards allocated were actually deserved. Thus, the guilt is of short-term duration. This is not the case with the underpaid. The resulting frustration and anger at receiving less than equitable treatment tend to last for longer periods and often result in overt behavior to reduce the degree of disequilibrium.

It has been observed that many organizations pursue a pay increase policy characterized by cells 4, 5, and 6. The employee of average contribution is accorded an average increase in pay, but those above and below average are allocated compensation amounts *not* significantly different. Thus superior personnel are moderately under-rewarded, leading to lower contributions or withdrawal from the firm. Inferior personnel are moderately over-rewarded, leading to little or no change in behavior but effecting acceptable levels of employee satisfaction. It is this condition that led Herzberg to conclude that pay *cannot* be an effective motivator of employee behavior.[9] Figure 14-1 and equity theory would suggest that the problem may be one of improper design of compensation systems, rather than the fundamental inability of pay to motivate.

To cope with possible feelings of inequity, various organizations follow a practice of imposing secrecy with respect to compensation received. This is particularly true for salaries of executives and other personnel not covered by union contracts. Seventy-seven percent of a group of 500 managers operating on all levels in a wide variety of organizations agreed that management pay rates are best kept secret.[10] In a related study of 563 managers operating in organizations practicing salary secrecy, each was asked to estimate the average yearly earnings of (1) other managers at their own organizational level, (2) those one level above, and (3) those one level below. When these estimates were compared with actual salaries, it was clear that the secrecy policy had been successful in keeping the truth from the responding managers. However, the errors in estimating were not random. Managers *consistently* underestimated the pay of higher-level managers and overestimated the pay of both peers and those at the next lower level. In reply to questions concerning justice and equity, they felt that there was too small a difference between their own pay and that of peers and lower managers. Thus, even though pay is actually geared to consistency within the firm, a policy of secrecy will often lead to dissatisfaction concerning perceived equity. Those managers who did possess an accurate picture of other managers' pay were more satisfied with their own pay than those who did not.

[8]Robert D. Pritchard, Marvin D. Dunnette, and Dale O. Jorgenson, "Effects of Perceptions of Equity and Inequity on Worker Performance and satisfaction," *Journal of Applied Psychology*, vol. 56, no. 1, February 1972, pp. 75–94.

[9]See Chap. 19.

[10]Edward E. Lawler III, "The Mythology of Management Compensation," *California Management Review*, vol. 9, no. 1, Fall 1966, pp. 11, 17–19.

JOB EVALUATION

As a first step in the pursuit of equity, there should be established a consistent and systematic relationship among base compensation rates for all jobs within the organization. The process of such establishment is termed "job evaluation" and is not to be confused with job analysis, which is concerned with collection of data about jobs. In job evaluation, one attempts to consider and measure the inputs required of employees (skill, effort, responsibility, etc.) for minimum job performance, and to translate such measures into specific monetary returns. Equity will also be affected by individual treatment of employees within the total compensation system; but the prior establishment of consistent base rates, regardless of job incumbent, is the first step in the building of perceived equity.

The immediate objective of the job evaluation process is to obtain internal and external consistency in wages and salaries. Internal consistency is concerned with the concept of relative wages within the firm. If, for example, the supervisor is paid less than a subordinate, these rates are inconsistent. The scatter diagram of wage rates shown in Figure 14-2 depicts an internally inconsistent wage structure. The horizontal portion of the scale shows a hierarchy of jobs from low value to high value. The vertical portion shows the wage rates. Each dot shows the wage rate of a particular job. If these were internally consistent, the higher-worth jobs would be paid more than those deemed to be of lower value. The dots would form an upward-sloping line to the right. Of importance to internal consistency also are the specific amounts of wage differentials between any two jobs.

External consistency refers to a desired relativity of an organization's wage structure to that of the community, the industry, or the nation. The organization may choose to pay the going rate, more than the rate, or less. Wage and salary surveys are necessary for the determination of external consistency. It is here, also, that collective bargaining must enter the picture. Job evaluation and collective bargaining are not incompatible; they can and do exist within the same organization. Job evaluation would reduce the area of collective bargaining by systematizing the determination of internal consistency, which is concerned with proper wage differentials. Collective bargaining must still work to attain the objective of external consistency, the raising or lowering of the entire wage structure. Job evaluation should determine the *shape* of the wage structure and collective bargaining the *location* of the entire structure as a unit. Labor

Figure 14-2   Scatter diagram of wage rates showing inconsistent structure

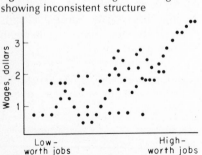

unions can also participate in the design and administration of the job evaluation system. In a sample of thirty-eight unions questioned in 1972, twenty-six had job evaluation provisions in their contract, with union leader preference for the point system described on page 304. [11]

Though internal and external consistency are the immediate objectives of job evaluation, its ultimate objective is employee and employer satisfaction with wages and salaries paid. Management wishes the employee to perceive that his or her compensation is fair and equitable. Management hypothesizes that development of rational consistency, both internally and externally, will increase the likelihood that compensation will be seen as just and equitable.

As a method of personnel management, job evaluation is not old. Early attempts along this line took place in the 1920s, and the period of most rapid growth occurred during the 1940s. The increasingly widespread adoption of job evaluation has been due to the growing size and complexity of modern organizations, as well as to societal requirements for justification of pay differentials accorded female employees and various minority groups. This demands a systematic and defensible approach to measurement and recording of job worth.

In establishing this systematic approach to measuring job worth, there are a number of necessary prerequisites. First, reasonably clear and accurate job descriptions and specifications must be available to provide data concerning the factors to be measured. Secondly, a decision must be made concerning what groups of employees and jobs are to be covered by a single evaluation system. Often, there are separate systems for production and maintenance, clerical and administrative, scientific and professional, and managerial employees. If all personnel are deemed to be in one market as they are all in one firm, there will have to be some means of relating these multiple systems to assure equitable treatment. A final prerequisite is the "selling" of the idea of systematic evaluation to all participants in the system. Selling the approach is the first step and the last step, and the insistence upon it is consistent with the concept that a correct salary must be satisfactory to both employee and employer. In most instances, it is a matter of employee education concerning goals and methods and adopting an open mind to alternative approaches, provided greater values can be proved.

JOB EVALUATION SYSTEMS

There are in use today four basic systems of job measurement. They fall into two categories. The first category covers the simpler methods, which make no use of detailed job factors. The job is treated as a whole, and job descriptions, rather than job specifications, are often utilized. In this category we place two systems sometimes known as the nonquantitative systems, (1) simple ranking and (2) grading.

The second category covers systems which use a more detailed approach. Job factors are selected and measured, and job specifications are definitely required. This category is known as the quantitative approach and includes (1) the point system and (2) the factor-comparison system. These systems are most widely used, with the point

---

[11]Harold D. James, "Issues in Job Evaluation," *Personnel Journal*, vol. 51, no. 9, September 1972, pp. 675–679.

system being utilized by approximately 75 percent of the firms that use job evaluation. The ranking system is used least frequently, with grading and factor comparison vying for second position. Many firms use more than one system. For example, a point system may be used for production employees and a grading system for clerical. In addition, an excellent way of ascertaining the accuracy of one system is to check its answer by applying *another* system to the same jobs; there should be a substantial amount of agreement between the answers obtained by the two systems. *Any one* of the four systems can be as accurate as any other system if applied with care and enthusiasm. One study compared the results of a point system, factor-comparison system, and ranking method and found the intercorrelation to be .94.[12]

SIMPLE RANKING

Since most of the business organizations of the United States are relatively small in size, as measured by the number of personnel, a simple and inexpensive system of job measurement has great potential usefulness. Ranking should involve the preparation of brief job descriptions, although some firms merely attempt to rank job titles. These descriptions are handed to a committee of judges, with instructions to place them in the order of worth, without respect to persons at present performing these jobs or to the present wage rates paid. No specific factors are selected for consideration.

Several techniques of ranking can be of value in this process of evaluation. First, the top and bottom jobs should be selected as bench marks for the remainder of the ranking process. They, at least, provide a point of departure on which there is generally full agreement among the judges. Secondly, the paired-comparison technique, previously discussed, can be applied. Each job can be compared with every other job, one at a time. A third technique is that of using a committee for the judging. Admittedly, there is a great deal of conjecture and some arbitrariness in any system of job evaluation, and the averaging of ranks by a group of informed evaluators often results in a more accurate judgment. It also makes it easier to sell the end result, since a committee is generally considered to be more objective and unbiased than any one individual. A fourth device that can be used in ranking is the organization chart, if one exists. Job evaluation ranks should not violate the organizational ranking of jobs depicted on the chart, or, if they do violate the chart, perhaps the chart should be modified.

The defects of the simple ranking system are many. Its greatest virtue, simplicity, is also a disadvantage, in that the measurement is somewhat crude. It is hard to measure whole jobs. In addition, there is no predetermined scale of values, or yardstick, for the judges to use. Each judge has her or his own set of criteria, and it is difficult to explain the results to a job incumbent. The end result of this system is a list of jobs in the order of worth, such as the following:

Rank	Job
1	X
2	Y

[12]Thomas Atchinson and Wendell French, "Pay Systems for Scientists and Engineers," *Industrial Relations*, vol. 7, no. 1, October 1967, p. 45.

3	M
4	N
5	A
6	B
7	C
8	D
9	U
10	R

Are we to assume that the difference between X and Y is equal to that between Y and M or between M and N? Obviously these differences are not necessarily equal. A fifth technique of ranking can be introduced here to correct this difficulty to some degree. The rank order can be spaced along a numbered line, as in Figure 14-3. X, the highest-ranked job, is placed at the far end of the abscissa. A judgment is now necessary concerning the closeness of X to Y, and Y is therefore located at some selected distance from X. Considering this space and the estimated closeness in job requirements of X and Y, how close is M to Y? The rank order given above is not violated in Figure 14-3. The only difference is that varied spacing is introduced to show varying differentials. One can turn these ranks and spacings into wage rates by making wage surveys of selected key jobs and computing a wage curve. For example, going rates have been determined for jobs U, B, A, and X. A wage line can be drawn that is closest to the four rates charted for these jobs. All other rates can be interpolated from this line. The process of making a wage survey is explained under the subject of the point system discussed later in this chapter.

JOB GRADING

In the ranking system there is no predetermined yardstick of values. In the job grading approach there is *one* such yardstick consisting of job classes or grades. Jobs are measured as whole jobs. A scale of values is created with which jobs and their job descriptions can be compared. This scale consists of grades and *grade descriptions*. For example, it may be determined that twelve job grades are to be utilized for a category of

Figure 14-3 Ranking along a numbered line

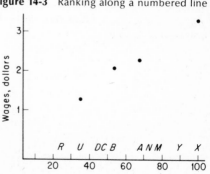

jobs. Twelve grade descriptions must then be prepared. Such descriptions must be sufficiently broad to include several jobs. In a sense, a grade description is a job-*class* description, as compared with a job description.

There are two approaches to writing grade descriptions which will create a single scale of values for measuring the worth of jobs. Jobs may first be ranked and natural classes determined. If, for example, X and Y jobs are in one class, and A, N, and M are in another, these job descriptions can be used to create the two grade descriptions. It is also possible to convert a factor-comparison system and a point system into a grade-description system through this same process. The second approach is to ask a committee to determine in advance a series of grade definitions. Such definitions can be checked by grading some known key jobs against them.

When the scale of values is established, the process of job evaluation through the grading system consists in reading the job description, reading the grade descriptions, and then allocating the job to one particular grade. All jobs within one grade are treated alike in the matter of base salary.

Job grading is considered to be an improvement over ranking in that a predetermined scale of values is provided. In addition, this method arrives at a series of classes or grades, which is precisely the point at which both the point and factor-comparison systems also arrive. The grading system merely goes there *directly* by evaluating the job as a whole job; the other two systems create job classes out of a detailed measurement of job factors. Evaluation under the grading system can be supported by the evidence of job descriptions and job grade descriptions. It is also a relatively simple and inexpensive system to operate.

The primary disadvantage of the job grading approach is that broad generalities must be used in defining grades. These somewhat vague statements often lead to heated arguments between the jobholder and management, but the definitions must be general in order to include several jobs, since whole jobs are being measured. Another difficulty is that the grading approach usually requires multiple systems for different types of jobs; for example, grade descriptions for office jobs differ widely from those for production jobs.

POINT SYSTEM

The most widely used job evaluation method is the point system. It, along with the factor-comparison system, involves a more detailed, quantitative, and analytical approach to the measurement of job worth. This system can best be described through the presentation and discussion of a series of steps for its design and installation. A suggested procedure is as follows:

1 Select job factors or characteristics.
2 Construct a scale or yardstick of values for each job factor.
3 Evaluate all jobs in terms of the yardsticks.
4 Conduct a wage survey for selected key jobs.
5 Design the wage structure.
6 Adjust and operate the wage structure.

Selection of the job factors

In contrast to the ranking and grading methods, which measure jobs as whole jobs, the point system is a more analytical approach and deals with job components or factors. A job factor is a specific requirement levied upon the jobholder, which she or he must contribute, assume, or endure. In general, there are four major job factors in use: (1) skill, (2) responsibility, (3) effort, and (4) working conditions. In another sense, these are the values for which an employer pays money. One buys a certain amount and level of skill and effort. One also buys the abilities to assume certain amounts of responsibility and to endure certain specific working conditions.

The number of factors used in any one system varies with the organization. Some use only the four listed above. More frequently, these four major factors are divided into a number of smaller factors; the most common number used is approximately ten or eleven. One of the most widely used point systems, National Electrical Manufacturers Association–National Metal Trades Association, utilizes the following factors.[13]

Skill	Responsibility	Effort	Working conditions
Education	Equipment or process	Physical	Work conditions
Experience	Material or product	Mental and visual	Hazards
Initiative and ingenuity	Safety of others		
	Work of others		

The measurement of skill is accomplished indirectly through the evaluation of the job requirements for education, experience, and initiative. Responsibility is more specifically evaluated through a measurement of the *amount* and *value of things* and the *number* and *kind of personnel* for which the job incumbent is accountable. In most instances, effort is divided into mental and physical energy required to be expended, though occasionally the requirement for emotional effort is considered important. Working conditions constitute one factor which labor and management are agreed is directly and specifically compensable. Its measurement is concerned with the necessity for enduring disagreeable and hazardous conditions.

The selection of specific job factors to be used in any one system must be made by the organization concerned, as each system should be tailored to specific requirements. At one time, the Xerox Corporation had four separate point systems for four nonexempt salaried groups: technical-support, clerical, equipment service, and field production personnel.[14] It was discovered that a common set of ten factors could be used to measure all four classes of jobs: education, training and experience, job complexity, accountability for efforts, internal contacts, external contacts, guidance of work of others, confidential information, work surroundings, and physical effort, In another organization, coverage of *managerial* jobs in a system resulted in the use of the

[13]National Electrical Manufacturers Association, *Job-rating Manual and Hourly Job-rating Plan*, 1953; and *Wage and Salary Administration*, National Metal Trades Association, Industrial Relations Policies and Practices Bulletin no. 3, Chicago, Ill.

[14]Jay R. Schuster, "Job Evaluation at Xerox: A Single Scale Replaces Four," *Personnel*, vol. 43, no. 3, May–June 1966, p. 17.

following factors: nature of decisions, consequences of decisions, internal and external relationships, and scope of authority and responsibility.[15] In various instances, statisticians have proved that the use of a limited number of key factors will provide the same final evaluation as the use of three times as many factors. Nevertheless, if employees perceive that twelve factors are more believable than four, then the former is the correct number for the system.

As the contents of jobs are altered by technology and automation, it is logical that job evaluation systems should change in response. Traditional approaches are difficult to apply because of the greater degree of interdependence among automated jobs. There must be greater concentration upon interrelationships. In addition, it is common practice to introduce a greater degree of flexibility in job assignments; jobs are enlarged and people are rotated from station to station. The rigidity of some job descriptions will have to be altered. In general, it is suggested that increased automation will cause greater job evaluation weights to be given to the value of the equipment, amount of discretion and initiative required, increased responsibility, increased tension, and required higher educational levels.[16]

Elliott Jacques has recommended that all job factors be discarded and replaced by a single index—the time span of discretion.[17] This is the length of time that elapses between the point at which a subordinate begins a task and the point at which the supervisor would normally examine performance against quantity and quality standards. He proposes the existence of an intuitive awareness of equity derived from an unconscious estimate of one's capacity, level of work to which assigned, and compensation received. As a single index, many researchers are doubtful that it will give satisfactory results. One study found that the time span measure and the results of the government grading system correlated .82.[18] In effect, the evaluation of the job is moved from the specialist in the personnel department to the supervisor as he reports the time spans of discretion. Doubts concerning its reliability are introduced inasmuch as there are multiple raters instead of a centralized core applying a common set of scales to all jobs. There is little evidence that following the time span will introduce greater perceived equity, though Jacques contends that this is the major element considered when the employee feels that justice is or is not being accorded.

With respect to pay systems for scientists and engineers, there is evidence of basing compensation upon *no* job factors directly. In a sample of 120 major companies in aerospace, chemical, electrical, petroleum, and research industries, 56 percent used maturity curves.[19] Pay is thereby governed by the number of academic degrees, the *years* of professional experience, and the *quality* of performance, all of which are personal factors and not job factors. It is assumed that management will assign the maturing scientist and engineer to progressively more difficult tasks, thereby introduc-

[15]Otis Lipstreu and W. J. D. Kennedy, "Pricing the Management Job," *Personnel*, vol. 44, no. 1, January–February 1967, p. 68.

[16]Julius Rezler, "Effects of Automation on Some Areas of Compensation," *Personnel Journal*, vol. 48, no. 4, April 1969, pp. 282–285.

[17]Elliott Jacques, "Objective Measures for Pay Differentials," *Harvard Business Review*, vol. 40, no. 1, January–February 1963, pp. 133–138.

[18]Atchison and French, op. cit., p. 53.

[19]Sang M. Lee, "Salary Administration Practices for Engineers," *Personnel Journal*, vol. 48, no. 1, January 1969, p. 36.

ing the job factors. This approach avoids the problems of having to define jobs in a precise fashion. A study previously cited discovered a correlation of .64 between a job grading system and results obtained by a maturity curve.[20] This same study indicated that there was *less* perceived equity on the part of engineers and scientists when the maturity curve was used. Most of the firms that reported using the curve indicated that it is a check upon other methods; 85 percent used job evaluation and 90 percent conducted periodic salary surveys.

Construction of the factor scales

For each factor selected as important, a yardstick or scale of values must be constructed to permit measuring the factor in each job. The first decision is that of deciding the *total number of points* that will be utilized in the entire system. A more important decision is a determination of the percentage of these points that will be allocated to skill, effort, responsibility, and working conditions.

In most systems, the factor of skill is allocated the greatest percentage of value. Responsibility is ordinarily second in importance, with effort and working conditions given approximately the same value. The NEMA-NMTA breakdown is as follows:

Factor	Number of points	Percentage
Skill	250	50
Responsibility	100	20
Effort	75	15
Working conditions	75	15

In the revised Xerox plan, a grouping of the ten functions would produce 55 percent for skill (education, training, experience, complexity), 40 percent for responsibility (accountability, contacts, guidance of others, confidential information), 2.5 percent for working conditions, and 2.5 percent for physical effort.

In recent years, there has been a definite tendency, in many plans, to *decrease* the importance of skill and *increase* that of responsibility. As suggested above, the reasons for this are the mechanization and automation which transfer more skill from humans to machines, thus decreasing the requirement for worker skill and increasing worker responsibility for equipment, processes, and results.

Just as a committee should select the factors to be used, so should the weights be determined. Assignment of relative values is largely subjective in nature. With the total value of each factor thus determined, yardsticks can now be derived. These yardsticks are composed of *points* and *definitions* of degrees of the particular factor. For example, let us consider the education factor of the NEMA-NMTA plan. The total value is 70 points of the 250 allocated to skill. Five degrees of education have been established with an arithmetic progression of 14 points. As Figure 14-4 indicates, a job requiring only the

[20]Atchison and French, op. cit., p. 53.

Figure 14-4 Scale of value for the education factor in NEMA-NMTA job-evaluation system

Points

14	28	42	56	70
Read, write, add, and subtract	Equivalent 2 years high school	Equivalent 4 years high school or 2 years plus 2-3 years trades training	Equivalent 4 years high school plus 4 years trades training	Equivalent 4 years university training

Definitions

ability to read and write will be allocated 14 points, while one requiring a college degree will be awarded the maximum of 70 points.

Thus, a scale of values for education has been derived which can be used to measure that factor in *any* job in the system. Similar yardsticks must be derived for all other factors. The more quantitative the definition of degrees, the higher the reliability of each scale. In one study, the following reliability coefficients were ascertained for the factors used in the NEMA-NMTA system: education, .94; experience, .96; initiative and ingenuity, .95; physical demands, .82; mental demands, .75; responsibility for equipment, .78; responsibility for materials, .77; responsibility for safety of others, .85; responsibility for work of others, .84; working conditions, .85; and hazards, .72. The reliability for system totals was .94, meaning that raters using this *same system* on the *same set of jobs* derived approximately the *same answers.*[21]

Evaluation of the jobs

If reliable scales for each factor have been constructed, and if detailed job specifications are available, the evaluation process has been greatly simplified. It consists of reading the job specifications carefully, comparing that information with degree of definitions on factor scales, and deciding at which degree the job falls on each factor. A totaling of the points for all factors will give the evaluation of the job in terms of points.

In practice, the evaluation of jobs is generally done by a committee, the members of which may have varying degrees of familiarity with the job to be rated. In one study of twelve raters evaluating five jobs on each of fourteen factors, it was determined that the degree of rater familiarity had a significant effect on five of these factors—adaptability, decision making, mental work, working conditions, and managerial requirements.[22] It has also been determined that the more detailed the job specification, the higher the ratings are likely to be. Reliable scales and detailed, but consistently written, job specifications will do much to prevent trouble and controversy in these rating meetings.

[21]C. H. Lawshe, "Simplified Job Evaluation," *Second Annual Industrial Management Conference Proceedings,* University of Missouri, Columbia, Mo. 1948, p. 19.
[22]Joseph M. Madden, "The Effect of Varying the Degree of Rater Familiarity in Job Evaluation," *Personnel Administration,* November–December 1962, pp. 42–46.

Conducting the wage survey

As a result of the preceding step, jobs have been evaluated and differentials established in terms of points. In effect, we have established the spacing of jobs on the horizontal axis of the chart shown in Figure 14-3, except that this time the *spacing is measured* rather than estimated. We now must translate these point values into monetary values. The basic means of accomplishing this translation is through the wage survey. At this point, the going rate enters the picture. Through the survey we hope to discover the going rate for various jobs and to key our entire structure to these rates.

The first step in a wage survey is to select key jobs, ones whose duties are clearly defined, reasonably stable, and representative of all levels of job worth. Thus, a sample of jobs is created. Secondly, a sample of firms in the labor market area must be chosen. The labor market for different jobs can vary from local to regional to national in scope. With both samples selected, the final task is to obtain appropriate wage information, being careful to ensure that the job comparisons being made are valid. Job content, the varying qualities of personnel on these jobs, and the total compensation program must be carefully analyzed, compared, and equated.

The data obtained from the survey are analyzed and averaged. Dollar values of key jobs can now be plotted on the wage chart, shown in Figure 14-5. By drawing a wage-trend line that is closest to all points plotted, we have a line that approximates the going rates for all jobs in the structure. This line can be drawn freehand or by using the "method of least squares." Wage rates for all other jobs can now be interpolated by reading up from the point values to the wage line.

The obtainment of current and accurate compensation data can be greatly facilitated by a computer-assisted data exchange. System Development Corporation has been active in forming a group of thirty firms which have agreed to contribute to a large, centralized compensation data base on a semiannual basis.[23] Standard job family and subfamily codes have been developed, and the system staff takes the lead in ascertaining comparability of company job descriptions with these codes. Data are

[23]Kenneth E. Foster, "Job Worth and the Computer," *Personnel Journal*, vol. 47, no. 9, September 1968, pp. 619–626.

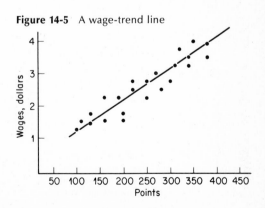

Figure 14-5 A wage-trend line

collected on rate ranges, actual high and low salaries, and number of job incumbents. Three reports can be requested by each company: (1) a complete breakdown of all rates within the requesting company, (2) compensation data for bench mark *key jobs* from all participating companies, and (3) detailed comparisons with selected companies with whom the requesting company has a mutual agreement. The last would include average ranges on all jobs, average salaries paid, and distribution of personnel within each range. It is apparent that such a comprehensive data base would enable the company to go far beyond the typical wage survey in ascertaining the detailed nature of various employee markets. The sample of job rates can be larger, more detailed, and tapped more frequently.

Designing the wage structure

In many instances, the design of the wage structure revolves around the establishment of job classes and rate ranges. Ordinarily, jobs are not treated separately but are grouped to form a job class. All jobs within a class are treated in the same way. In a point system, classes are established by dividing the point range into the desired number of classes; that is, from 120 points to 150 points could constitute one class, 150 to 180 would be the spread for another, etc. Almost all firms group jobs into classes for purposes of economical wage administration.

The firm has a choice of paying *flat rates* for each job class or *varying rates* within a rate range for each class. Flat rates would result in the wage structure shown in Figure 14-6a. Rate ranges would result in the creation of the structure shown in Figure 14-6b. If the structure consists of flat rates, there are usually a greater number of job classes, since promotion from one class to another constitutes the primary method of obtaining a higher base rate. Rate ranges permit varying compensation within the same job class. As was pointed out in Chapter 12, progression through the rate range can be through seniority, merit, or a combination of both. The distribution of wage rates obtained for each of the key jobs often provides clues as to where the upper and lower limits of the wage range should be located. A survey of 382 of *Fortune's* directory of the 500 largest industrial firms revealed that 42 percent use the flat-rate structure for blue-collar employees, as compared with only 2 percent for clerical and 1 percent for professional

Figure 14-6 Wage structures

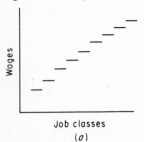

Job classes   Job classes
    (a)   (b)

employees.[24] Rate ranges in conjunction with formal appraisal systems were most common for the latter types of employees.

Adjusting and operating the wage structure

The wage structure that has been developed constitutes a *standard* according to which wages can be administered. Ideally, all wages paid should be within the limits established by the structure. In the beginning, there will be some out-of-line rates, "red-circle" rates, of those who are receiving *more* than the proper amount, as well as substandard rates of those receiving *less*.

It is a cardinal principle of wage and salary administration that no individual shall receive a cut in pay as a result of the installation of job evaluation. Consequently, the firm will live with the red-circle rate until it can be placed into the proper structure through such means as a general increase in the rate structure, promotion of the individual to a job of higher worth, or waiting until the job is vacated through transfer, retirement, or resignation. The substandard rate can be raised immediately to the minimum authorized level. All future pay-rate changes should be in line with the designed limits of the systematic wage structure. It should be noted that across-the-board increases of identical amounts for all jobs will soon destroy the relationships created by this job evaluation process. Adjustments in the total rate structure should be more closely akin to percentage increments in order to maintain equitable relationships.

FACTOR-COMPARISON SYSTEM

The fourth system of job evaluation is the factor-comparison system. In essence, it is an application of the person-to-person system of merit rating to job evaluation. The steps in this system are as follows:

1   Select job factors.
2   Select key jobs.
3   Determine correct rates of key jobs.
4   Rank key jobs under each job factor.
5   Allocate the correct rate of each key job among the job factors.
6   Evaluate all other jobs in terms of these factor yardsticks.
7   Design, adjust, and operate the wage structure.

The first step is the same as for the point system, the selection of job factors. The factor-comparison system uses fewer factors, usually not more than seven. The selection of key jobs and the determination of correct rates are similar to the steps described for the point system above. The fourth step constitutes a refinement of the

[24]William A. Evans, "Pay for Performance: Fact or Fable," *Personnel Journal*, vol. 48, no. 9, September 1970, p. 731.

ranking system. Instead of being ranked as whole jobs, the jobs are ranked by one factor at a time. For example, a committee of judges may rank five key jobs as follows:

Skill	Responsibility	Effort	Working conditions
A	B	E	D
B	A	D	E
C	C	B	C
D	D	C	B
E	E	A	A

The correct pay is then divided among the factors for each key job. Thus, if the pay for job A is $6, it is divided among skill, responsibility, effort, and working conditions, as the committee feels these factors are important in the job. The results of this allocation are portrayed in Figure 14-7.

We have now created a series of four scales or yardsticks. Each scale consists of *key job titles* and *money*, as contrasted with similar scales in the point system, which consisted of degree definitions and points. Other jobs are now evaluated by comparing them with the list of key jobs in each scale. If new job X is most similar to B in skill ($2.20), C in responsibility ($1.20), A in effort ($0.40), and B in working conditions ($.60), its correct rate is $4.40. If it is considered to be slightly different from any of these key jobs, varying amounts can be allocated and the new job X placed into the factor scale as a new level of that factor.

Factor comparison thus incorporates a job-to-job type of rating. It is a refinement of simple ranking in that comparisons are accomplished *job to job, by factors*, rather than as whole jobs. Instead of using money values today, most firms convert the dollar

Figure 14-7 Factor scales of a factor-comparison system

	$0.50	$1.00	$1.50	$2.00	$2.50	$3.00	$3.50	$4.00
Skill	E	D		C B			A	
Responsibility	E D		C		A B			
Effort	A	C B D	E					
Working conditions	A	B C E D						

Correct job rates	Skill	Responsibility	Effort	Working conditions
A – $6.00	A – $3.40	B – $2.00	E – $1.20	D – $1.00
B – $5.60	B – $2.20	A – $1.80	D – $0.90	E – $0.90
C – $4.40	C – $1.80	C – $1.20	B – $0.80	C – $0.80
D – $3.40	D – $1.00	D – $0.50	C – $0.60	B – $0.60
E – $2.80	E – $0.40	E – $0.30	A – $0.40	A – $0.40

amounts into points to avoid adjusting their scales to changing price and wage levels. The final step of designing and operating the structure involves substantially the same problems as described under the point system.

HUMAN RELATIONS EFFECTS OF JOB EVALUATION

In discussions of job evaluation, the implications for human relations are often overlooked. The technical parts of job evaluation are undeniably complicated, but the human problems which may be created by this process are equally complex.

As noted earlier, job evaluation is a systematic, rather than a scientific, process of establishing wages and salaries. It possesses a high degree of reliability, but its validity must be determined by ascertaining the impact upon employee satisfaction. One way to do this would be by collecting and analyzing data with respect to employee complaints and grievances concerning pay. Morale surveys could also be adapted to this purpose. In addition, realizing the impact of relative pay upon perceived equity, a comparison of organization pay rates with going rates in the local community should provide some evidence bearing upon probable validity. There is no basis for contending that job evaluation and wage/salary surveys are scientific and provide incontestable answers. Consequently, we must be heavily concerned with employee and labor union reactions to specific challenges to the system and its results.

A second difficulty arising from the installation of job evaluation is that it will usually promote an *immediate* increase in the number of grievances concerning wages. Job evaluation gives the wage structure a sharp definition that it did not have before and, in effect, turns a spotlight on wages. The formerly hazy structure has now become distinct. When this new clarity of structure is combined with the system's admitted lack of infallibility, it is obvious that grievances will be filed. It is not so certain that these same grievances were not already present prior to job evaluation; the sharp definition provided by job evaluation merely provides a basis on which the grievance can be filed. The solution to this problem is to *wait* and process all grievances judiciously and fairly. If the system has a reasonable degree of reliability and validity, the first burst of grievances will die down, leaving the level of satisfaction higher than it was before job evaluation.

Finally, there is often a conflict between worker values and management values in job evaluation. As indicated earlier, management generally considers, in rating a job, the general factors of skill, responsibility, effort, and working conditions. To these, workers would add the values of (1) the type of supervision received, (2) the congeniality of other workers, (3) the steadiness of the work, (4) the amount of overtime, and (5) the tightness of incentive standards. Obviously, no job evaluation system could ever encompass all the variables of a job that make it attractive to a worker. At times the job evaluation system may reverse the order of worth which the employees themselves have established. The solution to this type of problem usually lies in the managerial ability to be flexible rather than rigid. Where two jobs were reversed, it may be possible to consider both jobs to be in the same class and at least minimize the differences between workers and management. At one time, the management of a firm had assigned equal value to a number of jobs. Employees on the jobs saw great differences among them, and these differences varied from week to week. Instead of insisting that all jobs were equal, management was flexible enough to permit distinctions to be made among the jobs with respect to job assignment. The rates of pay were still equal, but job assignment was handled on a seniority basis, an assignment which was altered as conditions changed.

SUMMARY

The first and most difficult problem in wage and salary administration is the establishment of base compensation for the job. This problem is enormously complicated by such factors as supply and demand, labor organizations, the firm's ability to pay, variations in productivity and cost of living, and governmental legislation. In order to attract and retain needed personnel for the organization, employees must perceive that compensation offered is equitable in relation to their background inputs and relative contributions. Outside of haphazardly establishing or bargaining over each individual rate, the only usable method of solving this problem at present is job evaluation, a systematic and orderly process for establishing the worth of jobs.

There are four alternative methods of job evaluation: (1) simple ranking, (2) job grading, (3) the point system, and (4) factor comparison. The significant elements of these systems are summarized in Figure 14-8.

The introduction of a pay system is an event of major importance to employees, and its effects upon them cannot be ignored. It is a valid system if it results in a structure acceptable to both employee and employer. In general, structures which are internally and externally consistent have the greatest chance of effecting overall satisfaction. Under-reward, over-reward, and inconsistency of reward not only tend to lead to lower satisfaction but encourage behavior that often proves dysfunctional to organizational

Figure 14-8 Comparison of the attributes of the job evaluation systems

Attributes	Job evaluation systems			
	Simple ranking	Job grading	Point system	Factor comparison
Popularity	Least popular	2d or 3d	Most popular (75 percent)	2d or 3d
Type of comparison	Job-to-job	Job-to-category definition	Job-to-category definition	Job-to-job
Number of factors	None	None	Average of 11	Not more than 7
Type of yardstick	None	Single scale of job class descriptions	Multiple scales of points and factor degree definitions	Multiple scales of money (or points) and key job titles
Similarity to other job evaluation systems	Crude form of factor comparison	Crude form of point system	Refinement of job grading	Refinement of simple ranking
Similarity to performance appraisal systems	Corresponds to ranking system of appraisal	Corresponds to grading system	Corresponds to graphic scales	Corresponds to person-to-person system

objectives. A sound, systematic, consistent system of compensation determination will do much to promote equity and satisfaction, provided that such a system is understood and reasonably accepted by most employees.

DISCUSSION QUESTIONS

1　Contrast the impact upon employee satisfaction and behavior of over-reward and under-reward situations.

2　When all employees are paid fundamentally the same amount of compensation (cells 4, 5, and 6), what is the likely impact upon satisfaction and behavior? What effect would a secrecy-of-pay policy have upon the situation?

3　John Jones and Walda Sheean both worked the following hours this week: Monday, 10; Tuesday, 10; Wednesday, 10; Thursday, 8; Friday, 4. Walda is on contract work and is governed by the Walsh-Healey Act, while John's work is covered only by the Fair Labor Standards Act. The prevailing wage for this job has been established by the Department of Labor as $3 per hour. The firm's not-so-liberal policy is to pay each as little as the laws will permit. How many hours of overtime are there for each person? How much pay is there for each?

4　What is the nature and significance of productivity guidelines in establishing annual compensation increases?

5　What is the relationship between job evaluation and employee perceptions of equity?

6　Contrast the four systems of job evaluation with respect to the following: (a) type of scales used, (b) number of scales used, (c) type of comparison process, (d) nature of job analysis data required.

7　Explain how the factor-comparison system can be construed as a refinement of ranking.

8　Explain how the point system can be construed as a refinement of grading.

9　What human reactions and difficulties are often encountered with the introduction of a new job evaluation system? How can some of these be alleviated?

10　What is a maturity curve and how does it differ from job evaluation?

SUPPLEMENTARY READING

DEAN, Michael L., and William B. Wagner: "Labor's Hedge against Inflation: the CPI," *Personnel*, vol. 49, no. 3, May–June 1972, pp. 23–28.

GOODMAN, Paul S., and Abraham Friedman: "An Examination of Adams' Theory of Inequity," *Administrative Science Quarterly*, vol. 16, no. 3, September 1971, pp. 271–288.

JANES, Harold D.: "Issues in Job Evaluation: The Union View," *Personnel Journal*, vol. 51, no. 9, September 1972, pp. 675–679.

KLEIN, Stuart M.: "Pay Factors as Predictors to Satisfaction: A Comparison of Reinforcement, Equity, and Expectancy," *Academy of Management Journal*, vol. 16, no. 4, December 1973, pp. 598–610.

MINER, Mary G.: "Pay Policies: Secret or Open? And Why?" *Personnel Journal*, vol. 53, no. 2, February 1974, pp. 110–115.

PRITCHARD, Robert D., Marvin D. Dunnette, and Dale O. Jorgenson: "Effects of Perceptions of Equity and Inequity on Worker Performance and Satisfaction," *Journal of Applied Psychology*, vol. 56, no. 1, February 1972, pp. 75–94.

FIFTEEN
INCENTIVE
COMPENSATION – PERSON

Employee compensation can be used for two basic purposes: (1) to attract and retain qualified personnel in the organization, and (2) to motivate these personnel to higher levels of performance. The proper establishment of base pay for the job is directed toward the first purpose. In this chapter, we shall be concerned with the uses of money as a means of motivation toward improved performance. This is not to deemphasize or deny the importance of nonmonetary motivational techniques, such as praise, competition, and participation. These, along with others, will be covered under the operative function of integration. Even though we disclaim the existence of the purely economic person, it cannot be denied that money constitutes a powerful motivation for many people. It should take a high position in any list of motivational tools and is sufficiently complicated to deserve detailed coverage. Though many behaviorists downgrade the importance of the role of money, one noted psychologist stated, "Money is our mainspring of motivation in the firm."[1]

Though the discussion in this chapter will be primarily concerned with various types of incentive plans and arrangements for both operative and managerial personnel, we shall lead off with the necessary prerequisites for establishing money as a motivator. Specific problems and complexities of devising, installing, and administering incentive arrangements will also be discussed, thereby demonstrating the very complicated managerial processes involved in such programs. Finally, this chapter will deal with human reactions to motivational schemes, emphasizing again that the unexpected is to be expected.

---

[1]Mason Haire, "The Use of Motivational Techniques in Increasing Productivity in the Business Firm," *Michigan Business Papers*, no. 39, 1964, p. 37.

EXPECTANCY THEORY AND COMPENSATION

In his research concerning what motivates people, Herzberg discovered that money ranked among those factors that do *not* serve to motivate behavior. Rather, he concluded that satisfactory compensation could, at best, serve only to reduce dissatisfaction and preserve the peace. It is suggested that though this condition doubtlessly exists in many organizations, it could well be caused by the manner in which money is actually utilized by managerial personnel.

If money, or any factor, is to motivate behavior, employees must both desire it and believe that it will be forthcoming if they behave in the manner prescribed. Thus, the actual effect of its influence comes from employee assessment of (1) the value of money in meeting personal needs, and (2) the strength of expectancy that the prescribed behavior will actually result in the obtainment of the proffered reward. Vroom therefore suggests the following formula:[2]

$$\text{Motivational force} = \text{valence} \times \text{expectancy}$$

In determining the degree of valence or value of money to employees, one requires knowledge of current need levels. As will be discussed at greater length in Chapter 17, Maslow suggests that those persons whose survival needs are not reasonably well met are likely to place high value upon money as a means of gratifying physiological requirements. In addition, since people are rarely exclusively economic in their orientation, employees will have to compare positive monetary outcomes with all possible losses, e.g., social rejection if the incentive plan clashes with primary group norms. Despite its lower order of importance in certain groups, there is evidence that money is attractive and has real value for large numbers of organizational employees.

The greatest difficulty in monetary motivation lies in the expectancy portion of the formula. Employees will subjectively assess the likelihood that desired compensation will *actually* be forthcoming. This requires consideration of two major items: (1) personal capacity to perform the prescribed act, and (2) perception that such behavior will actually be rewarded. Obviously, if the person highly desires money and is offered $1 million to high-jump 10 feet, the motivational force is likely to be zero, since this is far beyond the current world's record. Supervisors can assist in increasing abilities through training, increasing confidence in capacities by encouragement, and removing organizational obstacles to employee performance.

Perhaps the greatest difficulty in regard to expectancy is convincing the employee that management can be trusted to pay off when the prescribed behavior is forthcoming. If the incentive scheme is so complicated that accountants have difficulty in understanding, then expectancy is likely to be low. If superior performance has been accorded little or only slightly higher pay increases in the past, then the assessment of instrumentality of monetary rewards is likely to be low. Organizations that use base pay supplemented by merit-rating schemes to determine periodic pay increases are less likely to breed high expectancies than those utilizing individual incentive plans. In a study of varying degrees of expectancy achieved in a firm of 2,000 employees, Schwab discovered that the perceived individual linkage of money with behavior was highest among those on individual incentive plans, next highest for those on group incentive,

---

[2]Victor H. Vroom, *Work and Motivation*, John Wiley & Sons, Inc., New York, 1964, p. 183.

and lowest for those on hourly pay plans.[3] Supporting the thesis that objectives have higher valence when attached to performance that requires effort, those on incentive systems tended to place higher values on money. Money-behavior instrumentality or linkage was measured by asking employees to choose one of the available choices in the following statement: "How much pay I get depends on (1) how much I produce, (2) my seniority, (3) my job level, (4) the union, (5) overtime and hours of work, and (6) my coworkers." The first choice would demonstrate the greatest linkage and trust in management to "put the money where the mouth is!"

Research in this same organization revealed that though employees on incentive plans were more highly motivated than those on hourly pay, the latter were *more* satisfied with the pay actually received.[4] Productivity was highest under the individual piece-rate system and lowest under the hourly. In separate measures of satisfaction, hourly paid personnel reported the highest satisfaction with pay received, individual-incentive employees next highest, and those on group plans reported the greatest dissatisfaction. Thus, it is suggested that one may have to choose between developing motivated employees or satisfied employees. In this chapter, we are concerned with motivation through money, and will now turn our attention to the specifics of various incentive schemes.

COMPLEXITIES OF INCENTIVE COMPENSATION SYSTEMS

The management that embarks upon a program of incentive compensation for all or any part of the personnel of an organization should be fully aware of the attendant demands and difficulties likely to be encountered. It should first be noted that nonincentive compensation, that is, payment on the basis of time expended, is the most commonly used arrangement for operative personnel. One of a continuing series of surveys of approximately eighteen million office and plant employees in major metropolitan areas revealed that almost all office employees and 86 percent of the plant workers are paid on the basis of time.[5] Payment on the basis of time is steadily increasing inasmuch as the preceding survey conducted seven years earlier indicated that 80 percent of plant workers were paid on an hourly basis. Variable compensation is more widely used for managerial personnel, with two-thirds to four-fifths of companies in various surveys reporting some type of executive bonus plan. Incentive compensation is very common for sales personnel, with the widespread use of commissions and bonuses based on sales quotas achieved. This type of compensation is relatively rare for professional and technical employees.

Among the complexities and difficulties that will be encountered in establishing an incentive arrangement are the following: (1) some acceptable and reasonably accurate measure of varying employee performance must be devised; (2) such measures should be related to desired organizational goals; (3) data concerning such varying performances must be collected daily, weekly, or monthly; (4) standards established should

---

[3]Donald P. Schwab, "Impact of Alternative Compensation Systems on Pay Valence and Instrumentality Perceptions," *Journal of Applied Psychology*, vol. 58, no. 3, December 1973, pp. 308–312.

[4]Donald P. Schwab and Marc J. Wallace, Jr., "Correlates of Employee Satisfaction with Pay," *Industrial Relations*, vol. 13, no. 2, February 1974, pp. 78–89.

[5]John Howell Cox, "Time and Incentive Pay Practices in Urban Areas," *Monthly Labor Review*, vol. 94, no. 12, December 1971, pp. 53–56.

be of uniform difficulty among the covered group; (5) total compensation of salary plus incentives should be consistent among incentive groups and between incentive and nonincentive groups; (6) performance standards must be adjusted periodically to account for both minor and major changes in work procedures; (7) union opposition must be expected and dealt with; and (8) varied employee reactions to the designed incentives must be anticipated. A review of this list should demonstrate why incentive compensation is applied to far less than half of the nation's working population.

Concerning the first item of an accurate measure of performance, time study is the management technique which can best supply a performance standard for operative production employees. A specific answer is derived from this study, e.g., 50 units of product produced per hour. Portions of the time study process can be characterized as scientific, but much of it is simply systematic. Certain assumptions and elements of arbitrariness can be challenged by both the employee and the union. There are problems of selecting a representative worker, selecting a representative sample of the work, allowing for variable delays, providing for the accumulation of fatigue, and trying to outwit the worker, as she or he is fully aware of the effect of the resulting standard upon total compensation. Many firms report that three-fourths of their total grievances issue from this process of establishing performance standards. In the sales area, time and duty analyses as well as past experience are used to establish quotas and standards. As indicated in Chapter 13, if merit-rating increases are to be given to stimulate improved performance, the design of the scale constitutes the task of devising a standard of desired performance. The resulting standards should be accurate, sufficiently objective to be compared with performance results, and reasonably acceptable to the employee. If not acceptable, it is obvious that incentive will be lacking.

Often there is a difference between what activities can be measured accurately and what activities contribute toward desired organizational goals. Some managements have discovered that employees have been motivated by a system to contribute to goals *not* considered desirable, e.g., a piece rate that pays off on quantity to the detriment of quality or an executive bonus based on short-run profits to the detriment of long-run goals of the firm. There is obviously a demanding administrative task of collecting the results of performance. Inspectors, cost-control clerks, supervisors, and the operatives themselves must report and attest to the accuracy of results achieved. It is not unknown for work produced during one period to be held in a "kitty" for reporting during another period when the employees feel that the compensation will be more acceptable to either them or management. Thus, management must deal with uncertainty as well as facts in controlling the activities of an organization. Administering an incentive compensation system is costly in terms of daily administration, as evidenced in both monetary expenditures and friction in human relationships.

Incentive compensation is designed to result in varying total compensation for different people on the same job. Performance standards must be established for different projects to be accomplished by the same person or different persons. Some project standards will constitute "gravy" jobs while others will be "stinkers." It is extremely difficult, if not impossible, to ensure that all standards established are of uniform difficulty.

As indicated previously, some personnel in a firm will be on incentives, while the majority may well be on time payment. It is not unknown for a skilled subordinate to receive greater compensation through incentives than the supervisor will receive. In one paint and varnish company, two of thirty salesmen earned more than $50,000 a year on straight commission, while the president's salary and bonus amounted to $42,000.[6] One salesman for a soft-drink distributor has averaged income over twice that of the president of the company for a period of four years. At times, a traditionally low-paid, low-skilled group can, through incentives, contribute to an imbalance between their total compensation and that of a high-skilled, high-salaried group. The resulting human conflicts and controversies are inevitable and bitter. Thus, management cannot legislate pay for a portion of the organization without considering the possible effects upon personnel *not* under that particular plan.

From the day a performance standard is established, it begins to deteriorate in quality and accuracy. Small changes are introduced which add up to substantial changes. A new method is devised by methods analysis, a new machine or system is installed, or a significant shortcut is discovered by the operative employee. All serve to contribute to the inaccuracy of the original standard. Changing this standard is difficult both technically and in terms of human relationships. Employees usually resist any changes which will tend to cut their income or increase the effort required. Some specific human reactions and difficulties in this regard will be discussed later in this chapter.

The traditional, official posture of organized labor is one of opposition. In practice, many unions accept incentive compensation and protest possible cuts in total pay should it be removed. One study indicated an *absence* of correlation between unionization and the presence of an incentive arrangement.[7] However, the typical desire of the union for labor solidarity, which often means uniform compensation for all personnel on a single job, leads it to harass firms that hold to the philosophy of incentive compensation. At the least, the union will stand guard over the process of establishing and administering standards, ready at any moment to process a grievance protesting a decision which leads to less compensation for its members.

Despite the difficulties and problems enumerated above, the fact is that a number of firms feel that the returns in motivation are worth the costs. In general, incentives will be used more frequently when labor represents a higher percentage of the costs of manufacturing. In the cigarette industry, for example, the labor cost averages 12 percent, and approximately 3 percent of the firms in the industry use wage incentives. This is to be compared with the footwear industry, where labor costs are 50 percent and an average of 71 percent of the firms use incentive compensation.[8] In work-clothing manufacturing, over 80 percent of production and related workers are paid under incentive wage plans.[9] Thus, it is believed that additional productivity will result, thereby effecting a reduction in labor costs per unit. Incentive wage plans are also a matter of tradition in various industries. In steel, for example, though labor costs amount to only 7.3 percent of the total, the usage of wage incentives stands at approximately 60 percent of the firms. When the work is machine-paced, incentives are either dropped or replaced by group incentives geared to enhancing equipment

[6]Richard C. Smyth, "Financial Incentives for Salesmen," *Harvard Business Review*, vol. 46, no. 1, January–February 1968, p. 111.

[7]Robert B. McKersie, Carroll F. Miller, Jr., and William E. Quarterman, "Some Indicators of Incentive Plan Prevalence," *Monthly Labor Review*, vol. 87, no. 3, March 1964, pp. 271–276.

[8]Ibid., p. 272.

[9]George L. Stelluto, "Report on Incentive Pay in Manufacturing Industries," *Monthly Labor Review*, vol. 92, no. 7, July 1968, p. 50.

utilization. In most of the manufacturing industries where production operations are heavily machine-paced, the proportion of production workers under incentive arrangements is less than 10 percent.[10]

INCENTIVE PLANS FOR OPERATIVES

A wide variety of incentive wage plans for operative production employees have been devised and used by manufacturing firms. In general, they can be classified into two categories: piece rates and time bonuses. Examples of these types are as follows:

I. Piece rates
　　1. Straight piecework plan
　　2. Taylor piecework plan
　　3. Group piecework plan
II. Time bonuses
　　A. Bonus based on *time saved*
　　　　1. Halsey plan
　　　　2. 100 percent time premium plan
　　　　3. Bedaux plan
　　B. Bonus based on *time worked*
　　　　1. Rowan plan
　　　　2. Emerson plan
　　C. Bonus based on *standard time*
　　　　Gantt task and bonus plan

The above classification is based on the fundamental elements of any wage incentive plan: units of output, standard time, time worked, and time saved. Using these elements, many organizations develop their own particular plans without using any of the examples given above. Thus, we may establish a standard output in pieces, e.g., fifty per hour, and elect to compensate the worker for each piece produced. Or a standard time may be established for a project, e.g., 12 hours, and the worker awarded a bonus if this standard is met or exceeded. If the job is done in 8 hours, the time saved would be 4 hours. We may pay a bonus percentage which is multiplied by the value of the standard time (12), or of time worked (8), or of time saved (4). The value of any one hour should be determined by job evaluation as described in the preceding chapter. In the previously cited survey, where 14 percent of plant workers were on incentive arrangement, approximately half were on piece rate and half received a bonus based on one of the three types of time.[11]

STRAIGHT PIECEWORK　This most commonly used incentive system involves a fixed price per unit of output based upon a combination of time study and job evaluation. Thus, if the standard is 50 units per hour, the base rate $3 per hour, and the employee produces 500 units in an 8-hour day, then the piecework rate is 6 cents and the total earnings are $30. Often, hourly earnings are guaranteed for the time worked, 8 hours, leaving incentive earnings of $6.

---

[10]Ibid., p. 51.
[11]John Howell Cox, op. cit., p. 54.

TAYLOR PIECEWORK PLAN   This plan, originated by Frederick W. Taylor, involved establishment of two piece rates: one for above-average output and one for average and below-average performance. Thus, with a standard of 60 units per hour, units produced up to 59 might carry a rate of 4 cents, while those at 60 or above carry 6 cents. The tremendous strength of the incentive is revealed by the pay of $2.36 one would receive if 59 units were produced as compared with $3.60 if the standard were met by producing *one more.*

GROUP PIECEWORK PLAN   At times, the work of a single individual cannot be differentiated from that of the group, e.g., in a soap-flake-packaging line of four operatives or a fuel-pump assembly line requiring three employees to complete one pump. In these situations, a standard can be set for the group. Below this standard, hourly rates are received. Above the standard, a group bonus is earned which can be shared equally or according to base hourly rates if they differ.

THE HALSEY PLAN   This is a time-saved bonus plan which is ordinarily used when accurate performance standards have *not* been established. The hours saved by an employee are computed by subtracting hours worked from standard time. The value of such time saved is then *shared* by the employee and the organization because of the admitted looseness of standard times. Thus, if 12 standard hours of work is completed in 8 hours, the employee may receive pay for the 8 hours plus that for 2 of the 4 hours saved. For example, 8 hours worked times $3 per hour equals $24 guaranteed pay. To this is added 50 percent of the value of the 4 hours saved, which is $6, making a total income of $30.

THE 100 PERCENT TIME PREMIUM PLAN   When accurate time standards are created through time study or work sampling, the employee may be awarded the *full value* of the time saved. Thus, in the above illustration, one would receive the guaranteed $24 plus 100 percent of the time saved of $12, making a total income of $36. This plan is identical in effect with the straight piecework plan, the only difference being that one is expressed in terms of standard hours and the other in standard units.

THE BEDAUX PLAN   This is also a time-saving bonus plan used when carefully established performance standards are present. It differs from the 100 percent plan in that the basic unit of time is the *minute*, termed a "B," and the employee is allocated *less* than 100 percent of the savings, e.g., 75 percent. The remaining 25 percent is awarded to those personnel who made meeting the standard possible—material handlers, setup personnel, and the supervisor. The idea of providing for the motivation of indirect help is an excellent one, but it is not good to take the funds for this out of the usual bonus earned by the employee.

THE ROWAN PLAN   This plan pays a bonus based on the time worked. An efficiency percentage is computed by dividing the time saved by the standard time; e.g., 4 hours saved divided by 12 standard hours equals $33^{1}/_3$ percent efficiency. The employee is paid the guaranteed amount, $24, plus a bonus of $33^{1}/_3$ percent of this $24, equaling a total income of $32. This system is used when performance standards are *very* poor and the management wishes to install an automatic brake upon total income. It is apparent that the employee cannot double total wages regardless of how "efficient" he or she is.

THE EMERSON PLAN Like the Rowan, this plan is based on an index of efficiency multiplied by the value of the time worked. The differences are (1) the index is computed by dividing standard time by the time actually worked; e.g., 36 standard hours completed in a 40-hour week equals 90 percent efficiency; (2) an arbitrary scale of bonus percentages is prepared for varying efficiencies; and (3) a bonus is often paid for efficiencies as low as 65 percent. This plan is sometimes used for clerical personnel on a weekly basis where present performance is so poor that bonuses based on 100 percent of standard would appear to be impossible of attainment. Thus to improve their *expectancy* that output standards can actually be met, personnel are gradually led up from the markedly substandard level of performance to a point where they receive a 20 percent bonus for 100 percent performance. Efficiencies beyond this are also accorded additional pay.

THE GANTT TASK AND BONUS PLAN This plan, created by Henry L. Gantt, is the only one that pays a bonus percentage multiplied by the value of *standard* time. As such, it will pay *more* than either straight piecework or the 100 percent time premium plans. It, like the Taylor system, provides for a substantial differential between standard and substandard work. If the employee does not make standard, the $24 per day (8 × $3) is received. If the employee does 8 standard hours of work during this 8-hour day, the value of this, $24, is received, plus a bonus of 20 percent times $24, or a total of $28.80.

The choice of incentive pay plans for operative employees is very large, particularly when it is realized that firms can devise their own using the basic elements of output, time saved, time worked, and standard time. The effecting of employee assessment of high expectancies will be materially increased if the plan possesses such characteristics as the following:

1 The plan should be simple, understandable, and calculable by the employee.
2 Earnings should vary directly with increased output and efficiency.
3 Earnings should be paid to the employee as soon as possible.
4 Work standards should be carefully developed through systematic studies or else provision made for deficiencies in the incentive plan.
5 Incentive rates should be guaranteed against change unless there is a change in method, equipment, or specifications of material.
6 The base hourly rate should be guaranteed to the employee regardless of daily output. Of course, if standards are consistently not met by an individual, he or she should be retrained, transferred, or severed. If they are consistently not met by the group, either the standard is technically incorrect or we are experiencing restriction of output.
7 The spread between normal incentive earnings and the base hourly rate should be sufficient to stimulate greater than normal effort from the employee. This is usually estimated to be from 30 to 40 percent above straight hourly earnings.

Because of the difficulties of adhering to such characteristics, some firms have abandoned individual incentives for what is termed "measured day work." Work standards are retained but employees are paid on an hourly basis. Comparisons of performance results with these standards are made for the worker and for the department, and pressure is exerted upon the employee and supervisor to meet these standards. Thus, supervision and pressure are substituted for money as the incentive to meet the standard.

HUMAN PROBLEMS OF INCENTIVE COMPENSATION

It is difficult enough to devise a technically workable incentive arrangement, but it is far more difficult to devise one that will truly elicit the behavior desired. People do not always act as management intends they should. A few live up to the "economic man" model, but more are concerned with acceptance by their associates. Space does not permit an extensive treatment of the human relations problems growing out of incentive systems, but four will be discussed briefly: (1) the ratebuster, (2) the reaction to changes in methods, equipment, and materials, (3) the reaction to lack of uniformity in tightness of standards, and (4) informal restriction of output. All these problems revolve around employee fear of management and a desire for security.

A *ratebuster* is an employee who produces far in excess of standard, and consequently in excess of the production of most of the members of a work group. Ratebusters are found even in situations where fair and accurate work standards have been established. There is a feeling among most employees that management will stand for paying only so much bonus, and that if one or more employees make excessive bonuses, the rates will be cut. There is great informal pressure upon all employees to conform to the production level of most of the group. It therefore follows that the employee who does not conform has to have a strong personality, and often a strong physique, in order to resist these pressures. Dalton discovered nine ratebusters in a group of eighty-four employees in a Chicago plant.[12] Among various characteristics, these men possessed the following: (1) they were family men who were not "joiners" of community organizations, (2) they came from families of higher socioeconomic level, (3) they were more likely to be nominal Protestants than Catholics, and (4) they were normally Republicans who read a conservative newspaper.

The ratebuster is usually ostracized by other workers and operates as if isolated; few if any close relationships are established with regulars or other "isolates." The values of additional money have been balanced against the values of group acceptance, with the decision going to the former. In theory, management should look with favor upon the ratebuster and pay double and triple wages when they are earned. In practice, management often prefers *not* to have a ratebuster, feeling that she or he is a disruptive influence in the shop; and indeed there have been times when the ratebuster has been transferred to other jobs in order to smooth relations. This type of management appears to want incentives, but only in limited amounts; they seem to join with the larger group of employees and bring pressure to restrict production of individuals. But if the standards are properly established, there is little justification for not paying the production genius all that is earned.

No firm is ever static and unchanging. Small and large changes in methods, equipment, and materials will be constantly introduced. The worker's desire for security and distrust of management call for an explicit policy to the effect that management will not cut the rate unless there is a substantial change in methods, equipment, and/or materials. The fear of rate slashing goes back to the Taylor era, when there was widespread cutting of the worst sort. If a change is substantial (and there is difficulty in defining this word "substantial"), there should be clear agreement between labor and management that the work standard can be revised. This revision usually

---

[12]Melville Dalton, "The Industrial 'Ratebuster': A Characterization," *Applied Anthropology*, vol. 7, no. 1, Winter 1948.

means an increase in total pay for the employee even though the unit rate is reduced. This compensation can be construed as a sharing with labor of gains in productivity and a purchase of the employee's cooperation. The worker expects to, and will, share in the gains of these technological changes, but not to the extent of receiving the same unit rate.

Sometimes a mistake has been made in a time-studied standard. This mistake can be one of two types, the creation of an excessively loose standard or an excessively tight one. The former error may be discovered if the greater bulk of employees make bonuses of over 50 percent of regular earnings when only the usual 25 to 30 percent was intended. The error is frequently undiscovered, however, because of restriction of output by the employees. Such errors can occur just as often as mistakes of the other type, an excessively tight standard. In the latter situation, the employee and the union usually demand a restudy in the hope of loosening the standard. In the case of the loose standard, management is bound by the policy of no change, unless there is a major change in conditions. For this reason some managements introduce work changes for the sole purpose of justifying a revision of standard. The practice is not desirable, but it often is the only feasible approach to the problem. It would admittedly be better if employees and unions would recognize that mistakes of this type may also merit a restudy; but there is always the tendency to hide such mistakes by a restriction of output.

An even more difficult problem lies in the many small and seemingly insignificant changes in method, equipment, and materials that occur in most firms. These changes are initiated by both management and labor, through informal and formal means. No one change appears to justify a change in the rate, but the cumulative effect of many changes can be disastrous. Often there is only one remedy: complete restudy of all jobs under the incentive plan. The accuracy of work standards has a tendency to deteriorate with the passage of time from the very first day of installation.

A third human problem issues from inconsistencies in the accuracy of standards. The supervisor has the additional problem of awarding easy and tough jobs on an equitable basis. If awarded on a systematic basis, such as seniority or taking turns, one must predict in advance the classification of each job. This often means a balance of its easiness in relation to how long it will last. A moderately tight job lasting four hours may be preferred to an easy one lasting twenty minutes.

Various factors have been identified as contributing to lack of uniformity in work standards. As indicated earlier, newly studied jobs are likely to have tighter rates while older ones have been affected by many small changes. Rates set during times of prosperity tend to be looser than those established during recessions; time study personnel are psychologically affected by their environment. The smaller the profit margin on an item, the tighter the rate is likely to be. Jobs that involve higher levels of skill tend to have looser rates since they cannot be as closely studied as low-skilled tasks. In departments where there is greater group cohesiveness, which leads to sanctions on the ratebuster and greater cooperation in informally sharing work and falsifying timecards, standards are likely to be looser. Sayles has observed that in departments with higher percentages of union membership the rates are likely to be looser in recognition of that threat.[13] Strategic, isolated, and dangerous jobs tend to be

---

[13]Leonard R. Sayles, "A Case Study of Union Participation in Technological Change," *Human Organization,* Spring 1952, pp. 5–15.

favored with looser rates. Thus, the causes are limitless and the possibilities for trouble and problems of administration are great.

In all the above discussion, the concept of restriction of output has been involved. This is the major defense of employees in the informal battle with management that takes place through the incentive wage device. The fact that the term "ratebuster" is used is an indication that there is restriction of effort. A tabulating of the average incentive earnings of the group can also show this restriction. Instead of a normal distribution of individual outputs, there is a rapid rise to the informally agreed-upon amount, whatever the employees feel management will "put up with"; and after that point few, if any, operatives make bonuses in excess of this level. Those who make above the allowed amount are ratebusters. In a study by Roy, two kinds of restricters were noted.[14] There was quota restriction on "gravy" jobs that the men did not want to kill. He estimated that an average of 1.39 hours were wasted daily in this manner. On "stinkers" where it was felt that meeting standard would be very difficult, the men hardly tried after this was ascertained. Instead of quota restriction, there was "goldbricking." Roy estimated the average percentage of standard met on goldbricking jobs as 56 percent.

Restriction of output is tangible evidence of the power of social over monetary desires, but it does not eliminate the value of monetary motivation. The entire group is producing at a level which is in excess of the amount produced under the formerly administered time rates. For example, in one corrugated container company, a stable firm operating in a stable industry, the conversion to incentive pay resulted in increased output for sixteen of eighteen operations.[15] In comparing the average plant efficiency in the ten months prior to incentive-plan installation (a process consuming twenty-six months) with that achieved in a ten-month period afterward, it was calculated that an overall increase of 58 percent was effected along with an increase in employee earnings of 25 percent. In more dynamic and uncertain environments, the development of effective incentive schemes is extremely difficult and often impossible.

MONETARY MOTIVATION OF MANAGERS

The wage plans discussed above are not adaptable to all groups of employees. Aside from time payment, which is very widespread in all occupations, most of these plans are used primarily among operatives in production. There are some plans, such as the Emerson, that are highly adaptable to office employees—typists, file clerks, and the like. Motivation of sales personnel through commission payments and bonuses of various types is extremely widespread. In comparison with operative production jobs, the determination of what constitutes desired behavior is somewhat more difficult. Firms often want *more* than just quantity sales, e.g., missionary work to develop new accounts, full-line selling, collection of market information, training junior sales personnel, etc. The design of the incentive scheme must link payoff with the model of behavior desired.

[14]Donald Roy, "Quota Restriction and Goldbricking in a Machine Shop," *The American Journal of Sociology*, March 1952, pp. 427–442.

[15]Donald L. McManis and William G. Dick, "Monetary Incentives in Today's Industrial Setting," *Personnel Journal*, vol. 52, no. 5, May 1973, pp. 387–392.

Perhaps the most complicated incentive design task is that related to motivating managerial personnel. Members of management are subject to stimulation by monetary techniques like any other group of people. Though informal pressures exist among managers, the individual usually shows a greater willingness to distinguish himself or herself from the group. Consequently managers are frequently highly responsive to motivational devices, particularly those of the monetary type.

As in the cases of operative employees and salesmen, the place to begin the design of an executive incentive compensation system is with the types of behavior desired by the organization. Cassell suggests that this will differ significantly by organizational level and type of work.[16] For the top executive, the emphasis should be on entrepreneurial behavior emphasizing risk taking. These people can drastically influence the direction of the enterprise and should be encouraged to innovate, originate action, and assume the necessary risks for organizational growth and development. Consequently, incentive compensation should be geared to profits, degree of market penetration, acquisitions, and new-product development. However, it is important to recognize that such incentives cannot be established and administered by formulas emphasizing equal treatment, as is so often the case for lower-level executives. Each executive's behavior should be subjected to hard and detailed scrutiny, and nonformulistic decisions made as to the extra compensation deserved.

The most typical incentive arrangement for executives is payment of annual bonuses geared to profits. A typical plan would specify that after achievement of 6 to 8 percent return on invested capital, 10 to 12 percent of the additional profits will be paid into an executive bonus fund. Because of the complex and dynamic nature of the top executive job, allocation of individual bonuses should be geared to intensive, person-by-person reviews that culminate in varying amounts each year, depending upon specific accomplishments. An alternative method would be a ritual allocation of percentage increase equal to the ratio of the bonus fund to total executive salaries. Though this would make for easier decision making, it materially reduces the linkage between behavior and payoff. Bonus systems for executives are quite common in such industries as automobiles, retail chains, department stores, electrical appliances, office equipment, textiles, and chemicals. They are relatively rare in public utilities, banking, mining, railroads, and life insurance. Where numerous short-term decisions can influence profit and a decentralized type of organization structure is utilized, the firm is more likely to adopt some type of executive bonus system.

For lower-level executives, the emphasis in desired behavior is often on smooth administration and cooperative relationships with others within the organization. Bonus systems may be based on department- or division-wide ratings of general quality of performance, and specific allocations to individual executives are often a percentage of base salary. It is desirable that the executive identify personal performance with that of the department. Such an approach preserves the basic salary structure while keeping a portion of the pay in flexible form. It does not pretend scientifically to evaluate and measure each executive's contribution, which is so greatly affected by a myriad of interdependent relationships with others.

Gearing the system to desired behavior must also consider the general nature of the people who are to be motivated. It has been suggested that the needs, and

---

[16]Frank H. Cassell, "Management Incentive Compensation," *California Management Review*, vol. 8, no. 4, Summer 1966, p. 16.

consequently the motivation, of executives will vary at different levels of age. Those below forty require cash, and thus salary is most important; pay deferred until after retirement would be pointless as a motivator. Those over fifty-five will be more interested in deferred income, stock options, and the like. Those between forty and fifty-five might better respond to a variety of compensations, including bonuses, stock options, paid-up life insurance, and some contribution to deferred income. Though this approach makes the administrative problems far more complex, perhaps extra compensation can be tailored to the needs of groups of executives on the basis of both organization level and age of the executive.

Because of the graduated income tax system in this country, attention has been switched from analyzing desired executive behavior to the goal of trying to increase the amount of compensation actually retained by higher-paid executives. In recent years, many different compensation methods have been introduced in reaction to income tax regulations. For example, pay deferred until after retirement is one way to reduce the income tax. In deferred stock payment, the shares of company stock are transferred to the executive after a stated time. One pays income tax at regular rates on the full market value of the stock when the transfer is completed. In restricted stock payments, the stock is transferred immediately, but it is made subject to restrictions which usually prohibit the manager from selling for some time. A recent change in internal revenue rules makes this taxable at the time the allocation is nonforfeitable, rather than when all restrictions are removed. The list of such devices is seemingly unlimited; Stayton and Lesher itemize some eight basic approaches used by 100 large companies.[17] As suggested above, "The most devastating effect of the graduated income tax on executive compensation strategy has been to divert top management attention from the motivational aspects."[18]

Though steadily declining in favor, a widespread motivational device for higher executives is the stock option. The executive is given the option to purchase company stock at current market prices that may be exercised anytime within a five-year period. If several options are given, they must be exercised in chronological sequence. Once the stock is obtained, it must be held for three years before sale in order to merit capital gains treatment. One is also taxed on paper gains at the time of exercising the option. These more stringent regulations concerning stock options, qualified as company expenses, were introduced in 1969 and have led to a marked decrease in their popularity; 49 percent of one sample of large companies had such plans in 1972 as compared with 93 percent in 1969.[19] There is growing interest in the "nonqualified" stock option which permits establishment of any option price, exercise within a ten-year period, sale of shares after holding for only six months, and exercise of multiple options in any order desired. Paper profits at exercise are taxable as current income (50 percent maximum) while capital gains (35 percent maximum) apply if the stock is held for over six months. It has been concluded by some experts that stock

[17]John P. Stayton and John L. Lesher, "Recent Developments in Deferred Compensation," *Business Horizons*, vol. 12, no. 2, April 1969, pp. 75–76.

[18]Arch Patton, "The Impact of Taxes on Executive Compensation Strategy," *Business Horizons*, vol. 9, no. 1, Spring 1966, p. 95.

[19]George H. Foote, "Performance Shares Revitalize Executive Stock Plans," *Harvard Business Review*, vol. 51, no. 6, November–December 1973, p. 121.

options are inferior in effect to cash salary in all but the highest-income classes. A seriously declining stock market makes them even more unattractive.

There are other alternatives besides salary, bonuses, and stocks of various types. Postponement of portions of salary until after retirement is attractive when inflationary rates are not excessive. This helps the executive through reducing the levels of taxable income and benefits the firm in that it can utilize and invest saved funds more effectively than can the individual. Attention is turning in some quarters to performance objectives, a high-level variation of MBO. A challenging objective is established, e.g., there will be cumulative growth in earnings per share of 10 percent during the next four years. If achieved, the executive will receive a previously committed award of 1,000 shares of stock, one-half of which is in cash so that taxes may be paid on the total. Finally, with inflation and high individual tax rates, the popularity of various "perks" or perquisites has increased. Among these are use of company automobiles, club memberships, personal financial planning services, use of company airplanes, annual physicals at plush health resorts, and major medical insurance with no deductibles. Many of these are not taxable as income received.

The total amount of compensation for different levels and types of executives will vary by industry and company size. In a survey of 3,157 manufacturing companies conducted by the Executive Compensation Service of the American Management Association, the Chief Executive Officer typically receives the top money.[20] With this designated as 100 percent, the corresponding percentages for varying executive jobs in smaller firms ($2 million to $5 million in sales) were as follows: Chief Operating Officer, 90 percent; Executive Vice-President, 62 percent; top Marketing Executive, 60 percent; top Manufacturing Executive, 54 percent; top Financial Executive, 51 percent; and top Personnel Executive, 34 percent. For larger firms ($200 million to $500 million in sales), they were: Chief Operating Officer, 81 percent; Executive Vice-President, 60 percent; top Marketing Executive, 40 percent; top Manufacturing Executive, 45 percent; top Financial Executive, 48 percent; and top Personnel Executive, 32 percent. Those interested in personnel management as a career should note the relatively lower compensation in both sizes of firms. Within this broad manufacturing grouping, firms in electrical equipment and chemicals pay significantly more than do those of comparable size in building materials, food, and paper and allied products.

Members of the lowest level of management are also involved in monetary motivation systems. The job of the first-level supervisor, in particular, is subject to measurement. Among the various measurement criteria that can be used are (1) total production of the department, (2) quality reject rate, (3) meeting of production schedules, and (4) meeting of the departmental budget. Going back to Figure 5-6 in Chapter 5, we can see that these are standards of performance covering quantity, quality, time, and costs. First-level supervisors can be awarded bonuses based on a total or partial measurement of their performance. Though they have a less close relationship with profits of the firm than do the higher executives, a few firms follow the practice of sharing profits with first-level supervisors. In many such instances, the profits to be shared are the profits from production and are unaffected by the other factors in and out of the business that can affect net profits.

[20]Jay Engle, "Top Management: Hot Topic in Corporate Compensation," *The Personnel Administrator*, vol. 19, no. 1, January–February 1974, p. 35.

SUMMARY

Money is an important and widely recognized motivational tool. The rise of the human relations school has placed it in a more balanced perspective but has not destroyed its basic significance. It is important to be aware of how the dollar can be utilized to stimulate the type of activity desired. In general, motivation force will equal the value of money to the person multiplied by the degree of expectancy that it will be forthcoming if the desired act is performed. Assessment of expectancy is affected by self-determination of capacity to perform and by a degree of trust in management assuring that money will actually be allocated. Such trust requires understanding of the incentive scheme and consistent linkage of money and desired behavior.

Incentive compensation is fraught with complexities involving such problems as accurate establishment and maintenance of work standards, collection of performance data, maintenance of consistency in total income, and maintenance of work standards in the light of change. There are limitless alternatives in the selection or creation of an incentive plan for operative employees. All, however, involve the standard elements of output, time saved, time worked, and standard time.

Despite the wide variation in the details of wage-incentive plans, they should hold certain characteristics in common, criteria that have to do with simplicity, flexibility, study of conditions, and fairness to the employee.

Adhering to these criteria is important in avoiding or minimizing some of the human relations problems exemplified by restriction of output and resistance to improvements in methods, equipment, and materials. In general, these problems issue from a basic distrust of management and a desire for security and protection. Ensuring that the incentive arrangement conforms to the criteria of good design and operation is one excellent way to reduce the fears of the employees. In addition, it is usually necessary to guarantee that there will be no rate reduction unless there are substantial changes in conditions. It is important to live up to the spirit of this guarantee as well as the letter.

Design of incentive arrangements for managerial personnel is highly complex. There are a variety of behavioral goals as well as a wide assortment of possible monetary arrangements. Basic salary, bonuses geared to profits, stocks, performance shares, and a variety of "perks" can be utilized to effect a relationship between organizational goals and executive behavior.

DISCUSSION QUESTIONS

1 Define and distinguish between equity and expectancy with respect to the subject of compensation.
2 What factors affect the assessment of expectancy in the motivation formula?
3 What factors affect the assessment of valence in the motivation formula?
4 Jane Jones produced 1,000 units of product in an eight-hour day. The work output standard established by time study is 100 per hour. If the base hourly rate is $3, how much income would she receive under (a) straight piecework, (b) 100 percent time premium, (c) the Rowan plan, and (d) the Gantt plan with a 10 percent bonus?
5 What is the relation between job evaluation, time study, and incentive wage plans?

6 What are some alternative types of incentive compensation that have been used for top-level executives?

7 George, Carla, and Roger work as a team on a group piecework system. The hourly rates are $6, $4, and $3, respectively. For each unit of output, the complete team is allocated $5. If today, in their usual eight-hour day, the team produced 26 units, what would be each person's pay if the bonus is divided equally? If it is divided according to base pay?

8 What factors tend to contribute to relatively loose incentive output standards for various jobs?

9 Briefly discuss the major human problems issuing from the administration of incentive payment schemes.

10 Discuss the Emerson efficiency index in terms of expectancy theory.

SUPPLEMENTARY READING

CAMMANN, Cortlandt, and Edward E. Lawler III: "Employee Reactions to a Pay Incentive Plan," *Journal of Applied Psychology*, vol. 58, no. 2, October 1973, pp. 163–172.

MCCONKEY, Dale D.: "The 'Jackass Effect' in Management Compensation," *Business Horizons*, vol. 17, no. 3, June 1974, pp. 81–91.

PITTS, Robert A.: "Incentive Compensation and Organization Design," *Personnel Journal*, vol. 53, no. 5, May 1974, pp. 338–344, 348.

SALTER, Malcolm: "Tailor Incentive Compensation to Strategy," *Harvard Business Review*, vol. 51, no. 2, March–April 1973, pp. 94–102.

SASSER, W. Earl, and Samuel H. Pettway: "Case of Big Mac's Pay Plans," *Harvard Business Review*, vol. 52, no. 4, July–August 1974, pp. 30–46, 156–158.

SCHWAB, Donald P., and Marc J. Wallace, Jr.: "Correlates of Employee Satisfaction with Pay," *Industrial Relations*, vol. 13, no. 1, February 1974, pp. 78–89.

SIXTEEN
SUPPLEMENTARY
COMPENSATION – GROUP

Monetary compensation assumes many different forms in modern business enterprises. The two most commonly found forms, the base rate and incentive wages, have been discussed in the two preceding chapters. In this chapter we shall discuss additional forms of monetary remuneration, among them the guaranteed annual wage, employee profit sharing, production-sharing plans, employee stock ownership, and suggestion systems. Though these forms of compensation cannot constitute a substitute for a fair and competitive base wage or salary, there is growing evidence that they are beginning to be substituted for individual incentive systems. Perhaps the basic force behind this trend is the increased mechanization and automation of work processes, making it more difficult to identify and measure the particular contributions of individuals. In addition, labor unions have leaned toward supplementary compensation for larger groups in place of individually oriented incentive arrangements that tend to reduce union solidarity. Behavioral management theorists have also contributed to the acceptance of group compensation plans in their emphasis upon the cooperative power of the informal organization and primary work groups.

All of the above-mentioned forms of supplementary group compensation will be briefly discussed in this chapter. Each constitutes a difficult and complex arrangement in itself, and more detailed coverage will be found in the literature. In the brief space here, only the philosophies behind these plans will be covered, along with some discussion of salient features.

GUARANTEED ANNUAL WAGE

The guaranteed annual wage is a form of compensation that has received much attention and publicity in recent years. Much of the publicity has resulted from the drive of certain labor unions in the old Congress of Industrial Organizations to obtain from employers some form of guaranteed wage for rank and file employees. As the union leadership says, the employee must eat and live fifty-two weeks a year, whether or not work is actually available in the firm. One has great need for some form of stable income. The amount of the base rate is therefore not at issue here, but rather the steadiness of its payment throughout the year. Recent studies of morale have indicated that employees are often more interested in the security provided by steadiness of income than they are in the actual amount.

Obviously, an annual wage of some type has great appeal for the employee, for the fear of a layoff is very real and grave. Not all the values of continued employment go to the worker, however. Among the returns to the business enterprise of a steady employment of resources are increased efficiency resulting from uninterrupted operations, avoidance of the expenses of layoff and rehiring, higher employee morale, lower training costs, lower unemployment compensation taxes, and greater employee acceptance of changes introduced by management. Realization of such values has led many businesses to attempt to effect greater stabilization of operations and employment. In essence, the business must combat the effects of seasonal and cyclical fluctuations as well as the effects on employment of the introduction of technological changes, vagaries in shipments of supplies, strikes in related industries, etc. Firms engaged in producing consumer goods rather than industrial products seem to have the greatest success in effecting some degree of stability. Much, however, can be done in all companies to develop more stable operations. Perhaps the most fundamental contribution would be the application of sound principles of scientific management to every phase of the enterprise. Proper planning, organizing, directing, and controlling of the work to be done, with the emphasis upon planning for the future, will do much to reduce fluctuations in the level of operations. This means sound planning in production, sales, finance, personnel, and other functions of business. In addition to good basic management, specific methods that have been used to advantage are as follows: (1) producing to stock during slack seasons, (2) diversifying the product line to permit dovetailing of production, (3) stimulating sales in slack seasons by special discounts, contests, and consumer education, (4) effecting transfers of personnel to accommodate intraorganizational fluctuations in output, (5) training employees to be able to do various types of jobs, thus creating a flexible organization that can adjust to variations in output, (6) elimination of overtime and retrieval of any work previously subcontracted, (7) absorption of the usual attrition of the work force without replacement, and (8) shorter workweeks and temporary plant shutdowns to adjust inventory.

The first and most important problem is to effect a stability of operations which, in turn, will result in a greater stability of employment. This is the basic desire of both labor and management. If *employment* stability cannot be had, *wage* stability may still be sought. Much of the writing and work in this field in the last three decades has centered around wage stability rather than employment stability. There have been at least three main approaches to the solution of this problem: (1) unemployment compensation established by the government, (2) guaranteed annual wage plans initiated by private enterprise, and (3) supplemental unemployment compensation plans that were started at the behest of labor organizations. Each of these three plans will be discussed below.

Unemployment compensation

Though a few states had passed unemployment compensation legislation prior to 1935, it was not until passage of the federal Social Security Act that such compensation became widespread in the United States. The original act provided for a payroll tax on employers of 3 percent of the first $3,000 pay of each covered employee. The Employment Security Amendment of 1970 changed both the tax rate and base to 3.2 percent of the first $4,200 of pay. The federal law provides an incentive to states to pass suitable unemployment compensation legislation. If state laws and administrations meet certain standards, most of the tax monies (2.7 percent) can be retained by the state. The remaining 0.5 percent is also usually returned under special conditions, e.g., extended benefits for employees when the unemployment rate is unusually high, and benefits paid that cannot be charged to the employer's account. The present law covers over 80 percent of the work force.

In the states, reserve accounts are established for each employer and the applicable tax rate may increase or decrease, depending upon the firm's experience. In Minnesota and Vermont, for example, the tax rate can rise to 5 percent for employers with unusually bad experiences. Overall, the average tax collection throughout the nation has been less than 1 percent of total wages in covered employment. Since total fringe benefits are currently estimated to be approximately 30 percent of total compensation, it is apparent that the unemployment compensation feature is a relatively inexpensive one.

If a person is laid off by the firm, she or he is eligible for unemployment compensation for a twenty-six-week period. If the nation's unemployment rate is above 4.5 percent, an additional thirteen weeks of compensation is provided, the monies for which are not charged to the employer's reserve account. In general, the employer's fund is not charged if the person quits, is discharged for cause, is on strike, or refuses suitable employment in other firms. The Employment Security Amendment of 1970 provides, however, that total refusal of the state to pay unemployment compensation can be based on only two reasons: (1) discharge for misconduct in connection with work and (2) fraud in connection with filing a claim. Thus, the employee who merely quits or refuses suitable work cannot be denied *some* compensation. Most states provide for a penalty in these cases, e.g., a five-week waiting period instead of the usual one, or a 25 percent reduction in maximum benefits. Though the employer's fund is not charged in these instances, the fact that the government will still pay compensation from other tax monies (the 0.5 percent portion of the 3.2 percent) indicates that this is becoming a form of welfare payment.

It is estimated that unemployment benefits actually received amount to only one-fourth to one-third of wages lost during the payment period. Though the federal government has established a goal for the states of a minimum payment of two-thirds of the average weekly wage, only five of the fifty-two states and territories have met this standard. Thirty-seven, however, have maximum benefits amounting to over 50 percent of the average weekly wage.[1] Specific rules and administrations vary from state to state, and some labor unions have established a classification of state administrations ranging from "tough" to "easy."

Guaranteed annual wage plans initiated by private companies

Some progressive managements have long been aware of the value of stable operations and steady employee earnings. The number of managements that have been willing and

[1] Joseph A. Hickey, "State Unemployment Insurance Laws: Status Report," *Monthly Labor Review*, vol. 96, no. 1, January 1973, p. 37.

able to create and administer a private plan to stabilize employment and/or earnings is relatively few. Perhaps the three best-known plans of this type are the systems of the Procter and Gamble Company, George A. Hormel Company, and the Nunn-Bush Shoe Company. It will be noted that all three companies are engaged in producing a consumer good.

Most of the private annual wage plans have three basic characteristics: (1) they guarantee a certain number of weeks of employment and/or wages, (2) they restrict the number of employees who are covered, and (3) they suspend the operation of the plan under conditions of extreme emergency, such as fire, flood, explosion, and strikes. The Procter and Gamble plan, for example, guarantees employment for forty-eight weeks each year to employees who have two or more years of service. There is no guarantee that the wage rate will not be lowered in the event that an employee must be transferred to another job. Stability of operations and employment has been effected by educating the consumer to buy more steadily, producing to stock during slack sales periods, and transferring personnel from job to job as operations fluctuate. The Hormel plan guarantees a certain amount of wages rather than employment. Fifty-two paychecks a year will be paid to eligible employees, with a minimum weekly pay for thirty-eight hours. Total wages for the year are established on the basis of the sales forecast. This total pay is divided into fifty-two equal amounts. Actual working hours frequently vary from week to week, but the pay received does not. Overages and underages of time worked relative to pay received are balanced periodically. The Nunn-Bush plan is similar to that of Hormel, providing for a guarantee of fifty-two paychecks. The guarantee to employees is based on the concept that labor will receive 20 percent of the value of products sold. Thus, the percentage of sales is guaranteed to labor, but the dollar amount is not. Examples of other companies that have similar guaranteed annual wage plans are William Wrigley, Jr., Armstrong Cork, and Sears, Roebuck, and Company. It will again be noted that all companies named produce and sell consumer goods. The first requirement for a guarantee of this type is a reasonable degree of stability of operations, and this stability is usually more easily obtained in consumer goods industries than in those which deal in producer goods.

Supplemental unemployment compensation

In the last two decades there has been much interest in the idea of extending the concept of the guaranteed annual wage to larger numbers of workers, in producer goods as well as consumer goods industries. All people live and eat fifty-two weeks a year, and employment security has become more important to many employees and labor unions than has base or incentive compensation. In the vanguard of this movement have been three labor unions: the United Auto Workers, the United Steel Workers, and the Ladies' Garment Workers. In a survey of 1,773 major labor contracts during 1963–1964, it was found that 247 provided for supplemental unemployment compensation.[2] The United Steel Workers was involved in 81 of these contracts, the United Auto Workers in 66, and the Ladies' Garment Workers in 40. Though these plans were frequently referred to as "guaranteed annual wage" plans, their makeup is more

---

[2]"Supplemental Unemployment Benefit Plans in Major Agreements," *Monthly Labor Review*, January 1965, pp. 19–26.

accurately described by the terms "supplemental unemployment compensation" or "supplemental unemployment benefits."

In all cases the plan is financed solely by the company, usually at the rate of 10 cents per hour worked. A trust fund is established into which these monies are paid, and the size of this fund is a major factor in determining the amount of benefits to be paid. Employees earn credits at the average rate of one-half per week worked, and these are cashed in upon layoff at the rate of one credit for one week of compensation. In most cases, an employee can accumulate a maximum of only fifty-two weeks of credit. If the trust fund is low in funds, more than one credit may be required for each week of benefits.

In most plans, the unemployed individual must qualify for state unemployment compensation. Payments from both sources usually amount to 50 to 80 percent of weekly wages, but the United Auto Workers Union has negotiated an arrangement that pays 95 percent of normal wages less a small charge ($7.50) for job-related expenses that would not be incurred by the laid-off employee. An automobile worker with seven years of seniority is entitled to this 95 percent of normal pay for up to a year. A worker with one year of seniority is eligible for 95 percent for thirty-one weeks.

Many people have claimed that instead of being a true guaranteed annual wage plan, these arrangements merely constitute an additional fringe benefit of a dime an hour, which the employees have chosen to receive in this form rather than as a part of the wage. Certainly many of the high-seniority employees, who are unlikely to receive any benefit from this fund, are not enthusiastic about such arrangements. It is estimated that these plans cover about 4 percent of wage and salaried employees in the private economy.[3] This compares with 25 percent coverage for major medical insurance plans, and 75 percent for hospitalization benefits. As state unemployment compensation laws are improved in benefit coverage, the need for this supplementary allotment will tend to decrease.

The tie-in with state unemployment compensation programs has posed a legal problem in many states. If the employee receives money from the fund, some states have ruled that she or he is not unemployed and therefore deserves no state unemployment compensation. Most states, however, have ruled that an unemployed person can receive payments from both sources. In those states that do prohibit simultaneous receipt of both types of benefits, arrangements are usually made for alternate receipt; that is, the unemployed person will first collect state unemployment compensation for a few weeks and then catch up with his benefits from the trust fund.

The most recent innovation in the use of the supplementary compensation fund is the provision for earnings protection for employees whose pay has been reduced while still employed. The steel industry and the United Steel Workers have agreed that whenever workers suffer a cut in earnings due to technological change or other causes, they will receive from the fund a transitional quarterly earnings supplement to bring them up to 85 percent of average quarterly income in the previous year. For example, when workers are transferred from old open-hearth furnaces to new oxygen furnaces, the increase in productivity results in fewer high-pay furnace jobs to be filled; many workers suffer significant pay cuts in moving to lower-paid jobs. Under the plan, a $4-an-hour worker moving to a $3-an-hour job would receive $3.40 an hour during the first quarter following the change, $3.27 in the second, $3.12 in the third, and finally the

[3]"Guaranteeing a Year of Work and Pay," *Monthly Labor Review*, vol. 91, no. 1, January 1968, p. iv.

$3 in the fourth and succeeding quarters.[4] Though originally intended for technological displacement, difficulties in defining eligibility have led to a decision to include *any* worker whose earnings go down. These additional benefits are to be financed by an extra 2 cents per hour worked being placed into the supplemental fund.

There is one final problem that worries many managements. If the total benefits are raised from 60 percent to 80, 90, or 100 percent of straight-time earnings, what happens to the incentive to seek work? Many would claim that the unemployed person would attempt to *avoid* return to work if thirty-nine to fifty-two weeks of regular earnings are assured while *not* working. Doubtlessly some individuals would be thus affected; some even lose their desire for work under a less than 40 percent average payment of state unemployment compensation. Though the trend in this country is to provide some minimum compensation for all, the difference between that and average income does not make the guarantees highly attractive. Those influenced by the "work ethic" would still find work attractive regardless of financial benefits. If the movement of the young toward an existentialist ethic continues and if the *lack* of movement by most organizations toward job enrichment is unchanged, then perhaps we will become increasingly concerned about the impact upon behavior of larger financial guarantees.

EMPLOYEE PROFIT SHARING

Employee profit-sharing plans constitute one of the more glamorous forms of monetary compensation used in business. The definition of employee profit sharing was formulated quite well by the International Cooperative Congress in 1897, as follows: "An agreement freely entered into, by which the employees receive a share, fixed in advance, of the profits."[5] Though the term "profit sharing" is not used precisely by many, a true plan generally involves a definite commitment on the part of management to pay, over and above a fair wage, extra compensation which bears a definite percentage relationship to company profits or declared dividends. This definition would exclude bonuses based on profits which are not assured on a continuing basis. It is desirable that the commitment be sufficiently exact so that the profit-sharing fund can be computed by anyone for any given profit amount.

There are two main types of employee profit-sharing plans: (1) cash or current distribution and (2) trust or deferred distribution. Under the current arrangement, benefits are distributed among participants in cash at least once each year. The deferred type involves a trust fund, the benefits from which are distributed in the event of death, retirement, or disability. Some managements prefer to place part of the profit share in trust and to distribute the remainder in cash each year.

There are varying estimates of the number of profit-sharing plans actually in existence. The major source of information is the Internal Revenue Service, which qualifies deferred-sharing trusts for tax exemption purposes. The Service requires that a qualified plan (1) cover a majority of plant and office employees, (2) stipulate a management commitment of periodic contributions to the fund based on profits, (3) be communicated to all covered employees, (4) contain a formula for allocating shares to employees, and (5) establish a definite method of distribution. As of 1968, the Service

---

[4]"Protecting the Paychecks of Victims of Technology," *Business Week*, Aug. 16, 1969, p. 98.
[5]David F. Schloss, *Methods of Industrial Remuneration*, Williams & Norgate, Ltd., London, 1898, p. 242.

had approved a total of 77,000 plans of the deferred type.[6] Estimates of abandonment would reduce this to approximately 60,000. In addition there are an unknown number of cash or current distribution plans. One author suggests that the total lies somewhere between 85,000 and 145,000 plans.[7]

The failure rate of these profit-sharing plans is very high during periods of economic difficulty. One study showed that up until World War II, the discontinuance rate ranged from 50 to 60 percent of the plans discovered by the research agency.[8] Since 1940 the failure rate has been much lower. Obviously, when there are no profits to share, difficulties of plan administration will be encountered.

Objectives of and objections to employee profit sharing

Employee profit sharing is a highly controversial form of employee remuneration. Its ardent advocates are found in the Council of Profit Sharing Industries, an association of employers founded in the 1940s. Among the values claimed for profit sharing are that it (1) effects an increase in productive efficiency through reducing costs and increasing output, (2) improves employee morale and reduces labor-management strife, (3) provides for employee security in the event of death, retirement, or disability, (4) constitutes a mechanism of employee economic education, (5) reduces turnover, and (6) improves public relations. A few managements also view profit sharing as a means of drawing labor and management closer together, thus inhibiting the development of a labor union. Other specific objectives can be tied into the mechanics of a plan. For example, one firm distributes profit shares solely on the basis of attendance, and its absenteeism rate is far below the industry average. Another distributes shares on the basis of employee savings, thereby contributing to employee security.

The opponents of employee profit sharing are equally vehement in their objections. Profit sharing is a type of compensation about which there is much emotion. One major objection is that such compensation is often a poor incentive to efficiency in production. In the first place, the extra income bears little relation to individual employee effort, for many factors besides labor affect profits. It is also difficult to gauge the varying contributions of individuals. In contrast with the participant in managerial profit sharing, the individual employee has even less effect upon the profits of the enterprise. Most plans do not attempt to distinguish among individuals on the basis of effort and contribution. Thus the incentive value is reduced. In the second place, the extra compensation is not paid soon after the employee effort is made. Cash plans usually pay yearly, and companies utilizing deferred distribution can only issue reports of account balances. Employee profit sharing, therefore, hardly qualifies as an incentive wage plan. A second major objection is that such plans often prove to be a morale depressant rather than stimulant. Employees often regard a reasonably steady profit share as a part of their regular income. When there is no profit share to be paid, they are greatly upset and frequently ask for abolition of the system accompanied by a raise in base pay. If employees cannot or do not distinguish between the regular wage and the profit share, the company is assuming great risk and receiving little or no return.

[6]"No Slowdown in the Growth of Profit Sharing Trusts," *Personnel Journal*, vol. 48, no. 6, June 1969, p. 464.

[7]Edgar R. Czarnecki, "Effect of Profit-Sharing Plans on Union Organizing Efforts," *Personnel Journal*, vol. 49, no. 9, September 1970, p. 765.

[8] National Industrial Conference Board, *Profit Sharing for Workers*, Studies in Personnel Policy, no. 97, New York, 1948, p. 35.

Concerning the value of increasing employee security, opponents of profit sharing maintain that a properly constituted pension plan will more adequately meet the security objective of employees. Under a pension plan, the benefit is a known amount and the company contributes enough money to produce this amount of pension. Under a deferred-profit-sharing trust, the contribution is variable, depending on profits, and the resulting retirement benefit is also variable. In defense of profit-sharing trusts, it can be stated that many firms cannot afford the high fixed cost of a pension plan. With profit sharing they can make a contribution to employee security without saddling the firm with an inflexible cost.

Probably the most telling argument against employee profit sharing is its high discontinuance rate. These discontinuances are caused by such factors as employee apathy to the profit-sharing appeal, lack of profits, insufficient shares, union opposition, and unintelligent plan administration. In the previously cited survey of discontinuance rates, approximately two out of five were abolished as a result of sale or merger of the company. The greater bulk were discontinued for a variety of reasons that could be encompassed under the label of "poor management." Employee profit sharing *can* work, but it is an extremely difficult form of remuneration to administer effectively, and therefore often constitutes a greater incentive to management than it does to the employees. It takes excellent management to make it work. Perhaps the activities that management undertakes to make it operate *actually* create the results; perhaps the profit share is a catalytic agent which permits the other parts of the personnel program to work more effectively. The requirements of effective plan administration will be discussed after a presentation of the mechanics of typical plans.

The framework of employee profit sharing

As we have said, employee profit-sharing plans are of two types, current and deferred distribution. Prior to 1940, there were three current plans to one of the deferred type in the United States. With a favorable change in tax regulations in the early 1940s plus the effects of the wage freeze of World War II, the number of deferred plans has greatly increased. It is believed that the deferred plans are in the majority today.

One of the first items to be established under a profit-sharing plan is that of specifying the nature and amount of the company contribution to the profit-sharing fund. It must be decided (1) whether the share shall be a percentage of profits or a wage dividend based on the stock dividend declared by the board of directors; (2) whether the percentage shall be fixed or on a sliding scale based on the amount of profits; (3) whether the percentage shall be computed before or after dividends to stockholders, taxes, and amounts to be reinvested in the firm; and (4) what shall be the amount of profits to be shared. One study showed that profits contributed under current-distribution plans constituted 16 to 25 percent of profits before taxes and that under deferred-distribution arrangements they amounted to 7 to 15 percent.[9] Most firms establish a set percentage to be applied to profits. A few, such as Eastman Kodak, authorize the board of directors to declare a wage dividend each time a stock dividend is paid. A percentage is applied to the employee's total yearly income to determine his or her wage dividend.

---

[9]Edwin B. Flippo, *Profit Sharing in American Business*, Ohio State University Bureau of Business Research, Columbus, Ohio, 1954, p. 38.

A second part of the framework of profit sharing is the determination of the personnel eligible for participation in the plan. The usual stipulation is a certain amount of seniority. Current-distribution plans usually specify a period of one year or less, while deferred plans ordinarily require from two to five years of service. Current-distribution plans tend to emphasize the objective of production incentive while plans of the deferred type stress security. Also of importance is deciding how these participating employees shall share in the profit-sharing fund. Two bases are widely used, earnings and service. Often they are used in conjunction with each other, as is shown in the example in Figure 16-1. Another common approach is to credit each employee with one point for a certain amount of salary, and with another point for each year of service. Thus, one employee may have 30 points from salary and 20 points from service for a total of 50. The value of one point is determined as shown in Figure 16-1. The total number of points of all employees is divided into the profit-sharing amount. The individual's share is then determined by multiplying the value of one point by the total of 50. Other bases of distribution that are sometimes used are merit rating, attendance, savings, and an equal sharing. Regulations of the Bureau of Internal Revenue for the deferred type do not allow tax deductions to the company for amounts in excess of a stipulated percent of total compensation otherwise paid.

A very few plans have provided for loss sharing as well as profit sharing. The few companies that have provided for scheduled cuts in wages geared to losses have never enforced these provisions. It is significant to note that all these companies have

Figure 16-1 Profit-sharing plan bases of distribution, Champion Paper and Fibre Company

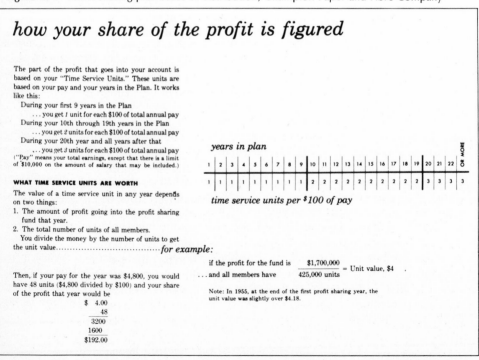

how your share of the profit is figured

The part of the profit that goes into your account is based on your "Time Service Units." These units are based on your pay and your years in the Plan. It works like this:

During your first 9 years in the Plan
  ...you get *1* unit for each $100 of total annual pay
During your 10th through 19th years in the Plan
  ...you get *2* units for each $100 of total annual pay
During your 20th year and all years after that
  ...you get *3* units for each $100 of total annual pay
("Pay" means your total earnings, except that there is a limit of $10,000 on the amount of salary that may be included.)

WHAT TIME SERVICE UNITS ARE WORTH

The value of a time service unit in any year depends on two things:
1. The amount of profit going into the profit sharing fund that year.
2. The total number of units of all members.
  You divide the money by the number of units to get the unit value.............................*for example:*

Then, if your pay for the year was $4,800, you would have 48 units ($4,800 divided by $100) and your share of the profit that year would be

```
$  4.00
      48
    3200
    1600
 $192.00
```

years in plan

1	2	3	4	5	6	7	8	9	10	11	12	13	14	15	16	17	18	19	20	21	22	OR MORE
1	1	1	1	1	1	1	1	1	2	2	2	2	2	2	2	2	2	2	3	3	3	3

time service units per $100 of pay

if the profit for the fund is $\dfrac{\$1,700,000}{425,000 \text{ units}}$ = Unit value, $4
...and all members have

Note: In 1955, at the end of the first profit sharing year, the unit value was slightly over $4.18.

abandoned the practice of employee profit sharing. Employee profit sharing is so difficult to administer effectively that it is safe to say that the firm that entertains the thought of loss sharing might just as well forget about this type of compensation.

Employee vesting of shares in deferred-distribution trust funds is provided for by many firms. Some object to vesting on the grounds of labor turnover, pointing out that if their employees lose shares upon quitting the firm, they are more likely to remain. Those that do provide for vesting usually establish a graduated type of ownership of shares, such as 10 percent of the share for each year of service. Company contributions to the profit-sharing trust are deductible as expenses on income tax returns. They are not taxable to the employee until the time the funds are actually received. In addition, any returns from fund investments, or from forfeitures of persons who resigned without full vesting, are distributed among participants on the same basis as the regular profit share. Plans that are discontinued are, of course, fully vested. No employer contributions can revert to the company.

Administration of employee profit-sharing plans

As we have emphasized earlier, the successful operation of employee profit sharing is difficult to effect. By successful operation is meant a situation in which profits are shared and the company derives a known return in production, cooperation, turnover, morale, or the like. Many firms go through the mechanics of computing and distributing profit shares, but receive little return. In general, it is easier to administer an employee profit-sharing plan in a small company, where the employees number in the hundreds or fewer. Proper administration is essentially a problem of *employee education*. A person must be convinced that the base wage is fair in relation to the going rate, and that any profit shares paid are over and above this rate. One must see the relation between efforts and the success of the enterprise, and must learn to accept profits as variable and the absence of profits as a challenge to increased effort. At the least, one should learn not to be shocked or disgruntled by variations.

In general, successful administration of employee profit-sharing plans encompasses the following activities and policies:

1 The sharing of profits should be accompanied by a feeling of employee-employer partnership. Tangible evidences of this feeling can be given by such activities as the joint administration of the plan, joint labor-management shop committees which consult on operating problems, the distribution of meaningful and understandable financial information, the establishment of an employee stock-ownership plan, the permitting of employee inspection of company books, and the distribution of information concerning production, shipments, receipts, etc.

2 An effective employee educational plan concerning the nature of profits and the profit-sharing plan is necessary if any cooperation is to be expected. This involves some teaching of basic economics. It also involves continuous education concerning the significant events affecting profits and profit sharing. All types of media of communication should be utilized, such as individual status reports, group meetings, letters from the company president, social occasions to dramatize the plan, and supervisory contacts.

3 The nonprofit year should be provided for in advance. Management should not allow itself or its employees to be surprised by the sudden decline or absence of profits and the profit share. The following is presented not as a formula for avoiding trouble during the nonprofit year but rather as a series of suggestions which have been found helpful in minimizing trouble at this time:[10]

a. If a company is especially fearful of possible adverse effects during nonprofit periods, it should adopt the deferred-distribution type of plan.

b. The conditioning of employees to the possibility of profitless years in advance, by education concerning the nature and functioning of profits under the economic system, tends to result in more desirable employee reactions.

c. If a company is desirous of stimulating employee cooperation and performance during the profitless period, it should adopt the current-distribution type. Whereas the deferred type seems to stimulate little reaction during the nonprofit period, the current type usually effects some result. It should be recognized, however, that the chances for loss are almost as great as the opportunities for gain.

d. The larger the average individual profit share paid to the employee during profitable periods, the more favorable will be the reaction of employees during the nonprofit periods.

e. It is essential to keep the profit share and the regular wage distinctly separate in the eyes of the employees.

f. The more education of employees that is undertaken on a continuous basis, the less trouble there is during a nonprofit period.

g. The adoption of some type of partnership attitude and program tends to induce more favorable employee reactions during nonprofit periods.

4 It should be recognized that labor organizations and employee profit-sharing plans are not necessarily incompatible. Though the traditional attitude of organized labor has been antagonistic, apparently this approach is currently being modified. Thus far, there is no legal requirement that management must bargain over a profit-sharing plan as there is in the cases of pensions and employee stock-ownership plans.

There is evidence of a growing labor union interest in the possibilities of profit sharing. Perhaps the largest union-negotiated profit-sharing plan is the one at American Motors, though it does not rank as an unqualified success. It is estimated that profit-sharing plans cover approximately 25 percent of all blue-collar workers employed by nonunion companies; however, only 6 percent of covered workers are in unionized firms.[11]

A recent statistical study suggests that employee profit-sharing plans may be used by companies to forestall organization of employees by labor unions. In a study of the five-year period, 1961 to 1966, one-half of the representation elections held were sampled.[12] In these it was found that 759 elections were held in plants having profit-sharing plans. Unions won 336 and lost 423, for a winning ratio of 44.3 percent. This compares with a 59.8 percent victory ratio for unions in all other elections held during this five-year period. After adjustment for such variables as size of company, geographic location, industry, and the particular unions involved, the difference in wins was determined to be statistically significant.

[10]Ibid., p. 129.

[11]"When Workers Share the Pie," *Business Week*, July 22, 1967, p. 118.

[12]Edgar R. Czarnecki, "Profit Sharing and Union Organizing," *Monthly Labor Review*, vol. 92, no. 12, December 1969, p. 61.

The primary conclusion of the above discussion is that management should not fall for the glamorous appeal of employee profit sharing and embark upon such a venture thoughtlessly. Profit sharing should not even be considered unless present relationships between labor and management are reasonably good. It can make something better out of something good, but it is quite ineffective in situations of poor labor-management relations. Management should also be thoroughly aware of all the work that is necessary to make employee profit sharing effective. As we have pointed out earlier, the effectiveness of the plan is very probably produced by its necessary administration, that is, by the activities of education and partnership, rather than by the profit share itself.

PRODUCTION-SHARING PLANS

Closely allied to profit sharing, but not properly classified as such, are production-sharing plans. Like profit sharing, these plans are designed to appeal to the cooperative instincts of large groups. Instead of sharing profits, however, savings resulting from a reduction in labor or production costs are divided among the employees. Since production savings are narrower in scope than company profits, there is a greater possibility of the individual's being able to relate his or her efforts to the results of a smaller group of persons.

In essence, these production-sharing plans constitute an attempt to share in productivity gains. Shultz classifies such attempts into four categories: (1) the General Motors type, where base compensation is automatically adjusted by the productivity index discussed in Chapter 14, (2) the longshoremen type, where management paid approximately $30 million for the right to eliminate wasteful and inefficient practices in the loading and unloading of ships, (3) the ad hoc type, where management and labor adopt a problem-solving approach of working out specific solutions to productivity innovations, and (4) the Scanlon and Kaiser plans.[13]

Perhaps the most famous production-sharing plan is that known as the Scanlon plan. This plan requires the computation of a *normal* labor cost per unit of product produced. If through more cooperation and greater efficiency labor costs can be reduced from the normal level, the entire amount saved is distributed among the workers in the form of a bonus. Lesieur, the heir-apparent to Scanlon, recommends that three-fourths of all savings be distributed with the remaining one-quarter retained by management.[14] One of the earliest successful installations of this plan was made by Scanlon, a United Steel Workers official, in the Lapointe Machine Tool Company of Hudson, Massachusetts. Individual incentives were scrapped in favor of the group incentive of the production-sharing plan. Scanlon claimed that individual incentive plans stimulated cutthroat competition to the detriment of the group, whereas group incentives effected constructive cooperation.

The Scanlon plan is more than a form of monetary compensation. Many authors classify it as a type of union-management relationship rather than a form of remuneration. Essential features of the plan are an attitude of labor-management cooperation

[13]George P. Shultz, "Sharing Gains in Productivity," *The Conference Board Record*, August 1964, pp. 43–45.

[14]Fred G. Lesieur and Elbridge S. Puckett, "The Scanion Plan Has Proved Itself," *Harvard Business Review*, vol. 47, no. 5, September–October 1969, p. 112.

and a system of processing suggestions. The processing of suggestions under the Scanlon plan involves the establishment of departmental production committees composed of the supervisor and a union representative. The supervisor and the union representative meet periodically to discuss individual suggestions and develop general production plans for the department. Suggestions that are either disapproved or outside the province of the department are submitted to a plant-wide screening committee which includes the top leadership of both union and management. There are *no* individual rewards for accepted suggestions. The group prospers through the production-savings bonus. The union is obviously highly involved and encourages suggestions. A contrast of managerial attitudes in eight firms that had abandoned a Scanlon plan with attitudes in ten firms that had retained their plans revealed a significant difference.[15] Those abandoning the plan had significantly lower estimates of employee judgment, dependability, initiative, and alertness. They were also more suspicious of policies encouraging employee participation in decision making. It is apparent that a Scanlon plan is more than a simple sharing of monetary rewards; it is also an indication of basic managerial philosophy.

At the Parker Pen Company, a unionized firm of 1,000 employees, bonuses have been paid in 142 months out of 168, and range from $5^{1}/_{2}$ percent to 20 percent of payroll.[16] At the Atwood Vacuum Machine Company, a unionized firm of 2,000 employees, bonuses have been paid in 163 periods out of 187, and range from 5 to 20 percent of payroll. Over 25,000 suggestions have been turned in by employees of the latter company. In both companies, the levels of bonuses awarded correlate highly with company profits. In both instances, the Scanlon plan replaced an individual incentive system. Under the new arrangement, workers appeared to take a broader interest in company well-being and tended to accept changes and improvements more readily. The number of written grievances dropped because of management's greater willingness to listen. Management was able to stress quality and efficiency in the interests of improving the return to all workers. General sharing led to improved cooperation from indirect workers such as toolroom employees, maintenance personnel, and materials handlers. The accent was on teamwork, both in terms of the spirit that pervaded the shop and in the formula for sharing the extra compensation.

The most publicized production-sharing plan in recent years is the Kaiser Long Range Sharing Plan. This arrangement provides for a sharing of savings in labor, materials, and supply, thus encouraging not only more efficient work but greater attention to the reduction of waste. Employees receive 32.5 percent of any savings as compared with expenditures for the base year. By 1967, over 5,000 suggestions had been submitted and 3,500 accepted and implemented. A specific goal of the plan was protection against layoff for reasons of technology. All covered employees are guaranteed forty hours of pay, fifty-two weeks a year, against the danger of unemployment due to mechanization and automation. In this manner, Kaiser hoped to reduce resistance to changes issuing from improved technology. A second specific goal was the reduction in the number of employees on individual wage incentive plans. The firm hoped to substitute group cooperation through production sharing for individual

---

[15]Robert A. Ruh, Roger L. Wallace, and Carl F. Frost, "Management Attitudes and the Scanlon Plan," *Industrial Relations*, vol. 12, no. 3, October 1973, pp. 282–288.
[16]Ibid., p. 113.

competition through incentive wages. In recent years, the average annual bonus has decreased to one-seventh of the amounts in earlier years. This led to a bargained guarantee of minimum earnings from the fund (10 percent of hourly earnings), to be provided in part by *not* draining the fund for vacations and supplemental unemployment benefits as in the past.[17]

EMPLOYEE STOCK OWNERSHIP

Employee stock-ownership plans had their beginning in this country around the turn of the century. By the 1920s the movement was well established. The Depression of the 1930s dealt these plans a severe blow, and most companies discontinued the practice. Approximately 20 percent of the firms listed on the New York Stock Exchange have some type of stock purchase plan. Such plans are more common among major insurance companies, commerical banks, gas and electric companies, and those with over one-half billion dollars in sales.[18] Employee stock-ownership plans resemble profit-sharing plans in that they grow and flourish during prosperity and are discontinued and die on a large scale during depression. These two types of compensation also have similar objectives, in that there is an attempt to promote an identity of interest between employee and employer by tying the employee to the company objective.

The typical employee ownership plan provides a mechanism through which certain eligible employees may purchase the stock of the company at a reduced rate. Eligibility is usually determined by wage level or years of service or both. Though a few firms offer the stock at the market rate, most cut the price 10 to 20 percent. A second typical feature is that provision is made for installment buying. The employee authorizes a payroll deduction, and stock is periodically purchased for her or him in the market by the company. A less widespread feature of these plans is the issuance of special nonvoting stock for employees at special prices. Most companies prefer to deal in their regular issues. A fourth feature of some plans is the granting of a stock option—a right to purchase a certain amount of stock in the future at a stated price. The stock-option feature is much more widely used in executive compensation plans than it is with the rank and file.

What does the company hope to gain from the creation of an employee stock-ownership plan? As stated above, one of the commonly cited objectives is to promote a mutuality of interests. The employee is encouraged to consider the viewpoint of the company as a stockholder. He or she is also led to read company literature received as a part owner which would probably be ignored as an employee. Other possible values stemming from employee stock ownership are the promotion of thrift and security, the creation of an added incentive to work productively and cooperatively, and the creation of an additional source of investment capital. The employees of Armco Steel Corporation, for example, own 5 percent of that firm's outstanding stock. It was acquired through employee contributions of from 5 to 8 percent of salary or wages received, supplemented by a company contribution of 50 cents on the dollar saved. Stocks are

---

[17]"Kaiser's Cost-Savings Plan Revised," *Monthly Labor review*, vol. 95, no. 5, May 1972, p. 66.
[18]Surendra S. Singhvi, "Motivation through Employee Stock Option Plans," *Personnel Administration/ Public Personnel Review*, vol. 1, no. 3, November–December 1973, p. 61.

held in trust until employees choose to withdraw from the plan or terminate with the company. Over 80 percent of Armco personnel participate in this thrift-stock purchase arrangement.

The high discontinuance rate of these plans during periods of economic difficulty has led many to be highly suspicious of the values of employee stock ownership. The objection of placing too many eggs in one basket is often cited. The employee is asked to invest savings as well as talent in one company, with a consequent lack of investment diversification. Instead of promoting organizational morale, these plans at times seem to contribute to its deterioration. Stock prices fluctuate, and the employee can see nothing in the daily operation of the company to justify such fluctuations. As long as the stock prices go up, morale is good; when they go down, the employee is likely to blame the company—the intermediary who purchased the stock for her or him. There seems to be an implied obligation for protection. For this reason, some firms have a plan feature which guarantees a certain repurchase price. The unhappy situation of the 1930s, when many employees were still paying for stock purchased at inflated prices prior to the stock-market crash, is one to be avoided.

Employee ownership of stock also resembles profit sharing in that the key to effective administration is education of the employee participant. One must understand the nature of stock, dividends, and the stock market. This education requisite is both a duty and an opportunity for the company. Stock ownership, like profit sharing, provides a basis for approaching the employee with company information.

A second essential feature of plan administration is that there should be absolutely no pressure and little promotion in the sale of stock. The company should advertise that the plan is available for eligible persons who may wish to invest, but there should be no special encouragement to buy. As with profit sharing, the philosophy and methods of administration are more important than the particular details of the plan. These forms of compensation can be compared to the frosting on a cake. They can improve upon the good but have little power to make good out of bad. Both should have a low priority in the creation of an effective personnel program.

SUGGESTION SYSTEMS

There is a great amount of confusion concerning the objectives and nature of suggestion systems. Perhaps this is because of the dual objectives of such plans, which in effect make them two different systems. There is first the suggestion system that is designed to encourage the submission of anonymous complaints and gripes. This type of system is more properly classified as a form of communication under the subject of morale.

The second type of suggestion system is more properly classified as a form of supplementary compensation. It is a system designed to encourage and reward the submission of ideas for improving operational efficiency. Even here, there are two divergent philosophies. Some firms run this type of system as a part of their human relations program. Their main objectives seem to be concerned primarily with human beings; that is, they aim to promote the employee's sense of personal significance and achievement. In these systems almost all the suggestions are related to personal needs, covering such subjects as water fountains, parking, and washrooms.

The second philosophy of administering suggestion systems of the idea type is the one we wish to stress here. The emphasis is upon encouraging the submission of valuable and practical ideas for the improvement of operational efficiency. The awards are usually 10 to 20 percent of the first year's savings rather than a flat fee of $5, $10, or $25, the amounts that are usually paid for personal-needs suggestions. The objective is to draw forth practical ideas of improvement where total value is in excess of the costs of administering the system. This is the traditional system of rewarding *individuals* for specific ideas. Behaviorists are more in favor of the Scanlon and Kaiser approaches where the *group* shares in all suggested new ideas through a production-sharing arrangement. There has been no research to indicate the more effective method. Traditionalists claim greater motivation of the individual and thus more ideas. Behaviorists claim more cooperation and less social pressure upon the one with the idea, and thus more ideas actually submitted.

With respect to these traditional suggestion systems, one survey of 473 firms revealed that 29 percent make formal provision for such plans.[19] Approximately one-half of these firms pay from 10 to 14 percent of the first year's savings, and one-tenth pay up to 20 percent.

Administration of suggestion systems

The establishment of any type of suggestion system levies certain administrative requirements upon management. In the first place, the plan must be introduced with a good deal of publicity and employee education. Means for writing and collecting the suggestions must be established. The suggestion box is the hallmark of the system. Suggestions must be processed promptly. A committee is usually established, since the evaluation of most ideas is a subjective process. In the type of system that emphasizes submission of productive ideas, the administration should be in the hands of line management rather than of the personnel department, for line personnel can more accurately evaluate the worth of an idea and determine a fair monetary award. In any event, the receipt of all suggestions must be promptly acknowledged, and those refused must be returned with explanations. Persons whose suggestions are accepted should be promptly rewarded in terms of both recognition and money. When rewarded on the basis of 10 to 20 percent of the first year's savings, it is not unusual to find awards running in the thousands of dollars.

Suggestion-system problems

A number of problems are usually encountered in the establishment and administration of a suggestion plan. There is frequently a considerable amount of apathy or outright opposition to the plan on the part of supervisors. Some of this hostility issues from a feeling that members of management should *give* orders and subordinate personnel *take* orders. Some supervisors have to be convinced that the rank and file employee can have ideas that are equal to or better than those of management. Usually some developmental work is necessary with supervisors upon the introduction of a suggestion system.

---

[19]National Industrial Conference Board, *Personnel Practices in Factory and Office: Manufacturing*, Studies in Personnel Policy, no. 194, New York, 1964, p. 58.

A second problem frequently encountered is the opposition of employees to the concept of a suggestion system. This opposition is somewhat similar to the informal pressures exerted under an incentive wage system. By definition, a good suggestion improves operational efficiency, in that it makes possible the same amount of work, or more, to be done with less effort. Jobs are threatened. Employees are reluctant to submit suggestions which may restrict or destroy their own jobs or the jobs of other workers. There have been occasions when the recipient of an award was forced to give a party for coworkers on the basis that they also had to bear part of the burden of the suggestion. It may be necessary for management to guarantee assistance to present employees who are seriously affected by the installation of a suggestion. As indicated above, the Scanlon and Kaiser plans avoid this problem by permitting all employees to share in savings from ideas. Kaiser guarantees that employees will not be laid off for one year as a result of such improvements.

Other minor problems are sometimes encountered in suggestion systems. For example, many employees have excellent ideas but are unable to express them in writing. It may be possible for certain members of staff and management to provide assistance in preparing suggestions. When a suggestion falls in certain staff areas, it is not unusual to see staff resentment like that of the supervisor described above. There is obviously an administrative cost in running the system. Like all other approaches and practices of good management, suggestion systems are not easy to administer effectively. Going through the motions of announcing a plan and tacking up the boxes is not enough to make the plan work. These systems do work and work well when a proper philosophy and a sufficient degree of energy and enthusiasm are applied. The National Association of Suggestion Systems and its members, which number in excess of 1,000, can testify that suggestion systems designed to increase efficiency can and do work in American business.

SUMMARY

In studying the various types of monetary compensation used in business, we find that it can assume a limitless number of forms. Money is an excellent motivational tool and has long been respected for its power. We have gradually learned more about how to utilize its influence in effecting the types of employee responses desired. The first and most basic form which monetary compensation must assume is a fair base rate. The most effective method for determining this rate is a combination of job evaluation, wage survey, and collective bargaining. In this way the worth of the job is established.

Recognizing that the value of different people on the *same* job will vary with the person, compensation techniques have been developed to reflect these different values. Merit rating or performance appraisal is preferred for some jobs, to compensate varying qualities of performance. Group and individual incentive systems are utilized to draw out above-average effort on the job. Competition of the individual against the work standard is emphasized in these incentive systems.

In addition to the values of competition, there are the returns of group coopera-tion. To stimulate this response on a broad scale, production-sharing and profit-sharing plans have been devised. The difficulty encountered is the problem of specifically relating the extra compensation to the varying contributions of individuals. The accent, however, is primarily upon cooperation toward a mutual objective. A still more indirect type of pressure toward group cooperation is exemplified by employee stock-ownership plans. If the enterprise prospers, its stock values are likely to increase. If employees can share in this increase in organizational value, it is believed that they will be more cognizant of the interests of the group as well as the interests of the entire economic system.

In seeking still other devices for encouraging desired employee behavior, suggestion systems have been established to enhance operational efficiency through the stimulation of practical and valuable ideas. In general, the appeal is directed toward the individual employee. Finally, one of the more significant aspects of monetary compensation, particularly to the rank and file employee, is its steadiness of payment. The desire for a secure income has led labor organizations in recent years to demand a form of the guaranteed annual wage. As yet, the negotiated plans are of the supplemental unemployment benefit type. It may well be that these plans in the future will supplement state unemployment compensation to a level of 100 percent of annual straight hourly earnings. Though these modern plans are primarily the result of a drive by organized labor, certain firms had designed and adopted true guaranteed annual wage plans long before. The hoped-for responses to this type of monetary compensation are a sense of loyalty to the firm and a feeling of security, which will permit greater concentration upon the job at hand.

DISCUSSION QUESTIONS

1   Compare and contrast the traditional suggestion system with the manner in which suggestions are administered under a Scanlon plan.

2   Compare and contrast the goals and methods of employee profit sharing with those of employee stock purchase.

3   Compare and contrast the problems of effecting employment stability with those of generating income stability.

4   Compare and contrast unemployment compensation with supplemental unemployment compensation.

5   What are the purposes of a system of unemployment compensation from the viewpoint of society? From the viewpoint of the employing firm?

6   What is the significance of dividing up the tax monies under employment compensation to the effect that 2.7 percent is allocated one way and 0.5 percent another?

7   Compare and contrast the goal and methods of employee profit-sharing plans with those of production-sharing plans.

8   What is meant by the statement that "an *employee* profit-sharing plan can constitute a greater incentive to management than it does to employees"?

9   How should the organization approach the problem of a profitless year under an employee profit-sharing plan?

10 What are some of the managerial problems involved in designing and administering a traditional employee suggestion system?

SUPPLEMENTARY READING

CZARNECKI, Edgar R.: "Effect of Profit-Sharing Plans on Union Organizing Efforts," *Personnel Journal*, vol. 49, no. 9, September 1970, pp. 763–773.

EDGELL, David L., and Stephen A. Wandner: "Unemployment Insurance: Its Economic Performance," *Monthly Labor Review*, vol. 97, no. 4, April 1974, pp. 33–40.

KRAUS, David: "Employee Stock Purchase Plans," *Business Horizons*, vol. 15, no. 4, August 1972, pp. 25–34.

MAHAN, Paul B.: "Unemployment Insurance: A Unique Self-Insured Group Plan," *Personnel Journal*, vol. 51, no. 10, October 1972, pp. 747–752.

RUH, Robert A., Roger L. Wallace, and Carl F. Frost: "Management Attitudes and the Scanlon Plan," *Industrial Relations*, vol. 12, no. 3, October 1973, pp. 282–288.

SINGHVI, Surendra S.: "Motivation through Employee Stock Option Plans," *Personnel Administration/Public Personnel Review*, vol. 1, no. 3, November–December 1973, pp. 61–66.

CASES FOR PART FIVE

THE CASE OF THE FRUSTRATED EXPERT: GEORGE GRIDLEY*

George Gridley secured his college training at a large state university. For his first two years, he followed a mechanical engineering curriculum; he then switched to commerce. His major course work centered on motion and time study.

Upon graduation he was hired by Wellington Corporation, a large Chicago firm employing 2,500 workers, to work in its standards department. In Gridley's words:

> I was really in a good spot when I graduated. You see, I'm both an engineering and commerce major. You can't beat that combination. I'm just a natural for a standards department because I have the business know-how together with my engineering. Wellington had the best spot for me so I took the job because I could get ahead fastest there. Their interviewer told me when he came over to school to interview us that I had a rare combination his company was glad to find. I went up to Chicago for some additional interviews. I liked them and they liked me, so I took the job.

Gridley reported for work two weeks after graduation, having arrived in Chicago three days before starting work in order to find a place to live. After the usual processing in the personnel department, he was taken up to the standards department to the office of its chief, Mr. McGuire, who had interviewed George before he was hired. McGuire kept George waiting for 10 minutes and then turned to him. George described this meeting.

*Robert Dubin, *Human Relations in Administration*, 2d ed., Prentice-Hall, Inc., Englewood Cliffs, N.J., 1961, pp. 475–478. Used with permission.

I just sat there in McGuire's office watching him work on some papers, not knowing quite what to expect. Finally, he turned to me and said, "Well, Mr. Gridley, are you all set to go to work?" He never did call any of us younger fellows in the department anything but "mister." He told me that there would be a department staff meeting that morning when he would introduce me to everyone. Meantime he gave me the company standards manual and told me I ought to spend several days getting familiar with it. He called his secretary and told her to take me to my desk and get me all the supplies I needed; that ended the interview. He certainly was a cold fish and all the time I worked for him I never could warm up to him. I didn't get any assignment at all the first week but just sat at my desk and worked over the manual. I got to know several of the fellows around me and we went to lunch together.

Gridley was finally assigned to work up the time study on a simple assembly of refrigerator door handles being assembled in a department in which Mason was foreman. When McGuire gave him the assignment, George was so glad to be working he failed to respond with any questions when given the opening by McGuire's query, "Any questions?"

I felt so glad at getting a real job at last that I just said, "I think I can handle this easily, Sir," and left his office. I went and got the drawings for the assembly and studied them for a few hours. Then I went down to Mason's department and told him Mr. McGuire had given me the assignment of working up the refrigerator door handle job. He said that was all right with him. Mason was a crusty old guy who didn't seem to have much education at all. Nobody could remember when he started with the company and he'd been a foreman a long time. I got out the drawings and wanted to talk to him about the job but he sort of brushed them aside and started asking personal questions about me. I figured maybe he couldn't read drawings too easily, so I didn't try that approach again. After I told him about myself and my education he said, "Well, this ought to be easy for you. Let's go over and look at the job."

There were 10 workers assembling the door handles, working for the second day on this job. The first thing that struck George about the job was the casual attitude that seemed to be evident, and the pronounced talking and minor horseplay that continued after Mason and Gridley came over to observe. Mason left almost immediately, saying to the group, "This is Gridley from standards on this new job. He's new with the company."

In talking about it later, Gridley recalled the subsequent developments of that day with some discomfort. He knew that under the union contract, work on a new job was paid for at a guaranteed rate, until the standards and price were set. Then the work went on an incentive basis. But he was scarcely prepared for the complete irreverence with which he was greeted.

Almost the first remark I heard from the group was, "Well, here is the genius who is going to show us how to bust this job wide open without any work at all." You can imagine how the others laughed and what a spot that put me in. I made some comment about "just doing a job" and began observing the assembly work. It seemed to me there was pretty poor discipline in a company where the workers made remarks like that. It got me so that I just automatically reached for a cigarette and started to light it. That same worker saw me and said, "Say, haven't they told you that only fireproof cigarettes are permitted here?" Then I remembered the no-smoking rule. I was so mad by then I just went off to the washroom and smoked. Those damned ignorant workers sure take a lot of pleasure in making life miserable for their betters.

That afternoon George went back to the department and began observing the operation, and made arrangements with Mason and the union steward to time the job on the following morning. Gridley made no suggestions for any assembly procedures changes, figuring he would time the job "as is" rather than force himself to discuss with Mason and the workers some changes he thought might be useful. The principal saving he could see was in proper flow of materials to each work station and he planned to take this into account in working out some standard procedures and estimated prices based upon them. The time study was made the next day as planned.

Gridley immediately took the data back to his desk and spent that day and the following preparing his report. After waiting still another day getting it typed up, he submitted it to McGuire. The figures showed a price of 60 cents a dozen for assembly. McGuire sat down immediately with the report and read it over. It took him only about 10 minutes to go over it, saying not a word to Gridley, who had been asked to wait. Then as Gridley reported:

> He finally looked up at me and said, "Mr. Gridley, this is a good job. From your report I feel your operating scheme is good and your time data shows consistent results. I have Mason's estimate on the job some place. Let me get it." He got out a file and found a memo sheet that had some handwriting on it. "Yes," he said, "here is his estimate. You know in this company we often have foremen estimate prices on simple jobs, just in case we can't handle them up here because of a work load. Then we let the foreman's estimate ride. Mason says 62 cents on that job. You never know how these foremen figure those things out. Mason has done a lot of these refrigerator handle assemblies in his department in the past. Since our study is so close to his figure, I think I'll let his stand. There is only a little better than three per cent difference. This is no reflection on you, understand that, Mr. Gridley. I just feel in this instance it would be valuable to the company and to our operations in the standards department to let Mason think his estimate and our study agree."
>
> Can you imagine anything like that? Here I really put out to give them a job and then McGuire goes ahead and uses some off-the-cuff estimate of a foreman who can't even read prints. That doesn't seem to me to be very good management. Does management really want brains around here or are they just going to run the company by-guess-and-by-gosh all the time?

THE CASE OF THE FLORAL ASSEMBLY LINE

In 1973, the Asbury Florist Corporation was started by James A. Asbury. He opened a small shop near a large state university of over 15,000 students. In the beginning the firm consisted of Asbury, Bill Hodges, who was a floral designer, and Alice Myers, who waited on customers. James Asbury had a small but reasonably profitable business.

In the early part of 1973, Asbury was approached by Warren Hamilton, a graduate student at the university, who had had a considerable amount of business experience. He pointed out that the school constituted a tremendous market for flowers, particularly corsages. He suggested that he could recruit a large number of student salesmen who would work on commission. Asbury felt that this could be done, but he was then concerned with how he could produce enough products to handle this potentially high sales level. Hodges was at the time producing about four corsages per hour, and considerably more time was taken on the more unusual floral displays. A large sales volume would require several more designers. Good designers were hard to find, and the wage rate was rather high. After some discussion and observation of the process of floral arrangement, Hamilton and Asbury decided that production methods could be changed. Many of the operations performed by the designer were purely routine and required little skill. If all such operations could be taken from him, leaving only the final

Figure 16-2 Organization chart, Asbury Florist, Inc.

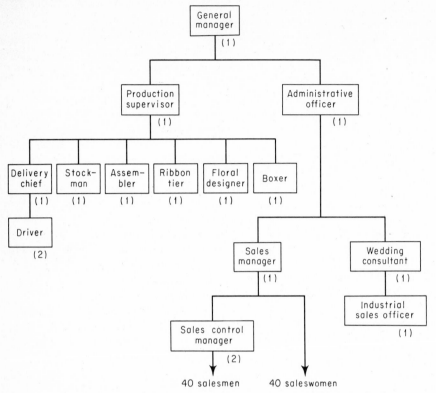

artistic arrangement, output per hour could be materially improved. The one job of designer was divided into five jobs: (1) a stock man, who controls the order slip and assembles the flowers, (2) the assembler, who prepares the flowers by wiring and wrapping with paraffilm strips, (3) the ribbon tier, who prepares bows and maline backing, (4) the designer, who quickly arranges the corsage flowers and attaches the ribbon and maline, and (5) the boxer, who places the corsage in a bag and box. These five persons would work in sequence along a table.

After a trial operation, it was found that the floral assembly line would work. The floral designer could turn out twenty corsages per hour if necessary. Students were hired for the unskilled jobs, and the commission salesmen were recruited. As time passed and sales improved, an industrial salesman was added to contact industrial firms for flower sales. A wedding consultant was also hired to develop that particular market. Since this entire operation was new and relatively unfamiliar to Asbury, wage rates for all personnel were individually negotiated. Some of the personnel in the higher positions contributed to the financing of the enterprise.

As of June 1973, the organization structure of Asbury Florist, Inc., was as indicated in the preceding chart. On the following pages are short job descriptions of the fourteen separate jobs in the firm. Job descriptions were not made of the duties of the commission salesmen and saleswomen. The wage rates of these fourteen jobs were as follows:

Position	Dollars per hour
Administrative officer	$4.50
Assembler	2.30
Boxer	2.30
Delivery chief	2.70
Driver	2.70
Floral designer	4.50
General manager	4.50
Industrial sales officer	Commission
Production supervisor	3.80
Ribbon tier	2.40
Sales control manager	Commission
Sales manager	4.50
Stock man	2.70
Wedding consultant	4.50

After operating under this wage structure for several months, Asbury realized that something would have to be done. The wages paid were somewhat inconsistent. There were very few jobs in his company that were comparable with jobs in other floral concerns, but on the ones that were comparable, he felt that his rates were in line. He made a quick telephone wage survey check of five floral concerns and discovered that the average hourly rate for floral designers was $4.75, for drivers, $3.50, and for boxers, $2.30. He decided to use these three jobs as a base for determining the rates for the other eleven jobs. He consulted with Warren Hamilton, who proposed that some type of simplified job evaluation be applied, since short job descriptions were available.

I. Job title: General manager   II. Job code: A

III. Number employed: One   IV. Date: June 19, 1973

V. Location: Central Office, Ashbury Florist, Inc.

VI. Job summary: Plans, organizes, controls, and coordinates the activities of the entire firm within limits established by the board of directors.

VII. Duties

  A. Daily

   1. Plans progress of business, new enterprises, business procedures, policies, and designs many of the necessary forms.
   2. Advises the administrative officer and wedding consultant on the preparation of sales promotional booklets and pamphlets.
   3. Organizes the entire company, assigns duties, and delegates authority.
   4. Recruits, selects, and trains the managerial force.
   5. Reviews all recommendations for dismissal of employees.
   6. Approves or disapproves all buying expenditures of sales manager and the expenditures of the production supervisor for flowers in excess of $100.
   7. Possesses final authority over expenditures under $1,000.
   8. Handles personally selling accounts in excess of $200.
   9. Supervises generally and consults daily with administrative officer and production supervisor.
   10. Spot-checks quality of production.
   11. Prepares retail price lists with the assistance of the production supervisor and administrative officer.

  B. Periodical: Prepares weekly report of progress of business to stockholders.

C. Occasional: None.

VIII. Job-knowledge requirements: Order procedure, flower code, wholesale and retail prices, characteristics of floral trade, and characteristics of most of the available floral arrangements.

IX. Supervision given: Generally supervises administrative officer and production supervisor.

X. Working conditions: Vary. Office, production room, and travels.

I. Job title: Sales control manager   II. Job code: B

III. Number employed: Two   IV. Date: June 19, 1973

V. Location: Administrative and sales department

VI. Job summary: Selects, trains, supervises, and compensates a force of 15 to 20 part-time commission salesmen.

VII. Duties

A. Daily

80 percent	1.	Selects and trains salesmen in own district.
	2.	Contacts salesmen regarding impending social affairs which they are to cover.
	3.	Transmits information to salesmen about price, product changes, and delivery.
	4.	Holds individual conferences with salesmen to train, orient, and inspire them to greater sales efforts.
	5.	Encourages salesmen to collect delinquent accounts.
5 percent	6.	Maintains a work sheet showing schedule and plans for all impending social affairs within district.

B. Periodical

15 percent	1.	Obtains settlement sheet of district sales and receipts from sales manager weekly, and discusses past week's activities.
	2.	Informs salesmen of delinquent accounts.
	3.	Receives commission weekly from administrative officer, from which the salesmen are paid the commission due them.

C. Occasional: None.

VIII. Job-knowledge requirements: Retail prices, flower code, flower characteristics, and delivery schedule.

IX. Supervision given: Supervises generally 15 to 20 part-time commission salesmen.
Supervision received: Very general from sales manager.

X. Working conditions: Vary.

I. Job title: Floral designer   II. Job code: C

III. Number employed: One   IV. Date: June 19, 1973

V. Location: Production department

VI. Job summary: Designs and fashions bouquets, corsages, sprays, wreaths, and fancy floral designs, determining what flowers to use or using flowers requested by customer.

VII. Duties

A. Daily

5 percent	1.	Receives order slip from stock man and reads code to determine flower combination desired.
70 percent	2.	Receives flowers from assembler and arranges specified flower combination into a design which varies at the discretion of the designer.*
15 percent	3.	Selects ribbon and attaches maline backing.
5 percent	4.	Clips wire ends and passes order with order slip to boxer.
1 percent	5.	Advises and consults with sales manager, wedding consultant, and industrial sales officer concerning characteristics of various flower combinations.

B. Periodical: None.

---

*Examples of flower combinations are sprays, vases, wedding bouquets, fans, special and standard corsages, baskets, boutonnieres, wreaths, blankets, artificial trees, floats, coronet crowns, candelabras, and centerpieces.

C. Occasional

1 percent   1. Decorates church interiors for wedding.

2 percent   2. Makes short talks about floral design before various public groups.

1 percent   3. Dyes flowers for special purposes.

VIII. Tools and materials used: Table, wire cutters, flowers, maline, ribbon, wire, dye, baskets, vases, arborvitae, picks, moss, pots, water vials, and floral tape.

IX. Supervision given: None.

Supervision received: General from production supervisor.

Work received from: Assembler and stock man.

Work delivered to: Boxer.

X. Working conditions: Inside, artificial light, concrete floor, damp.

I. Job Title: Production supervisor   II. Job code: D

III. Number employed: One   IV. Date: June 19, 1973

V. Location: Production department

VI. Job summary: Plans, organizes, and controls the activities of the production department, purchases flowers, and maintains the stock records.

VII. Duties

A. Daily

80 percent   1. Receives order slips and route sheet from wedding consultant and gives route sheet to delivery chief.

    2. Separates orders by date, delivery hour, type of flower, color, and combination, and places on control board.

    3. Supervises and checks production operation and delivery for effectiveness and idleness and adjusts working hours to the work load.

    4. Consults with general manager on plans for immediate future and reports progress.

    5. Inspects for proper "housekeeping" and examines product for quality from time to time.

    6. Records, selects, and trains production department personnel and records their working time each day.

    7. Supervises all maintenance work in the company.

5 percent   8. Determines proper stock level for 50 varieties of flowers and calls personally or by telephone to one of several wholesalers to replenish stocks.

    9. Purchases all production room supplies; is final authority on flower and supply orders not to exceed $200.

    10. Checks stock received from vendor against invoices and turns over invoices to administrative officer.

5 percent   11. Maintains stock record daily, showing amount received, amounts on hand, amount utilized, and scrappage.

B. Periodical: None.

C. Occasional

5 percent   1. Plans layout of production room and arrangement of work places.

5 percent   2. Performs various types of maintenance work, such as painting, construction of tables, etc.

VIII. Job-knowledge requirements: Current market prices of flowers, quality of flowers, flower characteristics of floral combinations, order procedure, production method, and flower code.

IX. Supervision given: Supervises closely stock man, assembler, ribbon tier, and boxer.

          Medium—delivery chief.

          General—floral designer.

Supervision received: Rather general from general manager.

X. Working conditions: Inside, concrete floor, artificial light, damp.

I. Job title: Boxer   II. Job code: E

III. Number employed: One_____   IV. Date: June 19, 1973_____

V. Location: Production department_____

VI. Job summary: Receives flower combination from floral designer, sprays with water, and boxes, attaching order slip and cards.

VII. Duties

A. Daily

10 percent   1. Makes up boxes from flattened-out cardboard.

20 percent   2. Lines interior of box with florist green wrapping papers.

20 percent   3. Receives flowers from designer, and sprays with water using cotton squares if necessary.

10 percent   4. Places flower combination into cellophane bag and/or box.

20 percent   5. Places artificial green grass, personal card, and corsage pin in box.

19 percent   6. Attaches address label, company label, and c.o.d. slip, if any, to box and passes to delivery chief with order slip.

1 percent   7. Assists in cleanup of production room.

B. Periodical: None.

C. Occasional: None.

VIII. Tools and materials used: Table, water spray, boxes, paper, flowers, corsage pins, artificial grass, cellophane bags, cotton, personal cards, address labels, and company labels.

IX. Supervision given: None.

Supervision received: Rather close from production supervisor.

Work received from: Floral designer.

Work delivered to: Delivery chief.

X. Working conditions: Inside, concrete floor, damp, artificial light.

I. Job title: Wedding consultant_____   II. Job code: F_____

III. Number employed: One_____   IV. Date: June 19, 1973_____

V. Location: Administrative and sales department_____

VI. Job summary: Collects information of approaching weddings, makes contacts, and handles flower arrangements and procedure for entire wedding. Also performs general office work.

VII. Duties

A. Daily

65 percent   1. Gleans information concerning future weddings from newspapers, salesmen, etc., and files.

2. Telephones brides and informs them of services offered and makes an appointment if possible.

3. Calls at home of bride to discuss wedding details.

4. Prepares a personal data card for each wedding.

5. Advises as to wedding gowns, colors, floral decorations, wedding procedure, etiquette, etc.

6. Attends wedding to supervise arrangements.

25 percent   7. Receives flower orders from customers by telephone and from sales manager.

8. Prepares c.o.d. slips, address labels, personal cards, and attaches to original copy of order, giving c.o.d. list to administrative officer.

9. Delivers original copies to production supervisor and files duplicates.

10. Receives original copies from production supervisor after delivery and checks against duplicates to guard against loss.

11. Files duplicates in permanent file and sends originals to sales manager.

10 percent   12. Answers telephone.

13. Performs general office work, such as typing letters and filing.

B. Periodical: None.

C. Occasional: None.

VIII. Job-knowledge requirements: Order procedure, flower code, flower prices, wedding procedures, and flower characteristics of wedding work.

IX. Supervision given: General to industrial sales officer.
Supervision received: Rather general from administrative officer.
X. Working conditions: Inside, office, agreeable.

I. Job title: Assembler   II. Job code: G

III. Number employed: One   IV. Date: June 19, 1973

V. Location: Production department

VI. Job summary: Cuts, strips, wires, and paraffilms* individual flowers before passing to floral designer.
VII. Duties
A. Daily

1 percent	1. Receives flowers from stock man.
20 percent	2. Breaks stems to 1 inch and strips leaves and outer petals.
5 percent	3. Attaches one green leaf to roses only.
35 percent	4. Wires flower by inserting wire through the calix, and bending to form substitute stem.
35 percent	5. Wraps paraffilm strips around calix and down around wire.
1 percent	6. Passes flower on to floral designer.
1 percent	7. Makes up boxes of cut flowers lined with arborvitae or ferns.
1 percent	8. Assists in cleanup of production room.

B. Periodical: None.
C. Occasional

1 percent   1. Makes up maline backing by bunching an 8- by 6-inch piece of maline in the center and wiring.

VIII. Tools and materials used: Table, wire cutters, scissors, flowers, green leaves, paraffilm strips, wire, and maline.
IX. Supervision given: None.
Supervision received: Rather close from production supervisor.
Work received from: Stock man.
Work delivered to: Floral designer.
X. Working conditions: Inside, concrete floor, damp, artificial light.

I. Job title: Driver   II. Job code: H

III. Number employed: Two   IV. Date: June 19, 1973

V. Location: Production department

VI. Job summary: Delivers flower orders to all parts of the city and collects money for c.o.d.s.
VII. Duties
A. Daily

5 percent	1. Receives load of orders and district assignment from delivery chief.
10 percent	2. Maps out a route from delivery addresses of load.
70 percent	3. Delivers orders and collects money for c.o.d.s.
5 percent	4. Checks in with delivery chief and turns over c.o.d. money or c.o.d. slip, depending upon whether or not the money was collected.

B. Periodical: None.
C. Occasional

10 percent   1. Performs various types of maintenance work, such as painting, constructing tables and shelves, making flower gardens, etc., under the supervision of the production supervisor.

VIII. Tools and materials used: Automobile or truck, simple maintenance tools, flower orders, and money.
IX. Supervision given: None.
Supervision received: Medium from delivery chief and production supervisor.
Work received from: Delivery chief.
Work delivered to: Customers.
X. Working conditions: Outside, vary.

*¼-in. strips lightly coated with paraffin.

I. Job title: Stock man   II. Job code: I

III. Number employed: One   IV. Date: June 19, 1973

V. Location: Production department

VI. Job summary: Prepares workplace for operation, takes order slips from control board, assembles specified flowers, and passes on to assembler.

VII. Duties

A. Daily

10 percent   1. Sets out wire, paraffilm, scissors, wire cutters, etc., on production line in preparation for work.

5 percent   2. Takes order slips from control board and thereby regulates the flow of production.

70 percent   3. Reads flower code and assembles flowers specified by obtaining them from icebox.

5 percent   4. Delivers flowers to assembler.

5 percent   5. Gives order slip with personal card, address label, and c.o.d. slip attached to floral designer.

5 percent   6. Takes inventory of flowers in icebox daily and reports to production supervisor.

B. Periodical: None.

C. Occasional: None.

VIII. Tools and materials used: Table, control board, scissors, cutters, paraffilm, wire, order slip with cards and labels, flowers.

IX. Supervision given: None.

Supervision received: Rather close from production supervisor.

Work received from: Production supervisor.

Work delivered to: Assembler and floral designer.

X. Working conditions: Inside, concrete floor, artificial light, damp, and coldness in the icebox.

I. Job title: Sales manager   II. Job code: J

III. Number employed: One   IV. Date: June 19, 1973

V. Location: Administrative and sales department

VI. Job summary: Selects, trains, and supervises part-time commission saleswomen, handles the sales records, bills customers, receives cash in payment of orders, and manages the retail florist shop.

VII. Duties

A. Daily

38 percent   1. Receives flower orders from salesmen and customers by telephone or in person.

2. Prepares order in duplicate, personal card, address label, and c.o.d. slip, and sends to wedding consultant.

3. Receives original copy of order from wedding consultant after delivery, and posts in daily sales journal.

4. Files cash order originals in permanent file and charge copies in temporary files pending payment.

5. Receives cash for orders in person or by mail, records in daily sales journal and accounts receivable ledger, and turns over amount daily to administrative officer; varies up to $250.

10 percent   6. Supplies information about current flower offerings and prices to sales control managers and commission saleswomen.

2 percent   7. Receives and refers complaints of customers to administrative officer.

3 percent   8. Assists commission saleswomen in solving small sales problems.

15 percent   9. Arranges retail store displays and waits on walk-in trade.

5 percent   10. Receives and files in tickler file information in regard to "remembrance service" and sends out reminder letters on proper dates.

B. Periodical

4 percent   1. Posts unpaid orders to accounts receivable ledger weekly.

1 percent   2. Prepares summary sheet of week's sales and receipts for each of two sales control managers.

5 percent	3. Prepares and sends out bills to unpaid accounts three times monthly.
3 percent	4. Prepares delinquent accounts list and sends to collection agency monthly.
1 percent	5. Prepares monthly report of industrial sales and sends to industrial sales officer.
2 percent	6. Prepares summary sheet of month's sales and receipts for each of 40 saleswomen.

    C. Occasional

9 percent	1. Recruits, selects, and trains part-time commission saleswomen.
1 percent	2. Buys office supplies for entire firm upon authorization of general manager.
1 percent	3. Receives information from convention bureau about future conventions coming to town and contacts convention organizer concerning floral arrangements.

VIII. Job-knowledge requirements: Salesmen-account numbers, flower code, flower prices, order procedure, flower characteristics.

  IX. Supervision given: Supervises generally two sales control managers and 40 part-time commission saleswomen.

    Supervision received: Rather general from administrative officer.

   X. Working conditions: Inside, office, agreeable.

   I. Job title: Ribbon tier   II. Job code: K

 III. Number employed: One   IV. Date: June 19, 1973

   V. Location: Production department

  VI. Job summary: Ties different-colored ribbon into a standardized bow.

 VII. Duties

    A. Daily

1 percent	1. Receives instructions from production supervisor as to amount and colors of ribbon bows needed for stock.
70 percent	2. Doubles ribbon into 7 or 8 loops and wires in the center to form a bow.
5 percent	3. Places bows into boxes by color and stacks on ribbon table in the production room.
20 percent	4. Makes up maline backing by bunching an 8- by 6-inch piece of maline in the center and wiring.
1 percent	5. Assists in cleanup of production room.

    B. Periodical: None.

    C. Occasional

3 percent	1. Paints floral baskets.

VIII. Tools and materials used: Scissors, table, ribbon, maline, wire, and boxes.

  IX. Supervision given: None.

    Supervision received: Rather close from production supervisor.

    Work received from: Production supervisor.

    Work delivered to: Floral designer via production ribbon table.

   X. Working conditions: Inside, artificial light, concrete floor, damp.

   I. Job title: Industrial sales officer   II. Job code: L

 III. Number employed: One   IV. Date: June 19, 1973

   V. Location: Administrative and sales department

  VI. Job summary: Telephones officials of industrial firms and party organizers, solicits flower orders, and follows up with a form letter.

 VII. Duties

    A. Daily

85 percent	1. Obtains names of industrial firms from telephone directory.
	2. Telephones officials of firms, introduces self and company, and informs them of special flower offers for industrial accounts.
	3. Follows up first call with a form letter summarizing information given over the telephone.
	4. Adds new firms as work load permits.
	5. Telephones each firm on growing list once each month.

6. Maintains a file of calls made recording name, time, and type of response.
7. Drops firms from call list only upon instructions of wedding consultant.

14 percent   8. Gleans information concerning parties, club meetings, and other social functions from daily newspapers.

9. Telephones organizers of social functions and solicits orders.

  B. Periodical

1 percent   1. Receives and analyzes monthly report from sales manager on amount of sales to industrial accounts.

  C. Occasional: None.

VIII. Job-knowledge requirements: Flower prices, discounts to industrial concerns, and flower characteristics.

  IX. Supervision given: None.

    Supervision received: Rather general from wedding consultant.

  X. Working conditions: Inside, office, agreeable.

  I. Job title: <u>Delivery chief</u>   II. Job code: <u>M</u>

  III. Number employed: <u>One</u>   IV. Date: <u>June 19, 1973</u>

  V. Location: <u>Production department</u>

  VI. Job summary: Separates flower orders by location and time, assigns loads to drivers, supervises delivery, and checks collection of c.o.d.s.

  VII. Duties

    A. Daily

85 percent   1. Receives orders from boxer and files order slip temporarily.

2. Separates orders by district and delivery time and enters order number on route sheet by district of city with driver's name.

3. Assigns drivers to districts and dispatches with loads at the proper times.

4. Checks deliveries made against order slips with driver upon his return and collects money for c.o.d.s.

5. Turns over money and order slips to administrative officer.

6. Returns orders not deliverable to production supervisor.

    B. Periodical: None.

    C. Occasional

5 percent   1. Instructs drivers as to delivery procedure.

5 percent   2. Delivers orders.

1 percent   3. Assists boxer in making up cardboard boxes.

4 percent   4. Performs general maintenance work under production supervisor.

  VIII. Tools and materials used: Order file, route sheet, automobile, flower orders, money, and general-maintenance tools.

  IX. Supervision given: Rather general supervision of two drivers.

    Supervision received: Medium from production supervisor.

    Work received from: Boxer.

    Work delivered to: Drivers, administrative officer, and production supervisor.

  X. Working conditions: Inside, concrete floor, damp, artificial light.

  I. Job title: <u>Administrative officer</u>   II. Job code: <u>N</u>

  III. Number employed: <u>One</u>   IV. Date: <u>June 19, 1973</u>

  V. Location: <u>Administrative and sales department</u>

  VI. Job summary: Handles all advertising, complaints of customers, office management, company payroll, all receipts and disbursals of cash, and special administrative tasks.

  VII. Duties

    A. Daily

30 percent   1. Prepares advertising copy for local newspapers.

2. Selects the advertising media.

30 percent	3. Supervises the office force.
	4. Receives c.o.d. list from wedding consultant and checks against cash or c.o.d. slips received from delivery chief.
	5. Assists wedding consultant in order writing and checking against deliveries.
20 percent	6. Adjusts customer complaints.
	7. Performs miscellaneous administrative duties such as dealing with company attorney about corporate matters, handling leases, creditor adjustments, etc.
	8. Administers the $25 petty cash fund.
10 percent	9. Receives all cash from customers, directly or through sales manager, deposits in bank, and files deposit slips.
	10. Pays all company obligations with general manager's approval.

    B. Periodical

7 percent	1. Receives time slips from production supervisor and prepares and pays company payroll bimonthly.
3 percent	2. Computes and pays, with assistance of sales manager, the commissions of the sales control managers weekly, and the saleswomen, monthly.

    C. Occasional: None.

VIII. Job-knowledge requirements: Order procedure, flower code, flower characteristics, income tax provisions, social security tax, workmen's compensation tax.

  IX. Supervision given: Generally supervises sales manager and wedding consultant.

    Supervision received: Rather general from general manager.

   X. Working conditions: Inside, office, agreeable.

THE CASE OF THE INEFFECTIVE INCENTIVE

George Morales had worked at the Adams Company for eight years in the extrusion press department. He had progressed from his break-in job of laborer to sawyer, leadout, and the top job of heater and press operator. The functions of the press operator are to operate the press, act as leadman of the crew, and arrange his work into an orderly sequence. George had spent most of his time on a press of 2,500-ton capacity, although presses of larger capacities were available.

An incentive system had been installed in the press area and was based on the load and extrusion cycles to determine the standard minutes. The actual time to perform the job was divided into the standard minutes to determine the efficiency of the crew.

George had performed satisfactorily for a long period of time in all classifications, particularly in that of operator. He was considered as having a pleasing personality and being an efficient operator with an average efficiency of 116 percent, an excellent coordinator of his four-man crew, and highly concerned with the quality of the work he and his crew turned out. He was in good health, and his attendance record was considered perfect.

The firm's profits has been decreasing the past eighteen months owing to the effects of stringent competition. Management decided to investigate the methods of performing the work in each department, the objective being to improve methods wherever possible to decrease costs. Some layouts in the press area were modified to the extent that crew sizes could be reduced. George's crew was reduced by one crew member.

About this time, George's attitude and performance changed markedly for the worse. His immediate supervisor found it necessary to caution him several times, first on the quality of his work, then his grouchy attitude which verged on insubordination, and finally his attendance. His supervisor could not determine any satisfactory reason for this situation. It appeared to him that George was just not trying or that he was not paying attention to what he was doing. The supervisor was also unable to determine the reason for the grouchy attitude, except George saying he "didn't feel good."

The supervisor didn't have much time to let the situation ride because the poor quality of George's work was beginning to show up in other process centers. This caused his own superior to get into the act. When the poor quality began reaching the final inspection department, "the roof fell in." The plant superintendent, the general superintendent, and the department supervisor were now on the supervisor's neck. An immediate meeting was held with the supervisor by the plant's top management where he unfolded his meager story. Since this was not an adequate explanation, it was decided to bring George into the meeting. While waiting for him to appear, the general superintendent convincingly advanced his theory that George was offering resistance to the change in methods. The department supervisor objected to his theory since no trouble had been experienced in prior similar situations. When George arrived, he was asked to state why his production had worsened, but he declined to offer any more information than that he had given to his supervisor. He was informed that he would have to improve immediately or be dismissed. He was told he would be given one week to make the transition in recognition of his long period of satisfactory service. The proper union officials were informed of all the facts and the proposition. The union officers were perplexed about the change in George but, being aware of his poor performance, reluctantly went along with the arrangement.

The department supervisor was the sole individual not in agreement with the rest. He first quizzed the immediate supervisor again and obtained no new information. He felt somewhat disappointed in him for not being closer to the man and having some idea of what had caused the sudden change. The department supervisor then talked to several union leaders and other members of the organization. None had any additional information. George had been part of the gang up to the time his work performance changed; since then he had become a lone wolf. The union and informal group leaders were aware of the seriousness of his situation if he did not change, and felt that they had let the department foreman down in not being able to shed any light on the case.

The first three working days of the week-long waiting period went by with no change. On the fourth day the department supervisor ran into George in the restroom. He asked him what he intended to do. George replied that he guessed they would just have to fire him. The department supervisor looked at his worried, strained face—the previously happy, handsome Mexican youth looked as though he had aged many years in a short time. The department supervisor knew that this man had married a beautiful girl of Italian and French descent, so he asked George what he and his wife were doing about this problem. This question caused George to break down completely; he even cried. A private place was found, and he and George talked. His beautiful wife had left him. This was the man's problem. He refrained from telling anyone of this because he had bragged so much of the good relationship he and his wife had, and now that she had left him, he was ashamed to mention it. The department head could do little but sympathize with him. Remarkably enough, George's performance improved the next day.

The department supervisor informed his superiors of what had happened. The plant superintendent was elated, but the general superintendent, while saying the department supervisor had done a good job, was very cool. The recovery for George was slow but positive. The general supervisor continued to "ride" both the department foreman and George about the slow recovery. The general supervisor's attitude was that this company was in business to make a profit and was not a psychological correctional institution. The general supervisor persisted in taking some disciplinary action. The department supervisor resisted and won out at the expense of some lowering of status in the eyes of his superior.

The operator fully recovered his composure in another few weeks and approached his jovial former self. He again talked and joked with his fellow workers. His efficiency returned to his prior average and his quality was again high.

PART SIX

INTEGRATION

It is important that our employee not only be *able* to work (development) but *willing* to work as well. This willingness is based largely on management's ability to integrate the interests and needs of its employees with the objectives of the organization. Therefore, we must first examine the nature of these employee needs (Chapter 17). Secondly, we must examine how these needs can be integrated in the climate of a business organization (Chapters 18 and 19). Perfect integration would lead to complete agreement and absence of conflict, a state which is highly unlikely. Consequently, we must examine the situations, exemplified by grievances and disciplinary action, in which either the organization or the employee is dissatisfied (Chapter 20). The process of stimulating willingness to work is largely a process of communication (Chapter 21). And finally, we must be concerned with the problem of integrating various *groups* of employees, particularly those taking the form of labor unions (Chapters 22 and 23).

SEVENTEEN
NATURE OF THE
HUMAN RESOURCE

In the sequence of operative personnel functions followed in this text, we have thus far procured our employee, developed the skill and ability to do the job assigned, and determined the manner and amount of monetary compensation. To some, our task would appear to be at an end. The employee would naturally perform the job well since she or he has been properly placed, trained, and compensated. In recent years, however, there has been a growing recognition of the need for particular efforts in dealing with the attitude of an employee. It is not enough that one is able to work; one must also be willing to work. This subject is of such importance and difficulty that this chapter and the following six are devoted to a discussion of the philosophies, approaches, and methods of stimulating a will to work productively and cooperatively.

IMPORTANCE OF HUMAN RELATIONS

As suggested by the title "Integration," there must be a reasonable merger of person and organization if effective action is to result. When the needs of human beings meet the needs of organization, conflict often occurs. It is the purpose of the chapters in Part Six to examine the fundamental nature of the human resource, integration of this resource with organizations, coping with the inevitable conflicts that ensue, and the various mechanisms and forms that these integrations and conflicts may take. Managerial activities in this regard are termed "human relations." The goal is effecting a reasonable integration leading to productive and creative collaboration toward mutual objectives. The manager will therefore require knowledge and skill in such underlying disciplines as psychology, sociology, anthropology, and ethology in attempting to understand and cope with problems in human relations.

The primary basis of management's activities in this field of interpersonal relations is a belief that they will contribute to the effective and economical accomplishment of organization objectives. This would establish human satisfaction as a *means* to the accomplishment of organizational ends such as productivity, innovation, and profit. If it could be proved that humanistic managerial approaches would *always* result in higher productivity and profit, it is certain that they would be adopted by most organizations fairly quickly. With respect to actual research, some studies have shown a positive relationship between satisfaction and output, but others have not. Results of these numerous studies have been summarized periodically by various researchers. Though most show a meaningful relationship between satisfaction and such variables as absenteeism and turnover, the one conclusion held in common has been that there is not a strong relationship between satisfaction and productivity. The studies reviewed by Vroom, for example, show a median correlation of plus .14 between satisfaction and output.[1] Fortunately, the correlation is on the *plus* side, but the level is low enough to lead some managers to doubt the validity of the relationship. Likert suggests that this low correlation is a result of research covering varying time spans; that is, some researchers introduce a humanistic factor and measure the results within weeks or months, while others measure after much longer periods.[2] He contends that changes in human relationships require considerable time to be absorbed and reflected in performance, though the reactions in terms of absenteeism and turnover occur more quickly. It should be noted, however, that more managers are convinced of an output payoff from humanistic approaches when dealing with technical, professional, managerial, and white-collar employees who are placed on jobs that cannot be highly structured and controlled by management. These employees have a greater measure of freedom and self-control, thereby increasing the importance of the relationship between their attitudes and resulting performances. Thus, some portions of the enterprise may be managed in terms of assuring employee satisfaction, although other portions are approached in a more regimented and autocratic manner.

Some observers and researchers contend that human values should be viewed as *ends* of the business organization rather than means to an end. If this is the case, it is usually the result of (1) outside pressures from government, (2) outside pressures from labor unions, or (3) "outside" pressures from the manager's personal code of ethics. Since private enterprise received its huge grant of authority from society through the mechanism of private property, that grant has been increasingly reduced by various administrative, judicial, and legislative decisions and acts. Society, in general, has not approved of industry's treatment of its employees. Consequently various laws, such as the Civil Rights Act, the Social Security Act, and the Fair Labor Standards Act, have been passed to dictate certain minimum standards of treatment. The management and ownership of business organizations have provoked such legislation by their manner of managing or mismanaging personnel. Therefore the improvement of human relationships and services within the firm can be looked upon as one means of lessening the inroads of such governmental actions. If the grant of private authority over personnel management is not to disappear completely, industry must learn to regulate itself in conformance with the general wishes of society.

---

[1]Victor H. Vroom, *Work and Motivation*, John Wiley & Sons, Inc., New York, 1964, p. 183.
[2]Rensis Likert, *The Human Organization*, McGraw-Hill Book Company, New York, 1967, chap. 5.

Fear of unionization is another somewhat negative stimulus toward management activity in the general field of human relations. If the halting of unionization is the *only* objective of such a program, such attempts will generally fail. However, a well-formulated human relations program in a nonunionized firm has frequently created a by-product in the form of an employee vote against labor organization. In many of these firms, the philosophy of management has included the concept of employee free choice. If the employees desire a union, management willingly accepts and works with it; if not, management will continue the sound program of human relations and integration of interests as in the past. The objective in this philosophy, however, is not specifically the inhibition of labor organization.

A fourth justification for managerial interest in human relations rests on moral grounds. Employees are human beings, just as are members of management and ownership, and are therefore entitled to certain human rights. They should be treated with the same respect for their dignity that any other human beings can claim. Human relations activities should be undertaken because they are morally right, and not because they will make money or keep out the union and the government. Though it is difficult to present to the "hard, level-headed businessman," we believe that the strength of moral justification may well exceed that of the other, previously mentioned three bases of action.

It should be emphasized that a human relations program does not require a soft treatment of employees with an abdication of managerial responsibility for running the firm. On the contrary, proper treatment of some employees requires punishment and other forms of negative motivation. Employees themselves have a definite obligation of good followership. A sound program certainly requires an atmosphere in which efficiency and accomplishment are encouraged and rewarded, employee self-development is emphasized, and employee obligations, as well as rights and privileges, are recognized. Neither completely autocratic nor democratic management is to be desired. The study and establishment of sound human relationships are difficult tasks and will result in varying approaches for different situations. Thus, it may well be that some human values are correctly viewed and utilized as constructive means to economic ends of the enterprise; that is, there are many overlapping interests. The larger the degree of overlap, the more rapid will be the development of human relations programs. Much of the work of behavioral scientists is concerned with discovering and proving that the degree of overlap is much larger than many managers now believe. However, if the approaches suggested by behaviorists are unsuccessful in terms of costs, quantity, quality, and creativity, it is likely that only the outside forces of union, government, and/or personal codes of ethics will produce changes in management practice more favorable toward human values. Our societal values are slowly but steadily changing, and private business institutions are increasingly being called upon to assist in the pursuit of values other than the economic.

NATURE OF HUMAN NEEDS

To observe the behavior of a person is one thing; to understand it is another; and to influence that behavior toward a certain direction is still a third problem. Understanding and influencing human behavior require knowledge of human needs. Most psychologists are in agreement that human behavior is not completely disorganized and without motivation. The human personality is composed of multiple elements which are related to effect some degree of apparent balance.

The needs of human beings can be classified into three categories: physiological, social, and egoistic. *Physiological needs*, often termed primary, are those that issue from the necessity to sustain life—food, water, air, rest, sex, shelter, and the like. The "economic man" model assumes that such needs are the sole needs of people. In addition to meeting these basic and fundamental needs, one also must be assured that they will *continue* to be met. Thus, security is a vital need of a high priority to most people. When threatened, as it is by mechanization, automation, and economic recession, it gives rise to much and strongly motivated activity.

The remaining two types of needs are often termed secondary since they are more nebulous and intangible. They vary in intensity from one person to another, much more than do the primary needs. In the *social* category are the needs of (1) physical association and contact, (2) love and affection, and (3) acceptance. Most people are gregarious and desire to live with other people. This nation is rapidly becoming a country of "city dwellers." Physical contact, however, is not enough. People feel a need for love and affection from at least a few other human beings. Thus, we form and maintain ties of family and friendships, relationships which are often vitally affected by policies and practices of the employing organization.

In addition to physical contact and affection, human beings feel a need for acceptance by and affiliation with some group or groups. It has long been noted that modern society has tended toward the formation of more and more groups and that a single individual is usually a member of multiple groups. In addition to formal groups, of which the business firm is one, there are many diverse and complex informal groups which can serve to enhance or frustrate the effectiveness of organized cooperation within the firm. The need for acceptance and social approval is also reflected in such factors as styles, fashions, traditions, mores, and codes. It is a strong need which provides one of the cornerstones of any organized society.

Egoistic needs are derived from the necessity of viewing one's self or ego in a certain manner. Among the identifiable egoistic needs are the following: (1) recognition, (2) dominance, (3) independence, and (4) achievement. Though a person needs reasonable acceptance by a group, one usually does not wish to merge with it to the point of losing personal identity. We are often caught between two somewhat conflicting needs, one of which requires merger, the other separation. If one accepts a promotion to supervisor, thereby gratifying a need of the ego, one must forgo the association of many old friends, thereby frustrating a social need.

As one matures, a need for dominance often becomes apparent. Dominance may well be a continuation of the need for recognition with the ultimate objective of achieving autonomy and independence. The drive for the formation of labor unions, for example, does not issue solely from physiological needs. In many instances, well-paid employees voted overwhelmingly for a union which could serve to provide them with the dignity of independence necessary to their self-esteem.

Many psychologists contend that the highest need of the human being is that of achievement or self-actualization. It encompasses not only the ability to accomplish, but the need for actual achievement of something in life. The job or task is the major source of satisfaction for this need. If frustrated internally, the employee may attempt fulfillment in off-the-job activities such as serving in community service organizations, perfecting a hobby, or developing his or her children.

Conscious or unconscious needs set up in an individual certain tensions which stimulate behavior that will relieve those tensions. The objective of behavioral acts is to gratify these needs. It is doubtful if any or all needs are ever completely and permanently satisfied, inasmuch as people seem constantly to raise their levels of aspiration as accomplishments develop. If the person is able to satisfy needs in a manner that is acceptable to both the self and society, one is termed "adjusted." If, on the other hand, the person is unable to satisfy a particular need, or is able to gratify it only in a manner which is unacceptable to society, she or he is termed "maladjusted." Thus, behavior is a process of adjusting to certain human needs. The goal of this adjustment process is satisfaction.

Maladjustment results when human needs are not attained, are attained with great difficulty, or are attained in a manner not approved by society. In some cases, satisfaction of the need is effected, but in an undesirable manner; in others, there is no satisfaction at all. Typical examples of behavior indicating maladjustment are frequent changes in jobs, withdrawal, daydreaming, jealousy, desire for excessive attention, excessive complaining, bragging, and lying.

Some needs cannot be satisfied in *any* manner by the individual; tensions are not relieved; and the result is termed "frustration." A well-known story will illustrate the essential nature of frustration. While two men were drinking in a bar late one night, they got into an argument over the meaning of the terms "irritation," "aggravation," and "frustration." In order to get his point across, one of the men offered to demonstrate the fundamental distinction among the terms. He walked to a telephone and dialed a number at random. After several rings, a very tired, sleepy voice said, "Hello!" Our man of empirical research said, "Hello! Is Joe there?" The sleepy voice growled that there was no one there by that name, and the connection was broken abruptly. "That," said our man, "is an example of irritation." After waiting a period of thirty to forty minutes, he dialed the same number again, and asked the same question, "Is Joe there?" The response this time was considerably more intensified. After much yelling and shouting, the connection was broken. "That is an example of aggravation." He waited a period of thirty or forty minutes to allow the "guinea pig" to go back to sleep, then dialed the same number, but this time said, "Hello. This is Joe. Any messages for me?" There was complete silence for a long minute before the explosion. That was frustration.

Frustration is often recognized by certain types of behavior such as aggression, regression, fixation, and resignation. *Aggression* usually occurs when the person is attempting to accomplish something that he or she is not capable of achieving. Our guinea pig in the above experiment is unable to get to the man in the bar. Since aggression usually involves an attack upon the obstructing barrier, it is highly likely that the telephone took a beating. A worker in the plant may take out his or her frustration on a machine by abusing it. One may also become angry with all associates and the world in general. This type of behavior is wasteful and destructive, and it should be recognized and alleviated by management.

Regression is a type of behavior that is exemplified when the person resorts to acts of an immature type. Unreasonable complaining and crying help to relieve some of this frustration, but such behavior has adverse effects upon associates. *Fixation* is an attempt to gratify a need in a manner which has been proved to be worthless. In searching for lost car keys, for example, we tend to look in the same place over and over again, even though we know they were not there the first time. *Resignation* involves complete surrender. Satisfaction of needs is impossible, but there is no unreasonable attack upon obstruction, resorting to tears, or repetition of valueless behavior. Resignation is one of the latter stages of frustration and in an extreme case borders on serious mental illness.

It is important for the manager to be aware of the nature of need-motivated behavior and to recognize the evidences of maladjustment and frustration. Though we cannot compare humans to machines, this process is similar to the knowledge an engineer has of a piece of equipment. If the manager observes a malfunction among personnel, behavior that is considered undesirable, she or he must have some knowledge of what makes human beings tick. But there is little that is cut and dried about the process of understanding human behavior, and for this reason the profession of personnel management is characterized by many of the features of an art.

HUMAN MODELS PROPOSED BY ORGANIZATION PSYCHOLOGISTS

It has often been stated, "Tell me your basic view of what people are, and I'll tell you how you will manage." The statement implies that managers do develop and utilize a basic "human model" in their general approach to subordinates. It also implies that there are multiple models of humanity rather than just one accepted by all. In this section, we shall review the models proposed by four major organization psychologists. In a survey of business firms, one researcher discovered that six psychologists were very well known by many businessmen: Abraham Maslow, Douglas McGregor, Chris Argyris, Frederick Herzberg, Rensis Likert, and Robert Blake.[3] The first four have proposed fundamental conceptions of the nature of human beings, each of which is briefly discussed below. It will be noted that though the details differ, there is much in common among the "self-actualized" human of Maslow, the "theory Y" person of McGregor, the "mature" being of Argyris, and the "motivated" person of Herzberg. The last two psychologists, Likert and Blake, have developed specific *leadership styles*, System IV and 9,9 management, that can be utilized if one wishes to manage on the basis of the human models proposed by the first four. These style frameworks will be discussed in the following chapter.

MASLOW'S NEED HIERARCHY

The need hierarchy proposed by Abraham Maslow is perhaps the most widely accepted model of the human being. He suggests the following order of priority of fundamental needs:[4]

1   Basic physiological needs

---

[3]Harold M. Rush, "Behavioral Science: Concepts and Management Application," *Studies in Personnel Policy No. 216*, National Industrial Conference Board, New York, 1969.

[4]A. H. Maslow, "A Theory of Human Motivation," *Psychological Review*, vol. 50, no. 4, July 1943, pp. 370–396.

2   Safety and security
3   Love
4   Esteem
5   Self-actualization

Since the physiological needs are classified as primary, they are, of course, given first priority. "Man lives by bread alone when there is no bread."[5] If a person is starving, only food occupies the mind. It is a curious thing, however, that as soon as one need is reasonably well satisfied, a second need becomes apparent; the person forgets that she or he was starving, and now starts to be concerned about a need which was formerly of less significance. In Maslow's hierarchy, one now becomes aware of the need for *safety and security*. Human beings are motivated by *unsatisfied needs*, not by those that have been gratified. The desire for safety and security is met by such things as an orderly society, job tenure, insurance, religion, and the like. People are never completely satisfied on any need level, but a reasonable amount of gratification of first-priority needs must be forthcoming if they are to perceive a lower-priority need. Maslow suggests that an average citizen might be 85 percent satisfied in physiological needs, 70 percent in safety needs, 50 percent in love needs, 40 percent in the self-esteem category, and 10 percent in self-actualization needs.[6]

Once the necessities for continued existence have been met, the three higher needs of lower priority come into prominence. The need for *love* includes the need for affection and the desire for association with others. The need for *esteem* includes the desire for social approval, self-assertion, and self-esteem. Gratification of the need for esteem contributes to a feeling of self-confidence, worth, and capability. The need for love precedes that for esteem. The final need indicated in the list, that of *self-actualization*, refers to the desire for self-fulfillment and achievement. A person desires actualization in that in which he or she has capabilities. This is the highest-level need and has lowest priority. It is not a motivator of behavior until and unless the needs of love, self-esteem, social approval, and self-assertion are fairly well satisfied.

This hierarchy of needs helps to explain certain mistakes of management as well as to justify certain other philosophies. For example, the firm that embarks upon an elaborate personnel services program without the basis of a fair and competitive wage structure is usually wasting its efforts and money. Basic physiological needs are usually met by a fair amount of money. It is also significant to note that company appeals for employee cooperation and loyalty fall on deaf ears when a reasonable degree of security has not been provided. Security from the arbitrary dictates of management is prerequisite to the stimulation of employee participation and pride in work.

Some field research has been done which tends to substantiate this hierarchical concept of need perception. In contrasting the levels of need satisfaction of lower- and middle-level managers, it was discovered that the former perceive significantly less need fulfillment in security, esteem, and autonomy.[7] Both groups perceived greater deficiencies in the low-priority categories (autonomy and self-actualization) than in the

---

[5]Ibid., p. 375.

[6]Abraham Maslow, *Motivation and Personality*, Harper & Row, Publishers, Incorporated, New York, 1954, chap. 5.

[7]Lyman W. Porter, "Job Attitudes in Management: I. Perceived Deficiencies in Need Fulfillment as a Function of Job Level," *Journal of Applied Psychology*, vol. 46, no. 6, 1962, pp. 375–384.

higher-priority categories (security and social approval). Contrary to expectations, both groups were equally dissatisfied in the self-actualization category. In a second study of managers in a steel plant, the researcher discovered that the higher-order needs of autonomy and self-actualization were more closely related to actual levels of perform-ance than were the lower needs.[8] The level of satisfaction generally increased with each higher level of management even though the lower needs of physiological, security, and social were being substantially met on all levels. Admittedly, the level of organiza-tion structure is not the only factor affecting need satisfaction, but the differences discovered lend some support to the existence of a hierarchy.

The Maslow hierarchy of needs, though widely publicized and accepted by theorists and practitioners alike, is basically a theoretical conception issuing from an attempted synthesis of much psychological research. Research in the United States tends to substantiate the existence of the hierarchy. That it may be culturally bounded is suggested by a research project that compared the need hierarchies of American and Mexican employees in plants owned by a common parent company where the jobs, product, and technology were identical.[9] One interesting finding was that although the self-actualization need for the Americans was highly deficient in satisfaction, as hypothesized by the Maslow hierarchy, it was the *second* most satisfied need for the Mexican employees. This difference was attributed to differences in culture and social structure between the two nations.

MCGREGOR'S THEORY Y

Philosophers have long been fascinated and puzzled concerning the apparent contra-dictory and dual nature of human beings. People appear to have a capacity for tenderness, sympathy, and love while at the same time they possess tendencies toward cruelty, callousness, hate, and malicious aggression. If we are basically the former, we need little external regulation. If the latter, we must be controlled for the good of ourselves and society.

Though this philosophical clash is age-old, Douglas McGregor is responsible for introducing the dual theme into management literature. After observing the actual practices of many traditional managers, he proposed that they were operating on a set of assumptions that he labeled "theory X": (1) the average human being has an inherent dislike of work and will avoid it if possible; (2) because of this human characteristic of dislike of work, most people must be coerced, controlled, directed, and threatened with punishment to get them to put forth adequate effort; and (3) the average human being prefers to be directed, wishes to avoid responsibility, has relatively little ambition, and wants security above all.[10]

In disagreement with the assumptions of theory X, McGregor feels that modern management is grossly underestimating the interest and capacities of its organization members. On the basis of psychological and social research results, he submits an

---

[8]John W. Slocum, Jr., "Motivation in Managerial Levels: Relationship of Need Satisfaction to Job Performance," *Journal of Applied Psychology*, vol. 55, no. 4, August 1971, p. 315.

[9]John W. Slocum, Jr., Paul M. Topichak, and David G. Kuhn, "A Cross-Cultural Study of Need Satisfaction and Need Importance for Operative Employees," *Personnel Psychology*, vol. 24, no. 3, Autumn 1971, p. 442.

[10]Douglas McGregor, *The Human Side of Enterprise*, McGraw-Hill Book Company, New York, 1960, pp. 33–34, 47–48.

opposing theory, called "theory Y," as a more realistic assessment of the capabilities of people.

1   The expenditure of physical and mental effort in work is as natural as play or rest.
2   People will exercise self-direction and self-control in the service of objectives to which they are committed.
3   Commitment to objectives is a function of the rewards associated with achievement.
4   The average human being learns, under proper conditions, not only to accept but to seek responsibility.
5   The capacity to exercise a relatively high degree of imagination, ingenuity, and creativity in the solution of organization problems is widely, not narrowly, distributed in the population.
6   Under conditions of modern industrial life, the intellectual potentialities of the average human being are only partially utilized.

If one accepted the McGregor human model, such managerial practices as the following would be seriously considered: (1) abandonment of timeclocks, (2) flexi-time, (3) job enrichment, (4) Management by Objectives with subordinates determining the objectives as well as appraising their own accomplishments, and (5) participative and democratic decision making concerning the general organizational environment. All are based on the concepts of *abilities being widespread* in the population and *trust* in each person to behave in a responsible manner. It is apparent that the person who feels the higher-order needs, such as esteem and self-actualization, is likely to behave in a manner similar to that incorporated into the "theory Y" model. Thus, management must structure the organizational environment in a manner that will further the release of this tremendous human potential. This model suggests that people are born basically good with considerable potential for growth; at the least, they are born neutral with a "blank page" to be written upon by society.

ARGYRIS'S MATURE HUMAN BEING

Though the human being may be "constructed" at birth with all the Maslow needs and "theory Y" potential embedded in embryonic form, Chris Argyris emphasizes that development from that point is naturally in the direction of maturation. He proposes several dimensions of maturation through which the person will develop to achieve good mental health. At the immature-infant end of this continuum are these seven characteristics: (1) being passive, (2) being dependent, (3) being unaware of self, (4) being subordinate, (5) possessing a short time perspective, (6) having casual and shallow interests, and (7) being capable of behaving in only a few ways.[11] On the other hand, natural movement with maturation would be toward behavior characterized by increasing activity, independence, an awareness of and control over self, aspiring to occupy an equal or superior position, having long-term perspectives, developing deeper interests, and being capable of behaving in many ways to satisfy needs.

Organizations need human resources to fill positions necessary to achieve organization objectives. Though one might contend that mature personnel are a prime

---

[11]Chris Argyris, *Personality and Organization*, Harper & Row, Publishers, Incorporated, New York, 1957, p. 50.

necessity, Argyris argues that many organizations are structured and managed in such a way that immature, infantlike behavior is required for retention and "success." Employees are asked to submit to orders, plans, policies, procedures, and rules as given. They are asked to work in an environment where they have little control over their lives, are expected to be passive and dependent upon authority, and are asked to use a "few skin-surface shallow abilities."[12]

Faced with the incongruity of organizational demands and mature human needs, it is suggested that the employee will adapt to this environment by quitting the job that insults personal integrity, by attempting to advance to higher positions where there is more freedom and autonomy, or by being resigned to a frustrating situation and adopting an attitude of apathy and disinterest. This paints a rather gloomy picture of organizational requirements that will lead to widespread psychological failure for organizational members. McGregor tends to agree with this thesis as he poses the theory X and theory Y assumptions. Both he and Argyris suggest that industrial organizations are doing serious harm to human beings through management based on assumptions of employee immaturity and irresponsibility.

On the reverse side is the question of whether *all* employees are mature as defined by Argyris or theory Y types as defined by McGregor. Many have granted the importance of these concepts when dealing with more highly educated professional, technical, and managerial white-collar employees. But Strauss has suggested that the theories advanced by various behaviorists are more indicative of the need structure of highly educated behavioral theorists than they are of rank and file blue-collar employees.[13] Security may mean more to the industrial worker than to the highly educated professional. The former often values the freedom of thought permitted by a structured, repetitive, simple task which may be boring to others. Strauss indicates that the need to self-actualize may not be so widely spread in the population as hypothesized by Maslow, Argyris, and McGregor. One study of 83 workers (bench hands, testers, wiremen, machinists, toolmakers, electricians, etc.) in a firm of 8,000 employees revealed a positive correlation between need satisfaction and job structure. The higher the structure, the greater was the need satisfaction in such areas as achievement, affiliation, autonomy, and recognition.[14] Behaviorists would doubtlessly reply that such successful employee adaptation to oppressive and mechanical structures indicates that we have compounded the felony; not only have we forced employees to act in an immature manner, we have also conditioned them to *prefer* that type of behavior. Perhaps Dubin is taking a compromise position when he suggests that we can distinguish between necessary and voluntary behavior.[15] He feels that most people can and will adjust to tightly regimented work situations which Argyris contends would demand immature behavior. The resulting condition is one of indifference and apathy, which Dubin accepts as successful adaptation. No serious psychological damage is done, however, since the workday and workweek are becoming shorter and shorter. The employee can meet self-actualization needs *off* the job.

[12]Ibid., p. 66.

[13]George Strauss, "The Personality-versus-Organization Theory," in Leonard Sayles, *Individualism and Big Business*, McGraw-Hill Book Company, New York, 1963, p. 70.

[14]William P. Sexton, "Industrial Work: Who Calls It Psychologically Devastating?" *Management of Personnel Quarterly*, vol. 6, no. 4, Winter 1968, pp. 3–8.

[15]Robert Dubin, *Human Relations in Administration*, 3d ed., Prentice-Hall, Inc., Englewood Cliffs, N.J., 1968, pp. 72–76.

It should be apparent that most conditions are neither as bad as behaviorists contend nor as good as traditional managers claim. We are always operating in the gray area of optimizing multiple values under conditions of uncertainty. Only a fraction of the jobs in American business are of the highly mechanized, totally controlled type. To the degree that an open job market operates effectively, there will be some matching of varying human needs and organizational demands. One writer points out that 85 percent of American workers indicated that they were satisfied with their jobs, that fewer than 2 percent actually work on an assembly line, and that the typical employee does not even work for a manufacturing organization.[16]

Not all personnel are theory Y types despite arguments concerning how they got that way. Not all personnel are most motivated by the low-priority needs of Maslow. Not all organizations demand total obedience on narrowly defined tasks. But, certainly, not all organizations have examined their structures and management approaches to determine where some alterations could produce a better fusion between organizational and human values. In general, it can be contended that most managers in business have tended to underestimate the motivation and capabilities of their personnel. This is confirmed in surveys asking (1) whether managers believe in greater subordinate participation in decision making, and (2) whether managers believe that such participation will increase the quality of operation. The typical result is a "yes" to the first question and a "no" to the second. The implication is that greater employee involvement is the price of cooperation, submission, and acceptance, but only managers and other higher types can really make decisions that will improve the quality of the situation.

HERZBERG'S MOTIVATED EMPLOYEE

One of the more stimulating and controversial theories of human nature proposed in recent years is that developed by Frederick Herzberg and his associates.[17] It is consistent with the self-actualization of Maslow, McGregor's "theory Y," and the maturation process of Argyris.

Herzberg proposes that human beings have two basic needs: the need to avoid pain and survive and the need to grow, develop, and learn. As such, the analysis of employee job satisfaction would result in the formation of two separate continuums rather than the traditional one of satisfaction/dissatisfaction. The first continuum, ranging from dissatisfaction to no dissatisfaction, would be affected by environmental factors over which the employee has limited influence. Typical of these "hygienic factors" are pay, interpersonal relations, supervision, company policy and administration, working conditions, status, and security. Herzberg indicates that these factors do *not* serve to promote job satisfaction; rather, their absence or deficiency can create dissatisfaction. Their presence can only serve to eliminate dissatisfaction.

The second class of factors, referred to as "motivators," makes up a continuum leading from *no job satisfaction* to *satisfaction*. Examples from this class are the work itself, recognition, achievement, possibility of growth, and advancement. All of these

[16]Irving Kristol, "Is the American Worker Alienated?" *The Wall Street Journal*, Jan. 18, 1973.

[17]F. Herzberg, B. Mausner, and B. Synderman, *The Motivation to Work*, John Wiley & Sons, Inc., New York, 1959; and F. Herzberg, *Work and the Nature of Man*, The World Publishing Company, Cleveland, 1966.

are concerned with the work itself, rather than its surrounding physical, administrative, or social environment. If the worker is to be truly motivated, the job itself is the major source of that motivation. All of the other hygienic factors can serve only to "clean up" the environment and prevent dissatisfaction.

The method of research used in developing this theory was not the usual anonymous objective questionnaire. Rather, subjects were asked to recall a time when they felt exceptionally good or a time when they felt exceptionally bad about their work. These incidents or stories were analyzed to ascertain the particular factors mentioned as contributing to the exceptional satisfaction or dissatisfaction. A preponderance of the motivator factors dealing with the work itself were mentioned when the subject was describing a time of feeling exceptionally good. And the times of feeling very bad were marked by a significantly large number of hygienic factors.

This type of study has been duplicated by other researchers on many occasions. In a summary of twelve investigations encompassing 1,685 employees, incidents describing job satisfaction involved 81 percent motivator factors and only 19 percent hygienic factors.[18] In cases describing job dissatisfaction, 69 percent involved hygienic factors as compared with 31 percent motivator factors.

The Herzberg theory has been criticized by some as being method-bound; that is, individuals tend to blame environmental factors for job failure and consequent dissatisfaction and take credit for any job successes that occur. A few objective questionnaire studies are in agreement with the theory, but most are not. Others have criticized the Herzberg type of study as being primarily concerned with higher-level, technical jobs whose usual occupants are better educated and more interested in their work. However, this method has been used in studies of various types of jobs such as lower-level supervisors, hospital maintenance personnel, nurses, food handlers, agricultural administrators, accountants, Finnish supervisors, Hungarian engineers, and military officers. Herzberg contends that the work itself can be the basic motivating force for lower-level jobs as well as higher and more complex types.

The Herzberg theory is similar to the Maslow hierarchy in that the hygienic factors are related to the higher-priority physiological, security, and social needs, while the motivators correspond to the esteem, ego, and self-actualization needs. The Maslow hierarchy proposes a continuous, rather than disconnected, sequencing of felt needs, whereas the Herzberg theory would not require hygienic factors to be provided as a prerequisite to satisfaction on the job. There is widespread agreement that satisfaction will be higher when both motivational and hygienic factors are well taken care of. There is also evidence that when both are reasonably well met by organizations, the motivators are *more* powerful sources of satisfaction.[19] When they are not well met, hygienic factors are the *more* powerful source, thus tending to substantiate the Maslow hierarchical concept. Other research indicates that older employees as well as the blue-collar tend to value the hygienic factors more highly than do the younger or the white-collar. One study did not find that those individuals with a high level of motivators and a low level of hygienic factors were significantly more satisfied than

[18]Frederick Herzberg, "One More Time: How Do You Motivate Employees?" *Harvard Business Review*, vol. 46, no. 1, January–February 1968, p. 57.

[19]Hanafi M. Soliman, "Motivation-Hygiene Theory of Job Attitudes: An Empirical Investigation and an Attempt to Reconcile Both the One- and the Two-Factor Theories of Job Attitudes," *Journal of Applied Psychology*, vol. 54, no. 5, October 1970, pp. 452–461; and D. A. Ondrack, "Defense Mechanisms and the Herzberg Theory: An Alternate Test," *Academy of Management Journal*, vol. 17, no. 1, March 1974, pp. 79–89.

those who perceived the reverse.[20] In other words, a "good" job in a "bad" environment will not necessarily result in greater satisfaction than a "bad" job in a "good" environment. Except for highly unusual instances, employees are likely to be upset by the idea of performing a challenging job for low pay, in a shabby office, under negative leadership styles and inconsistent policies.

Herzberg would certainly not deemphasize the importance of the hygienic factors in successful management. He favors "good" environments. The primary impact of his theory is to direct management's attention to the task itself as the primary source of motivation. It rests upon the important human need to self-actualize through doing something interesting, challenging, and important in life. It certainly emphasizes the fact that a good environment is not enough. It asks that additional efforts be expended in the interest of greater motivation.

HUMAN MODELS OF ETHOLOGISTS

All of the models of the four organizational psychologists have one thing in common: the infinite human capacity to learn, grow, and achieve. It is a human model that is very attractive to the human ego. Humans constitute the greatest resource on this planet, ranking only slightly below the angels. In contrast with this orientation toward human nature, we now turn to the field of ethology, the study of animal behavior. Just as Herzberg cited the dual nature of humans (the need to survive and avoid pain and the need to grow), modern ethologists study humans as animals and humans as humans. They tend, however, to emphasize the first approach as a means of enlarging understanding of the second. Robert Ardrey credits Konrad Z. Lorenz, the Austrian naturalist, with fathering the field of modern ethology.[21] Ethology has been popularized in the last two decades through such writings as Lorenz's *On Agression*, Ardrey's *Territorial Imperative*, and Desmond Morris's *The Naked Ape* and *The Human Zoo*.

As the titles of the books indicate, the basic thesis is that humans are both animalistic and humanistic. Certain animal characteristics provide a framework that helps to shape the humanizing process. For example, Ardrey's thesis is that humans share with many animals an innate behavioral pattern that leads them to establish a basic area or territory as theirs and to defend it against invaders. This defense leads them to benign aggression, that is, aggressive acts against invaders that are biologically adaptive through contributing to the survival of the species. It ceases when the threat has been removed. Malignant aggression, however, appears to be a learned response that is specific to humans.[22] Humans will kill other humans for reasons that are *not* biologically adaptive.

In lower animals and insects, these innate behavioral patterns that are genetically transmitted are generally referred to as "instincts." Instincts can vary from a completely closed program of behavior, as in the cases of ants and bees, to a fairly open one that requires considerable learning after birth. Arguments abound over whether humans inherit any instincts whatsoever. Ashley Montagu, a well-known anthropologist, con-

[20]Richard Kosmo and Orlando Behling, "Single Continuum Job Satisfaction vs. Duality: An Empirical Test," *Personnel Psychology*, vol. 22, no. 3, Autumn 1969, pp. 327–334.

[21]Robert Ardrey, *The Territorial Imperative*, Atheneum Publishers, New York, 1966, p. 12.

[22]Erich Fromm, *The Anatomy of Human Distractiveness*, Holt, Rinehart and Winston, New York, 1973.

tends, "It is not human nature, but nurture that is the cause of human aggression."[23] As suggested above, there are two types of aggression, one of which may be caused by human nature, the other by human nurture. Pioneers in ethology have proposed five possible human instincts that are genetically transmitted: reproduction, hunger, fear, aggression, and grooming. Kefalas and Suojanen suggest that these can be remembered in the form of the five "f's": flirting, feeding, flight, fighting, and feeling.[24] These instincts do not constitute preprogrammed behavior as in the case of lower animals. Rather, they are shapers of learned behavior. Lower animals master their environment through an evolutionary change in genes. Humans master their environment more quickly and effectively through culturally learned behavior. Yet to contend that people are totally human without any genetically transmitted behavioral inclinations would result in an incomplete understanding of the nature of human beings. Both organization psychologists and ethologists can aid in designing a more realistic model of the complex human.

HUMAN MODELS AND BEHAVIORISM

To B. F. Skinner, the foremost proponent of behaviorism, there is little need to theorize over the basic nature of the human being. He seeks explanations of human behavior, not from within, but from without. The stimulus to human behavior can be observed and measured. The behavioral response of the human can also be observed and measured. One needs only to establish behavioral objectives and to engineer appropriate responses through a conditioning process. Thus, humans, if anything, are malleable mechanisms. They are without mystery and merit little concern for proposed felt needs of dignity and autonomy. "Operant conditioning shapes behavior as a sculptor shapes a lump of clay."[25]

The Skinner thesis is an even greater shock to the ego of humans than that proposed by the ethologists. Hart and Scott suggest that this blow to the central importance of humans ranks along with the discoveries of Copernicus, Darwin, and Freud.[26] Copernicus proved that the earth was *not* the center of the universe. The human being's centrality on the now lesser important earth was attacked by Darwin and his thesis that man is not unique and totally separate from animals. And then Freud contended that the individual was not totally master of the self, that the libido and the unconscious have a considerable impact upon behavior. Now Skinner indicates that human behavior can be totally controlled through an operant conditioning process.

In his book *Beyond Freedom and Dignity*, Skinner contends that humans can be controlled and shaped while simultaneously feeling free.[27] The basic engineering approach is to *reward* desired behavior while *ignoring* undesirable actions. Over a period of time, the reinforced behavior will tend to be repeated, while the unrewarded will tend to be extinguished and to disappear. Punishment of undesired behavior is to

---

[23]M. F. Ashley Montagu, *Anthropology and Human Nature*, Porter Sargent, Boston, 1957, p. 36.

[24]Asterios G. Kefalas and Waino W. Suojanen, "Organizational Behavior and the New Biology," *Academy of Management Journal*, vol. 17, no. 3, September 1974, p. 523.

[25]"Conversation with B. F. Skinner," *Organizational Dynamics*, vol. 1, no. 3, Winter 1973, p. 31.

[26]David K. Hart and William G. Scott, "The Optimal Image of Man for Systems Theory," *Academy of Management Journal*, vol. 15, no. 4, December 1972, p. 536.

[27]B. F. Skinner, *Beyond Freedom and Dignity*, Alfred A. Knopf, Inc., New York, 1971.

be avoided as contributing to feelings of restraint and to actions of rebellion. Thus, in time, the conditioner can effectively control human behavior without the human becoming aware of being controlled—thus "beyond freedom." Choice has, on the surface, remained with the positively conditioned subject, while the conditioner pulls the strings in an unobjectionable and unnoticed fashion.

At this point, total confusion concerning the fundamental nature of the human resource may have set in. One conclusion is obvious—the human being is a highly complex mechanism not subject to simplistic theories of management. Simultaneous belief in elements of all three approaches is not impossible. Herzberg's hygienic factors and Maslow's physiological and security needs may well be related to the animalistic nature of humans emphasized by ethologists. Ethology does not reject the learning and growth capacity possessed by human beings and so greatly emphasized by the organization psychologists. It merely asks for a broader study to include some of the genetically transmitted shapers of learning. One can also believe and utilize much of the Skinner thesis of shaping behavior without necessarily contending that there is no mystery about the human being. Many Skinner-oriented conditioning devices are totally compatible with participative management recommendations of Argyris and McGregor and the job enrichment programs of Herzberg. Obtaining immediate feedback of results on a newly enriched job is a form of immediate reward connected to job behavior. One major worry is nevertheless attached to the basic Skinner thesis. Who is the conditioner? What are his or her goals in shaping behavior? Skinner's response is that the conditioning technology is ethically neutral; it can be used by both good and evil conditioners.[28] This would not satisfy persons highly concerned with the proposed needs of humans for dignity, autonomy, and self-determination. We have seen instances where the power to decide was taken from a manager with the result that the subordinate's materialistic position was significantly worsened; the offsetting gain was greater autonomy and self-control over elements of life significant to the subordinate.

HUMAN BEINGS AND CULTURE

As emphasized in all the preceding human models, the behavior of humans is also heavily influenced by the culture of which they are a part. Culture is composed of the human-created elements of life—customs, beliefs, habits, codes, mores, and laws. Culture arises in part from the need for security, since it is established, conventionalized behavior that changes slowly and possesses great stability. No person and no organization can be isolated from this cultural environment. The various types of behavior possible in the pursuit of need satisfaction are restricted by the culture in which this behavior occurs.

The importance of culture in the administration of a business firm can best be exemplified by contrasting one country with another. In Japan, for example, the worker expects advice and guidance from the employer to a degree that would be resented in the United States, with the latter's emphasis upon freedom and equality. A Japanese worker expects to remain a worker and not pass to managerial levels, a situation which *used to* exist in this country. He or she expects to remain an employee of one particular

[28]"Conversation with B. F. Skinner," op. cit., p. 32.

firm for life—incompetency is no justification for dismissal. Promotion is strictly on the basis of seniority, and pay is largely controlled by tenure and family needs. To offset this great degree of security, the Japanese worker's sense of duty and need to avoid shame leads her or him to produce well. The employees work extremely well toward definite short- or medium-range goals, which leads to popular managerial use of slogans and mottos.[29]

With respect to managerial practices, it is suggested that the Japanese approach may be more compatible with large, crowded, complex organizations than the American way.[30] American cultural values of individuality and self-sufficiency often lead to competition and rivalry within the organization. Japanese management practices emphasize a cooperative "bottom-up" process of decision making as a fundamental way of management. As stated by one American manager, "Americans will disagree with their boss rarely but violently; the Japanese disagree often but politely."[31] The Japanese manager is a facilitator, communicator, and participant in group decision processes. Americans tend to be independent, entrepreneurial, competitive, decisive, and action-oriented. Obviously, both managerial cultures have their strengths, but cultures will undergo change slowly in response to alterations of the environment.

In identifying varying managerial cultures of the world, the Haire, Ghiselli, and Porter study of 3,641 managers of fourteen countries is perhaps the largest single research to identify common values and differences in beliefs and practices.[32] The study identified several significantly different clusters of nations. The United States and England formed one combination with similar views and approaches to subordinate participation, use of authority, and the like. A later separate study found that Australia could also be allied with this group.[33] Other clusters were a Nordic-European group of Denmark, Germany, Norway, and Sweden; a Latin-European group of Belgium, France, Italy, and Spain; and a developing-nation group comprised of Argentina, Chile, and India. Only Japan could not be grouped with any other of the nations included in the study.

Perhaps one of the most commonly cited examples of varying international cultural beliefs is the treatment of time. Most Americans are greatly concerned with the importance of time, as witnessed by the widespread availability and use of accurate clocks and watches, the precision of transportation time-schedules, and the pressing necessity to meet scheduled appointments. In various foreign cultures, time does not have this same high value. This does not necessarily mean that these peoples do not value efficiency and coordination. Often, their attitude toward time is a result of poorer transportation and communication facilities, greater degrees of patience, religious philosophies that deemphasize the importance of this day or hour, or a different hierarchical arrangement of values in life. Being five minutes late for an appointment in the United States calls for a brief apology; fifteen minutes' lateness requires an

[29]Masaaki Imai, "Shukko, Jomukai, Ringi—The Ingredients of Executive Selection in Japan," *Personnel*, vol. 46, no. 4, July–August 1969, p. 23.

[30]Richard Tanner Johnson and William G. Ouchi, "Made in America (under Japanese Management)," *Harvard Business Review*, vol. 52, no. 5, September–October 1974, p. 69.

[31]Ibid., p. 63.

[32]Mason Haire, Edwin E. Ghiselli, and Lyman W. Porter, *Managerial Thinking: An International Study*, John Wiley & Sons, Inc., New York, 1966.

[33]Alfred W. Clark and Sue McCabe, "Leadership Beliefs of Australian Managers," *Journal of Applied Psychology*, vol. 54, no. 1, February 1970, pp. 1–6.

extended apology for the purpose of communicating great concern and regret; and being thirty or more minutes late is best excused by an act of God. In other countries, being thirty to forty-five minutes late for appointments is not an unusual event and is not to be taken as an insult when it passes unmentioned. The symbol of "lateness" stands for vastly different things in differing cultures. It has been suggested that the American can adapt by scheduling additional work beyond the appointed hour; considering his or her attitude toward time, the foreign visitor will not be insulted by not being immediately ushered into the executive's office.[34]

Within the United States, there are many subcultures that can affect business operations. There is a subculture for each business organization as well as subcultures cutting across various firms. Engineers and scientists, for example, are hired by many business establishments and bring with them certain beliefs, values, and standards that can conflict with the subculture of the firm. For example, research scientists highly value freedom of investigation and research that meets certain quality standards. The XYZ firm may insist that the scientist punch a timeclock, even though she or he works best from 1 A.M. to 5 A.M., and research only those fields that will result in immediate profit for the enterprise even though the scientist's work turns up an interesting lead in another area. With this clash in cultural values, higher salaries may not serve to keep the scientist from leaving for government or university employment. It is necessary for the manager to study the characteristics, standards, and values of the subcultures whose members one wishes to employ.

SUMMARY

A study of the history of American business will show that the development of an interest in human relations is the most recent of a series of changing emphases. In the latter 1900s the primary emphasis, for example, was upon the function of finance. This was the age of the Goulds and Rockefellers. After the turn of the century, the emphasis swung to marketing and sales. The mass market was developed, along with the further refinement of such institutions as the mail-order house and the chain store. From marketing, the primary interest moved to engineering and production, a change that was and still is exemplified by such advances as automation, cybernetics, and operations research. It should be noted, however, that though the emphasis appears to swing from one function to another, continued developments occur in each of the areas mentioned.

Human relations has been defined as the area of management practice that is concerned with the integration of people into a work situation. It is concerned with motivating personnel to work together cooperatively and productively. In understanding the behavior of human beings, some knowledge of basic needs is necessary. If their satisfaction can be effected in a manner that contributes to organization objectives, then interests have been integrated. They may be classified as physiological, social, and egoistic. The goal of human behavior is adjustment to need-stimulated tensions in a way that will bring satisfaction. When needs are frustrated, employee behavior may be aggressive, regressive, fixated, or resigned.

[34]James A. Lee, "Cultural Analysis in Overseas Operations," *Harvard Business Review*, vol. 44, no. 2, March–April 1966, pp. 112–113.

Various models of human beings have been proposed by separate disciplines. Despite the separate labels of "self-actualization," "theory Y," "maturation," and "motivators," the organization psychologists put forth a highly optimistic view of human beings as possessing an infinite capacity for growth, development, and achievement. Ethologists contend that this capacity for growth rests on a foundation of genetically transmitted behavioral patterns. Behaviorism, proposed by Skinner, eschews interest in what is in the human and confines its attention to stimulus-response. Humans are malleable and behavior can be engineered. Obviously, one cannot engineer activities totally beyond the physical and mental limitations of the human, e.g., condition a person to pole-vault 100 feet in the earth's atmosphere.

Human behavior cannot be fully understood and accurately predicted apart from a knowledge of the various cultures in which this behavior takes place. The customs, traditions, codes, and laws that make up a culture circumscribe the freedom of management. To a large degree, the problem is one of predicting and adjusting to cultural requirements. But within a single organization, a culture should be developed that will facilitate effective cooperation and fulfillment of quality performance levels. Organization, procedures, and controls must be established by management to ensure coordinated activity. The human desire for stability and security will contribute to greater acceptance of the need for such restrictions.

DISCUSSION QUESTIONS

1   Compare and contrast the human models of Maslow and Herzberg.
2   Compare and contrast the human models of McGregor and Skinner.
3   How could the Skinner approach conceivably end up with a human state of "beyond freedom"?
4   What is ethology? What contribution can it make to understanding human beings?
5   Are the human needs proposed by Maslow simply a list or a hierarchy? What is the significance of this distinction?
6   What is the basic commonality of the human models proposed by Maslow, Argyris, McGregor, and Herzberg? How is this commonality labeled in each model?
7   Contrast the approach toward human relations as a means to organizational ends with the concept that human values are ends in themselves.
8   Contrast the American and Japanese cultures with respect to managing business organizations.
9   To manage as McGregor suggests, what, specifically, would one do?
10 What is the relationship between employee satisfaction and such variables as absenteeism, turnover, and productivity?

SUPPLEMENTARY READING

ARGYRIS, Chris: "Personality vs. Organization," *Organizational Dynamics*, vol. 3, no. 2, Autumn 1974, pp. 2–17.
COSTELLO, John M., and Sang M. Lee: "Needs Fulfillment and Job Satisfaction of Professionals," *Public Personnel Management*, vol. 3, no. 5, September–October 1974, pp. 454–461.
HART, David K., and William G. Scott: "The Optimal Image of Man for Systems Theory: A Review

Essay of B. F. Skinner, *Beyond Freedom and Dignity*," *Academy of Management Journal*, vol. 15, no. 4, December 1972, pp. 531–540.

HERZBERG, Frederick: "The Wise Old Turk," *Harvard Business Review*, vol. 52, no. 5, September–October 1974, pp. 70–80.

JOHNSON, Richard Tanner, and William G. Ouchi: "Made In America (under Japanese Management)," *Harvard Business Review*, vol. 52, no. 5, September–October 1974, pp. 61–69.

KEFALAS, Asterios G., and Waino W. Suojanen: "Organizational Behavior and the New Biology," *Academy of Management Journal*, vol. 17, no. 3, September 1974, pp. 514–526.

ONDRACK, D. A.: "Defense Mechanisms and the Herzberg Theory: An Alternate Test," *Academy of Management Journal*, vol. 17, no. 1, March 1974, pp. 79–89.

EIGHTEEN
MOTIVATION

As indicated in Chapter 1, the organic functions of management are planning, organizing, directing, and controlling. Discussions of the personnel manager's responsibilities for planning, organizing, and controlling the personnel program were presented in Chapter 5. Coverage of the third function of direction was postponed until this point inasmuch as it is a vital component of the operative function of integration. Just as the personnel manager should be more than ordinarily competent in organizing, he or she should be similarly superior in the direction function. This latter function is concerned with *stimulating action to take place*. Action is undertaken by people, and the personnel manager should possess unusual competence in the understanding and utilization of people in the pursuit of personal and organizational goals.

The separation and development of the management function of direction is the result of an increasing appreciation of the power of organizational members. We cannot assume that the existence of good plans and excellent organization will result in an automatic undertaking of assigned tasks, thereby leaving the manager with only the responsibility of controlling the activity that develops. Getting organization members to go to work *willingly* and *enthusiastically* is a problem that has been compounded by such factors as the increasing educational level of employees, greater utilization of professional personnel, advancing technology, and the power of labor organizations. It is a task that can be more important than planning, organizing, and controlling. On various occasions, highly motivated people have achieved success despite the absence of good plans or effective organizational structures. And, of course, the more highly motivated the subordinate, the less control is necessary to assure that work will be executed. However, motivation is *not* a substitute for planning, organizing, and controlling. One can work effectively toward the wrong goal.

EMPLOYEE WANTS

The various types of human needs discussed in the preceding chapter will be converted by employees into specific "wants" in the organization. Just as the definition of basic human needs is a highly complex task, it naturally follows that there are no easy assumptions concerning what employees really want from the organization. In various surveys, the following are some of the more typically specified wants:

1 *Pay.* This want helps in satisfying physiological, security, and egoistic needs. As discussed in the preceding section of this text, the design of a monetary compensation system is exceedingly complex since it serves to satisfy multiple needs and cannot alone motivate the whole person.

2 *Security of job.* Because of current threats from technological change, this want is high on the list of priorities for many employees and labor unions. The underlying need of general security is also high on the list of priorities in the suggested need hierarchy of Maslow.

3 *Congenial associates.* This want issues from the social need of gregariousness and acceptance. Management can aid the process by carefully planned and executed induction programs, provision of means to socialize through rest periods and recreational programs, and promoting the formation of work teams through proper workstation layouts and human-related work procedures.

4 *Credit for work done.* This want issues from the egoistic classification of needs and can be supplied by management through verbal praise of excellent work, monetary rewards for suggestions, and public recognition through awards, releases in employee newspapers, and the like.

5 *A meaningful job.* This want issues from both the need for recognition and the drive toward self-realization and achievement. This is a very difficult want to supply, particularly in large organizations having minute division of work and mechanically paced assembly lines. But, as discussed in Chapter 4, some research into the possibilities of job enlargement has indicated the possibility of integrating the need of employees for significant work and the need of the organization for productive, coordinated activity.

6 *Opportunity to advance.* As was discussed in Chapter 12, not all employees want to advance. Some feel the social needs more strongly than the egoistic ones. However, most employees like to know that the opportunity is there, should they desire to use it. This feeling is influenced by a cultural tradition of freedom and opportunity.

7 *Comfortable, safe, and attractive working conditions.* The want for good working conditions also rests upon multiple needs. Safe working conditions issue from the security need. The specific attributes, such as desks and rugs, constitute symbols of status denoting a hierarchy of importance. Many managements have discovered that the allocation of such status symbols can be quite as difficult as the allocation of money.

8 *Competent and fair leadership.* The want of good leadership can issue from physiological and security needs. Good leadership helps to assure that the organization and its jobs will continue to exist. In addition, the ego demands that one respect persons from whom orders and directions are to be received. It is very frustrating to be subjected personally to a command from an individual who is deemed unworthy and incompetent. Orders from persons who are generally respected do not do as much damage to the ego, despite our cultural tradition of equality.

9   *Reasonable orders and directions.* The order is the official communication of organization requirements. In general, it should be related to the requirements of the situation, capable of being executed, complete but not unnecessarily detailed, clear and concise, and given in a manner that stimulates acceptance. Unreasonable orders incapable of accomplishment serve only to increase insecurity and frustration. Unreasonable orders that work contrary to the best interests of the organization may lead to a form of malicious obedience; the employee takes great delight in following them to the letter in the hopes of harming the superior who merits little respect.

10   *A socially relevant organization.* As indicated in Chapter 3, the trend toward greater social expectations of private organizations has impact upon such an organization's employees' expectations. This want issues from human needs of self-esteem, and levies a highly challenging responsibility upon the organization's management.

MOTIVATION

Just as the employee has certain wants that the organization is expected to supply, the organization has certain types of behavior that it wishes to elicit from the employee. The managerial responsibility for eliciting this behavior is usually termed "direction" or "motivation." In essence, it is a skill in aligning employee and organizational interests so that behavior results in achievement of employee wants simultaneously with attainment of organizational objectives.

The motivational force formula proposed by Vroom, briefly introduced in Chapter 15 in relation to monetary incentives, provides the framework for the motivation function. It will be recalled that the formula suggests that the motivational impact upon an employee of an attempted managerial influence is heavily influenced by the employee's assessment of (1) the anticipated *valence* or value of the perceived outcome of the prescribed behavior and (2) the strength of the *expectancy* that the behavior will actually result in a realization of the outcome.[1]

Valence

To ascertain what the employee values, we must analyze basic human needs and survey current employee wants. The significance of the Maslow hierarchy is that a person will not perceive the values of the lower-priority needs until those of higher priority have been reasonably well satisfied. If one happens upon a man about to expire from exhaustion and thirst in the burning desert, water and rest are the only wants that have value to him. If you say, "I have been following your crawling tracks for ten miles, and since the world's record is eleven without water, would you like to try?" it is not likely that such world recognition will motivate his behavior. Once he has received water, food, and rest, and is assured that they will continue, things will look somewhat different; it is then that he may regret *not* having tried. This fictitious illustration is extreme, but it does illustrate how degrees of value depend upon one's location within the need hierarchy.

There are a number of organizationally controlled incentives that may have value for employees of organizations. We have discussed at length in the preceding section

[1]Victor H. Vroom, *Work and Motivation*, John Wiley & Sons, Inc., New York, 1964, chap. 2.

the use of money as a reward. In addition, there are such rewards as: (1) praise, either public, private, or both; (2) promotion to jobs of higher responsibility; (3) leader's personal interest; (4) status symbols; (5) consultation and solicitation of subordinate participation in managerial decision making; (6) feeling of accomplishment; and (7) peer acceptance and approval. Some of the rewards are highly controllable by the leader while others are more under the control of one's self and one's associates. Leaders can encourage peer acceptance but cannot command it. Leaders can construct job assignments and work environments that should permit a feeling of real accomplishment, but they cannot directly effect the feeling. Leaders can, of course, more fully control the payment of money, issuance of praise, allocation of status symbols, solicitation of participation, and demonstration of personal interest in subordinates. Concerning the last item, it is quite difficult to fake purposefully an interest in others. The story is told of the company president who had learned of this motivational approach and resolved to apply it. He had made up a set of cards showing the special interests and hobbies of his employees. Before making a tour of the office or production floor, he would memorize two or three names, faces, work locations, and the special interest or hobby of each employee. This system appeared to be working, or so the president thought. One day, however, he casually remarked to one employee, "The company is might proud of your bowling scores, Jim." Jim replied, "Mr. Smith, you've been looking at the wrong cards. I'm the fellow who likes gardening. The bowling champ is over there."[2] It is said that the card system was thereupon immediately destroyed.

Expectancy

Though the employee may highly value the proffered reward, its availability will have little impact upon behavior if he or she does not perceive (1) personal capacity to behave in the manner prescribed, and (2) a definite linkage between the behavior desired and the valued payoff. Various studies have demonstrated that self-perceptions of capability can be enhanced by leader and peer views concerning one's capability. Thus, performance is in part a function of the expectations which significant others have of one's competence and ability. In one study of low-level office employees in a federal government agency, reported views of superiors' estimates of personal abilities correlated .93 with performance evaluations actually accorded.[3] In experiments with school children, teachers' prophecies concerning scholastic success tended to be self-fulfilling.[4] This was truer in the first and second grades than at the upper levels. If a teacher felt that a student would do poorly or perform very well, the prophecy was fulfilled. And it is not necessarily a matter of assessing varying levels of ability. In a study of the performance of automobile salesmen in New England, it was discovered that ten of the top fifteen salesmen were in three (out of approximately two hundred) dealerships in the region.[5] Approximately half of these men had previously worked for

[2]Lawrence Stessin, "The Gimmick Craze in Employee Communications," *The Management Review*, vol. 46, no. 9, September 1957, pp. 83–84.

[3]Abraham K. Korman, "Expectancies as Determinants of Performance," *Journal of Applied Psychology*, vol. 55, no. 3, June 1971, pp. 218–222.

[4]Robert Rosenthal and Lenore Jacobson, *Pygmalion in the Classroom*, Holt, Rinehart, and Winston, Inc., New York, 1968, pp. 74–81.

[5]J. Sterling Livingston, "Pygmalion in Management," *Harvard Business Review*, vol. 47, no. 4, July–August 1969, pp. 87–88.

other dealers *without* having superior sales records. It could, of course, be a matter of superior training and organization of the more successful dealerships, but certainly the expectancy of success that was communicated to the salesmen had a motivational effect.

It is believed that expectancy can be more effectively controlled in the early years of experience. Just as the first- and second-grade students were more responsive to teacher expectations than those of upper grades, the beginning employee or manager is more susceptible to the expectations of his superior. In one study at American Telephone and Telegraph Company, it was found that what the company expected of recent college graduates was the most critical factor in their subsequent performance.[6] If a superior feels and communicates that it will take twenty years of experience to be a competent manager, it will probably take that long. When one bank manager did not believe that it took so long to gain the necessary skills, a young assistant developed to the point where he became a branch manager at the age of twenty-five, as compared with most managers, who were in their forties and fifties. In developing his own assistant, the youthful branch manager communicated similar expectations with similar results.[7] The expectations of superiors are communicated daily in many subtle and overt ways.

With respect to perceptions of linkage between behavior and reward, this takes us into the subject of behavior modification, a field that has developed as a result of B. F. Skinner's view of the nature of humans as discussed in the preceding chapter. Whether one accepts Skinner's philosophical view or not, the fact is that managers have always used a conditioning process in attempting to influence subordinate behavior.

BEHAVIOR MODIFICATION

In the management of employee expectancies to effect desired behavior, the basic view is that much, if not all, behavior is learned. Thus, management must first describe in specific terms the type of behavior desired, e.g., higher output, fewer quality rejects, customer complaints answered within one hour, etc. In effect, we would include not only the objectives proposed in a Management by Objectives program, but also the specific behavioral processes designed to produce those objectives.[8]

When the specific behavior is observed, it should be reinforced in a positive fashion. It is contended that any behavior that is not so rewarded will tend to disappear. Reinforcement through punishment is to be deemphasized or avoided because of its stimulation of subordinate anger, hostility, aggression, and rebellion. It has also been observed that behavior that has been conditioned through punishment not only tends to have relatively short-term effects but encourages innovative behavior to thwart and frustrate the manager, e.g., providing the absolute minimum required, producing only when supervised, malicious obedience, etc.

In reinforcing desired behavior in a positive fashion, it is important to allocate the

---

[6]"Some Determinants of Early Managerial Success," Massachusetts Institute of Technology, Alfred P. Sloan School of Management Organization, Research Program no. 81–64, 1964, pp. 13–14.

[7]Livingston, op. cit., p. 87.

[8]See Chap. 13.

reward *soon* after the behavior is effected so that the subordinate perceives a clear linkage. There has been much research concerning the schedule for allocation of rewards. The choices include (1) continuous reinforcement, or the giving of the reward every time the behavior occurs; (2) reinforcement on a fixed ratio schedule—e.g., each morning the manager says, "Keep up the good work," or "This group is the best in the company"; (3) reinforcement at a variable interval, that is, rewarding on a random time basis; and (4) reinforcement on a variable-ratio schedule, e.g., allocate a reward after a random number of units are produced.[9] When beginning to modify the behavior of a person, it is recommended that a continuous reinforcement schedule be followed. Each time success is achieved, rewards should be given. Most firms follow this schedule continually when administering incentive wage systems, e.g., *each* unit of output above standard is rewarded with 5 cents.

Research in the area of behavior modification suggests that the last-named schedule, variable ratio, is most successful in maintaining behavior over long periods of time. As some have pointed out, sitting and playing bingo for long hours at a time is not a task that is intrinsically rewarding in itself. The possibility of a reward on a variable-ratio basis tends to shape the bingo player's behavior. Though this schedule would tend to violate many managers' concepts of consistency and equity, it has been utilized in many organizational contests. For example, in one firm any employee who went injury-free for a three-month period was placed into a pool of candidates for a possible prize. At three-month intervals, telephone calls were placed at random to homes of those employees eligible. If the spouse could supply the safety slogan of the month, a major household appliance was won.

Research does indicate that an assured reward tends to diminish in value over time. Thus, motivation may be highest when there is a less-than-perfect relationship between effort and reward. When one throws darts, it is not very rewarding to stand only two feet distant from the target. The constant reward of the bull's-eye takes on diminishing value. As a result, the thrower stands back far enough so that hitting the bull's-eye is not consistently certain, yet not so far that there is little hope of scoring. Lawler suggests that when the probability of success is greater than .5, it tends to diminish the value of the outcome.[10]

In one well-publicized case of systematic behavior modification, the management of Emery Air Freight used the simple rewards of information feedback and praise to effect significant changes in employee behavior.[11] In responding to customer questions about service and schedules within a 90-minute period, performance moved from 30 percent accomplishment to 90 percent within a few days. Employees were provided feedback charts through which they could monitor their own behavior, and were praised by supervisors on first a fixed- and then a variable-schedule basis. Those who did *not* achieve the desired result were reminded of the goal and then praised for their honesty. This 90 percent achievement remained stable for over three years. In a second attempt, the use of large shipping containers by customers at the suggestion of

[9]Herbert J. Huebner and Alton C. Johnson, "Behavior Modification: An Aid in Solving Personnel Problems," *The Personnel Administrator*, vol. 19, no. 7, October 1974, pp. 32–33.

[10]Edward E. Lawler, III, "Job Attitudes and Employee Motivation: Theory, Research, and Practice," *Personnel Psychology*, vol. 23, no. 2, Summer 1970, p. 234.

[11]"At Emery Air Freight: Positive Reinforcement Boosts Performance," *Organizational Dynamics*, vol. 1, no. 1, 1973, pp. 41–50.

employees moved from 45 percent to 90 percent. Estimated savings to the company were placed at $650,000 per year.

STYLES OF LEADERSHIP

All managers develop a style of leading or motivating subordinates. A leadership style can be defined as a pattern of behavior designed to integrate organizational and personnel interests in pursuit of some objective. As suggested in role analysis, the specific execution of that responsibility can take many forms. As a consequence, there have been developed various frameworks or schemes that depict the types of leadership styles from which a manager may select the one most appropriate to personal, subordinate, and organizational needs.

One of the commonly cited frameworks consists of a simple continuum from total autocracy to almost total democracy. This continuum would consist of the following: (1) coercive autocracy, where the leader *tells* and if necessary threatens; (2) benevolent autocracy, where the leader tells *and* explains, utilizing positive reinforcement if the behavior is forthcoming; (3) manipulative autocracy, where the leader "cons" subordinates into thinking that they are significantly participating as he or she is pulling the strings behind the scenes—in effect, a sophisticated autocrat; (4) consultative leadership, where employees feel and believe that their inputs are truly desired and can have impact upon the decision; and (5) a laissez-faire approach, where the leader wishes to join the group as a fellow participant and do what the group wants to do. Obviously, in the last style, the organization superiors still hold the leader accountable for decision results, thus limiting the degree to which this industrial democracy can be practiced.

The introduction of such a scheme of leadership styles does not require that the leader acquire and develop a single one among the available choices. In a study of 143 British managers, it was found that all but ten used three or more styles, depending upon the nature of the decision.[12] When the decision was important to the organization but not the subordinate, managers tended to be autocratic, with or without explanation. When it was important to subordinates but not to the organization, leaders tended to consult, encourage joint decision making, or actually delegate the decision to them. When the decision was not important to either, leaders tended to save personal time by autocratically deciding or allowing determination by subordinates. When the subject was one of importance to both, the greater majority tended to *consult* with subordinates prior to making the decision themselves. In contrasting style preferences in different portions of organizations, the greatest tendencies toward more subordinate participation were observed within the personnel department and among levels of general management, the least were reported in production and finance units, while sales and purchasing units were in the middle between these two extremes.

The implication that leadership style selection should be heavily influenced by forces in the subordinates, leaders, and the situation has led various theorists and consultants to establish situational frameworks. Prominent among these are the frameworks of Reddin and Fiedler. On the other hand, two of the best-known behavioral scientists, Rensis Likert and Robert Blake, propose that there is only one best

---

[12]Frank A. Heller, "Leadership, Decision Making, and Contingency Theory," *Industrial Relations*, vol. 12, no. 2, May 1973, pp. 194–195.

universal style suitable for all personnel on all occasions. Each of these frameworks will be briefly described below.

Reddin 3-D theory

Following the research of Ohio State University, which suggested that two important leadership behaviors were *initiating* and *consideration*, Reddin proposes to identify style mixtures in four basic types of situations.[13] As indicated in Figure 18-1, styles and situations can be placed into a grid format utilizing the dimensions of Task Orientation and Relationships Orientation. Dividing the total area into four cells results in situations where the manager can be (1) separated from both task and human considerations, (2) highly related to the task with limited emphasis upon people, (3) highly concerned with people with limited attention being allocated to the task, and (4) highly concerned with integrating *both* task and human objectives. The scheme is labeled "3-D" inasmuch as in each of these four cells two types of styles are identified—one which is most effective in dealing with a situation and the other less effective. In Figure 18-1, these are indicated by the letters "I" for ineffective and "E" for effective, though their specific location is not necessarily as depicted by Reddin.

In cell 3, for example, the ineffective style is labeled "missionary," suggesting a disproportionate concern for people. A more effective balance, 3E, would be a "developer," where the orientation is more toward helping people develop skills that will ultimately pay off in task accomplishment. Managers working in personnel units tend to have styles located in this cell.

In cell 1, the ineffective style is "deserter," suggesting that one wishes *not* to be a leader. The more effective in this type of situation is 1E, "bureaucrat," displaying a dedication to enforcing the procedures and rules of the organization. If these procedures are correct, the style is effective. In large organizations, various positions may require this type behavior to ensure minimum levels of uniformity. In cell 2, the less effective style is "autocrat," while the more effective is "benevolent autocrat." It

---

[13]William J. Reddin, *Managerial Effectiveness*, McGraw-Hill Book Company, New York, 1970. For a review of research efforts utilizing the Ohio State factors, see Abraham K. Korman, "'Consideration,' 'Initiating Structure,' and Organizational Criteria: A Review," *Personnel Psychology*, vol. 19, no. 4, Winter 1966, pp. 361–379.

Figure 18-1 Leadership styles framework

Reddin 3-D styles

1-I Deserter	3-I Missionary
1-E Bureaucrat	3-E Developer
2-I Autocrat	4-I Compromiser
2-E Benevolent autocrat	4-E Executive

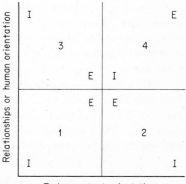

Task or output orientation

will be recalled above that managers in production units ordinarily display autocratic tendencies. Only in cell 4 is the inner position *not* the effective one. The less effective style here is termed "compromiser," involving integration through trade-off and "split-the-difference" approaches. The more effective style is termed "executive," emphasizing teamwork, coordination, and confrontation to discover the law of the situation. In much testing of style tendencies throughout the world, Reddin has discovered that higher-level managers tend toward the "executive" style. In any event, there are four acceptable styles depending upon the situation.

Fiedler's contingency theory

The contingency theory developed by Fred E. Fiedler is also a situational approach.[14] The framework is made up of eight significantly different situations and *two* basic types of leadership styles. In identifying the eight situations, three major elements are analyzed: (1) leader-member relations, (2) task structure, and (3) position power of the leader. Measurement of leader-member relations is done on a group atmosphere scale indicating the degree to which the leader feels accepted by subordinates. The atmosphere may be friendly or unfriendly, relaxed or tense, and threatening or supportive. Task structure is measured by evaluating clarity of goals, verifiability of decisions made, specificity of solutions, and multiplicity of options available for solving problems. The position power of the leader is determined by the degree of influence he or she has over rewards and punishments, as well as by amount of official authority. Through mixing these three elements, the following eight situations can be identified.

Situation	Leader-member relations	Task structure	Position power
1	Good	Structured	High
2	Good	Structured	Low
3	Good	Unstructured	High
4	Good	Unstructured	Low
5	Poor	Structured	High
6	Poor	Structured	Low
7	Poor	Unstructured	High
8	Poor	Unstructured	Low

These eight situations vary in accordance with the degree of leader influence and control over the group. There is maximum influence in situation 1 and very little in situation 8. Research evidence indicates that a *task-oriented, controlling leader* will prove most effective when the situations are either very easy (1, 2, and 3) or very difficult (6, 7, and 8). The more *permissive, considerate* leader performs more effectively in the intermediate situations of medium difficulty. In Fiedler's approach, the two leadership styles are measured by asking one to rate her or his Least Preferred Coworker on seventeen bipolar adjective scales, e.g., pleasant to unpleasant. A high-score LPC leader is seen as being personal relations-oriented, and the low-score LPC leader is more task-oriented.

[14]Fred E. Fiedler, *A Theory of Leadership Effectiveness*, McGraw-Hill Book Company, New York, 1967.

There have been over forty studies dealing with the Fiedler contingency theory, and most seem to be supportive of the concept that leadership styles should be adapted to situational elements. Arguments about specifics of the theory are prevalent in the literature. There has, for example, been little research in situation number 6. In any event, the concept that leadership styles are *contingent* upon situational variables is both highly plausible and consistent with both the continuum and Reddin frameworks.

Management Grid

Moving to the universalists' frameworks, the Management Grid of Robert Blake and Jane Mouton is one of the most widely known style schemes among business managers.[15] If Figure 18-1 were relabeled using "concern for people" for relationships oriented, and "concern for output" for task orientation, we could then number each from 1 to 9. The grid is thus a 9 × 9 checkerboard and a score of 1 denotes low concern and a score of 9 shows high concern. On this basis, five basic styles have been identified as follows:

1,1 The leader whose style exhibits little concern for either people or output. Reddin uses the term "deserter" and agrees that it is typically ineffective.

9,1 The manager who stresses output and operating efficiency with neglect or unconcern for human components. Reddin entitles this "autocrat."

1,9 The manager who is thoughtful, comfortable, and friendly, and who exhibits little concern for output. Human considerations are placed before organizational requirements. Blake and Mouton have referred to this as "country-club" management, while Reddin uses "missionary." Both agree that it is ineffective.

5,5 The manager who attempts to balance and trade off concern for work in exchange for a satisfactory level of cooperation, a "compromiser."

9,9 The manager who seeks high output through the medium of committed people, a commitment achieved through mutual trust, respect, and a realization of interdependence. Reddin terms this "executive" and agrees that it is more effective than "compromiser" in situations calling for integration.

In the view of Blake and Mouton, *only* the 9,9 style represents a successful integration of organizational and human values in *all* situations. They assume that both values can be maximized simultaneously, and they rest their scheme on the philosophical implications of the human models proposed by Maslow, McGregor, Argyris, and Herzberg, the organizational psychologists.

Blake and Mouton have been successful in converting leadership styles toward the 9,9 corner of the grid. Their total program of organization development encompasses six phases, the first two of which concentrate on altering styles. In one large organization, comparisons were made of managers who had received no Grid training versus those who had been exposed in phases 1 and 2 to both structured insight and team-development training techniques. Among those with no Grid experience, 28 percent described their personal styles in 9,9 terms.[16] For those completing phase 1, the

[15]Robert R. Blake and Jane S. Mouton; Louis B. Barnes and Larry Greiner, "Breakthrough in Organization Development," *Harvard Business Review*, vol. 42, no. 6, November–December 1964, p. 133.

[16]Howard A. Hart, "The Grid Appraised—Phases 1 and 2," *Personnel*, vol. 51, no. 5, September–October 1974, p. 52.

responses rose to 36.4 percent. Almost one-half of those undergoing team development in phase 2 gave a 9,9 response.

Likert's continuum

The second universalist framework of leadership styles was developed by Rensis Likert, formerly Director of the Institute for Social Research at the University of Michigan.[17] It consists of a classical-behavioral continuum of styles ranging from autocracy to participation in the manner described above. Four basic styles are envisaged: System I—Exploitative Autocracy, System II—Benevolent Autocracy, System III—Consultative Leadership, and System IV—Participative Group Leadership. Only the last style or system is deemed best in the long run for all situations.

System III requires that group members be consulted prior to the decision being reached, but it does not involve them in the actual process. System IV's emphasis is upon a *group* participative role with full involvement in the process of reaching a conclusion. Subordinates feel free to discuss things with their leader, and the leader displays supportive, rather than condescending or threatening, behavior. It is contended that the entire organization should be designed along System IV lines, with work being performed by a series of overlapping groups. The group leader provides a linking pin between his or her group and other units that are higher in the organization. Decision making is widespread throughout the enterprise, with the power of knowledge usually taking precedence over the power of authority. If well executed, it is contended that the informal and formal organization can be one and the same—all social forces support efforts to achieve organizational goals.

The frameworks of both Likert and Blake/Mouton rest on the philosophical human models of self-actualization, "theory Y," maturation, and motivator factors. In contrast, the situationalists suggest that organizations, technologies, problems, and personnel will differ, and the successful style is one that adapts to these constraints and contingencies. A key factor in the choice of style is subordinate participation, a subject to be discussed in the following section.

DEGREES OF PARTICIPATION

Where situations permit, some form of subordinate participation in decisions that affect them and the firm is likely to be a valued reward based on the human needs of self-esteem and self-actualization. Anticipated returns to the organization would include higher-quality decisions when subordinates possess relevant information unavailable to managers, greater acceptability of resulting decisions, and greater identification with the organization and its goals.

The degree of subordinate participation is usually limited by such variables as ability levels, interest levels, amount of time available, skill of the leader, and the area of freedom available. Knowledge, ability, and interest vary among personnel, and the leader cannot transform everyone overnight into the "theory Y" image. Organizational restraints always exist in terms of time available to reach a decision, as well as subjects

[17]Rensis Likert, *The Human Organization*, McGraw-Hill Book Company, New York, 1967.

Figure 18-2 Degrees of participation

	Degrees		
Factor	Low	Moderate	High
Scope of usage	Narrow, minor matters	Selected subjects	Everything of real concern
Frequency of use	Rarely used	Occasional or periodic meetings	Consistently, "way of life"
Persons involved	Select few Top management	Select groups or committees	All supervisors All employees
Part taken	Communication heard	Consulted (consulta- tive management)	Group decision (demo- cratic management)

Source: Robert E. Schwab, "Participative Management: The Solution to the Human Relations Problem?" Speech before the Cincinnati chapter of the Society for the Advancement of Management, Oct. 2, 1952.

about which group decisions can be made. Figure 18-2 portrays one way of looking at the alternative degrees available.

Concerning scope of subject and frequency of use, it was determined in one study that the significance of the subject was a more important factor in producing employee satisfaction than sheer quantity of participative acts.[18] A high quantity of participative interactions on trivial matters is more indicative of manipulative autocracy than of true involvement. In a survey of 3,453 subscribers to *Harvard Business Review*, only one-third of this managerially sophisticated group would agree that employees should be allowed to vote on certain policy issues.[19] If confined solely to subordinate managers ("persons involved" in Figure 18-2), the percentage rose to about half. Subscriber approval of employee voting was as follows: 29 percent on mandatory retirement policies, 37 percent on possible plant relocation, 29 percent on individual relocation, 16 percent on accepting controversial defense contracts, and 15 percent on establishing hiring policies for minority groups. Two-thirds of these respondents would not bind management to the results of the vote, thus allocating it to the "consulted" degree for "part taken" in Figure 18-2.

As a final observation on Figure 18-2, a reading of the columns would indicate the extremes of participation. An extremely high position would be that on "everything of real concern" as a "way of life" the leader should allow "all employees" to make a "group decision." Except for a small and sophisticated primary work group, one might wonder how such an organization could exist. Multiple management, a program discussed in Chapter 11, would rank on the moderate degree for scope, moderate on frequency, moderate on persons involved (middle management), and between mod- erate and high on part taken (95 percent of recommendations were accepted). The Scanlon plan, discussed in Chapter 16, would be moderate on scope, moderate on frequency, high on persons involved, and probably moderate on part taken.

[18]J. B. Ritchie and Raymond E. Miles, "An Analysis of Quantity and Quality of Participation as Mediating Variables in the Participative Decision Making Process," *Personnel Psychology*, vol. 34, no. 3, Autumn 1970, pp. 347–359.

[19]David W. Ewing, "Who Wants Corporate Democracy?" *Harvard Business Review*, vol. 49, no. 5, September–October 1971, pp. 25–28.

PERSUASION

Many observers of private business organizations have concluded that the currently dominant style of leadership is that of benevolent autocracy. We have moved from a position of coercive autocracy to one of benevolency in response to governmental decrees, union powers, and adaptation to higher-skilled and more sophisticated employees. Nevertheless, the typical management wishes to "call the shots" but realizes that subordinate acceptance is crucial to continuing cooperation. As such, this form of autocracy calls for skills of persuasion or indoctrination.

Indoctrination is the process of presenting one viewpoint to a person in the hope that it will be accepted. The indoctrinator has decided what she or he wants the person to believe, and presents the one doctrine persuasively and effectively. The objective is acceptance of the doctrine. The term "propaganda" is frequently applied to an indoctrination process that incorporates the use of half-truths and lies. Organizations often apply the term "educational" to processes that are indeed indoctrinational in nature. There is nothing essentially wrong with indoctrination so long as we maintain our freedom of speech and freedom of press. We are all subjected to such attempts daily. Though they are usually called "selling," "persuading," or "arguing," they all consist fundamentally in one person or group trying to convince another of the correctness of a view. Acceptance of some values to be held in common is essential to organized activity.

There are a number of principles of indoctrination. Many of these appear to be obvious and dictated by common sense, but their statement is necessary to present the full nature and scope of the indoctrination process. More complete statements of these principles will be found in other sources.[20]

PRINCIPLE OF REPETITION   The more frequently one repeats a doctrine or idea, the more likely it is to be accepted. This principle also involves the idea of continuity; that is, indoctrination is a never-ending process. Industrial management has a number of doctrines that it would like accepted by employees to a reasonable degree. Among these doctrines are the following:

1   The free-enterprise system can and does contribute greater values to consumers and members of the system than any other economic system.
2   There is a necessary and legitimate foundation for the making of a profit.
3   The profits made by industry in general and this company in particular are reasonable and necessary for the welfare of the economy.
4   Management, labor, and capital must cooperate in organized activity for the benefit of all.

PRINCIPLE OF TRUTHFULNESS   The truer the doctrine, the more likely it is to be believed. This is a particularly important principle in the United States, where we have a maximum of freedom of speech and press. Untrue doctrines will certainly be attacked by the press, labor unions, and other spokesmen. In addition, management must realize that it must live with its employees continuously. If you have duped them once, it will take a long time to regain their trust.

[20]Ralph C. Davis, *The Fundamentals of Top Management*, Harper & Row, Publishers, Incorporated, New York, 1951, pp. 593–600.

PRINCIPLE OF SIMPLICITY   The more simple and understandable the doctrine, the more likely it is to be accepted. Understanding is prerequisite to acceptance. What we cannot understand we automatically suspect.

PRINCIPLE OF THE PRESTIGE OF THE INDOCTRINATOR   The greater the prestige of the indoctrinator, the more likely we are to accept what he says. If the President of the United States makes some statement, a large percentage of the population will accept it without checking, solely because of the person who said it. The implication that this principle has for management is that the more confidence employees have in their leadership, the more likely they are to accept new ideas and to try new methods.

PRINCIPLE OF THE PRESTIGE OF THE DOCTRINE   The greater the prestige of the doctrine, the more likely it is to be believed. People tend to accept with a minimum of questioning the beliefs that have been accepted by a majority of the people with whom they are associated. Their acceptance is evidence of the human need of social approval.

PRINCIPLE OF EXCLUSION OF OPPOSING IDEAS   This is a very powerful principle and one which we in this country find highly objectionable. If you are able to keep people from being exposed to opposing ideas, repetition of your own idea over a period of time will result in what some term "brainwashing." The power of this principle is evidenced by the first act of new dictators and despots, the seizure of the communications systems of a country.

At one time, this principle was applied to management with respect to the doctrine of the desirability of joining labor unions. Under the Wagner Act, to coerce, threaten, or reward employees in the matter of whether or not to join a union constituted an unfair labor practice. This provision, as gradually interpreted and applied by the National Labor Relations Board, was finally held to mean that management could *not* legally present an opinion concerning this issue. In view of the usual power and authority of management over employees, an opinion was interpreted to be an implied threat. The amendment to the Wagner Act, passed in 1947 as the Taft-Hartley Act, gave back to management its freedom of speech concerning this doctrine.

These principles of indoctrination are highly practical and pertinent to modern labor relations. In one case brought before the National Labor Relations Board, the labor union had complained that the company had convened all employees for an indoctrination session one hour before the labor-representation election.[21] The union contended that the election, which it had lost, was unfair since the union had not had equal time to present its case just prior to the election. The Board agreed that holding the election on company property had given the company an unfair advantage, that a new election should be held, and that a period of silence should be declared twenty-four hours prior to the new election. In this manner the union could indoctrinate in the union hall and the company on its property, but nothing was to be said about the issue immediately before the election. The National Labor Relations Board, under the authority of the Wagner and Taft-Hartley Acts, issues directives which regulate the manner of company and union indoctrination with respect to employee

[21]Peter A. Davis, "Before the NLRB Election: What You Can and Can't Do," *Personnel*, vol. 44, no. 4, July–August 1967, pp. 9–10.

choice in selecting representatives. Among the great number of such directives are the following:

1   The company must turn over to the union a list of names and addresses of employees eligible to participate in the representation election, in order that the union may be able to contact all employees.[22]

2   A company may declare its unalterable opposition to unions, but may not term them "enemies" or "communists."

3   A company may tell employees that wage raises, if secured by the union, *might* require a reduction of overtime.

4   A company may say that it believes union dues to be a waste of money.

5   A company may describe experiences of other plants that relocated to avoid unionization, so long as this is not used as a threat.

6   The company must accept union sound-car broadcast appeals for votes near plant entrances after the 24-hour ban discussed above; they are construed merely as a "reminder" to vote.

7   A company may not forbid distribution of union literature in nonworking areas during nonworking time.

8   Information leaflets may be included in pay envelopes even during the 24-hour ban, provided that they do not contain promises or threats. Specifically, part of the wage due can be given separately with a note that this amount (union dues) will be subtracted from the paycheck in the event that the union wins.

9   The company cannot usually prevent employees from wearing campaign buttons. Exceptions are in cases where the buttons will distract or interfere in production process, when they will detract from the dignity of business operations, and when customers have voluntarily complained in writing.

10 Management may *never* wear campaign buttons.

The minds and attitudes of employees are of great importance to any organization. Although management should not seek to control those minds, it should be active in utilizing them in participative programs, as well as in attempting to increase the acceptability of official decisions. Persuasion, coupled with the power issuing from authority, is an attractive style to many managers of private organizations. Offsetting power sources in the forms of government and labor unions have led to style changes in the direction of bargaining and compromise. Organization psychologists would strongly recommend moving further to considerations of power issuing from employee knowledge and goodwill. This subject of power, along with other important components of the emerging informal organization, is the subject of the next chapter.

SUMMARY

The needs that a human being brings to the organization are made evident in terms of specific wants such as money, security of job, congenial associates, credit and praise, a meaningful job, opportunity to advance, good working conditions, reasonable orders, a relevant organization, and competent and fair leadership. These wants provide an array of motivational tools that managers may utilize to motivate behavior toward

---

[22]*Excelsior Underwear, Inc.*, 156 NLRB No. 111, 1966. See Earle K. Shawe, "The National Labor Relations Board and Employee Free Choice," *Personnel Administration*, vol. 30, no. 4, July–August 1967, pp. 46–50.

desired directions. Motivational force is greatest if the want is highly valued, if the person feels capable of performing as specified, and if he or she perceives that the reward will actually be allocated. Behavior modification suggests that a continuing positive reinforcement schedule is preferred at the beginning of any new program, to be followed by a reward schedule of a variable-ratio type. Ignoring undesirable behavior is preferred to punishment.

Leaders must align and integrate member efforts and interests with the goals of the organization. Style frameworks portraying available choices include those of the situationalists such as Reddin and Fiedler, as well as those of the universalists Likert and Blake/Mouton. The latter style schemes propose to implement the human models of the organization psychologists Maslow, McGregor, Argyris, and Herzberg. The total conversion of the organization to this set of values is termed "organization development."

Following the recommendations of organization psychologists would entail heavy utilization of participative philosophies of leadership. The fact that most agree that the typical leadership approach is the "tell and sell" benevolent autocratic style prescribes consideration of skills of persuasion and indoctrination. Regardless of what the leader prescribes, orders, permits, or manipulates, the members of the enterprise will develop an unofficial organization of their own, the subject of the next chapter.

DISCUSSION QUESTIONS

1   Explain the role of leader and peer expectations in altering subordinate perceptions of expectancies in the Vroom formula.
2   In behavior modification programs, what are the available types of reward schedules? What is the role of punishment?
3   Define and distinguish between human needs and employee wants.
4   Itemize leadership-style frameworks that could be classified as (a) situational or (b) universal. What is the meaning of this classification?
5   Compare and contrast the style frameworks of Reddin's 3-D with Blake/Mouton's Management Grid.
6   What are the philosophical underpinnings of the 9,9 style and System IV?
7   Describe the varying situations that provide the framework for Fiedler's contingency theory.
8   Apply the degrees of participation model to both multiple management and the Scanlon plan.
9   In the event that a manager wishes to convince subordinates of the desirability of a new company policy favoring hiring of the culturally disadvantaged, how would you go about applying the principles of indoctrination?
10 In what way does the National Labor Relations Board regulate company and union rights of indoctrination?

SUPPLEMENTARY READING

GREINER, Larry E.: "What Managers Think of Participative Leadership," *Harvard Business Review*, vol. 51, no. 2, March–April 1973, pp. 111–117.
HELLER, Frank A.: "Leadership, Decision Making, and Contingency Theory," *Industrial Relations*, vol. 12, no. 2, May 1973, pp. 183–199.

LUTHANS, Fred, and Robert Kreitner: "The Management of Behavioral Contingencies," *Personnel*, vol. 51, no. 4, July–August 1974, pp. 7–16.

MITCHELL, Terence R.: "Motivation and Participation: An Integration," *Academy of Management Journal*, vol. 16, no. 4, December 1973, pp. 670–679.

SCHNEIER, Craig Eric: "Behavior Modification in Management: A Review and Critique," *Academy of Management Journal*, vol. 17, no. 3, September 1974, pp. 528–548.

SCHRANK, Robert: "Work in America: What Do Workers Really Want?" *Industrial Relations*, vol. 13, no. 2, May 1974, pp. 124–129.

STINSON, John E., and Lane Tracy: "Some Disturbing Characteristics of the LPC Score," *Personnel Psychology*, vol. 27, no. 3, Autumn 1974, pp. 477–485.

NINETEEN
THE EMERGING INFORMAL ORGANIZATION

Earlier in this text, we discussed the concept of the formal organization. It was described as the official structure of relationships that serve to combine people, functions, and physical factors together in order that they may be directed by management toward a common objective. Personnel management assists in the organizing process, not only in providing expert advice, but also in procuring and placing personnel into officially designated slots known as "jobs." Once these artificial slots are peopled by human beings, the organization comes alive and is filled with a myriad of informal or unofficial relationships. Some of these are of the "feeling" type: Joe likes John, respects Georgia, detests Jim, and is indifferent to Joan. Obviously, these feelings will affect the manner in which official duties are executed. Other informal relationships pertain to performance behavior that is not officially prescribed in the manual, job description, procedure, or approved policy. If the appointed supervisor's actions and attitudes do not inspire cooperation and respect in subordinates, the workers may turn to another person for the leadership they desire. Thus, we often see the emergence of informal leaders who can and do influence both official and unofficial activities. There may be a number of such leaders. One may establish and control the mores of the shop, arbitrate disputes, and the like; another may be the spokesman or spokeswoman in presenting group requests to the formal leader.

In this chapter, we shall examine the nature of the informal organization that inevitably *emerges* from interpersonal relationships among specific individuals and groups. As Figure 19-1 suggests in a somewhat humorous fashion, some managers believe that the formal organization totally controls behavior and are oblivious to the many deviations that will occur. The author does not mean to suggest that the informal organization consists solely of drinking and sleeping on the job, gossip, sabotage, backstabbing, and aggressive attacks on others. These undoubtedly do occur at times.

Rather, the emerging informal organization is viewed as the basic means through which the greater bulk of the organization's work is accomplished. There is literally no way that any manager can specify in advance all activities and interactions necessary for effective accomplishment of organization goals. We are dependent upon the flexible and thinking human being to transform rational formal plans into realistic goal accomplishment.

NATURE OF THE INFORMAL ORGANIZATION

As suggested above, management does not have the option of destroying or abolishing the informal organization. Wherever people are, informal relationships will spring up. As indicated in Figure 19-2, these relationships emerge from the formal gathering of

Figure 19-1   Formal and informal organization structure

Source: Ross Martin Company, *Systemation Letter*, copyright 1959, Tulsa, Okla. By permission.

inputs from the environment to create the official structure of the enterprise. The organization, designated as the "processor," is a mechanism designed to transform inputs from the environment into outputs desired by other portions of the outer environment. The variety and quality of the inputs, such as human resources, management philosophies, and available technology, will directly affect the design of the official processor. We have noted earlier how economic conditions as well as specific governmental legislation and orders can lead to the creation of specific organizational activities.

Within the processor, the first duty of the manager is to determine the necessary activities required for goal accomplishment. This task was described extensively in Chapter 3, but major elements would include the design of *jobs* for all personnel, the gathering of groups of jobs into *units* such as departments or divisions, and the establishment of the formal ties of authority, responsibility, and accountability. When these jobs and units are filled with particular people with varying personalities, an informal organization will emerge. The informal additive counterpart of the job is that of role. It is additive in that the role includes not only the official job content but also the behavioral expectations of others with whom the incumbent must deal. The informal counterpart of the official unit is the primary work group. Such small and cohesive groupings of people who are attracted to each other are considerably affected by formal requirements for working in certain locations. The informal counterparts of authority, responsibility, and accountability are the relationships of status, power, and politics. Power, for example, is a broader concept than authority. It deals with total influence, only *one* source for which is authority. These five concepts (role, primary group, status, power, and politics) constitute the greater bulk of this chapter.

The planned and intended outputs of the organizational processor would certainly include productivity in the form of a product or service desired by society. In addition, organizational psychologists would also content that human growth and self-actualization should be concomitant goals for a human society. Nothing ever works totally as planned, and one would be wise to be aware of possible dysfunctional outputs. We have noted earlier that rational incentive plans often do not prevent output restriction by primary groups. And many organization psychologists contend that business firms have been successful in producing the unintended consequences of human frustration, apathy, and indifference. The manager must constantly work with both the formal and the informal organization to promote intended outputs and to

Figure 19-2 Formal and informal organization

diminish those of the dysfunctional type. As Davis states, "The most desirable combination of formal and informal organization appears to be a predominant formal system to maintain unity toward objectives, along with a well-developed informal system to maintain group cohesiveness and teamwork."[1]

VALUES AND LOSSES OF THE INFORMAL ORGANIZATION

Both formal and informal organization have values and costs. Formal organization is designed to make possible the effective execution of a high volume of planned tasks by multiple personnel. As such, it is adapted to yesterday's problems, which are also presumed to be a large portion of tomorrow's tasks. But tomorrow's problems are not always foreseeable and controllable, so that a more flexible managerial attitude toward organization structure and organizational behavior is required.

Management must establish basic, general guides in the forms of goals, policies, procedures, and structures. At the same time, it must develop means for combatting the pressures and habits through which people become prisoners of these guides. Essential to this are the recruitment and retention of inquiring, motivated, and innovative personnel. Equally essential is the creation of an environment in which these personnel can thrive. This requires a tolerance for reasonable deviations from organization guides, a measure of freedom in which the limits of a job can be reworked, an absence of overt and covert thought control, and provision for conflict and dissent. In classical management literature, conflict seems to be the antithesis of good organization. Cooperation, subordination, and coordination are the values to be derived from functional definition, commensurate authority and responsibility, single accountability, and an absence of gaps and overlaps in responsibility. Those who emphasize this approach assume that this cooperation and subordination are geared to a correct and true specification of goals. If this assumption is not true, if there is disagreement about goals, then dissent and conflict can lead to organizational reexamination, renewal, and revitalization. Such renewal activities in turn will have to be incorporated into the formal system if the enterprise is to derive maximum utilization of its personnel; yet this incorporation must not mean the end of further "constructive dissent."

On the other hand, objections and contributions of particular organization members do not always magically represent truth and correctness. The manager is an organization member who *also* has certain skills and information that are often not possessed by others. This position is unique in that he or she must *judge* the quality of the contributions of others. The manager has the formal responsibility for decisions and is accountable for the resulting action. But even when criticism is rejected and subordination is required, one would do well to defend the prescribed course of action through information and explanation, rather than to rely solely upon authority. The ability to direct and control without sacrificing the values of freedom and dissent may be tantamount to eating one's cake and having it, too. It is, nevertheless, the managerial stance necessary for an effective integration of formal and informal organizations.

To delineate more specifically the values of informal organization, it should be

---

[1]Keith Davis, *Human Relations at Work*, 3d ed., McGraw-Hill Book Company, New York, 1967, p. 232.

pointed out that the informal organization makes possible the accomplishment of the great bulk of the organization's work. If personnel were restricted precisely to the formal contacts established by the chart and manual, the organization would become a straitjacket rather than a harness. If all the rules, policies, regulations, job descriptions, and standard procedures were followed to the letter and not altered or supplemented in any manner, irreparable harm would probably be done to the organization. In one company, for instance, a form of employee slowdown was instituted by a group who agreed to follow rigidly all formal regulations. In a short while output was far below the usual norm. In the absence of the perfect prediction of the future, management must rely upon informal contacts and cooperation to effect the greater portion of operating results.

Informal organization often serves as a "patch" that can be applied to offset formal organization deficiencies. At times a particular job incumbent cannot really fulfill requirements even though systematic personnel management has properly recruited, placed, inducted, and trained the person for that job. In such cases, the person may seek help from others, including peers and subordinates. The manager who is deficient in planning, but excellent in organizing, directing, and controlling, recruits an assistant whose skills compensate for this deficiency. The manager whose responsibility, contrary to formal organization principles, exceeds authority seeks to resolve the discrepancy by increasing *informal* influence through friendly persuasion or exchanges of favors. The manager who shares authority over a subordinate with other managers, contrary to the principle of single accountability, seeks to develop an informal arrangement in order that coordinated direction may be effected. It is naive to think that the formal organization will automatically work as intended. In reality, there must be informal reshuffling and re-relating in order to advance the work of the organization. Care must be taken, of course, to ensure that such reshuffling is actually in the best interests of the organization.

Some of the informal groups established by employees provide great social and psychological values to members of the group. There is a satisfaction in being accepted as a part of an informal social group organized at the place of work. Pleasure in work is added to the satisfaction of doing the formal job well. This is why freedom of work and movement within the organization is so highly valued by most people. Not only does the accorded freedom show respect for the person concerned, but it permits one to talk, or gossip if you will, and make numerous contacts with various people. Informal relationships are highly satisfying to gregarious people and thus constitute a social value which contributes to the development of good morale.

Other values of the informal organization have been cited by various authors. Among them are the values of providing faster and sometimes more complete information and of stimulating better management on the part of the formal superior. The informal channel of communication known as the grapevine has received much attention in recent years. Rumors as well as facts fly along this medium. Management has often had to supplement formal channels of communication in order to provide subordinates with official information more speedily, in competition with the grapevine. The grapevine also contributes to the social values of work. Gossip is satisfying to both men and women. When the grapevine stops transmitting information—facts or fiction—*then* it is time to begin worrying. Listening to as well as feeding the grapevine is a management skill well worth developing. In a study of a grapevine in one organization, it was discovered that of the rank and file employees, 33 percent were isolates who did not participate in the grapevine, 57 percent functioned as dead-enders who listened but did not pass on information, and only 10 percent were liaison individuals who passed on the information to one or more people.[2] All of the personnel in managerial positions functioned as liaison individuals. Most of the interchange was *within* formal organizational groupings, rather than between different departments. The fact that a limited number of individuals form the major links in a grapevine indicates that it can be fed and tapped with some degree of success.

The fact that management is aware of the power held by associates, equals, or subordinates, through their willingness or reluctance to give cooperation and enthusiasm, should stimulate them to be more concerned with how they manage. Instead of relying upon the brute force of formal authority, managers are tending to consult with others on plans, explain actions more fully, motivate subordinates to comply with orders, and emphasize a "we" approach. The influence held by the group must be respected. Thus, a fuller recognition of the nature and importance of the informal organization serves to stimulate a greater concern for the human relations implications of management decisions and actions.

The losses suffered through informal organization are particularly apparent when a head-on conflict with formal organization takes place. The supervisor who abdicates her or his position to the shop steward on an informal basis must be reeducated and strengthened or replaced. Though management recognizes the values of the contributions of informal leadership, it cannot accept the informal leader as the sole leader. The ultimate to be desired is that the formal leader and the informal leader should be the same person. Occasions have arisen when management was forced to alter informal relationships for the good of the organization. Two instances might be cited. A supervisor who rode to work with one of his female subordinates was asked to find other means of commuting when she attempted to take over the supervisory job through him. He had a tendency to follow her advice on departmental matters instead of higher management's, even to the point of accepting her intervention in the processing of grievances. Management chose to reestablish the man as supervisor rather than to replace him. In the second instance, a laundry manager was confronted with a demand by eight of his employees to discharge a particular person, on the basis that she was not wanted by the eight. Though cliques can often work for the benefit of the organization, this manager believed that there was no sound reason for this dismissal. When the clique threatened to resign en masse, the laundry manager gave in and let the employee go. He then proceeded to break up this group by moving them to various parts of the organization. Though they clung to their informal relationship for several months thereafter, the strength of the ties gradually diminished. This illustrates the part that geographical proximity can play in the matter of establishing and maintaining informal relationships.

It is possible to overemphasize informal organization so much that the formal organization is destroyed. If all work is conducted on the basis of personality, informal contacts, and social meetings, chaos and disorder can result. The disorder can be avoided only when all personnel are so in tune with each other that all actions mesh automatically. Though such a high development of the art of informal organization has

[2]Harold Sutton and Lyman W. Porter, "A Study of the Grapevine in a Governmental Organization," *Personnel Psychology*, vol. 21, no. 2, Summer 1968, p. 226.

been observed on a few occasions, it is very unlikely that it could be continued for any length of time. Turnover will introduce new people and new relationships. Informal organization must of necessity always remain small. It takes formal organization to relate large groups of people to a single objective.

ROLE AND PRIMARY GROUPS

Though alluded to earlier in relation to job analysis, the concept of role is broader than that of a job. A role would consist of the total pattern of expected behavior, interactions, and feelings for a job incumbent. If a person is officially designated as a supervisor, she or he is often expected to dress, talk, act, and identify as a manager. Thus, in an autocratically managed enterprise, a permissive supervisor would experience role conflict even though there is agreement that one must plan, organize, direct, and control. The manner in which one undertakes these functions is made evident in daily activities, interactions, and communications.

In role theory, various special concepts will add to the understanding of the nature of a role. A *role set* is composed of all persons and groups with whom an individual must have interactions. As suggested above, the organizational superior will have one set of behavioral expectations. On the other hand, subordinates will expect their boss to represent and protect them from threats and pressures from above. Various staff specialists will expect cooperation and collaboration with special studies within the firm. When the supervisor attends community meetings, he or she may go as an employee of the organization and fulfill the role of its representative. It is probable that he or she will develop friends within the enterprise and that they may make various demands which may or may not coincide with the official role. A friend from outside the organization may appear in the form of an applicant for a vacancy within the supervisor's unit. And, of course, one's spouse and children have certain behavioral expectations of one in one's additional roles as husband or wife and mother or father. All of these, and more, would constitute the role set.

Role demands would be the specific official and unofficial expectations projected by members of the role set. These are communicated through orders, requests, pressures, and reactions. Since frequent interactions tend to increase favorable interpersonal feelings, some managers treat their subordinates impersonally and distantly in order to reduce their role demands.

Role ambiguity is concerned with the degree of clarity with which role demands are communicated. One of the advantages of classical theory is the specificity of its attempts at programmed behavior. Job descriptions, policies, procedures, performance standards, and organization charts are all designed to clarify official expectations regarding activities and interactions. If the role is ambiguous, the employee will not know if work output will be acceptable. He or she will not know how much authority is possessed in a particular case. One will be disciplined or rewarded for behavior when one least expects it. The employee does not know how this job is linked to others in the enterprise. Role ambiguity is reduced if the requirements are clear and the person is able to correctly predict the outcomes of his or her behavior.

Finally, *role conflict* exists if compliance with expectations from one member of the role set makes compliance with those of another impossible. Katz and Kahn identify four basic types of role conflict: person-role, interrole, intersender, and intrasender.[3] Person-role conflict exists if, for example, a superior asks a subordinate to do something that would conflict with his or her personal code of ethics, e.g., falsify a report, play politics, etc. Interrole conflicts exist when external and internal roles an individual must play are incompatible, e.g., the job requires long hours of overtime and extended traveling which conflict with role requirements as a father or mother. Intersender conflict is sometimes purposely designed into the organization structure. It was noted in an earlier chapter that a project member is under the control of two bosses, the project manager temporarily and the functional supervisor more permanently. The principle of single accountability was developed specifically to avoid intersender role conflicts. Staff departments are frequently subjected to intersender conflicts, e.g., maintenance receives many requests for repairs, all of which are to be done tomorrow. Imbalance among the capacities of interdependent units always provides many opportunities for intersender conflict. Finally, there is the distinct possibility that even though there is single accountability, the single sender of role expectations may be inconsistent. Thus intrasender conflict may exist when orders are given to improve efficiency but not to fire anybody, or when the government issues decrees to settle a strike but not raise prices. Research has indicated that the amount of role conflict is significantly related to job anxiety *positively* and to job satisfaction *inversely*.[4] But no matter how carefully the official organization is designed, the multiplicity and complexity of roles that must be played by personnel would preclude the complete elimination of conflict. Thus, we are dependent upon the informal activities, interactions, and sentiments to reconcile many conflicts and provide the basis for much of the coordination that is effected.

Because of the human need for association and acceptance, people tend to form or join small primary work groups within the formal organization. Often the official location of desks and machines will provide the initial impetus to formation. Employees have varying types of personalities and bring with them into the organization varying levels of status, aspirations, and values. A social group will develop when a small number of people share common values and develop a pattern of relationships solidifying the group. Norms of behavior are developed and social pressures brought to bear upon group members to conform. As a result, there develop such membership categories as "regulars," "deviants," and "leaders."

A *regular* member accepts and conforms to most of the group norms. Examples of common norms are (1) help one another, (2) do not "squeal" on other members to management, (3) hold down production so that all can meet the output norm, and (4) take pride in executing work in a creative fashion. A *deviant* will reject one or more of the norms, yet still retain membership. He or she will be the recipient of many group interactions to bring behavior back into line, e.g., sarcasm, needling, ostracism, etc. A *leader* makes a special contribution in preserving the solidarity of the group, e.g., special help for weaker members, reducing intragroup tensions, confronting the official supervisor with group wishes, etc. Organization members who belong to no primary work group are usually termed "isolates." Often they show psychological

---

[3]Daniel Katz and Robert L. Kahn, *The Social Psychology of Organizations*, John Wiley & Sons, Inc., New York, 1966, p. 184.

[4]Henry Tosi, "Organization Stress as a Moderator of the Relationship between Influence and Role Response," *Academy of Management Journal*, vol. 14, no. 1, March 1971, p. 16.

allegiance to a reference group existing outside the immediate formal organization, e.g., the machine operator who aspires to owning and operating a separate business.

Cohesion of the primary work group is the degree of attraction that the group has for each of its members. It is exemplified by such attitudes and actions as loyalty, a feeling of responsibility for group endeavors, defending against outside attack, friendliness, and a tendency to think in terms of "we" instead of "I." If the norms of a cohesive work group can be aligned with the goals of the formal organization, the manager has a tremendously powerful instrument at his or her disposal. On the other hand, if the norms are directly contrary to organization objectives, considerable harm can be done. As indicated above, the laundry manager felt that his only alternative was to set out to break up the highly cohesive group of shirt pressers. Though some managers prefer to "divide and conquer" as a basic style, one should realize that this approach sacrifices the considerable potential that lies in cohesive work groups aligned with organizational goals.

STATUS

Status is a relationship which issues largely from informal organization but which is also closely geared to the formal. Status is one's social rank. Most of us desire the respect and acceptance of others, and we need also to believe in the higher status of our superiors. Formally, they are our superiors on the organization chart; informally, we desire to respect them so that we can take their orders without losing face or diminishing our feeling of importance. If we believe our formal superior is incompetent, thereby imputing low status, we dislike to follow her or his instructions. Status is also of value in communication. We recognize occupational status when we accept the advice of a physician instead of that of a lawyer in matters of medicine, though we are personally acquainted with neither person. We may respect more the advice of an electrical engineer on a power-plant failure than that of an electrician, thus reflecting a status hierarchy within an occupation. Status is a basic ingredient of our society. It enables people of differing ability to work together cooperatively, since unequals do not work well as equals. We require recognition of our abilities and backgrounds.[5]

Management is often unaware of the establishment of status hierarchies, and its edicts often upset these informal relationships. Maier's instance of the truck-seating problem is a case in point.[6] The employees had developed a seating arrangement, the status symbol, on the basis of seniority, the status cause. The low-status position in the truck was by the tail gate, and the occupant of this position had to open and close the tail gate. A management order was issued, for safety reasons, directing that personnel sitting in the cab of the truck were to operate the tail gate. This, in effect, meant the performance of a low-status task by a high-status individual, since the cab was the highest symbol of status and was therefore occupied by a person with the greatest seniority. One can imagine the difficulties that would ensue. Management's worst mistake is to be caught completely unaware of the existence of an informal

---

[5] Chester I. Barnard, "Functions of Status Systems in Formal Organizations," in Robert Dubin (ed.), *Human Relations in Administration*, 3d ed., Prentice-Hall, Inc., Englewood Cliffs, N.J., 1968, pp. 302–314.

[6] Norman R. F. Maier, Allen R. Solem, and Ayesha A. Maier, *Supervisory and Executive Development*, John Wiley & Sons, Inc., New York, 1957, pp. 49–67.

organization established by the employees. They must be conscious of the concept of status among operative personnel as well as in management. The best command or order is one that gets the job done with the least upset of the informal hierarchies.

In addition to seniority as a cause for status, there are a number of other sources, such as organization level, income, skill, occupation, sex, race, and age. The symbols of status constitute a particularly thorny problem. In striving for status, many try to obtain the symbol when the basis or cause of the status is absent. Anything can constitute a symbol if one person or group has it and others do not. The following have served as status symbols at one time or another:

1 Washrooms
2 Uniforms
3 Privilege of not punching the timeclock
4 Type and location of desks
5 Type of rug
6 Type and number of paintings, plants, water bottles, and other fixtures
7 Size and location of office, as well as the number of windows and the view
8 Freedom to leave the workplace
9 A secretary or secretaries
10 Type of company automobile

Some managements have sought to solve the problem of status symbols by attempting to equalize all symbols. In a Crown Zellerbach Corporation building, for example, the walls were arranged so that offices for executives could be built within a square inch of one another in size. It is doubtful if this particular approach will solve successfully the problem of status and status symbols. It is not possible to equalize all symbols for all personnel. Any difference that does exist will gradually assume the position of a status symbol. Thus, there may be a status location or corner in the room or building, or status may be determined by one's geographical distance from the president. Obviously we cannot all stand in one spot. Though one symbol may be eliminated through an equating process, another will rise to take its place if the basis for status differentiation still remains.

Status and status symbols can be used to advantage by a management. The acceptance of status as an object of desire for most people is an admission that other factors besides money can serve to motivate them. To reduce the battling and struggle for particular status symbols, it may be necessary to formalize the major levels of such symbolism. One large oil corporation has divided its management personnel into five levels for the purpose of distributing privileges and symbols. In the matter of company cars, the top level can choose among such cars as Cadillac and Imperial, while the lower group must confine their choice to the more inexpensive models of Chevrolet, Plymouth, and Ford. It is generally accepted that the higher salaries of the higher positions in the organization serve to stimulate the type of behavior that will be recognized by promotion. It must be realized that the symbols and trappings that go with such high positions can be equally powerful in motivating desired behavior. Thus the informal relationship of status can be utilized in a manner that develops desired attitudes and promotes an integration of interests along the lines of the organization objective.

POWER AND POLITICS

Power can be defined as the capacity to apply *"any force that results in behavior that would not have occurred if the force had not been present."*[7] As such, it includes, but goes beyond, the capacities provided by the formal organization. *Authority* is a major, but not exclusive, source of power. Thus, authority that has been artificially created by the organization is "institutionalized power."

There are many other sources of influence or power that accrue to members of formal organization. *Rewards and punishments* can be meted out to influence behavior. The primary group, for example, can either reward a person through acceptance and liking or punish a member through rejection and giving the "silent treatment." We often speak of the power of *knowledge*. Though a staff unit is formally established to give only advice, its superior knowledge in a highly technical area often generates almost total acceptance of the advice.

In complex organizations, the ability to *control significant dependencies or contingencies* is a source of power. If, for example, a central purchasing staff has been formally created, the operating departments are dependent upon this staff for obtainment of the right kind of material at the right time. If materials represent a particularly crucial contingency, as they do now in this world of shortages, then the purchasing agent has enhanced power. The private secretary to a major official has power because of access to influence over incoming and outgoing communications to a central authority. Persons responsible for negotiating with crucial members of the outer environment of the enterprise also possess significant power, e.g., those dealing with financial institutions and governmental agencies. In any job, if there are no others assigned to execute it, the incumbent has more power than if there were several other alternative people.

Finally, the particular *personality* and characteristics of an individual will affect the degree to which other persons would wish to identify with him or her. If one is liked and respected, we are more willing to acknowledge influence. If he or she is associated with persons occupying high and visible power positions, we are more inclined to pay greater attention. In two studies requiring ranking of influence actually accorded to varying power sources among sales personnel and engineers, the typical order was as follows: (1) expertise, (2) authority, (3) reward, (4) referent or identification, and (5) coercion or punishment.[8] In both cases, the person who *knows* was accorded greatest influence, and the one who *threatens* was responded to least. The power source of contingency control, quite difficult to assess reliably, was not included in these studies.

As power is actually used in the organization, we become involved in a political process. As defined by Pfiffner and Sherwood, politics is "the network of interaction by which power is acquired, transferred, and exercised upon others."[9] A less objectionable term for politics is "accommodation." For example, one staff engineer had been

[7]David Mechanic, "Sources of Power of Lower Participants in Complex Organizations," in David R. Hampton, Charles E. Summer, and Ross A. Webber (eds.), *Organizational Behavior and the Practice of Management*, Scott, Foresman, Glenview, Ill., 1968, p. 426.

[8]John M. Ivancevich and James H. Donnelly, "Leader Influence and Performance," *Personnel Psychology*, vol. 23, no. 4, Winter 1970, p. 543; and John W. Slocum, Jr., "Supervisory Influence and the Professional Employee," *Personnel Journal*, vol. 49, no. 6, June 1970, p. 485.

[9]John M. Pfiffner and Frank P. Sherwood, *Administrative Organization*, Prentice-Hall, Inc., Englewood Cliffs, N.J., 1960, p. 311.

experiencing considerable difficulty with a particular line supervisor. Rather than utilizing an appeal to a common superior to force cooperation through authority, the engineer chose to (1) try to get to know him on a friendly basis, (2) eat lunch with him several times, (3) offer a staff study of a problem that was bothering the supervisor, and (4) finally, when nothing worked, bide his time and not push things. One day, the engineer was asked to investigate a work stoppage in the supervisor's department. The department was flooded with water and would be out of operation for a period of time. Though finding that the cause of the stoppage was the responsibility of the supervisor, the engineer chose to cover for him by issuing a rather innocuous report of the situation. Though the morals of some would not approve this "covering lie," the engineer reasoned, or rationalized, that the enterprise would be further advanced through the political process of accommodation. The supervisor "owed" him one, and he chose to "collect" on future staff study cooperation from the supervisor. The dangers lie in the possibility of moving too often and too far from a management norm of honest reporting, as well as possible deleterious effects on future supervisory behavior in living up to responsibilities.

Politics is a fact of life in all organizations. In areas of vital importance where judgmental criteria are not objective and where conflicts will develop, arenas of political interchange will be established. Examples of such political arenas are line and staff relationships, promotion to higher positions, union and management relationships, and the establishment and enforcement of controls such as budgets and production schedules. The line and staff arena will be discussed below. Though the neat, logical, and complete theories of formal, traditional management are highly attractive, it is naive to insist that political action does not take place in any organization. As in the case of any informal relationship, it can be overdone and work contrary to the formal goals of the organization. In such cases, new formal systems and orders may be required to control and regulate it toward acceptable ends. But it must still be recalled that if the official edicts were *all* that were followed, the organization would meet a quick and early end. The realistic manager knows that she or he must live and work with both the formal and the informal.

INFORMAL LINE AND STAFF RELATIONS

It will be recalled that in Chapter 5 certain principles of line and staff relationships were presented. These principles proposed to define the correct *formal* relationships, that is, (1) that staff should advise rather than command, (2) that staff should serve and not demand to be served, (3) that line should use and consult with staff, and (4) that line should not unduly dominate the thinking of staff. These principles are sound and rest upon a logical base. It is our purpose here to point out that the relationships between line and staff are *not* usually as logical as textbooks would have you believe. In fact, students who have studied business solely from textbooks, which usually present best practice rather than usual practice, are often shocked by the politics, bickering, fighting, and confusion which they encounter on their first jobs.

When particular people, with particular desires, aspirations, and personalities, are placed into those square blocks on the formal organization chart, the organization becomes alive with the likes, dislikes, hopes, fears, backgrounds, and ambitions of these particular people. What takes place is not always logical or predictable. To begin with, there is a built-in conflict between staff and line positions, which forms the basis of much disagreement. This conflict arises from at least three causes: (1) differences in types of personnel in line and staff positions, (2) the effect of staff work on the line, and (3) staff methods of operation.

Staff positions are often filled by personnel who are younger and better educated than line personnel, and who possess less experience, at least in line work. They also seem to have a manner of dress, customs, habits, and preferences that are markedly different from those of line personnel.[10] The youth of the staff specialists conflicts with the higher status of the age of line personnel. Older people dislike accepting advice, however good and valid, from younger personnel. When this difference is compounded by differing levels of education and experience, there is ample opportunity for conflict regardless of particular personalities. As viewed by the line, the better-educated but younger staff deals in impractical theory. Often these two groups do not and cannot communicate well because of varying social habits, manner of dress, and speech vocabulary. If we continue to fill these two classes of positions with two different types of personnel, any integration of interest and action will be difficult to effect.

The second cause of line-staff conflicts has to do with the essential nature of staff. As we indicated in Chapter 4, staff is developed when it can add to the economy and effectiveness of operation. Thus staff is always trying to increase efficiency. Efficiency often means doing *more* work with the same personnel or doing the same work with *fewer* personnel. This results in changes in line operations, and it may even result in the elimination of jobs and loss of personnel. Major modifications in the customary manner of conducting line operations may be effected. Here again line senses the implication that the expert staff *knows* more about the line work than the more experienced line personnel. The implied superiority makes the staff innovations doubly difficult to take.

Not only is the net effect of staff work generally objectionable to line personnel, but the staff manner of operation often causes trouble. Being specifically trained and educated for a task, the staff specialist tends to work on a logical and scientific basis. The line terms this approach cold and impersonal. In addition, staff personnel know that they are on trial and that they must justify their function in the organization. They tend to press hard for results to show that they and their functions are of value.

The student of personnel management must recognize that conflicts do and will occur among various groups in any organization, and the line-staff conflict is an excellent example of this type of problem. There are several possible answers to this problem, answers that will tend to promote an integration of interests. Among these possible solutions are the following.

1 *Line and staff rotation.* Serving in various positions makes one appreciate the values of cooperation and coordination.
2 *Staff-line accommodation.* Some term this method playing politics, but it is frequently necessary to buy the cooperation that should be forthcoming automatically. Various devices have been used, such as winking at the enforcement of minor policies originated by staff, delaying the introduction of new and approved systems and ideas at the request of certain line officials, and covering for the mistakes of others. For

---

[10]Melville Dalton, "Conflicts between Staff and Line Managerial Officers," in Hampton, Summer, and Webber, op. cit., pp. 385–395.

example, understanding quality specialists have helped line personnel to hide or reclaim damaged products without the knowledge of higher management. In return, immediate-line supervisors have been quite cooperative and helpful in working on staff quality control projects. Much danger is involved in defining the degree of staff-line accommodation that is desirable. It is useless to deny that such accommodations happen; in fact, one must admit that the return to the organization is frequently in excess of the cost. When people energize the mechanical structure of an organization, a great deal of interpersonal adjustment must take place. One cannot always abide by regulations, policy, and procedure. Such accommodation, however, often borders very closely on blackmail and bribery, and extreme care must be used in its application. There has to be an underlying code of ethics for any person or group. Staff-line accommodation is a *fact* of informal organization which exists in all complex firms.

3 *Education of each group in the culture of the other.* The staff specialist must learn to approach the line official from the latter's viewpoint and frame of reference. One must accept the task of salesmanship and persuasion; one may have to dress the new idea in terms of the old to make unlearning less painful; one must learn to talk the language of the line and reduce the amount of technical jargon used. One should place faith in the evolutionary rather than the revolutionary changes. As visualized by organization psychologists, the ideal relationship would be adoption of a consultative role by staff. This would require deemphasis of police and surveillance activities as well as elimination of unwelcome entry into operating department activities. If the staff specialist is to succeed, he or she must demonstrate that knowledge and service can work to the benefit of the using agency. There must be established a continuing relationship involving *joint* study of operations and an absence of threatening reports to higher line superiors. Similarly, the staff consultant should be free to withdraw from situations in which one feels that one cannot be helpful.[11]

CHARTING THE INFORMAL ORGANIZATION

Since we have formal organization charts, there is a feeling that we should also have informal charts. Because of the fluid nature of informal relationships, these charts can use various approaches. In one type of chart the emphasis is upon the clique, a "small exclusive group of persons with a common interest."[12] Dalton classifies cliques into three types, the vertical, the horizontal, and the random. The vertical clique usually refers to an association of a superior and a small number of the subordinates in a single department, as depicted in Figure 19-3a. Formally, employees B and D are equal to A, C, E, F, and G. Informally, they are closer to the supervisor and have more influence and informal authority.

The horizontal clique cuts across organizational lines and usually includes only formal equals, as shown in Figure 19-3b. These cliques usually form in an attempt to resist a proposed organizational change or in an attempt to secure a change which the members of this informal group deem desirable. This type of clique has a tendency to

---

[11]See Douglas McGregor, *The Professional Manager*, McGraw-Hill Book Company, New York, 1967, Chap. 7; and Sharon L. Lieder and John H. Zenger, "Industrial Engineers and Behavioral Scientists: A Team Approach to Improving Productivity," *Personnel*, vol. 44, no. 4, July–August 1967, p. 72.

[12]Melville Dalton, *Men Who Manage*, John Wiley & Sons, Inc., New York, 1959, p. 55.

Figure 19-3a The vertical clique

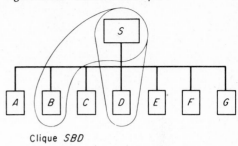

Clique *SBD*

be weak because of the necessity for crossing organization lines. When the particular occasion causing the formation of the horizontal clique passes, it either disappears or lies dormant until a new emergency occurs. The third type, the random clique, issues from an attraction based on friendships, social satisfaction, or kinship.

A second type of charting is concerned primarily with the nature and frequency of contacts among members of the organization. For example, in Figure 19-4, employee *P* has bypassed the formal superior on numerous occasions, and this informal relationship has been supported by a return of such contacts by *B*. The solid lines on the chart show the formal relationships, and the dotted lines depict the informal contacts. Such charts, though based exclusively on the concept of contacts, can supplement the formal organization chart in the portraying of the relationships that actually exist.

ASSESSING ATTITUDES

If the informal organization has been well aligned with the formal, there are likely to develop attitudes characterized by (1) willing cooperation, (2) loyalty to organization and its leadership, (3) voluntary conformance to rules, regulations, and orders, (4)

Figure 19-3b The horizontal clique

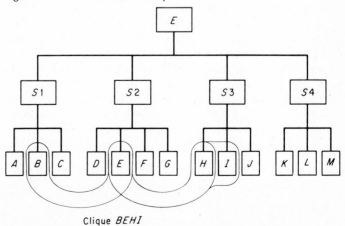

Clique *BEHI*

Figure 19-4 An informal organization chart

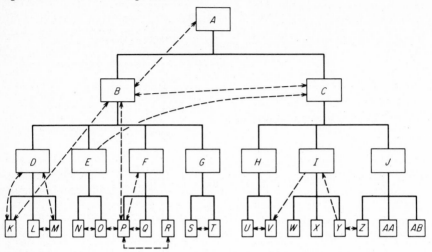

organizational stamina, or the ability to "take it" during times of difficulty, (5) employee interest in job and organization, (6) reasonable display of initiative, and (7) evidences of pride in the organization.[13] Though evidence of these characteristics can be observed and assessed by organizational managers, a more systematic measurement can be undertaken by means of a morale or questionnaire survey.

There are many standard measurement devices for measuring the degree of employee satisfaction. If a common device is utilized, firm-to-firm and sometimes nationwide comparisons can be made. Science Research Associates has prepared a standard list of fourteen subjects for employee scaling, as depicted in Figure 19-5. Results are analyzed on a selective basis, with the national average being placed at the fiftieth percentile. In one year, office workers reported higher satisfaction with working conditions and lower contentment with pay, and production workers indicated higher satisfaction with pay and security and lower approval of colleague friendliness, supervisory-employee relations, and opportunities for growth.

One of the more valid standard measures of employee satisfaction is the Job Descriptive Index, for which norms have been developed on the basis of 2,000 male and 600 female workers.[14] Employees are not asked to scale their satisfaction on various subjects; rather they report only "yes," "no," or "?" to numerous questions about their work. The raw scores for the fiftieth percentile on the basic five categories of Work, Pay, Promotions, Supervision, and Coworkers for male employees are 38, 30, 18, 44, and 46, respectively. For females, they are 37, 28, 14, 42, and 44.

An individually tailored morale survey instrument can be developed by the organization's personnel unit or a hired consultant. There are two main types of morale

---

[13]Ralph C. Davis, *The Fundamental of Top Management*, Harper & Row, Publishers, Incorporated, New York, 1951, p. 552.

[14]Patricia Cain Smith, Lorne M. Kendall, and Charles L. Hulin, *The Measurement of Satisfaction in Work and Retirement*, Rand McNally and Company, Chicago, 1969, pp. 83 and 106.

Figure 19-5 How three employee groups feel about their jobs

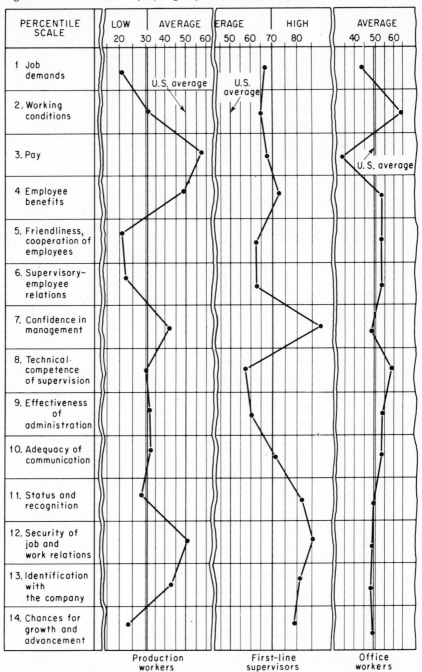

Production workers   First-line supervisors   Office workers

Source: *Factory Management and Maintenance*, vol. 114, no. 2, February 1956, pp. 130–136. By permission.

surveys, the attitude survey and the opinion questionnaire. In the attitude survey, questions are asked of the employee, and multiple-choice answers are provided that are scaled or weighted according to some set of values. For example, employees may be asked the following question, and they are to check the answer that they believe is most applicable.

What do you think of the way promotions are handled in this company?

1   I think that if you work hard and use your ability, you will get ahead in this company.
2   You have to know someone and have "pull" to get ahead.
3   There are no promotions in this company.
4   If you can stick around long enough, you'll get ahead here.
5   The giving of promotions is, for the most part, very fairly done.
6   Usually the best man gets promoted, but at times "pull" will win out.

The six answers to this question have been scaled according to their desirability to the organization. For example, choice 1 may be scaled at 6.2 points while choice 2 may have a value of 0.5 point. Needless to say, the construction of a good attitude scale requires the services of a trained industrial psychologist.

The opinion questionnaire is more widely used because of its greater simplicity. The employee is asked a similar question with multiple answers, but there are no scaled values. The survey analyst would merely report that 55 percent of the responses were for answer 1, 5 percent for 2, 2 percent for 3, etc.

In administering the questionnaire to employees, the accent is on anonymity. No questionnaire is to be numbered or signed. Frequently outside consultants are hired to give a feeling of independence and trust to the survey. Questionnaires are usually filled out on company time and company premises and deposited in a locked ballot box supervised by the consultant. Only summarized results are reported to the firm by the consultant. The employee must feel absolutely free and safe to answer the questions truthfully.

The analysis of the results of morale surveys can be as easy or as difficult as the company wishes to make it. In the scaled-attitude survey, scores are obtained which can be analyzed in various ways. Scores are often derived for the following categories:

1   Total survey score for the organization
2   Total score for each department
3   Total score for men and women
4   Total score for levels of seniority and organization position
5   Scores for each question
6   Scores for each question for each category of personnel

The scores derived from an attitude survey are significant only in relative, rather than absolute, terms. A total score of 70, for example, has no significance except insofar as it can be compared with similar scores. If a similar survey had been taken in the past with a total score of 65, we know attitudes are improving. If our survey is a standard one, such as that of the Science Research Associates mentioned earlier, we can compare our score with those of our industry and of the nation. If department scores show an array of 90, 75, 70, 65, 30, and 75, we know that there are particular difficulties in the department scoring 30 and unusually good morale in that scoring 90. These scores are significant, therefore, only in relative terms.

Individual subjects of discussion can be analyzed to determine where the attitude is good and where it is unsatisfactory. It has been suggested that the best discussion can be obtained when members of management are asked to *predict* scores on specific employee wants. If they are wrong, analysis can be directed toward *why* management does not know what the employees feel and believe. Thus, values in communication analysis can be added to the usual values to be derived from a survey of morale.

The revelation of conflicts calls for investigation and analysis. The mere act of conducting a survey often has a favorable effect upon employees, but this good effect will be lost if management does not attempt to follow up and alleviate the troubles discovered. Operative as well as managerial personnel can be assigned to task forces to discuss the results and prepare suggestions for alleviating difficulties. Conducting an opinion or morale survey can provide much information of value to an organization, but, by the same token, it imposes a serious responsibility to do something about the results.

SUMMARY

Research into the area of human relations begun by Mayo and Roethlisberger in the 1920s has opened management's eyes to numerous other facets of the employer-employee relationship which had largely been ignored prior to that time. Though the existence of an informal organization had been observed by most people, such relationships were not subjected to serious and systematic study until recent decades. The informal organization is composed of the relationships that are established by the particular people filling the formal organization structure depicted on the chart. These relationships are highly personal, somewhat unstable, and restricted to relatively small groups of people. The informal organization cannot be absolutely abolished, but it can be influenced when its objectives do not coincide with formal organization objectives. These informal relationships produce values for the organization, such as (1) providing social satisfaction for members of the group, (2) supplementing and filling in the gaps of formal organization orders and policies, (3) helping to patch up formal-organization-position deficiencies, (4) providing an additional channel of communication through the grapevine, and (5) causing management to be more concerned with the impact of its edicts upon subordinate personnel.

Five particularly important concepts in the field of informal organization are roles, primary groups, status, power, and politics. Roles are determined by the behavioral expectations of significant members of one's role set. Cohesive primary work groups have tremendous potential for good or bad—that is, for results functional to the organization as well as for effecting dysfunctional outputs. Shrewd allocation of status symbols that denote social rank can help to elicit satisfaction and create effective interpersonal relationships.

The realistic manager must also be aware of the difference between official authority and actual capacity or power to get things done. He or she will also recognize that all persons in an organization have a degree of power, thus emphasizing human relations skills in developing cooperation. Obedience, based on formal authority, is steadily decreasing in importance as a result of the increasing sophistication of the work force and the increasing inroads made upon management by labor unions and governmental agencies.

One of the more important political arenas within the business firm is that of line and staff relationships. Conflicts between these two groups can be reduced through such means as line-staff rotation, line and staff accommodation, and education. The health of the resulting emerged informal organization can be assessed through charting and studying actual contacts and associations, as well as through periodic surveys of employee satisfaction. The managerial goal is reasonable reconciliation and integration of both the formal and the informal in the pursuit of organizational objectives.

DISCUSSION QUESTIONS

1   Define and distinguish between job and role. Between formal unit and primary work group.
2   Why is the informal organization designated the "emerging" organization?
3   Distinguish among role conflicts that are intrasender, intersender, interrole, and person-role.
4   Contrast the formal concepts of authority and responsibility with the informal concepts of status and power.
5   In the Maier truck situation, indicate the significant status source, significant status symbols, and actions undertaken to reconcile conflicts that arose.
6   What is meant by the statement that authority is institutionalized power?
7   What are the various sources of line and staff conflict? What suggestions have been made to reduce this conflict?
8   Discuss the concept that scores on morale or opinion surveys are significant only in relative terms.
9   What are primary group norms? How can people be classified in relation to these norms?
10 Itemize and indicate the nature of significant sources of power in organizations.

SUPPLEMENTARY READING

DE LA PORTE, P. C. Andre: "Group Norms: Key to Building a Winning Team," *Personnel*, vol. 51, no. 5, September–October 1974, pp. 60–67.

EMERY, Fred E.: "Bureaucracy and Beyond," *Organizational Dynamics*, vol. 2, no. 3, Winter 1974, pp. 3–13.

GANNON, Martin J.: "The Proper Use of the Questionnaire Survey," *Business Horizons*, vol. 16, no. 5, October 1973, pp. 89–94.

MORANO, Richard A.: "Opinion Surveys: The How-to's of Design and Application," *Personnel*, vol. 51, no. 5, September–October 1974, pp. 8–15.

SIROTA, David, and Alan D. Wolfson: "Pragmatic Approach to People Problems," *Harvard Business Review*, vol. 51, no. 1, January–February 1973, pp. 120–128.

ZALEZNIK, Abraham: "Power and Politics in Organizational Life," *Harvard Business Review*, vol. 48, no. 3, May–June 1970, pp. 47–60.

ZENGER, John H., and Dale E. Miller: "Building Effective Teams," *Personnel*, vol. 51, no. 2, March–April 1974, pp. 20–29.

TWENTY

HUMAN AND ORGANIZATIONAL CONFLICTS

The process of integrating interests requires both preventive and curative activities. Despite the best of management practices in acting and communicating, conflicts between employees and the organization will occur. A total absence of conflict would be unbelievable, boring, and a strong indication that such conflicts are being suppressed. One of the characteristics of a mature group is its willingness and ability to bring suppressed conflicts to the surface where they may be discussed with a greater opportunity of resolution. It would be naive to insist that all conflicts can be eliminated in some manner or other, but their exposure and discussion will contribute greatly toward their reduction. Conflict per se is neither bad nor contrary to good organization. Disagreements and dissatisfactions can lead to reexamination of basic assumptions and practices, to the end that adjustments can be made to improve overall organizational effectiveness.

Thus, the first step in the resolution of conflicts is their discovery and exposure. There are many upward channels of communication that can be developed for the purpose of bringing dissatisfactions to the surface. After a brief discussion of these channels, greater attention will be given to the grievance procedure, which is perhaps the most significant means of discovering and resolving employee complaints and dissatisfactions. On the other hand, there is the distinct possibility that the organization will become dissatisfied with a particular employee. Though the Skinner approach to operant conditioning of behavior would preclude the use of punishment, typical practice of most organizations includes programs of negative disciplinary action ending up with the maximum penalty of discharge from the organization. Finally, the chapter will conclude with a discussion of the alternative methods of dealing with conflict. Certain basic methods have been used in all types of conflicts, whether they are between individuals, between groups, or between the organization and an individual or group.

THE DISCOVERY OF CONFLICTS OF INTEREST

There has been a trend toward increasing the number of upward channels of communication. Part of the impetus for this trend comes from a growing recognition of the importance of good organization morale. Credit can also be given to the growth of labor unions, which exemplified a need for additional communication channels. In any event, the voice of the employee is much louder today in American business than formerly. Some would view this vociferousness as evidence that the amount of disagreement and trouble has been on the increase. On the other hand, it may be that such trouble has always existed, but that now it can rise to the surface and be observed.

GRIEVANCE PROCEDURE   The most important channel through which to communicate dissatisfactions to management is a properly constituted grievance procedure. Such a channel presumes that the individual has the courage to submit a complaint to the supervisor for discussion. One contribution to communication that the labor union has made is the provision of some of this needed courage. Because of the importance of this means of discovering conflicts of interest, a large portion of this chapter will be devoted to the processing of grievances.

DIRECT OBSERVATION   Not all conflicts will be voiced to other people. A good supervisor knows the customary behavior of subordinates, and when significant changes in that behavior occur, he or she is concerned with possible motives. Often such motives are apparent, as in the case of an individual who failed to receive an expected promotion. Though she said nothing, her work and work habits deteriorated rapidly. Such a conflict is difficult to resolve, but if productivity is not to be adversely affected, the person's disappointment must be somehow alleviated.

In addition to direct observation of individual human behavior, the study of various records and statistics can often give clues to general areas of trouble. Analysis of the number of formal grievances filed by a department, regardless of their content, may disclose additional unvoiced conflicts. In a comparison of the characteristics of grievants with nongrievants in one manufacturing company, it was discovered that the former were more likely to be (1) better educated, (2) younger in terms of seniority, (3) more active in the union, (4) lower paid, and (5) have higher absenteeism and tardiness rates.[1] Absenteeism and lateness are often construed as symbols of conflict which go along with heavier use of the grievance procedure. Younger and better-educated employees are more likely to question the status quo, using any means available. In addition, analysis of accident rates, requests for transfer, resignations, and disciplinary cases may reveal general patterns which are not apparent in any one instance.

---

[1]Howard A. Sulkin and Robert W. Pranis, "Comparison of Grievants with Non-grievants in a Heavy Machinery Company," *Personnel Psychology*, vol. 20, no. 2, Summer 1967, pp. 111–119.

SUGGESTION BOXES The usual type of suggestion system has been discussed in Chapter 16. The type referred to here may be called a gripe box. The company that establishes an anonymous gripe system is concerned with the problem of bringing *all* conflicts of interest to light. Anonymity may provide the courage to submit a dissatisfaction which will otherwise go unvoiced.

This means of stimulating the submission of disagreements makes it very difficult to accomplish the objective of resolving the disagreement. Since management does not know the identity of the individual, discussion is out of question. Management can only investigate and then either correct the condition, trusting that the aggrieved person will observe, or publicize the facts which call for no change. Consequently, a gripe box *cannot* be a basic means of discovering disagreements. It can, however, be a supplementary device which is evidence of a sincere desire to discover and eliminate trouble.

OPEN-DOOR POLICY The open-door policy is commonly announced but seldom works. As it is usually established, a higher-level executive announces that the door is always open to anyone who would like to discuss anything with her or him. But try to get past the supervisor, the first sergeant, or the secretary! This technique of discovering dissatisfaction appeals only to people with "brass," and these could well use the established grievance procedure. Most employees recognize the policy for the window dressing it is. They are acutely aware of the organizational obstacles as well as of their own deficiencies in dress, speech, and manner, which make it impossible for them to walk through the door. The policy sounds good and democratic, but it is generally ineffective.

On the other hand, a true open-door attitude toward subordinates on the part of the immediate supervisor is very helpful in improving communication. If the supervisor is receptive to relatively free talk from subordinates, there is an opportunity to promote good organization morale. When the policy requires a jumping of organization levels, however, the immediate supervisor is often suspicious of any circling of his or her position in order to go in the open door of the higher executive.

PERSONNEL COUNSELORS Some of the larger organizations hire trained psychologists to act as counselors for employees. Ordinarily these counselors are members of a staff personnel department. The rationale for a counseling system is somewhat similar to that for the gripe box. When employees do not wish to go to a superior, they can go to a person outside of the chain of command who will protect their identity and confidence. It takes time to build up an atmosphere of impartiality and trust about the personnel counselor, who is often considered a member of management in a staff capacity. This approach to integrating and reconciling conflict will be discussed at greater length in the following chapter.

EXIT INTERVIEW If the conflict or disagreement is so great that the employee resigns, the exit interview provides one last opportunity to discover the nature of the complaint. The exit interview, however, is very difficult to conduct effectively. The nondirective type of interview is usually preferred. If the employee is quitting because of some dissatisfaction with the company, he or she is usually very reluctant to discuss it. There is little to be gained from burning bridges behind one. No matter how you might enjoy "leveling" with the interviewer and saying what you really think of the boss or the organization, references for the next job must come from the present organization. Consequently the exit interviewer must exercise great skill in getting to the true reason for the resignation, and often, the interview itself does not reveal the reason. Resignation statistics gathered by departments over a period of time frequently uncover general sources of difficulty.

In a survey of 426 companies in manufacturing, approximately 70 percent required an exit interview upon separation from the firm.[2] The announced objective of the interview included possible improvement of personnel practices, counseling of the employee, attempting to identify weak supervisors within the firm, and general public relations values. A few companies have found that an exit questionnaire mailed after three months have passed produces a substantial amount of information. By this time the ex-employee usually has another job and no longer fears a poor reference. He or she can then be approached in a positive fashion and be asked for the benefit of past experiences in improving working conditions in the company. By the time an exit interview occurs, it may be too late to salvage a particular employee, but information can still be obtained that will prevent others from leaving for reasons within the control of the organization.

THE OMBUDSMAN OR OMBUDSWOMAN   An organizational "patch" that is attracting increasing interest among management theorists is the ombudsman or ombudswoman. This is a special position in that one acts, not as the right arm of the president of an organization, but rather as an additional set of ears. In effect, one operates a complaint office to which individuals may go when they feel that they have exhausted the more usual means of receiving an acceptable hearing. An ombudsman or ombudswoman has only the right of acceptance or rejection of such complaints. In the event of acceptance, the holder of this unusual position has rights of investigation and recommendation to responsible organization officials. Failing satisfactory resolution of the conflict in this direct manner, a recommendation can then be made to the president of the organization. The ombudsman in the Danish government, for example, accepted and investigated only 15 percent of the citizen complaints submitted.[3] Specific recommendations to the top official were made in only 5 percent of the cases investigated. In most instances, either the investigation did not substantiate the complaint, or lower officials voluntarily adjusted the matter upon the advice of the ombudsman. This new position has been recommended to private business firms as a further indication of corporate interest and concern for the feelings of employees with respect to justice and fairness of treatment. Relatively few firms, however, have felt the need for this additional channel. The position is beginning to appear more frequently in the organizational structures of various colleges and universities.

MISCELLANEOUS CHANNELS   Numerous other channels of upward communication have been utilized at one time or another as a means of bringing conflicts of interest to light. *Group meetings* or gripe sessions are conducted by some supervisors who have the

[2]National Industrial Conference Board, *Personnel Practices in Factory and Office: Manufacturing*, Studies in Personnel Policy, no. 194, New York, 1964, p. 20.

[3]Isidore Silver, "The Corporate Ombudsman," *Harvard Business Review*, vol. 45, no. 3, May–June 1967, p. 78.

courage and balanced perspective to solicit complaints publicly. An individual acts differently in the company of others than when alone, and a group meeting may stimulate the submission of gripes which otherwise may be repressed. *Unsolicited employee letters* sometimes constitute an additional channel. One firm utilized a blackboard in a manner similar to the gripe-box method. The complaint or rumor was written on one side, and the management wrote an answer opposite it on the other. In addition to interviews of the exit type, *scheduled interviews* of present employees can be conducted to attempt to discover the source of difficulty. For example, the morale-survey score may show one department far out of line from the rest. The survey has identified the area, and the interview may be used within the area to pinpoint the trouble further. Of course, *collective bargaining* is a highly formalized method of discovering the discontents of employees. This subject is discussed in Chapter 23. Finally, on rare occasions, *the informer* has been used. The employment of labor spies is not to be recommended, but this technique utilizes a basic principle of communication. In order to understand people, they must be studied where they stand, in their customary social and physical environment. Though an employer may have the best intentions in utilizing an informer, that is, of wanting to know what employees truly believe without thought of reprisal or punishment, the practice is highly objectionable to all concerned. More orthodox techniques will produce more value in the long run.

THE PROCESSING OF GRIEVANCES

The definition of a grievance often varies from company to company and from author to author. The broadest interpretation of the term is exemplified in the following definition: A *grievance* can be "any discontent or dissatisfaction, whether expressed or not and whether valid or not, arising out of anything connected with the company that an employee thinks, believes, or even 'feels,' is unfair, unjust or inequitable."[4] This definition would cover dissatisfactions which possess any one or all of the following characteristics:

1 The grievance can be either unvoiced or stated by the employee.
2 It can be written or unwritten.
3 It can be valid and legitimate, untrue, or completely ridiculous.
4 The discontent must arise out of something connected with the company.

Thus, the only major restriction in this definition is that a discontent can be termed a grievance *only* if it is concerned with company policy or actions. Its form of expression or its validity is unimportant in the definition of the term. Whether or not a particular employee has a grievance is up to her or him, and not to the supervisor or any other member of management.

The broad definition of a grievance has its value as far as basic managerial philosophy is concerned. The manager has to be concerned with *all* discontents, regardless of a personal opinion of their validity. One has to watch for unexpressed dissatisfactions. Thus it is the basis for a sound approach to the development of good morale.

[4]Michael J. Jucius, *Personnel Management*, 5th ed., Richard D. Irwin, Inc., Homewood, Ill., 1963, p. 450.

In the business world, however, the term "grievance" is usually more restricted in its meaning. Many managements distinguish between a "complaint" and a grievance. A *complaint* is a discontent or dissatisfaction which has not, as yet, assumed a great measure of importance to the complainant. Complaints are often submitted in a highly informal fashion. An employee may complain that it is too hot in the shop, that another employee will not cooperate, or that one has been assigned a distasteful job. There are many more complaints than there are grievances. A complaint becomes a grievance when the employee feels that an injustice has been committed. If the supervisor ignores the complaint and the dissatisfaction grows within the employee, it usually assumes the status of a grievance. A grievance, in business organizations, is *always* expressed, either verbally or in writing. If a discontent is unexpressed, it does not constitute a grievance under the labor contract or in the general parlance of union and management leaders. This does not mean that management should not be concerned with unexpressed discontents, but obviously such dissatisfactions cannot be handled through a grievance procedure. A grievance is usually more formal in character than a complaint. It can, of course, be either valid or ridiculous, and must grow out of something connected with company operations or policy. In many instances it must involve an interpretation or application of provisions of the labor contract. Negotiation through the grievance procedure is often considered to be a continuation of the collective bargaining which theoretically stopped with the signing of a new contract.

The grievance machinery

A grievance machinery or procedure is usually thought of in connection with a company that deals with a labor union. Though the union must be given a considerable amount of credit for stimulating the installation of such procedures, all companies, whether unionized or not, should have established and known methods of processing grievances. This channel of communication is vital to all organizations, and the managements who have waited for the demands of a labor union have been remiss in their obligations. Employees should know where they stand in matters pertaining to the justice or injustice of their treatment. They should be aware of the fact that they are not totally and irrevocably under the thumb of an immediate superior. Though they must rely primarily upon executive justice, they should have access to a judicial type of justice when they feel that it is necessary. The mere fact that such a procedure exists is satisfying, even though an employee never has an occasion to use it.

In a survey of 1,717 labor contracts covering over 7 million workers, all but 20 had specific clauses detailing formal grievance procedures.[5] This represented an increase over the 94 percent reported in 2,850 contracts surveyed in 1950. With respect to procedures *voluntarily* established solely by management, Scott reports that approximately 11 percent of 793 firms provided these means of appeal beyond the immediate supervisor.[6] The most popular channel involved a combination of line and staff officials, the latter usually being members of the personnel department.

The primary value of a grievance procedure is that it can assist in minimizing discontent and dissatisfaction which may have adverse effects upon cooperation and

---

[5]Rose T. Selby and Maurice L. Cunningham, "Grievance Procedures in Major Contracts," *Monthly Labor Review*, October 1964, pp. 1125–1130.

[6]William G. Scott, "Employee Appeal Systems," in Edwin B. Flippo (ed.), *Evolving Concepts in Management*, Proceedings of the Academy of Management, Chicago, 1965, pp. 120–125.

productivity. The procedure also has value in that it serves as a check on arbitrary management action. Being aware of the right of employee appeal should help supervisors to avoid the tendency toward corruption and arbitrariness that power and authority often bring. It therefore tends to emphasize a need for skill in dealing with people over and above a skill in using authority and force.

The details of a grievance machinery vary with the organization. It may have as few as two steps or as many as ten, depending primarily upon the size of the organization. The first and last steps are almost always the same for all organizations, particularly for those that are unionized. In the discussion that follows, the intermediate steps will be summarized for purposes of concise coverage. Though a labor union is not essential to the establishment and operation of a grievance procedure, one is assumed in the illustration in Figure 20-1. The following four steps of the machinery are presented:

1 Conference among the aggrieved employee, the supervisor, and the union steward
2 Conference between middle management (e.g., superintendent, general supervisor, and plant manager) and middle union leadership (e.g., committee representative, committee of stewards, and business agent)
3 Conference between top management and top union leadership
4 Arbitration

Each of these steps and problems pertaining thereto will be briefly discussed.

Figure 20-1 A grievance procedure

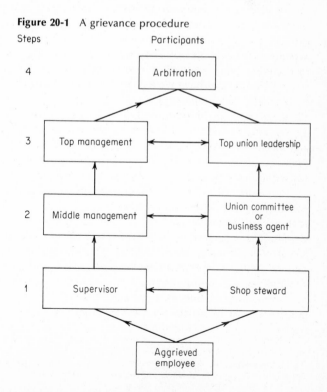

INITIAL STEP   The greatest opportunity for the settlement of a complaint or grievance lies in the initial step of the procedure. The higher the discontent rises through the organization, the more difficult it is to resolve. The give-and-take of the shop is lost and saving face becomes more important at higher levels. Unfortunately, some managements and unions view the procedure as a game or a form of organized warfare. Score is kept of the number of wins and losses.

In the unionized concern, the first step of the procedure usually involves three people: the employee with the unresolved complaint which has now become a grievance, the supervisor, and a representative of the union. The supervisor, as always, is a key individual and can do much to reduce the number of grievances that get past to higher steps in the machinery. Proper training and the adherence to a basic problem-solving process, to be discussed in the following section, will do much to resolve trouble on the shop level. In one large organization that handles up to 3,000 grievances per year, the percentage settled at this first step was increased from 33 to 54 percent after a training program that included both supervisors and union stewards.[7] In addition, the number of grievances filed per 100 employees was reduced from seventeen to seven during an eight-year period.

The shop steward can also do much to reduce the flow of greivances. He or she is usually an elected representative of the union and a full-time employee of the company. Being on the payroll of the firm, the shop steward must receive permission to take time off to process grievances. It is customary for the company to pay for time spent in grievance processing. The fact that one is an elected official has implications for the grievance procedure. An astute steward will consider a number of interests in electing to push or not to push a particular grievance. One must, of course, consider the interest of the grievant in terms of equity. But in addition, one should consider the possible effects upon other employees if a precedent is established, the interests of the union in any immediate negotiations it may have in process, the political interests of present and would-be officers if a union election is in the offing, and whether or not a victory would stimulate a tremendous work load of "me, too" grievances by other employees.

There is a considerable amount of informal byplay between the union steward and members of management, as is illustrated by an incident which occurred in one company. A representative of the personnel department, who was active in the grievance procedure, was walking through a department. Suddenly the shop steward rushed up to him, shouting and waving his arms. When the representative from personnel finally got the gist of the shouting, he realized that the steward was blasting him concerning a grievance that had arisen in this department. The confusing thing was that, earlier in the day, this grievance had been settled in the second step in favor of the union, but the settlement had not yet been generally announced. The steward was well aware of these facts. It was apparent that he was doing a little "politicking" for the benefit of his employee constituents, who were watching with great interest. He could not lose since (1) he was telling management what to do in no uncertain terms, and (2) tomorrow management would announce a win for the union in this particular grievance. Not to be outdone by the steward, the personnel representative hurried back to the grievance file and selected another which he felt was going to be conceded

---

[7]J. C. Pettefer, "Effective Grievance Administration," *California Management Review*, vol. 12, no. 1, Winter 1970, p. 18.

to the union. Returning to the department, he threw his arm around the shoulders of the shop steward, and told him that he liked him so much that he was going to concede another grievance. While the personnel specialist was talking, the shop steward was fiercely whispering, "Get away from me! The boys are watching!" Obviously, it is not good union politics to be too closely identified with management. The personnel representative was attacking the status of the steward as revenge for being used as a political foil.

Lower-management officials are not above utilizing the grievance procedure as a means of convincing superiors of the inappropriateness of particular orders and policies. There are occasions when an unrealistic top-management order causes chaos among the work force, and lower managers are unable to have the order rescinded or altered. In such instances, application of the order as quickly and clumsily as possible will ultimately lead to a decision against management by an outside arbitrator. The record will show that the lower manager did not reject the plan; the arbitrator did.

It is also interesting to note that the union steward has a legal obligation to represent *all* employees in his jurisdiction, regardless of whether or not they are union members. In accordance with a basic principle of organization, the authority given to a union to represent all employees, whether they are members or not, must be equated with a responsibility to represent properly their interests, individually as well as collectively. As a practical matter, the nonunion employee generally does not expect or get individual representation.

If the supervisor, the aggrieved employee, and the steward are unable to work out a settlement of the grievance and thus effect an integration of interests, the dispute is placed on paper and is sent to a higher step in the procedure. Contract limits for the entire procedure run from one week to a year, but most stipulate periods shorter than two months.[8]

INTERMEDIATE STEP As Figure 20-1 indicates, the next step on the management side of the machinery is to submit the dispute to middle management. In a large organization there are a number of intermediate steps. Superintendents, general supervisors, and plant managers are typical of the management personnel involved. It is important to ensure that the line management assumes prime responsibility for the settlement of a grievance. In many firms, however, the personnel department is injected into the procedure as a decision-making power. This violates a basic principle of line and staff relationship, in giving a personnel representative authority to reverse and overrule a supervisor. Certainly the labor relations specialist should study grievances and advise and counsel line management in their handling, but the power to decide should rest in the line.

On the union side, intermediate levels are represented by higher personnel in the union hierarchy. In some unions a committee representative supervises several shop stewards and constitutes the second step; in others, a committee of shop stewards may be involved; and in still others the business agent, a full-time negotiations specialist of the union, takes over the intermediate and sometimes the final step. The presence of a business agent may explain why management is often outmaneuvered by the union. Business agents are specialists in union-management negotiations. It is their full-time

---

[8]Robert W. Fisher, "When Workers Are Discharged—An Overview," *Monthly Labor Review*, vol. 96, no. 6, June 1973, p. 6.

job. The line manager often considers grievance processing a minor, incidental, and distasteful duty. This lack of specialization and interest on the part of line management has led to the situation in which the staff personnel department is given authority to make decisions about grievances. Specialization of the union is met with specialization of management. Thus the law of functional growth often leads to a separation of the grievance-handling function from the line and often to a violation of the principle of staff advice. In one survey of personnel department rights concerning grievances or discharges, 26 percent of 185 companies required compulsory consultation while 22 percent gave the department the final decision for the company.[9]

FINAL COMPANY-UNION STEP   The final step to be undertaken by the company and union is a discussion of the grievance between representatives of top management and top union officials. For management, it may be the president in important grievances, a vice-president, or a high-level industrial relations executive. For the union, it may be the president of the local union, the union executive committee, or a representative of the international union when the case is so important that its settlement may establish a precedent in the industry. It is very difficult to secure an integration of interests at this high level. The grievance has usually become an issue which has political implications. Nevertheless, this step must be a last attempt for the two parties to come to some agreement by themselves.

ARBITRATION   If the grievance has not been settled by top management and top union leadership, three possibilities remain: (1) the union can temporarily or permanently drop the issue; (2) the union can call a strike if the contract permits (sometimes there are unauthorized wildcat strikes over a grievance); or (3) the case may be submitted to an impartial arbitrator. In 94 percent of 1,717 major agreements surveyed, arbitration was substituted for the strike as the final step in the grievance procedure.[10] Arbitration is usually handled by either a single individual or a panel of three, consisting of a representative of labor, one of management, and an impartial third person.

An arbitrator is an outside third party who is brought in to settle a dispute. He or she has the authority to make a decision. The arbitrator may be hired for a particular case or may be appointed as a permanent official for the industry or the company and the union. Naturally, the person must be acceptable to both union and management. Salary is usually paid by both, since it is important that no undue influence be brought to bear on his or her deliberations. The American Arbitration Association maintains a list of arbitrators for consideration by managements and unions, as does also the Federal Mediation and Conciliation Service. Often college professors, lawyers, and retired businessmen serve in such a capacity. The average time consumed from the point where an official request for arbitration is filed until handing down of the award is 168 days.[11] When we add the typical internal grievance processing time of approximately two months, it is apparent that considerable time is consumed in resolving this type of conflict. Total cost of arbitrating a single case in 1971 was $600; when the additional costs of internal processing are added, one firm estimated minimum costs of $1,500 for

[9]*Employee Conduct and Discipline*, The Bureau of National Affairs, Inc., Washington, D.C., 1974.
[10]"Processing of Grievances," *Monthly Labor Review*, November 1964, pp. 1269–1272.
[11]"The Demand for Arbitrators Outruns Supply," *Business Week*, Jan. 8, 1972, p. 62.

the entire process.[12] Once the decision of the arbitrator has been made and issued, both parties must accept it and abide by it; otherwise the contract has been violated. Provisions of the contract can be enforced in court if either party is so inclined.

The fact that over 90 percent of all labor contracts provide for this industrial judicial system gives cause for optimism and encouragement in the field of labor-management relations. It is astounding to realize that this judicial complex has been largely created in only thirty years. The arbitrator is bound in her or his deliberations to the provisions of the contract. One can only interpret the agreement, not write new contract provisions. The results of other arbitration cases are sometimes considered, but precedent does not have the power and influence that it has in our regular court system.

Mediation is distinguished from arbitration in that a mediator is a third party who enters a dispute with no power of decision. One can only suggest, coax, recommend, or merely keep the two parties talking to each other. Only 2.6 percent of the contracts surveyed revealed a provision for mediation.[13] It is widely used in the negotiation of new contracts and in the settlement of strikes. In such instances, both labor and management refuse to delegate the authority of decision to an outside party. In the case of a grievance, a dispute arising within the realm of a present contract, such a delegation of authority to decide is much more acceptable to both parties.

A manager's steps in handling a grievance

At any one stage of the grievance machinery, the dispute must be handled by some member of management. In the solution of a problem, the greater burden rests on management. As indicated earlier, the clearest opportunity for settlement is found at the first stage before the grievance has left the province of the supervisor. For this reason, many firms have specifically trained their supervisors in how to handle a grievance or complaint properly. Needless to say, other levels of management could also profit by the same training, since some grievances do progress to later stages of the procedure.

One of the most widely adopted grievance-handling procedures is that presented in the Training within Industry Program in its job relations training. The dispute or grievance constitutes a managerial problem, and the scientific method is usually most productive in arriving at a satisfactory solution. As applied to grievances, directions for this procedure could be as follows:

1 *Receive and define the nature of the dissatisfaction.* The manner and attitude with which the supervisor receives the complaint or grievance is very important. We seek agreement, an integration of interest. Needless barriers should not be thrown up. As a principle applicable to this step, the supervisor should assume that the employee is fair in presenting the complaint or grievance. Statements should not be prejudged on the basis of past experience with this or other employees. The supervisor should not be too busy to listen and should not give an impression of condescension in doing so. Research indicates that the supervisor's basic leadership style can do much to reduce the number of grievances. In one study, the incidence of grievances correlated

[12]J. C. Pettefer, "Effective Grievance Administration," op. cit., p. 13.
[13]"Processing of Grievances," *Monthly Labor Review*, op. cit., p. 1271.

negatively with supervisory inclination toward "consideration" for people (−.51), and correlated positively with a style characterized by "initiating structure" (.71).[14] Thus supervisors who were heavily task-oriented, as contrasted with people-oriented, tended to experience a significantly greater number of grievances being filed in their units.

Instead of trying to deal with a vague feeling of discontent, the supervisor should attempt to define the problem properly. Sometimes the wrong complaint is given or received. The supervisor must be wary in defining the grievance, otherwise it may be necessary to "solve" it over and over again. He or she must listen carefully and with empathy, in order to make sure that the true complaint or grievance is being voiced.

2   *Get the facts.* Obtaining the facts about a complaint or grievance requires some effort. Facts must be separated from opinion and impressions. In gathering facts, one quickly becomes aware of the importance of keeping proper records, such as performance ratings, job ratings, attendance records, and suggestions. In addition, with the increasingly legalistic bent that is characteristic of modern labor-management relations, the supervisor is wise to keep records on each particular grievance. One may be called upon to testify, in later steps in the procedure, if the grievance is not resolved here. It is equally important that the supervisor possess and exercise some skill in interview, conference, and discussion. We are dealing with human minds and interests, and discussion is basic not only to the gathering of facts, but also to the effecting of a meeting of minds.

3   *Analyze and decide.* With the problem defined and the facts in hand, the manager must now analyze and evaluate them, and then come to some decision. There is usually more than one possible solution. The manager must also be aware that the decision may constitute a precedent within both the department and the company. A wrong decision may have to be lived with in other cases in the future.

It would be foolish to deny the existence of frequent "horse trading" between shop stewards and supervisors in the handling of these problems. Some grievances are very important to the steward's political position. He or she may trade a favorable decision from the supervisor for unusual cooperation in the future. At times the union leadership may wish to preserve good relations with the company in order to be able to negotiate more important disputes that are coming up. In the meantime, small but legitimate grievances may get little or no attention from the steward. On the other hand, management frequently encourages the establishment of informal agreements and compromises in the first stage of the grievance machinery in order to confine the difficulty to that level. Trouble between line management and staff specialists sometimes arises because of concessions made by supervisors to the union in the areas of prime interest to the staff. It is not unusual for an immediate supervisor to have to walk a narrow path, hemmed in by union, upper management, and staff specialists.

4   *Apply the answer.* Even though the solution decided upon by the superior is adverse to the employee, some answer is better than none. Employees dislike supervisors who will take no stand, good or bad. They will often accept unfavorable decisions when such decisions have a legitimate foundation that is explained to them. In the event of an appeal beyond this stage of the machinery, the manager must have

---

[14]E. A. Fleishman and E. F. Harris, "Patterns of Leadership Behavior Related to Employee Grievances and Turnover," *Personnel Psychology*, vol. 15, no. 1, Spring 1962, pp. 43–56.

the decision and reasons therefor properly recorded. If a decision favorable to the employee is reached at any stage of the machinery, the privilege and responsibility of communicating the answer to the employee should be delegated to the immediate supervisor. There is too often a tendency to let the supervisor communicate all the bad news and to allocate the favorable contacts to some other member of higher management or staff.

5 *Follow up.* The objective of the grievance procedure is to resolve a disagreement between an employee and the organization. Discussion and conference are important to this process. The purpose of its follow-up phase is to determine whether the clash of interest has been resolved. If follow-up reveals that the case has been handled unsatisfactorily or that the wrong grievance has been processed, then redefinition of the problem, further fact-finding, analysis, solution, and follow-up are required.

Among the common errors of management encountered in the processing of grievances are (1) stopping too soon in the search for facts, (2) expressing a management opinion prior to the time when all pertinent facts have been discovered, (3) failing to maintain proper records, (4) resorting to executive fiat instead of discussion and conference to change minds, and (5) settling the wrong grievance—a mistake which may in turn produce a second new grievance. Follow-up is the step in the procedure that tells us when a mistake in handling has been made. The objective of perfect organization morale is never attainable, but the systematic processing of complaints and grievances will do much to promote an integration of interests.

DISCIPLINARY ACTION

In addition to the confusion over the meaning of a grievance, there is also a certain ambiguity in the term "disciplinary action." A broad interpretation would consider the words to mean any conditioning of future behavior by the application of either rewards or penalties. This approach would include positive motivational activities, such as praise, participation, and incentive pay, as well as negative motivational techniques, such as reprimand, layoff, and fines. Both types of activities seek to condition employee behavior in order to achieve good discipline in the organization.

The more commonly accepted definition of the term, and the one to be used in this text, is that disciplinary action is confined to the application of penalties that lead to an inhibition of undesired behavior. Thus, disciplinary action is usually considered to be negative motivation. Though the majority of employees do conform to orders, policies, and regulations, a minority still require the stimulus generated by penalties. Employees do not respect supervisors who are lax in the enforcement of all rules and regulations. Any attempt to curry favor and be "one of the group" is usually accepted on the surface but is actually met with rejection, which is accompanied by a growing attitude of disrespect toward the supervisor. On the other hand, an autocratic and excessively severe enforcement of policy and regulations is to be avoided. One of the most difficult tasks of a supervisor is the effective administration of negative disciplinary action. It is our purpose in this portion of this text to discuss a general manner of approaching the problem, before presenting a series of commonly accepted principles of disciplinary action. Our general objective is still that of developing an integration of interests. The approach has shifted, however, to a utilization of *negative* means to achieve that integration.

Basic elements of the disciplinary-action process

The first element of the disciplinary process must be location of the responsibility for the administration of disciplinary action. There is general agreement that it must be a line responsibility. A staff personnel agency can and should provide advice and assistance, but disciplining subordinates is so close to the essential nature of leadership and command that it should not be taken away from the supervisor. Unfortunately, there has been a trend in recent years to reduce the authority of the supervisor in disciplinary matters, a trend which is due partly to the increasingly legalistic approach to personnel problems as specified by government and labor contracts. Higher managements feel that supervisors are not cognizant of all the implications of the law or of the labor contract. They have therefore reduced or sometimes removed the power to discipline and have either placed it higher in the line of hierarchy or delegated it to a staff specialist who is an expert in the labor law. Undeniably, some restriction of the grant of authority to supervisors to discipline must come with the advent of greater and greater government and labor union interference. But it must also be realized that the power to discipline, even though it is rarely used, is essential to the maintenance of a management position.

The second element of a disciplinary-action program must be a clarification of what is expected of an employee in the way of behavior. This requires an establishment of reasonable rules and regulations which contribute to effective operation. These are not rules that are established solely to provide a basis for punishment. A no-smoking rule in a department working with inflammable materials is not made to harass the employee. The objective of disciplinary action is not to inflict punishment. Rather, a certain type of behavior is desired, and the employee is informed of the nature of that behavior and the reason for it. If it requires a penalty to produce that type of behavior, then disciplinary action must be administered. Rules and regulations are established in such areas as attendance, safety, theft, insubordination, intoxication, fighting, dishonesty, solicitations, smoking, and housekeeping. In addition, there are often written or implied rules governing aspects of private life, such as loose morals, destructive criticism of the organization, and garnishment of wages.

In specific cases appealed to the outside arbitrator in grievance processing, the general approach has been a functional rather than a geographical analysis of the act. If the off-the-job act adversely affects the enterprise, management can legally invoke organizational disciplinary action. For example, off-the-job Communist activities are punishable only when the employer can provide tangible proof of damage to the company. In off-the-job fighting, the employer can discipline when supervisory personnel are involved in order to preserve the authority hierarchy. Criminal convictions will be upheld by arbitrators as a cause for discharge if it is determined that they will either jeopardize the company's relations with customers or create substantial doubts about the safety of fellow employees.[15]

It is also interesting to note that employees who are union members are subject to union disciplinary powers. Over 90 percent of 158 union contracts covering over 16 million workers provide for disciplinary action by union locals. Examples of such union offenses are engaging in work speed contests, buying without the union label,

---

[15]John W. Leonard, "Guidelines for Off-the-job Discipline and Discharge," *Personnel Administration*, vol. 32, no. 6, November–December 1969, pp. 39–43.

participating in wildcat strikes, working for less than union scale, disclosing union secrets, refusing to parade on Labor Day, and encouraging establishment of piece-rate incentive systems.[16] A court decision upheld the right of the labor union to discipline members for exceeding the union-established quota of production output. Though contrary to the values of economy and efficiency, the court determined that preservation of solidarity to protect the labor organization had higher priority.

A basic problem in all such codes is that of informing employees, so that they have an opportunity to act in the desired manner. Many of the rules should be apparent to most employees, but the unusual ones must be covered in indoctrination sessions given by either the personnel department or the supervisor. In addition, it is important that the rules be enforced fairly consistently over a period of time. If the no-smoking rule has not been enforced for several months, it is unfair and contrary to the labor agreement, according to many arbitrators, suddenly to start picking up violators on some Monday morning.

With reasonable authority possessed by the supervisor, and the employees well apprised of what is expected of them, the basis of disciplinary action has been established. When an offense takes place, it is important to establish and maintain proper records concerning the nature of the event, the participants, and the surrounding circumstances. Record should also be made of any action taken by the supervisor. Such written evidence is highly important, should the event be the basis for a grievance filed by the employee. Thus, in modern management's increasingly legalistic environment, written records constitute a third basic element of a well-organized disciplinary-action program.

In taking disciplinary action, the attitude of the supervisor is extremely important. One should be objective in collecting facts. One should approach the problem, if possible, with a nonjudicial attitude. Jumping to conclusions is particularly dangerous in the area of disciplinary action. Making a mistake in the handling of a grievance may mean that the grievance has not been solved and that it is still with us. Making a mistake in disciplining someone who does not deserve it could well mean a permanent destruction of the morale of the employee and a general loss of respect for the supervisor. Prejudging the offense, even in terms of general attitude and manner of collecting facts, can be quite destructive of future cooperation, particularly when the facts later show that no action was merited.

Disciplinary-action penalties

If the facts and policies warrant the application of a penalty, the supervisor must choose one from the number he or she is authorized to use. It is not unusual for the list of rules to specify also the corresponding penalties for their violation. Ordinarily, there are varying penalties for first, second, and third offenses of the same rule. Among the penalties available in business are:

1 Oral reprimand
2 Written reprimand
3 Loss of privileges

[16]David A. Swankin, "Union Disciplinary Powers and Procedures," *Monthly Labor Review*, February 1963, pp. 125–132.

4	Fines
5	Layoff
6	Demotion
7	Discharge

The penalties are listed in the general order of severity, from mild to severe.

For most cases, an oral reprimand is sufficient to achieve the desired result. The supervisor must know her or his personnel in determining how to give a reprimand. For one person, a severe "chewing out" may be necessary in order to get attention and cooperation; another person may require only a casual mention of a deficiency. If the offense is more serious, the reprimand may be put in written form. Since a written reprimand is more permanent than an oral one, it is considered a more severe penalty.

For such offenses as tardiness or leaving work without permission, fines or loss of various privileges can be used. The fines usually have some relationship to the work time actually lost. The loss of privileges includes such items as good job assignments, right to select machine or other equipment, and freedom of movement about the workplace or company.

The more severe penalties of layoff, demotion, and discharge are usually outside of the grant of authority to the immediate supervisor. Disciplinary layoffs can vary in severity from one to several days loss of work without pay. The use of demotion as a penalty is highly questionable. If the employee is properly qualified for the present assignment, he or she will be improperly placed on a lower job. In addition, demotion for disciplinary reasons results in loss of face and the possible creation of a permanently dissatisfied employee. Demotion should be used only in a case where an employee does not meet present job requirements or in the event of a cutback in the work force.

Discharge is the most severe penalty that a business organization can give to its members. Discharge for cause makes the ex-employee ineligible for unemployment compensation in most states. It should be used only for serious or habitual infractions of company rules and policies. In a survey of 185 companies, immediate discharge without warning was reported as the penalty by the following percentages of firms: 90 percent for theft, 88 percent for falsifying the application blank, 70 percent for possession of narcotics, 63 percent for possession of firearms, 62 percent for willful damage to company property, 58 percent for falsifying work records, and 54 percent for fighting on the job.[17]

Because of the Wagner and Taft-Hartley Acts, any recommended discharge should be reviewed by those familiar with labor law. If the discharge could reasonably be interpreted as a means of halting union activity in the firm, it cannot be justified legally. Arbitration records reveal that cases involving discharge and discipline constitute the most prevalent single type of grievance. In approximately one-half of these cases, the company's decision is reversed or softened. In an analysis of 391 such instances, the major reasons for reversal were (1) the desire of the arbitrator to give the griev-ant a second chance because the offense was an isolated incident in a generally satis-factory work record (27 percent), (2) inconsistency of the company in enforcement of rules (19 percent), and (3) determination that the punishment was too harsh in terms of in-

[17]*Employee Conduct and Discipline*, op. cit.

dustrial practice generally (14 percent).[18] Other less frequent reasons were the commission of procedural faults by the company in processing, management being partly at fault in the incident, retroactive application of a new rule, and discipline of union stewards or officers for actions in connection with their official union business.

Members of the Young Presidents Organization have reported that one of the most difficult tasks as president of an organization is to separate someone from a job. There is a general reluctance to tackle this very unpleasant task, and situations have dragged on for as long as two to three years before a deserved discharge was given by an executive. Other employees always tend to sympathize with the underdog even though clearly in the wrong. Some executives have developed unusual means of eliminating a person without an outright discharge. The flow of work may be altered so that it goes around the particular employee; thus, the employee may become bored or take the hint and submit a resignation. The job may be abolished and the duties scattered about among other employees; then, after the person has left the organization, the duties can be reassembled and a new employee hired to fill the job. Resignations have been negotiated. An opportunity to resign is traded for the threat of discharge. In higher positions, the undesired person may be "kicked upstairs" and promoted out of the way; he or she may be made a special consultant and never be consulted. And, as is so common in the civil service, a manager may effect a transfer of the individual to some other department: the "hot potato" is pitched to someone else. The fact that managers have devised so many devious ways to separate a person from a job without utilizing an outright discharge is tangible evidence of the repugnance with which they approach the task of discharge.

Guides to disciplinary action

Experience and some research have provided a number of guides to assist the manager in undertaking negative disciplinary action. Among the more commonly cited concepts are the following:

Disciplinary action should be taken in private. Perhaps the most commonly cited guide of disciplinary action is that such action should be administered to the person in private. Our purpose is to condition behavior, not to punish. Holding a person up to public ridicule often has the opposite of this desired effect. There are isolated occasions, fortunately exceptional, when an employee's skin is so thick that only a public reprimand will get through. In general, the purpose will be better accomplished if any penalty is exacted in private. This is not to say that the grapevine will not be working, passing either correct or incorrect information about the act. But even so, the grapevine cannot take away the penalized person's pride or dignity, for no one knows for sure that a penalty has been given, whereas a public reprimand leaves no doubt. In addition, a public reprimand generally stimulates resentment toward management among the employees not disciplined.

An application of a penalty should always carry with it a constructive element. There is little in the penalty itself that is constructive. The individual should be told clearly and precisely the reasons for the action that is to be taken. The employee should

18Morris Stone, "Why Arbitrators Reinstate Discharged Employees," *Monthly Labor Review*, vol. 92, no. 10, October 1969, p. 48.

also be told how to avoid such penalties in the future. Negative motivation should be handled in a positive manner.

Disciplinary action should be applied by the immediate supervisor. Even though an act meriting disciplinary action has been observed by the superior of the immediate supervisor, any action that is taken should be carried out by the supervisor. In this manner we avoid violating the principle of single accountability and in addition we preserve the status of the supervisor. The authority to discipline is essential to the maintenance of a managerial position and to the respect of subordinates for the manager.

Promptness is important in the taking of disciplinary action. The desire for promptness should not lead to quick but unfair punishments. Yet, on the other hand, if punishment is delayed too long, the relationship between the penalty and the offensive act becomes hazy. The penalty not only tends to lose its positive effect on behavior but also seems to stimulate greater resentment than if it were applied earlier. The longer the delay, the more one forgets and the more one feels that punishment is not deserved.

Consistency in the administration of disciplinary action is highly essential. This guide of disciplinary action has in it an interesting contradiction. The characteristic of consistency can be applied to the cause (the penalty) or to the effect (the employee reaction). As applied to the penalty, it would require equal treatment under the code. If two persons are caught smoking in a no-smoking area, both are given identical penalties, assuming that neither has more offenses in the past than the other. The fact that one has a strong personality and the other is somewhat timid would have little to do with it. If consistency is to be applied to the effect, the concept of individual differences tells us that two people react differently to the same action. A reprimand for one may have the same effect as a two-day layoff for another.

Despite the significance of the individual-differences concept, the practical supervisor must emphasize the consistency of penalty. Not only must one be concerned with the offenders; one must also be aware of the possible reactions of other employees. Charges of favoritism would surely arise if different penalties were awarded based solely on the psychological differences of the recipients. Reports of manager practice indicate that consistency in penalty application is more common than a clinical or judicial approach that could result in varying penalties for similar offenses.[19] This consistency can take the form of a "legalistic" approach where a rule is a rule, or a "humanitarian" approach where the rule is not enforced through disciplinary action. In the latter case, rules are viewed as educational devices, and violations are deemed accidental and unintentional. Encouragement is preferred to punishment as a means of conditioning employee behavior.

An immediate supervisor should never be disciplined in the presence of his own subordinates. The concept of privacy would forbid the disciplining of anyone in the presence of others. It is doubly important in the case of managers, who must preserve a position of status and power in addition to the formal authority granted by the organization. The importance of this guide should be obvious, but the author has observed more than one occasion when it was violated. The grapevine will be active

[19]Fremont A. Shull, Jr., and L. L. Cummings, "Enforcing the Rules: How Do Managers Differ?" *Personnel*, vol. 43, no. 1, March–April 1966, p. 36.

enough when managers are disciplined, without their status being completely destroyed by public action.

After the disciplinary action has been taken, the manager should attempt to assume a normal attitude toward the employee. This is an important but difficult guide to follow. If the manager continues to regard the employee with great suspicion after the action has been taken, the employee may oblige by providing the trouble expected. It is better to assume that the incident is closed after the penalty has been inflicted, with advice as to how to alter behavior in the future. Certainly the disciplined employee is aware that the supervisor remembers what has happened, and the supervisor will be interested in seeing if the person's behavior has been successfully conditioned. But one should not go about seeming to wait and hope for the next offense. This attitude merely antagonizes people to the point of hurting themselves through further improper behavior.

When management is dissatisfied with the behavior of an employee, its goal is to effect a change more consistent with organization requirements. Penalties or punishments constitute only one means of doing this, and should be used as a last resort. The attitude of all levels of management is extremely important in the implementation of this desired behavioral change. The attitude of the immediate supervisor should be one of counseling and understanding, rather than "police and punish." One company even goes so far as to suspend for one day *with full pay* in order that the employee may think through personal problems. Should this approach and these activities fail, it might well be that the next best action is discharge. Fines, demotions, loss of privileges, and long suspensions rarely convert a bad performer into a good one. After a sincere effort has been made through casual warnings, counseling interviews, and perhaps a short suspension with pay, then unions, arbitrators, management, and sometimes the employee might well agree that discharge is the next logical event.

CONFLICT RESOLUTION

In dealing with the specific subjects of processing grievances and administering disciplinary action, a variety of approaches have been noted. At this point, we wish to catalog methods of conflict resolution and to indicate the approach advocated by behavioral scientists. Conflict occurs when two or more people or groups perceive that they have (1) incompatibility of goals, and (2) interdependence of activity. Unless one believes in a utopian world where all interests are additive, overlapping, and compatible, one must admit to possible conflicts accompanied by deliberate behavior characterized by interference and blockages. Employees and organizations need each other and are therefore interdependent. Employees and organizations have some values that conflict, e.g., the ego versus control, self-actualization versus division of labor, and freedom versus efficiency. Thus, managers of organizations must accept the inevitability of conflict, recognize those reactions that are helpful to organizational renewal, and seek to minimize behavioral reactions that interfere with and block attainment of legitimate goals.

In Figure 20-2, the reconciliation of conflict between party 1 and party 2 can be approached in seven ways: (1) win/lose fashion, where one party *forces* the other to concede; (2) withdrawal and retreat from argument—"Silence is golden"; (3) smooth-

Figure 20-2 Methods of conflict resolution

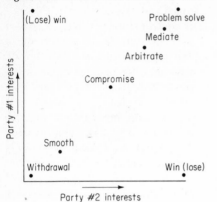

ing or playing down the differences—"We're one big happy family"; (4) compromising, splitting-the-difference, and bargaining in search of intermediate acceptable positions; (5) submission to an outside third party for decision—an arbitrator; (6) inviting an outside third party to mediate and help the two primary parties reach a reconciliation; and (7) problem solving or confrontation through an open exchange of information and working through of the differences so that both can win. It should be apparent that the basic behavioral approach in this regard is the last—the traditional "win/lose" or "lose/lose" approach should be replaced by the behavioral "win/win" philosophy.[20] It is illustrative of the ideal 9,9 leadership-style world, where after the conflict is resolved, both parties are fully satisfied with the results—their values, after all, were overlapping. As usually practiced, confrontation is characterized by such elements as an open and trusting exchange of views and facts and acceptance of the concepts (1) that conflict is caused by relationships among people and is not in the person, (2) that rarely is one completely right and the other completely wrong, and (3) that granting concessions is not a sign of weakness or capitulation.

Even without contending that confrontation and problem solving will always result in solutions that simultaneously maximize both parties' positions, this approach will usually effect better resolutions than the other six. In a study of five methods used in an engineering department of a large corporation, opinions of seventy-four managers were obtained concerning their relative efficacy. Correlations were computed between methods used and resolution effectiveness, with the following results: (1) withdrawal, −.19; (2) smoothing, +.20; (3) compromising, −.08; (4) forcing win/lose, −.26; and (5) problem solving, +.26. Only the last two were significant statistically.[21] A second study of fifty-three managers from various organizations was undertaken, where these people were asked to write descriptions of both good and bad conflict resolutions that they

[20]Robert R. Blake and Jane Srygley Mouton, "The Fifth Achievement," *Personnel Administration*, vol. 34, no. 3, May–June 1971, pp. 49–57.

[21]Ronald J. Burke, "Methods of Resolving Superior-Subordinate Conflict: The Constructive Use of Subordinate Differences and Disagreements," *Organizational Behavior and Human Performance*, vol. 5, no. 4, July 1970, pp. 400–403.

had experienced. In coding these narratives by the five methods, 58.5 percent of the effective resolutions utilized the confrontation approach and 24.5 percent used forcing a win/lose decision. Of the ineffective, none used confrontation while 79.2 percent used forcing. Withdrawal was utilized in about 10 percent of the ineffective stories.

Despite the behavioral views of the efficacy of the problem-solving, confrontation approach, the facts of organized life do indicate that we are often unable to achieve the answer that maximizes competing values simultaneously. We can agree that withdrawal or avoidance, as well as smoothing over real conflicts, are not viable methods of handling this type of problem. However, compromise is often the result of collective bargaining processes between two groups of equal power, e.g., labor and management, the United States and Russia. Neither may be completely happy, but coordinated activity is allowed to continue. When the two parties are unable to reach a solution, either through problem solving or compromise, third parties may enter the scene. In Figure 20-2, arbitration is placed just above compromise to indicate what often happens in such proceedings: the arbitrator, whose salary is equally shared, will over a period of many cases tend toward a balanced position in his or her awards. The mediator, who has no power of decision, is located closer to the problem-solving position in the figure, indicating the greater possibility of *three* parties being able to discover that elusive position of simultaneous maximization. When time for conflict resolution is limited or when basic values are directly conflicting, methods of resolution that are less than the best are often considered to be the "practical" approach.

SUMMARY

Despite the best efforts of all, conflict among people and between people and organizations will occur. It is important to discover these clashes of interest as quickly as possible through such means as gripe boxes, direct observation of behavior, analysis of records, an open-door attitude, personnel counselors, morale surveys, exit interviews, ombudsmen and ombudswomen, and grievance procedures.

A grievance is a complaint which the employee feels is serious enough to justify some type of formal submission and action. It may be ridiculous and without foundation, or real and justified, but whether or not it is a grievance is up to the employee and not to the management. The usual steps in a grievance procedure are (1) conference among the aggrieved employee, the supervisor, and the union steward, (2) conference between middle management and middle union leadership, (3) conference between top management and top union leadership, and (4) arbitration. The manner of processing the grievance on any one level should follow the sequence of functions found in the scientific method, that is, (1) receive and define the grievance, (2) get the facts, (3) analyze and decide, (4) apply the answer, and (5) follow up. The grievance procedure is the most fundamental method of discovering and resolving disagreements, since it both follows the chain of authority and provides for conference and discussion.

Just as the individual makes certain demands upon the organization, so the organization expects certain things from its members. Codes of behavior are established. For those individuals who do not choose to conform to the codes, even though the values and rewards of conformance have been demonstrated by management, negative disciplinary action must be applied. The supervisor should seek to condition behavior and not merely to punish. In the application of penalties, the following guides have been found to be valuable: (1) disciplinary action should be administered in private; (2) an application of a penalty should always carry with it an explanation of what constitutes proper behavior; (3) disciplinary action should be applied by the immediate supervisor; (4) promptness is important in the taking of disciplinary action; (5) consistency in penalty is highly essential; (6) an immediate supervisor should never be disciplined in the presence of his or her own subordinates; and (7) after the disciplinary action has been taken, the manager should attempt to assume a normal attitude toward the employee.

The basic method of conflict resolution advocated by behavioral scientists is problem solving and confrontation, a stance that approaches the 9,9 leadership style in the Management Grid. Other commonly used approaches are withdrawal, smoothing, compromise, mediation, arbitration, and forcing. Each of these approaches either does not deal with the conflict or results in answers that are not fully satisfying to both parties. In our discussion of integrating interests thus far, we have *assumed* that we can and are communicating with the employee. Such an assumption is often dangerous unless one is really aware of the fundamental nature of the communication process, a subject which will be examined in the following chapter.

DISCUSSION QUESTIONS

1   Describe the method of conflict resolution preferred by behavioral scientists. How does it relate to the subject of leadership styles?

2   Ignoring the forced win/lose approach to conflict resolution, describe the continuum of methods ranging from withdrawal on the one extreme to confrontation-problem solving on the other.

3   In what way does an ombudsman or ombudswoman operate to discover and alleviate employee dissatisfactions?

4   Distinguish between a complaint and a grievance. What relation is there between the number of such dissatisfactions and the style of leadership utilized?

5   Describe the role of the union steward with reference to his or her role set of employees, supervisors, and union leaders.

6   Describe the role of the immediate supervisor in processing grievances with respect to subordinates, union stewards, superiors, and the personnel department.

7   Can employees be disciplined for acts committed off the job? What has been the general approach of the courts?

8   What is the nature of the concepts of consistency and privacy in administering disciplinary action?

9   Discuss the use of mediation and arbitration in a grievance procedure. Which is more commonly used? Why?

10 What are the specific difficulties of dealing with employee dissatisfactions obtained through the exit interview? The open-door policy? Suggestion or gripe boxes?

SUPPLEMENTARY READING

BLAKE, Robert R., and Jane Srygley Mouton: "The Fifth Achievement," *Personnel Administration*, vol. 34, no. 3, May–June 1971, pp. 49–57.

FISHER, Robert W.: "When Workers Are Discharged—An Overview," *Monthly Labor Review*, vol. 96, no. 6, June 1973, pp. 4–17.

JENNINGS, Ken: "Employee Loyalty: Relationship between Theory and Practice," *Personnel Journal*, vol. 52, no. 20, October 1973, pp. 864–873.

ROBBINS, Stephen P.: *Managing Organizational Conflict*, Prentice-Hall, Inc., Englewood Cliffs, N.J., 1974, chaps. 7 and 8.

ROSEN, Benson, and Thomas H. Jerdee: "Factors Influencing Disciplinary Judgments," *Journal of Applied Psychology*, vol. 59, no. 3, June 1974, pp. 327–331.

SULLIVAN, Dennis M.: "Employee Discipline: Beware the 'Company Position,'" *Personnel Journal*, vol. 53, no. 9, September 1974, pp. 692–695.

TWENTY-ONE
COMMUNICATION AND COUNSELING

Up to this point in our discussion of the integration function, we have been concerned with the problem of producing good organization morale through a promotion of constructive agreement and a resolving of destructive conflict. We have spoken of education, indoctrination, motivation, grievance procedures, and disciplinary action, and have assumed that in all these processes communication is taking place. This is a dangerous assumption to make and has led to confusion, bewilderment, and, at times, chaos. It is our purpose to examine in this chapter the process of communication which must take place between one human mind and another. This process is fundamental to all aspects of life and is vital to the function of integration. The chapter will conclude with a discussion of employee counseling, a complex communication form that requires highly sophisticated skills to execute properly.

NATURE AND IMPORTANCE OF COMMUNICATION

The term "communication" has many and varied meanings. To some it denotes the means or media of passing information, as for example the telephone, telegraph, or television. To others it has to do primarily with the channels of communication in the organization, such as the grapevine, the formal chain of command, the complaint box, and the grievance procedure. The definition to be discussed in this chapter has to do with the *act* of imparting ideas and making oneself understood by others. Communication is the act of inducing others to interpret an idea in the manner intended by the speaker or writer. The term is derived from the Latin word *communis*, which means "common." If we effect a communication of ideas, we have established a common meeting ground for understanding. If we speak or write, and the idea received by the listener or reader is not that intended, we have not communicated and thus do not hold this single idea in common. We have merely spoken or written. There was either no reception or an imperfect reception of the ideas intended by the would-be communicator.

Perfect communication between two people has probably never been achieved. The story is told of the old man who strolled along talking to himself, and who, when asked why he did it, gave two reasons: "I like to talk to myself, first, because I like to talk to a smart man, and second, because I like to hear a smart man talk." This is probably as close to perfect communication as one can get; the sender and the receiver are bound up in one person and one mind. Even here, some would say, the fact that the old man is talking to himself is evidence that he is confused and does not actually understand himself. But the story does demonstrate the basic purpose of communication, that of transmitting perfectly from one mind to another the intent of the speaker or writer.

Communication is a very important subject to any manager. Managing is getting things done through others, a task which obviously requires the manager to communicate with other people. Both traditional and behavioral managers are interested in developing good communication. The former wishes to assure that orders are understood and that the downward channels are open. The manager also desires to receive accurate information concerning the effectiveness of execution. Behaviorally inclined managers would add the values derived from knowing subordinate attitudes and feelings toward the job, firm, supervisor, and environment. Not only would they emphasize the importance of establishing numerous upward channels of communication, they would attempt to create an "open" organization in the interest of developing creativity and self-control among all organization members.

All estimates concerning the percentage of time allocated to communication processes are quite high, ranging from 75 to 90 percent of our working hours. "Five percent of this communication time is spent in writing, 10 percent in reading, 35 percent in talking, and 50 percent in listening."[1] It might also be added that we often communicate unknowingly as others observe our actions and facial expressions and derive inferences or conclusions from them. The fact that we all send and receive communication signals constantly leads us to assume that we are experts in the process. However, the lack of understanding and acceptance and the wealth of confusion and disagreement which follows are tangible evidence that the signals being sent are not received in the form intended by the sender. If no one is listening or if no one understands what is being said or written, then there is no communication.

CHANNELS AND STRUCTURE

Within an organization, many communication signals will be sent through formally designated channels. Traditional management is noted for insisting that channels be followed in order that work can be coordinated and unity of command preserved. Behaviorists, such as McGregor and Argyris, would recommend less structuring in

---

[1] Aurelius A. Abbatiello and Robert T. Bidstrup, "Listening and Understanding," *Personnel Journal*, vol. 48, no. 8, August 1969, p. 593.

communication. All personnel are deemed to be capable and responsible, and greater participation in management decision making should be sought.

In research conducted by Bavelas, Guetzkow, Simon, and others, it has been discovered that structuring communication flow will lead to the efficiency desired by traditional managers.[2] However, less structuring will lead to greater individual job satisfaction. Subjects in the experiments expressed greater interest and enjoyed the process more under conditions of free interchange. In addition, where there was less structure, there tended to be more ideas and suggestions of an innovative type, a finding which has been emphasized by behaviorists. Thus, some control of communication is essential to efficiency through division of work, coordination of effort, and preservation of unity of direction. However, the resulting regimentation is somewhat detrimental to morale and employee satisfaction and also represses a tendency toward innovation.

As in most problems in management, multiple values are desired, a fact which makes compromises necessary. Management desires efficiency, innovation, *and* high morale. There has to be some formalization of communication flow. Pfiffner and Sherwood suggest that formalized channels should be set up between organization levels, but among personnel at the same level, the information flow should be circular and more free.[3] Thus, this modified structural system would resemble a series of chain links rather than a single unbroken line. It has also been noted that when communications are left largely unstructured among a number of personnel, over a period of time they will introduce a significant amount of structuring on their own. Out of the daily person-to-person interaction will develop a set of stable relationships that will facilitate effective action. In the experiments of Bavelas referred to above, it was found that under conditions of free interchange, subjects would introduce a definite structure of information flow after a number of trials. Some type of balance must be struck between a relatively free exchange of information, which contributes to morale and innovation, and controlled exchanges, which contribute to coordination and unity of command.

In the preceding chapter, a number of formal channels of communication were discussed through which subordinates could communicate *upward* to superiors. Provision for such formal channels is deemed necessary in order to discover clashes of interest, reconcile conflicts, and coordinate efforts. A more complete list of such upward channels of communication would include the following: (1) face-to-face contacts, (2) supervisory "cracker barrel" group meetings, (3) special organization-wide elected councils that meet with top management periodically, (4) "speak up" programs where employees are given a telephone number to call, (5) anonymous-complaint boxes, (6) annual employee meetings parallelling annual stockholders meetings, (7) a grievance procedure, (8) morale questionnaires, (9) exit interviews, (10) open-door policy, (11) the labor union, (12) the grapevine, (13) ombudsmen and ombudswomen, and (14) employee counseling programs.

On the other hand, management must establish *downward* channels through

[2]Alex Bavelas, "Communication Patterns in Task-oriented Groups," *Journal of Acoustical Society of America,* vol. 22, pp. 725–730, 1950; and Harold Guetzkow and Herbert A. Simon, "The Impact of Certain Communication Nets upon Organization and Performance in Task-oriented Groups," in Albert H. Rubenstein and Chadwick J. Haberstroh (eds.), *Some Theories of Organization,* The Dorsey Press, Inc., and Richard D. Irwin, Inc., Homewood, Ill., 1960, pp. 259–277.

[3]John M. Pfiffner and Frank P. Sherwood, *Administrative Organization,* Prentice-Hall, Inc., Englewood Cliffs, N.J., 1960, p. 306.

which information and commands can flow. Many of the same channels can be used for both upward and downward communication. Among the downward channels would be the following: (1) the chain of command, (2) posters and bulletin boards, (3) company periodicals, (4) letters to employees, (5) employee handbooks, (6) information racks, (7) a loudspeaker system, (8) pay inserts, (9) the grapevine, (10) annual reports, (11) group meetings, and (12) the labor union.

COMMUNICATION FILTERS

In large firms, some channels are long, running through several levels of organization. This emphasizes a significant problem in communication, the filtering that takes place at each level. As information is sent up to management, the sender is well aware that it can be used for two purposes: (1) to aid in coordinating and controlling the organization toward basic goals and (2) to evaluate him or her and the quality of performance. Usually, the sender does not object to the first purpose. But concerning the second, one will be influenced by selfish motives of wanting to appear well in the eyes of superiors who control the future. This introduces a filtering effect through conscious and unconscious withholding, interpreting, and altering of facts to be transmitted. The higher the management position in an organization, the more uncertainty its holder must deal with.

There have been many managerial attempts to reduce both the number and the thickness of the authority filters that clog organization communication channels. It should be apparent that decentralization and broadening spans of control of various managers should serve to flatten organization structures, thereby reducing the number of authority filters. One organization reduced the number of managerial levels from eight to four, with a consequent speeding-up of the communication process. Such reorganizations are drastic and require considerable efforts in the areas of retraining and establishing realistic control standards.

Another approach would be the application of a "patch" upon the organization to eliminate some communication filters. The ombudsman or ombudswoman was briefly discussed in a preceding chapter. He or she would serve as a means whereby a rank and file employee could go directly to a representative of the top official in the organization. Some organizational presidents have created an information assistant position for the purpose of centralized gathering of important information to be used in periodic briefings. In one steel company, the occupant of this position succeeded to the presidency.

The consultant can also be used as a means of reducing communication filters. In one manufacturing company, there was a steady decrease in productivity for no reason that could be ascertained by management.[4] The hired consultant employed a "listen to the employee" technique through a systematic interviewing of all 600 employees over a six-month period. The results of these many interviews indicated that many employees felt strongly that work standards were too high, that older employees resented the high wage scales of the new, and that temporary transfers to new jobs to avoid layoff were widely resented. In each case, management believed that they had communicated effectively. In particular, management felt that the temporary transfers would be widely

[4]A. A. Imberman, "To Avoid a Strike," *Personnel Journal*, vol. 48, no. 11, November 1969, pp. 890–894.

applauded by employees in preference to short-term layoffs. On the advice of the consultant, a concerted action and communication program was undertaken, including such elements as the following: (1) all employees with less than six months service were put through a training routine that had been previously neglected under a rapid expansion program; (2) methods specialists were hauled out of their offices and set to roaming the floor to be available for employee questioning; (3) vacations were lengthened for older employees, since high wage scales were necessary for new employees in a tight labor market; (4) service clubs for older employees were begun, along with a new plant organ, both to develop the social life of the plant and instill a sense of pride in company products; (5) a rotation system was set up to handle the temporary transfer problem and the layoff alternative was explained; and (6) many small corrections were made, such as improved lighting, ventilation, and quality of sand-wiches in the vending machine. Perhaps all of these troubles could have and should have been discovered by regular managers, but lack of skills and time often contribute to the creation of problems that appear obvious from the 20/20 hindsight of an outsider. After introduction of the above-described programs, there was a significant improve-ment in the level of productivity as well as a decrease in grievances and absenteeism.

It should also be apparent that most regularly constituted staff positions perform an information-collection function which can bypass intervening levels of line organiza-tion. Behaviorists have questioned the compatibility of the staff role of consulting and advice with the role of police and surveillance. If staff is widely used for policing activities, it will not be voluntarily sought out in the solution of lower-managerial problems.

The development of a total management information system with the aid of the large memory bank of a computer can also assist in providing more accurate informa-tion to multiple levels of management. As indicated in Chapter 5, the tapping of such a data bank by higher management would result in the elimination of many reports from multiple organizational layers, thereby resulting in a decrease in the number of communication filters.

Perhaps the most important approach toward the filter problem is the development of leadership skills among all supervisors. If supervisors can acquire the skills of openness and receptiveness, the thickness of the authority filter can be reduced. It will be recalled that one of the major goals of sensitivity training is development of attitudes of openness and support as well as the skill of effective listening. That this is a problem in many business organizations is made evident by various surveys conducted by Opinion Research Corporation among 2,147 supervisors, engineers, and white- and blue-collar employees in eight companies.[5] Among the various findings were: (1) over half of all employees believe that telling one's supervisor everything one felt about the company would probably get them into a "lot of trouble"; (2) almost three-quarters of all employees feel that management is not interested in employee problems; (3) most employees rate their supervisor as "good" on job knowledge and operating problems, but only one-third say that she or he is "good" on being easy to see with a problem, and one-quarter allocate the supervisor a level of "good" on handling complaints and encouraging suggestions; (4) less than one-quarter feel that management usually takes prompt action in connection with employee complaints; (5) almost three-quarters of

[5]Alfred Vogel, "Why Don't Employees Speak Up?" *Personnel Administration*, vol. 30, no. 3, May–June 1967, pp. 20–22.

the supervisors feel that they need more training in communication practices, particularly in how to listen.

That such training is worth the effort is suggested by a study in six offices of a large public utility.[6] In relating the perceived degree of openness between supervisor and subordinate to employee satisfaction, a clear-cut effect was discovered. The greater the openness of either superior or subordinate, or both, the greater the degree of employee satisfaction with the company, the job, and the supervisor. Equal degrees of openness on the part of both tended to result in greater satisfaction, as contrasted to situations where one or the other was more open. Though not proved, it was suggested that an open attitude on the part of the subordinate was a direct result of such an attitude on the part of the supervisor.

JOHARI'S WINDOW

In developing supervisory skills to effect openness and interpersonal trust, a conceptual device originated by Joseph Luft and Harry Ingham provides a basis for understanding the basic process involved.[7] As indicated in Figure 21-1, the model consists of portraying the varying degrees of information held in common between two people, as well as methods that can be utilized in increasing the size of one's "window." Cell 1 of the figure denotes the "arena" of communication, that is, information held in common and known simultaneously by oneself and others. Cell 2, labeled

[6]Ronald J. Burke and Douglas S. Wilcox, "Effects of Different Patterns and Degrees of Openness in Superior-Subordinate Communication on Subordinate Job Satisfaction," *Journal of the Academy of Management*, vol. 12, no. 3, September 1969, p. 326.

[7]Joseph Luft, *Of Human Interaction*, National Press Books, Palo Alto, Calif., 1969.

Figure 21-1 The Johari Window: a model of interpersonal processes

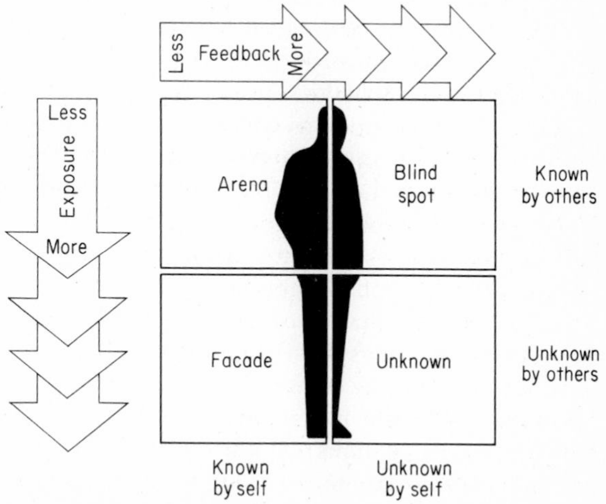

Source: Jay Hall, "Communication Revisited," *California Management Review*, vol. 15, no. 3, Spring 1973, p. 58. Used with permission.

the "blindspot," is information known by others but not by oneself. One of the purposes of sensitivity training is to reduce the size of the "blindspot" through providing increased honest feedback from others about one's personal style. The old phrase, "Even your best friend will not tell you," is indicative of the existence of such a class of information. And often when we are told, we refuse to believe if the information attacks our self-image.

Cell 3, termed the "facade," is a class of information known to ourselves but *not* to others. It is the protective front that all people find necessary to some degree in order to defend the self. The final cell is that information which exists but is unknown to all. Hall suggests that this is indicative of a hidden potential, the unconscious, or the "data base of creativity."[8]

Communication will be enhanced if Cell 1, the "arena," is increased in size. This can be effected through two processes: (1) exposure of self to others and (2) soliciting feedback from others. Exposure requires an open, candid, and trusting approach where one "lets it all hang out." Feedback requires an active solicitation of feelings, opinions, and values from others. For these processes to be fully developed, reciprocity is required. An attempt to use one to the exclusion of the other often generates resistance from associates in the long run.

In research conducted by Hall, it was discovered that interpersonal styles of exposure/feedback correlated with types of leadership styles as depicted on the Management Grid.[9] In a study of 200 managers, classified into the five leadership styles of deserter (1,1), autocrat (9,1), missionary (1,9), compromiser (5,5), and problem-solving integrator (9,9), measurements were taken of the size of their reported "arenas" in Johari's Window. The greater bulk of the 1,1 managers possessed a relatively small "arena," characterized by personal behavior of aloofness, coldness, and indifference. The 9,9 managers had the largest "arena," involving a balanced and heavy use of both exposure and feedback processes. The 5,5 manager also exhibited a balanced utilization (as did the 1,1), but the size of the "arena" was intermediate, lying between the 1,1 and 9,9. Autocratic managers, 9,1, tended to overuse exposure, resulting in the creation of a large blindspot. They did not solicit feedback from subordinates and colleagues as much as they were willing to convey their own opinions, orders, and values. The missionary style, 1,9, tended to emphasize feedback to the detriment of exposure, with the "facade" assuming greater importance.

Effective organizational communication requires a maximum of information held in common among personnel required to work together toward common goals. If active solicitation of feedback is to result in accurate information being supplied, a necessary concomitant is willingness to expose oneself to others. Openness, trust, honesty, and candor are tracks that run on a *two*-way street.

THE COMMUNICATION PROCESS

All people have "arenas" in Johari's Window, whether large or small. The processes of exposure and feedback can be further analyzed by the specific skills of sending

---

[8]Jay Hall, "Communication Revisited," *California Management Review*, vol. 15, no. 3, Spring 1973, p. 58.

[9] Ibid., pp. 64–66. Measurement of "arena" sizes was effected through the *Personnel Relations Survey*, authored by Jay Hall and Martha S. Williams of Teleometrics International, Conroe, Tex.

information to others, as well as by the methods of receiving feedback that facilitates accurate perception. Thus, the communication process can be portrayed as having three basic elements: (1) the sender of the signal, (2), the media by means of which the signal is sent, and (3) the receiver. The sender can be anyone who attempts to transmit some type of meaning or intent to another person. As we said earlier, it is impossible to effect a perfect transfer of meaning. We must encode our intent or meaning into *symbols* and send the symbols to the other person. The major symbols of communication are (1) words, (2) actions, (3) pictures, and (4) numbers. As indicated in Figure 21-2, the communicative skills of sending are speaking, writing, acting, and drawing, while those of receiving are listening, reading, and observing. A person who would improve communicative skills as a manager must develop in these areas.

The media consist of the channels of communication and the particular mechanism that is being utilized to transmit the signals. The receiver must obtain the symbols which have been sent and decode them to form an idea. If the signal is confused and unclear, or if the symbols used do not mean the same thing to both the sender and the receiver, communication is not achieved. We shall now examine in greater detail the symbols used in communicating as well as the problem of the receipt and interpretation of these signals.

Communication symbols: words

As Korzybski has written, language can be compared to a map which purports to represent a certain area or territory.[10] Just as the map is *not* the territory itself, a word is *not* the object or idea it represents. We have less difficulty in effecting a transfer of meaning when the words used represent tangible objects, such as a chair, a building, or a street. But it is much more difficult to transmit the intent of the sender when words representing intangible concepts are used, such as "management," "labor," "liberal," "attitude," or, for that matter, "communication." We do not even have the advantage of using only *one* map to represent the objects and/or ideas. The speaker has her or his own frame of reference and selects words that it is hoped will convey the meaning intended. The listener has a slightly different map, even though both may be referring to a common dictionary. The term "management" may have a favorable connotation to one and a highly objectionable one to another, depending upon background, education, associates, and experience. After we examine the complexities of the communication process, we are often amazed that we communicate as well as we do.

[10]Alfred Korzybski, *Science and Sanity*, 3d ed., The International Non-Aristotelian Library Publishing Co., Lakeville, Conn., 1948, p. 58.

Figure 21-2 The communication process

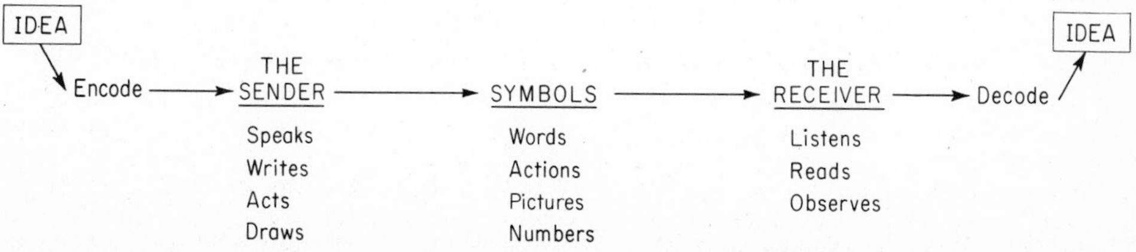

The English language further complicates the process of communication by assigning several meanings to one word. Upon first coming into contact with someone who is attempting to learn the language for the first time, a person is impressed by the multitude of acceptable definitions of a single word. The term "team," for example, has several uses and connotations. In one plant, a female employee was insulted because her supervisor had asked her to "pull with the team"; she felt that she was being compared to an animal. In another instance, the plant superintendent opened his talk to a group of supervisors by stating that he wished "to discuss production problems from your level." He was referring to organizational levels, whereas the supervisors chose to interpret the remark as condescending, implying a stepping down to a lower level of status and competency. Needless to say, the plant superintendent spoke and thereby communicated, but he did not convey the meaning he intended. He had already thrown up a block or barrier to true communication with these supervisors.

Words constitute the most important symbols used in the communication process. They can be transmitted orally and be received by listening, or they may be given in written form and be received by reading. Thus speaking, writing, listening, and reading constitute fundamental communication skills. A manager spends almost all her or his time in using one or the other of these skills.

Though more of a manager's time is spent in oral communication, it is important also to study carefully the nature of effective writing. The act of placing words on paper lends them a greater permanence than does the act of speaking. Sheer size of an organization plus the inevitable phenomenon of turnover compels us to communicate by means of the written word. In oral communication we can rely upon oral response or observation of the expression on the listener's face to determine whether we have transmitted the meaning intended. In written communication we do not have that advantage and, thus, must redouble our efforts to ensure that the reader will receive, as closely as possible, our original intent.

"Bafflegab" and "gobbledegook" are terms that have been coined to describe unnecessarily complex writing in which a hundred words are used to say what could have been said in thirty. Pompous, vague, and intangible words are used whenever possible with a heavy sprinkling of five- and six-syllable words. Several mechanical systems have been developed which enable writers to estimate the readability of their material. The Flesch system incorporates an analysis of average sentence length and number of syllables per 100 words.[11] The average sentence length is multiplied by 1.015 and the total number of syllables per 100 words is multiplied by 0.846. The sum of these two figures is then subtracted from 206.835 and the result is a score ranging from 0 to 100. The 90 to 100 range is rated "very easy" and can be handled by those with a fourth-grade education. The range of 60 to 70 is "standard" and is equivalent to seventh- or eighth-grade education. Scores from 0 to 30 are rated "very difficult" and require a college degree for comprehension. That which is rated "very easy" can be read and understood by over 90 percent of our adult population. The "very difficult" can be understood by only 4 percent. The Air Materiel Command of the United States Air Force was surprised to discover that more than 90 percent of its personnel found it hard to read and understand directives of higher headquarters. It is apparent that

---

[11]Bergen Evans, "Our Changing Language," *Machine Design*, July 20, 1967, p. 192.

subordinate understanding is prerequisite to acceptance of and compliance with orders and directives.

A system similar to that of Flesch is the "fog index" by Robert Gunning.[12] This index is obtained by adding the average number of words in a sentence to the number of words with three or more syllables in a hundred-word passage. Multiplying this figure by 0.4 gives a result which corresponds roughly to the number of years of formal schooling a person would require to read the passage with ease and understanding. With this index, most best-selling books test at seventh- or eighth-grade reading level, the Bible at sixth- or seventh-grade, air force regulations at the sixteenth-grade, and air force numbered letters at the eighteenth-grade level. Most adults prefer to read at least two grade levels below their ability level. The publishers of best sellers are more shrewd in written communication than are most managements.

Soon after the appearance of the Flesch scale, Davis analyzed the readability of seventy-one employee handbooks and discovered that 92 percent of them were too difficult for their intended readers. In a follow-up study of twenty-nine of these same company handbooks fifteen years later, little or no improvement was noted.[13] As judged by the scale, eighteen of the twenty-nine handbooks were lacking in appeal for those employees who were not college graduates. It is apparent that the subject matter of a handbook is not as appealing as a novel or a popular magazine. This, combined with a readability level that is beyond the wishes or capability of most employees, will assure that only publication, rather than communication, is accomplished.

How to improve our ability to communicate meaning through the use of words would go far beyond the limits of this text. The point emphasized here is that we must become aware of the difficulties of true communication. We must not assume that when we are talking or writing we are actually communicating with the listener or reader. Consciousness of the importance of the proper use of words should encourage us to seek improvement in the skills of speaking and writing.

Some, however, feel that our attention to the mechanics of communication has led to a deemphasis of the importance of the *idea* to be communicated. This is not our intention. Obviously, if the person who proposes to communicate does not really know what it is he or she wants to transmit, there can be no communication. One must have a clear, coherent, and rational concept to transmit. Perhaps one of the causes of obscurity and gobbledegook in business communication is that the person who is speaking or writing does not know what to do or say and is trying to hide behind the smoke screen of language. Language can be used to communicate, but it can also be used to confuse and mislead.

Clarity of concept and effective organization of thoughts, however, do not ensure good communication. The person who has something to say does not always get it across. To the study of the content of a concept to be communicated must be added the study of the process of communication. The sender must recognize and understand the nature and importance of the symbols one has for use. Whether or not a communication of ideas is effected is up to *two* people, not one. The person who shouts for help on a desert island is not communicating unless there is someone to hear.

[12]Robert Gunning, "How to Improve Your Writing," *Factory Management and Maintenance*, vol. 110, no. 6, June 1952, p. 134.

[13]Keith Davis, "Readability Changes in Employee Handbooks of Identical Companies during a Fifteen-Year Period," *Personnel Psychology*, vol. 21, no. 3, Winter 1968, pp. 413–420.

Communication symbols: actions

The manager must recognize the fact that he or she communicates by actions as well as by words. If the actions belie the words, the former will carry the weight of meaning to the receiver. If a supervisor suddenly stops beside a worker, pulls out a notebook, and enters a short notation, the employee may think, "What have I done now?" Yet the supervisor may have been only scribbling a list of groceries to bring home that evening. A manager must realize that she or he is a center of attention to subordinates. All observable acts communicate something to the observer whether intended or not by the supervisor.

When unexplained actions by management occur, a vacuum of meaning is thereby created which is usually filled by the receiver's own interpretation of the actions. For example, the manager who removes various machines from the production floor is communicating, whether realizing it or not. If he or she does not tell the subordinates why the machinery is being removed, they will supply the missing signal by creating one of their own. One of the most frequently heard rumors in industrial plants is that of a possible shutdown or transfer of the plant to another city. The manager may have no intention or desire to communicate a possible shutdown to the employees, but unexplained actions, coupled with the fear of insecurity, often lead to such a communication of meaning. Actions *do* speak louder than words. They also communicate many varying meanings, depending upon the background and position of the observer.

Communication symbols: pictures

Comic pages, motion pictures, and television have demonstrated the power of pictures in conveying meaning and understanding to other people. Business has also made extensive use of pictures to communicate understanding. Blueprints, posters, charts, motion pictures, and graphs can and do convey more meaning in certain situations than could be transmitted by volumes of words. Some business managers (and textbook writers) have discovered that the people they hope to reach do not like to read long, uninterrupted passages of writing. Important, comprehensive, and accurate reports have been given little attention because of the complexities of reading. The writer did not communicate, not because the signal was not clear and accurate, but because the reader did not avail herself or himself of the signal. The same report, organized in conformance with the exception principle and supplemented by summarizing graphs, charts, and pictures, conveys more meaning in less time. Often the better-illustrated reports bring the greater results because of the stimulus they give to reader receptivity. This is not necessarily logical, but logic does not always communicate. It may be that in the future college textbooks will be printed in red, white, and blue colors with pictures on each page, in order to attract and to lead the reader to open her or his mind to the signal accompanying their illustrations. The preparation of some military manuals has already reached this level of illustration. It is possible to overdo this type of thing, and preparing comic books for the education of business managers and college students is likely to meet the barrier of resistance to communication through insult. However, it is folly to ignore the power of pictures in communicating, and a judicious use of charts, graphs, and other illustrative material will make a substantial contribution to the process of transmitting meaning.

A chart or graph has the advantage of depicting many relationships of a complex type in one picture. Contrasts can be seen and grasped more clearly. Trends can be more easily recognized. In addition, they have the showmanship that stimulates the reader receptivity discussed above. Among the various types of charts and graphs that are used in business are the curve, bar, column, circle, pie, pictorial, map, organization, ranking, and frequency distribution. Pictorial illustration is especially effective in communicating with groups of people. Oral communication and actions are the symbols that are used more often in the ordinary daily contacts among individuals.

Communication symbols: numbers

Perhaps our discussion of the language symbol should have included a consideration of figures or statistics in their role as communication symbols. We have felt, however, that numbers have a peculiar character of their own which makes separate discussion and emphasis desirable.

It is generally true that people are greatly impressed with data which consist largely of figures and statistics. Words may flow around them and pictures appear interesting, but when a few figures are tossed into a presentation, acceptance and belief tend to rise. There is a pronounced tendency to accept figures as facts. There is a worship of the number.

Darrell Huff has made a contribution in his book, *How to Lie with Statistics*, in demonstrating how people can be purposefully misled by adroitly selected numbers.[14] Unscrupulous persons can profit through the communicative power of the number symbol and transmit meaning in a manner which engenders acceptance. For example, biased samples of a population are easily devised through skillful selecting or influencing of the sample. The arithmetic mean can be used to portray a central tendency when it suits the communicator's purpose in a particular situation. One may shift to the median to make an entirely different point in another problem. If a chart is not impressive enough, the bottom can be cut off and the spacing intervals widened, thus creating in Huff's terms a "Gee Whiz" chart similar to that depicted in Figure 21-3. Correlations between two sets of data can be used to confuse cause and effect without mentioning the possibility that a third factor may be influencing both sets. Undue emphasis can be given to small differences between two figures. For example, one applicant's test score was 84, another's, 83. If the communicator wishes to hire the first person, one makes much of the one-point difference, a difference which is probably insignificant in view of the current quality of testing.

Skillful use of numbers and statistics can be applied to lead or mislead. We are not suggesting that the manager should not use these particular communication symbols in dealings with others. On the contrary, he or she will find them to be one of the most valuable means of communicating. However, it is important to understand how such statistics can be misused, so that one is not fooled by another's attempted communication. It is also important for the communicator to use data properly and admit the deficiency of statistics when necessary. Numbers and statistics are very powerful tools of communication. It is to be hoped that the increasing sophistication of readers and listeners in this area will make it more difficult to "lie with statistics" in the future.

[14]Darrell Huff, *How to Lie with Statistics*, W. W. Norton & Company, Inc., New York, 1954.

Figure 21-3 The creation of a "Gee Whiz" chart for purposes of emphasizing a point

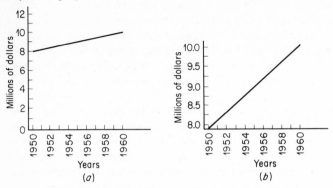

Source: Adapted from Darrell Huff, *How to Lie with Statistics*, W. W. Norton & Company, Inc., New York, 1954, chap. 5.

Listening

Sending is only a part of the process of communication. Some attention must be directed to the problem of receiving. Receiving communication signals is effected primarily through listening, inasmuch as most communication is of the oral type. Several firms, however, have undertaken to improve the reading skills of their managers in order to speed up and make more effective the process of communication.

We encounter several obstacles in the process of communicating, many of which have already been discussed. One that has not been mentioned thus far is the discrepancy between the speeds of speaking and of listening. It takes far less time to listen and think than it does to speak. We usually speak to others at a rate of from 120 to 160 words per minute. We can listen and think four times faster than that. It would appear that this speed should make listening all the easier. On the contrary, it presents an obstacle, in that it leads the listener to poor or marginal listening to the speaker, while thinking ahead to what *he* or *she* is going to say in reply. The listener is easily distracted because of this excess time. Good listening is not passive; one has to work at it to do it properly. Research indicates that usual listening efficiency will result in 50 percent retention immediately after a ten-minute talk, with a decline to 25 percent retention after 48 hours. "The biggest block to personal communication is man's inability to listen intelligently, understandingly, and skillfully to another person."[15]

Various types of listening have been identified as (1) marginal, (2) evaluative, and (3) projective. Marginal listening is, as the term implies, a process of giving the speaker a small degree of one's attention. This dangerous type of listening can lead to misunderstanding of the speaker and even insult to the person. The manager who pretends to listen to a subordinate while actually worrying about some other problem is asking for trouble. It is extremely difficult to fake sincere interest in the remarks of others, and the likelihood of actually insulting the speaker is high. It would be much

[15]Carl R. Rogers and F. J. Roethlisberger, "Barriers and Gateways to Communication," *Harvard Business Review*, vol. 30, no. 4, July–August 1952, p. 52.

better to postpone the meeting if the manager feels able to listen in only a marginal fashion at that time.

Evaluative listening is attentive rather than marginal. We give the speaker our full attention. As we hear what is being said, however, we utilize the time created by the slowness of speech and the rapidity of listening to judge and evaluate the remarks. We approve or disapprove of what he or she says from our own point of view. We often form mental remarks of rebuttal in anticipation of our own opportunity to speak. Thus, evaluative listening constitutes an obstacle in the communication process. Instead of ideas being transferred from speaker to listener, we end up with two ideas, the speaker's and the listener's, neither of which is really communicated to the other. If we spend our time criticizing, approving, or disapproving the remarks of the speaker, we actually are devoting little time and effort to the task of really understanding what she or he wants to say. This is particularly true when the ideas being communicated are loaded with emotion. In such discussions there is often a great deal of talk and argument but little true listening, a situation which rules out any real communication.

Real communication takes place when the listener truly hears and understands the position and intent of the speaker. This requires a type of listening which is called "projective." While hearing the remarks of the speaker, the listener purposefully avoids any attempt to criticize, approve, or disapprove. We attempt to project ourselves into the mind of the speaker and really try to understand his or her viewpoint *without* evaluation at this time. Evaluation of the content of a speaker's remarks must come in any communication process, but it should not come until the listener has heard, studied, and understood the meaning of the remarks. Carl Rogers suggests a rule to be followed in a discussion, which will facilitate projective listening. "Each person can speak up for himself only *after* he has restated the ideas and feelings of the previous speaker accurately and to that speaker's satisfaction."[16] Following this rule would probably mean the end of most "bull sessions," inasmuch as a large portion of such discussions is composed of speaking rather than listening and of misunderstanding rather than understanding. The quality of empathy is essential to good listening. There is no necessity to agree with the statements of the speaker, but there is every need to try to understand them and the speaker's intent and attitude. Only in this way can you frame a reply that will *actually* respond to the speaker's remarks. The speaker attempts to communicate an idea. One must then listen with understanding to the response in order to adjust the next remark to the other person's response. We must not spend our time listening marginally while framing the next statement. We must not listen in a critical or evaluative sense so that we do not really understand the intent of the response. Effective listening is empathic listening, which enables one truly to understand and *then* to evaluate and respond in a manner that fits the statement.

Most training efforts have been directed toward increasing listening efficiency, thereby decreasing marginal listening. In one programmed-learning course, participants listen to a series of tape-recorded statements. The beginning statements are short and easy; later ones become progressively longer and more complex. Often the statements are technical in content, accented with anger, and delivered in a poorly organized fashion against a background of office noise. The student is asked to write a summary of the statement which can be compared with the summary in an instruction booklet. A study of several hundred supervisors indicated that before training the

[16]Ibid., p. 75.

average retention rate was 25 percent; after training the group average had increased to 90 percent.[17] A retest of the group one year later did not show a decline in this level of efficiency.

Reading skills are also important to the communication process. The amount of written material that a manager must plow through seems to increase yearly. Admittedly, the first and most constructive approach is to reduce the amount of such material and to organize what remains in a manner that will conserve the executive's time. The exception principle is basic to a reduction of this reading problem. Nevertheless, there still remains a substantial amount of communication through the written word. Some companies have undertaken training programs to teach excutives how to read. Some have emphasized speed of reading and have discovered that the normal reading speed can be doubled or tripled without too much loss of comprehension. Reading is a skill that can be taught and learned. But like all skills, if not used by the executive, it tends to fade, bringing a return to former reading habits. It is interesting to note that though some firms have proposed to teach the more tangible skill of reading, few, if any, have set out to teach the executive how to listen. Since we are able to listen long before we learn to read, skill in this area is largely taken for granted, and its absence may well be at the root of the problem of communication.

COUNSELING

In attempting to reconcile and integrate interests of personnel with the interests of the organization, one of the more sophisticated communication forms that are used is counseling. It would appear that a maximum of openness and candor could be effected between counselor and counselee. However, the degree to which this can be done is greatly affected not only by the counseling method utilized, but also by the position and skills of the counselor.

The view that the typical manager is autocratic, tough-minded, and opposed to counseling of any type is an erroneous one. Managers have long been aware of emotional conflicts in the workplace and have attempted in their own way to reduce the impact of such conflicts. They generally wish to know as quickly as possible the nature of the difficulty. From a "superior" knowledge of position and background, he or she immediately "understands" the problem, formulates the "correct" answer, and proceeds to persuade the employee to perceive this answer in the same way. This general approach is usually labeled "directive counseling."

Behavioral scientists, on the other hand, recommend relying more heavily upon the employee to solve his or her own problem. This would be consistent with the human models proposed by organization psychologists. Rather than acting as an initiator and problem solver, the counselor views her or his proper role as one of sympathetic and active listening. This approach is termed "nondirective counseling," and often requires skills and environments that are beyond those possessed by line managers. As a historical note, Western Electric is credited with developing one of the best-known counseling programs which grew out of the famous Hawthorne experiments of the 1920s and 1930s. It grew from its inception in 1936 to a maximum total of fifty-five professional counselors serving 21,000 employees in 1948.[18] With a change in

[17]Abbatiello and Bidstrup, op. cit., p. 596.

management in the early 1950s, the number of counselors was gradually reduced to zero in 1956. Dickson and Roethlisberger concluded that the program was highly successful in solving personal problems in a clinical, nondirective situation but the company policy of counselor nonintervention in managerial processes precluded organizational use of most personal information. The new management felt that immediate supervisors should reassume the responsibility for human relations, including the counseling function.

Directive counseling

After a preliminary statement of the nature of the difficulty by either the directive counselor or the employee, the former controls the discussion. He or she may seemingly permit the latter to volunteer solutions by directing a series of leading questions to the employee. For example, the employee's difficulty may be one of chronic tardiness. The directive counselor, after condemning the behavior, may ask why the employee has this difficulty. This will often result in a noncommittal response. The counselor then fires a rapid series of leading questions: Did you oversleep? Were you ill? Did you have car trouble? Is it the children? Are you overworking? etc. Not only does the process usually *not* lead to a discovery of the source of the trouble, it suggests to the employee possible excuses the manager-counselor might find acceptable.

The major tools of correction used by the directive counselor, upon discovering the nature of the difficulty, are advice, warning, exhortation, praise, and reassurance. All these actions emphasize the superior position of the counselor and the dependent one of the employee. The manager assumes full understanding of the fundamental nature of the difficulty and determines and attempts to implement changes in attitudes or actions which will resolve the conflict. For the most part, however, one provides advice which is in response to one's *own* needs rather than to the needs of the employee. At times, the directive counselor will make use of praise and reassurance in order to encourage the employee to overcome problems, or to realize that no problem really exists.

Nondirective counseling

The philosophical framework of nondirective counseling is consistent with the behavioral approach to management theory. It rests upon a fundamental respect for the individual—a belief in the person's ability to solve personal problems with the aid of a sympathetic listener—and emphasizes the role of the counselor as one of understanding rather than one of passing judgment. The goal is to facilitate development of self-insight.

In the nondirective counseling discussion, the roles of counselor and employee are more nearly equal; there is no attempt to create a superior-subordinate relationship. Carl Rogers has broken the nondirective counseling session into three parts: (1) the release of tension; (2) the development of insight; and (3) the formation of new plans and choices.[19]

[18]William J. Dickson and F. J. Roethlisberger, *Counseling in an Organization*, Harvard University Division of Research, Boston, 1966, pp. 4–7, 477.

[19]Carl R. Rogers, *Counseling and Psychotherapy*, Houghton Mifflin Company, Boston, 1942. See chaps. 6, 7, and 8.

The nondirective counselor assumes that the employee is in the best position to know and understand the problem. He or she must be essentially an interested and active listener, preferably one with the power to offer whatever help might be necessary. This requires a somewhat permissive, friendly atmosphere, with actions and statements which exhibit continuing interest but *not* judgment. Silence is also an invitation for the employee to speak further. At times the counselor may make a summary statement, being ever careful that it is truly reflective and not altered in any essential manner. Probing questions are more directive but are often helpful in obtaining a fuller statement—such questions as, "Could you tell me more about . . . ?" or "I'm a stranger to this situation; could you fill me in on . . . ?" The counselor should learn to listen for feelings as well as for words. The hope is that, as the employee verbalizes the problem, the situation will clarify itself and both will have a truer awareness of what lies behind the difficulty. The employee need no longer be defensive and can devote energies to discovering insights about herself or himself and the particular problem.

A difficult task for the counselor, particularly if a manager, is the handling of *negative* feelings. The employee may attack the organization, other employees, or the counselor. The natural tendency is to refute these accusations and demonstrate logically, or with the use of authority, that the employee is in error. If this should occur, the counselor has become directive. If one wishes to profit from the values of nondirective counseling, one must keep the self under restraint and accept these negative expressions as representative of the employee's feelings. Though it is difficult for many managers to accept, having to listen to negative expressions is *not* evidence of reduced managerial authority. If he or she but continues to listen, it is almost certain that these hostile expressions will diminish and the discussion will turn to more fruitful areas.

As a result of the new insight gained by the employee, he or she can develop new plans, actions, or attitudes. At this point the counselor may be of assistance by making sure that the employee has considered as many alternatives as possible. One may ask, "What would happen if you did what you suggest?" or "Have you considered such and such?" The expression of these probes must not, of course, reveal a bias toward any of the alternatives. There are occasions, however, when the counselor becomes convinced that resolution of the problem will require action by the *organization* rather than reorientation by the individual. In this event, it is helpful if the counselor has the authority to inaugurate such organizational changes. There is still a third possibility, that of arriving at no acceptable solution. In this event, the use of nondirective counseling might be condemned as worthless. But at least it can be said that listening does little actual harm and has the possibilities of doing considerable good.

Organization for counseling

In selecting the appropriate person to execute the counseling function, the two most apparent choices are either the immediate supervisor or a staff personnel counselor. In addition, there is a certain amount of counseling done by friends and acquaintances, as well as by outside professional personnel such as psychiatrists, psychologists, and representatives of religious organizations.

We have noted that nondirective counseling has many advantages over directive counseling. To achieve the necessary permissive, confidential, and nonjudgmental atmosphere, many have concluded that specialized staff personnel constitute the best organizational arrangement. A staff psychologist can set up a zone of neutrality, while the immediate supervisor must work within the framework of formal authority. On the other hand, the staff personnel counselor has little or no authority to institute organizational changes, a fact which is also apparent to the employee. The staff counselor must preserve the identity of the employee and can make only general reports to line management. In effect, then, communications are going up one channel—employee to personnel counselor—and possible action is taking place down another—supervisor to employee. For these reasons, the immediate supervisor is viewed by some as the most effective counselor. This was the conclusion of the new management of the Western Electric Company when it abolished its huge program of staff counseling.

When supervisors accept a counseling obligation, the temptation is to assume a directive role, for it is difficult to be directive on the plant floor and nondirective in the office. The supervisor protests that nondirective counseling is fine in theory but impractical in operation inasmuch as he or she is lacking in both skill and time. With the authority allocated to the position, one could never hope to create a truly free and permissive atmosphere.

Keith Davis has proposed as one answer to this dilemma a third type of counseling which he has termed "cooperative counseling," lying somewhere between directive and nondirective counseling.[20] Cooperative counseling begins with exclusive emphasis upon the nondirective approach. The employee is encouraged to voice difficulties, and the supervisor accepts as a first role that of listening actively, interestedly, and intelligently. In all actions, the supervisor must demonstrate an interest in and receptivity to subordinate problems, an attitude which in no way conflicts with her or his superior organizational position. When the supervisor is certain that the problem is understood, it is difficult to continue to allow the subordinate to talk. But it is essential for the supervisor to accept the concept that the subordinate must be allowed to speak without interference and with encouragement at the beginning of the session.

After the supervisor is certain that she or he has heard as much as the counselee will provide, a more directive role in counseling is assumed. One may reassure the employee that the problem is not really insoluble, or one may provide more information about the broader situation. If some action is necessary, he or she will take this as the employee's supervisor rather than as counselor. The supervisor must demonstrate a willingness to listen and a desire to come to some conclusion that helps the employee and is consistent with the needs of the organization. If the problem is a sensitive one, whose causes are outside the organization, e.g., trouble with family, the supervisor's role should be one of sympathetic listening *only*. Providing advice in this area is to be avoided. If the problem seems to require a major reorientation of values, the supervisor should recognize his or her lack of ability as a nondirective counselor and refer the employee to skilled help either within or without the organization.

Thus, the type of counseling that is appropriate to the immediate supervisor should be neither completely directive nor completely nondirective in nature. *It is employee-centered in the beginning and supervisor-organization-centered in the end.* It may not

[20]Keith Davis, *Human Relations at Work*, 4th ed., McGraw-Hill Book Company, New York, 1972, p. 431.

be as effective as the purely nondirective approach, but it will do less harm than the purely directive approach. At least the supervisor will have more information than he or she had before and will acquire a greater understanding of the needs of subordinates. A danger, of course, is that supervisors will become excessively employee-centered rather than maintaining a balance between the individual and the organization.

SUMMARY

The subject of communication is one of the broadest in the field of personnel management. It encompasses a consideration of the subjects to be communicated, media, channels, communicators, and the symbols of communication. In this chapter we have been primarily concerned with the *communication process*, that is, the transfer of meaning and understanding from one human being to another. This process breaks down fundamentally into three elements: the sender of the signal, the means by which the signal is sent, and the receiver.

No true communication is established unless the receiver actually understands the original meaning and intent of the speaker or writer. If you have been confused by this chapter, the author has written rather than communicated.

Since meaning and understanding cannot be physically transferred from one mind to another, we must rely upon symbols, which are substitutes for the actual idea, concept, or thing about which we propose to communicate. They constitute a map of the meaning we wish to convey. When the symbols are received, they constitute a second map for the receiver. Thus we not only must deal in symbols, but must realize that the same symbols often have slightly different meanings for sender and receiver.

The symbols of communication are four in number, namely, (1) words, (2) actions, (3) pictures, and (4) numbers. An understanding of both phonetics and semantics is essential for the modern manager. The receiver of these symbols is charged with the responsibility of listening or reading attentively. There are various types of listening, such as (1) marginal, (2) evaluative, and (3) projective. The chances of real communication between two persons are greatly enhanced when both realize the empathic values of projective listening. They are also increased when both parties are willing to utilize the processes of exposure and feedback in creating a larger "arena" in Johari's Window, thereby effecting greater degrees of openness, candor, and trust.

Counseling is one of the more effective approaches toward reducing conflict and integrating interests. Directive counseling, widely practiced by most managers, rests on the philosophy that the manager can best understand both the situation and the individual problems arising therefrom. Nondirective counseling rests on the belief that the individual can best understand his or her own emotional problems and work out an effective solution to them. This is done with the aid of a nondirective counselor whose major contribution is that of active and empathic listening. If the supervisor is to attain any of the values of the nondirective approach, she or he should attempt to use it in the early portions of the counseling interview. Given the limited possession of highly sophisticated counseling skills, as well as the contamination of the atmosphere by one's formal authority, the supervisor can only hope to improve a basically directive approach with greater initial attempts to listen, to display openness, and to encourage feedback.

DISCUSSION QUESTIONS

1 Outline Johari's Window, indicating its role in improving communication processes.
2 Which cells in Johari's Window are usually indicative of which leadership styles on the Management Grid?
3 Why do communication filters exist between organization levels? Between two friends?
4 What organizational approaches have been used to reduce the number and thickness of communication filters between organizational levels?
5 In what way is language similar to a map for a plot of ground? What problems of communication are thereby created?
6 What are the Flesch and "fog" indexes, and how can a manager make use of them in improving communication processes?
7 Why is projective listening recommended for improved communication? What are the other alternatives in listening?
8 What are the respective roles of counselor and counselee in both directive and nondirective counseling?
9 Contrast the roles of supervisor and professional staff specialist in executing a counseling function.
10 Contrast the values to the organization of structured information flow with the advantages of free-flow communication.

SUPPLEMENTARY READING

BEDEIAN, Arthur G.: "Superior-Subordinate Role Perception," *Personnel Administration/Public Personnel Review*, vol. 1, no. 3, November–December 1972, pp. 4–11.
FENN, Dan H., Jr., and Daniel Yankelovich: "Responding to the Employee Voice," *Harvard Business Review*, vol. 50, no. 3, May–June 1972, pp. 83–91.
HALL, Jay: "Communication Revisited," *California Management Review*, vol. 15, no. 3, Spring 1973, pp. 56–67.
HARRIMAN, Bruce: "Up and Down the Communications Ladder," *Harvard Business Review*, vol. 52, no. 5, September–October 1974, pp. 143–151.
ROBERTS, Karlene H., and Charles A. O'Reilly III: "Failures in Upward Communication in Organizations: Three Possible Culprits," *Academy of Management Journal*, vol. 17, no. 2, June 1974, pp. 205–214.
SUSSMAN, Lyle: "Perceived Message Distortion, or You Can Fool Some of the Supervisors Some of the Time . . . ," *Personnel Journal*, vol. 53, no. 9, September 1974, pp. 679–682, 688.

TWENTY-TWO

THE STATUS
OF THE
LABOR UNION

The nature and significance of the function of integration are well exemplified by the problem of labor-management relations. The successful manager of personnel is one who has effectively integrated the interests of the labor union with the interests of the company. The union represents a set of interests which appear, at least in the immediate sense, to be directly contradictory to the interests of the management and the company. The union proposes, for example, to restrict the freedom of the company in the decision-making process in various areas of personnel management. That this poses some difficulty is revealed in a comparative study of values held by both business managers and labor union leaders. In determining which of several goals are of dominant importance, over 1,000 business leaders came up with the following rank order: (1) organizational efficiency, (2) high productivity, (3) profit maximization, (4) organizational stability, growth, and leadership, (5) employee welfare, and (6) social welfare. Determining order of priority on the basis of reports from 136 union leaders, the sequence was as follows: (1) employee welfare, (2) organizational efficiency, (3) high productivity, (4) organizational stability, growth, and leadership, (5) social welfare, and (6) profit maximization.[1] It is apparent that though both groups allocate a low relative ranking to social welfare, they disagree markedly on employee welfare and profit maximization. Rank order correlation between the two lists is approximately .22.

Despite these differences, an integration of interests can be and often is effected. It is significant that both sets of leaders view organizational efficiency and high productivity as major avenues to *either* employee welfare or organization profits. Perhaps the

---

[1] George W. England, Naresh C. Agarwal, and Robert E. Trerise, "Union Leaders and Managers: A Comparison of Value Systems," *Industrial Relations*, vol. 10, no. 2, May 1971, p. 222.

major disturbing factor in this research is the relatively low level of importance attached to general societal goals.

In this and the following chapter, we propose to examine the role of the labor union in the industrial environment, as well as the process in which the role is made effective—that of collective bargaining. In this chapter, the following subjects will be discussed: (1) the nature of a labor union, including objectives, types, and current status, (2) the role of the union as established by law, and (3) the role of the union as established by the labor contract.

NATURE OF A LABOR UNION

A *labor union* or *trade union* is an organization of workers formed to promote, protect, and improve, through collective action, the social, economic, and political interests of its members. The philosophies of labor organizations have gradually changed with the times. In the early 1800s, the social theme of brotherhood and fraternity was of dominating importance. Coupled with this was often a great interest in "uplift unionism," a desire to remake society, as exemplified by proposed reforms in land, currency, and debtor laws. Today this social objective of the labor organization is still of real concern. It is one of the reasons often given for joining any organization, and the labor union is no exception.

The dominant interest with which the union is concerned is economic. In this area desires and demands for improved wages, hours, and working conditions are foremost. Since the early union movement in this country was unduly influenced by social objectives, it fell to Samuel Gompers and the American Federation of Labor to emphasize the concepts of business unionism and job consciousness over and above any interests in brotherhood and social legislation. Business unionism holds to the thesis that a union's major objective is to protect and improve the economic position of its members. If a union is to exist, its members must believe that this objective can be achieved more effectively through organized and collective action than through the individual. Certainly, the American Federation of Labor, as formed in 1886, constituted the cornerstone of the American labor movement.

For years, the AFL pursued a policy of nonparticipation in political action. In the last few decades, this policy has been radically modified. It is now a generally accepted objective of the modern labor union to seek to improve and protect the political status of the union, the union leader, and the union members. This objective was exemplified by the old Political Action Committee of the Congress of Industrial Organizations and by the Labor League for Political Education of the old AFL. These two organizations have been combined as a result of the AFL-CIO merger of 1956.

A particular employee often has a variety of reasons for wanting to join a union. Frequently, it is the only avenue toward obtaining a job. In three-fourths of the labor contracts of this nation, union membership is compulsory for job retention. Compulsory unionism, through the union shop, is very widespread in this country.

A second reason for joining a labor organization is one for which management can find no substitute, a sense of freedom from arbitrary management action. A theoretically perfect management could provide more-than-fair hours, wages, and working conditions, as well as institute a most complete and effective human relations and integration program. But there is no way other than through organized and collective force that an employee can feel independent enough to challenge the actions of formal superiors in management. Perfect management cannot give this desired sense of freedom and importance. Many managers have become bewildered when their employees, who had been given the best of everything, voted to organize a union at the first opportunity to do so. They condemn the employees as unappreciative, when in reality they are evidencing a desire to stand on their own feet and speak with a voice of authority rather than subservience. This is a need which exists in most adults, and if it is not satisfied through individual relationships with management, it must be taken care of in a collective manner. The ability to offer freedom from actual or potential arbitrary management decrees and actions concerning the industrial lives of employees is a primary source of strength for the labor union. The union must also be successful in delivering the economic goods. However, an effective management could do this alone and is often successful in warding off unionization by paying better-than-average wages and benefits. What the effective management finds it difficult to provide is this sense of independence, freedom, and power.

TYPES OF UNIONS

In general, there are two types of labor unions, the industrial and the craft. These are often referred to as vertical and horizontal, respectively. The industrial union is vertical in the sense that it includes all workers in a particular company or industry regardless of occupation. It thus constitutes a mixture of skills and lacks the homogeneity of the crafts. It represents the mass production worker or "common-man" approach to labor organization. This type of organization was promoted chiefly by the leaders of the CIO movement in 1936. Examples of this industrial type of union are the United Automobile Workers and the United Steel Workers.

The horizontal or craft union is an organization that cuts across many companies and industries. Its members belong to one craft or to a closely related group of occupations. Examples of this type are the unions that have organized the carpenters and the machinists. This is the kind of organization emphasized by the AFL from its inception. One of the basic weaknesses of the old Knights of Labor in the latter 1800s was its heterogeneity of membership, which led to lack of unity of action. Gompers worked to stress organization of groups with a high degree of common interests. A company management that deals with craft unions may have to negotiate with as many as eighteen different organizations, as contrasted with one if it deals with an industrial union. Any one of the craft unions may strike the plant and set up picket lines which will effectively shut off operations. It is a cardinal principle among unions to respect one another's picket lines.

The industrial union is not without its craft problems. When unskilled, semiskilled, and highly skilled employees are combined into one organization, internal clashes of interest can and do take place. For example, the industrial union is often prone to negotiate across-the-board increases in pay. If all jobs are raised a certain amount, say 25 cents per hour, the percentage pay differential between top and bottom jobs has been reduced. The skilled craftsman often feels that if the semiskilled worker obtains 25 cents, he should have 30 or 35 cents to maintain established relationships. There have been threats among the skilled in some industrial unions to carve out of the larger industrial union a craft union of the highly skilled. Yet it is difficult for the industrial union leadership not only to demand a larger increase for the skilled workers but also to back up this demand with the economic force of all, the skilled and the unskilled. Since the skilled constitute a minority in numbers, the unskilled and semiskilled are not enthusiastic about striking or threatening to strike for the exclusive benefit of a few who are already being paid more than they. The clash of industrial and craft union organizations is not one that is or will be easily solved. The merger in 1956 of the AFL, which emphasized craft unionism, and the CIO, which emphasized industrial unionism, has brought at best only an uneasy peace. There is a built-in conflict between these two types of labor organization.

CURRENT STATUS OF LABOR UNIONS

The history of the union movement in the United States dates back to the very beginning of this country.[2] Growth was relatively slow until the passage of federal acts in the 1920s and 1930s which gave the protection of law to the organizing process. As of the pre-World War I period, total union membership stood at approximately $2^1/_2$ million.[3] The prosperity of the war period, when combined with favorable governmental attitudes, particularly those of the federal government, served to stimulate a rapid and remarkable expansion of union membership to a total of approximately five million in 1920.[4] This doubling of the number belonging to labor unions served to stimulate a change in the philosophy of personnel management in many companies, a switch from the mechanical or commodity approach to one that has been labeled "paternalistic."[5] During the 1920s and early 1930s, there was an actual decline in the numerical strength of unions to a level of fewer than three million in 1933. With the passage of federal legislation protecting the right to organize without interference from the employer, as exemplified by the Wagner Act of 1935, the union movement started to grow very rapidly. In the twelve-year period from 1933 to 1945, the numerical strength of unions increased fivefold, from less than three million to approximately fifteen million.

The strength of the union movement in terms of membership is difficult to state with precision, though statistics are gathered by the Bureau of Labor Statistics on a biannual basis. The report for 1972 indicates that the total membership of national and international unions that had collective bargaining agreements with different employers in more than one state stood at approximately 20.9 million.[6] After an absolute net decline during the 1960s, the union movement in recent years has slowly but steadily increased in numbers—20.2 million in 1968, 20.7 million in 1970, and 20.9 million in the last-reported period. However, the percentage of the United States labor force that this represents stands at 21.8 percent, the lowest in the past three decades. The high percentage point for unionization was reached in 1953, when 27.1 percent of the labor force was organized.

Of the total union membership, 16.5 million are in unions affiliated with the

---

[2]See Thomas R. Brooks, *Toil and Trouble: A History of American Labor*, Delacorte Press, New York, 1964.

[3]Harry A. Millis and Royal E. Montgomery, *The Economics of Labor*, vol. III, *Organized Labor*, McGraw-Hill Book Company, New York, p. 132.

[4]Ibid., p. 163.

[5] See Chap. 2.

[6]Sheldon M. Kline, "Membership in Labor Unions and Employee Associations, 1972," *Monthly Labor Review*, vol. 97, no. 8, August 1974, p. 67.

AFL-CIO. Two of the three largest single unions are not affiliated with this national organization—the Teamsters, with 1.86 million members, and the United Auto Workers, with 1.39 million. The third major union, the United Steel Workers, with 1.4 million, remains an affiliate of the AFL-CIO.

The steady decline in the proportion of the labor force that is organized is attributed to various reasons. Beginning with increased automation in the 1950s, the traditional stronghold of manufacturing shows steady declines in membership. As indicated earlier in this text, the proportion of white-collar employees is now greater than that of blue-collar, and the latter constitute the heart of the union effort. Two-thirds of blue-collar personnel have been organized, as compared with less than 10 percent of the engineers and technicians. Union leaders are valiantly trying to increase the degree of unionization of the white-collar, with the percentage of such membership increasing from 12.2 percent of the total in 1962 to 16.5 percent in 1972. One particular group stands out in this regard: the proportion of government employees unionized has more than doubled in recent years. The three largest unions in this area are the American Federation of State, County and Municipal Employees, the American Federation of Government Employees, and the American Federation of Teachers. The latter two unions have increased their memberships by over 60 percent during a recent five-year period. In addition, there are a number of professional employee associations not strictly classifiable as labor unions. In 1972, total membership in this group stood at 2.2 million.

White-collar employees, particularly the professional and technical, have always been very difficult to organize into bargaining units. The professional employee has traditionally felt that unions were "unprofessional" in their exercise of control. They have doubts about professional freedom within the corporation without adding the specter of union control. With prosperity and a scarcity of highly skilled personnel, white-collar employees often feel that they can deal for themselves. If the union movement is to continue to grow, it must alter its policies and tactics to attract the interest of these white-collar employees who exhibit strong identification with their work. There will have to be less emphasis upon seniority and other popular trade-union, blue-collar appeals. It is apparent that management can make a large contribution to white-collar union membership by such practices as assigning professionals to subprofessional work, rigid task specialization, timeclocks, distorted salary structures, limited participation in decision making, insecure tenure, and impersonalization of employee-employer relationships. The increasing interest of such groups as nurses and teachers has convinced some white-collar employees that unions are socially, as well as economically, acceptable. "In 1967, for the first time, unions won more white-collar elections than they lost—567 out of 868, covering more than 15,000 workers."[7] However, the continued union preoccupation with the blue-collar worker is evident in the statistics of 1961 to 1966; 89 percent of the workers in previously unorganized units voting in elections were blue-collar workers, 4 percent were white-collar, and the balance were service industry and other workers.[8] The change in image, policies, and tactics comes hard for union leaders; but change is essential for survival and growth.

[7]Thomas P. Gilroy, "New Developments in the Labor Movement," *Personnel*, vol. 46, no. 1, January–February 1969, p. 50.

[8]Leo Troy, "Trade Union Growth in a Changing Economy," *Monthly Labor Review*, vol. 92, no. 9, September 1969, p. 7.

The AFL-CIO, with approximately 75 percent of the total membership, is obviously the core of the union movement. This organization is not a union; rather, it is a collection or federation of national and international unions. The AFL-CIO is composed of over one hundred national and international unions. The major source of power in the federation lies at the international-union level. The AFL-CIO exercises control over these international unions by establishing criteria for membership and expelling those who do not conform. In 1958, for example, the Teamsters union was expelled from the federation for not complying with certain ethical practices established by the organization. In 1968, the UAW withdrew voluntarily through its refusal to pay dues to the AFL-CIO.

An international union is composed of a number of local unions, the number ranging from 10 to 2,000. As indicated in Figure 22-1, the superstructure of the federation provides for interunion cooperation in such departments as building trades, industrial unions, maritime trades, metal trades, railway employees, and the union label. In addition, cooperation on a geographical basis is encouraged by state and local bodies. The president of the federation is usually regarded as one of the major spokesmen for organized labor in America.

Thus, the current status of the union movement can be summarized as follows: There are approximately 20.9 million members of national and international unions, of whom almost 17 million are in unions affiliated with the AFL-CIO. The AFL-CIO is a federation of autonomous unions joined together to promote unified and cooperative advancement of labor union interests. The remaining members are in national unions which are *not* affiliated. Two of these, the United Automobile Workers and the Teamsters, are the largest unions in the United States. In addition, there are a number of major independents, such as the United Mine Workers and the railway brotherhoods, and many smaller unaffiliated independents. After a gentle decline in absolute total membership during the decade of 1956 to 1966, the movement had reached its highest total enrollment in 1972. Within the United States, this constitutes 21.8 percent of the total labor force. Even though total membership has grown only from 15 to 21 million from 1945 to 1972, as compared with a fivefold growth from 1932 to 1945, it would be inadvisable to conclude that union growth is at an end. It also must be realized that these current union members are located in the most crucial industries in our nation, such as steel, railroads, automobiles, truck transportation, the maritime industries, and construction. One has only to visualize the power that *could* issue from a federation of transportation unions covering trucks, buses, trains, ships, and planes to conclude that the assessment of the strength of the labor union movement cannot be made in numbers alone.

LABOR LEGISLATION

The power and influence of favorable governmental attitudes have already been indicated in the discussion of the remarkable growth of the union movement during World War I and the late 1930s. Federal legislation cannot be ignored. We shall discuss briefly some of the more significant legislation, emphasizing the following turning points:

1   Early legislation

Figure 22-1 Structure of the AFL-CIO

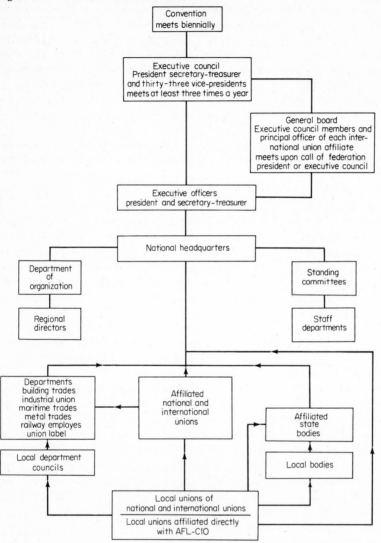

Source: U.S. Department of Labor, *Directory of National and International Labor Unions in the United States, 1971*, Bulletin No. 1750 (1970), p. 64.

2   The National Labor Relations Act of 1935 (Wagner Act)

3   The Labor-Management Relations Act of 1947 (Taft-Hartley Act)

4   The Labor-Management Reporting and Disclosure Act of 1959 (Landrum-Griffin Act)

These laws are all federal statutes which apply only to firms engaged in interstate commerce. Other business enterprises, whose activities are exclusively intrastate in nature, are regulated by state labor laws.

Early labor legislation

The field of business in which a favorable governmental attitude was first established toward labor organization was that of the railroads. As early as 1898, Congress passed the Erdman Act, which prohibited discrimination against workers by the interstate railroads because of union membership. This constituted an attempt to outlaw the yellow-dog contract, an agreement by which the employee was forbidden to join a labor union while in the employ of the company. This act was declared unconstitutional ten years later, on the ground that it was an invasion of the right of private property. It was not until 1926, with the passage of the Railway Labor Act, that public policy in favor of labor organization on the railroads was made effective. One of the objectives of this act was to forbid any denial, as a condition of employment, of the right of employees to join a labor organization. This act for the railroad industry was a forerunner of the Wagner Act for the remainder of the business economy.

The Norris-LaGuardia Act of 1932 incorporated the first statement of general public policy concerning labor unionization. This statement of policy attested to the belief that workers should have the right to organize into unions of their own choosing if they desire to do so. This doctrine received relatively limited protection in the act, which provided only for the outlawing of yellow-dog contracts and for a marked restriction upon the employer's freedom to utilize the labor injunction to halt work stoppages. In 1933, the federal government attempted to guarantee this right to organize by means of Section 7(a) of the National Industrial Recovery Act, which stipulated that every code of fair competition had to incorporate provisions protecting the right to organize. A National Labor Board was established to administer this portion of the act, with Senator Robert Wagner as chairman. This board passed from the scene in 1935, when the NIRA was declared unconstitutional. The provisions of the act pertaining to labor were reintroduced as a separate bill in that same year, and the National Labor Relations Act, or Wagner Act, became the law of the land.

National Labor Relations Act

In essence, the Wagner Act proposed to become the protective tariff of labor. It guaranteed the right of employees to organize by forbidding the employer to (1) interfere or restrain employees in the exercise of this right, (2) dominate or interfere with any labor union, (3) discriminate against anyone for union activity, (4) discriminate against any employee who gave testimony under the act, and (5) refuse to bargain collectively with representatives chosen by the employees. The National Labor Relations Board was established to administer the act. The board had two primary functions: (1) to prevent or correct any of the five unfair labor practices given above, and (2) to establish the appropriate bargaining units and specific representative organizations for the employees. In effect, this meant that the strike of the union to obtain recognition by the employer was now replaced by an orderly process of democratic elections. Workers or their representatives could petition the board for certification of a union as the sole collective bargaining agent. The representative had to demonstrate that there was a substantial number of employees in the company, usually 35 percent of the total eligible, who were interested in joining the labor organization. If a voluntary agreement to recognize a labor union could not be evoked from the employer or if there were doubts as to which of several organizations was to represent the employees, an election would be held to determine the authorized representing organization. A majority of those voting was required to name a bargaining agent. For example, if there was only one union concerned, two choices would appear on the ballot, the XYZ union and "no union." If over 50 percent of those voting indicated the XYZ union, that union was then certified as the official bargaining representative for all 100 percent. There was no requirement that all support the union or that all pay dues. There was a requirement that all work under the contract signed by the bargaining representative.

The Supreme Court of the United States has pointed out in a number of cases that the Wagner Act does not specifically say that an election must be held to select a bargaining representative. Majority status can be established by other means such as showing convincing support on a union-called strike or strike vote, or by union possession of cards from a majority of employees authorizing the union to represent them for collective bargaining purposes. The National Labor Relations Board has the power to designate the official bargaining representative, and can, with the assistance of court injunctions, compel an employer to bargain in good faith. The commission by the employer of an unfair labor practice can lead to official union designation even when an election is not actually held or, if held, is lost by the union.

Under the protection of this act, the union movement quintupled its strength in a decade. There was obviously a great desire to form organizations to represent employee interests in dealing with the employer. The employer, through various legal, formal, and informal means, had been successful in holding down the union movement. With governmental protection, the top was blown off. Strikes gave way to elections, which in the large majority of cases were won by the unions. Employees expressed an overwhelming desire to join organizations empowered to deal from strength with their employers. Many employers who had developed the most progressive types of personnel programs fell before the consent elections of the National Labor Relations Board. This phenomenon caused a major and serious reappraisal of labor-management relations policies across the country. Most managers have had to admit that the labor union is here to stay as a significant part of our business scene. With this admission and acceptance, new departures and policies must be examined and implemented to effect a constructive relationship among employee, employer, union member, and union leader.

The Labor-Management Relations Act

In the twelve years between 1935 and 1947, the labor movement enjoyed a tremendous growth. A large grant of authority had been delegated to the union by the American people. But just as some of the authority delegated to the business manager was revoked because of certain abuses, so in 1947, through the Taft-Hartley Act, some of the authority of the labor union was reclaimed by society. Certain unions and union leaders had abused their authority in such a way that it seemed detrimental to the public interest. To the unfair labor practices of employers specified in the Wagner Act were added in the Taft-Hartley the following unfair practices of labor unions: (1) to restrain or coerce an employee into joining or not joining a labor union; (2) to cause an employer to discriminate against an employee because of nonmembership in the union resulting from any action other than the nonpayment of dues to the union; (3) to refuse to bargain collectively with the employer; (4) to engage in secondary boycotts and jurisdictional strikes; (5) to require workers to pay exorbitant fees; and (6) to require an employer to pay for services not rendered, a practice known as "featherbedding."

Under the Taft-Hartley Act, the strongest degree of union security, the closed shop, was outlawed.[9] The union shop was permitted, but with the stipulation that any state may pass a law, contrary to this act, outlawing the union shop in that state. Approximately nineteen states, mostly nonindustrial, had such laws. Approximately five states repealed "right-to-work" laws in the early 1960s. The repeal of this provision of the Taft-Hartley Act has been high on the list of organized labor's political aims for many years.

A number of other provisions of the Taft-Hartley Act served to clarify the roles of unions and union leaders. Supervisors are not permitted to join employees' unions, and the employer may refuse to bargain with a supervisors' union. The employer has freedom of speech and may express an opinion against the desirability of employees' joining labor unions. Management may sue the union in a federal court for breach of contract. They may deduct dues from paychecks (the "checkoff") only when so authorized by the individual employee in writing. The union leader must file union financial reports and inform members how monies are spent. Any welfare fund, financed in whole or in part by the employer, must be administered by a joint employer-union board. A union leader who has not signed a non-Communist affidavit removes his union from the protection of the National Labor Relations Act.

Just as the union representative has rights of petitioning the National Labor Relations Board for a representation election, the employer may now petition for a similar election if it is felt that the union no longer represents a majority of the employees. A new election cannot be held, however, within twelve months of a preceding election. The NLRB retains the right to designate the appropriate bargaining area, industrial or craft, and to certify those employees who are eligible to vote.

One other major provision of the Labor-Management Relations Act of 1947 was that dealing with the handling of national emergency strikes. Excessively long strikes in basic industries, such as steel or coal, could cause great harm to the nation. In such a situation, the President of the United States is empowered to declare a national emergency and to ask for a federal court injunction to terminate the strike for a period of eighty days. If no agreement is arrived at, the injunction is dissolved at the end of eighty days, and the two parties are free to resume the work stoppage. If a national emergency is in fact still present, it is inconceivable that our governmental representatives will allow the nation to be seriously harmed to preserve the principle of free collective bargaining. In such an emergency, it is highly likely that further and more drastic laws, limiting the freedom of both management and union, would be passed by Congress.

The Labor-Management Reporting and Disclosure Act of 1959

In the latter part of the 1950s, a Senate Select Committee on Improper Activities in the Labor and Management field was set up under the leadership of Senator McClellan. Its purpose was to investigate and report upon criminal and other improper practices in the field of labor-management relations. In general, this committee concluded that the majority of labor unions were honest and that labor-management relations were

[9]This type of union security, as well as several others, will be defined and discussed later in this chapter.

conducted upon a sound basis. However, certain objectionable practices were uncovered, which the committee felt should be remedied by law. Among these practices were the following: (1) infiltration of labor organizations by gangster elements, (2) collusion between management and labor leaders in the signing of "sweetheart" contracts to the detriment of the employees, (3) a lack of democratic procedures in the organization and operation of some labor unions, (4) an abuse of the power of the international union to place selected locals under protective custody or trusteeship, (5) widespread misuse of union funds as exemplified by large loans without interest to union officials and poor audits of union accounts, (6) the use of labor spies by management, and (7) union picketing of organizations whose employees have no desire to join the union. The recommendations of this committee resulted in the passage of the Labor-Management Reporting and Disclosure Act of 1959, otherwise known as the Landrum-Griffin Act.

This act is appropriately titled. A large portion of it is devoted to the establishment of a series of reports to be filed with the Secretary of Labor by both unions and management.[10] Among these reports are the following:

1   Report by the union of its constitution and bylaws
2   Submission by the union of an annual financial report covering assets, liabilities, receipts, salaries of officials, and loans to any officer, member, or business enterprise
3   Report by the union of its administrative policies, such as those concerning initiation fees, dues, assessments, qualifications for membership, calling of meetings, ratification of contracts, etc.
4   Reports of officers and employees of a union that disclose any personal financial interest which conflicts with duties in the union
5   Report by the employer concerning any expenditure for the purpose of interfering with, restraining, coercing, or persuading employees in their right to organize
6   Reports by labor relations consultants covering any fees received from employers for the purpose of interfering with, restraining, coercing, or persuading employees in their right to organize

In addition to these reports, the act establishes a bill of rights for union members, which includes freedom of speech and assembly in union meetings, secret ballot on proposed increases in dues and assessments, the right to sue the union, safeguards against improper disciplinary action of members by the union, and equal rights to nominate candidates for union office, to vote, and to have a voice in the conduct of union business.[11] Restriction of the right of the international union to establish trusteeships over any of its locals is provided to safeguard the democratic process.[12] Persons who have been members of the Communist party or have been convicted of certain major crimes are prohibited for five years from the termination of membership, or from conviction, from holding office as a union official, labor relations consultant, or officer of an employers' association. The stipulation regarding Communist party membership was declared unconstitutional by the United States Supreme Court in 1965.

The final portion of the law deals with various amendments to the Labor-

[10]Title II, Public Law 86–257.
[11]Title I, Public Law 86–257.
[12]Title III, Public Law 86–257.

Management Relations Act of 1947.[13] Among the changes in the Taft-Hartley Act are the following: (1) a repeal of the requirement of a non-Communist affidavit for union officials, (2) the giving to states of jurisdiction over certain types of cases which the NLRB has refused to handle as not significantly affecting interstate commerce, (3) the prohibition of organizational picketing by a union when a rival union has been recognized by the employer or an NLRB election has been held in the last twelve months, (4) the safeguarding for twelve months of the right of an economic striker to vote in union-representation elections held while he is on strike, (5) the prohibition of "hot cargo" agreements in which the employers agree to stop handling, using, selling, transporting, or dealing in any of the products of another employer against whom the union is exerting economic pressure, and (6) the authorization of union shops in the construction industry, which require membership after the seventh day of employment rather than the usual thirty days.

In general, labor union leaders were very much opposed to the passage of the Landrum-Griffin Act. It served to limit further their authority over the operation of their own organizations. The AFL-CIO leadership felt that they could handle most of such abuses through their ethical-practices committee and through threatened or actual expulsion of the offending union from the AFL-CIO. But the widespread publicity given to the investigations of the McClellan committee for a period of two years had seriously weakened the power and prestige of labor unions in the eyes of the public and their elected representatives.

The law is extremely difficult to administer. It is a further inroad by government into the area of labor-management relations. It again emphasizes the fundamental truth that if labor unions and managements do not conduct themselves in a manner approved by society, a diminution of private authority will inevitably follow, with giant strides being taken toward a socialistic state. The public interest is and must be paramount. If the private interests of any party, labor or management, lead to a conflict with public interest, the latter will in the long run prevail. Unions and union leadership have just as much to lose by this invasion by government as does the employer. It behooves them both to approach the labor-management relations field with a greater concern and respect for sound ethical practices consistent with the public interest.

TYPES OF UNION SECURITY

One of the foremost objectives of a labor union is to establish and protect the existence and security of the organization. As we have shown above, the law has much to say about union security. Before proceeding with a presentation of a constructive management viewpoint on this matter, let us examine briefly the various types of union security. Discussion of these types will proceed from the least secure position for the union to the most secure.

RESTRICTED SHOP   This is a situation or attitude rather than a formal type of shop like the union or closed shop. It exists in many firms in one of two types, legal or illegal. The legal restrictive situation exists when the management does what it can to keep a union out without violating the Wagner, Taft-Hartley, or Landrum-Griffin Acts. Such a

---

[13]Title VII, Public Law 86-257.

management may try to buy the employees off by providing more in pay and benefits than could be obtained in competitive unionized firms. Or it may try to manage as perfectly as it knows how in the hope that the employees will not feel a need for organization. The illegal restricted shop would allow activities that are specifically prohibited by law, such as the use of yellow-dog contracts, the searching out and dismissal of persons who show any leanings toward unions, the threatening of employees, and the promising of rewards if unionization is voted down.

OPEN SHOP Technically, the restricted shop is an open shop. For our purposes here, however, a true open shop is one in which there is neither a union present nor a management program to promote or keep out a union. The employees are relatively free to decide whether or not they will exercise their legal rights of organization. In the open shop, the employees have not as yet decided to form a union. This does not mean that there are no union members in the company; it merely means that they are not in the majority. This type of shop is fair game for the union organizer.

SIMPLE-RECOGNITION SHOP The simple-recognition shop is one in which the management has recognized a union as the official and exclusive bargaining agent of all employees in its area of jurisdiction. The act of recognition is the first stage of security for the union. It is usually gained with the assistance of the National Labor Relations Board and may be derived from a consent election. If a majority of those voting favor the union, there is a legal requirement that the employer recognize and deal with the union. Union security lasts for a minimum of twelve months, inasmuch as the NLRB will not hold recognition elections in any one company more often than this. If 50 percent plus one of those voting favor the XYZ union, a simple-recognition shop exists. If, in the following month, 2 percent of these employees become disenchanted and leave the union, there is still a simple-recognition shop until the twelve-month period is up, when the employer may ask for decertification of the union. Though the union may have only 50 percent plus one of the employees as dues-paying members, it is authorized to bargain in behalf of all 100 percent. This is the source of the "free rider" argument of unions, the 49 percent who derive the benefits of organization but do not contribute financially to its support. Prior to 1935, a strike was the usual method of obtaining recognition. Since the Wagner Act, recognition has been handled in an administrative manner rather than in one relying upon economic and physical force.

AGENCY SHOP The agency shop is identical with the simple-recognition shop except for one item: *All* employees pay union dues whether or not they are members of the union. This eliminates the "free rider" argument. In our illustration, 51 percent of the employees are dues-paying members, but the other 49 percent are dues-paying nonmembers. These 49 percent are exempt from required attendance at union meetings, union disciplinary action, and the like. They are merely paying a fee for the services of organized representation.

PREFERENTIAL SHOP The preferential shop is one in which the union is recognized and union members are given preference in certain areas of employment. For example, in new hires, a union member is given preference over a nonunion member. The employer goes to the union first in trying to fill the position. Preferential treatment may also apply to transfer, promotion, and layoff. Many of these preferential shops, as operated, are in violation of the Taft-Hartley Act. Excessive preference for union members may in effect constitute a closed shop. The philosophy of the Taft-Hartley Act is to give all employees a chance, whether union members or not.

MAINTENANCE-OF-MEMBERSHIP SHOP This type of shop is a compromise between freedom to join or not join a union and compulsory unionism. It was a development of World War II, when the government had to arbitrate disputes to prevent work stoppages. There is no requirement that an employee join the union. Once the union is joined, the employee is frozen, or compelled to remain in the union for the life of the contract. Usually, when the contract expires, a short escape period is provided when employees may withdraw their membership. Once this period is ended, the lid goes on again, and the membership is maintained for the life of the contract. The employee is free to join the union at any time. Thus, there is an element of freedom and an element of compulsion.

UNION SHOP The union shop is a form of compulsory unionism. The employer may hire whom he or she will, but within a stipulated period the employee must join the union if he or she is to keep the job. In the Taft-Hartley Act, this period of grace could be no shorter than thirty days. Under the Labor-Management Disclosure Act, this period can be shortened to seven days in the construction industry only. Thus, in a union shop, assuming no new hires in the last thirty days, *all* employees are union members. There are no free riders and no dues-paying nonmembers. Most of the labor-management contracts in this country provide for the union shop.

CLOSED SHOP The highest degree of union security is the closed shop. It, like some restricted shops, is illegal under the Taft-Hartley Act. Under this arrangement, an employee must be a union member at the time of hiring. The union becomes the *only* source of labor for the employer. Though this arrangement is technically illegal, there are in practice a number of closed shops, particularly in the construction, maritime, and printing industries. The closed-shop clause does not appear in the contract, but it is present in effect through operating rules, customs, a union hiring hall, or management's willingness to use the union as a sole source.

If one considers all of the firms in the United States, it is evident that the majority are not organized; that is, they have restricted or open shops. This conclusion is based on the fact that only one-fifth of the total labor force and only one-third of those potentially organizable are now in unions. Of those that are organized, the union shop is by far the most commonly found type of union security. The last major national survey of union security provisions revealed that 74 percent of 1,631 major union contracts provided for a union shop.[14] This percentage has grown steadily from 49 percent in 1949, to 64 percent in 1954, to the figure given above. From the postwar peak of 25 percent, the maintenance-of-membership shop has declined to 7 percent of the contracts. Simple-recognition and agency shops make up the rest, with less than 1 percent being of the latter type. It has been found, however, that the agency shop is the

---

[14]"Union Security Provisions in Major Union Contracts, 1958–1959," *Monthly Labor Review*, December 1959, pp. 1348–1356.

preferred substitute for the union shop in those states with "right-to-work" laws. In Indiana, for example, the proportion of union shops in 1958 stood at 78 percent, which was in line with the national average.[15] With passage of a "right-to-work" law making the union shop illegal, this naturally fell to zero. However, from zero agency shops in 1958, the proportion rose to 91 percent just prior to repeal of the Indiana law in 1965. In 1968, the union shop was back up to 73 percent, with the agency shop holding at around 10 percent. It is therefore believed that the percentage of agency shops is considerably higher than the 1 percent discovered in 1959.

These figures show that compulsory unionism is a very common phenomenon in the American union movement. Thus, the majority of American employers who deal with unions have accepted, through collective bargaining, the principle of compulsory unionism. The law states that you *must* grant the simple-recognition shop if the union wins a majority of the vote. There is no law requiring an employer to grant the union shop.

A POINT OF VIEW

In viewing the progress of the labor union movement in the United States, a realist must conclude that the unions are a continuing part of our society. There is little or no chance that employers can regain the amount of authority they possessed during the 1800s. Thus, the basic attitudes toward the status of labor unions in general must move from an attempt to undermine and halt the union movement to a desire and attempt to work constructively with the union for the benefit of the entire organization. This does not mean that management must clasp the union to its bosom; such an attitude is not desirable, practical, or legal. It does not mean that a management cannot attempt to determine for itself, with the assistance of the NLRB, that a majority of its employees have chosen the union on a rational and informed basis. If a management is convinced that this is true, and has determined that the particular labor organization concerned is responsible and mature in its objectives and policies, then the employer should accept the union as a major working participant, in spirit as well as in procedure. A management has the obligation, however, to make the attempt to determine (1) whether the particular union can and will be a constructive and working organization and (2) whether the majority of employees truly want this union. If these questions are both answered in the affirmative, management should make the first move to create a situation of working harmony. If the answer to either question is in the negative, management has an obligation to oppose the union in any legal manner. The employees have the legal right to choose, and management has the legal right to present its viewpoint. The union must *earn* its right to represent the employees in negotiations with management through its policies, practices, and attitudes.

In the last decade, the number of recognition elections won by labor unions has been steadily declining. This is due to various reasons, such as the unfavorable publicity received by a few well-known union leaders, the increased militancy of management

[15]Mitchell S. Novit, "Right-to-Work: Before and After," *Business Horizons*, vol. 12, no. 5, October 1969, p. 64.

under the "free speech" provisions of the Taft-Hartley Act, the difficulty of organizing smaller companies since most of the large ones have been covered, interunion rivalry, and the difficulty of organizing white-collar workers, who now outnumber blue-collar employees. If a resurgence in union membership is to come, policies and practices will have to be adjusted to the needs and desires of white-collar employees.

Each manager must also determine his or her basic attitude toward the concept of compulsory unionism. Those who are against this concept in principle see it as the abolition of freedom for each individual to choose to join or not to join an organization in order to keep a job. In addition, they contend that a highly secure position for the union may well lead to an abdication of union leadership responsibility. If the union is impregnable, it tends to be less responsive to the desires of its members. On the other side, compulsory unionism ensures that all shall share equally in the support and financing of the labor organization which is authorized by law to represent all employees. Compulsory unionism ensures that attempts to undermine the union will be ineffective. But more important, it is certain that every union will work and fight as long as it does *not* have the secure status of the union shop. Lacking this degree of security, the union leadership is highly suspicious of every management action and is reluctant to cooperate in programs initiated for the good of the entire organization.

One point of view on this issue involves a compromise with the ideal of complete freedom on the part of the employees to choose to join or not to join a labor organization. If the employer discovers that a majority of the employees have voluntarily joined the labor organization, as many as 80 percent or more, and if the union gives signs of continued fight and a withholding of needed cooperation, and if the management desires to obtain some constructive good from the labor organization, it may well be that the granting of the union shop would be a highly desirable management action. The basic guide is once again a measure of contribution to the organizational service objective. If the organization gains substantially from this process in the long run, it may be necessary to sacrifice the freedom of choice of the remaining 10 to 20 percent of the employees.

In summary, accepting the concept of compulsory unionism is not necessarily antagonistic to the philosophy of an effective management in a free-enterprise system. Of course, if this concept is accepted in the process of collective bargaining, a subject discussed in the following chapter, it is not granted without some return in union concessions which will allow management to operate the firm in the interest of greater economy and effectiveness. The granting of the union shop is not a minor issue. If a management feels that the times and conditions are right for agreeing to this type of union security, it should certainly use its agreement to exact from the union whatever it feels to be desirable for the long-run benefit of the firm. Perhaps the greatest danger resulting from compulsory unionism is union leadership complacency. In addition, sometimes improper, unethical, and illegal activities result from such security for the union. Management must keep ever aware of the importance of the union leadership's actual representation of the best interests of the majority of the employees. The government also will play a role in ensuring that democratic processes are followed in the union, as well as in providing sufficient information to the union member, so that one can determine whether the organization is giving proper service.

SUMMARY

The role of the labor union in our society is a fairly secure one as measured by the degree of its growth and public support. From slightly less than three million in 1933, unions grew to some fifteen million members in 1945. In the last fifteen years, the pace of growth has slackened considerably, and the approximate current total is 21 million members. This figure shows that one-third of those who are potentially organizable have joined unions. It indicates that unions occupy a strong position in the economy, particularly when we realize that the overwhelming number of our key industries are almost completely organized. On the other hand, the slackening of the pace in the last twenty-five years indicates that all labor is not going to be organized overnight, as some had feared. The majority of the total, almost 17 million, are found in international unions affiliated with the AFL-CIO.

The status of the labor union within the company is largely affected by management attitudes and controlled by the type of union security arrangement that has been agreed upon. These positions can range from an illegal restricted shop to an illegal closed shop, including, according to degree of security, (1) the restricted shop, illegal and legal, (2) the open shop, (3) the simple-recognition shop, (4) the agency shop, (5) the preferential shop, (6) the maintenance-of-membership shop, (7) the union shop, and (8) the closed shop. Approximately 75 percent of all union security contract clauses provide for the compulsory unionism of the union shop.

With respect to the proper attitude of the modern manager toward the status of the labor union, we should have to say that it would be considerably affected by the situation and environment in which the union and company operate. In general, it is foolish to look toward the abolition of all unions and a return to the nineteenth century. It is also extremely doubtful that favorable governmental attitudes toward unions will change drastically. Modern managers must accept the fact that they must live and deal with a labor union. Whether or not they will recognize the union as sole bargaining agent is a decision which has largely been taken from them by the National Labor Relations Act and the NLRB. Whether or not one will consent to a degree of union security greater than simple recognition is a decision over which one has some control in the collective bargaining sessions. It is the thesis of this chapter that we need not be unalterably opposed to compulsory unionism. Given certain conditions, the long-run interests of the firm may be better served by acceptance of such a security arrangement.

The solution to the problem of establishing and maintaining equitable relationships among management, employees, and the union involves large elements of subjectivity. In this field there is no exact science. The answer to the problem, as expressed in our national policy, is that of collective bargaining. This process will be examined in the following chapter.

DISCUSSION QUESTIONS

1 Compare and contrast the values of labor union leaders with those of business managers in the areas of employee welfare, societal welfare, stockholder welfare, and organizational welfare.
2 Though union membership has increased in actual numbers, why is it declining in terms of percentage of the labor force?

3 Briefly trace the major changes in union membership figures that have occurred in this century. What possible causes could have effected these major movements?

4 Assuming "perfect management," what particular human need is still likely to lead to acceptance of a labor union?

5 Compare and contrast the philosophies of the National Labor Relations Act (Wagner) and the Labor-Management Relations Act (Taft-Hartley).

6 What is the major purpose of the Landrum-Griffin Act?

7 Identify the types of union security arrangements in order from complete union security to situations where there is little chance that a union may be formed.

8 Discuss the issue of compulsory union membership in terms of effect upon the company, the union member, the union, and society.

9 Define the following terms: "free rider," "right-to-work law," "craft union," and "industrial union."

10 Indicate how the "maintenance-of-membership" union security clause provides both an element of compulsion and an element of freedom for the employee.

SUPPLEMENTARY READING

BERQUIST, Virginia A.: "Women's Participation in Labor Organizations," *Monthly Labor Review*, vol. 97, no. 10, October 1974, pp. 3–9.

DUBIN, Robert: "Attachment to Work and Union Militancy," *Industrial Relations*, vol. 12, no. 1, February 1973, pp. 51–64.

ELLIS, Dean S., Lawrence Jacobs, and Gary Mills: "A Union Authorization Election: The Key to Winning," *Personnel Journal*, vol. 51, no. 4, April 1972, pp. 246–254.

ENGLAND, George W., Naresh C. Agarwal, and Robert E. Trerise: "Union Leaders and Managers: A Comparison of Value Systems," *Industrial Relations*, vol. 10, no. 2, May 1971, pp. 211–226.

PERLINE, Martin M.: "Organized Labor and Managerial Prerogatives," *California Management Review*, vol. 14, no. 2, Winter 1972, pp. 46–50.

ROSE, Joseph B.: "What Factors Influence Union Representation Elections?" *Monthly Labor Review*, vol. 95, no. 10, October 1972, pp. 49–51.

TWENTY-THREE
COLLECTIVE BARGAINING

It is the public policy of the United States that the determination of employer-employee relationships in firms engaged in interstate commerce shall take place through collective bargaining. To this end, the right of the employee to join and work through organizations is protected by the various labor statutes. Such labor organizations must be recognized by the employer if they include a majority of the personnel voting in a representation election. The National Labor Relations Act specifies that it is an unfair labor practice for the employer to refuse to bargain collectively with chosen representatives of a certified labor organization. The Labor-Management Relations Act specifies that it is an unfair practice for the representatives of a labor organization to refuse to bargain in good faith with the employer. Current national policy, therefore, not only states that collective bargaining is the approved answer to the employee-employer relationship problem, but that this policy is to be implemented through the National Labor Relations Board and the federal courts. If either side refuses to bargain in good faith, a charge of unfair practice can be brought before the Board. If the charge is sustained, an order can be issued by the Board to bargain properly. If such an order is not obeyed by either party, the Board can seek a federal court injunction, the violation of which constitutes criminal or civil contempt of court. Thus, it is evident that collective bargaining is the preferred method of working out employee-employer relationships in our free-enterprise system.

THE NATURE OF COLLECTIVE BARGAINING

Collective bargaining is a process in which the representatives of a labor organization and the representatives of the business organization meet and attempt to negotiate a contract or agreement which specifies the nature of the employee-employer-union relationship. The term "collective" merely indicates that the representatives are trying to negotiate an agreement for *groups* of persons. The National Labor Relations Act gives the legally authorized labor representative the right to bargain for *all* employees in the jurisdiction, whether members of the union or not. Bargaining is the process of meeting, presenting demands, discussing, presenting counteroffers, haggling, cajoling, threatening, and a whole host of other activities which go into the negotiation of an agreement. Obviously, the process of collective bargaining is not confined to the relationships between labor and management. Collective bargaining takes place, for example, when the representatives of one nation attempt to work out a treaty with another nation. In this text, we are concerned only with the relationships between employee and employer.

Collective bargaining is a process which imposes certain restrictions upon the employer. Unilateral action is prevented; on appropriate subjects, the management must bargain with the union. All employees in the jurisdiction must be treated equitably. The conditions of employment can be changed only at fixed intervals and with the agreement of the labor organization. The employer is no longer free to make and enforce employment decisions at will and has substantially less authority than under the open shop.

Despite the background of force provided by the laws governing collective bargaining, the validity of this approach is well grounded in facts and logic. Most of the decisions that pertain to employee-employer relationships are not of the objective, black-and-white type. For example, there is no formula that will tell exactly what a worker's wage should be. Job evaluation will provide certain data that help in establishing the internal relationships of one job to another, but subjective judgment must enter into the determination of the precise amount. In this and many other matters, we cannot be certain that the employer will arrive at the correct answer. For that matter, we are not certain that the decision made through collective bargaining will be right. But in matters involving equity and right treatment, the voicing of all interests will probably lead to a better decision. The collective bargaining process is not easy and is often exasperating. It is, however, the best answer available for a problem that defies quantitative measurement and exact answers.

THE PROCESS OF COLLECTIVE BARGAINING

The actual conduct of the collective bargaining process is very complicated but very interesting. Despite the wide variety of shapes that bargaining can take, there are certain fundamental procedures and stages of action that deserve consideration, among them (1) the prenegotiation phase, (2) the selection of negotiators, (3) the strategy of bargaining, (4) the tactics of bargaining, and (5) the contract.

The prenegotiation phase

The labor organization is an institution engaged in the full-time job of protecting and improving the status of the employee. The company, whose major objective is the production and distribution of an economic good, can ill afford to consider collective bargaining as a fringe duty which merits little special attention. Such an attitude may turn the bargaining process into a unilateral determination of relationships by the union. The company must match the union in time, effort, energy, skill, and enthusiasm if a true bargain is to be effected.

The prenegotiation phase of the process is vital. When the contract has been signed for one period, the prenegotiation phase begins for the next. Data of all types should be maintained religiously by management, including, of course, facts and figures in the more tangible areas of wages, hours, pensions, vacations, and similar types of remuneration. From sad past experience, firms are lengthening the prenegotiation phase in order to avoid last-minute crises that lead to undesirable contract provisions. For example, the typical negotiations between Armour and Company and the United Packinghouse Workers, along with the Amalgamated Meat Cutters, during the period of 1941 to 1959 involved such elements as the following: (1) negotiations usually began in July against a contract expiration date in August; (2) over 100 local union delegates and international representatives constituted the union bargaining team; (3) six to ten management representatives made up the company team; (4) a great deal of speech making took place to justify demands; (5) final marathon continuous bargaining sessions, lasting as long as seventy-two hours, were held; and (6) final settlements were actually reached through a much smaller committee of management and union personnel.[1] With the stimulus of mechanization and automation, the Armour Automation Fund Committee was inaugurated in 1959 to study the human problems involved. Over the years, the committee was utilized in stimulating a longer prenegotiation phase. In one year, for example, the committee was approached in mid-December by management to begin exploratory meetings concerning possible settlement for the following August. This resulted in a union-management meeting in February from which issued a basic two-page agreement among the eight negotiators. This "memorandum of agreement" was later ratified by local plant delegates. Thus, bargaining was accomplished neither in a fish bowl nor under crisis conditions.

It is also important for the company representatives to study very carefully the labor organization with which they are to bargain. Since most unions do business with many firms, copies of other contracts negotiated by this union should be secured and studied. This analysis will at least show some of the union's thinking as well as indicate its power. If the union is an industrial one, it is very likely that its leadership will have a social philosophy. It is also likely that the union representatives will have less power in the negotiations to commit the union than will the representatives of a craft union. The craft union is usually more interested in wages, hours, and working conditions than in anything else, and its representatives are usually delegated an ample amount of authority to execute an agreement with the company. Not only must the organization be analyzed, but the background and personality of the particular union negotiators must also be studied. Part of the bargaining process is acting, and part of it is bluff. If one knows little or nothing about the union and the people representing that organization, how can one tell whether the union will back up particular demands by a strike or whether it will consent to make further concessions? Collective bargaining, like management, is an art rather than a science. But it is an art that can be improved by serious study and preparation.

---

[1]Walter E. Clark, "The Problems and Benefits of Early Labor Settlements," *Personnel Journal*, vol. 47, no. 7, July 1968, pp. 482–485.

The negotiators

On the company side, the particular negotiator may be any one of a number of persons. It may be the industrial relations director, the head of the production area, an executive vice-president, or the company lawyer. The team or committee approach is frequently used, thereby broadening the base of participation. The practice of allowing all major division heads to participate and a few supervisors to observe on a rotating basis has great advantages in the area of communication and education.

The lawyer should have a place on the negotiating committee although he or she should not be the prime or sole negotiator. Lawyers have skills that management can well use, particularly a skill in evaluating the acts and statements of the labor representative so as to separate and identify feelings, facts, bluff, and conviction. However, collective bargaining is not essentially a legal process. Negotiators must have substantial and factual knowledge of working conditions and past management-employee relationships in order to be able to negotiate successfully. Excessively complicated legal phraseology should not be allowed to frustrate the application and interpretation of the contract that will result from the process.

Some consider it sound planning to keep the president of the firm out of the negotiation process. Because of the nature of the bargaining process, delays for the purpose of reevaluation of positions are often desirable. If the president is present on the bargaining team, she or he may be forced to give an instant yes or no on an issue that deserves more careful consideration. In addition, selecting someone other than the president as spokesperson places the two bargaining teams on an equal footing. The union representative must check with rank and file on tentatively accepted offers. The company representative must check with top management on union demands.

On the union side, the team approach is also customarily used. The team may consist of business agents, some shop stewards, the president of the local, and, when the negotiation is basic and vital, representatives of the international union. Always in the case of industry-wide bargaining, the chief spokesperson is a representative of the international, and often it is the president of that organization. Most of these union bargainers are full-time specialists in the art of bargaining and negotiating with various managements.

Strategy of bargaining

Because of the considerable importance of the labor agreement, it is essential for management to plan its strategy and tactics carefully in preparation for the bargaining sessions. Strategy is concerned with mapping out the plan and basic policies to be followed in the bargaining process. Tactics are the particular actions that are taken while at the bargaining table. Obviously, tactics should conform in general to the basic outline of the planned strategy. The labor union will also have a similar strategical plan and will execute tactical actions that will promote the accomplishment of union objectives.

Before management ever enters the conference room, certain elements of the basic plan must be worked out. The key personnel must agree on the *maximum concessions* that can be granted to the anticipated demands of the union. Often the union files its demands with the employer in advance of the first bargaining session.

Management must of course determine which demands they believe are serious objectives of the union and which constitute smoke screens to advance those serious objectives. The company must know how far it can go before it will seriously risk the possibility of a work stoppage. In another area, it is best for the management to avoid conceding at any time any *mutual agreement clauses* to the labor union. The union often tries to obtain the concession that promotion, transfer, change-of-work procedures, layoff, and similar decisions shall be made and applied only by mutual agreement of the two parties, management and the union. This serves to tie very effectively the hands of management. The contract may state the basic conditions necessary for promotion, layoff, and the like, but it is management's responsibility to make decisions and execute them on the basis of the contract. If the union believes that a particular decision is improper and contrary to the contract, it has access to the grievance procedure through which a protest can be filed. Requiring mutual agreement *before* the action takes place gives the union a complete veto which will rapidly bring action to a halt.

In addition to mapping out the basic bargaining limits, the company must specify or recognize, in the strategical plan, certain other important elements. First, the management must keep their eyes on the *entire package*. Other things must be watched besides immediate dollar outlay. A work-procedure concession may eventually cost the company more money than a demanded raise in the base rate. Secondly, management must plan to *keep company personnel informed* of the progress of the bargaining sessions. Supervisors should be informed, not only to emphasize that they are truly a part of management but also to enable them to appear well informed in competition with shop stewards and union members. It is important to realize that employees are company personnel as well as union members. The union should not be the sole source of information for the employees; the company also must present its analysis of the bargaining progress. In some situations, management may decide that the *public should be informed* of the issues in the bargaining conference. This is particularly important if a strike that will affect the public welfare is anticipated as a distinct possibility.

A final important element of management bargaining strategy is the adoption of a basic attitude of *not being afraid of a strike*. The union is fully aware of the fact that the strike is its most potent bargaining weapon. It is not opposed to using this weapon in its threat form, but neither management nor union likes to have a strike. A strike is also very seldom called at a moment's notice. There is a basic process, much of it psychological in nature, through which the union and its membership must go before a walkout can take place. Management should study this process and be able to predict when the strike weapon is being used as a threat and when it is an imminent event.

Tactics of bargaining

Although many authors have asked for more objectivity in collective bargaining, the fact is that bargaining, by its very nature, will involve acts and tactics that are calculated to mislead the other party. This does not mean that factual bargaining cannot be introduced nor blue-sky demands toned down. Bargaining does, however, require a shrewd study of the other side and an awareness of the impact of one's actions on all concerned.

A tactic of the General Electric Company has been declared by the National Labor Relations Board to constitute failure to bargain in good faith. It has been the policy of this company, variously labeled as "truth in bargaining" and "Boulwareism" (after the former vice-president who developed it), to work out a "firm and fair" set of offers and stick to them regardless of the length and intensity of negotiation meetings. The company also carried on an intensive publicity campaign with its employees to inform them of the benefits offered. The company contends that the NLRB decision requires it to follow tactics of "haggling-for-haggling's sake" and to hold back its maximum concessions until the very last moment in order to give the appearance of bargaining through "bluff and counter-bluff." The decision of the Board was appealed to the United States Circuit Court of Appeals at New York. In 1969, this Court upheld the position of the Board, indicating, "We hold that an employer may not so combine 'take-it-or-leave-it' bargaining methods with a widely publicized stance of unbending firmness that he is himself unable to alter a position once taken."[2] It was emphasized, however, that the Court was neither forbidding the "best offer first" bargaining tactic nor requiring "auction bargaining."

One of the commonly used tactics of the labor union is to attempt to get management to settle in a piecemeal manner. A very logical appeal is made to the effect that the present contract should be analyzed clause by clause, and that then each clause should be reevaluated, revised, and agreed upon *before* proceeding to the next. Management should avoid this type of bargaining. It must view the agreement in its entirety and bargain for the entire package. The desirable tactics are to give *tentative* agreement to each clause until the entire agreement is wrapped up, at which time final agreement can be given.

It is also excellent bargaining tactics to avoid all-night and excessively extended sessions. The labor agreement is one that both parties must live with for a year or more, and concessions engendered by fatigue and frustration are not likely to improve the tenor of labor-management relations.

Various critics of collective bargaining have decried horse trading and haggling as legitimate tactics and have argued that a presentation of facts and a problem-solving approach should be substituted for these devices. In a sense, it is claimed that the law of the situation should govern the agreement. We must agree with this position to the extent that the law of the situation can be recognized by both parties. There are many problems, however, for which the correct answer is either not known or, when known, is highly objectionable to one or the other of the parties. It is not realistic to insist there there should *never* be any trading of concessions. Though the 9,9 position of conflict resolution is theoretically possible, there are many occasions when one must retreat to positions more closely approaching the 5,5 compromise solution. If both parties could ascertain all of the facts, if both were completely objective, and if the facts did dictate a particular direction, then the objective problem-solving approach to conflict resolution could be utilized. Such a situation, at least in the present and forseeable future, is not likely to occur with any frequency.

The highly skilled collective bargainer on either side has the emotional control of an accomplished actor. There are times in the bargaining process when one will have to "give a performance." Shouting and table pounding are sometimes effective but can be

2"Labor Month in Review," *Monthly Labor Review*, vol. 92, no. 12, December 1969, p. 2.

overdone. Sometimes the union makes a demand that is completely within the limits of bargaining concessions that management had anticipated in the strategical plan. Rather than concede immediately according to the strategy, it is perhaps better tactics to resist for a time. The very nature of the bargaining process would lead to union suspicion and disappointment if management should give in immediately with little or no fight. On the next occasion the union would be sure to increase its demand since management had shown that it could meet the earlier one so easily.

In the event of a deadlock in the bargaining process, various tactics can be used. A subcommittee, composed of members of both sides, can be appointed to investigate the dispute while the main bargaining committee proceeds to other points. Or the designated point may simply be tabled until other clauses in the agreement have been worked out. In the event that the deadlock is very serious and could well lead to a work stoppage, appropriate governmental mediators should be notified. The mediation process is discussed in a later section in this chapter.

The contract

The labor-management contract stipulates in formal terms the nature of the relationship between management and labor for the ensuing year or years. The average contract runs for two or three years. It has been the unique history of the American labor movement to become involved in detailed specifications of union-management relationships. It has not been a class-conscious political movement geared toward changing the economic system, but rather one that has been oriented toward increasing union power in the operation of the business. In response, management attempts to protect its prerogatives by spelling out in unambiguous language those specific areas in which they have agreed to share power with the union. The unions retaliate by adding language to consolidate gains acquired. This approach may well be a broader, more fundamental feature of our society. It has been pointed out that, "The United States was the first nation in history to organize its governmental apparatus by written constitution, which fairly quickly came to be regarded as the true source of all authority."[3] It is also noted that the United States has four times the population of Great Britain, but twelve times as many lawyers. Such a legalistic approach to specification of relationships provides the basic foundation for the system of grievance arbitration discussed in previous chapters.

Most labor contracts include clauses covering the following subjects:

1 Union security (see the preceding chapter for the various types of union security)
2 Grievance procedures, including steps, time limitations, and provisions for arbitration (see Chap. 20)
3 Promotion, transfer, and layoff, covering particularly the nature and effect of seniority (see Chap. 12)
4 Wages, including shift and Sunday premiums, cost of living, and job evaluation (see Chaps. 14 to 16)
5 Hours of work, including absenteeism, overtime, holidays, and vacations (see Chapters 1 and 25)

---

[3]Martin Mayer, "Justice, the Law, and the Lawyer," *Saturday Evening Post*, Feb. 26, 1966, pp. 36–37.

6 Incentive wages and time study (see Chap. 15)

7 Discharge (see Chap. 20)

8 Safety and health (see the following chapter)

9 Management responsibilities (see Chaps. 3 to 5)

10 Miscellaneous clauses covering such subjects as severance allowances, military service, a saving clause which keeps the rest of the agreement valid should a court declare any one part invalid, and termination dates

As can be seen, the labor contract refers to most of the subjects discussed in this text. Obviously, the personnel manager in a firm that deals with a labor union will find her or his freedom somewhat restricted. The ideal approach, as depicted by textbooks, is often impossible when it meets the facts of the situation.

THE VARYING TYPES OF COLLECTIVE BARGAINING RELATIONSHIPS

Since the Wagner Act of 1935, a formal union-management relationship can be and often is created by law. What, then, are the varying types of informal relationships that can be established between this "new" organization and the company? In the first place, there is the possibility of *militant opposition*. Management can do all in its power to undermine and alienate the union. Since 1947, management can speak out against the union so long as threats and promises of reward are avoided. It can, in effect, attempt to operate a restricted shop. It is not likely that the union will take this approach with calmness. Militancy stimulates militancy. The union will do all it can to solidify its position. Union survival will take precedence over the interests of the union members and of the company. Obviously, such a relationship as this practically calls for open warfare.

Harbison and Coleman have discovered that three aditional management-union relationships can be established: armed truce, working harmony, and union-management cooperation.[4] *Armed truce* is the next logical phase after militant opposition, assuming that the union survives. The battle is over, for the moment. The contract that has been signed is a truce which presages further battle. Management emphasizes the approach of attempting to rewin the loyalty of its employees, who are coincidentally members of the union. Management attempts to preserve its traditional prerogatives in running the company while trying to delimit narrowly the areas in which the union can operate.

If the union manages to hang on, there is the possibility that the relationship will develop into one known as *working harmony*. It is difficult for most managements to accept at first the invasion of a union. After working with union representatives for a while, management often develops a respect for their skill and dedicated philosophies of unionization. Management may well conclude that the clock cannot be turned back but perhaps should be turned ahead; it may take the initiative in developing a sense of responsibility in the labor union leadership. The bargaining relationship becomes more mature. There is, at the least, a reduction in the number and severity of bargaining

---

[4]Frederick H. Harbison and John R. Coleman, *Goals and Strategy in Collective Bargaining,* Harper & Row, Publishers, Incorporated, New York, 1951.

threats and a greater reliance upon facts. In order to obtain a relationship of this status, a formal union-shop clause is necessary, inasmuch as the union will usually fight, and fight hard, until it achieves this measure of security. Working harmony must grow out of security on both sides. There is the hope and the possibility that the worker will learn to be loyal to *both* the union and the company.

In a relatively few instances, the relationship between union and management may grow from working harmony into one of *union-management cooperation*. Instead of attempting to apply pressure on each other in collective bargaining, the two parties try to apply pressure to common problems. Both union and management accept a common responsibility in such matters as increasing productivity, reducing waste, recruiting, and safety. In this stage of development, there may be the desired objective bargaining on the basis of facts, without the blue-sky demands, haggling, horse trading, and acting that are so characteristic of the usual collective bargaining sessions. The emphasis is upon joint problem solving. Unfortunately this relationship of joint union-management cooperation is rarely developed until the company is in serious danger of going out of business. When the handwriting is on the wall and both union and management can read it clearly, cooperation may then be entered upon so that both may survive.

In general, management gets the type of relationship that it wants from the union. There is a "mirror effect" in collective bargaining relationships. If management wants to fight, the union will accommodate them; a militant management begets a militant union. As the traditional dominant party in this relationship, management must take the initiative in promoting a more peaceful relationship.

This is not to say that there are no instances where a particular union leader loves to fight management just for the sake of fighting or to redress real or assumed slights and ills of the past. One instance has been noted where a strong and aggressive leader of a local union outlasted sixteen consecutive managers with the ultimate result of closing the plant.[5] Once management is assured that the union is reasonably responsible in its policies and actions and does in effect represent the majority of the employees, it has an obligation to make the *first* move toward working harmony. In most cases, it is probable that this initial overture will not come from the union. Management must accept the prime responsibility for the establishment of this relationship.

UNION BARGAINING PRESSURES

The labor union, as the other bargaining member, has certain strategies and tactics that it utilizes to extract greater concessions from the employer. Union representatives use most of the particular tactics described for the employer above. They haggle, horse-trade, act, demand more in the expectation of getting less, and make tentative agreements subject to ratification by the membership. In addition to these maneuvers there are certain stronger types of pressure which are sometimes used. These are strikes, picketing, and boycotts.

[5]Sumner H. Slichter, James J. Healy, and E. Robert Livernash, *The Impact of Collective Bargaining on Management*, The Brookings Institution, Washington, 1960, p. 954.

Strikes

A strike is a concerted and temporary withholding of employee services from the employer for the purpose of exacting greater concessions in the employment relationship than the employer is willing to grant at the bargaining table. The strike, or the potential strike, is a basic part of the bargaining process. The possibility of a strike is the ultimate economic force that the union can bring to bear upon the employer. It is the power which offsets the employer's right to manage the firm and lock out the employee. Without the possibility of a strike in the background, there can be no true collective bargaining. When the strike is prohibited by law, some other mechanism, such as arbitration, must be established as a substitute for collective bargaining.

There are various types of strikes. Among them are the following:

1   *Recognition strike.* This is a strike to force the employer to recognize and deal with the union. This type of strike has been largely replaced by the consent elections administered by the National Labor Relations Board.

2   *Economic strike.* This is the typical strike, based on a demand for better wages, hours, and working conditions than the employer is willing to grant.

3   *Jurisdictional strikes.* When two unions argue about which has jurisdiction over a type of work and attempt to exert pressure upon the employer to allocate it to one or the other, a jurisdictional strike may ensue. For example, both carpenters and metal workers wish to hang metal doors. If either group strikes to force the employer to grant the work to its members, this is a jurisdictional strike. The employer is caught in the middle between two warring unions. Under the Taft-Hartley Act such strikes are illegal.

4   *Wildcat strike.* Wildcat strikes are the quick, sudden, and unauthorized types of work stoppages. Such strikes are not approved by union leadership and are contrary to the labor agreement. They are sometimes viewed as a form of "fractional bargaining" by a subgroup of employees who have not achieved satisfaction through regular grievance processing or collective bargaining procedures. Rather than violations to be condemned out of hand, it has been suggested that they should be studied to determine whether existing procedures should be modified to make the bargaining relationship more realistic.[6]

5   *Sit-down strike.* When the employees strike but remain at their jobs in the plant, this is termed a "sit-down strike." Such strikes are illegal since they constitute an invasion of private property. Employees are free to strike for certain objectives, but they must physically withdraw from the company's premises.

6   *Sympathy strike.* If other unions who are not party to the original strike consent to strike in sympathy with the original union, this is termed a "sympathy strike." It is an attempt to exert an indirect pressure upon the employer. This type of strike is also outlawed by the Taft-Hartley Act.

When any type of strike occurs, the employer should have a well-thought-out plan for functioning during the work stoppage. Among other items, he must make provision

[6]David R. Hampton, "How Can Wildcats Be Prevented?" *Personnel*, vol. 43, no. 2, March–April 1966, pp. 51–59.

for the following: (1) making sure that the plant is left in good physical condition; (2) explaining the employer's side of the issue to the employees; (3) giving a statement to the press; (4) notifying suppliers and customers; (5) notifying the appropriate mediation services; (6) determining to what extent nonunion personnel will be maintained on the working staff; and (7) paying off striking workers for work completed in the past. There are few, if any, friendly strikes. Employers should do all in their power, short of violating law and public policy, to win the strike. Yet they must be aware of the fact that they have to live and work with these striking employees when the work stoppage is over. They should be wary of making permanent enemies of any large group of personnel. But if collective bargaining is to operate properly, there can be no automatic capitulation to union terms solely in the interest of maintaining harmony after the strike. If harmony and cooperation are the sole objectives, the employer should have given up before the strike stage was ever reached.

Picketing

The union desires to keep the plant completely closed during a strike. The patrolling of strikers in front of plant entrances—picketing—is the most effective device for accomplishing this objective. If the employer accepts the shutdown and makes no attempt to reopen the plant, picketing will be routine and peaceful. If the employer attempts to start a back-to-work movement, picketing can turn into violence as nonstrikers are attacked and cars damaged.[7] Peaceful persuasion through picketing is entirely permissible and legal, but violence is not. For this reason, the employer can often obtain court injunctions to limit the number of pickets that can be placed in front of any plant entrance.

Secondary boycotts

A secondary boycott takes place when a union, which is seeking a concession from employer A, places pressure on employer B to influence employer A to grant the concession. The union may attempt to make employers B, C, D, etc., refuse to deal with employer A until A falls in line with their demands. The "hot cargo" agreement is a particular type of secondary boycott. This is an agreement by which the employer agrees that the union does not have to work on materials that come from employers whose plants have been struck or who have not recognized a union. The Taft-Hartley Act sought to make such secondary pressures illegal and attempted to keep labor-management disputes confined to the primary parties. The Labor-Management Disclosure Act of 1959 strengthens this objective in the case of "hot cargo" clauses. This act did, however, authorize such boycott agreements in the construction and clothing industries.

It is difficult to state how far public policy should go in permitting various pressures to be placed upon employers by a union. The philosophy in recent years has seemed to be that of restricting the extreme applications of force, with the major exception of the

---

[7]Modern technology has obviated some personal clashes. A few plant managements have used helicopters to avoid patrolling pickets, leading to the suggestion by some that barrage balloons will have to be used to extend picket lines into the sky.

primary strike. The philosophies of both the Taft-Hartley and the Labor-Management Disclosure Acts have been to curb the union in some of its activities. On the other hand, the basic philosophy of the various branches of our federal government has been one of support for organizations that represent the views and interests of employees. As indicated earlier, there are few, if any, black-and-white, objective, and scientific answers to issues involving employer-employee relationships. In the absence of a "law of the situation," bargaining from strength, which includes strikes by the union and lockouts by the employer, is the adopted approach.

THIRD-PARTY RESOLUTIONS

When disagreements between labor and management become serious, a third party often enters the controversy. The third party may be a (1) fact-finder, (2) mediator, (3) arbitrator, or (4) mediator-arbitrator. *Fact-finders* may be appointed by the government or selected by the two parties. After investigation of the dispute, a report will be filed and made public. Not only are the two parties likely to modify extreme positions on the basis of additional facts, but the power of public opinion will be brought to bear. The major limitation of this approach is its lack of finality.

Mediation is a process by which the third party attempts to stimulate labor and management to reach some type of agreement. Mediators cannot decide issues; they can only listen, suggest, communicate, explain, and persuade. Among other re-quirements, effective mediators must (1) establish and maintain themselves as strict neutrals in the dispute, (2) exhibit confident belief that a solution is not only pos-sible but probable, (3) listen, (4) ask intelligent questions, (5) keep the two parties talk-ing, and (6) when asked, propose compromise solutions based on knowledge of the "rock-bottom" positions of both parties. Mediators are most heavily used in new-contract negotiations. They rarely enter the labor-management picture in grievance processing that occurs after the contract is signed.[8] Contracts constitute "new law," and the two parties are generally unwilling to allow third parties to make final decisions. Grievances involve interpretations of existing law, and both labor and management are willing to allow arbitrators to act as industrial judges.[9] Thus there is much contract medi-ation and grievance arbitration, and little grievance mediation and contract arbitration.

Most mediators are supplied by the state and federal governments. In the interest of preserving the neutrality of the Federal Mediation and Conciliation Service, that organization was removed from the supervision of the Secretary of Labor and now operates as a semi-independent body under the President. Mediators must be accepted and trusted by both parties; they must maintain the same relationship with both parties; they must be equally friendly and equally withdrawn. If one party proposes to drive them away, they must withdraw from the other party in like manner or, perhaps, withdraw from the dispute entirely.

Third parties can do much to promote an agreement.[10] They can at least keep the

---

[8] In a survey of 1,717 agreements covering 7.5 million workers, only 2.6 percent had provision for mediation of unsettled grievances by an outside third party. See "Processing of Grievances," *Monthly Labor Review,* November 1964, pp. 1269–1272.

[9] See Chap. 20 for a discussion of grievance arbitration.

[10] See William E. Simkin, "Code of Professional Conduct for Labor Mediators," *Labor Law Journal,* October 1964, pp. 627–633.

two parties talking. They can take the initiative in calling conferences and keep ever before the disputants the desirability and inevitability of reaching an agreement at some time or other. If both sides trust as they should, mediators know their basic, immovable positions. They therefore know whether an agreement is possible from these positions, although being careful to reveal neither one. At times, mediators permit themselves to be "used," to save face for one or both parties. The company or union representatives may take an undesirable, yet inevitable, contract clause back to their principals and label it a suggestion of the mediators, when in reality it was not. At times, the mediators are also abused. Through all of this use and/or abuse, the mediator must fill his or her role with stability, maturity, confidence, neutrality, and competence.

Arbitration is a process in which the third party collects the facts from the two primary parties and proceeds to make a decision which is usually binding on labor and management. As indicated earlier, over 90 percent of all collective bargaining agreements in the United States provide for arbitration as a last step.[11] Its use in new-contract negotiation as a sole final approach is relatively rare. A recent agreement in the steel industry, however, provides that all issues not agreed upon by a stipulated time will be submitted to an Impartial Arbitration Board peopled by one union representative, one management member, and three impartial arbitrators appointed by agreement of the parties.[12] Certain issues are excluded from this process, such as union membership, cost-of-living provisions, management rights, and uniformity of benefits throughout the industry. The purpose of this rather unusual approach is to avoid the periodic threatened strikes which result in excessive costs of stockpiling, closing down of furnaces, etc. Employees received a one-time bonus of $150 in recognition of these cost savings.

In most public employment, employees are not permitted to strike. In four states, strikes by government workers are permitted if the two parties have exhausted all fact-finding and mediation procedures, and if the strike would not endanger the public health and welfare. In the federal government, and all other states, the public strike is technically illegal. In these instances, there is room for arbitration as a substitute. In the states of Wisconsin and Michigan, fact-finding and mediation can be followed by "final offer" arbitration. The power of the arbitrator is restricted to selecting between the two final offers. The hope is that more realistic initial bargaining will take place, and that neither party will submit an extreme final offer, knowing that it may well be rejected. In Michigan, parties may modify "final offers" for a time in the interest of trying to have the decision made by the disputants. Arbitrators can also refuse to accept both, if both choices are highly objectionable. In this "either-or" procedure, the power of the arbitrator is somewhat reduced; he or she cannot "split the difference." This approach is recommended only when substantial and mature two-party negotiations have been developed. It is also recommended that it *follow* fact-finding and mediation efforts.

In other public jurisdictions, interest is growing in the possible use of a *mediator-arbitrator*. This is "mediation with muscle," since both parties know that if they do not come up with a resolution, their mediator will supply the final answer. Thus they will *not* deal with the mediator at "arm's length," nor do they adopt the semi-legalistic

[11]Rose T. Selby and Maurice L. Cunningham, "Grievance Procedures in Major Contracts," *Monthly Labor Review*, October 1964, pp. 1125–1130.
[12]I. W. Abel, "Basic Steel's Experimental Negotiating Agreement," *Monthly Labor Review*, vol. 96, no. 9, September 1973, pp. 39–41.

stance of pure arbitration. In experiences thus far, the overwhelming bulk of issues have been resolved through the mediation process, with only a few finally being decided by the mediator-arbitrator. In resolving eighty-nine issues in California nursing negotiations, only one had to be arbitrated. Of thirteen issues submitted for mediation-arbitration from a Pacific longshoremen's dispute, all were settled through mediation.[13]

As suggested in Figure 20-2, the third-party attempts at conflict resolution often fall somewhere between the 9,9 problem-solving approach and the 5,5 compromise condition. Pure mediation is most often utilized in new, private-contract negotiations. Some elements of arbitration tend to be adopted in new-contract negotiations for public employees. As illustrated by the new and revolutionary steel agreement, arbitration may enter the private sector on new contracts when both parties, rather than the government, feel that neither can afford a work stoppage.

CURRENT ISSUES IN BARGAINING

As times change, the dominant issues in collective bargaining tend to change. The issue of union recognition has been replaced by economic issues of wages, hours, and working conditions. With the advent of mechanization and automation, job security and supplementary employee benefits have assumed greater importance. Among the current issues of significance are the following: (1) work rules governing the establishment of crews and use of new methods and equipment, (2) subcontracting of work to other firms, (3) the shorter workweek, (4) job security through softening the impact of technological change, (5) benefits such as guaranteed annual wages, pensions, and insurance to supplement reasonably satisfactory wages and protect against the effects of technology, and (6) wage settlements deemed to be "noninflationary." Three currently significant issues are productivity bargaining, public employee bargaining, and coalition bargaining.

Productivity bargaining

The typical approach in labor-management bargaining is that labor makes demands and management makes counteroffers related to those demands, e.g., labor demands a 12 percent pay increase and the company offers 6 percent. Productivity bargaining would change the managerial stance to one of volunteering wage increases *provided* the union will accept new work practices that will enhance company efficiency and productivity. Certainly, in the United States we have a very difficult and pressing problem of increasing productivity to cope with general economic problems. There are some signs that particular labor unions are beginning to recognize that *other* matters besides employee benefits must be negotiated to improve general productivity.

In every plant, there are certain existing practices, formal or informal, that serve to inhibit organizational efficiency. In some, there are outright bars to the introduction of more productive methods. In the construction industry, for example, there are a variety of union rules that serve as a drag on productivity. Concerning one extreme instance, a

[13]Sam Kagel, "Combining Mediation and Arbitration," *Monthly Labor Review*, vol. 96, no. 9, September 1973, pp. 62–63.

master mechanic, earning $10 per hour, was entitled to pay for the full time that *anyone* was on the job servicing machinery, day or night, regardless of whether he was actually around.[14] In one year he collected $94,000 pay for 107 hours a week for 52 weeks, mostly at overtime rates. Leaders of construction unions are beginning to move to reduce, through productivity bargaining, some of the major drags on output. Among these inefficient practices are requiring electrician pay for only plugging in equipment when it is moved, requiring a plumber to attach hoses to faucets, restricting the width of paint brushes, restricting use of rollers in painting except at premium pay rates, barring the use of plastic pipe, and barring the use of prefabricated units or requiring that they be disassembled and reassembled on the job. In one instance, five different crafts were required to install a water fountain. In railroads, the definition of a "day's run" is still heavily influenced by the slower steam-engine travel speeds of decades ago.

In productivity bargaining, management may be forced to pay a one-time premium for the right to introduce efficiency-enhancing programs. Obviously, such bargaining cannot threaten the employee's security, and it must make use of the traditional processes of negotiating. But it is certain that it is time for both management and unions to consider and negotiate over methods whereby organizational productivity can be enhanced, and to understand that such bargaining is to be concerned not only with what one gets, but with what one must contribute.

Public employee bargaining

If labor unions and collective bargaining work well for employees of private enterprises, it is logical to suggest that they would be equally advantageous for public employees. As indicated in the preceding chapter, three of the fastest-growing unions are in the public area. A presidential executive order has provided the basis for encouraging union organization among federal employees. Observation of the effectiveness of labor union negotiations with private employers has stimulated widespread interest in such organizations among state and local government personnel.

Under Executive Order 11491 of 1969, a form of collective bargaining is provided for employees of the federal government. It provides for exclusive representation by a single union if approved by a majority of those voting. Bargaining units and eligibility for voting are decided by the Assistant Secretary of Labor-Management Relations, with provision for appeal to a Federal Labor Relations Council. The latter is peopled by the Chairman of the Civil Service Commission, the Secretary of Labor, and members of the Executive Office. Neither the union shop nor the agency shop is permitted; thus "free riders" are possible. Bargaining is restricted to issues not determined by legislation; compensation rates and fringe benefits are thus outside of the union-management relationship. In the event of an impasse in negotiations, arbitration is provided through a Federal Services Impasse Panel. This panel, made up of seven appointed experienced arbitrators, may impose a settlement. The strike is illegal, the penalty being a fine of not more than $1,000 or imprisonment for not more than one year and a day, or both.

Some have decried the prohibition of strikes by public employees as effecting a type of "second-class citizenship." Others feel that public employment offers unusual

---

[14]"The Unions Begin to Bend on Work Rules," *Business Week*, Sept. 9, 1972, p. 100.

degrees of job security, for which the employee should be willing to give up some other economic rights. In any event, experience has shown that when public unions feel strong public-opinion support, they will risk the illegal strike anyway, e.g., discovery that normal postal employee progress took twenty-one years to go from $6,100 to $8,500 led to public support of the illegal strike, which in turn led to legislation permitting resolution of strike issues.

In addition to the substitutes of fact-finding and variations of arbitration for the right to strike, theorists have suggested such other innovations as: (1) a "nonstoppage strike," where both participants continue operations but contribute monies to a fund equal to 10 percent of total cash wages; (2) a "graduated strike," where employees stop work during portions of the usual workweek, thereby decreasing but not stopping public services; and (3) a "partial strike," where the government designates essential services, such as police and fire, and gives to the remainder the right to strike.[15]

With reference to state and local governments, it is estimated that only one-third require or permit organized collective bargaining for public employees.[16] Some permit union and agency shops, in contrast to the federal pattern. Bargaining tends to be much broader and includes such issues as salaries, hours of work, and fringe benefits. Binding grievance arbitration is common, as is the provision of third parties to deal with impasses. Only four states have legislation permitting some public employees to strike. The law in Hawaii, for example, permits such strikes when (1) there is no danger to public health and safety (thus excluding police and fire), (2) both parties have exhausted mediation and fact-finding processes, and (3) the union has issued a ten-day notice of the strike. It is suggested that labor-management relations in public work is steadily coming to resemble the model followed in private institutions. Such a model includes emphasis on realistic two-party bargaining, recognition of exclusive bargaining agencies for employees, some degree of union security, provision for third-party machinery to handle impasses, grievance arbitration, and, in some cases, the right to strike. Some fear the effect of this process on the "merit system" administered by independent civil service commissions, particularly when recognizing the typical labor union preference for following seniority in decision making. As yet, it is too soon to determine how the civil service system and the collective bargaining system will be accommodated to each other.

Coalition bargaining

Specific bargaining units are recognized by the National Labor Relations Board upon petition by labor or management for a representation election. As a result, there is often no overall plan for a large company or a major industry that deals with numerous unions. Exceptions to this are the cases of the United Automobile Workers and the United Steel Workers. In the steel industry, there is three-tier bargaining: (1) industry-wide master contract bargaining by a committee of employers and the USW, (2) company-wide master contract bargaining by a single company and the USW, and (3)

[15]Merton C. Bernstein, "Two Alternatives to Traditional Strikes by Public Employees," *Monthly Labor Review*, vol. 95, no. 5, May 1972, p. 44.

[16]Felix A. Nigro, "Labor Relations in State and Local Governments," *Personnel Administration*, vol. 33, no. 6, November–December 1970, p. 42.

plant bargaining by plant management and a local of the USW to cover unique problems. There has been less intercompany cooperation in the automobile industry, and negotiations are often confined to the latter two tiers. In any event, there is a single labor organization with which the entire industry or major companies must negotiate. It is no accident that these two unions are among the most powerful in the country and can call strikes affecting the entire nation.

In most other instances, a number of bargaining units and unions have developed under the auspices of the NLRB. General Electric, for example, deals with 150 bargaining units represented by more than eighty unions; American Standard, Inc., negotiates with five unions, and Union Carbide must deal with twenty-six unions. In the copper industry, companies have extended their technology from mining to fabrication, resulting in numerous facilities involving different processes at widely separated locations. As a consequence of this, numerous bargaining units have also developed. The net result of this situation is a diminution of power of the multiple unions in opposition to a coordinated plan from a single, large, national company. In recent years, therefore, there has been a move toward coalition bargaining among cooperating unions, a situation viewed with alarm by management because it enhances union bargaining power. In one instance, "stranger," nonvoting members of the International Union of Electrical Workers' team appeared to bargain with General Electric. When company representatives refused to continue the negotiations, the union filed an unfair labor practice with the NLRB for refusal to bargain in good faith. The Board upheld the charge on the basis that each side could select its representatives without interference from the other. Appeals to the courts are pending. In most instances, the goals of coalition bargaining include standard fringe benefits for all personnel, standard wage increases, and a common expiration date for all contracts. Obviously, the last goal is for the purpose of achieving the power of a UAW or USW in calling a national strike. At present, the company can divide and conquer, or negotiate, as each smaller-unit contract expires. Company managements are fearful that such industry-wide bargaining would encourage greater government interference and pressures leading to political decisions in public-interest strikes. In one instance, the NLRB moved to redefine and broaden the bargaining unit by the election process, even though there is no authorization for such an act in the existing legislation.[17] In the past, the United States Supreme Court has upheld the duty to bargain unit by unit, without extending the agreed-upon terms to other employees.

Under the guidance of the Industrial Unions Department of the AFL-CIO, it appears likely that the move toward coalition bargaining will continue. If the actual presence of outside union representatives is prohibited, then the "road show" approach encouraging common agreement by the separate unions is likely to be the tactic adopted. Common expiration dates for multiple contracts is to be continually sought, or at least the time intervals will be steadily shortened. On the other hand, all employers are not against coalition bargaining, and some seek to encourage it in order to reduce the degree and number of inconsistencies and complications in dealing with multiple unions. In most instances, these are employers operating in a single location. The large, integrated employers with widely separated sites and differing technologies still seek the values of flexibility.

[17]George H. Hildebrand, "Cloudy Future for Coalition Bargaining," *Harvard Business Review*, vol. 46, no. 6, November–December 1968, pp. 126–127.

A PHILOSOPHY OF LABOR-MANAGEMENT PEACE

Every manager has a philosophy of labor-management relations, a philosophy based on experience and formal and informal education. The importance of the problem to the future of the American economy dictates that considerable and mature thought should be devoted to working out such a philosophy. This philosophy should not only advance the objectives of the particular organization but also be consistent with the continued development of a relatively free, competitive economic system.

The cornerstone of a constructive philosophy of labor-management peace must be that of *acceptance*. Management must accept the labor union as the official representative and watchdog of the employee's interests. The union must accept the management as the primary planners and controllers of the company's operations. The union must not feel that management is working and seeking the opportunity to undermine and eliminate the labor organization. The company must not feel that the union is seeking to control every facet of the company operation, thereby creating a partnership of authority but not of responsibility.

A second basic characteristic of the constructive labor-management philosophy is acceptance by both parties of the principle of *free collective bargaining* and *free enterprise* consistent with the advancement of the public interest. Neither should want to substitute outside force or governmental control for the usual pressure of the marketplace. The objective should be to improve one's lot under the present system rather than to change to another involving greater regulation and a shifting of ownership to the state. Both parties must recognize their obligation to handle this freedom in a manner consistent with the public interest and must realize that abuse by either side in effect calls for a different type of economic system.

A third element of a philosophy should be an emphasis upon a *problemsolving attitude and a deemphasis of the legalistic approach*. Such an approach is not, of course, possible until and unless the preceding two requisites have been established. There will be less interest in finding loopholes in the contract, in pulling "slick" deals to the detriment of the other party, or in relying solely upon the lawyer to develop and preserve the union-management relationship. A problemsolving philosophy would often entail a seeking of union help by the management. It also would require a union respect for management as the primary director of the organization.

Finally, both parties must be cognizant of *obligations to the principals* in the situation. For the union, the principal is obviously the union member, for whom the organization was formed. This obligation requires the adherence to democratic processes in order that the union may be truly responsive to its members. For management, the principal has traditionally been the stockholder. As indicated in Chapter 2 of this text, this philosophy is out of date. Management has many principals, among whom are stockholders, the public, customers, and employees. It might be similarly contended that the modern, mature union should also number among its principals the general public and the customers of the business firm. It is apparent that the employee is a principal of both union and management. This realization does not justify any attempt on the part of management to alienate the worker's allegiance to a responsible union. But it does lead to an awareness that the union member is also a company employee and that a relationship must be established that will further the interests of all parts of the organization and not just those of the stockholder alone, the consumer alone, the employee alone, or the public alone.

SUMMARY

Since collective bargaining has been established in our national policy as the basic method for the solving of labor-management problems, it is important to devote some attention to this process. Collective bargaining has its tactical and strategic implications as well as its national and local aspects. Both labor and management have an obligation to develop a philosophy and approach which will promote labor-management peace while advancing the objectives of a free economy.

The establishment of basic principles and philosophies of bargaining must be supplemented by practical procedures for implementing that philosophy. The collective bargaining procedure has certain fundamental phases: (1) the prenegotiation phase, (2) the selection of negotiators, (3) the strategy of bargaining, (4) the tactics to be used in the sessions, and (5) the writing of the labor contract. Labor-management relations have, in some cases, progressed from a status of *militant opposition* to *armed truce* to *working harmony* and finally, in rare cases, to joint *labor-management cooperation*. We do not believe that the final stage is either inevitable or even necessarily desirable if each party is properly to fulfill its basic function.

In the event of no agreement, various pressures are brought to bear upon management by the union, such as strikes, picketing, and boycotts. The basic management pressure is that of waiting until the absence of the payroll makes itself felt on every union member. There are often third-party pressures involved in these disputes, including fact-finders, mediators, arbitrators, and mediator-arbitrators. Negotiators in collective bargaining in the private sector generally prefer to use the mediator in new-contract bargaining and the arbitrator in grievance processing. In the public sector, where the strike may be prohibited, there is much more concern for innovation, entailing varied use of fact-finders buttressed by public opinion, arbitrators restricted to "either-or" decisions, and mediator-arbitrators engaged in both processes sequentially.

Both parties have a basic obligation to establish a constructive relationship of working harmony in the advancement of labor-management peace. Such a relationship would include (1) labor union and management acceptance of each other as responsible parties in the collective bargaining process, (2) acceptance by both parties of the free-enterprise system with its concomitant obligations and the authority of private ownership and private operation of business organizations, (3) an emphasis upon a problem-solving approach with a deemphasis upon excessive legalism, and (4) an awareness of basic obligations to principals, who include employees, stockholders, customers, and the public.

DISCUSSION QUESTIONS

1   Define and distinguish among mediator, arbitrator, and mediator-arbitrator.
2   Contrast the third-party machineries used in resolving labor-management disputes in the private sector with those in the public sector.
3   What is productivity bargaining? How do the roles of management and union in this type of bargaining differ as compared with traditional bargaining?
4   What is "Boulwareism"? Is it a "fair" tactic of bargaining?

5 Is a legalistic approach to union-management relations helpful or harmful in the view of society?

6 Compare and contrast the following methods of conflict resolution: compromise, problem solving, mediation, and arbitration.

7 Discuss the following concepts in terms of nature and use: grievances, new contracts, mediation, and arbitration.

8 Distinguish between a strike, a secondary boycott, and picketing.

9 What should be the role of the lawyer in collective bargaining processes?

10 What is the typical sequence of informal union-management relationships as they move from infancy to maturity?

SUPPLEMENTARY READING

BARRETT, Jerome T., and Ira B. Lobel: "Public Sector Strikes—Legislative and Court Treatment," *Monthly Labor Review*, vol. 97, no. 9, September 1974, pp. 19–22.

BLUM, Albert A., Michael L. Moore, and B. Parker Fairey: "The Effect of Motivational Programs on Collective Bargaining," *Personnel Journal*, vol. 52, no. 7, July 1973, pp. 633–641.

FOWLER, Robert Booth: "Normative Aspects of Public Employee Strikes," *Public Personnel Management*, vol. 3, no. 2, March–April 1974, pp. 129–137.

ROSOW, Jerome M.: "Now Is the Time for Productivity Bargaining," *Harvard Business Review*, vol. 50, no. 1, January–February 1972, pp. 78–89.

STERN, James L.: "Final Offer Arbitration—Initial Experience in Wisconsin," *Monthly Labor Review*, vol. 97, no. 9, September 1974, pp. 39–43.

TAGLIAFERRI, Louis E.: "Plant Operation during a Strike," *Personnel Administration*, vol. 35, no. 2, March–April 1972, pp. 47–51.

CASES FOR PART SIX

THE CASE OF TROUBLESOME CREATIVITY IN THE IRWIN
MANUFACTURING COMPANY*

In August of 1964, B. A. Warner, personnel director of the Irwin Manufacturing Company, was trying to decide what action he should take with regard to Dan Johnson, an employee of the company. Johnson had submitted an acceptable suggestion but, before submitting the idea, had given it a trial run, thus violating a long-standing rule that no change could be put into effect without the prior approval of the engineering department.

Irwin Manufacturing Company produced electrical equipment and was located in a large city in the Midwest. It had been formed in 1919 by Mr. A. B. Baker, father of the present president and grandfather of two of the vice-presidents. The company organization is shown in Exhibit 1. The company had a reputation for being a "good place to work." Employees were not unionized. Most of the company's products were mass-produced to very close tolerances. They were sold in forty-eight states by a sales force numbering almost 400. These salesmen worked out of fifty-three company-owned branches and sold on commission. Home office employment was in the neighborhood of 1,300.

Dan Johnson had started with Irwin as a drill-press operator in 1953, shortly after arriving in Chicago from his former home and birthplace, Kentucky. Irwin was the first place to which he had applied, and he was offered the job on the spot. During his time with Irwin, he had received frequent pay increases. Exhibit 2 contains a record of Johnson's wage progress.

*Garret L. Bergen and William V. Haney, *Organizational Relations and Management Action*, McGraw-Hill Book Company, New York, 1966, pp. 517–522. Used with permission.

In 1958, five years after Johnson joined Irwin, he was promoted to setup man in the newly formed spring department. This department came about as a result of a large government contract. After the contract expired, the volume of Irwin's regular products had expanded enough to make it unnecessary to transfer Johnson back to his job as drill-press operator. As setup man, he was responsible for the setting up of the automatic equipment in his department as well as the supervision of the ten female spring loopers who also worked in the department. The springs were automatically formed by machine. They were then moved to benches where spring loopers, using special pliers, formed the ends. Johnson also operated a special-purpose engine lathe designed to manufacture heavy-duty springs. This engine lathe was not in constant use. When needed, it was usually scheduled for reasonably long runs.

In reviewing Johnson's personnel folder, Warner noticed that this was the third time he had violated the same rule. Other details concerning Johnson are noted in Exhibit 3. Dan's latest violation was a serious one, according to company engineers. If it had not been detected, serious damage might have resulted.

Johnson's idea concerned the forming operation of a certain heavy-duty spring— performing it in one step rather than two, thus eliminating one complete job element. He designed a special tool bit to accomplish the form. Before submitting his suggestion, Dan decided to try out his idea. He ran 5,000 of these heavy-duty springs. After inspecting them and seeing nothing wrong with the results, he moved them to the assembly area, where they would eventually become parts of machines which sold for $250.

They remained unnoticed in the assembly area for almost a week, until it came time to use them in final assembly. At this point, an inspector observed the difference and placed a stop order on the parts, pending investigation. Product engineers were called in, and they immediately called for Joe Poppy, Johnson's immediate supervisor. When Poppy expressed ignorance of the situation, Johnson was called in. He readily admitted making the change and commented, "Why, only yesterday, I mailed in the suggestion form." This occurred on the eighteenth of the month. Dan was told to return to his department until disposition of his case had been determined.

Company engineers explained to Warner that they could not be sure at the time if Johnson's idea was a good one. They feared that his form job set up a stress concentration that might fail under repeated loadings. They further explained that if this were so, it was fortunate that the inspector had caught the mistake. Otherwise, the springs would have been assembled into machines, which could develop trouble in the field and require expensive servicing.

On the afternoon of the eighteenth, Warner asked Bill Kay, a personnel assistant, to interview Johnson to learn more about his background. Bill Kay's comments follow:

A very likable, sincerely motivated worker. . . . Realizes he did wrong. When reminded that he had previously been warned about trying ideas out without approval, he expressed regrets and could offer no explanation. He said he was only sorry he didn't have more of an education, as he would like to study spring engineering and design. He also related an unhappy experience that happened to him about a month ago. As one of the engineers was walking through the department, Dan had stopped him and inquired if there were any books he could borrow to explain the theory of spring design. The engineer replied, "What would a hillbilly like you want with a book? Stick to your comic books and leave the technical publications alone." Dan said he didn't mention the incident to anyone, but he thought the girls in the department had overheard the engineer's remarks. He would not give the name of the engineer. Dan said his home life was fine. He spent two evenings a week in Boy Scout activities and bowled on another night in the company league. When asked why he had refused to attend foremanship training classes, he said he hated to spend another evening away from his family. Dan ended the interview with the hope that he would be given another chance.

Bill Kay

Late in the next day, Kay interviewed Joe Poppy. Poppy said he was in favor of firing Johnson. He explained that only this morning, his boss, Karl Metz, had "chewed him out" about Johnson. Neal Baker, vice-president and sales manager, had heard about the incident and called Metz on the carpet. Mr. Baker had expressed horror at the thought that 5,000 defective machines might have gone out to customers. Poppy also said Johnson did a fairly good job as supervisor of women but that he could no longer tolerate his constant experimenting.

Warner was reviewing the case after lunch on the nineteenth, in preparation for a meeting with Poppy and Metz to decide Johnson's fate, when the phone rang. It was Ralph Brown, product engineer, who reported that Johnson's idea was thoroughly sound. Based on this evidence, he was recommending a $50 suggestion award.

Exhibit 1   Irwin Manufacturing Company: Partial organization chart

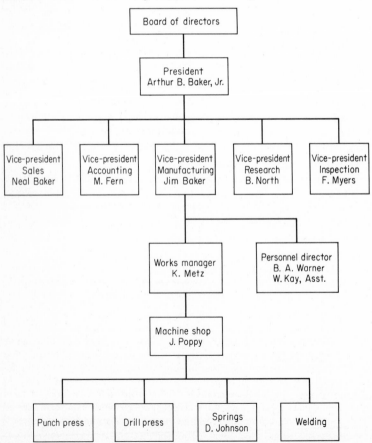

Warner hung up the phone wondering what effect this should have on his decision. Company policy provided that even if Johnson were discharged, he would still be in line for the award.

Exhibit 2 Irwin Manufacturing Company: selected data on Dan Johnson
Personal: 38 years old, married, two children. 1 year high school.

Salary:	Effective date	Hourly wage	Effective date	Hourly wage
	4/29/53	$1.60	5/1/59	$2.35
	8/26/53	1.70	1/3/60	2.45
	11/18/53	1.80	1/18/61	2.55
	6/3/54	1.90	9/30/61	2.65
	12/15/54	2.05	8/12/62	2.80
	9/18/57	2.15	2/10/63	2.90
	3/29/58	2.25	11/1/63	2.95

Exhibit 3 Irwin Manufacturing Company: comments on back of personnel record card

Date	Comment
6/15/58	Discussed importance of not initiating changes without approval. While walking by, noticed Dan grinding tool bit. Upon inquiring, learned he was trying out a new idea. Carefully explained the function of the suggestion system. *Joe Poppy*
2/9/60	Ran 11,000 defective parts. Failed to use lubricant. Said he was experimenting and couldn't understand why the lubricant was needed. *J. Poppy*
9/15/60	Offered chance to attend foremanship training. Refused. *K. Metz*
9/16/62	Same as comment of 9/15/60. *K. Metz*
10/8/62	Ran 6,000 defective springs. Failed to use specified tool bit for cutoff. His own design resulted in a burr. Warned he would not get another chance. *J. Poppy*
9/18/63	Offered chance to attend foremanship training. Refused. *B. Warner*

Exhibit 4 Irwin Manufacturing Company: suggestion record—Dan Johnson

Date	Award	Date	Award
6/15/58	$10.00	12/18/62	$15.00
8/11/59	5.00	2/12/63	25.00
9/6/59	15.00	8/2/63	15.00
3/4/60	20.00	1/14/64	10.00
7/21/61	5.00	2/16/64	10.00

Note: No record of the total number of suggestions submitted is available, as the suggestor only identifies himself if he wins an award.

THE CASE OF THE CONFUSED MANAGEMENT

National Labor Relations Act

Prior to 1970, the Stacy Refinery, a subdivision of the Ajax Oil Company, was known as a great place to work, the country-club firm of the town of Holloway. The firm offered most of the employee services known to experts in personnel management. Wages were better than competitive; pensions were provided, as were also a guaranteed

Work constructively with union for the benefit of the organization

annual wage, a credit union, a medical clinic, and insurance of all types. Once each year the entire plant took off for a holiday with their families at a local amusement park at the expense of the company. Most of the 4,000 employees of the refinery were members of the plant independent union, known as the Employees Independent Federation. There was no union shop. Relationships between management and the union had been quite cordial in the past, though a few employees had grumbled about the union being overly influenced by management. The high employee benefits and the low union dues, however, had served to prevent much employee dissatisfaction with the union and the management.

Oil company refinery operations are usually low-profit or even losing propositions, but the profit made on other processes had more than offset the absence of earnings here. After 1970, however, competition in the oil industry became so intense that the Ajax home office could no longer ignore refinery costs. Change finally came to Holloway. The payroll was cut by 40 percent. In the early fifties, Stacy was considered to be *the* place to work, and there was a long waiting list for jobs. The waiting list no longer existed in 1971. The country-club atmosphere disappeared, to be replaced by what some employees termed a "military barracks" atmosphere. Many of the same benefits existed, but they were no longer better than the competition. Now work procedures have been tightened up all along the line, and Stacy is no longer a "great place to work." Several foremen have indicated that they are confused, that the company seems to be veering wildly from easy paternalism to a get-tough approach. The top management of the refinery has admitted that things are not going too smoothly.

Great employee dissatisfaction has grown as a result of the drastic shift in management philosophy in 1971. Other unions have for many years looked longingly at Stacy because of its large size. The Oil Chemical and Atomic Workers in particular would like to represent these employees in their dealings with the refinery management. The top officers of the plant's independent union have been aware of this constant outside union interest, but they have, in the past, won several National Labor Relations Board elections. Now, they are not so sure that they can hold the loyalty of the majority of employees, as a result of the switch in management philosophy. The Teamsters union has also shown an interest in organizing the employees of Stacy. As a result of these rumblings, the top officers of the independent union have attempted to work out an arrangement whereby they can disassociate themselves from management control.

Recently, the jurisdiction of the independent union was challenged by a petition of the Oil Chemical and Atomic Workers submitted to the NLRB. An election was scheduled to take place in the Stacy refinery. On the ballot were the following choices: (1) the Employees Independent Federation, (2) the Oil Chemical and Atomic Workers, (3) the Teamsters, (4) the Operating Engineers Union, an organization that represented the employees of three other nearby refineries, and (5) no union. To combat this outside pressure, the top officers in the Employees Independent Federation pledged themselves to an alliance with the Teamster organization, should they win the election. Management cannot remain silent on the sidelines during the battle that is shaping up. Management has been reasonably happy with the EIF in the past, but does not look forward to their alliance with the Teamster organization. The top managements of Ajax and Stacy are now in the process of working out a management position in the coming four-way union battle. The present problem is considered to be a serious emergency. The Stacy management contends that more is at stake here than just taking a position in the present controversy.

THE CASE OF THE REBELLIOUS FOOTBALL TEAM *Motivation through participation Leadership style*

The 95th Fighter Group of the United States Air Force is located near a small town of 3,500 people. The installation has over 1,200 men. Entertainment facilities are inadequate, and the base commander has made special efforts to provide recreation for his men. Football, baseball, bowling, basketball, and other sports are followed with a great deal of interest, and many men belong to base leagues in the sports. League champions are awarded trophies and prizes. Higher command has complimented the base commander on his athletic program as a morale builder. The percentage of base personnel participating in some sport runs as high as 75 percent.

Capt. George Olsen, the adjutant of the 18th Fighter Interceptor Squadron, came on the base in August. He was a graduate of Ohio State University, where he had had an above-average scholastic record, been commander of his ROTC unit, president of his fraternity, and very active in intramural athletics. After college, Olsen entered the service immediately and chose to go into administration and personnel, though he had passed all examinations necessary for pilot training. Before coming to this base, he had had six years of experience as a personnel officer and adjutant.

Olsen asked for and was given permission to organize and coach a squadron football team. Practice started the first week in September with a turnout of thirty players. There were about twenty airmen and ten officers. Among the candidates, six had had college football experience, three of whom were chosen to assist Olsen in the coaching. Lieutenant Jones, a pilot, had been a first-string guard at North Carolina; he worked with the linemen. Captain Green, a flight leader in the unit, had been on the squad at West Point; he coached the ends. Lieutenant Smith, the squadron assistant adjutant, had played for a small college in Pennsylvania and was made backfield coach. Olsen and Smith roomed next to each other in the bachelor officers' quarters and spent many hours in the evenings diagramming plays and planning overall strategy.

The base paper picked the 18th as potential league champions on the basis of available experienced talent. Olsen agreed that his team had a good chance to win, but was disturbed by the team's way of looking sensational in scrimmage on several plays and then turning a bit lackadaisical. He and Smith determined that they would have to drive the team harder and have anyone loafing on a play run a couple of laps. The next day, at practice, Captain Olsen felt that Lieutenant Burns was "dogging" it on a blocking assignment and ordered him to take a couple of laps. Lieutenant Burns laughed at first but jogged around the field when he saw that the coach was serious. As the opening day approached, Olsen was disturbed when the number of turnouts dropped to around eighteen, but he concluded that this was probably all for the good since it showed those who were serious about playing. Lieutenant Burns said he had a sprained ankle and missed practice for nearly a week. He said that he would be ready to go for the first game, however.

The first opponent was the base maintenance squadron, with the 18th being favored by two touchdowns. Olsen was disappointed to find that Captain Green and three others of the starting lineup had gone on a cross-country flight that morning and would not be back in time for the game. With a makeshift lineup, the team held a 14-to-0 lead at the half. Burns made three long runs, although Olsen kept reminding him to hustle it up. He told Smith between halves that Burns would be the best back in the league if he would just put out on every play. During the second half, Olsen was dissatisfied with Airman Rolf, who appeared to be tiring. Olsen took his place at right end. The score was now 14 to 7, but Olsen had full confidence in his team. The opponents made a couple of long gains around his end, but Olsen certainly did not feel that he was at fault when maintenance scored again. When he later dropped a pass from the halfback, he made a mental note to talk to Millis about sometimes throwing the ball so hard that no end could handle it. Maintenance scored again to win the game. The coach's urgings in each huddle just did not seem to lift the team.

At practice the next Monday, Olsen praised his team for a good effort, but singled out several players who he felt had put out less than full effort. He was particularly critical of Burns, who had left the game with a slight ankle injury early in the fourth quarter. The next game was with the toughest competition in the league, the 27th Interceptor Squadron. Olsen was shocked when his team lost 27 to 0. He had pulled Millis and Burns out of the game when he felt that they were guilty of calling some of their own plays rather than following the regular plays on the cards that he and Smith had prepared. That evening, at Smith's suggestion, he posted a notice suspending Burns and Millis from the team. The next day, on the urging of several team members, he relented and reinstated them.

At the first meeting the following week, Olsen blew his whistle to start practice. No one moved. He blew it again. The team merely gathered in a group around him. Captain Green started to speak for the group. He said that the team had got together the night before and decided that elected co-captains should be named to call plays and run the team during the game. He said that the team had decided to scrap the complicated multiple offense that Olsen had used. Green went on to say that if Olsen wanted to go on leading calisthenics and acting as an advisor, that would be all right. The elected co-captains, however, would be in charge of the team. Olsen said that if they did not appreciate all he had done for the team, he guessed he'd better get out completely. He walked off the field. The deposed coach read in the base paper the next day that Burns and Millis had been elected co-captains.

Olsen did not see the games that followed but told Green one night at mess that he was glad to see the team had built up a won-and-lost record of 7 and 2. Green persuaded Olsen that there were no hard feelings and that he should come out and see the game the following day. They were playing for the championship. In the account of the game the next day in the base paper, Olsen read:

In a game marked by keen desire on the part of both squadrons, the 3rd FIS nosed out the 18th FIS 21 to 20 yesterday afternoon when John McCarthy caught a pass in the end zone during the last thirty seconds of the game. The pass barely eluded the outstretched fingers of Jerry Burns of the 18th, who made a gallant effort to deflect the ball. The 6-foot-4-inch McCarthy had been outstanding on offense all afternoon.

After reading the account, Olsen told Smith that though it was a well-played game, he felt that many defensive halfbacks would have deflected the winning pass without trouble.

THE CASE OF THE STAFF ENFORCER

Communication

Ron Powell, twenty-eight years of age, is a job and wage analyst in the Industrial Relations Department within the Transport Division of Acme Aircraft. The Division produces a line of twin-engined passenger planes for the commercial market, and a militarized version of the same plane for the U.S. Air Force. The production work force was fairly stable at 6,000 employees working two shifts in such areas as fabrication, sub-assembly, final assembly, and support functions. Ron had been in the IR Department for seven months, being the junior person in the unit. However, he had been with Acme for six years, serving in the Final Assembly unit as leadman on the electrical checkout crew, and in the Electrical Planning unit as a planner. While in the latter position, he heard of the opening in Industrial Relations.

While working for many years on the night shift in final assembly, he took advantage of the opportunity to return to college and get a degree in Business Administration. He had been looking for a way to utilize this knowledge, and saw the job and wage analyst opening as a golden opportunity to do so. Movement into the position was much easier than he had anticipated. It was a salaried position with a good pay increase. Wage and salary personnel wore a candy-striped badge with a star on it, to which hourly workers, who wore mustard-colored badges, attached a good deal of prestige.

The Wage and Salary Section within IR was composed of six analysts and a section head. Two covered jobs in engineering, three maintained surveillance over the fabrication and assembly departments, and one was assigned to technical and office positions. There were approximately 1,000 employees per analyst. After receiving six weeks' training under one of the more experienced analysts, he was assigned to the sub-assembly and final assembly units.

Jim Hardy, thirty-nine years of age, was the Wage and Salary Section Head. He had been with the company for sixteen years, and in W&S for ten. Having no formal education beyond high school, he had risen through the ranks from punch press operator to General Supervisor. Ten years ago, when Acme suffered a severe cutback, he was saved by transfer to IR. His work in W&S had gained him a great deal of respect from Division management.

Hardy laid down a few simple but firm rules for his analysts to follow. The overall thrust was to be fair to all concerned. Among the specific rules were:

1 Every employee must be working under the proper job class and in the proper pay range for that class.

2 The work in each unit is to be evaluated on a regular basis, and classified by labor grade in accordance with the skill and knowledge required.

3 The number of employees in each class is to be kept in line with the available type of work in each unit.

4 All requests for classification changes, lateral or upgrading, are to be personally investigated by the analyst and substantiated on the basis of work actually being performed.

5 All requests for merit increases are to be personally discussed with the department supervisor initiating the request, to verify justification.

6 All job classification changes and merit rate increases required approval of the W&S Section.

7 The use of "name dropping" of higher-management authorities by analysts to exercise control will not be condoned.

Until about six weeks ago, Ron had enjoyed the independence with which he was allowed to work. Hardy occasionally stopped in his office cubicle for a short chat to inquire if there were any problems, and to remind Ron to keep an eye out for any changes in work patterns in his units. The other analysts said that when he called you to *his* office and closed the door, that's when you really found out what he was like. Though the work had been proceeding at a reasonable rate, recently Ron found himself reluctant to leave the office and spend time out in the units. Employees had begun to approach him, wanting to know when they were going to get an "A" classification. All Ron would say was, "That's a matter between you and your supervisor." His old acquaintances, however, seemed to be avoiding him.

One day Ron was stopped as he was leaving the plant after work by an irate employee who said that his supervisor had told him that he had put him in for a raise, and that W&S had turned it down. He demanded an explanation even though Ron could remember seeing no such request. Ron told him that if he had a "beef," he should see his shop steward. After he said it, he realized that that hadn't been too swift an answer, but he had been caught by surprise. When he told Hardy of the episode the next morning, all the latter said was, "Yeah, there's some real weak supervisors out there. You had better have a serious talk with them."

Ron's current problem is processing six requests for classification changes for personnel. All six were for upgrading to "A" class; all had come in on the same day two weeks ago from the same general supervisor—four from the Final Assembly Unit and two from Electrical Harness Assembly. Final Assembly presented a special challenge. In other departments where people worked on machines, one could look at the type of parts being manufactured and spot-check to see if they were making their own set-ups. Even in sub-assembly, when people worked at a regular station or bench, it wasn't too difficult to determine the level of work being performed. However, in Final Assembly, where people worked in groups all over the aircraft, inside and out, and frequently changed tasks, it was practically impossible to determine who was doing "A" work. Watching at close hand for any period of time was out—analysts were supposed to stay in the background. It was forbidden to talk to workers about the work they were doing without an invitation from the supervisor to do so. Even in this case, a shop steward had to be present. In Final Assembly, the analyst was forced to put his trust in the decisions of the unit supervisor. Ron was especially concerned about these latest change requests since Hardy had recently commented, "Final Assembly is top-heavy; don't let it get out of hand."

In the Electrical Assembly unit, most of the employees were female. The change requests were for two women on the second shift. The "A" classification called for working from blueprints to make up harness peg boards, or assembly work on certain harnesses where the soldering of plugs was especially difficult or critical. The "A" jobs were easy to spot, especially since they tended to be only in one area of the assembly floor. Ron had been keeping an eye on the situation for two weeks. The two employees had been moved into the "A" area, but it was clear to him that they were still doing "B" work. The supervisor had said that they were helping out on some of the "B" work in which the unit had fallen behind.

The time had come to make a decision on all six requests for class upgrading. Ten working days were allowed for investigation by the analyst. Ron decided to go over and talk to Dick Perry, general supervisor of both units.

Ron. Mr. Perry, I'd like to talk to you about these classification changes.

Perry. What's to talk about? I signed them, didn't I?

Ron. Well, if you get too many more "A" classifications than you have "A" work for, some of them are going to be working on "B" work all the time. That could cause some problems. Some of the other "B" people may think that they should have the "A" classification too—you know how aggressive the shop stewards are. We could end up with a bunch of grievances. This is especially true for the girls in Electrical Assembly. I'd like to see them put on some "A" work for a few weeks before they are considered for the classification. That's company policy.

Perry. Dammit! Don't quote me company policy! Was there any question in your mind that I was running this department when you used to work for me?

Ron. No.

Perry. Well, I'm *still* running it—not Wage and Salary. I promote whoever I please, whenever I please. I know my supervisors, and they know their people and what they're doing. I'm not going to stand for your questioning their judgment. I'm not afraid of the union either. I know the Head of Industrial Relations, "Red" Folsom, personally, and I'll just go to see him about this.

Ron. Well, if you know him personally, I sure can't stop you from talking to him. I just hope he realizes that I'm trying to do my job.

Saying that, Ron snatched up the request forms and left Perry's office. At his first opportunity, he went into Hardy's office to explain what had happened. He expected Hardy to close the door. But Hardy just said, "Well, if that's where you think he was headed, you might start gathering up your personal belongings and putting them in a cardboard box. I hope not. I have a meeting with 'Red' this afternoon and then we'll know."

Ron heard no more about it that day. When three days had passed, he figured that maybe he had passed the crisis. Then, in walked the labor relations specialist who told him that three grievances had been filed from units in Ron's area: one from Final Assembly, and the two from Electrical Harness. Ron thought, "What now?! What kind of support will I get from Perry? Will he help kill them at the first step? If they get further, losing a grievance could only be bad news for a new analyst."

As matters turned out, Perry was able to kill the Final Assembly grievance at the first step. Grievances for the two female employees went to a 3rd step hearing. In this hearing, the labor relations specialist gave one of the women a blueprint to interpret. She started to cry, and the company agreed to keep both employees in the "A" area, but they were to be given "A" classification only after a six weeks' training program.

Ron still had his job. He hadn't received a closed door session from Hardy, who let him know anyway that he didn't think that the situation had been handled very smoothly. Hardy hoped that Ron had learned something from it. Ron guessed he had learned something, but he wasn't sure what. In retrospect, he wondered if he shouldn't have gotten an engineering, rather than business, degree.

THE CASE OF THE UNWANTED EMPLOYEE

The Arrow Spring Company manufactures springs, wire parts, and metal stampings to meet customer specifications. It is a medium-sized company in its field and employs approximately 175 men and women. The company was established by the present owners just prior to World War II, and many of the employees have been with the firm since its inception. Mr. Miller, a brother-in-law of one of the two owners, is general manager and has managed the plant for the last several years since the owners retired from active participation in management.

The Arrow Company has always stressed the "one big family" philosophy in its approach to personnel management. Many of the workers are related to one another and some to the owners. A union represents the employees, but it is neither strong nor militant. Turnover is low. Much of the work is of the unskilled and semiskilled variety. The plant is located in a district heavily populated by blacks, but the only jobs in the company filled by blacks are janitorial in nature.

In 1960, the owners and Mr. Miller decided to open a branch plant in the northern part of the state. A capable man was selected from the sales staff of the parent organization to head the new plant. In getting together his initial staff, he hired two men away from a competing firm in the city where Arrow is located. One was a black named Scott, and it was rumored that he had to be taken in order to get the other man, who was not black. This was claimed by the competing firm who lost the two men. Immediately after the two men were hired and began work for Arrow, the second man quit and returned to his former company, with no apparent explanation. Scott remained and was placed in the company, awaiting completion of the northern plant.

The particular department to which Scott was assigned occupied half of a 70-foot-long room. The area had more people than any other similar space in the plant. Many women were doing small handwork in this department. Scott's job was to aid the department head and setup man in getting machines ready for work as well as doing some of the more difficult skilled work.

The plant superintendent had told all the department heads, including Mr. Yancy, who headed the department next to the one where Scott was located, that Scott was going up north and would be in the home plant only three or four weeks. There was no complaint at the time, as it was realized that the situation was temporary.

As the northern plant neared completion, one of the owners suddenly decided that he wished to get back to active work and take over the new plant. This was a surprise to all but had to be accepted. Shortly after, he selected his own general manager, a decision which relegated the previous selection to the position of northern sales manager. The latter resigned immediately.

While the above events were occurring, Scott had proven himself to be a good worker and very capable. But as the three weeks grew to six, so grew the resentment in the plant. Yancy was especially bitter. He had been an employee for twenty years, knew the owners very well, and was one of the best men in the state in his special work of spring manufacture. He was pleasant and well liked by all employees. Everybody knew him, and he was a close friend of many of the older personnel. Yancy, however, was intolerant of blacks. He got along quite well with the black janitors, but he rejected any attempt by a member of that group to presume himself equal to him. Yancy had been reared in the Deep South. He never insulted Scott or even said much about Scott to the other employees. But he resented being in the same area with him and using the same drinking fountain and washroom. He put up with the situation for approximately six weeks until he learned that Scott would not go north because of the change in management of the northern plant. Then Yancy told the plant superintendent that if Scott was not removed from the plant in three days, he wanted to be fired. This was not said in a loud or violent manner, but quietly and definitely.

The plant superintendent did not care to discriminate against or be intolerant of any race, but he valued the work of Yancy quite highly. When in three days Scott had not left, Yancy asked to be fired. The superintendent refused, whereupon Yancy submitted his resignation. The superintendent told him that his resignation would be considered to be a leave of absence and that he could return at any time he wanted. Yancy said he would never come back until Scott was removed.

The general feeling in the plant was rather mixed before Yancy's action. Most workers were apathetic since they did not come into contact with Scott very much. Those who objected did so mildly among themselves. There were no harsh words spoken to Scott. The general manager remained in the background, saying nothing on the subject except to the plant superintendent. They both had followed the "no blacks" rule in the past, not because of any personal intolerance but rather because of the family feeling among the employees. Now that by accident they had Scott, neither felt justified in discriminating against him. They were in the middle and tried to wait things out, hoping that Scott could be taken up north or that Yancy would not quit. They missed on both counts.

Word sped quickly through the plant when Yancy quit, and everyone was shocked, from management to the most unskilled worker. The many who had never even noticed Scott before were suddenly aware of the problem that had arisen. Why should a new employee, relatively unskilled compared with Yancy, be kept and Yancy be allowed to go? The head of the family was disowning a popular son and bringing in a stranger who could never really be one of the family because of his race. Sentiment in the plant was first, pro-Yancy, second, anti-Scott, and third, anti-black.

Yancy did not take another position and waited for the general manager's decision. The union, though Scott was a member, did not enter into the problem at any point. All of the shop stewards were outwardly pro-Yancy. The owners did not express their sentiments and made no comment, with the exception of a statement that Scott would not be taken to the northern plant.

PART SEVEN

MAINTENANCE

The final function in personnel operations is to maintain that which has been established, that is, an effective work force with the ability and the willingness to perform the tasks necessary to accomplish organization objectives. Maintenance would naturally encompass a continuation of all operative functions discussed thus far. But, in addition, special attention should be devoted to maintaining the employee's physical and mental health (Chap. 24) as well as desired attitudes toward the job and the organization (Chap. 25). And finally, personnel research (Chap. 26) is an absolute necessity for advancing as well as maintaining the art of personnel management.

TWENTY-FOUR
SAFETY AND HEALTH

In the sequence of personnel operative functions established as the outline for this text, we now come to a consideration of the maintenance function. Thus far, we have procured personnel, developed their abilities to perform, provided for adequate and equitable compensation, and integrated individual and group interests with organizational objectives. It would seem that we now have what we want: sufficient personnel who are able and willing to do the work of the organization. There remains, however, the function of maintaining what has been established; that is, we wish to maintain the abilities and attitudes requisite for organizational effectiveness. This would, of course, imply a continuation of all activities discussed thus far. But, in addition, there are other activities which serve specifically to maintain the abilities and attitudes of our personnel. Health and safety programs, for example, serve to maintain their physical condition, while employee service programs of various types assist in maintaining desired attitudes. In this chapter, we propose to examine the nature and significance of company safety and health programs. Though the head of a safety and health unit is often an engineer, it is typically placed within the personnel department since people are the major component in most accident situations. As will be pointed out later, people-caused accidents outnumber the technically caused four to one. In addition, the increased concern with preservation of the mental health of employees would also dictate that a safety and health unit be closely associated with a personnel department.

BACKGROUND OF SAFETY AND HEALTH PROGRAMS

The modern safety movement is believed to have started around 1912 with the First Cooperative Safety Congress and the organization of the National Safety Council. Just prior to this time, in 1906, the Massachusetts Board of Health had started the industrial health movement by appointing health officers to inspect factories, workshops, schools, and tenements. The early movement was interested primarily in acquainting the general public with the fact that there existed in business a high incidence of industrially caused accidents and diseases. From 1912 to 1968, remarkable advances were made in reducing the rate and severity of such accidents and diseases. In recent years, as indicated by Figure 24-1, the curves have begun to rise slightly. The National Safety Council estimates an annual industrial death toll of 14,000, with disabling injuries approximating 2.2 million.[1] The Occupational Safety and Health Administration estimates that there may be 100,000 "hidden" deaths each year caused by exposure to such substances as asbestos, lead, silica, carbon monoxide, and cotton dust. It is apparent that we are not fully aware of the potential impact of modern technology upon the health of our work force.

There were several reasons for the considerable progress in the field of safety during the 1912–1968 period. Some attributed such improvements to the humanitarianism of business. Preserving human life is an objective which requires no explanation. However, it is significant that little planned and constructive attention had been directed to the problem prior to 1912. Did industry suddenly become humanitarian in the twentieth century? One must conclude that economics had much to do with the safety movement. It was about this time that state workers' compensation laws were passed, which imposed financial responsibility upon the employer to compensate personnel injured on the job as well as to pay for the expenses of hospitalization. The first state workers' compensation law was passed in 1911. These laws will be discussed in a later section. It was also about this time that the National Safety Council began its campaign of educating employers in regard to the hidden and indirect costs of an accident. Thus the employer became acutely aware of the direct and indirect expenses of operating an unsafe plant. This is one area in which there is an obvious integration of employee-employer interests; the employee does not want to be injured and the employer does not wish to incur the costs of injuring him or her.

---

[1]Fred K. Foulkes, "Learning to Live with OSHA," *Harvard Business Review*, vol. 51, no. 6, November–December 1973, p. 58.

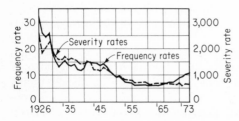

Source: National Safety Council, *Accident Facts*, 1973 ed., p. 28.

Figure 24-1   Accident rates, 1926–1973
Note: The injury frequency rate of NSC reporters declined rapidly to 1932, increased in World War II, then reached a low in 1961. The 69 percent increase to 10.55 in 1973 from the 6.26 average of 1962–1964 was partly due to changes in reporters and industry representation.

The severity rate followed a similar pattern. The 1973 decline of 5 percent from 1962–1964 was not affected by changes in industry representation.

COSTS OF AN ACCIDENT

Under workers' compensation laws, there is an immediate cost of an accident, namely, the insurance premium paid to cover the employer's financial liability for medical and compensation benefits for the injured. On the average, these premiums cost about 1 percent of the total payroll. An employer who has to write a check for these premiums and knows that they can be reduced by preventing accidents becomes acutely aware of the out-of-pocket cost of the accident. The experience of a plant of the Olin Mathieson Chemical Corporation provides a case in point. The composite premium rate for North Carolina companies from 1953 to 1959 was approximately $1 per $100 of payroll. After the introduction of a comprehensive and systematic safety program, the cost to the Olin Mathieson plant in this state for the same period was 50 cents per $100 of payroll.[2]

If all other accompanying costs of an accident can be labeled indirect, it is estimated that these costs are four times as great as the out-of-pocket costs of the insurance premiums and suit settlements. Among the indirect costs identified by the National Safety Council are the following: [3]

1 *Costs of damage to equipment, materials, and plant.* Many accidents entail considerable damage to physical property. Such costs are more evident to the employer than many of those that follow.

2 *Costs of wages paid for time lost by workers not injured.* No accident has yet occurred after which other people did not stand around, watch, and discuss the details. When this happens during working hours, the employer is absorbing wages paid for which there is no production. Besides, if the accident results in the death of a fellow employee, there is usually a considerable loss in production because of the lowering of employee morale.

3 *Costs of wages paid to the injured employee.* Technically, the employer owes no wages to the employee who is injured, since she or he is no longer working and future compensation comes from the insurance company under workers' compensation laws. Most states require a waiting period of one week before compensation can be paid, and some employers continue the injured employee's wage during this time. A survey of 427 companies revealed that 14 percent provided some type of supplementary pay to legally authorized workers' compensation payments.[4] At the very least, the employee is paid for the remainder of the workday during which he or she was injured.

4 *Costs of supervisors and staff in investigating, recording, and reporting.* One part of a constructive safety program is concerned with the effort to make people learn from mistakes. Each accident is an opportunity to learn, in order that similar ones may be prevented in the future. Obviously a large amount of paper work must be undertaken to provide records for management, the state industrial commission, the National Safety Council, and, most recently, the Occupational Safety and Health Administration of the federal government.

5 *Costs of replacing the injured employee.* If the employee is severely injured and

---

[2]N. H. Collisson, "Management and an Occupational Health Program," *Archives of Environmental Health*, February 1961, p. 119.

[3]See National Safety Council, *Accident Prevention Manual*, 4th ed., National Safety Council, Chicago, 1959, pp. 10–10 to 10–16.

[4]National Industrial Conference Board, *Personnel Practices in Factory and Office: Manufacturing*, Studies in Personnel Policy, no. 194, New York, 1964, p. 109.

must be permanently replaced on the job, the company will incur all of the many costs of labor turnover. If she or he does return to the job, the company has the costs of (1) adjusting during the absence and (2) decreased production from the employee immediately after returning. Most people are "gun-shy" after suffering an accident, and a certain adjustment period usually follows a return to work.

6 *Miscellaneous costs.* Other costs are even less apparent than those listed above. Among them are (1) any overtime caused by the accident, (2) any loss of profits due to canceled orders resulting from the delay in normal work procedures, and (3) the costs of maintaining a first-aid dispensary for accidents that do not technically result in lost work time.

The reason for the 4 to 1 ratio of indirect to out-of-pocket costs of accidents should now be apparent. As employers become fully educated in regard to the true costs of an accident, they become more concerned with its prevention.

ACCIDENT CAUSES

Most students of safety are convinced that accidents do not just happen. An accident is an unplanned incident, and for each such incident there is usually a specific cause or causes if one could but discover them. In passing, it is important to note that an accident does not have to result in injury to a person or damage to property to be called an accident. Where damage or injury does not result, it is often termed a "near accident." The manager who ignores near accidents and is concerned with only those unplanned incidents that result in damage or injury is shortsighted indeed.

The causes of accidents can be separated into two categories, technical and human. Technical causes are connected with deficiencies in plant, equipment, tools, materials, and the general work environment. The elimination of these causes is effected largely through engineering. Human causes are connected with deficiencies in the individual, such as improper attitudes, carelessness, recklessness, inability to perform the job, daydreaming, alcoholism, and the use of drugs on the job. It is estimated that there are four accidents caused by human deficiencies to every one that is caused by technical or mechanical defects. Thus a safety program must concentrate more on the personnel aspects than it does on the technical. It is impossible to create a completely safe plant where no one could possibly injure himself or herself.

Among the technical causes of accidents are improper lighting, poor machine guarding, and excessive noise. Some studies have shown that all types of materials handling are the source of the greatest number of technically caused injuries in industry. Poor housekeeping, lack of color contrasts, and inadequate ventilation have also led to accidents or industrial diseases. Certainly engineering is an essential phase of a comprehensive safety program, as is indicated by the fact that most safety experts are called "safety engineers."

There is an increasing appreciation in industry of the importance of the human factor in accidents. Accident-prone individuals are the cause of a large proportion of the total number of accidents. Some researchers attribute much of this proneness to defective human personality. Some studies have shown accident repeaters to be impulsive and irresponsible people who are compelled toward accidents. Others attribute accident proneness to physiological deficiencies, such as poor reaction times and inadequate muscular coordination. Undoubtedly accident repetition comes from both causes. In recent years it has been observed that some people are accident-prone for a time and then seem to get over it, with a consequent radical reduction in the accident rate. It has been noted that although a few accident-prone people are responsible for a large share of the accidents in a short period of time, the membership of this group will change.[5] Thus, it is doubtful that any person is born accident-prone with little hope for improvement. The solution to this problem is not one of dismissing the accident-prone individual, though the effect on the total accident rate of the company makes this action very attractive to many managers. The obvious answer of transferring to safer jobs is sometimes successful. The exclusion of an accident-prone person from the organization through an effective selection procedure is also a possibility. It must be noted, however, that no valid test of accident proneness has yet been developed.

The accident-prone individual is only one human cause of accidents. Some managements have discovered a direct relationship between accident frequency and seniority, the longer-service personnel having the fewer accidents. Others have discovered a relation between the type of motivation employed by management and the frequency of accidents; the tension caused by driving, negative supervisors tends to increase the likelihood of accidents. Certainly there are many accidents caused by horseplay, carelessness, exhibitionism, alcoholism, boredom, and fatigue. The manager who is concerned with safety must be fully aware of the nature and importance of the human factor in the causing of accidents.

MEASURES OF ACCIDENTS

In order that management may become aware of progress or lack of progress in the field of accident prevention, it is important to establish some type of measure. If the same measure is used by other companies, it is possible to determine whether or not one is competitive with other firms in the industry. The two measures of frequency and severity, established by the National Safety Council, are very widely recognized and followed in business. The frequency rate is the number of lost-time accidents per million man-hours worked. The severity rate is the number of days lost because of accidents per million man-hours worked. Expressed as a formula, the frequency rate is

$$\frac{\text{Number of lost-time accidents} \times 1,000,000}{\text{Number of employee-hours worked during period}}$$

The severity rate can be expressed as

$$\frac{\text{Number of employee-days lost} \times 1,000,000}{\text{Number of employee-hours worked during period}}$$

These measures of accidents are arbitrary, but so long as all firms use the same indexes, the results are valuable. Figure 24-2 shows the injury rates for various industries in 1973. On the average, all industries had 10.55 lost-time accidents per million employee-hours worked, resulting in an average loss of 654 employee-days per million employee-hours worked.

[5]Wayne K. Kirchner, "The Fallacy of Accident Proneness," *Personnel*, November–December 1961, pp. 34–37.

The new program instituted under the Occupational Safety and Health Act of 1970, to be discussed in a later section, has inaugurated a new set of measures for the 5 million business establishments covered by the law. Injuries and illnesses to be counted include (1) fatalities, (2) cases involving lost workdays, and (3) cases involving no lost workdays but necessitating action beyond immediate first aid, e.g., transfer to another job. The measurement base for all these injuries and illnesses is 100 full-time employees, as depicted in the following formula:

$$\frac{N}{H} \times 200,000$$

N stands for the number of injuries and illnesses; H for the total hours worked by all employees during the year; and 200,000 is the hours that 100 employees will work during the year, assuming a forty-hour week and fifty weeks.

With OSHA measurement, there were 10.9 recordable injuries and illnesses per 100 full-time workers during 1972, the lowest being 2.5 in finance, insurance, and real estate firms and the highest being 19.0 in construction. Instead of a severity rate, the measure is the average workdays lost per "lost-day case." In both construction and manufacturing, the 1972 figure was fifteen days. The average rate for the private nonfarm sector was fourteen days.

WORKERS' COMPENSATION LAWS

Prior to the twentieth century, industrial organizations were liable for damages for industrial accidents only to the degree that their liability could be proved in court. The injured employee was required to sue the employer for damages. In these suits the employer could use three common-law defenses: (1) contributory negligence, (2) the fellow servant rule, and (3) the assumption of risk. If employers could prove that the employee was partially at fault or that another employee had contributed to the accident, they could escape liability. If both of these first two defenses failed, one could argue that the employee had been informed of the dangers in the job and had indicated willingness to assume the risk.

Under the above existing conditions, the injured employee was not likely to win very many damage suits. In the early part of the twentieth century, several state workers' compensation statutes were passed. United States Supreme Court approval of such laws in 1917 served to stimulate the rest of the states to pass similar legislation. At present, all fifty states have workers' compensation laws.

Under the philosophy of workers' compensation laws, the employer is financially liable for all accidents arising out of, and in the course of, employment, regardless of whether or not the employee was specifically at fault. The employer insures against this risk with either a private or a state insurance agency. Approximately 80 percent of all firms are insured with private insurance companies. Large employers may have the option of insuring themselves. It must be noted that there are fifty different state laws and that exact provisions will differ markedly from state to state. Many states provide for some incentive to reduce accidents through schedule and experience rating. *Schedule rating* is a means of obtaining reduced premiums through the establishment and

Figure 24-2 Frequency and severity rates, 1973

Frequency Rate *disabling injuries* *per 1,000,000 person-hours*		Severity Rate *time charges (days)* *per 1,000,000 person-hours*	
Automobile	1.60	(24)*110	Storage & warehousing
Aerospace	2.22	(46)117	Electrical equipment
Electrical equipment	2.52	(31)156	Communications
Textile	4.09	(110)176	Automobile
Chemical	4.25	(27)275	Wholesale & retail trade
Steel	4.45	(76)311	Textile
Storage & warehousing	4.66	(147)326	Aerospace
Communications	5.00	(57)331	Machinery
Machinery	5.81	(93)397	Chemical
Sheet metal products	6.19	(34)404	Tobacco
Federal civilian employees	6.54†	(60)417	Rubber & plastics
Petroleum	6.73	(17)457	Air transport
Electric utilities	6.93	(77)475	Sheet metal products
Rubber & plastics	7.00	(30)488	Leather
Shipbuilding	7.08	(45)490	Printing & publishing
Fertilizer	7.89	(41)491	Glass
Gas	8.17	(66)540	Gas
Cement	9.11	(141)626	Steel
Nonferrous metals & prod.	9.31	(96)630‡	Federal civilian employees
Mining, surface	9.75†	(41)638	Food
Pulp & paper	9.78	(92)653	Shipbuilding
Wholesale & retail trade	10.22	(62)654	All industries
All industries	10.55	(24)671	Meat packing
Printing & publishing	10.83	(103)690	Petroleum
Glass	11.84	(76)712	Nonferrous metals & prod.
Tobacco	12.03	(75)736	Pulp & paper
Foundry	12.70	(59)747	Foundry
Iron & steel products	13.43	(61)822	Iron & steel products
Construction	13.59	(32)877	Transit
Marine transportation	14.08	(67)978	Wood products
Railroad equipment	14.23	(151)1,047	Electric utilities
Wood products	14.62	(62)1,131	Clay & mineral products
Food	15.70	(144)1,308	Cement
Leather	16.11	(95)1,335	Marine transportation
Quarry	17.67†	(96)1,361	Railroad equipment
Clay & mineral products	18.34	(140)1,365	Mining, surface
Lumber	21.11	(68)1,432	Lumber
Mining, undgrd., except coal	25.26†	(114)1,544	Construction
Air transport	26.99	(200)1,578	Fertilizer
Meat packing	27.51	(103)1,825†	Quarry
Transit	27.60	(175)4,431†	Mining, undgrd., except coal
Mining, underground coal	35.44†	(145)5,154†	Mining, underground coal

*Figures in parentheses show average days charged per case

† 1972

‡ 1969

Rates compiled in accordance with the American National Standard Method of Recording and Measuring. Work Injury Experience, ANSI Standard Z16.1–1973 (R-1967).

Source: National Safety Council, *Accident Facts*, 1974 ed., p. 26.

maintenance of a safe physical plant. *Experience rating* is a means of obtaining reduced premiums through having a low accident record.

The benefits to injured employees are of two types, substitute compensation for regular pay and medical benefits. Most laws specify that only one-half to two-thirds of the average wage will be paid as a substitute for regular compensation. However, many states have maximum limitations that result in employees receiving less than one-half of the average wage normally received. As in the case of unemployment benefits, there is some indication of a movement toward a percentage limitation with reference to the state's average weekly wage. The National Commission on State Workers' Compensation Laws recommends establishment of 100 percent of the state's average weekly wage for those on temporary disabilities and 66 $2/3$ percent for those on permanent total disabilities. Only a few states have met these high standards. States also place dollar limitations on medical benefits, particularly in such areas as facial disfigurement, furnishing artificial appliances, and rehabilitation retraining.

Payments in the various states also vary according to the duration of the disability. There are four main types of injuries. *Temporary total* disabilities, which constitute approximately 95 percent of all injuries, occur when employees are totally off the job for a restricted number of days. Usually they are compensated for this full time, less the one-week waiting period. A *permanent total* disability occurs when the employee lives but will never work again. Many states provide compensation in this instance for life, but some restrict duration to 300 to 700 weeks. A *permanent partial* disability occurs when the employee is permanently disabled but can return to work. Examples of such injuries are loss of an eye, arm, leg, or toe. Most of the laws establish a specific schedule of benefits for each specific injury without respect to occupation. There is little consistency among the states in this regard. The loss of an arm in Wyoming is valued at $6,800; losing the same arm in Pennsylvania would merit one $38,540.[6] The final type of injury is *death*. Permanent partial injuries constitute about 4 percent of injuries, permanent totals less than $1/10$ of 1 percent, and deaths about $9/10$ of 1 percent.

The workers' compensation law is usually administered by a state industrial commission, which investigates and makes the injury award. An injured employee who feels that he or she has received improper treatment by the commission has the option of appealing to the courts. The overwhelming majority, however, accept the commission's decision.

The philosophy of these laws has thus far been to compensate personnel for loss of wages sustained as a result of an industrially caused injury. Recent cases concerning loss of hearing have altered this philosophy to some extent. Some employees have received compensation for injury to hearing even though their earning capacity was never impaired and no wages were lost. Bethlehem Steel Corporation, for example, settled some $5 million in damage suits for $328,500; needless to say, this company has developed one of the more advanced noise abatement programs in industry. Many companies also began to add a hearing test to the hiring procedure as a defensive measure to prevent claims for hearing losses that did not result from employment in the hiring company.

Another type of injury with which we must be concerned in the future is an injury resulting from exposure to radiation hazards. Thus far, because of the care of the Atomic Energy Committee installations, such exposures have been few. It is anticipated that these will increase in the future as we have greater applications of atomic energy to industry and the utilization of more hazardous material. The number of potentially

---

[6]Jonathan R. Laing, "Payments to Workers Disabled on the Job Seem Certain to Rise," *Wall Street Journal*, Feb. 25, 1974, p. 1.

exposed workers is rapidly increasing. A major difficulty with these radiation injuries is that they often lie latent from seven to fifty years. Bone tumors, skin cancers, and lung cancers may arise years after exposure and years after the worker has left the job and the company.

Finally, the largest cloud on the workers' compensation horizon is the increasing likelihood that industry will be asked to underwrite the costs of emotional breakdowns issuing from job stresses. Since these injuries are not covered by existing legislation, employees turn to state courts to ask for compensation. In some instances the courts have denied compensation: an elevator operator suffered a neurotic reaction as a result of spending a half-hour in an elevator with a dying man, but his claim was turned down. However, the trend is in the other direction. A Texas ironworker was awarded compensation for psychoneurotic reactions that prevented his continued employment as an ironworker after seeing a buddy plunge to his death.[7] And in a more far-reaching decision, a Michigan court held that compensation was due an assembly-line machine operator who was unable to keep up with the speed of the line. He was criticized by his supervisor, suffered a mental breakdown, and was awarded workers' compensation under a temporary disability classification. It appears that the trend is in the direction of making an employer responsible for any and all human ills that may arise out of employment. Just as the past approach emphasizing physical injuries stimulated a marked and steady reduction in accident frequency and severity rates, a move toward compensation for emotional breakdowns issuing from employment may well stimulate a management effort to reduce mental stresses on the job.

OCCUPATIONAL SAFETY AND HEALTH ACT

Because of rising social concern with respect to industrial accidents and injuries, a far-reaching and revolutionary piece of federal legislation was passed in 1970—the Occupational Safety and Health Act. Basically, the approach is one of setting comprehensive and specific standards, governmental policing of company practices and workplaces, and enforcement through citations, fines, and other penalties. Just as a traffic police officer can inspect traffic flow at random and issue citations for violations, the OSHA compliance officer can inspect industrial businesses at random and issue a "ticket" on the spot.

The act covers approximately 60 million employees working for 5 million establishments. It applies to firms engaged in interstate commerce having one or more employees. Standards governing physical conditions and work practices are published in a voluminous *Federal Register*. Many are taken from existing organizations, such as the National Fire Protection Association, while others are developed through research by the newly formed National Institute for Occupational Safety and Health located in the Department of Health, Education, and Welfare. Standards are set for such items as minimum allowable exposure to health hazards (noise, sulphur dioxide, asbestos, cotton dust, etc.), as well as for plant conditions that present injury hazards (guards, rails, ladders, etc.).

[7]"Workmen's Compensation and New Job Hazards," *Monthly Labor Review*, vol. 91, no. 4, April 1968, pp. iii and iv.

Enforcement of these standards lies in the hands of the Occupational Safety and Health Administration located in the Department of Labor. States that submit qualified programs can take over administration of them, receiving a federal grant equal to 50 percent of their costs. It is expected that some thirty states will qualify by 1975. With respect to inspections, the compliance officer is not permitted to give advance notice of his or her arrival at the work site. Representatives of both employees and employers will accompany the officer on the "walkaround" inspection. Employer discrimination against the employee-chosen representative is prohibited, but the company is not required to pay for time expended during the inspection. When citations for violations are issued, the employer may appeal within fifteen days to a Review Commission and ultimately to the U.S. Circuit Court of Appeals. Thus far, only one out of four inspected employers has received a "clean bill of health." Total penalties amassed during the first two years amounted to over $10 million. Civil and criminal penalties authorized under the act are $10,000 and six months in prison. However, specific fines can be applied for each day of violation if not corrected.

Considering the number of firms as compared with the number of inspectors, the odds of receiving a random inspection are quite low thus far. OSHA is directing its attention first to five major target industries with high injury rates—roofing and sheet metal, meat processing, lumber and wood products, mobile homes and campers, and stevedoring. In addition, priority is given to inspecting in response to valid employee complaints; individual identification of the complainant to the employer is not required.

Thus, workers' compensation state laws and the federal OSHA program provide a double incentive to the employer. Workers' compensation uses the stimulus of lower insurance premiums, while OSHA emphasizes prevention of injuries and illnesses through unannounced inspections and monetary fines. Many feel that the major long-term impact of OSHA will be in the health, rather than accident, area.

THE SAFETY PROGRAM

Effective action in any field calls for advance planning. Once management's interest in safety has been stimulated, there remains the task of mapping out a program. Such a program can be most complex and varied in its attack, or it can be made very simple. Any particular safety program could be composed of one or more of the following elements:

1 Support by top management
2 Appointing a safety director
3 Engineering a safe plant and operation
4 Educating all employees to act safely
5 Accident analysis
6 Safety contests
7 Enforcing safety rules

Each of these procedures will be discussed briefly to indicate its relationship to the objective of preventing industrial accidents.

Support by top management

As in every other area, top management must lend a safety program its active support in order for it to survive and be effective. Management must give more than just lip service. The subject of safety and the protection of human life makes good material for public pronouncements and speeches before various social groups. Supervisors and superintendents are the first to know, however, whether or not top management really means what it says. Research in twenty-two firms revealed a strong relationship between top management support and reduced worker injuries.[8] Management support was characterized by personal attendance at safety meetings, periodic personal inspections, insistence on regular safety reports, and inclusion of safety figures and achievements on the agenda of the company's board of directors' meetings.

A safety director

To get any program off the ground, some one person must be given primary responsibility for its installation and maintenance. If the company is too small to justify staff differentiation of the function from the line, it is still important to assign some one person the additional duty of promoting the safety effort. Many have stated that safety is everybody's business, and so it is. But in organizational parlance, everybody's business often turns out to be nobody's business. The responsibility for pushing the safety effort should be centralized at some point, either line or staff.

In the larger firm, a staff safety director, often entitled a "safety engineer," is usually appointed. Such a person should be as much inclined toward the personnel approach as toward engineering. In some firms the relationship between the safety director and line employees is functionalized; that is, the director has the authority to issue and enforce orders in the functional field of safety. On the other hand, there is strong evidence that the greatest potential progress in safety lies in the area of education. Consequently, many safety directors prefer *not* to have functional authority so that they will not be tempted to use it. They view their job as largely one of education and positive motivation, and are inclined toward a deemphasis of its involvement with negative enforcement. A survey of 116 firms revealed that the impact of OSHA resulted in a substantial number (one-third) creating a new safety officer position; in two instances, they were allocated vice-presidential status.[9]

Engineering

Sound and forward-looking engineering must certainly be an essential requirement of any safety effort. Recognition of this fact is indicated through the schedule rating established by many state workers' compensation laws. Workplaces should be clean, well lighted, and properly ventilated. Mechanical devices for material handling should be provided. All dangerous equipment should be safeguarded insofar as possible. But, to illustrate again the inevitability of the human factor in engineering a safe plant, there

---

[8]Rollin H. Simonds, "OSHA Compliance: 'Safety is Good Business,'" *Personnel*, vol. 50, no. 4, July–August 1973, p. 35.

[9] Bureau of National Affairs, "Impact of OSHA on Personnel Management," *Bulletin to Management No. 1204*, American Society for Personnel Administration, Mar. 8, 1973, p. 1.

is probably no engineered safeguard that some employee cannot alter or circumvent if he or she gives sufficient thought to it. On punch presses, for example, two buttons are often provided, both of which must be hit simultaneously to permit the press to descend. This supposedly ensures that the worker will not get a hand caught by the press. It is not unusual to find that the employee has taped one button down so that she or he can work the press with one hand instead of two. Safety glasses are often required in departments involving metal working, but lenses have been removed from these glasses so that the employee appears to be wearing them but does not have to look through sweaty lenses. There can be no 100 percent safe plant as long as we have human beings to operate it. Safety precautions usually entail some delay or extra effort, and people are often prone to shortcut the engineered device. Engineering cannot be the sole or major approach to safety. The remaining two E's, education and enforcement, are essential to the completion of the safety equation.

In recent years increasing attention has been given to what has been termed "human engineering." Human engineering is "engineering for human use." It refers to the process of designing tools, materials, equipment, and workplaces in such a manner that they can be effectively operated by a human being, with all her or his limitations and abilities. The first objective of human engineering is to improve performance. This is naturally associated with motion study and work simplification. The second objective, however, is to protect the individual's physical and mental condition through making the work more comfortable, less fatiguing, and less hazardous. The psychologist, physiologist, and anthropologist contribute their knowledge of the capacities and limitations of people to the engineering function of design, and machines are constructed which can be safely and efficiently operated by the average person. Curiously enough, many mechanisms have been designed with little consideration given to the people who have to operate them. Some have been designed so that it was impossible for them to be operated according to specifications. In missile and aircraft design particularly, the development of a human factors staff group has been growing in recent years. Such groups, peopled largely by industrial psychologists and physiologists, must work right along with the design engineers long before the final design has been created.

Education

A large part of the safety program must be devoted to the process of educating the employee to act, think, and work safely. There are many avenues that this education can take, among which are the following:

1   Induction of new employees
2   Emphasis of safety points during training sessions, particularly in on-the-job training
3   Special efforts made by the first-level supervisor
4   Establishment of employee safety committees
5   Holding of special employee safety meetings
6   The use of the company periodical
7   Charts, posters, and displays emphasizing the need to act safely

Any or all of the above approaches can be used effectively. If safety is a major goal in an organization, the time to begin safety education is in the hiring process. Part of the induction procedure can be devoted to the safety policies and rules of the company. Certainly all training should be accompanied by warnings concerning dangerous points of job operations. Leadership is often by example, and the first-level supervisor must make concern for safety apparent through both word and deed.

The use of safety committees is highly effective in employee education because of the emphasis upon participation and responsibility. Such committees have, of course, operational objectives, which may include accident investigation and periodic safety inspections of the various company departments. It is significant to note, however, that personnel placed on such committees usually demonstrate a marked reduction in their own accident records. In addition, the committee member can exert a salutary influence on other employees. Receiving suggestions, aid, or advice from a colleague is often more effective than receiving them from a supervisor. The holding of regular safety meetings provides the basis for a reduction in workers' compensation insurance premiums in some states. It has been observed that companies holding such periodic educational sessions usually experience a reduction in their accident rate.

The National Safety Council has long advocated the use of films, posters, charts, and displays to bring various warnings and precautionary measures before employees. It is interesting to note how safety posters, for example, have changed over the years. Several decades ago, such posters were quite gory in effect, often showing human limbs flying in midair, blood gushing, and a considerable amount of human agony. Now the approach is often a light one. The employee is "kidded" into thinking about what he or she is doing and, as a result, remembers to operate in a safer manner. Displays, such as shattered safety goggles and crushed safety shoes, are often effective in emphasizing the possible results of industrial accidents. Needless to say, safety education is a continuous process, and the approach to the employee must be constant and varied.

Accident analysis

When an accident does happen, prevention thus having failed, management should take the opportunity to learn from this mistake. The accident should be studied in all of its aspects: the person, the job on which the accident occurred, the tools and equipment involved, the particular act, the department in which it happened, and the manner in which the employee was injured. Analysis should be undertaken with a view to future prevention. A study of environment and equipment may indicate need for engineering correction. A study of the person may indicate a case of accident proneness. A study of the department may show a high level of accident ratings issuing from faulty supervision. If possible, the various aspects of any accident should be categorized and company experience tabulated under these categories. Analysis of this record may show underlying causes which may not be apparent in any one accident.

Safety contests

Safety contests could be considered as one form of employee education, but they are sufficiently different in approach to merit separate discussion. There is a good deal of controversy over the merits of the safety contest. It usually happens that the accident level drops during the period of the contest, only to rise again after it has ended. This result is to be expected, since the contest prizes serve to stimulate great effort in the direction of accident prevention. It is to be hoped, however, that the habit of acting safely, gained during the contest period, will remain to some degree. Furthermore, it is to be hoped that the new accident level, though higher than during the contest, will be lower than in the precontest period.

There are various bases that can be established for a safety contest. Frequency and severity rates are rather obvious indexes around which a departmental contest can be arranged. It is necessary, however, to handicap certain departments whose physical working conditions are not in line with the rest of the plant. Other bases that can be used are the number of hours worked without a lost-time accident, attendance at safety meetings, good housekeeping, safety essays, and safety suggestions.

The incentive provided by some safety contests has led to abuses. Serious accidents have *not* been reported, and as a result inadequate medical attention has been received by the injured. The accident record becomes all-important, temporarily, and actual events are misrepresented in order that they may show up favorably on the record. Any minor injuries will certainly receive scant attention during the competition period. All incentive arrangements, from the profit system to safety contests, have in them the stimulus to undesirable as well as desirable action. But if, on balance, the good that is stimulated outweighs the ills accompanying the system, then the use of incentive arrangements is justified.

Enforcement

Undoubtedly the fundamental approach to a safety program must be positive in nature; but it is naïve to argue that disciplinary action has no place. Individuals differ, and for some only the negative approach will stimulate the desired behavior. Reprimands, fines, layoffs, and discharge have their proper place in an effective safety program. Principles and procedures governing the administering of disciplinary action have been discussed in Chapter 20.

THE HEALTH PROGRAM

The prevention of accidents is a major part of the function of employee maintenance, but constitutes only one segment of a comprehensive program. The employee's physical condition can be harmed through disease, stress, and strain as well as through accidents. It is important for the firm to be concerned with the general health, both physical and mental, of its employees for both economic and humanitarian reasons. Many state workers' compensation laws provide for compensation for specific occupational diseases. A major part of the OSHA effort is being directed toward prevention of illnesses issuing from the workplace environment. Particularly difficult problems have been highlighted in industries using asbestos, vinyl chloride, benzene, fiber glass, and silica. Moreover, poor employee health leads to a high level of absenteeism and a low level of productivity. The investment in training and organizational experience in key personnel should be protected by systematic and regular examinations of both personnel and plant. The employee also benefits materially from a company health program through losing fewer days of work and pay, working within more pleasant surroundings, and experiencing a lengthening of the number of years that he or she is able to work. The justification of a systematic health program is very much like that of a safety program.

Physical health

There is considerably more industrial activity in the field of safety than there is in the field of health. When health and medical programs are provided, it has been customary in too many firms to attach this function to the safety unit, as indicated in Figure 24-3. Too often the health portion of the program consists solely of a group of medical personnel, who administer physical examinations in the hiring process. The Occupational Health Institute would add to the placement physical examination the following requirements for a properly organized health program:[10]

1 A stated health and medical policy
2 The performance of periodic physical examinations on all employees exposed to health hazards
3 The availability of facilities for voluntary periodic physical examinations for all employees
4 A competent medical consulting staff
5 Systematic attention to sanitation, safety precautions, and industrial hygiene
6 A chief medical officer who reports to a responsible member of management
7 A well-equipped dispensary for emergency cases and physical examinations
8 Properly qualified medical and nursing personnel

With respect to periodic physical examinations, a survey of 426 firms revealed that slightly less than 30 percent provided for such examinations for operative employees.[11] Most indicated that such examinations were required for special groups such as older employees, handicapped workers, and those operating vehicles or in dangerous environments. It is more common to require periodic physical examinations of executives because of stresses issuing from such sources as overwork, conflicting obligations, too much responsibility, ambiguity of position, uncomfortable social roles,

[10]*Management Record*, July 1954, p. 268.
[11]NICB, op. cit., p. 117.

Figure 24-3 Organization of health and safety, 1

and insecurity.[12]   Often, such examinations are encouraged through the practice of combining them with a paid vacation at plush health resorts. There are also problems involving a conflict of interest for a physician who must preserve the confidence of the doctor-patient role and also report to management concerning the present and future fitness of the person for work. In most instances, however, there is a considerable amount of mutual interest between the person and the organization with respect to health.

It is apparent from the list of specifications laid down by the Occupational Health Institute that only the larger firms would qualify. In the above-cited survey of 426 companies, only 30 had full-time doctors in attendance, 211 had full-time nurses, 2 had psychiatrists, 4 provided full-time dentists, 1 an optometrist, 12 had industrial hygienists, and 90 provided full-time first-aid personnel.[13] The companies with comprehensive health programs are the large corporations; Du Pont, at one time, employed 90 full-time physicians, 150 nurses, 1 psychiatrist, and 50 industrial hygienists to service 110,000 employees.[14] However, the vast majority of companies that employ fewer than 500 workers have no in-plant health services. It must be emphasized that approximately two-thirds of the nation's labor force are employed in such plants.

In line with both an economic motivation and a social responsibility, the larger companies are undertaking a broader "whole person" approach toward industrial health. Some are studying the chronic diseases, such as cancer and heart trouble, and approaching them as a total complex or system involving both industrial and nonindustrial sources. In one company, it is estimated that nonoccupational illnesses account for more than 70 percent of its absenteeism. Payments in the form of sick leave or health fringe benefits may run ten times the amount expended under workers' compensation laws. It is maintained that environmental health must stem from *inside* industry, inasmuch as outside doctors cannot possibly know what goes on inside the plant. Though many maintain that generalized medical research is not industry's business, analysis could well suggest a profit-motivated base for such programs, along with an obligation in the social-responsibility area.

With respect to the field of industrial hygiene referred to in item 5 above, some firms have made an effort to elevate the hygienist to an organization position superior to that of the safety director. As indicated by Figure 24-4, he or she may be placed in a position coordinating safety and medical services. The reasons for this move are several. First, as actually practiced, safety is often backward-looking. The safety engineer learns through mistakes—accidents or diseases. It is quite typical for a serious accident to generate a tremendous amount of activity *after* the fact. The industrial hygienist is trained to adopt the preventive approach, to spot obvious and incipient dangers, and to request the appropriate specialty to eliminate those dangers. Secondly, a well-qualified industrial hygienist must undergo one or two years of college training in such subjects as physiology, psychology, air analysis, toxicology, and the radiological aspects of industrial health. He or she thus has the background that stimulates analysis and prevention of health and accident hazards.

The industrial hygienist usually analyzes health problems in terms of stress and

---

[12]Merrill T. Eaton, "Executive Stresses Do Exist—But They Can Be Controlled," *Personnel*, March–April 1963, pp. 8–18.
[13]NICB, op. cit., p. 136.
[14]"Industry Doctors Try New Approach," *Business Week*, May 13, 1967, p. 82.

Figure 24-4 Organization of health and safety, 2

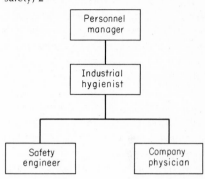

strains. The sources of occupational stress are four in number: chemical, physical, biological, and social. Occupational stresses result in certain strains being placed upon the human body and mind. The total strain is often greater than the sum of the individual stresses. When the stress is too great, the human body or mind breaks down. Thus, the emphasis is upon the elimination or control of the sources of occupational stress.

Measures for the prevention and control of occupational stress can be applied to the following: (1) the *source* of the stress, (2) the *media* of stress transmission, and (3) the *individual* subjected to the stress. In most health problems, research and correction should be applied in the order given. For example, the industrial hygienist has discovered a machining process that is throwing off a large volume of dustlike particles in the air. The first problem is to discover whether or not the process constitutes a health hazard. One must analyze the size of the particles to determine whether they are small enough to be breathed into the lungs or are large enough to cause them to be coughed out of the throat. One must analyze the rate of fallout of such particles in the various parts of the room. Assuming that a health hazard is found to exist, the first approach is to tackle the source. Too often firms have reversed the process and concentrated solely on the worker who has been protected to the degree that she or he may look like a creature from Mars with safety helmet, goggles, shoes, and special clothing. If the source of the stress can be eliminated, there is no need to restrict the movements and actions of the employee. It may be possible for the process to be changed or for people to be completely eliminated from the offending area. If there is no person, there is no stress on the person.

Failing the elimination of the source of stress, the next approach is to analyze the transmitting media. Can a baffle, screen, or some other type of protection be established to keep the particles away from the person? Can the air be washed and cleaned? The final step is that of protecting the worker. If neither the source nor the media can be corrected, the human being must be safeguarded. One may be forced to breathe through an oxygen mask.

All potential health hazards can be analyzed in this fashion. Stresses from noise, vibration, infrared rays, radiation, and fumes should be eliminated at the source. Failing this, the transmitting media should be controlled. And failing this, the person must be armored against the stress. As we indicated earlier, the modern industrial hygienist is becoming interested not only in the chemical, physical, and biological sources of stress, but also in the sociological sources. This would tend to place him or her in the field of human relations along with the psychologist and sociologist. The primary objective, however, is the reduction or elimination of stresses that will result in physical or mental damage to the human being.

Mental health

In recent years, an increasing amount of attention has been devoted to industrial mental health. It is difficult to determine how far a business firm should go in such matters as this. As indicated previously, various state court decisions are assigning liability to employers for emotional stresses engendered by employment.

The rationale for a company mental health program is the same as for programs designed to maintain physical health. In the first place, American business is responsible for creating many of the tensions and pressures of modern life, which in turn often lead to mental breakdowns. Secondly, mental difficulties of various types are reflected in the firm's productivity and profit records. Mental illness takes its toll through alcoholism, high accident rates, high tardiness rates, high labor turnover, and poor human relationships, which may be due to such attitudes as oversuspicion of one's associates and unusual sensitivity. Studies have shown that the emotionally ill have more accidents and safety violations, file more grievances, and are discharged more often than healthy workers. The threats of skill obsolescence created by industry's constant drive toward change can seriously affect the worker's sense of security and, in turn, the effectiveness of personal functioning on the job. And if the firm is truly interested in the physical health of employees, it must unavoidably be concerned with their mental outlook as well. The connection between mental and physical health has long been accepted by both physicians and psychiatrists.

Despite the logic of the above, mental health ranks third behind safety and physical health as an area in which private industrial managements expend resources. It will be recalled that the outstanding pioneering effort of Du Pont included ninety physicians but only one psychiatrist. When efforts have been made, as they have in Du Pont, Eastman Kodak, and Metropolitan Life Insurance Company, significant improvements have resulted. The fact that a company psychiatrist is on the premises will often result in visits, when a referral to someone across the street will often be ignored. If an employee-client cannot accept the fact that the company psychiatrist is not a "spy" for management, it will, of course, be best for outside referrals to be made.

The rehabilitation of the alcoholic employee is perhaps the best example of what private firms can do in regard to mental health programs. It is estimated that 5 to 10 percent of the national work force at all levels is affected by a drinking problem. One study indicates that the alcoholic employee was absent 19.4 days annually, as compared with 5.8 days for the nonalcoholic.[15] Because of this cost, plus those issuing from increased accidents and reduced efficiency, over fifty major corporations conduct rehabilitation programs in this field. Because of the alcoholic's overriding concern for job security, such programs are usually more effective than pleas of family and friends;

[15]Merrill T. Eaton, "Alcohol, Drugs, and Personnel Practices," *Personnel Journal*, vol. 50, no. 10, October 1971, p. 755.

some studies have shown recovery rates of between 65 and 85 percent, as compared with a general public recovery rate of 30 percent or less.[16]

Most of the successful alcoholic rehabilitation programs do *not* attempt to turn the immediate supervisor into a diagnostician. The supervisor concentrates upon worker behavior and makes no attempt to play psychologist. Just as a supervisor who observes a worker's shortness of breath would not offer a personal diagnosis of emphysema, neither should one suggest or even mention the word "alcoholism." The supervisor's role is one of performance observation and accurate record keeping. One should note changes in behavior such as marked fluctuations in work pace, changed patterns of attendance, increased number of warnings, new and "innovative" excuse patterns, and substantial declines in performance ratings. Such behavior triggers supervisory concern regardless of any specific possible reason. The recommended pattern in Hughes Aircraft Company requires that the supervisor discuss this undesirable performance pattern with the employee.[17] If the behavior changes, well and good. If not, the record is submitted to a counselor of the personnel unit. If deemed desirable, a meeting of all three—supervisor, employee, and counselor—is suggested to the employee. The worker is free to refuse and take a chance on ultimate discharge. If the idea is accepted and the meeting held, the supervisor presents the factual behavior and then departs. The counselor "lays it on the line" and suggests that discharge is imminent if performance is not improved. The hope is that the employee will volunteer the reason for the difficulty and ask for help. If it is the alcohol problem, she or he is retained on the payroll and referred to an appropriate outside agency, Alcoholics Anonymous or a hospital, for help in rehabilitation. The counselor follows the case for a year after referral to determine the extent of rehabilitation. Hughes estimates a success rate of 75 percent. Though most define the problem in terms of those who must be discharged, the greatest costs issue from those employees who are still in the early stages of the disease. In many instances, the gradual, creeping deterioration of performance efficiency takes ten to fifteen years to reach a level 25 percent below normal.

A related, but newer, problem is that of employee use of drugs on the job. In a study of 95 subjects in a drug rehabilitation center, ninety-one reported use of drugs while on the job, forty-eight reported they had sold drugs to other employees, and sixty-eight indicated forms of criminal behavior, including stealing materials, payroll forgery, etc.[18] That the problem does involve a significant portion of the work force is indicated by a survey of over seven million workers in the state of New York. Use of heroin was reported by 1.3 percent, of LSD by 2.6 percent, of methedrine by 2 percent, and of marijuana by 12 percent.

Though it would appear that the same approach could be taken to drug use as to alcoholism, fewer firms are willing to put forth a significant rehabilitation effort. Some claim that alcoholics do not proselyte for alcoholism; they can be helped while keeping them on the job. The drug user often wants to share his or her discovered escape route from the world with other workers. In addition, users may have to sell drugs to finance their personal habit. It is also suspected that the management does not understand the

---

[16]Wilbur J. Cohen, "Revolution in Mental Health," *Personnel Administration*, vol. 32, no. 2, March–April 1969, p. 7.

[17]"Business Dries Up Its Alcoholics," *Business Week*, Nov. 11, 1972, p. 169.

[18]Jerome Siegel and Eric H. Schaaf, "Corporate Responsiveness to the Drug Abuse Problem," *Personnel*, vol. 50, no. 6, November–December 1973, p. 9.

"drug culture" as well as the "alcohol culture." The typical alcoholic is older and has had longer service. The typical drug user is younger and has not built up a service record in the firm. Finally, many managements are discouraged with the low success rates of drug rehabilitation. In any event, the typical reaction to discovery of a drug user on the job is immediate discharge. Even the more humane managements will force an immediate leave of absence, with the right of return if successful rehabilitation is effected.

SUMMARY

The following comparison is perhaps a dangerous one to use in a "human relations era," but it nevertheless serves to summarize the essence of this chapter. An organization utilizes many factors to execute the work load. When a machine is purchased, it is selected and installed on the assumption that it fits the function to be performed. As the daily operations of the company take place, this machine is subjected to certain accidents and pressures and general wear and tear. The intelligent manager does not ignore the requirements for both preventive and curative maintenance. One hopes to preserve and extend the useful life of this machine.

It is to be hoped that the manager will take a similarly enlightened view toward another factor of business, the industrial employee. The worker is similarly selected and placed on a job, the performance of which makes an effective contribution toward company objectives. He or she is similarly subject to accidents, pressures, and general wear and tear. We maintain the machine because it is profitable to the organization to do so. We maintain the person, not only because it is profitable to the company to do so, but also because our care is humane and profitable to the person. With respect to physical injuries and occupational diseases, state workers' compensation laws require company responsibility and financial liability. The new standards and hosts of compliance officers from the Occupational Safety and Health Administration add the "police and penalize" approach to injury and illness reduction. The costs and disturbances of such laws are only a fraction of the true expense of ignoring employee physical and mental maintenance. Among the costs of an accidental physical injury are (1) damage to equipment, materials, and plant; (2) wages paid for time lost by workers not injured; (3) wages paid to the injured employee over and above those required by law; (4) investigation, recording, and reporting of the accident; (5) possible replacement of the injured employee; and (6) possible costs of overtime and lost orders. Among the costs of mental disturbances are (1) excessive number of accidents (and thus all of the preceding costs); (2) excessive absenteeism; (3) excessive labor turnover; and (4) excessive emotional costs for both the subject employee and all other personnel with whom she or he comes into contact.

Full realization of the economic and human costs of inadequate health and safety programs has led many organizations to undertake a more systematic approach to the effecting of personnel maintenance. Such programs can include one or more of the following elements:

I. Safety
    A. Top management support of special safety effort
    B. Appointing a safety director
    C. Engineering a safe plant and operation

    D. Educating all employees to act safely

    E. Accident analysis

    F. Safety contests

    G. Enforcing safety rules through disciplinary action

II. Health

    A. Physical

        1. Preplacement physical examinations

        2. Periodic physical examination for all key personnel

        3. Voluntary periodic physical examination for all personnel

        4. A well-equipped and staffed medical dispensary

        5. Availability of competent medical consultants

        6. Systematic and preventive attention devoted to industrial stresses and strains

        7. Periodic and systematic inspections of provisions for proper sanitation

    B. Mental

        1. Availability of psychiatric counseling

        2. Cooperation with outside psychiatric specialists and institutions

        3. Education of company personnel concerning the nature and importance of the mental health problem

        4. Development and maintenance of a proper human relations program

Over and above any economic costs, evading the maintenance responsibility will inevitably lead to increasing governmental interference and control of private company operations. The preservation of the physical and mental status of the nation's citizens is a social objective which transcends any company objective of producing economic goods, profits, wages, salaries, and the like.

DISCUSSION QUESTIONS

1 Compare and contrast the philosophies of the workers' compensation laws with the Occupational Safety and Health Act.

2 What are the rights of employees under the Occupational Safety and Health Act?

3 Compare and contrast the typical programs of dealing with the alcoholic with those established for dealing with the drug user.

4 Describe the role of the immediate supervisor in an advanced program of alcoholic rehabilitation.

5 Compare and contrast the measures of accidents proposed by the National Safety Council with those required by OSHA.

6 Rank the following in the order of private-industry concern and activity, indicating reasons therefor: (1) mental health, (2) safety, (3) physical health.

7 Outline the elements of a comprehensive educational program in the field of safety.

8 Contrast the industrial hygienist with the safety engineer as the head of the health and safety effort.

9 What is the nature and philosophy of workers' compensation laws?

10 Suppose that you have been designated to investigate an excessively high injury frequency rate in one department of the firm. Indicate how you would approach this research task.

SUPPLEMENTARY READING

COLLIER, Joe: "Federal Role in Job Safety and Health: Inspection and Enforcement at the Workplace," *Monthly Labor Review*, vol. 96, no. 8, August 1973, pp. 35–42.

FOULKES, Fred K.: "Learning to Live with OSHA," *Harvard Business Review*, vol. 51, no. 6, November–December 1973, pp. 57–67.

HOLLOMAN, Charles R.: "Mental Health on the Job: Whose Responsibility?" *Business Horizons*, vol. 16, no. 5, October 1973, pp. 73–80.

PARKER, Philip H.: "Washington State's Employee Alcoholism Program," *Public Personnel Management*, vol. 2, no. 3, May–June 1973, pp. 212–215.

SIEGEL, Jerome, and Eric H. Schaaf: "Corporate Responsiveness to the Drug Abuse Problem," *Personnel*, vol. 50, no. 6, November–December 1973, pp. 8–14.

SIMMONDS, Rollin H.: "OSHA Compliance: 'Safety Is Good Business,'" *Personnel,* vol. 50, no. 4, July–August 1973, pp. 30–38.

TWENTY-FIVE

EMPLOYEE BENEFITS

The maintenance function of personnel is concerned with preserving the physical and mental condition of employees, a condition that has been created or established by proper procurement, development, compensation, and integration and will be further maintained by the same means. But over and above this type of maintenance are activities devoted specifically to the preservation of employee health and attitudes. Health and safety programs, discussed in the preceding chapter, contribute to the maintenance of the employee's physical condition. Employee benefit programs, the subject of this chapter, contribute to the maintenance of employee morale. It can be said, of course, that these benefit programs serve to create and stimulate morale, and thus can be classified under the integration function. Obviously, there is some creation and stimulation in the maintenance function just as there is some maintenance in all other operative personnel functions. But the primary emphasis in employee benefit programs has been on maintaining an employee's favorable attitude toward the work and work environment. Clearly defined purposes and objectives are often lacking in the typical employee benefit program administered by private business firms.

There is some evidence to sustain the conclusion that employee benefit programs act more as maintenance factors than as motivators. It will be recalled that the research of Herzberg placed these programs in the maintenance category on the dissatisfaction to no-dissatisfaction continuum.[1] In another study of 550 white-collar employees, it was concluded that the average employee was aware of about one-half the benefit program features—this despite an unusually comprehensive and active program of communication with respect to employee benefits available.[2] One of this firm's most costly and widely publicized benefits, a disability wage plan, was essentially unheard of by 60

[1] See Chap. 17.
[2] Arthur A. Sloane and Edward W. Hodges, "What Workers Don't Know about Employee Benefits," *Personnel*, vol. 45, no. 6, November–December 1968, p. 32.

percent of those responding to the questionnaire. When asked if they felt that they knew enough about these programs, over three-quarters replied that they did. In a second study in another company, 249 new hires were queried concerning their knowledge of benefits explained during a comprehensive induction program.[3] A correlation between knowledge and attitudes toward the company's fringe benefit program proved to be quite low. The conclusion of the researchers was that an attempt to motivate employees through a fringe benefit program is probably futile.

Despite the absence of motivational effects, employee benefit programs make up a significant portion of most personnel department budgets. Currently, they approximate 30 percent of total payroll; predictions by experts of the Institute for the Future indicate that this will rise to 50 percent in 1985.[4] Clearly, the maintenance features of personnel programs consume the greater bulk of the monies available. Practical operational values to the employing organization may include attraction and maintenance of a work force in competition with other organizations, preservation of some degree of labor-management peace in collective bargaining arrangements, and maintenance of acceptable levels of general morale. Many observers are highly concerned with the markedly increased demands for hygiene and pain-avoidance measures as compared with a lesser concern for attitudes dealing with employee motivation to contribute to productivity. As indicated earlier, a few union leaders feel that we may have moved too far in the direction of increased benefits with too little concern for maintaining, if not increasing, the productivity from which these benefits are ultimately derived.

NATURE OF EMPLOYEE BENEFITS

Employee benefits are provided under a variety of titles in industry. Some refer to them as "service programs"; others characterize them as "non-wage" payments; still others emphasize the costs and label them "hidden payroll." Typically, they have been most often referred to as "fringe benefits." In the broadest sense, such "fringes" can be construed to include all expenditures designed to benefit employees over and above regular wages and direct monetary incentives related to output. As major categories, such benefits can include the following:

1 *Payment for time not worked.* Examples in this area would include paid rest periods, paid lunch periods, wash-up time, clothes-change time, get-ready time, vacations, holidays, sick leave, personal leave, voting time, and jury duty. There is seemingly no end to the innovative determination of new reasons for not working for pay. Perhaps the ultimate is a newly negotiated "to-hell-with-it" benefit: a certain number of days are provided for the occasion when the employee simply doesn't *feel* like going to work.
2 *Hazard protection.* There are a certain number of hazards that must be commonly faced by all. Income maintenance during these periods is the purpose of fringes

---

[3] James L. Sheard, "Relationship between Attitude and Knowledge in Employee Fringe Benefit Orientation," *Personnel Journal*, vol. 45, no. 10, November 1966, p. 616.

[4] T. J. Gordon and R. E. LeBleu, "Employee Benefits, 1970–1985," *Harvard Business Review*, vol. 48, no. 1, January–February 1970, p. 93.

designed to protect against the hazards of illness, injury, debt, unemployment, permanent disability, old age, and death. Pensions, protecting against loss of income after retirement, currently cost firms from 5 to 10 percent of annual payroll, an amount equal to about one-fourth of company profits. It is estimated that this single cost alone will ultimately rise to 20 to 30 percent of total pay.[5]

3   *Employee services.* All people must have certain services available on a continuing basis, e.g., housing, food, advice, recreation, etc. The trend toward the organization's providing such routine and ordinary services is exemplified by such fringe benefit programs as cafeterias, paid legal services, career counseling, educational tuition, aid in housing, medical services, low-cost loans, annual physical examinations, use of organization vehicles for personal reasons, day-care centers for children, and paid memberships in certain private organizations.

4   *Legally required payments.* Our society, through its government, has decreed that certain minimum levels of company expenditures will be made in the area of protecting employees against the major hazards of life. Thus, regardless of company policy, organizations covered by federal and state laws must pay for unemployment compensation, workers' compensation insurance, Old-Age and Survivor's Insurance under social security, and Medicare.

In view of the above discussions, it is little wonder that the term "fringe" is deemed no longer appropriate. In following changes in 146 companies, Foegen noted that the percentage of payroll allocated to employee benefits rose from 17.9 percent in 1949, to 25.6 percent in 1959, to 31.7 percent in 1969.[6] A report of the U.S. Chamber of Commerce indicated that the average worker received $3,230 in fringe benefits in 1973.[7] In manufacturing, the percentage of total payroll allocated to fringes ranged from 35.7 percent in petroleum to 23.6 percent in clothing. In nonmanufacturing, the range was from 35.6 in banking to 24.6 in retail department stores. Predictions for the future indicate greater expenditures and efforts in such fields as group purchasing of all types (e.g., group automobile insurance and legal services), longer vacations, no employee expense for major medical coverage, increased dental coverage, increased coverage for psychiatric difficulties, pension portability, cost-of-living adjustments of pensions after retirement, annual physical examinations, earlier retirement ages, and possible retraining when severed from the organization.[8] As suggested above, we appear to be limited only by our ingenuity; one firm provides a free jet flight anywhere in the world on the tenth anniversary of service with the firm.

After establishing a managerial philosophy and approach to the offering of employee benefits, we shall examine in more detail certain selected optional and required benefit programs. It is apparent that a complete coverage would be far beyond a text of this type. We will emphasize *economic programs* designed to protect against major hazards of life, *recreational programs* designed to improve the quality of life, and *facilitative services* designed to ease the ordinary routines of life.

[5]Donald G. Carlson, "Responding to the Pension Reform Law," *Harvard Business Review,* vol. 52, no. 6, November–December 1974, p. 144.

[6]J. H. Foegen, "Fringe on the Fringe," *Personnel Administration,* vol. 35, no. 1, January–February 1972, p. 18.

[7]"Tomorrow," *U.S. News and World Report,* Nov. 4, 1974, p. 8.

[8]T. J. Gordon and R. E. Lebleu, "Employee Benefits, 1970–1985," op. cit., pp. 96–101.

A PHILOSOPHY OF EMPLOYEE BENEFITS

The growth of employee benefits has been rampant, particularly since World War II, and apparently no end is in sight. Some managers are beginning to fear that instead of a governmental, socialistic welfare state, we are in the process of creating a private industrial welfare society. The role of the individual seems to be growing smaller and smaller.

There are a number of reasons behind the flourishing growth of employee benefits. It will be recalled that the period of the 1920s, labeled the "era of paternalism," saw a widespread adoption of such benefits as company housing and company stores. The paternalistic approach fell into disrepute, supposedly as a result of the employee's desire for "industrial adulthood." The Depression of the 1930s also served to eliminate many employer-financed services. Since World War II, we have entered the era of the "new paternalism." The services of the 1920s pale into insignificance when compared with those of the present. The attitudes of both employees and the general public toward service programs have changed considerably. The tremendous amount of social legislation of the 1930s, particularly the Social Security Act, has led many to believe that the private firm is morally responsible for the lives of its employees. It is no longer a service initiated by a fatherly, benevolent employer, but a requirement imposed by government, competition, or the labor union. Thus, we end up with the same or more benefits than in 1920, but they come by virtue of a new paternalistic philosophy, inasmuch as the employer is often *forced* into being paternal. The employee's life is being consumed by the company, but not always at the company's volition. The employee has been conditioned by the Depression, the government, and the union to demand and expect an unlimited number of services and benefits from the employer. In summary, the rapid growth of such programs can be traced to such sources as: (1) a changed employee attitude, (2) labor union demands, (3) governmental requirements, (4) competition that forces other employers to match benefits to attract and keep labor, and (5) periodic wage controls which freeze wages but permit the offering of services as a substitute for wage increases. High company income tax rates have also stimulated the offering of services, since they can be bought with cheap dollars.

What should be the philosophy of the manager in the realm of employee services? In a private-enterprise economy, the basic guiding principle should be that no employee benefit should be undertaken unless there is some return to the organization that is at least equal to its cost. This is not to say that government should not have the right and the obligation to impose employee services upon a private company if society feels that it is for the general interest and welfare. This imposition does result in a modification of the free-enterprise system. The manager must, however, make decisions in the area of freedom that is left, and the basic guide must be a comparison of costs of service with possible tangible and intangible returns to the company.

The returns of employee benefits to the company can take various forms, many of which are not subject to quantification. Among the values often cited are:

1   More effective recruitment
2   Improved morale and loyalty
3   Lower turnover and absenteeism
4   Good public relations

5 Reduced influence of unions, either present or potential

6 Reduced threat of further government intervention

Particular employee benefits will produce varying values. One example in each of the three categories will illustrate the nature of expected returns. In the economic category pensions are expected to produce values in several areas. The employer *hopes* for improved productivity and morale as a result of lessening employee worry over security. A more tangible value is improved recruitment, since pensions are a part of job sales appeal, as is demonstrated by many newspaper want ads. Some firms have installed pensions to offset the influence of union demands, while still other firms feel that these plans make good advertising and public relations. Thus, the pension benefit can be justified on many and varied grounds. Often these values are only rationalizations, as the employer seeks to find reasons for a decision made on other grounds.

In recreational services the return to the company is still more intangible. What values are derived from company picnics, employee country clubs, and sports programs? The first intangible value is that of improved morale. This is the most typical defense of company-sponsored recreational activities. On occasions, however, a company has studied the personnel who participate most in the company sport program and, in one case, discovered a relationship between productivity and participation. The only difficulty, however, was that the relationship was inverse: The most enthusiastic sports participants were among the poorer producers. This served to create grave doubts of the organizational value of such programs. Recreational services do, however, serve as excellent recruiting devices, particularly for certain classes of employees. Some employers have attempted to rationalize sports on the basis of their contribution to employee health and consequent indirect benefit to productivity. However, a case can be made for the opposite, particularly when excessive injuries to employees result from participation in company sports activities. The values of recreational services are largely intangible and are extremely difficult to quantify. Many feel that such activities are essential to making the company a "good place to work" and let the analysis drop at that point.

There are many facilitative services. To take one example, what values to the company are created by establishing a company cafeteria? Although again morale enters into the analysis, the more important result in this particular service is improved nutrition. Too often industrial employees eat poorly balanced meals when cafeteria service is not available. Improper eating may be reflected in productivity, particularly in the late afternoon. If the manager feels that work is being adversely affected through improper nutrition, there is economic justification for establishing some type of cafeteria service.

The dollar return from employee benefits is almost impossible to measure. It is safe to state that the overwhelming majority of all employee benefits are taken on faith rather than justified in dollars and cents. The correct management philosophy should have an economic orientation, modified by the influences of government and labor unions. We should prefer to be able to prove a positive return to the organization; but we cannot deny that fear of present or potential unions and of possible governmental interference has led many managers further into the area of employee benefit programs.

PRINCIPLES OF EMPLOYEE BENEFIT PROGRAMS

The cardinal principle of employee benefit programs has been set forth above; that is, the benefit must make a contribution to the organization at least equal in amount to its cost. In addition to this basic guide, there are several other generalizations that are applicable. Among these principles are the following:

1   The employee benefit should satisfy a real need.
2   Benefits should be confined to activities in which the group is more efficient than the individual.
3   The benefit should be extended on as broad a base as possible.
4   There should be an attempt to avoid connotations of benevolent paternalism in the granting and administration of these benefits.
5   The costs of the benefit should be calculable, and provision should be made for sound financing.

The first principle, that of satisfying a real need, would appear to be too obvious to need statement. However, many times benefits have been installed, only to be met with employee apathy or outright resistance. The ego in some managers has led them to believe that they know what is best for their employees. In one case, a company manager who felt that employees needed a sports program budgeted money, purchased facilities, and hired a company athletic director. When the whistle was blown to play ball, nobody wanted to play. Employee apathy sometimes turns into a demand that monies spent for employee benefits be given to them in the paycheck. It was found in one survey that the more dissatisfied employees tend to prefer pay to benefits of all types.[9]

The manager takes a step forward when realizing that one must go to the employee to determine the latter's real needs. Even here, there is danger. When questioned about certain proposed services, employees almost always show a favorable reaction. Managers have interpreted this as evidence of real need, when often the employee meant only that it would be "nice" to have such a service. Extreme care and serious research should go into the decision of whether or not to offer a particular employee service. More evidence is required than an unfounded bias of the manager or a casual questioning of the employee.

The benefits selected should be those that can be best handled by a group approach. For example, life insurance purchased as a group can be obtained at a significantly lower price than the same insurance purchased by the individual. Thus, group life insurance meets the requirements of principle 2. On the other hand, there is a serious question as to whether the needs of employees in the recreational field could not better be left to the individuals. This is particularly true if the firm is located in a metropolitan area where numerous private facilities are available. The philosophy behind this principle is a desire to preserve some of the individualism and freedom of our society. In the study cited above, it was discovered that there are large differences in the values placed upon a particular benefit by different types of employees.[10] These

[9]S. M. Nealey, "Pay and Benefit Preference," *Industrial Relations*, October 1963, pp. 17–28.
[10]Ibid.

values varied on the basis of sex, age, marital status, number of children, type of job, and income level. As a result, it has been suggested by some that a package total value be determined, and each employee be allowed to select benefits from a list to equal the authorized dollar expenditure.[11] This "cafeteria system" would permit a choice of those benefits most suitable to the employee's position in life, but the administration difficulties would be increased considerably.

If the organization is to derive maximum benefit from the employee service, as many as possible of its employees should participate. A recreational program participation of less than 10 percent of the total number of employees will produce little of the real or imagined returns of such programs. A pension plan that covers only a small group will not meet the security needs of the majority of the employees. If employee benefits are to contribute anything to the organization, they must be available to, and used by, a substantial portion of the organization.

We have spoken frequently of paternalism, both the old and the new. The old paternalism of the benevolent dictator-manager is out of date. The extended use of employee benefit programs today issues largely from demands made of the employer by employees, unions, competition, or government. The problem still remains, however, of properly relating employee contributions to the organization and the services. Many feel that there is no return to the organization in the form of productivity or morale because the employee takes the service as his due or is totally unconscious of its costs. To make the employee aware and properly appreciative of the service, various firms have applied the principle of sacrifice. The employee is required to pay for some portion of the service received. Some have even gone so far as to advocate a 50–50 sharing of expenses, though most require only a token payment. The trend, as evidenced by collective bargaining settlements, is certainly in the other direction. More and more contracts are being written which call for full payment of the service by the employer. Thus, the particular service will probably be less and less appreciated by the employee. If the employee takes it for granted, morale is benefited only in the sense that the service prevents a deterioration of morale which would have occurred had the service *not* been offered. There is little or no positive gain. As more and more employee services are fully financed by the company, the manager must assume a greater burden of employee education in order to make this fact clear.

The last principle cited is that the costs of the employee benefit must be calculable and its financing be established on a sound basis. This is particularly important in the matter of employee pensions. Sound actuarial estimates must be made, and adequate provisions for financing must be established before conceding the service over the collective bargaining table. These services are not cheap to administer, as is revealed by periodic surveys of personnel management budgets. This is one of the highest single costs of the entire budget of expenditures. Too often a company considers the advisability of a particular employee service on the basis of meeting competition, only to find later that unless the plan is abandoned the firm will be seriously damaged. Employee service programs are a part of the so-called fringe benefits, and, as noted above, the costs of such benefits can hardly be termed a fringe.

[11]Mason Haire, "The Use of Motivational Techniques in Increasing Productivity in the Business Firm," in Floyd A. Bond (ed.), *Business Schools and Economic Growth*, Michigan Business Papers, no. 39, University of Michigan, 1964, p. 33.

Figure 25-1   Economic needs and services

Source of economic need	Economic employee service program
Retirement	Pensions, public and private
Death	Life insurance
Illness	Health and accident insurance
Debt	Credit union

ECONOMIC BENEFITS PROTECTING AGAINST HAZARDS

There are various major hazards in one's regular life. As briefly portrayed in Figure 25-1, the major ones are reduced income issuing from retirement, survivor's welfare in the event of employee death, interruption of income caused by illness and injury, and unpredictable financial requirements leading to the incurring of debt.

Pensions

Since World War II we have seen a rapidly accelerating growth in the number of employee pension plans. The Social Security Act of 1935 probably had more to do with this growth than any other single factor. The public pensions issuing out of the Old Age and Survivors' Insurance portion of this act, when coupled with the benefits of a private pension plan, made possible a fairly reasonable retirement income. Prior to this act, few employers felt that they could afford a sufficient pension to make the attempt worthwhile. A second factor stimulating this rapid adoption of private pensions was the pressure brought to bear on the employer by labor unions. The 1948 National Labor Relations Board decision in the Inland Steel Company case forced employers to bargain over the subject of pensions.[12] Prior to that time, private pensions were installed largely at the initiative of management, since the subject was not considered to be appropriate for collective bargaining. Union demands for pension benefits increased markedly after the Board decision. A third factor stimulating the adoption of private pensions was the wage freeze of World War II. The adoption of a pension plan as a fringe benefit was permissible since it was not considered to be inflationary in its effect upon the economy.

PUBLIC PENSIONS   The Social Security Act of 1935 provided for the first broad government program in the field of industrial pensions. The benefits derived from the Old Age and Survivors' Insurance are financed by both employee and employer. In 1975, the tax rate was set at 5.85 percent of the first $14,100 of wages, levied on both employer and employee, making a total of 11.7 percent paid into the fund. The tax rate is scheduled to rise to 6.05 percent each in 1978. The base amount on which the tax is figured has been rising at a markedly accelerated rate in recent years. Self-employed persons ordinarily pay three-quarters of the total tax assessed against the individual and the organization. The fund not only finances payments to retirees and eligible survivors but also contributes to medical care for the aged. The latter provides for hospitalization of those

---

[12]*Inland Steel Co. v. NLRB 77*, NLRB 1 (1948).

over sixty-five years of age and doctors' fees for those electing to contribute an additional small monthly fee.

Benefits are paid to a retiree, his or her dependents, or survivors if insured under the law. One is *currently* insured if having worked in covered employment during one and one-half years out of the last three. One is *fully* insured if having worked in such employment for ten years. No retirement or disability payments are made if the employee is not fully insured. Some survivors' payments are made if the employee was only currently insured. Thus, if the employee hopes to retire and collect OASI benefits, he or she must be *fully* insured.

Retirement, disability, and survivors' benefits are calculated on the basis of one's average monthly earnings up to the taxable amount. When the law was first passed in 1935, the taxable wage was $3,000. This was later raised at different times to $3,600, $4,200, $4,800, $6,600, and the now applicable $14,100. It is safe to state that the taxable base will continue to be increased in the years ahead.

Retirement benefits in the future will be adjusted automatically upward when rises in the Consumers Price Index exceed 3 percent. Such benefits are reduced if the retiree continues to work in covered employment and receives money in excess of a relatively low amount. The current limit is approximately $2,500 per year. Income from savings, investments, pensions, and insurance does not affect benefits. People who are totally dependent upon wages and have no investments are those who need to work to supplement retirement benefits. There are excellent arguments for lifting all restrictions on earnings after the age of sixty-five.

The present Social Security Act covers over 90 percent of those who are gainfully employed. It constitutes the foundation of retirement pensions for the business personnel of this country.

PRIVATE PENSIONS   The benefits provided by OASI are inadequate retirement income. In many instances, private companies have initiated supplementary pension plans, the benefits of which, when added to OASI, constitute an income on which a retiree can live. As we said earlier, the labor union has had much to do with the widespread adoption of company plans. It is estimated that such plans covered 28 million workers in 1973, approximately half of the private nonfarm work force.[13] Unlike the 50–50 sharing of costs in OASI, the employer completely finances approximately 75 percent of these plans.

In recent years, there has been much concern over the assurance that private pension benefits accumulated will actually be paid. Many plans have gone bankrupt, leaving employees with only their Old Age and Survivors Insurance benefits, an amount in most cases too little to support themselves and their families. As a result, the Employee Retirement Security Act of 1974 was passed to ensure that employees of private pension plans will actually receive *something* at retirement. A basic provision of the act was to establish the Pension Benefit Guaranty Corporation in the Department of Labor. Employers with pension plans are required to pay a premium of $1 per participant to guard against plan bankruptcy. In the event of plan failure, employees will receive benefits from the Guaranty Corporation of their vested (owned) portion of

[13]Peter Henle and Raymond Schmitt, "Pension Reform: The Long, Hard Road to Enactment," *Monthly Labor Review*, vol. 97, no. 11, November 1974, p. 3.

the fund, up to $750 a month or 100 percent of average wages during the highest-paid five years of employment, whichever is less.

A second major feature of the act requires that employee vesting or ownership of pension amounts be provided. Though no employer is required by the act to inaugurate a new private pension plan, all private plans (estimated to range from 300,000 to 400,000) must have one of the three following vesting options: (1) 100 percent vesting after ten years of service, (2) 25 percent vesting after five years, grading up to 100 percent after fifteen years of service, or (3) 50 percent vesting when age and service equals forty-five, grading up to 100 percent five years later. Thus, the act requires that employees be given ultimate ownership of their pension accounts and insures these accounts against plan failure. Employers are liable for any insurance benefits paid upon plan failure up to 30 percent of the company's net worth.

Other provisions of this revolutionary act emphasizing employee security include the following: (1) prohibits eligibility requirements of more than one year of service or an age greater than twenty-five years, (2) requires annual funding of the full cost of current benefit accruals plus amortization of past benefit liabilities, (3) restricts investment of pension funds in company securities to no more than 10 percent, (4) permits transferability of vested amounts from the company to other companies or private individual retirement funds, and (5) permits employees of companies who do *not* have private pension plans to set up Individual Retirement Accounts. The limit on income tax deductions for such private accounts is 15 percent of employee compensation up to $1,500 each year. Self-employed people can establish such plans with limits on deductions of $7,500 a year or 15 percent of such income, whichever is less.

For some employers, these more stringent regulations to ensure the health of pension plans will require increased expenditures. For those who do not presently have such plans, these regulations may serve to discourage interest. However, the stipulations concerning the creation of Individual Retirement Accounts provide an additional avenue to explore in helping to provide some measure of income security on retirement, e.g., raise salaries and urge employees to set up such private accounts.

Life insurance

Life insurance is probably the oldest form of company-sponsored employee benefit. Group life premiums are considerably smaller than those of insurance purchased by the individual. The return to the company of this particular economic service comes from relieving the employee of worry about the security of his or her dependents. Relief from worry should enable a person to devote greater attention to the job and the company.

Health and accident insurance

Accidents and industrial diseases growing out of the job are compensable under state workers' compensation laws, as was explained in the preceding chapter. Illness and accidents that are not industrially caused are a source of worry and financial strain upon the employee. Various forms of health and accident insurance are provided, some completely company-financed and others whose costs are shared with the employee. Ordinary medical insurance policies are written by many private insurance companies. Blue Cross and Blue Shield are popular health plans in many areas of the country. Of increasing interest to many employees and employers are major medical insurance plans. Ordinary medical insurance adequately covers illnesses and injuries whose costs run under $500. Major medical plans are designed to cover illness in which costs run up to $10,000. Usually, such insurance is written as coinsurance, with the agency paying 80 percent and the insured the remaining 20 percent. This is the type of illness where insurance is almost a necessity. The individual would have a greater chance of adequately handling a lesser illness without the benefit of insurance. Through collective bargaining, labor unions have been instrumental in the constant widening of the health services to be financed by the employer. Among the more recent additions are dental care, prescription drugs, vision care, and mental health services. With respect to the last cited, the United Auto Workers Union has bargained for a plan under which the patient pays nothing for the first five visits to a psychiatrist's office, 15 percent of the cost of the next five, 30 percent of the third five, and 45 percent of all other visits. In contrast with many insurance plans that include a deductibility feature, this formula is designed to make the first treatments free on the theory that early treatment should be encouraged.

Credit union

A credit union is an organized group of people who pool their money and agree to make loans to one another. Thus one value of fostering a credit union is the relief from worry over short-term financial insecurity. A second value is the reduction in employee compensation garnishments by loan agencies when the employee fails to meet loan obligations. Garnishment proceedings are always objectionable to the employer and in some companies constitute grounds for discharge. However, federal legislation in 1970 prohibits discharge because of garnishment for any *one* indebtedness; some states prohibit discharge for reasons of garnishment regardless of number. In addition, the federal law stipulates that the portion of wages available for garnishment must not exceed 25 percent or an amount related to current minimum-wage levels, whichever is less. Again, the accent is on governmentally protected minimum degrees of employee economic security.

This type of employee service illustrates well the principle cited earlier, that employee services should be offered only when they can best be executed by a group rather than an individual. If an individual sought a short-term unsecured loan, he or she would pay interest rates in excess of 30 percent. If that same individual joined a credit union and sought a short-term unsecured loan from this union, the annual interest rate would be no more than 12 percent. Thus, in this instance, the group is more effective than the individual.

RECREATIONAL PROGRAMS

All people are in need of occasional diversion. Many managements are of the opinion that employee amusement is better left to the individual employee, but sometimes a case can be made for company-sponsored activities. With the trend toward decentralization of plant locations, many firms have located in small towns and find that recreational facilities are inadequate. Others find that when facilities are available, the costs are too high for the majority of the employees. Business managers are interested in seeing that recreational facilities are available to employees for several reasons. Worker attitudes improve when the routine of everyday living is broken occasionally. In addition, a more agreeable informal atmosphere is promoted through the contacts and relationships built up in particular recreational events. The employee not only gets to know other employees, but also has contact with members of management in a climate unaffected by the chain of command. This may provide a basis for accepting management as a group of individual human beings, rather than as some impersonal, threatening, dollar-motivated set of dictators.

Recreational programs may be divided into two types, (1) sports and (2) social events. In the sports category, activities can be further classified into "varsity" and "intramural" sports. Varsity sports are those in which a team is selected to represent the firm in competition with other institutions. This type of activity violates the principle of establishing a broad base of participation, but it may return values in improved public relations and in employee pride, particularly if the team is successful. Intramural sports, participated in by a greater number of employees, is the more desirable activity to undertake. Various firms have provided facilities and/or organization for golf, bowling, softball, tennis, swimming, and the like. It is not unusual to see a company purchase a recreational area, complete with golf course, swimming pools, and tennis courts. Such recreational facilities are of great value in employee recruitment.

FACILITATIVE EMPLOYEE SERVICE PROGRAMS

Facilitative services are activities which employees must normally take care of themselves in everyday living. Just as executives have certain perquisites, the trend is in the direction of providing regular employees with special assistance in some of the routine portions of life. Each facilitative service proposes to meet some continuing need. The justifications for the services will be given briefly below; the technical details of organizing and administering such activities are left to other books with more specific objectives than this one. We are concerned only with the general purposes of a service and with its relevance to a philosophy of personnel management.

CAFETERIAS The justification of the company restaurant or cafeteria has already been specified in the introduction to this chapter. The major values lie in the improvement of nutrition and consequently, it is presumed, of morale.

HOUSING The home life of the employee has a considerable effect upon performance at work. Many managers are concerned with assisting the employee to locate in a suitable home. This is particularly necessary when one is new in the area and requires assistance in finding a suitable rental. The employee will buckle down to work with greater concentration much faster when she or he is assured of proper housing.

It has also been discovered that employees who own their homes are more stable in the matter of labor turnover. Consequently some managements have provided financial assistance in aiding certain key employees to purchase homes.

EMPLOYEE PURCHASE The old company store, where the employee redeemed the scrip paid for work, had a very poor reputation in the past. The old type of store is justifiable only when no private stores are available or when the few stores that do exist take advantage of a monopoly situation. Many firms do, however, make available to their employees their own products at discount prices. This provides returns in morale and also stimulates the employee to use and "identify with" the products on which he or she works.

A serious question arises concerning the desirability of a company's opening its purchasing department to miscellaneous employee purchases. When a company purchases consumer goods from other firms, it can obtain them at discount prices for its employees. The anticipated return to the company is that of improved morale, but the potential dangers often outweigh this value. Among these dangers are the following: (1) the employee holds the company responsible for any deficiency or malfunction in the product purchased; (2) he or she requests installment financing of the purchase; (3) the company incurs the ill will of the community retailers who sell the same products bought through the purchasing agent; and (4) the purchasing agent looks upon the scheme with disfavor, since the agent is forced to purchase unfamiliar goods from unfamiliar sources.

MEDICAL SERVICES   The justification for a company's entry into the medical business is substantially the same as that for providing health and accident insurance. The difference here is that not only financing but also the medical services are provided. In effect, the company is in competition with private medical practices and hospitals. An example of this service is the Kaiser Medical Clinics started on the West Coast by Henry J. Kaiser. These clinics have been opened to the employees of numerous other organizations besides those of the plants of the Kaiser Corporation. The rationale for providing medical services directly involves a number of arguments. First, private services in the community may be limited. Secondly, group medical clinics may provide services at a lower fee than that charged by private practitioners. And thirdly, the clinic approach often results in better employee health. One is free to go to the clinic at any time at little or no charge per visit.

Under the Health Maintenance Organization Act of 1973, employers covered by the Fair Labor Standards Act and having twenty-five or more employees must include in any health benefits plan the option of membership in a qualified health maintenance organization available in the community. The total contribution to a health benefit plan being made by the employer does not have to be increased. The major requirement is that an on-going clinical-type organization must be included in the list of available alternatives, if such does exist within fifteen miles of where most employees reside. The health maintenance organizations generally charge higher rates inasmuch as they provide a complete service emphasizing preventive health care. It has been found that when HMO's are available, there are strong increased annual employee enrollments issuing from high satisfaction with such services in terms of both economics and health.

LEGAL AND FINANCIAL COUNSELING   It is not unusual for employees to get into some type of legal or financial touble. When a person is in that sort of trouble, productivity and morale are affected adversely. Many maintain that such problems as these are private problems to be handled by the individual. But if the individual will not seek a lawyer or a financial consultant, because he or she either does not know one or cannot afford such services, the provision of a company-sponsored service may work to the firm's advantage.

Ordinarily, business firms do not have a large number of lawyers who can give legal counseling on a broad scale. In addition, a corporation lawyer is not ordinarily expert in giving special aid and counsel in the types of cases in which individuals are usually involved. The lawyer can, however, determine if they are in need of detailed legal advice and stimulate them to seek that advice. The contribution of the firm in this area must be somewhat limited.

If employees become involved in financial trouble, they may have access to the credit union, employee savings and loan association, or some other similar service offered in the firm. Not infrequently the trouble is more deeply rooted—a chronic inability to handle money. The employee is in need of advice as well as financial assistance. Some firms make a practice of providing a wide range of counseling assistance, but the overwhelming majority do not. Counseling is a service that is on the fringe of the employee benefit program, which, in turn, is a fringe itself.

EMPLOYEE EDUCATIONAL SERVICES This is one type of employee benefit program which rests on a sound foundation of company and employee mutual interest. Employee educational programs are rapidly increasing in number year by year. It is to both the employer's and the employee's advantage for the latter to improve the level of his or her formal education. To stimulate ambition, the employer may agree to finance tuition for any college course in which a satisfactory grade is received. Occasionally, agreements have been worked out with colleges to give a credit extension class on company property. In this arrangement the employee has less freedom of choice concerning courses and majors that he or she may wish to pursue. The employee education that is being financed must usually take place in night or Saturday classes. Supplementing these courses, a company library may be established to enable the employee to do the necessary research work. With the growing interest in the study of management among managers, the addition of a business library to the usual technical and science libraries of industrial firms will become more widespread.

SUMMARY

Employee benefit programs can be compared to the mythological animal that immediately grew two heads when one was chopped off. There seems to be no end to the number, variety, and adaptations of such service programs. As an example, one local union demanded that when a retired company employee dies, a representative of the department be given time off with pay to attend the funeral. The limit on this arrangement is four hours' time off, unless the representative is asked to act as pallbearer, in which case one may get the whole day off with pay.

One could reason that the forces governing the determination of wages and other compensation will result in a certain size of compensation package. If the employee desires to take 30 percent of this package in the form of guaranteed annual wages, pensions, insurance, and the like, that is her or his privilege. This presumes that the compensation package can be scientifically determined and that the employee is actually substituting a fringe for a portion of the base wage. Such precision of measurement is, of course, impossible.

The typical approach to the problem of what employee benefits to offer is to attempt to prove or deduce specific and general values to the organization as well as to the employee participant. In general, all such plans should conform to such principles as the following: the benefit should provide organizational value at least equal in amount to its cost; it should meet a real need; group effort should be more efficient than individual; maximum employee participation should be engendered; benevolent paternalism should be avoided; the costs of the benefit should be calculable and provision made for sound financing.

Non-wage payments take a variety of forms, including pay for time not worked, economic benefits to protect against major hazards, recreational and social programs to enhance quality of life, and provision of numerous perquisites and privileges. Society appears to be most concerned about protecting against major economic hazards issuing from interruptions or stoppages of employment, as judged by passage of such laws as the Social Security Act and the Employee Retirement Income Security Act. There is obvious great concern with employee health, as exemplified by workers' compensation laws, the Occupational Safety and Health Act, and the Health Maintenance Organization Act. Perhaps the greatest degree of employer-initiated benefits lies in the recreational and facilitative services area, e.g., counseling, housing, tuition, sports, etc. Labor unions have been most prominent in steadily increasing the amount of pay for time not worked, e.g., holidays, vacations, rest periods, etc. In sum, the average employee working in a firm engaged in interstate commerce and organized by a labor union is likely to be on the receiving end of a multitude of benefits, many of which she or he becomes aware of only when the need arises. Professional personnel managers should be concerned with enhancing organizational returns for this major investment in employee attitudes.

DISCUSSION QUESTIONS

1 What major classes of benefits are usually included in the term "fringe benefits"?

2 Why are fringe benefits no longer properly considered to be fringes?

3 What are the rationalized organizational returns of a cafeteria? Of a private pension program? Of a recreational program?

4 What is the nature and rationale of the Employee Retirement Income Security Act of 1974?

5 What types of employee benefits tend to be required by government? What types tend to be voluntarily offered by employers?

6 Discuss the role of employee benefits as motivators versus their role as maintenance factors.

7 With respect to employee benefits in the health area, what are some of the varying types of services available?

8 What is a "wage garnishment," and what legal restraints are placed on it?

9 What specific principle of employee benefit programs best applies to the purchase of employee life insurance?

10 What unusual employee benefits are predicted for the future?

SUPPLEMENTARY READING

CARLSON, Donald G.: "Responding to the Pension Reform Law," *Harvard Business Review*, vol. 52, no. 6, November–December 1974, pp. 133–144.

DAVIS, Harry E.: "Pension Provisions Affecting the Employment of Older Workers," *Monthly Labor Review*, vol. 96, no. 4, April 1973, pp. 41–45.

FOEGEN, J. H.: "Fringe on the Fringe," *Personnel Administration*, vol. 35, no. 1, January–February 1972, pp. 18–22.

MABRY, Bevars: "The Economics of Fringe Benefits," *Industrial Relations*, vol. 12, no. 1, February 1973, pp. 95–106.

SMITH, Alexander F.: "Employer-Assisted Education: A Case of Corporate Apathy," *The Personnel Administrator*, vol. 18, no. 5, September–October 1973, pp. 23–28.

SULLIVAN, John F.: "Indirect Compensation: The Years Ahead," *California Management Review*, vol. 15, no. 2, Winter 1972, pp. 65–76.

TWENTY–SIX

PERSONNEL RESEARCH AND CHANGE

There is no field of management that will not benefit from systematic and purposeful research. Certainly the field of personnel management is in great need of more systematized knowledge and sound principles. There should be less "by guess and by gosh" and more accurate prediction of human behavior in an industrial environment. There should be less taking on faith and more proof of operating results. If personnel management is to obtain and retain the status of a legitimate management field and profession, research must provide the foundation.

Research can be defined as systematic and purposive investigation of facts with the object of determining cause-and-effect relationships among such facts. From research we hope to establish principles which define the relationship between two or more phenomena. The manager then attempts to use these principles in his philosophy, approach, attitude, and specific practices as a manager.

Research by itself is sterile if nothing is done with its results other than to publish them in journals and books. The personnel manager has an obligation, not only to assist in implementing research, but, more important, to see that usable results are actually implemented in his or her organization. This chapter will conclude with the basic change process, as well as fundamental humanistic challenges that must be faced in the future.

NATURE OF PERSONNEL RESEARCH

Personnel research is more difficult and frustrating than many of the types of research in the physical sciences. The human factor is extremely hard to delimit. It is unlikely, and probably undesirable, that human beings will ever be completely predictable in their behavior. Yet every event need not be a complete surprise to the observer. Known relationships usually exist between a particular causal act of management and a resulting reaction or act from an employee. Following the currently known principles of personnel management will serve to increase the odds of success. It will not ensure a home run every time the personnel manager comes to bat.

Personnel research finds its roots in a number of disciplines. Various types of psychological research can be applied in the personnel field, particularly those dealing with what is known as industrial psychology. The products of sociological research are also useful to the personnel manager, as are the findings of the economist, particularly in the function of compensation. The psychologist, however, dominates in numbers. Of the sixty-five personnel researchers with doctorates employed by fifty major business firms, sixty-one possessed a degree in psychology, three had degrees in sociology, and one was unspecified.[1] Of the sixty-two researchers with master's degrees, twenty-seven were in psychology, six in sociology, five in business, one in economics, and twenty-three were unspecified. The median size of the personnel research unit was seven. Berry estimates that these fifty firms constitute 60 percent of the business organizations that have research departments. Outstanding in this regard are General Electric, International Business Machines, Texas Instruments, and Du Pont.

Personnel management can be compared to engineering in the sense that it utilizes the knowledge of many disciplines and synthesizes multiple approaches to solve a particular, practical problem. There is, of course, personnel research per se, which might be termed business research. However, a particular business research project may well involve aspects of psychology, sociology, and economics. It is essential to recognize that the application of the basic disciplines must take place in a business environment, a fact which serves materially to alter the conclusions derived from a "purer" experimental situation.

In classifying personnel research as a function of personnel management, it is immediately apparent that there is or should be research in procurement, development, compensation, integration, and maintenance. There is much to be learned about each of these functions. A fundamental purpose of research is to improve the philosophy and practice of personnel management. Because of the deteriorative effects of time, a second objective of personnel research must be that of discovering ways to maintain abilities and attitudes of personnel at good or high levels on a continuing basis. Thus, research can be stimulating in the sense that it raises the level of performance, and it can be construed as a form of maintenance in that it contributes to the continuity of effective personnel management. In any event, personnel research is essential to the creation and maintenance of professional personnel management.

Types of personnel research

Two general types of research are usually identified as (1) basic or exploratory and (2) operational or applied. Exploratory research is concerned with the discovery of knowledge for its own sake. The scientist builds conceptual models and tests various hypotheses against them. From observation of life one extracts a single or a restricted

---

[1]Dean F. Berry, *The Politics of Personnel Research*, University of Michigan Bureau of Industrial Relations, Ann Arbor, Mich., 1967, p. 55.

number of basic variables in human conduct and studies them intensively with little or no concern as to whether or not the results of the investigation can be applied by some manager. Many of the published results of such research would appear highly theoretical and of little practical applicability to the business manager. Yet these are the generalizations which mark advances in the field, both in theory and in practice. Much of the pure research in personnel is accomplished by governmental institutions and colleges or universities. Relatively seldom does a private firm engage in pure personnel research. The incidence of pure physical science research among private business firms is uncommon enough, but research concerning personnel is even more rare.

Operational or applied research is directed toward the solution of particular business problems. The payoff of such research is immediate, observable, and tangible. The extent of such operational research can vary from the very elaborate, lengthy, and expensive studies of the Western Electric Company in the 1920s to a fairly quick analysis of company records to find the cause, for example, of excessive absenteeism. This type of research is obviously based on the products of pure research. The pure scientist indicates the possibility of certain fundamental generalizations governing relationships among various factors. The individual company manager may take the scientist's idea and test it in a particular situation. The operational environment is never identical with that under which the exploratory research was conducted. The findings of such research are not therefore invalidated; they are applicable under the conditions specified and must consequently be adapted to the operational situation in which the particular manager is located. Operational research can be elaborate, expensive, and carefully controlled. It can be conducted by the business manager, social engineer, or research scientist. Such research can also be performed every day by every manager in a somewhat less rigidly controlled manner. It is a type of research that no firm or manager can afford to do without, but its results are not so broadly applicable as those of exploratory research.

In the terms of Byham, both of the above-described types of research would be classified as "behavioral science based."[2] The researcher seeks to discover basic relationships that can lead to improved personnel decision making in such areas as increasing job satisfaction, assessing managerial potential, and increasing organizational effectiveness. Byham indicates, however, that most companies perform "descriptive" personnel research when they collect statistics to keep management informed about the existing personnel situation, e.g., turnover data, wage surveys, absenteeism rates, etc. It is the former that is seldom found but has the potential for introducing significant changes in management practices.

The researchers

A wide variety of people and institutions engage in either pure or applied research. Among these researchers are (1) colleges and universities, (2) governmental agencies, (3) private research organizations, (4) company personnel departments, and (5) the line manager. In the study cited above, it was estimated that $25 to 55 million of personnel research was being done each year, with the federal government providing 67 percent

[2]William C. Byham, *The Uses of Personnel Research*, American Management Association Research Study 91, New York, 1968, p. 9.

of the funds, foundations 16 percent, business and industry 13 percent, and state governments 4 percent.[3] This research was done by the following agencies: 39 percent by private research organizations, 34 percent by colleges and universities, 22 percent by the federal government, and 5 percent by business.

Colleges and universities are set up to operate in both the pure and the applied phases of personnel research. It is common to see bureaus of business research which engage in personnel projects as well as in investigations in the other fields of business management. Among the outstanding university centers of personnel research are the Institute for Social Research of the University of Michigan, the Personnel Research Board of Ohio State University, the Institute of Industrial Relations of the University of California, and the Behavioral Sciences Group of Carnegie Institute of Technology. The funds for such research agencies come from the university, business firms, and foundations of various types. The bureau often undertakes a great variety of applied and operational research projects for individual firms. A portion of the income from such projects may be set aside to finance pure or basic research to be conducted by various faculty members. Basic research is also financed through grants made by various foundations, such as the Ford Foundation. The objective of such basic research is to advance the frontier of knowledge without particular and immediate regard for its operational use.

Various *governmental agencies* conduct basic and applied research. Units in the Department of Labor are particularly interested in research dealing with personnel management. For example, the *Dictionary of Occupational Titles* and various occupational descriptions were prepared by the United States Employment Service for the general use of industry. Particular departments, such as the Department of Defense, do basic and applied research appropriate to their particular problems. For example, the findings of Air Force research in studying human reactions to various types of environmental stimuli have their uses in business situations.

Private research organizations take a number of different forms. Some are employers' associations that accomplish particular projects of special interest to an industry. For example, industry wage and salary surveys may be conducted by an employers' association on a continuing basis. In addition, there are the larger employer groups like the National Association of Manufacturers and the Chamber of Commerce of the United States. These latter groups number research among their vital functions. Other associations are established strictly for the purpose of conducting business research—such organizations as the National Industrial Conference Board, The Brookings Institution, RAND Corporation, and the Stanford Research Institute. And finally, there is the management consultant. He or she is doing and selling operational research of a type, particularly when *not* attempting to sell a ready-made system which proposes to solve the same problem in any firm with which the consultant comes into contact.

Individual companies also do personnel research, particularly of the operational or applied type. One of a series of surveys showed that 3 percent of the total expenditures made by personnel departments were applied to research. A later survey by the same group indicated that manufacturing firms, having a total personnel department manpower ratio of 0.77, allotted 0.02 to research activities.[4] For banking,

---

[3]Cecil E. Goode, *Personnel Research Frontiers*, Public Personnel Association, Chicago, 1958, pp. 18–21.

[4]Roberta J. Nelson, George W. England, and Dale Yoder, "Personnel Ratios, 1960: An Analytical Look," *Personnel*, November–December 1960, pp. 18–28.

finance and insurance companies, the ratios were 0.95 and 0.04, respectively. Though small, all figures indicate increases over surveys of preceding years.

It has been pointed out that some personnel managers are reluctant to allocate much money to personnel research. They are fearful that such research may reveal that a particular pet project that was taken on faith is actually not justified. They are unwilling to take any money away from an elaborate and "crucial" training program to determine whether or not the training is doing any good. The days of depending upon faith and the vague pronouncement, "It's good for morale," are rapidly coming to an end. If personnel managers are to continue to demand and receive a reasonable share of the budget, they will have to learn to talk the language of dollars and cents, profits and costs. They will have to look toward research to preserve and advance the function of personnel management.

Just as the *individual manager* finds the functions of procurement, development, compensation, and integration inescapable to some degree, one must also consider research to be an inevitable part of the job of manager. If one has the normal amount of curiosity and energy, one will want to know *why* certain things seem to be happening or *how* to effect certain desired results. Trial and error is a form of operational research, but a most expensive form when used exclusively. The essence of scientific management in any field (and personnel is no exception) is systematic study and investigation of phenomena affecting business decisions. The fact that personnel is a very intangible and elusive area is no excuse for depending upon luck, faith, and good guesses. If management is to be labeled a profession, the manager must incorporate a research philosophy into his or her basic approach to business problems. The line manager must not conclude that all personnel research must be done by a staff personnel department. Many important facts and relationships are available only to the immediate supervisor.

Sources of information

It is important in all research to be aware of the possible sources of information concerning any particular subject. There is a danger, in operational research, that the manager will conclude that all information must come from the environment of one's particular department and firm. In effect we close our eyes to all work done by others. We are at the beginning, the dawn of civilization.

The professional manager must learn to read and to make reading a part of his or her everyday operation. One should not confine such reading solely to the edicts and policies of the firm. It is impossible to list all the books available in personnel management, or even a small fraction thereof. It would be equally impossible for the manager to read or even skim them all. Some services provided by such organizations as the American Management Association will condense, summarize, and recommend publications to be read in the field of personnel. These should suggest the sources that the manager will find interesting and useful in the job of manager.

Periodicals and magazines are an excellent source of research information and ideas. Again, the manager cannot read them all, but one should incorporate a few as a part of one's regular reading routine. The following are some of the periodicals that are of general value in the personnel field:

Academy of Management Journal	Advanced Management Journal
Administrative Science Quarterly	American Journal of Sociology

California Management Review   Labor Law Journal
Conference Board Record   Management of Personnel Quarterly
Employment Service Review   Management Review
Fortune   Monthly Labor Review
Harvard Business Review   Organizational Dynamics
Human Organization   Personnel
Human Relations   Personnel Journal
Industrial and Labor Relations Review   Personnel Psychology
Industrial Management Review   Psychological Abstracts
Industrial Relations   Public Personnel Management
Journal of Applied Behavioral Science   Training and Development Journal
Journal of Applied Psychology

Research methods

All research involves the application, in some manner, of the scientific method. There are various specific forms that individual research projects can take, among them (1) controlled experiments, (2) surveys, (3) historical studies, (4) case studies, and (5) simulations.

CONTROLLED EXPERIMENTS   The controlled experiment is relatively rare as conducted by private concerns. Perhaps the most famous experiment of this type was the Hawthorne study of the Western Electric Company, begun in 1927. This study, conducted by Elton Mayo and his associates, was and is a classic in the field of personnel research. An earlier study, begun in 1924, was designed to isolate and discover the effect of lighting and other physical factors on employee output. Regardless of the level of lighting, output improved. These confusing results led to introduction of behavioral scientists from Harvard, and the study of the five "girls" in the relay assembly test room began. In this group there was an attempt to keep all variables constant and then to introduce one variation into the situation. The ensuing output result could, they thought, be attributed to the single variant factor. In this manner, changes that sought to introduce rest periods, new pay systems, different work schedules, and the like, led to immediate and significant improvements in group output. To validate further the discovered relationships between these variables and output, conditions were returned to their original status, in the expectation that productivity would drop. To everyone's surprise, output did *not* drop but continued to improve. Obviously, all the conditions of the experiment had not been rigidly controlled. What was not controlled were the minds and attitudes of the participant workers. They liked working in the experimental room with an observer rather than a supervisor; they felt rather important as a result of the special attention allocated and the involvement in decision making. Regardless of what was introduced, they attempted to produce more.

One of the continuing elements of this project that is reflected in all experiments is the so-called "Hawthorne effect." In analyzing results from the controlled introduction of a variable, one must be cautious in determining what degree of the result can be attributed to the experimenter or to the insertion of *anything new* into the environment. One must be careful in reaching conclusions about results from short-term studies where the "Hawthorne effect" may still be in operation. Other observers maintain that though this effect may have been present in the Hawthorne studies, the true cause of output improvement was the significant and real participation of the employees in making decisions about their work lives. Despite the contention of recent writers that the researchers departed from the scientific method and twisted their findings to favor the human component, these landmark experiments led to the development of a second school of management thought, the humanistic or behavioral approach.[5]

A variation of the controlled experiment is used quite frequently in industry. For example, one group of personnel is given training of a certain type. Though all conditions are not kept constant and the control is much less exact, the work of the trained personnel is compared with that of the untrained, the latter constituting the control group. Certain tentative conclusions can then be drawn concerning the value of the training given. But here again, all variables are not controlled. If the trained group does better, is it because of the skill of the trainer, the skill and attitude of the trainees, the feeling of importance at being singled out for training, or a peculiar combination of environmental circumstances which may not be duplicated again? This is what makes personnel management the exciting and frustrating field that it is.

SURVEYS The survey is a commonly used research method. It usually takes the form of a questionnaire or structured interview. Its object is to determine present practices or approaches and to attempt to relate certain results to particular causes. Like all other research methods, it rests upon the scientific method. For example, we may wish to know certain things about employee profit sharing. Can such plans survive a profitless year? If so, how many profitless years? What can management do to help ensure survival? Certain hypotheses must be established around which survey questions can be phrased. Perhaps elaborate employee education will help the firm through the profitless years. Perhaps the payment of large regular shares will help do the job in times of crisis. Perhaps the use of the deferred type of plan will result in less employee objection when there are no profits to share. But maybe the deferred arrangement will also result in no additional effort on the part of the employee to ensure a profitable result in the next year.

These are some of the hypotheses that can be formulated concerning the factors which may determine employee reactions in profitless years. Now, what criteria can be established so that we can judge the correctness of such hypotheses? One criterion might be the objective evidence of continued operation of the plan during many profitless periods. Another criterion might be employee attitudes during these periods. A third might be measures of productivity during the profitless periods. At this point, the actual survey is taken. Companies are asked questions concerning the possible causes of, as well as the facts that will indicate employee reactions to, the absence of profits. Correlations between possible causes and observed effects are then computed. As a result, certain generalizations deducible from the survey study can be made. Examples of these are: (1) the greater the number of educational efforts, the more favorable the reaction of employees in terms of attitudes and productivity; (2) the larger the regular share paid, the greater the effort made by employees during the nonprofit

---

[5]Alex Carey, "The Hawthorne Studies: A Radical Criticism," *American Sociological Review*, vol. 32, no. 3, 1967, pp. 403–416.

period; and (3) the use of the deferred-distribution plan tends to result in no employee reaction, good or bad, during the nonprofit period.

Such generalizations can be of value in suggesting to the individual manager what one might do in reference to this particular problem. In effect, we propose to use the efforts of *many* companies which appear to have solved this problem successfully. The key to success in the survey method of research is the ability to ask the right questions.

HISTORICAL STUDIES   There is a wealth of useful information in the files of most firms, including valuable records about personnel. Suppose, for example, a manager wishes to do research on a problem of high labor turnover. He or she can study turnover experience on the basis of such variables as sex, age, department, home ownership, marital status, and stated cause for leaving. One may find, for example, that turnover is high among female employees, the very young, employees of department D, employees who rent their homes, and unmarried personnel. Such results may lead to a revision of procurement policies and further investigation, in greater detail, of discovered trouble spots. The personnel problem of absenteeism can be attacked in the same manner, as can also the problem of high accident rates. The approach is to determine the fundamental factors which affect the problem and then to collect evidence on these factors from historical records. This presumes, however, that the manager has kept the appropriate records to begin with.

CASE STUDIES   The case-study approach is considered by many to be a separate method of research. Quite frequently, however, case studies result only in the creation of further hypotheses requiring additional research to validate. This method can be contrasted with the survey method. Surveys are usually extensive, in that a few carefully designed questions are asked of a large number of firms. Case studies are intensive, in that a great number of subjects are investigated in detail in a relatively limited number of firms. Complete case studies often suggest a great many more hypotheses than can be used by a single researcher as he prepares a survey questionnaire or designs a controlled experiment. Any conclusions drawn from a relatively limited number of case studies are, of course, of a highly tentative nature. The experiment in the test relay room at Hawthorne was followed by extensive observation of work behavior in the bank wiring room. From this intensive case study the concept of "informal organization" was developed.

SIMULATION   In recent years, simulation of performance has become an increasingly popular method of research in many fields. In political science, for example, there is some research through simulation to determine the factors affecting conflicts of interest and possible means of reconciling and integrating these conflicts. A simulation of the world situation through the formation of nations with varying degrees of power and resources provides the stage for introducing new variables. For example, when power forces were more equally divided among these simulated nations, the ties of alliance began to break down. Similar simulations have been used in business environments for studying problems of production control, inventory control, purchasing, and marketing. Role playing is a specific type of performance simulation which has been used to research human behavior. The advances in computer technology will make possible greater use of business simulations to determine and predict the effect of introduced new variables.

Research needs in personnel management

There is literally no end to the number of things we need to know about personnel and personnel management. In this text we have attempted to survey the field in a broad fashion. The approach has been taken that *all* managers of necessity direct and manage personnel in addition to directing a particular technical function. The five operative personnel functions are fundamental and inescapable. For example, every manager should have some conception of, and be able to participate in, the procurement function. At the minimum, one must accept and work with the new employee. In most organizations, line managers play a larger role entailing interviewing to determine whether the bolt (applicant) fits the nut (organization). One also requires some appreciation of the nature and value of more specialized personnel measurements such as psychological tests and performance simulations.

Every manager, line or staff, must participate in the development function. The trend is certainly in the direction of centering more of the developmental activities around the workplace. Supervisory coaching holds out great potential promise as the single most effective development technique. Even if a firm follows the policy of attempting to delegate all development to a staff personnel department, the supervisor must have knowledge of what is occurring in development, in order to be able to integrate the training of the employee with the work of the department.

The compensation function is sufficiently technical for much of it to be delegated to a technical staff department. But even here, the manager cannot escape personal responsibilities. In job evaluation, for example, the line manager should serve on the evaluation committee when the jobs in his or her particular department are being evaluated. And what supervisor can avoid dealing with incentive pay plans when one is in operation in the department? Though some of the aspects of compensation are operationally outside the supervisor's jurisdiction, compensation is, nevertheless, a fundamental personnel function of all managers.

Attempts to delegate completely the integration function to staff departments would be laughable if it were not for the ensuing tragic consequences. Integration, or human relations, is an important and unavoidable function of every manager. The human relations specialist can only train, educate, and advise. The real job must be done by the manager.

As in the first four functions, the maintenance of personnel must be of concern to the supervisor as well as to the specialist in personnel. Safety programs do not work if the supervisor does not do her or his part. Only in employee service programs can the function be almost completely delegated to the staff specialist. But even here, the supervisor should be intelligent and expert if the firm is to reap the anticipated return of such services. And, as we are attempting to emphasize in this chapter, every manager who purports to be a professional manager must have an inclination toward practical research. In understanding individual and group behavior displayed in the context of work, the professional manager exhibits both curiosity and the initiative to find out "why?" Perhaps one cannot use the elaborate techniques of large staff-research projects, but one can learn to think along the lines of the scientific method and devise general approaches and practices which will make performances more effective.

As indicated above, there are many specific things to be learned in personnel management. The following list, classified by function, is only a sketch of the territory that should be covered by new and continuing research:

1. Procurement
   a. Managerial job analysis
   b. Improvement of the reliability of interviews
   c. Practical and valid measures of personality
   d. Measures of leadership potential
   e. Establishment of more realistic criteria for validating selection devices
2. Development
   a. Valid and union-acceptable measures of merit and ability
   b. Effective management development
   c. Developing organizations as well as individuals
   d. Integration of supervision and coaching
   e. Bridging the gap between off-the-job development and on-the-job performance
3. Compensation
   a. The proper role of wage-escalator clauses
   b. Overcoming restriction of work under incentive wage systems
   c. Incentive wage plans that will increase quality as well as quantity
   d. Improved methods of selecting and weighting job evaluation factors
   e. A systematic and acceptable method of interchanging job rating information
   f. Determination of the effect of all types of pay upon employee motivation
   g. Determination of the effects of the guaranteed annual wage on the will to work
   h. Determination of the effects of profit sharing on productivity
4. Integration
   a. Communication symbols and skills
   b. Determination of the active needs of employees
   c. More practical techniques of charting the informal organization
   d. Determination of the effect of the union shop on union responsibility
   e. Objective collective bargainng
   f. Reducing employee alienation
5. Maintenance
   a. Determining the psychological impact of work and the workplace upon employees
   b. Discovery and alleviation of industrial diseases
   c. Determination of the appropriate degree and mix of employee benefits

With respect to actual practice in personnel research, the survey of forty-four companies by Byham revealed the following subjects were being actively researched: 98 percent were conducting research in selection, 75 percent in opinion measurement, 30 percent in training and development, 20 percent in appraisal, 18 percent in motivation, 16 percent in organizational effectiveness, and less than 10 percent in such areas as managerial obsolescence, counseling, and recruitment.[6] Berry's survey of fifty companies is in general agreement, with the four dominant subjects being selection, training and development, attitudes and leadership, and measurement devices.[7] In a third survey of 319 personnel administrators, the areas where they see the greatest usefulness of research are employee motivation (60 percent), managerial selection (59 percent), and managerial training (59 percent).[8] The single greatest need was for more useful research in motivation. The single smallest need was in job evaluation. Over three-quarters of these personnel managers believed that an industrial psychologist could increase productivity and satisfaction within their companies.

---

[6]Byham, op. cit., p. 14.

[7]Berry, op. cit., p. 72.

[8]George C. Thornton, III, "Image of Industrial Psychology among Personnel Administrators," *Journal of Applied Psychology*, vol. 53, no. 5, October 1969, p. 437.

THE PERSONNEL MANAGER AS CHANGE AGENT

Assuming that research indicates that changes should be made in areas pertaining to personnel, the personnel manager must assume some responsibility for the effective introduction of change. It is one thing to intellectually determine that change is necessary and to lay out its dimensions. It is quite another to translate the plan into action. As Selznick indicates, "We are inescapably committed to the mediation of human structures which are at once indispensable to our goals and at the same time *stand between* them and ourselves."[9]

In general, two basic approaches can be taken in effecting organizational changes. First, a change in *structure* and/or *technology* can be introduced which brings considerable pressure to bear upon organizational members. If, for example, the content of a job is altered, a new machine purchased for use, or a new form designed for collecting control information, participants must respond in some manner to these objective changes. Secondly, a *therapeutic approach* can be taken where organization members are counseled and encouraged to alter their behavior in line with some proposed model. Assuming, for example, that management concludes that the organization culture should be changed to one that is more trusting, supportive, authentic, and participative, change tactics of both types are often used. In the structural area, job enrichment, wider spans of control, and decentralization of authority have all been used to generate more real participation. In the therapeutic area, individual members have been sent to stranger "T-group" or sensitivity training sessions to stimulate more individual openness and supportiveness. Within the firm, organization development sessions with job-family groups have been held to stimulate teamwork and to work on interpersonal problems.

Arguments abound as to the most appropriate approach to effecting change. With the limited formal authority of staff personnel managers, there has been a considerable use of therapy rather than structural changes. It requires relatively little authority to implement training programs designed to affect attitudes. It requires a considerable amount of authority to alter the "guts" of the organization—its jobs, technology, and operating procedures. It is highly probable that structural changes are more lasting; there is less opportunity for backsliding. But certainly structural changes without some accompanying behavioral therapy are often nullified by informal deviations from the prescribed change.

The personnel manager as a change agent must move through the basic stages of change introduction. As outlined by Lewin, they are (1) unfreezing the present status quo, (2) moving to the new level of change, and (3) refreezing the organization at the new level.[10] Each of the stages will be briefly discussed in the following sections.

Unfreezing the status quo

If people are not truly involved and committed to a proposed change, the long-term impact upon their behavior is likely to be minimal. Thus, the first stage in effecting changes is to generate self-doubts as to the appropriateness of present practices.

[9]Philip Selznick, "Foundations of the Theory of Organization," *American Sociological Review*, vol. 13, 1948, p. 33.

[10]Kurt Lewin, "Frontiers in Group Dynamics," *Human Relations*, vol. 1, 1947, p. 34.

Admittedly, a manager with authority can command that a change be effected and enforce its implementation through threats, punishments, close supervision, and the like. Once embarked on this road, the manager finds that continuation of the change demands constant and close surveillance. A more permanent and substantial change can be induced if the person truly wants and feels a need to change. Certainly, the lack of formal line authority by the personnel manager is likely to lead to emphasis on the latter approach.

Generating receptivity to change often calls for pressures, both external and internal. External pressures from the environment are typically most powerful. If the firm is about to go out of business because of stringent competition, organization members are more inclined to receive and implement *any* change that has a chance of contributing to organizational survival. At times, personnel managers bring outside experts into the organization to generate self-doubts about current practice; e.g., assessment and normative evaluation of leadership styles by well-known consultants, such as Robert Blake and Rensis Likert, may lead to greater receptivity to change. Certainly, two of the major external sources of pressure of significance in the personnel field are government and the labor union. Personnel managers often point to legal requirements for changes in all the areas covered in this text—discrimination, safety and health, compensation, etc. And the steady strong pressures of organized labor have led to a strengthening of the personnel manager as a change agent in the organization.

The personnel manager must also understand the necessity for obtaining top management support for changes proposed in his or her area. It is no accident that the first session of most training programs is attended and supported by significant higher officials. Systematic accumulation of operating and organizational data concerning performance will also help to convince participants of the desirability of change. In one instance, the personnel manager was convinced from such data that a change was necessary—more older females should be hired in the firm. Middle-level supervisors resisted and did not believe. Rather than argue, persuade, or threaten, the manager asked the supervisors to collect their own data, perhaps with the idea that older females should be avoided. When the data were collected, supervisors discovered, to their surprise, the same favorable situation as the personnel manager, and all resistance to the idea faded. Sometimes a "fact" is not a "fact" until one collects it oneself.

Finally, in unfreezing present behavior of people, it has been found that temporary isolation is often conducive to receptivity. Sensitivity training laboratories as well as team development sessions are usually conducted at a site apart from the workplace and at a time when only the one subject is being considered. Religious organizations as well as the military have discovered and utilized isolation as a means of opening up the person to change, e.g., basic training, monastic orders, etc.

The action plan

If sufficient individual, group, or organization self-doubt has been generated, the personnel manager moves to the next stage—the change itself. Research as well as experience has demonstrated that the impact of change is more social and subjective than it is technical and objective. The first concern of most people is possible alterations in interpersonal and social relationships that the change will require. As a consequence, a significant role must be established for the changee in the creation of action plans. Plans that are technically perfect and not acceptable to those expected to carry them out are not likely to effect long-lasting results.

The most effective action plans involve a reciprocal relationship between change agent and changee. Rather than a one-way flow of suggestions or commands, the change agent does well to observe the norm of reciprocity. The roles of agent and changee should be blurred, rather than sharp. Suggestions should be made on a tentative basis, and changees should be encouraged to contribute and participate in final determinations. In an analysis of eighteen studies of organization change by Greiner, it was discovered that successful changes utilized patterns involving sharing approaches—that is, change agents sought participation of changees in decision making.[11] In the less successful change attempts, the approaches were either highly autocratic or highly democratic. The five less successful autocratic attempts utilized decrees, replacement of key personnel when decrees did not work, and ordered structural changes without participation. The two less successful democratic approaches used sensitivity training and self-generated fact-finding. The eleven successful attempts involved the techniques of group decision making on problems defined by the change agent, or group definition of the problem and subsequent problem solving with the aid of the change agent.

The personnel manager as change agent can also make use of a number of organizational devices to encourage internal acceptance of the change. Guarantees of security to present personnel are often a requirement for effective acceptance, e.g., no one will be laid off as a result of technological innovation, or base pay is guaranteed when new incentive plans are introduced. Certainly, the personnel manager will have to work with and through the normal political processes of the organization. Superiors will have to be persuaded, interacting parallel staff units will have to be informed and coordinated, and the labor union cannot be ignored. Welcoming the union as a significant participant in proposed changes will do much to reduce real or pretended political resistance. The personnel manager should consider any resistance to change to be a "red flag" denoting need for investigation and analysis, rather than regarding it as a symbol of immaturity, "theory X," or chronic unenlightenment.

Like all specialists, the personnel manager must be wary of excessive personal ownership of change ideas. The "pet idea" can lead to minds closed to significant, or even minimal, alteration by others. Change introduction becomes one of "managing the personal image" rather than one of managing the process of change implementation. Finally, one must be ever on guard against apparent contradictions in philosophies. There have been various instances where participative management has been introduced in an autocratic manner. In effect, "This company is going to be managed in a democratic and participative manner, and those that don't like it can get out!" or "I order you to be independent!" If one subscribes to the concept that changees must truly want to change, then greater measures of patience and tolerance must be forthcoming.

[11]Larry E. Greiner, "Patterns of Organization Change," *Harvard Business Review*, vol. 45, no. 3, May–June 1967, pp. 120–122.

Refreezing the new status quo

One of the early discoveries in sensitivity training was that the impact upon participants lasted only a short while after their return to the organization. The on-going culture of the operating organization was not supportive of the individually induced changes toward openness, empathy, and trust. Thus, attempts toward fundamental changes of this type in attitude and behavior inevitably lead to the conclusion that the total culture must be altered, thereby fostering an organization development approach. In some instances of job-enrichment structural changes, there was too little consideration of the impact of the changed job upon surrounding and interacting personnel and units. In one case, the supervisor felt that his job had been "raped," leaving him with little to do; he therefore reacted by practicing close supervision over the "enriched" incumbent in order to fill his time, thus generating a situation completely contrary to the philosophy of job enrichment. In another, the computer service center was totally unprepared to respond to new requests for information from incumbents on newly enriched jobs. It has been observed that profound and long-lasting changes are most likely to be effected if the total system can be designed from scratch. For example, the new plants built in Sweden by Volvo and at Topeka, Kansas, by General Foods involved total design, startup, and operation in a manner consistent with the behavioral, participative model. In this way, all of the interacting subsystems can be aligned to reflect the model desired, e.g., all personnel use a single entrance, all park in the same lot, performance of operations is on a group basis, pay is allocated to groups, etc. When attempting such changes in an existing plant, they tend to take the form of "paste-ons" which ultimately "fall off" if surrounding personnel and interacting systems are not intelligently attuned and aligned.

Finally, the change will be thoroughly digested only if the rewards system of the organization is geared to the new form of behavior. An employee's job may be substantially enriched in terms of content and self-supervision, but if the change is not accompanied by properly enriched pay, working conditions, and recognition, dissatisfaction is likely to ensue. Individuals and groups who comply with the change in spirit as well as deed must be recognized and rewarded by the organization. In some instances, managers have successfully used the "Hawthorne effect" to make the changes stick. The considerable television publicity and public attention allocated to the General Foods plant in Topeka has helped perpetuate in the personnel a feeling of importance and significance, generating a widespread desire among employees to see the change succeed.

CHALLENGES OF THE FUTURE

Contrary to the feeling of some that the personnel field is "bankrupt," we believe that increasing attention must and will be given to human problems in the years ahead. In a postindustrial society such as ours, human problems tend to take on greater degrees of importance and to occupy the center stage. On the basis of present trends and anticipated developments in the field of personnel management, we anticipate increased attention being allocated to the following:

1   Reducing employee alienation within organizations

2 Increasing human and organizational creativity and productivity

3 Expanded personnel manager roles in helping the private organization to meet its ever-increasing social responsibility

4 Expanded personnel manager roles in designing organizations

As Walton states, "Managers don't need anyone to tell them that employee alienation exists," as evidenced by "blue-collar blues," salaried dropouts, dislike of jobs, resentment of bosses, aggressive acts of sabotage and demonstrations, and escape through tardiness, absenteeism, turnover, and inattention to work.[12] The roots of this alienation lie in a clash between changes in basic social forces and the relatively few responding changes in design and management of organizations. Today's employees are better educated and more affluent; they display less obedience to arbitrary authority and greater concern for self-expression in place of competitive winning. On the other hand, typical organizations emphasize traditional career patterns, task specialization, authoritarian hierarchies, and monetary reward systems. Thus, a major challenge for the future is developing basic methods of reconciling clashes of values, thereby reducing the amount of employee alienation. The injection of constitutional rights of citizenship within the employing organization will help to reduce feelings of *helplessness*. The gradual movement toward job enrichment should assist in reducing feelings of *meaninglessness*. Facilitating the development of viable primary work groups should help reduce feelings of *normlessness*. Personnel managers must continue to seek approaches that will more effectively integrate human and organizational values.

Recent significant declines in the general level of productivity, accompanied by significant increases in the level of inflation, have highlighted an extremely serious need for greater productivity and creativity. Personnel managers have an obligation to help general management tap the vast reservoir of human capability that is present within all organizations. This would include not only moving to productivity bargaining with organized labor, but also promoting multiple and varied programs of real subordinate participation on real issues. Real participation on fake issues, and fake participation on real issues constitute pallid attempts at manipulative autocracy, thereby continuing the situation where the bulk of the burden for productivity rests solely on management. Organization development enthusiasts count as their basic goal the conversion of autocratic hierarchical organizations into viable, authentic, open, and problem-solving organisms. Personnel managers must continue to seek ways to involve the brains as well as the bodies of all organization members in the pursuit of meaningful organizational goals.

As suggested earlier in this text, the personnel manager has a considerable burden placed upon him or her in helping the private organization define and execute its proper social role in total society. Certainly, the unavoidable minimum is to comply with the continuing flow of social legislation designed to protect and promote the interests of society's citizens who happen to be organizational employees. The professional manager must go beyond this and propose programs and policies that meet social obligations that are not as yet defined by law. This is a difficult challenge

---

[12]Richard E. Walton, "How to Counter Alienation in the Plant," *Harvard Business Review*, vol. 50, no. 6, November–December 1972, p. 70.

inasmuch as he or she must do this while still recognizing the necessity of operating within the cost/effectiveness framework of a profit-seeking enterprise. Increased personnel research with respect to various social issues (employment of the culturally disadvantaged, employee freedom of speech, movement of females into responsible managerial positions, etc.) may well demonstrate a considerable overlapping of social interests *and* the economic interests of the firm.

Finally, if the above challenges are successfully met, it will undoubtedly have a considerable impact upon the design of organization structures. The personnel manager, who faces both outward to the social environment and inward to the technological environment, has skills and knowledge that can be utilized in creating organizational designs that can be effective on both fronts. The personnel unit already has expert knowledge about jobs through job analysis, and about personnel capabilities through various programs of hiring, training, and appraisal. Though the basic responsibility of organizational design must continue to rest with top managers, the personnel manager has an obligation to place this existing store of knowledge at their disposal, as well as to provide counsel and advice in aligning the basic organizational thrust with major trends in societal values.

SUMMARY

Systematic and purposive research is an obvious and continuing necessity in the field of personnel management. Exploratory and operational personnel research is done by such persons and institutions as colleges and universities, governmental agencies, private research organizations, personnel departments of private companies, and individual managers. Since the main variable in personnel research is that of people, it is very difficult to do exacting and lengthy research. Controlled experiments, surveys, historical studies, case studies, and simulations are five possible approaches to personnel research. There is much to be learned about the procurement, development, compensation, integration, and maintenance of personnel. These fundamental functions are universal for all who propose to be managers.

When research develops results capable of utilization by the organization, the personnel manager's task is one of introducing change. All staff personnel must have skills of change introduction, and the personnel manager should again have an unusual expertise because of a basic understanding of people. The status quo must be unfrozen through the generation of doubt about current practices. Moving to the new level should entail significant changee participation to stimulate improvements, adaptations, and the acceptance necessary for effective implementation. The new level should then be refrozen through various means, not the least of which is the organization's reward system.

Very serious challenges to the personnel manager exist in the future. There is widespread concern for increased employee alienation and reduced productivity and creativity. Personnel managers have a special obligation to assist in coping with these essentially human problems. Perhaps the significant pressures issuing from basic social forces will generate sufficient top management self-doubt to unfreeze the current status quo and allow constructive changes to be introduced.

DISCUSSION QUESTIONS

1 If one wanted to be a personnel researcher in a larger business organization, what type of academic preparation would best prepare one for the job? Why?

2 Who finances most of the nation's personnel research? Who does most of this research?

3 Suppose that you are interested in ascertaining the effects of job enrichment upon employee attitudes and output; describe how a controlled experiment could be set up.

4 What is the "Hawthorne effect"? Can it be overcome?

5 Suppose that you are interested in reducing the existing levels of turnover and absenteeism; describe how a historical study could be designed to provide needed information.

6 Suppose that you are interested in ascertaining the effects of different styles of leadership upon employee output and attitudes; describe how a questionnaire survey could be set up to produce the desired information.

7 In introducing changes in organizations, contrast the structural with the therapeutic approach. With which approach is the personnel unit more likely to be involved?

8 In what ways can the existing status quo be unfrozen by a change agent?

9 If the introduced change is to be truly internalized, what general approach is indicated?

10 What is the nature of the personnel manager's challenge to reduce employee alienation?

SUPPLEMENTARY READING

GRUBER, William H., and John S. Niles: "How to Innovate in Management," *Organizational Dynamics*, vol. 3, no. 2, Autumn 1974, pp. 30–47.

HIRSCHOWITZ, Ralph G.: "The Human Aspects of Managing Transition," *Personnel*, vol. 51, no. 3, May–June 1974, pp. 8–17.

NOSOW, Sigmund: "The Use of the Pilot Study in Behavioral Research," *Personnel Journal*, vol. 53, no. 9, September 1974, pp. 683–688.

PAUL, Robert J.: "Constructing Personnel Research Programs," in Joseph J. Famularo, ed., *Handbook of Modern Personnel Administration*, McGraw-Hill Book Company, New York, 1972, chap. 81.

PERROW, Charles: "Is Business Really Changing?" *Organizational Dynamics*, vol. 3, no. 1, Summer 1974, pp. 31–44.

ROKEACH, Milton: "Long-Range Experimental Modification of Values, Attitudes, and Behavior," in William A. Hunt, ed., *Human Behavior and Its Control*, Shenkman Publishing Company, Cambridge, Mass., 1971, pp. 93–105.

CASES FOR PART SEVEN

THE CASE OF THE MISGUIDED MISSILE

The Jones Paper Products Company is a firm of approximately 2,200 employees. Its employees are organized by a national papermakers union which is affiliated with the AFL-CIO. Relations between company management and union have been reasonably good and peaceful. The Jones Company attempts to take a modern, enlightened approach to personnel management, and its personnel department has subsections in employment, training, compensation, labor relations, employee services, and safety. Total personnel in the department is twenty-one.

Joe Roscoe has been employed by the Jones Company for two years. He joined the organization immediately after being discharged from the service. His job consists of removing various paper products from a machine, weighing these products, and transporting them to a storage area. At present, Joe works on the shift which begins around midnight and ends at 7:30 A.M. A skeleton crew works this shift, and Joe's supervisor is responsible for a very large area. Joe is on his own a good deal of the time, which is one of the attractive things about the job. In addition, an individual incentive bonus system has been set up, based on the tonnage of paper moved. He has found that he can make bonus and still have time to rest and read magazines occasionally. Sleeping is too risky.

One morning at about three o'clock, Joe was struggling with a load of paper, attempting to get it to the weighing scale. For some reason, the load simply would not move. He pushed, shoved, sweated, and swore. Suddenly he discovered that one of the metal weights of the scale had jammed against one of the wheels. This irritated him considerably, and he grabbed the metal weight and flung it without looking. It fractured the skull of a fellow employee, who was immediately rushed to a hospital, where he remained for several weeks. Joe, of course, was very upset by the event and went to the hospital with the injured employee. He was very much relieved when the doctors pronounced him out of danger.

As we said, the Jones Company has a safety section. This section consists of the safety director and two assistants. The safety director had been offered a functional type of authority over all personnel in matters affecting safety. He had refused this authority, preferring to work only in a staff capacity. His main thesis was that a man could not be *made* to act safely; he had to be persuaded, shown, and educated. The safety director did not want the temptation of organizational authority.

Joe's night supervisor filed disciplinary charges against him for the incident described above and recommended discharge. A committee hearing was held, at which the supervisor and Joe both testified. After all the facts were revealed, the safety director was asked for his recommendation. He argued that Joe should not be discharged. He felt that the Jones Paper Products Company was largely at fault in this incident. In the first place, Jones was remiss in not providing adequate supervision on the night shift. Had a supervisor been in the area, Joe would probably have been more restrained in his actions. Secondly, the Jones management should be fully aware of the effects of an incentive wage plan. The purpose of this plan is to stimulate an increase in employee output. The company wants its employees to respond, and Joe did respond. Naturally he was upset when he found that his progress was hindered by the scale weight. Thus the company incentive wage program was a contributing factor in the accident. Thirdly, Joe has a plant reputation of being a hothead. He is a good, steady employee, but he has been known to have a low boiling point. Plant management was aware of this side of his personality as were also most of his associates. Management was therefore at fault in coupling a temperamental employee with adverse working conditions. The safety director recommended that some lighter penalty should be given to Joe, that discharge was too severe.

The disciplinary committee listened attentively to the advice of the safety director. They concluded that the seriousness of the incident more than offset any of the extenuating circumstances offered by him. Joe was fired. The union immediately filed a grievance.

THE CASE OF THE COMPREHENSIVE BENEFIT PROGRAM

The Atlas Paper Corporation is a firm of some 3,500 employees whose plant is located in a medium-sized Midwestern city. This plant makes various types of paper and paper products with a concentration on the higher-quality grades. Though there have been many attempts on the part of the two national unions in the paper industry to organize the Atlas employees, all such attempts have failed by a wide margin.

The personnel department of the Atlas company has most of the usual functions associated with a large-sized organization. The total number of employees in this department is seventy-five, far in excess of the number found in most firms. One section of this department is devoted exclusively to the origination and administration of employee services and benefits. Among the benefits offered are the following:

1 A committee of twenty-eight persons elected by the workers to set up a recreation program, with activities which include softball teams, basketball teams, bowling, rifle clubs, camera clubs, and girls' social clubs.
2 Banquets for old-timers
3 Awards for years of service

4   A credit union, which loans over $2 million a year

5   Special events, such as a yearly picnic for all employees and open house in the plant

6   Construction of company houses, which are rented to employees

7   Sales of tickets to outstanding sports events in the community

8   Free assistance in making out income tax returns

9   Club rooms for men, women, and older retired employees

10 A servicemen's organization, through which gifts are sent to employees in the military services

11 Maintenance of a company-owned picnic park, which is always open to Atlas employees and their families

12 An employee profit-sharing plan, to which is contributed 15 percent of Atlas's profits each year

13 Hospital, surgical, and medical benefits

14 Temporary disability benefits

15 Death benefits

16 Pensions

17 Group life insurance

18 Financing of tuition for college courses

19 Patrolling of the company parking lot, not only to protect employee cars but also to discover and change flat tires

In addition to the above-listed services, a bonus system operates, which includes shift bonuses, group production incentive bonuses, and individual incentive bonuses. Over five hundred of Atlas's employees have been with the firm for more than twenty years and over one thousand have been there for over ten years. Atlas is considered to be *the* place to work. Needless to say, the benefit program is a large item in the annual budget.

In the same city there is another firm engaged in the manufacture of various metal products. This firm also has approximately 3,500 employees. The total number engaged in the personnel department is five, consisting of the personnel manager, his assistant, and three clerks. The firm is organized by a strong national union. The employee service program consists of those benefits required by law, such as unemployment compensation and Old Age and Survivors' Insurance, plus certain standard benefits written into the labor agreement, such as supplementary pensions and group life insurance.

An outside consultant in personnel management was struck by the contrast between the two organizations. She wondered if the metal products firm's organization was not out of balance. Her associate suggested that the Atlas Corporation's structure might also be out of balance.

THE CASE OF THE UNFETTERED EMPLOYEE

Dan Walton was hired for a summer job as a carpenter's helper by a home building firm. On reporting to his supervisor, the verbal assignment given was, "Just stay busy. I can't be concerned with everything you do. Just don't let any superintendents catch you standing around." The following is the sequence of events as related by Dan.

I was primarily engaged in supplying the framing crew of carpenters with adequate material to allow them to proceed from one structure to the next without any delays. I was relatively naive concerning union procedures that designated what I would be allowed to perform, as well as the basic work responsibilities that my employer would expect me to fulfill. My supervisor, who was in charge of fifteen carpenters and three laborers, was not concerned with individual performances as long as the completion schedule was met, and therefore offered little guidance in assigning tasks to be performed.

Our crew, the framing division, arrived at the residential site after the foundation had been poured. At the time of our arrival the bricklayers would also have the walls up on the houses. The first task of our crew was to have an individual chalk out the location of the walls from a blueprint. The laborers would then supply the dwelling with "studs" and "longs," which were the types of lumber used to build the internal frame for the walls of the house. The laborers would at this time stand planks around the outside brick walls which would be attached to the top of the brick walls to seal the walls. The roofing segment would then attach sheets of plywood to complete our division's tasks. The laborers would then sweep out the dwelling and gather all the scraps of lumber into piles which would be dumped by the cleaning crew.

At first I relied on the other two laborers to teach me the basic procedures of our operations, but they had specific duties which they did not want infringed upon and at times resented my encroachment on their standard tasks.

The carpenters also offered little help. As certain duties had to be completed I was randomly instructed by various carpenters to either assist or perform a particular task related to the general responsibilities of the crew. Meanwhile my supervisor as the occasion arose would similarly instruct me in the operation of some type of machinery or the desired performance of some necessary operation.

Upon arriving at work one morning my supervisor, Herb, informed me that I would have to remove all of the unused lumber and various other supplies that had not been used from the streets. Herb stated that a paving company would be arriving the next day to grade the streets and could not be delayed by the obstruction of our materials. He then told me to stack the leftover "studs" in three-foot-by-three-foot stacks, which I should then bind together with a binding instrument. He then instructed me to take the forklift, since the usual operator was on vacation, and pick up the bounded stacks of studs, and place them on the flatbed truck. He also stated that I should then drive the truck to the main yard and unload the truck, using the forklift to remove the stacks of lumber.

As my initial reaction I told Herb that I didn't know what a binding tool was, let alone how to operate it. He assured me that the instructions on the case would be self-explanatory. I then proceeded to stack the lumber into the three-foot-by-three-foot stacks as had been suggested. I soon realized that the reason many of these studs had not been used was because they were severely warped. After the stack was about two feet high the stack would then, because of the warped material, tumble to the ground. I soon became very discouraged and frustrated at the continual collapsing of the stacks of studs. A carpenter named Bob, who had been watching me and sensing my frustration, came over to where I was working and told me that after the stack had reached about a foot and a half, to place pieces of wood crossways on the top of the stack so the next tier of the stack would have a foundation. The idea sounded very logical and I wondered why I had not thought of it.

My next duties would be to load the stacks onto the truck with the forklift. I was apprehensive about running the forklift, even if the operator was on vacation. I had seen previously even the most experienced operators drop loads before, and I could only imagine the difficulties a novice would have. I decided to tell Herb that I did not really think I should operate the forklift. Herb's reaction was, "If you can drive a truck, you can drive the fork; just go play around with it before you move anything."

I walked down to the yard where the forklift was kept and climbed up on the machine. I finally got it started, but with all the various levers, it was confusing as to which sequence they were to be used in operating the machine. A carpenter named Al came into the yard at the same time to pick up a supply of nails. He then offered to demonstrate the operation of the machine. He suggested bits of advice that he thought were pertinent to the machine's operation. Al stated that first of all, the rear wheels turned on a forklift, which is different from most vehicles, and that this was important to remember when operating the machine. He also stated that it was important to keep the lift slightly tilted toward the machine when moving the stacks to counterbalance any sway in the load that might cause the load to shift and fall off the lift. He then explained the sequence in which the levers had to be operated to properly maneuver the machine. As I drove the forklift out of the yard I was confident that I would be able to operate the machine, thanks to Al's help.

After loading the stacks of lumber onto the truck it was about time to go home. Most of the other members of the crew had already started cleaning up for the day, and although I had not yet unloaded the stacks of lumber from the flatbed truck, I did feel I had accomplished a great deal. I decided that I might as well drive the forklift back to the yard. As I started toward the yard, Herb came over and said he would drive the forklift back, and that I could drive the boom truck which the beam crew had been using to set the trestles on the houses.

As I walked over to the boom truck, I noticed that the telescopic boom was fully extended and holding up one of the trestles that had not been hung yet. I started up the engine of the truck and tried to figure out which handle would slacken the line so I could detach it from the beam. I finally succeeded in detaching the line. I then brought the line and boom back onto the truck and attempted to apply the safety brace which keeps the boom from bouncing and being bent when the truck is moving. It was difficult to set the brace because it required someone holding the brace while the boom was lowered on top of it. I decided to lower the boom and wedge the brace under the boom. As I drove back to the yard I hit a bump which jarred the brace loose and it fell from under the boom. At this same time a car drove up to the truck and a man got out and introduced himself as the business agent of the operating engineers. He said he would help me put the brace in properly. He also stated that since I was a laborer, I was not allowed to operate machinery. He suggested that I tell my foreman that I had been instructed by the business agent of the operating engineers to not operate any machinery.

I thanked the business agent for his help and drove the truck to the yard. When I arrived I saw Herb, but I decided that it was not my duty to tell my supervisor what to do, since he rarely helped me perform my assigned tasks. So I jumped in my car and headed home.

NAME INDEX

SUBJECT INDEX